Family Law for Paralegals

Eighth Edition

Family Law for Paralegals

Eighth Edition

J. Shoshanna Ehrlich

Professor
Women's, Gender, and Sexuality Studies Department
College of Liberal Arts
University of Massachusetts Boston

Published by Wolters Kluwer in New York.

Wolters Kluwer Legal & Regulatory U.S. serves customers worldwide with CCH, Aspen Publishers, and Kluwer Law International products. (www.WKLegaledu.com)

Cover image: Cienpies Design/Shutterstock

To contact Customer Service, e-mail customer.service@wolterskluwer.com, call 1-800-234-1660, fax 1-800-901-9075, or mail correspondence to:

Wolters Kluwer
Attn: Order Department
PO Box 990
Frederick, MD 21705

Printed in the United States of America.

1 2 3 4 5 6 7 8 9 0

ISBN 978-1-5438-0166-8

Library of Congress Cataloging-in-Publication Data

Names: Ehrlich, J. Shoshanna.
Title: Family law for paralegals / J. Shoshanna Ehrlich, Professor, Women's, Gender, and Sexuality Studies Department, College of Liberal Arts, University of Massachusetts—Boston.
Description: Eighth edition. | New York: Wolters Kluwer, 2020. | Includes bibliographical references and index.
Identifiers: LCCN 2019021422 | ISBN 9781543801668
Subjects: LCSH: Domestic relations—United States. | Legal assistants—United States—Handbooks, manuals, etc.
Classification: LCC KF505.E35 2020 | DDC 346.7301/5—dc23
LC record available at https://lccn.loc.gov/2019021422

About Wolters Kluwer Legal & Regulatory U.S.

Wolters Kluwer Legal & Regulatory U.S. delivers expert content and solutions in the areas of law, corporate compliance, health compliance, reimbursement, and legal education. Its practical solutions help customers successfully navigate the demands of a changing environment to drive their daily activities, enhance decision quality and inspire confident outcomes.

Serving customers worldwide, its legal and regulatory portfolio includes products under the Aspen Publishers, CCH Incorporated, Kluwer Law International, ftwilliam.com and MediRegs names. They are regarded as exceptional and trusted resources for general legal and practice-specific knowledge, compliance and risk management, dynamic workflow solutions, and expert commentary.

To Alan, Emma, my father, and the memory of my mother

Summary of Contents

Contents		*xi*
Preface		*xxv*
Acknowledgments		*xxvii*
Chapter 1	**Marriage and Cohabitation**	1
Chapter 2	**Premarital and Postmarital Agreements**	61
Chapter 3	**Domestic Violence**	93
Chapter 4	**The Law of Divorce, Annulment, and Legal Separation**	155
Chapter 5	**Child Custody**	195
Chapter 6	**Child Support**	269
Chapter 7	**Spousal Support**	327
Chapter 8	**Division of Marital Property**	371
Chapter 9	**Jurisdiction**	421
Chapter 10	**The Divorce Process**	445
Chapter 11	**Determining Parentage**	551
Chapter 12	**Child Abuse and Neglect**	603
Chapter 13	**Adoption**	643
Glossary		*697*
Index		*713*

Contents

Preface   *xxv*
Acknowledgments   *xxvii*

Chapter 1   Marriage and Cohabitation   **1**

Marriage: Regulating the Relationship   2
   Common Law Origins   2
   The Civil Law Tradition   4
   Married Women's Property Acts   4
   The Move to Legal Equality   6
Entrance into Marriage: Choosing a Spouse   7
   Loving v. Virginia   8
   Marital Rights of Same-Sex Partners   9
      The Renewed Struggle for Marriage Equality   10
      The Backlash: The Campaign to Preserve Marriage as a Heterosexual
         Institution   10
      Marriage Equality in the States   10
      Marriage Equality: The Law of the Land   11
      The Backlash Against Obergefell   14
   Restrictions on the Entry into Marriage   15
      Incest   16
      Multiple Marriages   17
      Marital Age   18
Marriage Formalities   20
   Obtaining a Marriage License   20
      Consequences of Failing to Comply with Licensing Requirements   22
Common Law Marriage   22
   Formation Requirements and Consequences   23
   Interstate Recognition   24
The Legal Rights of Cohabiting Couples   24

Opening the Door to the Courthouse: The Landmark
Case of *Marvin v. Marvin*   25
Chapter Summary   28
Key Terms   29
Review Questions   29
Discussion Questions   30
Assignments   30
Cases for Analysis   31
Loving v. Virginia   31
Obergefell v. Hodges   34
Marvin v. Marvin   44
Brush & Nib Studio, LC v. City of Phoenix   49
Endnotes   57

Chapter 2   Premarital and Postmarital Agreements   61
The Traditional Approach to Premarital Agreements   61
The Growing Acceptance of Premarital Agreements   63
Legal Requirements   64
Threshold Considerations   64
The Fairness Requirement   64
Requirements of Procedural Fairness   66
Requirements of Substantive Fairness   69
The Interdependence of Procedural and Substantive Fairness   71
Common Types of Provisions   71
Property   72
Spousal Support   72
Child Custody and Child Support   73
Postmarital Contracts   73
Chapter Summary   74
Key Terms   75
Review Questions   75
Discussion Questions   76
Assignments   76
Cases for Analysis   77
Posner v. Posner   78
Simeone v. Simeone   80
Bedrick v. Bedrick   85
Endnotes   92

Chapter 3   Domestic Violence   93
The Traditional Approach   93
Early Reform Impulses   95

Present Legal Approach to Domestic Violence   96
Obtaining Civil Orders of Protection Under Abuse   97
   Prevention Laws   97
   Qualifying Relationships   97
      Dating Relationships   99
      Same-Sex Couples   102
   Covered Conduct   102
   Available Remedies   104
      Refraining from Further Abuse   105
      Vacate and Stay-Away Orders   105
      No-Contact Orders   106
      Custody and Visitation   106
      Protection of Pets   107
      Support and Monetary Compensation   107
      Treatment/Counseling   108
      Electronic Monitoring   108
      Relinquishment of Firearms   109
      Statutory Obligations of Police Officers   110
   Court Procedure: Obtaining Protective Orders   111
   Enforcement of Protective Orders   125
      Supplementing the Enforcement Process: Criminal Anti-Stalking Laws   127
      Cyberstalking   129
   Specialized Domestic Violence Courts   130
   The Federal Response to Domestic Violence: The Violence Against
      Women Act   131
      Select Provisions of VAWA   132
      The Violence Against Women Reauthorization Act of 2013   133
Chapter Summary   135
Key Terms   136
Review Questions   136
Discussion Questions   137
Assignments   137
Cases for Analysis   138
   Fowler v. Fowler   138
   Silva v. Carmel   144
   Huch v. Marrs   147
Endnotes   150

Chapter 4   The Law of Divorce, Annulment, and Legal Separation   **155**
Historical Overview   155
   Religious Underpinnings   156
      Marriage as an Indissoluble Bond   156
      The Protestant Reformation   156
      The English Experience   157

The American Experience   157
   Divorce in the Colonies   157
   The Rising Tide   158
Fault Divorce: Common Grounds and Defenses   159
  Divorce Grounds   159
   Adultery   159
   Desertion/Abandonment   161
   Cruelty   162
  Defenses   162
   Connivance   162
   Condonation   163
   Recrimination   163
   Collusion   163
No-Fault Divorce   164
  The Underpinnings of Reform   164
  No-Fault Laws   166
   No-Fault Grounds   166
  The Divorce Counterrevolution   168
   The Debate over No-Fault Divorce   168
   Legal Reforms   170
   Premarital Counseling   171
   Covenant Marriage   172
The Law of Annulment   174
  Distinguished from Divorce   174
  Grounds   175
   Void Marriages   175
   Voidable Marriages   176
  Consequences of an Annulment Decree   176
   Children   176
   Spousal Support and the Division of Property   177
   Revival   177
Legal Separation   178
  The Nature of the Action   178
  Distinguished from an Action for Separate Maintenance 179
Chapter Summary   179
Key Terms   180
Review Questions   180
Discussion Questions   181
Assignments   182
Cases for Analysis   183
  Berry v. Berry   183
  In the Matter of Blanchflower   186
  Lawrence v. Lawrence   189
Endnotes   192

Chapter 5   Child Custody   **195**

Evolving Legal Standards   196
  Paternal Preference   196
  Shift to Maternal Custody   197
  The Modern Best Interest Test   197
    Formulating the Test   198
    Applying the Test   199
    Factoring Parental Characteristics/Identities into the Best Interest Test   207
  Critiques of and Alternative Approaches to the Best Interest Standard   214
    Gender Bias   214
    Lack of Predictability   214
    The Primary Caretaker Presumption   215
    The American Law Institute's Approximation Rule   216

Custody and Visitation Arrangements   218
  Physical and Legal Custody Distinguished   218
  Sole and Joint Custody Distinguished   219
  A Closer Look at Shared Custody Arrangements   219
  The Joint Custody Controversy   220
  Legal Status of the Noncustodial Parent   222
  Visitation Rights   223
    The Visitation Schedule   223
    When Unrestricted Visitation Is Not in a Child's Best Interest   225
  Parenting Plans, Parenting Coordinators, and Parent Education
    Programs   226

Post-Divorce Custody and Visitation Disputes   230
  Disputes About Custody   230
  Disputes About Visitation   231
  Relocation Disputes   232
    Virtual Visitation   233

The Custodial and Visitation Rights of Grandparents and Stepparents   236
  Grandparents   236
  Stepparents   240

Chapter Summary   241

Key Terms   242

Review Questions   242

Discussion Questions   243

Assignments   244

Cases for Analysis   245
  Mary Ann P. v. William R.P., Jr.   246
  Danti v. Danti   250
  Miller v. Miller   258

Endnotes   264

Chapter 6   Child Support   **269**

Historical Overview   270

Administrative Framework for the Establishment and Enforcement of Child
    Support Orders   271
    The Federal Office of Child Support Enforcement   271
    At the State Level: The IV-D Agency   271
    Eligibility for IV-D Services   272
    Locating Absent Parents   273

Child Support Guidelines   274
    Guideline Formulas   275
        Percentage of Income   275
        Income Shares   275
        The Melson Formula   276
    Determining What Income Is Subject to the Child Support Obligation   276
        Defining Income   276
        Setting the Income Base   277
    Consideration of Specific Factors   278
        Income of the Custodial Parent   279
        Income of a New Partner   279
        Income/Resources of the Child   279
        Multiple Families   279
        Extraordinary Expenses   280
        Health Insurance   281
        Custody and Visitation Arrangements   282
    Financial Disclosure   283

Enforcing the Child Support Obligation   290
    Support Enforcement at the State Level   290
        Income Withholding   290
        Liens   291
        Credit Reporting   292
        Licenses   292
        The Federal Offset Program   292
        Federal Tax Offset   292
        The Passport Denial Program   293
    Interstate Cases   293
        The Uniform Interstate Family Support Act   294
        The Full Faith and Credit for Child Support Order Act 295
    Enforcement Under State Law Procedures   295
        Criminal Nonsupport   296
        Contempt   296
    Enforcement by Private Child Support Collection Agencies   298
    Modification and Adjustment of Support Awards   299
    Modification Based on Changed Circumstances   299
    The Review and Adjustment Procedure   300

Duration of the Parental Support Obligation   300
  Termination of Support Prior to Majority   300
    Emancipation   301
    Parental Death   301
    Adoption/Termination of Parental Rights   302
  Extension of Support Beyond Majority   302
    The Adult Student   302
    Mental and Physical Disabilities   304
Tax Implications of Child Support Awards   304
Chapter Summary   305
Key Terms   306
Review Questions   306
Discussion Questions   308
Assignments   309
Cases for Analysis   310
  McLeod v. Starnes   310
  Colonna v. Colonna   313
  Yerkes v. Yerkes   317
Endnotes   322

Chapter 7   Spousal Support   **327**
Historical Overview   327
  English Roots: Alimony and Fault   327
  Alimony on the Eve of the No-Fault Reform Era   328
Impact of No-Fault Reform   329
  Property Division as the Primary Distributive Event   329
  Shifting the Focus from Moral to Economic Considerations   330
  Degendering the Support Obligation   330
  Shifting from an Assumption of Female Economic Dependence to an
    Assumption of Economic Self-Sufficiency   330
  Critique of the "Clean Break" Approach   331
Support Determinations   333
  Factors to Be Considered   333
  Searching for Greater Certainty: Alimony Guidelines and the American
    Law Institute's Compensatory Principle   335
    Spousal Support Guidelines   336
    ALI's Compensatory Principle   337
  Different Approaches to Structuring Spousal Support   337
    Permanent Alimony   338
    Lump-Sum Support   339
    Rehabilitative Support   340
    The Backlash Against "Permanent" Spousal Support Awards   341

The Professional Degree Cases   342
   The Degree as Property   342
   Spousal Support Options   343
Medical Insurance   344
Post-Divorce Modification and Termination of Support   345
  The General Concept   345
  Modifiability and Termination of "Permanent" Support   346
   Remarriage   346
   Cohabitation   347
   Change in Financial Circumstances   347
  Modifiability of Specific Types of Support   348
   Lump-Sum Support   348
   Rehabilitative Support   348
   Reimbursement Alimony   349
  Agreement of the Parties to Prohibit Modification   349
Enforcement of Support Awards   349
  Contempt   349
  Other Enforcement Measures   350
Bankruptcy and the Support Obligation   350
Tax Consequences   351
Chapter Summary   351
Key Terms   352
Review Questions   353
Discussion Questions   354
Assignments   354
Cases for Analysis   356
  In re Marriage of Line Nang Baccam   356
  S.M.C. v. W.P.C.   360
  Loutts v. Loutts   363
Endnotes   368

Chapter 8   Division of Marital Property   **371**
Historic Overview of the Two Marital Property Systems   371
  The Common Law Approach   372
  The Community Property Approach   372
The Two Marital Property Systems Today   373
The Property Distribution Process   375
  Defining Property   376
   The Tangible/Intangible Distinction   376
   Divorce and the Family Pet   377
   Unvested Pensions, Accrued Leave Time, and Professional
    Goodwill: Are They Property?   380
   And What About the Virtual World?   383

Classification of Property   384
  Defining Marital and Separate Property   384
  The Significance of Timing   385
  Looking Beyond Definitions: The Complexities of Classification   387
  Transmutation   391
Valuation   392
  Valuation Methods   392
  The Role of Experts   393
  Time of Valuation   393
Distribution   394
  The Standard for Division: Equal or Equitable?   394
  Consideration of Specific Factors   395
  Effectuating the Distribution   396
Tax Consequences of a Property Distribution   399
Chapter Summary   400
Key Terms   401
Review Questions   401
Discussion Questions   403
Assignments   404
Cases for Analysis   405
  Olesberg v. Olesberg   405
  Schmitz v. Schmitz   409
  Castle v. Castle   412
Endnotes   418

Chapter 9   Jurisdiction   **421**
Overview of Subject Matter and Personal Jurisdiction   421
  Subject Matter Jurisdiction   421
  Personal Jurisdiction   422
Jurisdiction and the Divorce Action   423
  Does the Court Have Jurisdiction to Dissolve the Marriage?   423
  Does the Court Have Jurisdiction to Award Support?   424
  Does the Court Have Jurisdiction to Divide Property?   425
  Does the Court Have Jurisdiction to Determine Custody?   426
    Jurisdictional Requirements Under the UCCJA and the UCCJEA   427
    Initial Custody Determinations   427
    Modification Jurisdiction   429
    Declining Jurisdiction   430
    Jurisdictional Requirements of PKPA   431
International Child Abduction   431
Chapter Summary   433
Key Terms   434

Review Questions	434
Discussion Questions	435
Assignments	435
Cases for Analysis	436
Goodin v. Department of Human Services	436
Seekins v. Hamm	438
Endnotes	442
Chapter 10 The Divorce Process	**445**
The Initial Client Interview	445
The Emotional Context	446
Conducting the Client Interview	447
The Role of the Paralegal	447
Ethical Considerations	447
The Ethical Framework	448
Specific Practices	448
Developing Good Listening Skills	450
The Interview Itself: A Three-Stage Approach	452
The Divorce Action: Initial Steps and Discovery	457
The Initial Steps	457
The Complaint	457
Filing the Complaint	461
Service of Process	463
The Defendant's Response	468
The Component Parts of an Answer	472
Admissions/Denials	472
Affirmative Defenses	472
Counterclaims	472
Discovery	476
General Purpose	476
Scope of Discovery	476
Discovery Methods	477
Discovery Difficulties	486
The Middle Phase: Moving Toward Resolution or Trial	487
Motions for Temporary Relief	488
Overview of Motion Practice	488
Specific Divorce Motions	490
Sample Motion and Supporting Affidavit	493
The Role of the Paralegal	493
Alternative Approaches to Dispute Resolution	496
Negotiation	496
Mediation	498
Arbitration	503

The Collaborative Divorce Approach   504
Unbundled Legal Services   506
Reaching Resolution: The Separation Agreement   508
Drafting the Agreement   508
The Role of the Paralegal   509
Sample Separation Agreement and Comments   509

The Divorce Hearing   526
The Uncontested Case   526
Dissolving the Marriage   527
Approving the Separation Agreement   527
The Contested Case   528
The Pretrial Conference   528
The Trial   529
Trial Preparation and the Role of the Paralegal   529

Post-Divorce Proceedings   530
Post-Trial Motions   530
Motion for a New Trial   530
Motion for Relief from Judgment   530
Appeals   531
Overview of Appellate Practice   531
Appellate Procedure   532
The Role of the Paralegal   532
The Complaint for Modification   533
The Complaint for Contempt   536

Chapter Summary   540

Key Terms   541

Review Questions   542

Discussion Questions   544

Assignments   544

Endnotes   547

Chapter 11   Determining Parentage   **551**

The Emerging Legal Status of Children of Unmarried (Heterosexual) Parents 552
Common Law Status: A Child of No One   552
Early American Reform Efforts   552
The Roots of Reform   552
Creating Limited Family Rights   553
Legitimation   553
The End of Legal Innovation   554
Constitutional Developments   554
The Equal Protection Challenge to Differential Treatment   554
The Legal Status of the Unwed Father   555

Establishing Paternity   560
   The Adjudication of Paternity   561
   Voluntary Acknowledgment of Paternity   566
   Following the Determination of Paternity   568
Paternity Disestablishment   569
   Considering Best Interest: Conflicting Approaches   571
   What Makes a Man a Father?   571
Determining Paternity When the Genetic "Father" Is a Sperm Donor   572
   Donor Insemination and the Heterosexual Couple   572
   Donor Insemination and the Single Woman   574
Same-Sex Couples and the Establishment of Legal Parenthood   576
   The "Other" Mother: The Traditional Legal Approach   576
   The Extension of Parental Rights Based on Marriage and Consent   577
   De Facto Parental Status   579

Chapter Summary   581

Key Terms   582

Review Questions   582

Discussion Questions   583

Assignments   584

Cases for Analysis   584
   In re the Paternity of A.R.R.   585
   Paternity of Cheryl   591
   McLaughlin v. Jones   595

Endnotes   599

Chapter 12 Child Abuse and Neglect   **603**

Historical Overview   604
   The Colonial Period   604
   The Emergence of the Privatized Family   605
   Child Rescue: Preventing Cruelty to Children   605
      The Rescue of Mary Ellen   605
      The Emergence of Societies for the Prevention of Cruelty to Children   606
      The Rediscovery of Child Abuse and the Initial Legislative Response   607
The Child Protective System   608
   Defining Abuse and Neglect   608
      Physical Abuse   608
      Sexual Abuse   609
      Emotional Abuse and Neglect   610
      Neglect   610
      Medical Child Abuse   613
      Forced Child Marriage   613
      Drug Use by Pregnant Women   614

The Reporting of Suspected Abuse or Neglect   615
Screening and Investigation   616
Substantiated Cases: Federal Law and the "Reasonable Efforts"
   Requirement   617
   Reasonable Efforts Prior to Removal   618
Removal of a Child   619
   The Dependency Proceeding   619
   Permanency Planning   620
   Legal Orphans and the Reinstatement of Parental Rights   621
The Federal Statutory Framework: The Indian Child Welfare Act (ICWA)   622
Chapter Summary   623
Key Terms   624
Review Questions   624
Discussion Questions   625
Assignments   626
Cases for Analysis   627
   Tennessee Department of Children's Services v. Tikindra G. 627
   In the Interest of A.W.   633
Endnotes   638

Chapter 13 Adoption   **643**
Historical Overview   643
Approaches to Adoption   645
   Agency Adoptions   646
   Independent Adoptions   646
   Safe Haven Laws   648
The Adoption Process   649
   Adoption Based on Parental Consent or Relinquishment   649
      Parental Consent to a Private Placement Adoption 650
      Relinquishment to an Agency   650
      What If a Parent Changes His or Her Mind? 651
   Adoption Based on the Involuntary Termination of Parental Rights 652
   The Adoption Placement   653
      The Home Study   653
      Configuration of Relationships During the Placement 654
      The Social Study   655
   The Adoption   655
      Judicial Review and Approval   655
Lifting the Shroud of Secrecy: Post-Adoption Contact
   and Access to Records   656
   Open Adoption   657
   Access to Adoption Records   658

Adoption in Specific Situations   659
    Stepparent Adoptions   659
    Adoption by Gay Men and Lesbians   660
    Single-Parent and Joint Adoptions   661
    Co-Parent Adoption   661
    Unwed Fathers   662
    Transracial Adoption   669
Adoption Abrogation and the Tort of Wrongful Adoption   672
Chapter Summary   673
Key Terms   674
Review Questions   674
Discussion Questions   676
Assignments   677
Cases for Analysis   678
    Alma Society, Inc. v. Mellon   678
    In re Adoption of A.M.H.   682
    In re the Termination of Parental Rights to ARW   689
Endnotes   693

Glossary   697
Index   713

Preface

Welcome to the study of family law. This book is intended to provide you with a thorough working knowledge of this exciting area of the law. Along with its in-depth topical coverage, the book also addresses the important skills that a family law paralegal is likely to need in an active law office, such as client interviewing and legal drafting. However, in my view, it is not enough for a textbook simply to cover the topics and skills that a student will need in order to work effectively in a law office. Extending beyond that, a fundamental premise of this book is that paralegals are an integral part of the legal community and are entitled to a voice in the ongoing policy debates over contemporary efforts to reconfigure the legal contours of traditional family relationships. To help you enter into these discussions in an informed and engaged way, this book looks at both the historic understandings of the family and the critical legal issues facing us today regarding the future direction and definition of the family. This coverage will deepen your understanding of contemporary family law issues and enable you to consider emerging issues in a thoughtful way.

This book is divided into 13 chapters, each of which follows the same basic format. Most chapters begin with a brief historical overview of the subject matter of that chapter. By grounding your knowledge of the present in the past, you will have a more complete understanding of how the law has developed, which, in turn, will enhance your understanding of contemporary legal issues. In the text of each chapter, key terms are bolded. These terms are listed at the end of the chapter and defined in a glossary at the end of the book. At the end of the chapters, you will also find a chapter summary, review questions, discussion questions, assignments, and cases for analysis. The chapter summary provides you with a quick overview of what was covered in the chapter; it is not intended to be a substitute for the chapter content. To help orient yourself, you may find it helpful to read the summary before you read the chapter. The review questions follow the order of the chapter and are designed to help you determine how well you understood the chapter. They are a useful self-testing device. The discussion questions frame some of the more controversial and less settled aspects of the law discussed in the chapter. The assignments are designed to help you apply and further develop your understanding of the law. Last, each chapter (with the exception of Chapter 10) includes cases for analysis. These cases point to interesting and sometimes controversial aspects of the law. They are included to deepen your knowledge of the law, acquaint you with landmark decisions, and help you to develop your analytical and critical reading skills. Please note that cases have been edited for clarity and brevity. To this end, most internal citations have also been deleted.

Visit the product page at WKLegaledu.com for *Family Law for Paralegals* for additional resources for students and instructors.

In using this book, you should keep a few important points in mind. First, although every effort has been made to ensure that this book is current, the law is always changing, and that which is current today may be obsolete tomorrow based on a new court decision or statute. Second, this book is written for a national audience and is not geared to the law of any particular state. In the course of your studies, you may want to learn more about the law of your state. Third, although I hope that this book will continue to be a resource for you when you leave school, it should be clear from the above two points that when working on an actual case, this book should not be your primary source of legal information. No book can substitute for the legal research required to ensure a current and comprehensive understanding of the applicable law in your jurisdiction. Good luck, and I hope you enjoy your entry into this fascinating area of the law.

July 2019   *J. Shoshanna Ehrlich*

Acknowledgments

This book has benefited greatly from the contribution of many wonderful people who have given generously of both their time and their expertise. And although I certainly hope that this book is free of errors, if any do exist, I take full responsibility for them.

First, I would like to acknowledge the contribution of my students at the University of Massachusetts Boston. You keep me on my toes and encourage me to keep growing as a teacher and a writer. I cannot imagine being part of a more inspiring community of learners.

I would specifically like to thank the generation of students—from UMass Boston and elsewhere—who have enriched this book with their outstanding research assistance. They include: Janice Babcock, Stephanie Bonvissuto, Hui Chen, Abigail Dickson, Alexi Ehrlich, Kayla Getchell, Vicki Kelleher, Barry Kilroy, Jolie Main, John Martin, Andrea Martinez, Sarah Mcdougall, Darryl Palmer, Veronica Santos Puim, Sabah Uddin, Lizzy Wolozin, and Frank Woods. It has truly been a pleasure to work with all of you.

I would also like to extend a special thanks to David Kelly, who worked tirelessly on the first three editions of this book. Through this close collaboration, David has been a constant source of both wisdom and encouragement.

Many of my former colleagues at UMass Boston's College of Public and Community Service have contributed to the development of this book. In particular, I would like to thank Sarah Bartlett, Brad Honoroff, David Matz, Terry McLarney, David Rubin, and Ann Withorn. I would also like to recognize the ongoing support, encouragement, and friendship of my current colleagues in the Women's, Gender, and Sexuality Studies Department at UMass Boston. It is a joy to be part of such a supportive and enriching academic community.

Thanks also to the following individuals who have helped to shape this book through their careful review of various chapters in its early stages: Jacquelynne Bowman, Lynne Dahlborg, Janet L. Dolgin, Frederick M. Ehrlich, Judith Lennett, Jennifer Levi, Mary E. O'Connell, Paula Roberts, Alan Stoskopf, Stephen N. Subrin, and Joan Zora. This book has been improved immeasurably by the contribution of their expertise. I also want to extend special thanks to Jamie Ann Sabino, who has contributed more than she realizes to this book.

On a more personal note, a number of special people in my life deserve mention. To my husband, Alan Stoskopf, and my daughter, Emma Stoskopf-Ehrlich, thank you for your love and support throughout the years. I could not ask for more—you are my center. To my father, Fred Ehrlich, thank you for being there; and to the memory of my mother, who loved the written word. Thank you also to my siblings and dear friends for being such an important part of my life.

I would also like to thank Betsy Kenny of Aspen Publishers for her work on this book. Betsy has been there from the first edition, and this book has greatly benefited from her contribution. I would also like to thank the editorial team for all of their hard work in bringing this book to fruition, including Mary Sanger, Sarah Hains, and Renee Cote.

Chapter One

Marriage and Cohabitation

When people think about marriage, they usually think of it as a private, intimate relationship shaped by the love, commitment, and needs of two individuals. However, this understanding of marriage as an essentially private relationship fails to account for the fact that the state also has an interest in marriage—an interest that is grounded in the belief that the exclusivity, permanence, and procreative potential of the marital bond promotes social cohesion and stability. To promote this interest, states traditionally have exercised considerable control over marriage, and as an important corollary, have traditionally denied legal recognition to unmarried couples in order to buttress the privileged status of marriage.

Although the modern trend has been away from state control over marriage in favor of greater individual autonomy, state laws continue to structure the relationship. They determine who is eligible to marry, what the rights, entitlements, and obligations of spouses are during the marriage, and what their continuing responsibilities are toward one other should the marriage fail. In short, marriage is a legally transformative act. For example, upon marriage:

- each partner becomes formally connected to the family of the other. One literally acquires a "family-in-law." Mirror relationships are created such that the mother of one spouse becomes the mother-in-law of the other.
- spouses acquire the right to a wide range of entitlements, such as Social Security and workers' compensation benefits, health insurance coverage, beneficial immigration status, and statutory rights of inheritance.
- spouses acquire a mutual duty to support one another. Historically, this obligation was imposed only upon husbands, but this obligation is no longer gender-linked.

Moreover, as we will see in Chapter 4, if a marriage ends, state laws provide a structured framework within which competing claims to support and property can be resolved. Although one does not usually think of divorce as a "benefit" that comes with marriage, it is important to recognize that divorce provides married couples with a structured dissolution process that is not available to unmarried couples.

Reflecting the continued privileged nature of the marital relationship, the law draws a clear line between married couples and cohabiting ones. However, since, as discussed in this chapter, marriage equality has become the law of the land, this distinction has lost some of its practical significance as same-sex couples now enjoy the same right that heterosexual couples have long enjoyed — namely, the option of deciding whether or not they wish to formalize their relationship through marriage. Nonetheless, given that many couples do choose to live together rather than marry, it remains important to understand the key legal distinctions between these relationships; accordingly, we take up the subject of cohabitation at the end of this chapter.

Marriage: Regulating the Relationship

The modern legal approach to marriage is to permit spouses to shape the contours of their own relationship, but this is a fairly recent development. Historically, the law carefully defined the mutual rights and obligations of husbands and wives based upon highly gendered notions of appropriate marital conduct.

Common Law Origins

Our original marriage laws were based upon English **common law**.[1] As eloquently expressed by William Blackstone, a famed English legal commentator, a defining aspect of this tradition was the legal subordination of married women:

> By marriage, the husband and wife are one person in law; that is, the very being or legal existence of the woman is suspended during the marriage, or at least is incorporated and consolidated into that of the husband; under whose wing, protection, and *cover*, she performs everything. . . . Upon this principle, of a union of person in husband and wife, depend almost all the legal rights, duties, and disabilities, that either one of them acquire by the marriage.[2]

It is worth noting that this doctrine of **marital unity** by which a husband and wife are regarded as a single legal person bears a striking similarity to the biblical concept of the unity of the flesh.

Outwardly manifested by the requirement that she take her husband's last name as her own, marriage altered a woman's legal status; rights that she possessed as a single woman were transferred to her husband in exchange for his support and protection. Upon marriage, a woman lost the right to own **personal property**, property she owned at the time of marriage or subsequently acquired became her husband's. As owner, he could sell, destroy, or bequeath it, just as he could his separately acquired property. This property could also be taken by a husband's creditors in order to satisfy his debts. In short, as her person merged into her husband's so too did her property merge into his. **Real property**—land and whatever is grown on or fixed to it—was treated differently, as title did not pass to the husband. The husband did, however, acquire the exclusive right to manage and control the realty together with the right to all rents and profits derived from it. Although the nominal owner, a married woman could not convey her realty without the consent of her husband.

A married woman was regarded as unable to think for herself and thus lacked authority to act as an autonomous legal person. As a result, she lost the right to perform a variety of legal functions. Any **contracts** that she entered into were null and void. She also lost her **testamentary capacity**—the ability to make a will—and any wills she had made prior to marriage were automatically revoked. She could not sue or be sued in her own name. As the owner of her legal claims, her husband had to be joined as a party and was entitled to collect any damages.

Of profound consequence, a married woman also lost the right to her own labor. A husband acquired the right to his wife's services both at home and as performed for third parties. Because her labor belonged to him, he acquired an interest in the fruits of her labor, and monies paid to her for services she rendered became his. A husband's right to his wife's labor was characterized as a property interest. If his wife was injured by a third party, the husband was considered a victim in his own right and could sue for the loss of his wife's ability to perform her marital responsibilities. Damages frequently included compensation for the loss of her companionship, including sexual companionship, and her domestic services. Married women had no corresponding rights to their husband's services. As explained by Blackstone: "[T]he inferior hath no kind of property in the company, care, or assistance of the superior, as the superior is held to have in those of the inferior."[3] In exchange for the loss of her legal persona, a married woman was entitled to be supported by her husband, and he became responsible for her debts, including those she came into the marriage with. This exchange of services for support lay at the heart of the common law marital relationship, and this core feature of marriage survived well into the twentieth century, long after other common law marital requirements had been replaced by more modern rules.

Charged with this support duty, the husband was unquestionably considered the legal head of household with the right to make all major family decisions. Of particular significance was his unilateral right to decide where the family should live. A wife was required to follow her husband wherever he chose to go unless his choice was clearly unreasonable or intended as a punishment.

The Civil Law Tradition

Eight states did not follow this English common law model. These states, known as **community property** or civil law states, are Arizona, California, Idaho, Louisiana, Nevada, New Mexico, Texas, and Washington. Based upon patterns of colonization and territorial acquisitions, these states were influenced by Spanish civil law and, in the case of Louisiana, by Spanish and French law.

At least in theory, the status of married women was different in these states. Here, a wife's legal identity did not merge into her husband's. Instead, each spouse retained his or her separate identity, and marriage was viewed as a partnership. Subject to limited exceptions, property acquired during marriage was considered community property and belonged to both partners. However, the marital partners were not regarded as equals. A husband was given complete authority over the community property, including his wife's earnings; he could spend community assets freely, potentially leaving his wife with nothing to show for her contribution. Thus, in terms of her daily reality, the difference for a married woman between the common law and the civil law approaches would not have been as great as the doctrinal distinctions suggest.

Married Women's Property Acts

Beginning in the late 1830s, states began passing laws known as the **Married Women's Property Acts**, which led to a gradual improvement in the legal status of married women.[4] Interestingly, the first such Acts were enacted in the South and appear to have been motivated by economic concerns, rather than by a desire to emancipate married women. Prompted by the economic panic of 1837, in which many southern plantation owners faced bankruptcy and loss of property—including slaves—to their creditors, legislators passed laws giving married women rights of ownership over their own property, which served to protect it from being seized by their husbands' creditors. Husbands, however, retained their common law right of management and control over their wives' property.

In other regions of the country, most notably the northeast, the passage of these Acts responded more directly to concerns being voiced by the newly emerging women's rights movement about the legal subordination of married women. Although individual women had spoken out previously, 1848 marks the birth of the organized women's movement. That was the year women and men came together at Seneca Falls, New York, for the first women's rights convention in this country.

Although winning the right for women to vote soon became their focus, the reformers also sought legal equality for women within the domestic sphere. They attacked marriage laws as an abuse of male power, which relegated women to the status of children. As stated by Elizabeth Cady Stanton, an outspoken leader of the movement:

> . . . A man marrying gives up no right, but, a woman, every right, even the most sacred of all, the right to her own person. . . . So long as our present false marriage relation continues, which in most cases is nothing more or less than legalized prostitution, women can have no self respect. . . . Personal freedom is the first right to be proclaimed, and that does not and cannot now belong to the relation of wife. . . .[5]

Reformers demanded: "(1) full control over their property with the powers to contract, will, and sue regarding it; (2) the right to their own wages; (3) recognition of the wife's joint right to the earnings of the co-partnership; and (4) equal guardianship of their children."[6] Striking at the heart of the traditional marital relationship and the husband's privileged position within the home, these demands were seen as radical and were often greeted with scorn and apprehension that women were seeking to rule their husbands.

However, over the last half of the nineteenth century, states responded to these demands in halting fashion. Bit by bit, laws were passed extending property rights to married women and lifting many of the common law disabilities, although no state, with the exception of Maine, gave married women full control over their property. By the turn of the twentieth century, married women had many more rights than they had previously possessed, and in some states, they could own property, enter into contracts, and sue and be sued in their own name. Some states also passed "earnings" laws, giving a married woman a property right in the labor she performed outside the domestic realm, thus entitling her, rather than her husband, to the earnings. Despite these reforms, in no state were married women considered the legal equals of married men. Significantly, despite the passage of the earnings statutes, husbands still had a property right in their wives' domestic services,[7] and they remained firmly ensconced as the legal head of the household. Thus, the essential nature of the marital relationship remained unaltered by these Acts; the reformers' vision of true legal equality between husband and wife remained but a distant dream.

The Move to Legal Equality

As discussed in the previous section, historically our marriage laws reflect a highly gendered vision of the marital relationship. Rights and responsibilities were assigned based on deeply held beliefs about the proper role of women and their subordinate status. Although these underlying beliefs were challenged in the nineteenth century, leading to some legal reforms, the defining exchange of services for support continued to structure the marital relationship.

So powerful was this vision of woman as homemaker and man as provider that couples were unable to legally redistribute their roles through private, consensual agreements. By way of illustration, in 1940, a federal district court in Michigan refused to uphold an agreement between a husband and wife in which the husband agreed to quit his job and follow his wife in her travels in exchange for a monthly sum of money:

> As a result of the marriage contract . . . the husband has a duty to support and to live with his wife and the wife must contribute her services and society to the husband and follow him in his choice of domicile. The law is well settled that a private agreement between persons married or about to be married which attempts to change the essential obligations of the marriage contract as defined by the law is contrary to public policy and unenforceable.
>
> Even in the states with the most liberal emancipation statutes . . . the law has not gone to the extent of permitting husbands and wives by agreement to change the essential incidents of the marriage contract.[8]

Beginning in the late 1960s, this gendered approach to marriage was again challenged. With the emergence of the second women's rights movement, women again began to fight against laws that limited their rights based on fixed notions of appropriate female behavior. Reformers sought to eliminate all remaining common law marital restrictions, including laws that required a woman to take her husband's last name and to follow him in his choice of domicile, and that limited a married woman's right to freely dispose of her property or carry on a trade. Additionally, as married women assumed a greater role in the workplace, reformers challenged the still powerful exchange of support for services requirement, arguing that it confined women to the home and fostered economic dependency.

Gradually, courts began striking down most of the remaining gender-specific marital laws. Based mainly on the **equal protection clause** of the fourteenth amendment to the Constitution, courts held that it was improper for states to assign rights and responsibilities based on fixed assumptions about the proper roles of men and women. Illustrative of this approach, in 1979, the United States Supreme Court invalidated Alabama's alimony law because it only imposed a support obligation on men:

> [T]he "old notion" that "generally it is the man's primary responsibility to provide a home and its essentials," can no longer justify a statute that discriminates on the basis of gender. "No longer is the female destined solely for the home and the rearing of a family, and only the male for the marketplace and world of ideas. . . ."
>
> Legislative classifications which distribute benefits and burdens on the basis of gender carry the inherent risk of reinforcing stereotypes about the "proper place" of women and their need for special protection. Whereas here, the State's . . . purposes are well-served by a gender-neutral classification . . . the State cannot be permitted to classify on the basis of sex.[9]

In reviewing these marital laws that fixed the rights and obligations of spouses based on gender, courts were also influenced by the Supreme Court's decision in Griswold v. Connecticut. This 1965 case, which struck down a Connecticut statute prohibiting the use of contraceptives by married couples, enunciated a broad right of marital privacy.[10] Drawing on this right of privacy, courts limited the authority of states to structure the terms of the marital relationship. This was now regarded as a matter to be determined by individual spouses based on their own needs and desires.

Today, marriage is no longer considered a status relationship where marital roles are assigned by law without regard for individual choice, and the law no longer assigns married women a subordinate role. Legally, marriage now more closely resembles a contractual relationship in which rights and obligations are chosen according to the needs and desires of the particular couple. Of course, legal or formal equality does not necessarily result in actual equality, and many still view marriage as an institution that has not escaped the legacy of a highly gendered past.

Entrance into Marriage: Choosing a Spouse

Although state laws no longer define marital rights and obligations based upon assumptions regarding the proper role of men and women, the law still plays a role in shaping our understanding of marriage by imposing certain restrictions on an individual's choice of marital partner. Some of the most common restrictive laws, such as those that ban marriage between relatives or impose a "one-spouse-at-a-time" requirement, have stood the test of time based on the view that they serve important state interests. However, other state limitations, specifically those that prohibited interracial marriage and those banning same-sex partners from marrying, have been struck down by the Supreme Court.

We begin this section by looking at the Supreme Court's landmark 1967 Loving v. Virginia decision[11] invalidating Virginia's anti-miscegenation law on both due process and equal protection grounds. From there, we look at the struggle of same-sex couples for marriage equality, which ultimately culminated in the Court's landmark 2015 Obergefell v. Hodges decision.[12] We then turn our attention to the most common marriage restriction laws that remain in effect today.

Loving v. Virginia

In 1967, the United States Supreme Court, in the case of Loving v. Virginia,[13] struck down Virginia's anti-miscegenation law, which prohibited interracial marriage between white and "colored" persons. Reflective of their racist origins, anti-miscegenation laws date back to the time of slavery and were once in effect in a majority of states. When *Loving* was decided, Virginia was one of 16 states that still prohibited interracial marriage. Virginia's law was challenged by a couple who had been convicted of violating the ban on interracial marriage. They were given a one-year jail sentence, which was suspended on the condition that they leave Virginia and not return for 25 years.

On appeal, Virginia's highest court upheld the Lovings' conviction, concluding that the law was a valid exercise of state authority over marriage, and that Virginia could legitimately seek to "preserve the racial integrity of its citizens" and prevent "the corruption of blood" and a "mongrel breed of citizens."[14] The Supreme Court disagreed. Focusing on the racial hatred that had motivated passage of anti-miscegenation laws, the Court held that Virginia had violated the equal protection clause of the fourteenth amendment by restricting an individual's choice of marriage partner based on racial classifications.

The *Loving* Court also held that, under the **due process clause** of the fourteenth amendment, marriage is a *fundamental right*. Accordingly, it made clear that "the freedom of choice to marry [may] not be restricted by invidious race discrimination. Under the Constitution, the freedom to marry, or not marry a person of another race resides with the individual and cannot be infringed by the State."[15] Given this tight link between the freedom to marry and invidious *race* discrimination, which the Court stressed was "subversive of the principle of equality at the heart of the

Fourteenth Amendment," commentators subsequently wondered if the protected right to choose one's marital partner would extend to other situations or instead be limited to race-based marriage bans.

In a series of rulings, the Court subsequently made clear that, although the right to marry is not absolute, the fundamental right to choose one's marital partner extends beyond the matter of race. For example, in the 1987 case of Turner v. Satley, the Court invalidated a Missouri law prohibiting inmates from marrying, subject to limited exceptions such as in the case of pregnancy or the birth of a child, on the grounds that the state's interest in rehabilitation and security did not justify divesting prisoners of the fundamental freedom to enter into marriage with a person of their choosing.[16]

Marital Rights of Same-Sex Partners

Gay men and lesbians have been fighting for the right to marry since at least the early 1970s, when a number of same-sex couples who sought and were denied marriage licenses brought lawsuits in state courts challenging the fairness of restricting marriage to heterosexual couples. Citing *Loving*, they argued that this restriction was discriminatory and impermissibly interfered with their fundamental right to marry a person of their own choosing. In short, as in *Loving*, they argued that the denial of a marriage license violated their rights to equal protection and due process of the law under the applicable state constitutions.

In this early round of cases, courts did not take these assertions seriously. They consistently concluded that the fundamental right to choose one's marital partner does not extend to same-sex partners because marriage has always been between a man and a woman, thus placing same-sex partners outside the reach of the due process clause. The courts similarly concluded that because same-sex couples are critically different from male-female couples, particularly with respect to procreative potential, denying same-sex couples marital rights did not violate the equal protection clause because this clause only requires like treatment of persons who are similarly situated. Courts also made clear that a number of important state interests—such as encouraging procreation and protecting the traditional family—were of sufficient magnitude to offset any potential limitation of rights. Rejecting the *Loving* analogy, courts refused to consider the possibility that the exclusion was based on anything other than legitimate differences, such as bias against gay men and lesbians.[17]

Following these defeats, gay rights activists turned to other approaches, such as domestic partnership initiatives (discussed below), to obtain recognition of their relationships and access to family benefits. Some also hoped that a more gradualist approach would lead to a greater acceptance of gay couples, which in turn would eliminate social hostility to the idea of same-sex marriage.

The Renewed Struggle for Marriage Equality

In the late 1980s, prompted in part by the AIDS epidemic and bolstered by gains in civil rights protections for gay men and lesbians, activists again began to focus on securing equal marriage rights. This time, based on challenges brought by couples in Hawaii and Alaska, it looked as if the courts were poised to extend marital rights to same-sex couples. However, while the cases were winding their way through the legal system, marriage-rights opponents waged successful campaigns to amend their respective state constitutions to define marriage as being between one man and one woman, thus effectively bringing the court challenges to an end.[18]

The Backlash: The Campaign to Preserve Marriage as a Heterosexual Institution

When it looked as if marriage equality might become a reality in Hawaii and Alaska, opponents launched a fierce campaign to formally encode the traditional meaning of marriage as an exclusive relationship between a man and a woman into law at both the state and federal levels. At the federal level, in 1996, Congress, fearing the potential spread of marital rights for gay and lesbian couples from the shores of Hawaii to the mainland, enacted the Defense of Marriage Act (DOMA).[19] DOMA included two distinct sections. One section of the Act authorized states to withhold recognition from same-sex marriages that were celebrated in states where they were permitted. The other section declared that for purposes of federal law, marriage was to be strictly defined as a legal union between one man and one woman.

Following the lead of the federal government, a majority of states enacted laws or amended their constitutions to define marriage as exclusively being between a man and a woman. Frequently referred to as "mini-DOMAs," these measures, in addition to banning marriage between same-sex partners, also generally withheld recognition from marriages that were validly entered into in a sister state that permitted these unions.

Marriage Equality in the States

In 2003, in the groundbreaking case of Goodridge v. Department of Public Health, the Massachusetts Supreme Judicial Court ruled that same-sex couples have a constitutional right to marry.[20] Refusing to disaggregate the tangible benefits of marriage from its symbolic value, the Court focused on the profound importance of the marital relationship, stating:

> Without question, civil marriage enhances the "welfare of the community." It is a "social institution of the highest importance." Civil marriage anchors society by encouraging stable relations over transient ones. . . .
>
> Marriage also bestows enormous private and social advantages on those who choose to marry. Civil marriage is at once a deeply personal commitment to another human being and a highly public celebration of the ideals of mutuality, companionship, fidelity, and family. . . . Because it fulfills yearnings for security, safe haven, and connection that express our common humanity, civil marriage is an esteemed institution, and the decision whether and whom to marry is among life's momentous acts of self-definition.[21]

In deciding for the plaintiffs, the court rejected the state's assertion that the marriage ban was necessary to ensure a favorable setting for procreation and child rearing, concluding that there is no reasonable connection between protecting the welfare of children and barring same-sex couples from marrying. The court also rejected the state's argument that allowing same-sex partners to marry would trivialize or destroy "the institution of marriage as it has historically been fashioned" stating instead that "[i]f anything, extending civil marriage to same-sex couples reinforces the importance of marriage to individuals and communities . . . (and) is a testament to the enduring place of marriage in our laws and in the human spirit."[22] In order to remedy the discrimination, the court concluded that the common law definition of marriage should be modified to mean "the voluntary union of two persons, as spouses, to the exclusion of all others," thus making Massachusetts the first state in the nation to permit same-sex couples to marry.[23]

Making it clear that Massachusetts was not an outlier, in less than a decade after the *Goodridge* decision was handed down, marriage equality had become a reality in eight states as well as in the District of Columbia. In some jurisdictions, this was similarly accomplished by a ruling from the state's highest court, while in others it was accomplished by way of a legislative enactment or voter-approved ballot initiatives.

Marriage Equality: The Law of the Land

In 2013, in the case of United States v. Windsor,[24] the Supreme Court invalidated the section of DOMA that defined marriage for purposes of federal law as being exclusively between a man and a woman. As the basis of its decision, the Court concluded that the denial of federal recognition to relationships that states had "deemed . . . worthy of dignity in the community equal with all other marriages" in accordance with "evolving understandings of the meaning of equality," injured the very group of people they were seeking to protect by placing "same-sex couples in an unstable position of being in a second-tier marriage."[25] The Court made clear that this differentiation was demeaning to same-sex couples and humiliating to their children by making it "more difficult for them to understand the integrity and closeness of their own family and its concord with other families in their community and in their daily lives."[26]

Although *Windsor* did not speak directly to the constitutionality of state marriage bans, the decision nonetheless accelerated the pace of change as state and federal courts relied upon its powerful language to strike down state marriage bans. Thus, for example, in concluding that "Virginia's same-sex marriage bans impermissibly infringe on its citizens fundamental right to marry," the federal appeals court relied on *Windsor* for the proposition that laws that evince "disrespect for the 'moral and sexual choices' that accompany a same-sex couple's decision to marry" are constitutionally infirm.[27] In a similar vein, in striking down that state's marriage ban, the federal trial court in Colorado cited *Windsor* for the underlying principle that laws that "degrade or demean" same-sex couples by withholding recognition of their marriages violate the constitutional guarantee of equal protection.[28] Accordingly, by the time the *Obergefell* case reached the Supreme Court a majority of states had embraced marriage equality.

The groundbreaking case of Obergefell v. Hodges was brought by 14 same-sex couples and two men whose partners had died. The plaintiffs were from the states of Ohio, Tennessee, Michigan, and Kentucky, which all had laws defining marriage as being exclusively between one man and one woman. They argued that their rights had been violated under the fourteenth amendment of the United States Constitution either because their state had barred them from marrying or had failed to recognize the validity of a marriage entered into in another state.

James Obergefell's story poignantly captures the impact of the same-sex marriage ban on the lives of the parties. James had been with his partner, John Arthur, for more than two decades. When John was diagnosed with amyotrophic lateral sclerosis (ALS) in 2011, the parties decided to marry before he died. Since their home state of Ohio did not allow marriage between same-sex partners, they flew to Maryland in a medical transport plane. Because John was so ill, they married inside of the plane while it sat on the tarmac. After his death three months later, the state of Ohio refused to list James as the surviving spouse on the death certificate, which meant, as the Supreme Court put it, that they "must remain strangers" even in death.[29]

In its landmark ruling in favor of the plaintiffs, the Court began by explaining that the "history of marriage is one of both continuity and change."[30] It thus noted that marriage had once been viewed as an "arrangement by the couple's parents based on political, religious, and financial concerns," and that in the not too distant past, "a married man and woman were treated by the State as a single male-dominated legal entity."[31] Paralleling these developments, the Court also underscored the changing legal and social status of gay men and lesbians, remarking that until recently, "many persons did not deem homosexuals to have dignity in their own distinct identity."[32]

Citing *Loving*, the Court held that the well-established constitutional rule that marriage is fundamental applies with "equal force to same-sex couples" based on four essential principles, namely that:

1. "the right to personal choice regarding marriage is inherent in concept of individual autonomy" and is "among the most intimate that an individual can make";
2. marriage dignifies the commitment of two persons by offering "the hope of companionship and understanding and assurance that while both still live there will someone to care for the other";
3. marriage safeguards "children and families by affording material benefits and protections to children as well as by offering them 'permanency and stability' and the security of knowing that their families are accepted"; and
4. "marriage is the keystone of our social order."[33]

In so holding, the Court rejected the argument made by the defending states that the plaintiffs were not seeking to "exercise the right to marry but rather a new and nonexistent 'right to same-sex marriage.'"[34] In repudiating this assertion, the Court thus made clear that there is but a single category of marriage that includes both heterosexual and same-sex couples alike.

As in *Loving*, the Court also held that the ban on same-sex marriage violates the equal protection clause. Explaining that the rights of liberty and equality, as respectively embedded in the due process and the equal protection clauses, often worked hand in hand, it concluded that restricting the freedom of gay men and lesbians to marry the person of their choosing also abridged "central precepts of equality" that constituted a "grave and continuing harm" in an established realm of fundamental importance.[35]

A complex question that courts have begun to grapple with since *Obergefell* is whether or not the decision has retrospective application so as to enable the backdating of a couple's marriage to the date that they "would have married, but for the existence of a legal barrier to doing so."[36] This is not simply an abstract question as some entitlements, such as Social Security dependency benefits, are calibrated based upon the length of a marriage, while others depend on whether or not a couple was married at the time the right to the benefit actually accrued. In thinking about whether *Obergefell* should be applied backwards in time, two considerations are particularly important. First, when a statute, such as a state law banning marriages between two same-sex partners, is declared unconstitutional, it is generally treated as being *void ab initio*. In short, it is regarded as being "wholly void and ineffective . . . from the time of its enactment, and not from the date of the decision striking the statute[;] it is as if the statute had never been passed, and never existed."[37] Second, Supreme Court jurisprudence supports a general presumption of **retroactivity** in all civil cases, except in limited circumstances, such as where, for example, to do so would defeat the ownership rights of a purchaser of real estate.[38]

A number of courts that have addressed this issue have concluded that *Obergefell* should be applied retroactively in order to accomplish the goal of marital parity (see also the mention of retroactivity in the section on common law marriage below). For example, in a Texas automobile accident case, the Court allowed a woman to seek wrongful death benefits as a spouse following the death of her partner of 18 years based on the reasoning that the failure to do so would defeat the Court's ruling that same-sex couples must be afforded access to marriage on the same terms as heterosexual couples.[39]

The Backlash Against Obergefell

Needless to say, many people around the country greeted the hard-won victory in *Obergefell* with a tremendous sense of both relief and joy that marriage equality for same-sex couples was at long last the law of the land. However, in keeping with the view expressed by Chief Justice Roberts in dissent that the universal meaning of marriage is "the union between a man and a woman" and that the right announced by the majority had "no basis in the constitution,"[40] the decision has also generated considerable pushback. Perhaps most prominently, some wedding-related businesses, including bakers, florists, and photographers, have refused to provide services to same-sex couples based upon a religious opposition to such marriages. Seeking to encode a right of refusal into law, a number of states have enacted measures (or are considering doing so) that seek to insulate religious objectors from being sued under state public accommodation laws in jurisdictions that, in addition to barring businesses that offer goods or services to the public from discriminating on grounds such as race or sex, also bar discrimination based on sexual orientation and/or gender identity.

In support of their asserted right of refusal, these merchants seek shelter in the first amendment's right to freedom of religion, which they argue protects them from being compelled to engage in conduct, such as baking a cake or designing an invitation for a wedding ceremony, that is contrary to their religious beliefs. As a corollary, some have further argued that the first amendment's guarantee of free speech protects them from being forced by antidiscrimination laws to communicate messages they do not believe in. As a Colorado baker argued, "wedding cakes inherently convey a celebratory message about marriage" and requiring him to provide a wedding cake for a gay couple would compel him to "convey a celebratory message about same-sex marriage in conflict with [his] religious beliefs."[41]

These refusals present a clash of deeply cherished constitutional rights — namely, on the one hand, the right to equal treatment and on the other, the right to freedom of religion and speech. To date, most lower courts have come down on the side of same-sex couples who are seeking access to wedding-related services on the same basis as heterosexual couples. For example, an Arizona appeals court recently explained in a case involving a studio that did not want to make custom goods for same-sex weddings that "[p]rohibiting places of public accommodation from discriminating against customers is not just about ensuring equal access, but about eradicating the construction of a second-class citizenship and diminishing humiliation and social stigma."[42] Or as succinctly put by the Supreme Court of Washington in State of Washington v. Arlene's Flowers involving the refusal of a florist to provide flowers for the wedding of two gay customers, the case was "no more about access to flowers than civil rights cases in the 1960s were about access to sandwiches."[43] To date, the Supreme Court has yet to issue a definitive ruling on this issue; however, there is a good chance it will do so over the next few years, so stay tuned.[44]

Restrictions on the Entry into Marriage

Although the right to marry is now constitutionally protected, as noted above, the Supreme Court has nonetheless made clear that the right is not absolute, and may be restricted in order to advance compelling state interests. To this end, all states still have laws in effect that place limitations on the marriage right. Most commonly, these measures prohibit family members from marrying one another; restrict parties to one spouse at a time; and establish marital age requirements.

Incest

All states have criminal **incest** laws that make it a crime for family members within a certain degree of kinship to engage in sexual relationships with one another. Running along parallel lines, marriage restriction laws generally prohibit these same relatives from marrying.

These laws have religious roots, and can be traced back to the book of Leviticus. At one time, based on the view that a husband and wife were a single person, incest laws applied equally to persons related by marriage (affinity) and those related by blood (consanguinity); in effect, the blood relatives of one spouse were treated as the blood relatives of the other. Today, most states no longer prohibit marriages between persons related by affinity but retain the prohibition against marriage between stepparents and stepchildren to protect children from sexual exploitation.

In terms of specific prohibitions, all states forbid marriage between a parent and child, a grandparent and grandchild, and siblings of whole or half blood. Most states treat sibling relationships created through adoption as a blood relation, and thus prohibit marriage between adopted siblings, and most, if not all, states prohibit marriage between an uncle and a niece and between an aunt and a nephew. With respect to first cousins, the trend is in favor of lifting this restriction, and currently only about half of the states have a complete bar on first cousin marriages. Most of the remaining states permit such marriages, although some only allow it under certain circumstances, such as where the parties are above reproductive age.[45]

This gradual trend in favor of allowing first cousin marriages reflects the fact that concerns about the genetic risks of "inbreeding" have turned out to be less significant than once believed, at least where first cousins are concerned. According to a report of the National Society of Genetic Counselors, studies indicate that "the increased risk for a significant birth defect in offspring of a first-cousin union range between 1.7 and 2.8% above the risk of the general population."[46] Nonetheless, some states permit first cousins to marry only where the parties are over procreative age or provide evidence of genetic counseling.

Although incest laws are religious in origin, other explanations have been advanced to support such restrictions, which, at least with respect to the parent/child and sibling relationship, have near universal reach. From a sociological perspective, these restrictions have been explained as necessary to preserve the family unit by preventing it from being torn apart by sexual rivalries. From a political perspective, these restrictions have been explained as necessary to early survival and community building, as they compelled families to establish alliances outside their own immediate kin group. Genetic concerns about the dangers of inbreeding and the transmission of negative recessive traits also have played a significant role in the continuation of incest restrictions. Child advocates see these rules as necessary to protect children from sexual exploitation by family members and to provide them with a safe, sexually neutral environment in which to mature. Finally, there is the "yuck" factor—most people react with disgust at the thought of crossing the incest bar, although it is hard to know if this reaction is a cause or a result of the taboo.

Given that marriage is a fundamental right, some commentators have questioned the appropriateness of state laws that prevent consenting adults from marrying one another based on family ties. As expressed by one author:

> All too often . . . society is merely trying to save the individual from conduct that society finds repulsive. State intervention into adult decision-making must be restricted to those instances where the danger of imminent bodily harm is readily demonstrable and marriage between adults related by consanguinity or affinity does not meet this requirement.[47]

Although there has been some loosening of incest-based restrictions, as in the case of first-cousin marriages, there does not appear to be a growing trend in favor of eliminating this category of marriage restriction laws.

Consideration

Despite the internal logic of this argument, it is hard to imagine that states would eliminate incest prohibitions in order to enhance individual autonomy. What role do you think morality or public repugnance should play in the preservation of legal proscriptions that limit a fundamental right?

Multiple Marriages

All states prohibit a person from having more than one spouse at a time. The term **bigamy** describes the situation where a person enters into a second marriage while his or her first marriage is still in effect; the term **polygamy** applies to the situation where an individual (most commonly a man) has multiple spouses at the same time. A marriage contracted in violation of the "more than one spouse at a time" prohibition is void and may subject the participants to criminal prosecution.

Like incest prohibitions, these laws have religious underpinnings: Monogamy is a central tenet of the Judeo-Christian belief structure. However, unlike the incest taboo, the prohibition against multiple spouses has far less universal reach. For example, in this country, Mormon settlers in what is now Utah regarded the taking of multiple wives as a matter of divine right based on a revelation of the religion's founder, Joseph Smith.

In 1890, the Mormon Church repudiated the practice as a condition of Utah's admission as a state; however, since then, Mormon fundamentalists have revived the practice.

Although rooted in religious principles, the prohibition of multiple spouses has been justified on a number of other grounds. Perhaps most important, it has been regarded as essential to preserving the integrity of families by limiting an individual's financial and emotional commitments to a single spouse and their offspring. Other concerns include the potential coercion of women, the neglect of children, and the Mormon practice of older men taking girls as young as 14 to be one of their multiple wives.

In light of the Supreme Court's ruling in *Loving* that marriage is a fundamental right, some commentators have questioned the continued validity of the state's interest in prohibiting individuals from having more than one spouse at a time. For example, they point out that these laws do not really promote the state's interest in protecting the integrity of families, since the same concerns about financial and emotional instability are present with remarriage (or as it is sometimes called, sequential polygamy) and no limits are placed on the number of times a person can remarry and reproduce with each successive spouse.

Marital Age

Complex rules govern the ability of young people to marry. Most states set a minimum age, referred to as the **age of capacity**, below which a young person may not marry. Commonly, this age is 14. Some laws contain exceptions for circumstances such as pregnancy, but the exception usually confers a conditional (rather than absolute) right of marriage since most states require a minor to first obtain parental and/or judicial consent. Most states also set an age at which a person becomes eligible to consent to his or her own marriage. This is referred to as the **age of consent**, and it is usually set at 18—the age of majority.

For young people below the age of consent and, where applicable, above the age of capacity, the right to marry is usually conditional upon obtaining parental and/or judicial consent. Generally, states allow older minors to marry with the consent of a parent, but for younger minors, the consent of a parent and a judge may be necessary. In some states, if a parent withholds permission, a minor may petition the court for approval. These laws were designed to serve at least two state interests. First, by requiring parental participation and approval, they support the traditional authority of parents over their children. Second, and perhaps more importantly, they are thought to protect minors from making ill-advised decisions with potentially long-term harmful consequences for themselves and future offspring.

Although the parental/judicial consent requirement is intended to be protective of young people, it is important to recognize that most states do not actually require that their wishes be taken into account. Moreover, in many jurisdictions there is no formal requirement that the court make a determination that the marriage is in the best interest of the minor; accordingly, a "judge may simply confirm that the child's parents consent to the marriage without any independent questioning or investigation."[48] As a result, a teen may be compelled to enter into a marriage that is against her wishes or not in her best interest. The risk of this occurring is compounded by the fact that only a small handful of states require the appointment of counsel for minors in these cases.

Despite the fact that the law has moved in the direction of granting minors greater legal autonomy, challenges to these laws have not generally been successful. One important reason for this is that unlike other decisions, such as whether to terminate a pregnancy, the marriage decision can be postponed without any lasting, negative consequences. Moreover, unlike anti-miscegenation laws, or laws prohibiting marriages between same-sex partners, age-restriction laws are not an absolute barrier to marrying one's chosen partner; they simply require deferral of the marriage date.

There is a general assumption in this country that child marriages are not a frequent occurrence here. However, it occurs more frequently than people typically imagine is the case. According to the Tahirih Justice Center, more than "200,000 children under age 18 were married between the years 2000 and 2015" in this country.[49] The Center further reports that early marriage is "more common among those who are of lower socioeconomic status, socially conservative, liv[ing] in rural areas, and living in Southern states," and participants are "likely to come from very religious families . . . [with] the practice cut[ting] across many faiths." Importantly, "the religious institutions or denominations may not promote or condone child marriage"; rather, devout parents may press their daughter (typically it is a daughter) into an early marriage in order to "'safeguard a moral standard.'"[50]

A detailed discussion of the concerns commentators have raised about youthful marriage is beyond the scope of this book; however, a few points are in order as the law has slowly begun to respond to some of them. One important consideration is that 90 percent of teen marriages involve a young woman marrying an adult male, who may well be decades older than she is. Not uncommonly she may be pregnant and be coerced into the marriage by her parents, despite her own wishes to the contrary. In short, her gender in combination with her age may make her particularly vulnerable to parental pressure, particularly in communities in which premarital pregnancy and abortion are frowned upon. In fact, as will be discussed in Chapters 3 and 12, the law has begun to regard forcing a minor into marriage against her wishes as abusive behavior, which may entitle her to some kind of protection through abuse prevention or child protective laws, although as we will see, these are novel approaches to the issue. Layering on to concerns about parental coercion is the risk of coercion at the hands of a prospective spouse, particularly if he is considerably older than his prospective spouse; however, there is considerable disagreement over whether significant gaps in age render a relationship inherently unequal. Separate and apart from this uneasiness about the potential for coercion, significant concerns have been raised about a range of adverse impacts that early marriage may have on young women, including lower educational attainment, mental health complications, and a higher risk of domestic violence.[51]

As a result, a number of states are considering revising their marriage consent laws. One option under consideration would be to raise the minimum age of marriage to 17 or 18, with no parental or judicial consent exception. Another approach would be to require a far more searching judicial inquiry before consent can be given, including careful consideration of the minor's best interest in accordance with detailed statutory guidelines. In this regard, the Commonwealth of Virginia has adopted an interesting hybrid approach, which sets the minimum age of marriage at 18 unless a minor, who must be at least 16, has successfully petitioned the court for emancipation — a declaration that requires a searching inquiry into the minor's best interest and her capacity for making an informed decision regarding entry into marriage.[52]

Marriage Formalities

State control over marriage, particularly in structuring the terms of the marital relationship, has diminished over time. However, as clearly evidenced by the requirement that a couple must obtain a license in order to be recognized as legally wed, marriage continues to be a state-sanctioned and regulated relationship.

Thus, although we tend to think of a marriage ceremony as a private event, it is actually compliance with state licensing procedures, rather than saying "I do," that makes one married.

Obtaining a Marriage License

Although the requirements vary from state to state, the differences are generally minor. Allowing for variation, the following discussion provides an overview of the steps a couple must follow in order to establish a valid marriage and the rationale behind the requirements.

First, a couple must obtain a marriage license (Exhibit 1.1). Licenses are usually issued by a county or municipal officer, such as a clerk. Application is made by providing information under oath about age, prior marriages, and possibly also the legal relationship between the intended spouses. In some states, the clerk simply approves or denies the license based on the information as it appears on the face of the application. In other states, the clerk has some responsibility to assess whether the information provided is correct—for example, by requiring the production of a birth certificate or a divorce decree. This application process is a mechanism for enforcing a state's substantive restrictions on who can marry, as the information enables a clerk to determine if, for example, the applicants are underage, married to someone else, or close relatives. Disclosure of these circumstances would result in denial of the license. It also enables a state to collect vital statistics about its citizens as it does with birth and death certificates. Additionally, all states now require both parties to provide their Social Security numbers, which, in the event of divorce or separation, can be used to track down an absent parent for child support collection purposes.

Most states impose a waiting period, ranging from 24 hours to five days, between the time of application and the issuance of the license, although in some states, the waiting period is between issuance of the license and performance of the ceremony. It is hoped that this pause will deter couples from rushing into marriage, as it gives them time to reflect on the seriousness of their decision.

As a condition of eligibility for a marriage license, a few states also require that a doctor perform a blood test and certify that neither party has a venereal disease. The rationale of this requirement is to protect the health of the noninfected spouse and potential offspring. The measure assumes, however, that the parties have not had premarital intercourse and in recognition of changed social reality, many states have abandoned this requirement. Other less common requirements include the provision of birth control information, premarital counseling for couples under a certain age, and the distribution of information regarding the availability of AIDS and HIV testing.

Once the license is issued, a marriage ceremony must be performed by an authorized person. States usually authorize religious leaders as well as civil officers, such as justices of the peace, to perform marriage ceremonies. Beyond perhaps requiring an oath or acknowledgment of consent to become husband and wife, the presence of witnesses, and a statement by the officiator to the effect that the parties are now lawfully wed, states do not generally regulate the form, content, or manner of the ceremony. Following the ceremony, the license must be recorded in a timely manner. This is usually done by the person who officiated at the wedding.

Exhibit 1.1   Marriage License

Consequences of Failing to Comply with Licensing Requirements

In most states, a technical failure to comply with an entry requirement (e.g., if the ceremony is performed by someone claiming to be authorized to perform weddings but who, in fact, lacked such authority) will not invalidate the marriage. The public policy in favor of marriage will usually override any such procedural flaw. In states that recognize common law marriages, a common law marriage rather than a formal marriage may be the result, but, as discussed below, this distinction has no real practical significance.

Common Law Marriage

A **common law marriage** is created by the conduct of the parties in the absence of a formal ceremony. A well-established English practice, most

American colonies accepted common law marriage as a practical reality in a new country whose scattered populace made access to religious and civil officials difficult. But by the close of the nineteenth century, common law marriage came under increasing attack. Reformers complained that the modern American family had lost its moral footing and that overly relaxed marriage and divorce laws were leading to social decay and promiscuity. They feared that by treating these "irregular" relationships like true marriages, the law was condoning immoral conduct, especially on the part of women, as it was mostly economically dependent wives who sought to establish the existence of a common law marriage following the death of their spouses. As a result of these challenges and increased urbanization, most, but not all, states abolished common law marriages.

Formation Requirements and Consequences

Typically, the following elements must be shown in order to establish a valid common law marriage:

- the existence of a mutual agreement to become "husband and wife" (see below);
- cohabitation; and
- reputation in the community as husband and wife or the parties holding themselves out as "husband and wife."

Because it can be difficult to prove that the parties agreed to become spouses, especially since many disputes over whether a valid common law marriage existed arise after the death of one partner, some courts will infer agreement from the fact of cohabitation and reputation, thus obviating the need for direct proof. It should also be noted that even if these elements are present, a common law marriage cannot be established if there is an existing legal impediment to marriage formation, such as that one of the parties is already married to someone else.

Although the above elements have traditionally been framed in terms of becoming a "husband and wife," in the wake of the *Obergefell* decision, state courts that have considered the issue have concluded that common law marriages between same-sex partners must be afforded recognition on the same basis as those between heterosexual partners. Taking this a step further, some courts have applied *Obergefell* retroactively in order to backdate a couple's common law marriage to the time of its inception. For example, a South Carolina court held that two women who had lived together for almost three decades had in fact entered into a valid common law marriage in the late 1980s despite the existence of a marriage ban. In reaching this result, the judge reasoned that since *Obergefell* invalidated the same-sex marriage ban on constitutional grounds, the prohibition should not be regarded as a legitimate legal impediment to the formation of a common law marriage.[53] In short, as discussed above, the court regarded the marriage ban as void from its inception.

Once a valid common law marriage is established in a state that permits entry into such marriages, the parties are considered married for all intents and purposes. As a result, they are entitled to all of the benefits afforded to spouses, and dissolution of the relationship cannot be accomplished informally, but rather requires the filing of a divorce action. Accordingly, it is very important to distinguish common law marriage from "mere" cohabiting relationships; cohabitation may give rise to certain entitlements, but it does not lead to the creation of a spousal relationship.

Interstate Recognition

What happens if a couple establishes a common law marriage in a state that allows them and then moves to a jurisdiction in which one cannot establish a common law marriage? Will their marriage be accepted in the second state or will they be considered married in their home state and unmarried in the second state? Almost all states will recognize the marriage as valid so long as the parties satisfied the requirements of the state in which they were originally domiciled. This comports with the general rule that a validly contracted marriage will be recognized in all states, including a state that it could not have been entered into in the first place, unless it is in breach of that state's public policy.

The question of recognition becomes more complex when a couple from a state that does not allow common law marriages spends time in a second state that does, satisfies the requirements for establishing a common law marriage there, and then returns home. Some states will not recognize the marriage unless the parties have established a new domicile in the second state. Other states are looser and will extend recognition simply based on visits made to a jurisdiction that allows common law marriage. Other states take a middle position and will accept the marriage if the parties had sufficient contact with the second state to give rise to evidence of their relationship and reputation in that community.

▪ The Legal Rights of Cohabiting Couples

As noted in the introduction to this chapter, states traditionally have drawn a bright line between marriage and other forms of intimate association.

This fixed demarcation has long been considered necessary in order to safeguard the state's interest in marriage as a vital social institution. Placed outside the realm of sanctioned family life, unwed couples have accordingly been excluded from the rights and privileges of marriage. Needless to say, this exclusion had the greatest impact on same-sex couples who, until recently, did not have the option of formalizing their relationships through marriage.[54]

Even though, as we have seen in this chapter, marriage equality is now the law of the land, many couples, both same-sex and heterosexual, choose not to marry for a variety of reasons. Sometimes **cohabitation** is simply a trial run for marriage, but some people may opt to cohabit because they wish to keep the state out of their relationship, or because they wish to avoid the trappings of a historically paternalistic relationship. There may also be financial advantages to cohabitation over marriage, such as the preservation of Social Security benefits from a prior marriage.

Although the moral and corresponding legal opprobrium that once attached to cohabitation has faded to a pale shadow of its former self, and the courthouse is no longer closed to cohabiting partners seeking relief following the dissolution of their relationship, as discussed in this final section of the chapter, the law continues to privilege marriage over cohabitation.

Opening the Door to the Courthouse: The Landmark Case of Marvin v. Marvin

Before 1976, courts generally refused to get involved in dissolution disputes between cohabiting partners over money and the allocation of accumulated property. Judges did not want to appear to be sanctioning nonmarital sexual relationships, and they worried that recognizing rights between cohabiting partners would diminish the importance of marriage. However, in 1976, in the landmark case of Marvin v. Marvin,[55] the door to the courthouse was opened for the first time to cohabiting partners seeking to sort out their affairs upon the dissolution of a relationship.

Actor Lee Marvin and Michelle Triola lived together for more than seven years, accumulating assets worth more than $1 million in the name of Marvin alone. Following their breakup, Triola sued for support and a share of accumulated assets, based on what she said was an express agreement between the parties that she would give up her musical career and provide domestic services to Marvin in exchange for his financial support and a shared interest in accumulated assets. Marvin, on the other hand, argued that any agreement between the parties was void because it was inextricably bound up with the sexual aspect of their relationship—a traditional barrier to the enforcement of these claims.

Focusing on what it saw as the inherent unfairness of Marvin's position, the California Supreme Court held that unless sexual services are the sole contribution that one party makes to the relationship (thus making the relationship akin to prostitution), the fact that cohabiting partners are engaged in a nonmarital sexual relationship should not prevent the enforcement of agreements between them: "Although we recognize the well-established public policy to foster and promote the institution of marriage, perpetuation of judicial rules which result in an inequitable distribution of property accumulated during a nonmarital relationship is neither a just nor an effective way of carrying out that policy."[56]

In *Marvin*, Triola based her claim to support and a division of assets on the fact that the parties had entered into an express contract, which is an actual, articulated agreement. In holding that these agreements should be honored, the *Marvin* court recognized that most cohabiting couples do not formalize their relational expectations, and it urged other courts to consider a variety of contractual and equitable approaches when seeking to resolve claims stemming from a failed cohabiting relationship.

Presently, virtually all states have opened the door to the courthouse to cohabitating partners who are seeking to resolve support and property disputes at the dissolution of their relationships.[57] In resolving disputes between cohabiting parties, courts typically look to see if they had entered into some kind of agreement about property and support rights, although courts in some states have not limited themselves to a contractual remedy. For example, trust theories have been used to distribute property from one partner to the other, based on a showing that the titled partner was either actually holding it for the benefit of his or her partner or had engaged in some kind of fraud or overreaching.

Most couples do not sit down and negotiate a contract regarding the support and property rights they will have if they break up; courts therefore often infer agreements based on the conduct of the parties during their relationship, much as a court might infer an agreement to pay based on the acceptance of a paper that is delivered to one's door on a daily basis.[58] In contract parlance, an agreement that is inferred from conduct is referred to as an implied-in-fact contract. In the context of cohabitation, a court might find an implied agreement to share accumulated assets because a couple made purchases from a shared account or commingled their possessions. Some courts might also consider a partner's nonfinancial contribution (e.g., homemaking services) that preserves and enhances the value of the couple's property as evidence of an intent to share in the accumulation.

Courts have been more reluctant to find implied support agreements based on two traditional barriers. First, it has long been assumed that household services have no real monetary worth. Second, there is a long-standing legal presumption that household services are provided gratuitously or as a gift without expectation of compensation. These barriers, however, are breaking down. Based in part on the work of economists who have estimated what it would cost to purchase the services of a homemaker in the marketplace, courts have begun to recognize that household services have economic value and that they usually are not provided as a gift but rather, as acknowledged by the *Marvin* court, with the expectation that the parties intended a fair exchange.

In resolving disputes between cohabiting couples, most courts, however, have been reluctant to treat cohabitation as a status relationship. Accordingly, in contrast to a divorce case where the post-dissolution rights and obligations flow from the existence of the relationship itself, in most states, a cohabitant who seeks support or a share of accumulated assets must establish that his or her claim is grounded in a prior agreement (either express or implied) of the parties. In short, rather than creating a formal legal status for cohabitants, what courts have done is to have removed "a relationship-based impediment to their contractual freedom."[59] However, a distinct minority of jurisdictions have taken this extra step and now treat cohabitation as a status relationship. Accordingly, parties may be found to have post-dissolution obligations to one another based on the existence of the relationship itself.

Although the majority of states continue to use "contract as the conceptual underpinning for claims between intimate partners,"[60] in 2002, the prestigious American Law Institute (ALI) recommended, in its influential *Principles of the Law of Family Dissolution* ("Principles"), that status replace contract as the dominant paradigm. Accordingly, upon dissolution, cohabitants who have shared a "primary residence and a life together as a couple" for a significant period of time would be treated like a married couple with respect to post-relationship rights and obligations.[61] It should be noted that the Principles make no distinction between same-sex and heterosexual couples.

Family law experts are divided over the ALI recommendation.[62] Supporters argue that a status approach is a fairer way to resolve disputes because most couples simply do not think about their relationship in contractual terms. As a consequence, if there is no agreement to enforce, the economically more vulnerable partner may end up with nothing—a particularly harsh result in the context of a long-term relationship structured along traditional gender lines. Supporters also argue that this approach advances the goal of equality by honoring a broader range of relationship choices in accordance with how people are actually living their lives, rather than simply privileging marriage above all other forms of intimate associations.

Others, however, worry that recognizing cohabitation as a formal status will weaken the institution of marriage. One fear is that recognition will blur the distinction between cohabitation and marriage, thus detracting from the unique nature of the marital bond and making it more likely that couples will simply choose to live together because marriage will no longer seem so special. Another concern is that the imposition of post-relationship obligations may contravene the actual intentions of the parties, who, in choosing cohabitation over marriage, may have purposefully been seeking to avoid the legal consequences of marriage.

Chapter Summary

Although we generally think of marriage as a purely private matter, states have actively sought to shape and preserve marriage as a vital social institution. Although laws no longer mandate prescribed roles based on highly gendered notions of proper marital conduct, states still regulate who can marry and the formalities that must be complied with to establish a valid marriage. However, marriage is now recognized as a fundamental right, and laws that burden an individual's right to marry will be subjected to careful judicial review. Laws limiting the marital rights of minors have typically withstood constitutional scrutiny, but based on concerns about forced child marriages, states are revisiting entry into marriage requirements with a view toward protecting young women from coercion.

Since the 1970s, gay men and lesbians have actively fought for the right to marry, and in 2003, in a historic first, the Massachusetts Supreme Court ruled that it was unconstitutional to bar same-sex couples from marrying. A majority of other states soon followed suit, and in the landmark 2015 *Obergefell* decision, the United States Supreme Court made marriage equality the law of the land. In an effort to avoid the effect of the ruling, some merchants have refused to offer wedding-related services to same-sex couples, thus triggering legal battles that pit the right to equality against first amendment rights of religion and free speech.

Most states have abolished common law marriage. However, most, if not all, states will recognize a common law marriage that was entered into in a state that still permits them. Post-*Obergefell*, same-sex couples should have the same rights vis-à-vis common law marriage that are extended to heterosexual couples.

States continue to draw clear lines between marriage and cohabitation; however, in contrast to the past when the courthouse door was shut to cohabiting couples, virtually all states allow a partner to seek support and property rights upon the dissolution of a cohabiting relationship. Recovery is typically rooted in contract theories.

Key Terms

Common Law

Marital Unity

Personal Property

Real Property

Contracts

Testamentary Capacity

Community Property

Married Women's Property Acts

Equal Protection Clause

Due Process Clause

Retroactivity

Incest

Bigamy

Polygamy

Age of Capacity

Age of Consent

Common Law Marriage

Cohabitation

Review Questions

1. What was the status of married women under common law?
2. What were a husband's legal responsibilities under common law?
3. How was marriage seen in the community property states?
4. What prompted the passage of the Married Women's Property Acts?
5. What reforms did the Acts accomplish? What aspects of the common law marital relationship did they leave untouched?
6. When and how was the transition to gender-neutral marriage laws accomplished?
7. What did the Supreme Court decide in the case of Loving v. Virginia? Why is this case so important?
8. Describe the historic trajectory of the fight for marriage equality for same-sex couples, including a description of DOMA.
9. What did the Massachusetts Supreme Judicial Court say about marriage equality in the case of Goodridge v. Department of Public Health?
10. What was the basis of the U.S. Supreme Court's ruling in Obergefell v. Hodges?
11. What is the concept of retroactivity in relationship to the *Obergefell* decision?
12. How has resistance to the decision manifested itself? What legal rights are at issue on both sides here?
13. What kinds of marriage restriction laws are in effect today?
14. What types of arguments support these restrictions?
15. What concerns have been raised in relationship to marriages involving minors? What kinds of reforms are being considered?

16. What steps must a couple follow to create a formal marriage? What purposes are served by these requirements?
17. What is the effect of a technical failure to comply with these requirements?
18. What is a common law marriage?
19. What elements are necessary to establish a valid common law marriage?
20. Why did courts traditionally deny relief to cohabiting couples upon dissolution of their relationship?
21. What was the result of the *Marvin* decision?

Discussion Questions

1. Some commentators have suggested that all restrictions on an individual's right to marry are unconstitutional. Do you think states should be able to impose restrictions on a person's choice of a marital partner? What arguments support your position?
2. The dissenting Justices in *Obergefell* claimed that the plaintiffs were not seeking to "exercise the right to marry," but were instead seeking to exercise a novel and nonexistent right to enter into something called a same-sex marriage. Is this a valid critique of the plaintiffs' claim and of the majority's response to it?
3. Do you think someone who owns a business that offers services, such as baking cakes, catering, and creating floral arrangements, should be permitted to refuse service to same-sex couples seeking to get married? Support your position.

Assignments

1. Assume that you are working as a paralegal for an attorney who is considering representing two siblings who are seeking the right to marry each other. Both are in their 60s. She has asked you to find any law review articles that have been written on the subject and to write an interoffice memo in which you identify any arguments that she might be able to raise on their behalf. She would also like for you to identify the counter-arguments that are likely to be raised. Although these potential clients are not of procreative age, the attorney would nonetheless like you to address any additional concerns that would be raised if the couple were still able to have biological children, as procreation is likely to be a major concern of any court.

2. Assume your firm has agreed to represent a lesbian couple in their action against a florist who has refused to sell them flowers for their wedding. Your supervising attorney is pretty clear about the arguments she can raise on their behalf, but she would like a clearer sense of the arguments that the florist might be able to raise. Since this is a case of first impression in your state, she would like you to look into the cases that have been decided in other jurisdictions as the basis of your analysis.

3. Assume that a client who is in the process of ending a long-term cohabiting relationship has come to the firm where you work. Your supervising attorney has asked you to research the law in your state regarding the rights of cohabiting partners and then write up your results in a short in-house memorandum. The purpose of the memo is to provide the attorney with an overview of the law in your jurisdiction.

Cases for Analysis

The following landmark decision represents the first time that the United States Supreme Court invalidated a state law restricting entry into marriage. Although now more than 30 years old, the decision still dominates legal debates over the validity of contemporary marital restriction laws, such as those prohibiting same-sex partners from marrying.

LOVING v. VIRGINIA
388 U.S. 1, 87 S. Ct. 1817, 18 L. Ed. 2d 1010 (1967)

Mr. Chief Justice WARREN delivered the opinion of the Court.

This case presents a constitutional question never addressed by this Court: whether a statutory scheme adopted by the State of Virginia to prevent marriages between persons solely on the basis of racial classifications violates the Equal Protection and Due Process Clauses of the Fourteenth Amendment. . . .

In June 1958, two residents of Virginia, Mildred Jeter, a Negro woman, and Richard Loving, a white man, were married in the District of Columbia pursuant to its laws. Shortly after their marriage, the Lovings returned to Virginia. . . . [A] grand jury issued an indictment charging the Lovings with violating Virginia's ban on interracial marriages. . . . [T]he Lovings pleaded guilty to the charge and were sentenced to one year in jail; however, the trial judge suspended the sentence for a period of 25 years on the condition that the Lovings leave the State and not return to Virginia together for 25 years. He stated in an opinion that:

"Almighty God created the races white, black, yellow, malay and red, and he placed them on separate continents. And but for the interference with his arrangement there would be no cause for such marriages. The fact that he separated the races shows that he did not intend for the races to mix."

After their convictions, the Lovings took up residence in the District of Columbia. . . . [T]hey filed a motion in the state trial court to vacate the judgment and set aside the sentence on the ground that the statutes which they had violated were repugnant to the Fourteenth Amendment. . . . [T]he . . . judge denied the motion . . . and the Lovings perfected an appeal to the Supreme Court of Appeals of Virginia. . . .

The Supreme Court of Appeals upheld the constitutionality of the antimiscegenation statutes and . . . affirmed the convictions. The Lovings appealed this decision. . . . The two statutes under which appellants were convicted and sentenced are part of a comprehensive statutory scheme aimed at prohibiting and punishing interracial marriages. The Lovings were convicted of violating sect. 20-58 of the Virginia Code:

"*Leaving State to evade law.*—If any white person and colored person shall go out of this State, for the purpose of being married, and with the intention of returning, and be married out of it, and afterwards return to and reside in it, cohabiting as man and wife, they shall be punished as provided in sect. 20-59. . . ."

Section 20-59, which defines the penalty for miscegenation, provides:

"*Punishment for marriage.*—If any white person intermarry with a colored person, or any colored person intermarry with a white person, he shall be guilty of a felony and shall be punished by confinement in the penitentiary for not less than one nor more than five years.". . .

Virginia is now one of 16 States which prohibit and punish marriages on the basis of racial classifications. Penalties for miscegenation arose as an incident to slavery and have been common in Virginia since the colonial period. The present statutory scheme dates from the adoption of the Racial Integrity Act of 1924, passed during the period of extreme nativism which followed the end of the First World War. . . .

I

In upholding the constitutionality of these provisions . . ., the Supreme Court of Appeals of Virginia referred to its 1955 decision in Naim v. Naim, 197 Va. 80, 87 S.E.2d 749. . . . In *Naim*, the state court concluded that the State's legitimate purposes were "to preserve the racial integrity of its citizens," and to prevent "the corruption of blood," "a mongrel breed of citizens," and "the obliteration of racial pride," obviously an endorsement of the doctrine of White Supremacy. *Id.*, at 90, 87 S.E.2d, at 756. The court also reasoned that marriage has traditionally been subject to state regulation without federal intervention, and, consequently, the regulation of marriage should be left to exclusive state control by the Tenth Amendment.

[T]he State does not contend in its argument before this Court that its powers to regulate marriage are unlimited. . . . [T]he State contends that, because its miscegenation statutes punish equally both the white and the Negro participants in an interracial marriage, these statutes, despite their reliance on racial classifications, do not constitute an invidious discrimination based upon race. . . .

[T]he Equal Protection Clause requires the consideration of whether the classifications drawn by any statute constitute an arbitrary and invidious discrimination. The clear and central purpose of the Fourteenth Amendment was to eliminate all official state sources of invidious racial discrimination in the States. . . .

There can be no question but that Virginia's miscegenation statutes rest solely upon distinctions drawn according to race. . . . Over the years, this Court has consistently repudiated "distinctions between citizens solely because of their ancestry" as being "odious to a free people whose institutions are founded upon the doctrine of equality." Hirabayashi v. United States, 320 U.S. 81, 100 (1943). . . . [I]f they are ever to be upheld, they must be shown to be necessary to the accomplishment of some permissible state objective, independent of the racial discrimination which it was the object of the Fourteenth Amendment to eliminate. . . .

There is patently no legitimate overriding purpose independent of invidious racial discrimination which justifies this classification. The fact that Virginia prohibits only interracial marriages involving white persons demonstrates that the racial classifications must stand on their own justification, as measures designed to maintain White Supremacy. We have consistently denied the constitutionality of measures which restrict the rights of citizens on account of race. There can be no doubt that restricting the freedom to marry solely because of racial classifications violates the central meaning of the Equal Protection Clause.

II

These statutes also deprive the Lovings of liberty without due process of law in violation of the Due Process Clause of the Fourteenth Amendment. The freedom to marry has long been recognized as one of the vital personal rights essential to the orderly pursuit of happiness by free men.

Marriage is one of the "basic civil rights of man," fundamental to our very existence and survival. Skinner v. Oklahoma, 316 U.S. 535, 541 (1942). See also Maynard v. Hill, 125 U.S. 190 (1888). To deny this fundamental freedom on so unsupportable a basis as the racial classifications embodied in these statutes, classifications so directly subversive of the principle of equality at the heart of the Fourteenth Amendment, is surely to deprive all the State's citizens of liberty without due process of law. The Fourteenth Amendment requires that the freedom of choice to marry not be restricted by invidious racial discriminations. Under our Constitution, the freedom to marry, or not marry, a person of another race resides with the individual and cannot be infringed by the State.

These convictions must be reversed.

QUESTIONS

1. On what grounds did the state of Virginia seek to justify its miscegenation laws?
2. Why did Virginia claim that its miscegenation laws did not "constitute an invidious discrimination based on race"? Why did the Court disagree with Virginia on this point?
3. Based on your reading of the text, who generally has the authority to regulate the marriage?
4. In striking down Virginia's miscegenation law, the Court relies on two clauses of the fourteenth amendment. Identify these clauses and explain how the Court used them to invalidate the law.
5. How does the Court characterize the right to marry?

————————

In the following landmark decision, the United States Supreme Court holds that laws banning same-sex partners from marrying violate the due process and the equal protection clauses of the fourteenth amendment. The decision, accordingly, made marriage equality the law of the land. As you will see, the majority's opinion drew a biting dissent.

OBERGEFELL v. HODGES
576 U.S. ___, 135 S. Ct. 2584, 192 L. Ed. 2d 609 (2015)

Justice KENNEDY delivered the opinion of the Court.

The Constitution promises liberty to all within its reach, a liberty that includes certain specific rights that allow persons, within a lawful realm, to define and express their identity. The petitioners in these cases seek to find that liberty by marrying someone of the same sex and having their marriages deemed lawful on the same terms and conditions as marriages between persons of the opposite sex.

I

These cases come from Michigan, Kentucky, Ohio, and Tennessee, States that define marriage as a union between one man and one woman. . . . The petitioners are 14 same-sex couples and two men whose same-sex partners are deceased. The respondents are state officials responsible for enforcing the laws in question. The petitioners claim the respondents violate the Fourteenth Amendment by denying them the right to marry or to have their marriages, lawfully performed in another State, given full recognition. . . .

II

Before addressing the principles and precedents that govern these cases, it is appropriate to note the history of the subject now before the Court.

A

From their beginning to their most recent page, the annals of human history reveal the transcendent importance of marriage. The lifelong union of a man and a woman always has promised nobility and dignity to all persons, without regard to their station in life. Marriage is sacred to those who live by their religions and offers unique fulfillment to those who find meaning in the secular realm. Its dynamic allows two people to find a life that could not be found alone, for a marriage becomes greater than just the two persons. Rising from the most basic human needs, marriage is essential to our most profound hopes and aspirations. . . .

The centrality of marriage to the human condition makes it unsurprising that the institution has existed for millennia and across civilizations. Since the dawn of history, marriage has transformed strangers into relatives, binding families and societies together. . . . There are untold references to the beauty of marriage in religious and philosophical texts spanning time, cultures, and faiths, as well as in art and literature in all their forms. It is fair and necessary to say these references were based on the understanding that marriage is a union between two persons of the opposite sex.

That history is the beginning of these cases. The respondents say it should be the end as well. To them, it would demean a timeless institution if the concept and lawful status of marriage were extended to two persons of the same sex. Marriage, in their view, is by its nature a gender-differentiated union of man and woman. This view long has been held—and continues to be held—in good faith by reasonable and sincere people here and throughout the world.

The petitioners acknowledge this history but contend that these cases cannot end there. Were their intent to demean the revered idea and reality of marriage, the petitioners' claims would be of a different order. But that is neither their purpose nor their submission. To the contrary, it is the enduring importance of marriage that underlies the petitioners' contentions. This, they say, is their whole point. Far from seeking to devalue marriage, the petitioners seek it for themselves because of their respect–and need–for its privileges and responsibilities. And their immutable nature dictates that same-sex marriage is their only real path to this profound commitment. . . .

B

The ancient origins of marriage confirm its centrality, but it has not stood in isolation from developments in law and society. The history of marriage is one of both continuity and change. That institution—even as confined to opposite-sex relations—has evolved over time.

For example, marriage was once viewed as an arrangement by the couple's parents based on political, religious, and financial concerns; but by the time of the Nation's founding it was understood to be a voluntary contract between a man and a woman. . . . As the role and status of women changed, the institution further evolved. Under the centuries-old doctrine of coverture, a married man and woman were treated by the State as a single, male-dominated legal entity. . . . As women gained legal, political, and property rights, and as society began to understand that women have their own equal dignity, the law of coverture was abandoned. . . . These and other developments in the institution of marriage over the past centuries were not mere superficial changes. Rather, they worked deep transformations in its structure, affecting aspects of marriage long viewed by many as essential. . . .

These new insights have strengthened, not weakened, the institution of marriage. Indeed, changed understandings of marriage are characteristic of a Nation where new dimensions of freedom become apparent to new generations, often through perspectives that begin in pleas or protests and then are considered in the political sphere and the judicial process.

This dynamic can be seen in the Nation's experiences with the rights of gays and lesbians. Until the mid-20th century, same-sex intimacy long had been condemned as immoral by the state itself in most Western nations, a belief often embodied in the criminal law. . . .

For much of the 20th century, moreover, homosexuality was treated as an illness. When the American Psychiatric Association published the first Diagnostic and Statistical Manual of Mental Disorders in 1952, homosexuality was classified as a mental disorder, a position adhered to until 1973. . . . Only in more recent years have psychiatrists and others recognized that sexual orientation is both a normal expression of human sexuality and immutable. . . .

In 2003, the Supreme Judicial Court of Massachusetts held the State's Constitution guaranteed same-sex couples the right to marry. See *Goodridge v. Department of Public Health*, 440 Mass. 309, 798 N.E.2d 941 (2003). After that ruling, some additional States granted marriage rights to same-sex couples, either through judicial or legislative processes. . . .

III

[The Court has long held] the right to marry is protected by the Constitution. In *Loving v. Virginia*, 388 U.S. 1, 12, 87 S. Ct. 1817, 18 L. Ed. 2d 1010 (1967), which invalidated bans on interracial unions, a unanimous Court held marriage is "one of the vital personal rights essential to the orderly pursuit of happiness by free men." The Court reaffirmed that holding in *Zablocki v. Redhail*, 434 U.S. 374, 384, 98 S. Ct. 673, 54 L. Ed. 2d 618 (1978), which held the right to marry was burdened by a law prohibiting fathers who were behind on child support from marrying. The Court again applied this principle in *Turner v. Safley*, 482 U.S. 78, 95, 107 S. Ct. 2254, 96 L. Ed. 2d 64 (1987), which held the right to marry was abridged by regulations limiting the privilege of prison inmates to marry. . . .

It cannot be denied that this Court's cases describing the right to marry presumed a relationship involving opposite-sex partners. The Court, like many institutions, has made assumptions defined by the world and time of which it is a part. . . .

Still, there are other, more instructive precedents. This Court's cases have expressed constitutional principles of broader reach. In defining the right to marry these cases have identified essential attributes of that right based in history, tradition, and other constitutional liberties inherent in this intimate bond. . . . And in assessing whether the force and rationale of its cases apply to same-sex couples, the Court must respect the basic reasons why the right to marry has been long protected. . . .

This analysis compels the conclusion same-sex couples may exercise the right to marry. The four principles and traditions to be discussed demonstrate that the reasons marriage is fundamental under the Constitution apply with equal force to same-sex couples.

A first premise of the Court's relevant precedents is that the right to personal choice regarding marriage is inherent in the concept of individual autonomy. This abiding connection between marriage and liberty is why *Loving* invalidated interracial marriage bans under the Due Process Clause. . . . Choices about marriage shape an individual's destiny. As the Supreme Judicial Court of Massachusetts has explained, because "it fulfils yearnings for security, safe haven, and connection that express our common humanity, civil marriage is an esteemed institution, and the decision whether and whom to marry is among life's momentous acts of self-definition." *Goodridge*, 440 Mass., at 322, 798 N.E.2d, at 955. . . .

A second principle in this Court's jurisprudence is that the right to marry is fundamental because it supports a two-person union unlike any other in its importance to the committed individuals. . . .

As this Court held in [Lawrence v. Texas, 539 U.S. 558 (2003),] same-sex couples have the same right as opposite-sex couples to enjoy intimate association. *Lawrence* invalidated laws that made same-sex intimacy a criminal act. . . . But while *Lawrence* confirmed a dimension of freedom that allows individuals to engage in intimate association without criminal liability, it does not follow that freedom stops there. Outlaw to outcast may be a step forward, but it does not achieve the full promise of liberty.

A third basis for protecting the right to marry is that it safeguards children and families and thus draws meaning from related rights of childrearing, procreation, and education. . . . States, some of marriage's protections for children and families are material. But marriage also confers more profound benefits. By giving recognition and legal structure to their parents' relationship, marriage allows children "to understand the integrity and closeness of their own family and its concord with other families in their community and in their daily lives." *Windsor, supra*, at ___, 133 S. Ct. 2675, 186 L. Ed. 2d at 828. Marriage also affords the permanency and stability important to children's best interests. See Brief for Scholars of the Constitutional Rights of Children as *Amici Curiae* 22-27.

As all parties agree, many same-sex couples provide loving and nurturing homes to their children, whether biological or adopted. . . .

Excluding same-sex couples from marriage thus conflicts with a central premise of the right to marry. Without the recognition, stability, and predictability marriage offers, their children suffer the stigma of knowing their families are somehow lesser. They also suffer the significant material costs of being raised by unmarried parents, relegated through no fault of their own to a more difficult and uncertain family life. . . .

Fourth and finally, this Court's cases and the Nation's traditions make clear that marriage is a keystone of our social order. . . .

For that reason, just as a couple vows to support each other, so does society pledge to support the couple, offering symbolic recognition and material benefits to protect and nourish the union. Indeed, while the States are in general free to vary the benefits they confer on all married couples, they have throughout our history made marriage the basis for an expanding list of governmental rights, benefits, and responsibilities. . . .

There is no difference between same- and opposite-sex couples with respect to this principle. Yet by virtue of their exclusion from that institution, same-sex couples are denied the constellation of benefits that the

States have linked to marriage. This harm results in more than just material burdens. Same-sex couples are consigned to an instability many opposite-sex couples would deem intolerable in their own lives. As the State itself makes marriage all the more precious by the significance it attaches to it, exclusion from that status has the effect of teaching that gays and lesbians are unequal in important respects. It demeans gays and lesbians for the State to lock them out of a central institution of the Nation's society. Same-sex couples, too, may aspire to the transcendent purposes of marriage and seek fulfillment in its highest meaning.

The limitation of marriage to opposite-sex couples may long have seemed natural and just, but its inconsistency with the central meaning of the fundamental right to marry is now manifest. With that knowledge must come the recognition that laws excluding same-sex couples from the marriage right impose stigma and injury of the kind prohibited by our basic charter. . . .

The right to marry is fundamental as a matter of history and tradition, but rights come not from ancient sources alone. They rise, too, from a better informed understanding of how constitutional imperatives define a liberty that remains urgent in our own era. Many who deem same-sex marriage to be wrong reach that conclusion based on decent and honorable religious or philosophical premises, and neither they nor their beliefs are disparaged here. But when that sincere, personal opposition becomes enacted law and public policy, the necessary consequence is to put the imprimatur of the State itself on an exclusion that soon demeans or stigmatizes those whose own liberty is then denied. Under the Constitution, same-sex couples seek in marriage the same legal treatment as opposite-sex couples, and it would disparage their choices and diminish their personhood to deny them this right.

The right of same-sex couples to marry that is part of the liberty promised by the Fourteenth Amendment is derived, too, from that Amendment's guarantee of the equal protection of the laws. The Due Process Clause and the Equal Protection Clause are connected in a profound way, though they set forth independent principles. Rights implicit in liberty and rights secured by equal protection may rest on different precepts and are not always coextensive, yet in some instances each may be instructive as to the meaning and reach of the other. In any particular case one Clause may be thought to capture the essence of the right in a more accurate and comprehensive way, even as the two Clauses may converge in the identification and definition of the right. . . .

The Court's cases touching upon the right to marry reflect this dynamic. . . .

Indeed, in interpreting the Equal Protection Clause, the Court has recognized that new insights and societal understandings can reveal unjustified inequality within our most fundamental institutions that once passed unnoticed and unchallenged. To take but one period, this occurred with respect to marriage in the 1970's and 1980's. Notwithstanding the gradual erosion of the doctrine of coverture, . . . invidious sex-based classifications in marriage remained common through the mid-20th century. . . . These classifications denied the equal dignity of men and women. One State's law, for example, provided in 1971 that "the husband is the head of the family and the wife is subject to him; her legal civil existence is merged in the husband, except so far as the law recognizes her separately, either for her own protection, or for her benefit." . . . Responding to a new awareness, the Court invoked equal protection principles to invalidate laws imposing sex-based inequality on marriage. . . . The Equal Protection Clause can help to identify and correct inequalities in the institution of marriage, vindicating precepts of liberty and equality under the Constitution.

. . . It is now clear that the challenged laws burden the liberty of same-sex couples, and it must be further acknowledged that they abridge central precepts of equality. Here the marriage laws enforced by the respondents are in essence unequal: same-sex couples are denied all the benefits afforded to opposite-sex couples and are barred from exercising a fundamental right. Especially against a long history of disapproval of their relationships, this denial to same-sex couples of the right to marry works a grave and continuing harm. The imposition of this disability on gays and lesbians serves to disrespect and subordinate them. And the Equal Protection Clause, like the Due Process Clause, prohibits this unjustified infringement of the fundamental right to marry. . . .

These considerations lead to the conclusion that the right to marry is a fundamental right inherent in the liberty of the person, and under the Due Process and Equal Protection Clauses of the Fourteenth Amendment couples of the same-sex may not be deprived of that right and that liberty. The Court now holds that same-sex couples may exercise the fundamental right to marry. No longer may this liberty be denied to them. . . . [T]he State laws challenged by Petitioners in these cases are now held invalid to the extent they exclude same-sex couples from civil marriage on the same terms and conditions as opposite-sex couples. . . .

IV

The respondents . . . argue allowing same-sex couples to wed will harm marriage as an institution by leading to fewer opposite-sex marriages. This may occur, the respondents contend, because licensing same-sex marriage severs the connection between natural procreation and marriage. That argument, however, rests on a counterintuitive view of opposite-sex couple's decisionmaking processes regarding marriage and parenthood.

Decisions about whether to marry and raise children are based on many personal, romantic, and practical considerations; and it is unrealistic to conclude that an opposite-sex couple would choose not to marry simply because same-sex couples may do so. . . .

Finally, it must be emphasized that religions, and those who adhere to religious doctrines, may continue to advocate with utmost, sincere conviction that, by divine precepts, same-sex marriage should not be condoned. The First Amendment ensures that religious organizations and persons are given proper protection as they seek to teach the principles that are so fulfilling and so central to their lives and faiths, and to their own deep aspirations to continue the family structure they have long revered. The same is true of those who oppose same-sex marriage for other reasons. In turn, those who believe allowing same-sex marriage is proper or indeed essential, whether as a matter of religious conviction or secular belief, may engage those who disagree with their view in an open and searching debate. The Constitution, however, does not permit the State to bar same-sex couples from marriage on the same terms as accorded to couples of the opposite sex. . . .

V

No union is more profound than marriage, for it embodies the highest ideals of love, fidelity, devotion, sacrifice, and family. In forming a marital union, two people become something greater than once they were. As some of the petitioners in these cases demonstrate, marriage embodies a love that may endure even past death. It would misunderstand these men and women to say they disrespect the idea of marriage. Their plea is that they do respect it, respect it so deeply that they seek to find its fulfillment for themselves. Their hope is not to be condemned to live in loneliness, excluded from one of civilization's oldest institutions. They ask for equal dignity in the eyes of the law. The Constitution grants them that right.

The judgment of the Court of Appeals for the Sixth Circuit is reversed.

It is so ordered.

Chief Justice ROBERTS, with whom Justice SCALIA and Justice THOMAS join, dissenting.

. . . Although the policy arguments for extending marriage to same-sex couples may be compelling, the legal arguments for requiring such an extension are not. The fundamental right to marry does not include a right to make a State change its definition of marriage. And a State's decision to maintain the meaning of marriage that has persisted in every culture throughout human history can hardly be called irrational. In short, our Constitution does not enact any one theory of marriage. The people of a

State are free to expand marriage to include same-sex couples, or to retain the historic definition.

Today, however, the Court takes the extraordinary step of ordering every State to license and recognize same-sex marriage. Many people will rejoice at this decision, and I begrudge none their celebration. But for those who believe in a government of laws, not of men, the majority's approach is deeply disheartening. Supporters of same-sex marriage have achieved considerable success persuading their fellow citizens—through the democratic process—to adopt their view. That ends today. Five lawyers have closed the debate and enacted their own vision of marriage as a matter of constitutional law. Stealing this issue from the people will for many cast a cloud over same-sex marriage, making a dramatic social change that much more difficult to accept.

The majority's decision is an act of will, not legal judgment. The right it announces has no basis in the Constitution or this Court's precedent. The majority expressly disclaims judicial "caution" and omits even a pretense of humility, openly relying on its desire to remake society according to its own "new insight" into the "nature of injustice." . . . As a result, the Court invalidates the marriage laws of more than half the States and orders the transformation of a social institution that has formed the basis of human society for millennia, for the Kalahari Bushmen and the Han Chinese, the Carthaginians and the Aztecs. Just who do we think we are?

Understand well what this dissent is about: It is not about whether, in my judgment, the institution of marriage should be changed to include same-sex couples. It is instead about whether, in our democratic republic, that decision should rest with the people acting through their elected representatives, or with five lawyers who happen to hold commissions authorizing them to resolve legal disputes according to law. The Constitution leaves no doubt about the answer.

I

Petitioners and their *amici* base their arguments on the "right to marry" and the imperative of "marriage equality." There is no serious dispute that, under our precedents, the Constitution protects a right to marry and requires States to apply their marriage laws equally. The real question in these cases is what constitutes "marriage," or—more precisely—*who decides* what constitutes "marriage"?

The majority largely ignores these questions, relegating ages of human experience with marriage to a paragraph or two. Even if history and precedent are not "the end" of these cases, I would not "sweep away what has so long been settled" without showing greater respect for all that preceded us. . . .

A

As the majority acknowledges, marriage "has existed for millennia and across civilizations." . . . For all those millennia, across all those civilizations, "marriage" referred to only one relationship: the union of a man and a woman. . . .

This universal definition of marriage as the union of a man and a woman is no historical coincidence. Marriage did not come about as a result of a political movement, discovery, disease, war, religious doctrine, or any other moving force of world history—and certainly not as a result of a prehistoric decision to exclude gays and lesbians. It arose in the nature of things to meet a vital need: ensuring that children are conceived by a mother and father committed to raising them in the stable conditions of a lifelong relationship. . . .

The premises supporting this concept of marriage are so fundamental that they rarely require articulation. The human race must procreate to survive. Procreation occurs through sexual relations between a man and a woman. When sexual relations result in the conception of a child, that child's prospects are generally better if the mother and father stay together rather than going their separate ways. Therefore, for the good of children and society, sexual relations that can lead to procreation should occur only between a man and a woman committed to a lasting bond.

Society has recognized that bond as marriage. And by bestowing a respected status and material benefits on married couples, society encourages men and women to conduct sexual relations within marriage rather than without. . . .

As the majority notes, some aspects of marriage have changed over time. Arranged marriages have largely given way to pairings based on romantic love. States have replaced coverture, the doctrine by which a married man and woman became a single legal entity, with laws that respect each participant's separate status. Racial restrictions on marriage . . . were repealed by many States and ultimately struck down by this Court.

The majority observes that these developments "were not mere superficial changes" in marriage, but rather "worked deep transformations in its structure." They did not, however, work any transformation in the core structure of marriage as the union between a man and a woman. If you had asked a person on the street how marriage was defined, no one would ever have said, "Marriage is the union of a man and a woman, where the woman is subject to coverture." The majority may be right that the "history of marriage is one of both continuity and change," but the core meaning of marriage has endured.

It is striking how much of the majority's reasoning would apply with equal force to the claim of a fundamental right to plural marriage. If "[t]here is dignity in the bond between two men or two women who seek to marry and in their autonomy to make such profound choices," why would there be any less dignity in the bond between three people who, in exercising their autonomy, seek to make the profound choice to marry? If a same-sex couple has the constitutional right to marry because their children would otherwise "suffer the stigma of knowing their families are somehow lesser," why wouldn't the same reasoning apply to a family of three or more persons raising children? If not having the opportunity to marry "serves to disrespect and subordinate" gay and lesbian couples, why wouldn't the same "imposition of this disability," serve to disrespect and subordinate people who find fulfillment in polyamorous relationships?

QUESTIONS

1. As explained by the Court, how has the institution of marriage changed over time?
2. What are the four principles and traditions that the Court relies upon in support of its conclusion that same-sex couples have a fundamental right to marry?
3. According to the Court, why is marriage such an important institution?
4. Why does the Court ultimately conclude that it is unconstitutional to ban same-sex partners from marrying?
5. Identify the objections that the dissenting Justices raise in response to the majority opinion.

As discussed in the text, the following landmark decision helped to open the doors of the courthouse to unmarried couples seeking to untangle their interests following the dissolution of a relationship.

MARVIN v. MARVIN
18 Cal. 3d 660, 557 P.2d 106, 134 Cal. Rptr. 815 (1976)

During the past 15 years, there has been a substantial increase in the number of couples living together without marrying. Such nonmarital relationships lead to legal controversy when one partner dies or the couple separates. . . .

. . . Plaintiff avers that in October of 1964 she and defendant "entered into an oral agreement" that while "the parties lived together they would combine their efforts and earnings and would share equally any and all property accumulated as a result of their efforts whether individual or combined." Furthermore, they agreed to "hold themselves out to the general public as husband and wife" and that "plaintiff would further render her services as a companion, homemaker, housekeeper and cook to . . . defendant."

Shortly thereafter plaintiff agreed to "give up her lucrative career as an entertainer [and] singer" in order to "devote her full time to defendant . . . as a companion, homemaker, housekeeper and cook"; in return defendant agreed to "provide for all of plaintiff's financial support and needs for the rest of her life."

Plaintiff alleges that she lived with defendant from October of 1964 through May of 1970 and fulfilled her obligations under the agreement. During this period the parties as a result of their efforts and earnings acquired in defendant's name substantial real and personal property, including motion picture rights worth over $1 million. In May of 1970, however, defendant compelled plaintiff to leave his household. He continued to support plaintiff until November of 1971, but thereafter refused to provide further support.

In the case before us plaintiff, basing her cause of action in contract . . . maintains that the trial court erred in denying her a trial on the merits of her contention. Although that court did not specify the ground for its conclusion that plaintiff's contractual allegations stated no cause of action. . . .

Defendant first and principally relies on the contention that the alleged contract is so closely related to the supposed "immoral" character of the relationship between plaintiff and himself that the enforcement of the contract would violate public policy. He points to cases asserting that a contract between nonmarital partners is unenforceable if it is "involved in" an illicit relationship. . . . A review of the numerous California decisions concerning contracts between nonmarital partners, however, reveals that the courts have not employed such broad and uncertain standards to strike down contracts. The decisions instead disclose a narrower and more precise standard: a contract between nonmarital partners is unenforceable only to the extent that it explicitly rests upon the immoral and illicit consideration of meretricious sexual services. . . .

Although the past decisions hover over the issue in the somewhat wispy form of the figures of a Chagall painting, we can abstract from those decisions a clear and simple rule. The fact that a man and woman live together without marriage, and engage in a sexual relationship, does not in itself invalidate agreements between them relating to their earnings, property, or expenses. Neither is such an agreement invalid merely because the parties may have contemplated the creation or continuation of a nonmarital relationship when they entered into it. Agreements between nonmarital partners fail only to the extent that they rest upon a consideration of meretricious sexual services. Thus the rule asserted by defendant, that a contract fails if it is "involved in" or made "in contemplation" of a nonmarital relationship, cannot be reconciled with the decisions. . . .

The principle that a contract between nonmarital partners will be enforced unless expressly and inseparably based upon an illicit consideration of sexual services not only represents the distillation of the decisional law, but also offers a far more precise and workable standard than that advocated by defendant. . . .

In summary, we base our opinion on the principle that adults who voluntarily live together and engage in sexual relations are nonetheless as competent as any other persons to contract respecting their earnings and property rights. Of course, they cannot lawfully contract to pay for the performance of sexual services, for such a contract is, in essence, an agreement for prostitution and unlawful for that reason. But they may agree to pool their earnings and to hold all property acquired during the relationship in accord with the law governing community property; conversely they may agree that each partner's earnings and the property acquired from those earnings remains the separate property of the earning partner. So long as the agreement does not rest upon illicit meretricious consideration, the parties may order their economic affairs as they choose, and no policy precludes the courts from enforcing such agreements.

In the present instance, plaintiff alleges that the parties agreed to pool their earnings, that they contracted to share equally in all property acquired, and that defendant agreed to support plaintiff. The terms of the contract as alleged do not rest upon any unlawful consideration. We therefore conclude that the complaint furnishes a suitable basis upon which the trial court can render declaratory relief. . . . The trial court consequently erred in granting defendant's motion for judgment on the pleadings. . . .

As we have noted, both causes of action in plaintiff's complaint allege an express contract; neither assert any basis for relief independent from the contract. In In re Marriage of Cary, *supra*, 34 Cal. App. 3d 345, however, the Court of Appeal held that, in view of the policy of the Family Law Act, property accumulated by nonmarital partners in an actual family relationship should be divided equally. Upon examining the *Cary* opinion, the parties to the present case realized that plaintiff's alleged relationship with defendant might arguably support a cause of action independent of any express contract between the parties. . . .

Reviewing the prior decisions which had denied relief to the homemaking partner, the Court of Appeal reasoned that those decisions rested upon a policy of punishing persons guilty of cohabitation without marriage. The Family Law Act, the court observed, aimed to eliminate fault or guilt as a basis for dividing marital property. But once fault or guilt is excluded, the court reasoned, nothing distinguishes the property rights of a nonmarital "spouse" from those of a putative spouse. Since the latter is entitled to half the " 'quasi marital property' " . . ., the Court of Appeal concluded that, giving effect to the policy of the Family Law Act, a nonmarital cohabitator should also be entitled to half the property accumulated during an "actual family relationship." (34 Cal. App. 3d at p. 353.)

Cary met with a mixed reception in other appellate districts. In Estate of Atherley, *supra*, 44 Cal. App. 3d 758, the Fourth District agreed with *Cary* that under the Family Law Act a nonmarital partner in an actual family relationship enjoys the same right to an equal division of property as a putative spouse. In Beckman v. Mayhew, *supra*, 49 Cal. App. 3d 529, however, the Third District rejected *Cary* on the ground that the Family Law Act was not intended to change California law dealing with nonmarital relationships. If *Cary* is interpreted as holding that the Family Law Act requires an equal division of property accumulated in nonmarital "actual family relationships," then we agree with Beckman v. Mayhew that *Cary* distends the act. . . .

But although we reject the reasoning of *Cary* and *Atherley*, we share the perception of the *Cary* and *Atherley* courts that the application of former precedent in the factual setting of those cases would work an unfair distribution of the property accumulated by the couple. . . .

The principal reason why the pre-*Cary* decisions result in an unfair distribution of property inheres in the court's refusal to permit a nonmarital partner to assert rights based upon accepted principles of implied contract or equity. We have examined the reasons advanced to justify this denial of relief, and find that none have merit. . . .

First, we note that the cases denying relief do not rest their refusal upon any theory of "punishing" a "guilty" partner. Indeed, to the extent that denial of relief "punishes" one partner, it necessarily rewards the other by permitting him to retain a disproportionate amount of the property. Concepts of "guilt" thus cannot justify an unequal division of property between two equally "guilty" persons.

Other reasons advanced in the decisions fare no better. The principal argument seems to be that "[equitable] considerations arising from the reasonable expectation of . . . benefits attending the status of marriage . . . are not present [in a nonmarital relationship]." (Vallera v. Vallera, *supra*, 21 Cal. 2d at p. 685.) But, although parties to a nonmarital relationship obviously cannot have based any expectations upon the belief that they were married, other expectations and equitable considerations remain. The parties may well expect that property will be divided in accord with the parties' own tacit understanding and that in the absence of such understanding the courts will fairly apportion property accumulated through mutual effort. We need not treat nonmarital partners as putatively married persons in order to apply principles of implied contract, or extend equitable remedies; we need to treat them only as we do any other unmarried persons. . . .

. . . The argument that granting remedies to the nonmarital partners would discourage marriage must fail; as *Cary* pointed out, "with equal or greater force the point might be made that the pre-1970 rule was calculated to cause the income-producing partner to avoid marriage and thus retain the benefit of all of his or her accumulated earnings." 34 Cal. App. 3d at p. 353. Although we recognize the well-established public policy to foster and promote the institution of marriage . . . perpetuation of judicial rules which result in an inequitable distribution of property accumulated during a nonmarital relationship is neither a just nor an effective way of carrying out that policy.

In summary, we believe that the prevalence of nonmarital relationships in modern society and the social acceptance of them, marks this as a time when our courts should by no means apply the doctrine of the unlawfulness of the so-called meretricious relationship to the instant case. As we have explained, the nonenforceability of agreements expressly providing for meretricious conduct rested upon the fact that such conduct, as the word suggests, pertained to and encompassed prostitution. To equate the nonmarital relationship of today to such a subject matter is to do violence to an accepted and wholly different practice.

We are aware that many young couples live together without the solemnization of marriage, in order to make sure that they can successfully later undertake marriage. This trial period, preliminary to marriage, serves as some assurance that the marriage will not subsequently end in dissolution to the harm of both parties. We are aware, as we have stated, of the pervasiveness of nonmarital relationships in other situations.

The mores of the society have indeed changed so radically in regard to cohabitation that we cannot impose a standard based on alleged moral considerations that have apparently been so widely abandoned by so many. Lest we be misunderstood, however, we take this occasion to point out that the structure of society itself largely depends upon the institution of marriage, and nothing we have said in this opinion should be taken to derogate from that institution. The joining of the man and woman in marriage is at once the most socially productive and individually fulfilling relationship that one can enjoy in the course of a lifetime.

We conclude that the judicial barriers that may stand in the way of a policy based upon the fulfillment of the reasonable expectations of the parties to a nonmarital relationship should be removed. As we have explained, the courts now hold that express agreements will be enforced unless they rest on an unlawful meretricious consideration. We add that in the absence of an express agreement, the courts may look to a variety of other remedies in order to protect the parties' lawful expectations.

The courts may inquire into the conduct of the parties to determine whether that conduct demonstrates an implied contract or implied agreement of partnership or joint venture . . . or some other tacit understanding between the parties. The courts may, when appropriate, employ principles of constructive trust . . . or resulting trust. . . . Finally, a nonmarital partner may recover in quantum meruit for the reasonable value of household services rendered less the reasonable value of support received if he can show that he rendered services with the expectation of monetary reward.

Since we have determined that plaintiff's complaint states a cause of action for breach of an express contract, and, as we have explained, can be amended to state a cause of action independent of allegations of express contract, we must conclude that the trial court erred in granting defendant a judgment on the pleadings. The judgment is reversed and the cause remanded for further proceedings consistent with the views expressed herein.

QUESTIONS

1. What was the oral agreement between the plaintiff and the defendant?
2. Why did the defendant claim that any contract entered into by him and the plaintiff would violate public policy? How does the court respond to his argument?
3. What does the court decide about the enforceability of agreements between unmarried couples regarding their economic affairs? What consideration is to be given to the sexual nature of the relationship?
4. The *Marvin* court discusses an earlier decision, In re Marriage of Cary. What did *Cary* hold? Why does the *Marvin* court reject that decision?
5. How does the *Marvin* court address the concern that granting rights to unmarried cohabitants will undermine the institution of marriage?
6. What role do moral considerations play in the decision?

The following case is a prime example of the legal arguments that business owners have been making in support of their right of refusal to provide wedding-related goods and services to same-sex couples. Note that the lawsuit is brought against the City of Phoenix, rather than against a merchant who denied service.

BRUSH & NIB STUDIO v. CITY OF PHOENIX
488 P.3d 426 (Ariz. 2018)

Duka and Breanna Koski ("Appellants") are the owners of Brush & Nib Studio, LC ("Brush & Nib"). Appellants filed a pre-enforcement action against the City of Phoenix ("Phoenix") challenging the constitutionality

of Phoenix City Code 18-4(B) ("Section 18-4(B)") and seeking a preliminary injunction to bar enforcement of the ordinance. Appellants appeal the
superior court's denial of their preliminary injunction and grant of summary judgment in favor of Phoenix. For the following reasons, we affirm
as modified. . . .

Brush & Nib is a for-profit limited liability company, which sells
pre-fabricated and design artwork for home décor, weddings, and special events. Appellants provide retail goods and services to the public and
acknowledge they operate a place of public accommodation as defined in
Phoenix City Code §18.[63]

Appellants are devout Christians and believe their work is inextricably related to their religious beliefs. Appellants' goods and services include
both customer-directed projects (work created through a consultation
between Appellants and their customer) and pre-fabricated merchandise
(work created without Appellants' knowledge of how the items will be
used or who will use those products). Appellants believe their customer
directed and designed wedding products "convey messages about a particular engaged couple, their upcoming marriage, their upcoming marriage
ceremony, and the celebration of that marriage." Appellants also strongly
believe in an ordained marriage between one man and one woman, and
argue that they cannot separate their religious beliefs from their work. As
such, they believe being required to create customer-specific merchandise
for same-sex weddings will violate their religious beliefs.

Appellants want to be able to legally refuse to create custom-made
merchandise for all same-sex weddings. Additionally, Appellants desire to
post a public statement explaining their religious beliefs. Appellants' proposed statement, in part, would notify potential customers that "Brush &
Nib Studio won't create any artwork that violates [their] vision as defined by
[their] religious and artistic beliefs and identity," which includes "artwork
that demeans others, endorses racism, incites violence, contradicts [their]
Christian faith, or promotes any marriage except marriage between one
man and one woman." Appellants have not posted this statement because
they believe it would violate Section 18-4(B). Instead, Appellants sought a
preliminary injunction to bar Phoenix from enforcing Section 18-4(B) and
a declaration that Section 18-4(B) violates the Arizona Constitution's free
speech clause, religious toleration clause, equal protection clause, due process clause, and the *Arizona Free Exercise of Religion Act ("FERA")*. . . .

ANALYSIS

Arizona courts have long upheld the public's right to participate in society
without fear of discrimination. . . .

Currently, nineteen states have enacted public accommodation anti-discrimination laws which include sexual orientation and gender identity as protected classes. . . . Arizona's public accommodation antidiscrimination statute, however, does not specifically include sexual orientation as a protected class. Accordingly, several Arizona cities have enacted broader ordinances to prohibit discrimination based on sexual orientation in places of public accommodation. . . . Phoenix's Code, Section 18-4(B), as amended in 2013, prohibits discrimination in places of public accommodation based on sexual orientation. . . .

On appeal, Appellants raise a myriad of constitutional issues, arguing that Section 18-4(B) is unconstitutional, both on its face and as-applied, and that any enforcement of Section 18-4(B) would violate their *First Amendment* right to free speech and free exercise of religion under state law. Appellants are not the first to attempt to use their religious beliefs to justify practices others consider overtly discriminatory. . . .

While this case may be the first of its kind in Arizona, Brush & Nib is only one of numerous national litigants who seek to preserve and define their religious freedoms in the face of ordinances which prohibit places of public accommodation from discriminating based on sexual orientation. . . .

[O]ur inquiry is whether Section 18-4(B), which requires that Appellants provide equal services to customers regardless of sexual orientation, infringes their *First Amendment* rights, not whether Appellants have a free speech right to operate their stationery store.

FS   The Arizona Constitution guarantees that "[e]very person may freely speak, write, and publish on all subjects, being responsible for the abuse of that right." *Ariz. Const. art. II, §6.* Appellants assert that the Arizona Constitution provides broader free speech protections than the United States Constitution. Even assuming this to be true, Appellants do not explain how, in this case, our analysis under Arizona's free speech clause would differ from our analysis under federal free speech jurisprudence. Thus, we analyze Appellants' free speech claim pursuant to federal law. . . .

Appellants argue Section 18-4(B) compels them to speak in favor of same-sex marriages. We disagree. Although Section 18-4(B) may have an incidental impact on speech, its main purpose is to prohibit discrimination, and thus Section 18-4(B) regulates conduct, not speech. . . .

. . . Section 18-4(B) requires that places of public accommodation provide equal services if they want to operate their business. While such a requirement may impact speech, such as prohibiting places of public accommodation from posting signs that discriminate against customers, this impact is incidental to properly regulated conduct. . . .

We do not doubt that "words" are generally considered pure speech. Or that, in some instances, an ordinance may infringe a stationery store's *First Amendment* right, if for example, . . . the ordinance completely bars the store's ability to create stationery or to operate its business. Nor do we doubt that a law prohibiting a baker from writing certain words on a cake may implicate the *First Amendment*. None of these hypothetical *First Amendment* violations are currently before us, and they do not affect the outcome of this case. The case before us is one of a blanket refusal of service to the LGBTQ community and not a *First Amendment* challenge to a specific message requested by a specific customer.

Simply stated, if Appellants, as an economic entity, want to operate their for-profit business as a public accommodation, they cannot discriminate against potential patrons based on sexual orientation. It bears repeating that Section 18-4(B) regulates conduct, not speech. Accordingly, the conduct at issue is not the creation of words or images but the conduct of selling or refusing to sell merchandise—either pre-fabricated or designed to order—equally to same-sex and opposite-sex couples. This conduct, even though it may incidentally impact speech, is not speech. Further, allowing a vendor who provides goods and services for marriages and weddings to refuse similar services for gay persons would result in "a community-wide stigma inconsistent with the history and dynamics of civil rights laws that ensure equal access to goods, services, and public accommodations." *Masterpiece Cakeshop, Ltd., 2018 U.S. LEXIS 3386 at *20.*

Although Section 18-4(B) regulates conduct, this is not the end our inquiry. Next, we must determine whether the conduct regulated by Section 18-4(B) is inherently expressive. . . . Conduct is entitled to full *First Amendment* protections if the "speaker" intended to convey a particularized message by the conduct and if, given the surrounding circumstances, there was a strong likelihood that the speaker's message would be understood by those who viewed it. . . . Like many similar cases decided in other jurisdictions, we find Appellants' act of creating design-to-order wedding announcements, invitations, and the like is not inherently expressive. . . .

The mere fact that Section 18-4(B) requires Appellants to comply with the law does not render their creation of design-to-order merchandise for same-sex weddings expressive conduct. The items Appellants would produce for a same-sex or opposite-sex wedding would likely be indistinguishable to the public. Take for instance an invitation to the marriage of Pat and Pat (whether created for Patrick and Patrick, or Patrick and Patricia), or Alex and Alex (whether created for Alexander and Alexander, or Alexander and Alexa). This invitation would not differ in creative expression. Further, it is unlikely that a general observer would attribute a company's product or offer of services, in compliance with the law, as indicative of the company's speech or personal beliefs. . . . The operation of a stationery store—including the design and sale of customized wedding event merchandise—is not expressive conduct, and thus, is not entitled to *First Amendment* free speech protections.

The law has long recognized a state's authority to "create rights of public access on behalf of its citizens. . . . Thus, "[p]osting language on a website telling potential customers that a business will discriminate based on sexual orientation is part of the act of sexual orientation discrimination itself; as conduct carried out through language [and] this act is not protected by the First Amendment."

Although Appellants are prohibited from posting discriminatory statements about their intent to refuse services for same-sex weddings, they may post a statement endorsing their belief that marriage is between a man and a woman and may post a disclaimer explaining that, notwithstanding that belief, Section 18-4(B) requires them to provide goods and services to everyone regardless of sexual orientation. Or they may post a disclaimer that the act of selling their goods and services to same-sex couples does not constitute an endorsement of their customers' exercise of their constitutional right to marry or any other activities. . . .

Phoenix clearly has a substantial interest in discouraging discrimination in places of public accommodation. The way to effectively accomplish this goal is to explicitly prohibit places of public accommodation from discriminating. . . .

IV. EXPRESSIVE ASSOCIATION

Appellants additionally argue Section 18-4(B) compels expressive association. . . . The right to associate, or not associate, "is crucial in preventing the majority from imposing its views on groups that would rather express other, perhaps unpopular, ideas." . . . The right to associate, however, is not absolute and "may be curtailed if necessary to further a significant governmental interest like eliminating . . . public evils." . . .

Although the *First Amendment* "fully protects expression about philosophical, social, artistic, economic, literary, ethical, and other topics . . . it does not protect every communication or every association that touches these topics." . . . Importantly, a state does not lose its ability to regulate commercial activity merely because the activity has a speech component. A law, however, will be found to violate the right to "expressive association" if it requires the inclusion of an unwanted member, and that inclusion would significantly affect the group's association.

We are unpersuaded by Appellants' argument that Section 18-4(B) infringes their freedom of association by requiring that they provide equal services to same-sex couples. Appellants operate an economic entity and a place of public accommodation; as such, they are prohibited from discriminating against customers based on a protected class. Further, although Appellants argue they created Brush & Nib pursuant to their religious beliefs, this alone does not bestow on Appellants the unfettered right of expressive association in their business. . . . [T]he primary purpose of Brush & Nib is not to convey a particular message but rather to engage in commercial sales activity. . . . [The] requirement that Appellants provide equal goods and services does not infringe their primary goal of operating a business; if anything, such mandate is more aligned with their commercial interests by requiring services be provided to a broader customer base. . . .

Appellants remain free to disclaim and/or post their belief that their religion only recognizes marriage between one man and one woman. That said, however, Appellants cannot deny access to their goods and services based on potential customers' sexual orientation. . . .

VI.   FREE EXERCISE OF RELIGION

Appellants argue Section 18-4(B) burdens their free exercise of religion under state law by requiring them to create "custom artwork to celebrate and promote . . . marriage[s] outside of God's design for marriage as an institution between one man and one woman."

FERA protects an individual's exercise of religion from undue governmental interference. . . . Under the statute, the "government shall not substantially burden a person's exercise of religion even if the burden results from a rule of general applicability" unless the rule is both "[i]n furtherance of a compelling government interest [and is] [t]he least restrictive means of furthering that compelling governmental interest." . . . Pursuant to *FERA*, a party must establish that her act or refusal to act is motivated by her religious belief, that the religious belief is sincerely held, and that the governmental action substantially burdens the exercise of religious beliefs. . . .

On appeal, Phoenix does not dispute that Appellants' desire to refuse to create wedding-related merchandise for same-sex weddings and to post an explanatory statement is motivated by their religious beliefs, nor does Phoenix dispute the sincerity of Appellants' beliefs. . . .

Appellants have failed to prove that Section 18-4(B) substantially burdens their religious beliefs by requiring that they provide equal goods and services to same-sex couples. Appellants are not penalized for expressing their belief that their religion only recognizes the marriage of opposite-sex couples. Nor are Appellants penalized for refusing to create wedding-related merchandise as long as they equally refuse similar services to opposite-sex couples. Section 18-4(B) merely requires that, by operating a place of public accommodation, Appellants provide equal goods and services to customers regardless of sexual orientation. Appellants are free to discontinue selling custom wedding-related merchandise and maintain the operation of Brush & Nib for its other business operations. What Appellants cannot do is use their religion as a shield to discriminate against potential customers. . . .

Even if Appellants had met their burden of proof to demonstrate that Section 18-4(B) places a substantial burden on their religious exercise, Section 18-4(B) is still constitutional because Phoenix has a compelling interest in preventing discrimination, and has done so here through the least restrictive means. . . . Appellants, however, argue that Phoenix does not suffer from pervasive sexual orientation discrimination, as evident from the historic lack of lawsuits to date, and that Phoenix could have used other means to achieve its goal, such as posting lists of businesses that will provide services for same-sex weddings. Other courts have addressed this "go elsewhere" argument and found it unpersuasive. We agree with those courts. *See Arlene's Flowers, Inc., 389 P.3d at 566, ¶ 77* (rejecting Arlene's "go elsewhere" argument and finding that the "case is no more about access to flowers than civil rights cases in the 1960s were about access to sandwiches"). Prohibiting places of public accommodation from discriminating against customers is not just about ensuring equal access, but about eradicating the construction of a second-class citizenship and diminishing humiliation and social stigma. The least restrictive way to eliminate discrimination in places of public accommodation is to expressly prohibit such places from discriminating.

VII. EQUAL PROTECTION

Appellants' final argument is that Section 18-4(B) violates their right to equal protection under state law because Section 18-4(B) "favor[s] artists who support same-sex marriage and punish[es] those who oppose it." We disagree.

Arizona's equal protection clause provides that "[n]o law shall be enacted granting to any citizen, class of citizens, or corporation other than municipal, privileges or immunities which, upon the same terms, shall not equally belong to all citizens or corporations.". . .

Appellants have not alleged they are members of a suspect class; instead, they argue they are treated differently than other similarly situated businesses because "[a]rtists who support same-sex marriage can operate their businesses in accordance with their beliefs" whereas Appellants purportedly cannot. Even assuming this to be true, it does not render Section 18-4(B) unconstitutional. Section 18-4(B) applies to all places of public accommodation and all business owners equally, regardless of their beliefs. Contrary to Appellants assertions, Section 18-4(B) does not infringe their fundamental rights by requiring that they provide equal goods and services to all customers regardless of sexual orientation. As such, the provisions of Section 18-4(B) must only be rationally related to a legitimate governmental purpose. As previously demonstrated, Phoenix has a legitimate governmental purpose in curtailing discriminatory practices, and prohibiting businesses from sexual orientation discrimination is rationally related to that purpose. Thus, Section 18-4(B) does not violate Appellants' equal protection.

QUESTIONS

1. Why did Brush & Nib bring this case against the City of Phoenix?
2. What was Brush & Nib looking for as a result in the case?
3. What arguments did it make in support of its position?
4. Explain how the court responded to each of the arguments that Brush & Nib made.
5. What did the court conclude about the posting of a sign?

Endnotes

1. The term "common law" refers to English case law, much of which enforced long-standing customs and traditions. Most colonies and subsequent states accepted the precedential value of these English decisions. *See* Morton J. Horwitz, The Transformation of American Law 1780-1860 ch. 1 (1992).

2. William Blackstone, Commentaries on the Laws of England 441-442 (15th ed. A. Strahan ed., 1809) (citations omitted).

3. William Blackstone, Commentaries on the Laws of England 142 (Clarendon Press 1983).

4. This section is based mainly on the following works: Norma Basch, In the Eyes of the Law: Women, Marriage, and Property in Nineteenth Century New York (1982), and Elizabeth Bowles Warbassee, The Changing Legal Rights of Married Women 1800-1861 ch. 1 (1987).

5. Letter from Elizabeth Cady Stanton (July 25, 1857) to Susan B. Anthony, *quoted in* Elisabeth Griffith, In Her Own Right: The Life of Elizabeth Cady Stanton 103 (1984).

6. Warbassee, *supra* note 4, at 273.

7. *See* Riva Siegel, The Modernization of Marital Status Law: Adjudicating Wives' Rights to Earnings, 1860-1930, 82 Geo. L. Rev. 2127 (1994); Riva Siegel, Home as Work, 103 Yale L.J. 1073 (1994).

8. Graham v. Graham, 33 F. Supp. 936, 938-939 (E.D. Mich. 1940).

9. Orr v. Orr, 440 U.S. 268, 279-280, 283 (1979), quoting Stanton v. Stanton, 421 U.S. 7, 10, 14-15 (1975).

10. Griswold v. Connecticut, 381 U.S. 479 (1965).

11. 388 U.S. 1 (1967).

12. 135 S. Ct. 2584 (2015).

13. Loving v. Virginia, 388 U.S. 1 (1967).

14. *Id.* at 7, citing Naim v. Naim, 197 Va. 80, 90, 87 S.E.2d 749, 756 (1955).

15. *Id.* at 12.

16. Turner v. Safley, 428 U.S. 78 (1987).

17. *See, e.g.,* Jones v. Hallahan, 501 S.W.2d 588 (Ky. Ct. App. 1973), and Baker v. Nelson, 291 Minn. 310, 191 N.W.2d 185 (1971).

18. In 1993, the Hawaii Supreme Court concluded that imposing a "different-sex" requirement on the choice of marriage partner violated the equal protection clause of the state constitution. It remanded the case to the trial court to give the state an opportunity to try to show that the different-sex requirement served a compelling state interest. After a hearing, the trial court judge concluded that the state had not met its burden; while the case was back up on appeal, a constitutional amendment giving the legislature the authority to restrict marriage to male-female was approved. *See* Baehr v. Miike, 852 P.2d 44 (Haw. 1993), and Baehr v. Miike, Civil Action No. 91-1394 (Haw. Cir. Ct. Dec. 3, 1996). In Alaska, the constitution was amended following a trial court decision holding that the "choice of a life partner is personal, intimate, and subject to the protection of the right to privacy" for both same-sex and heterosexual couples. *See* Brause & Dugan v. Bureau of Vital Statistics (Alaska Super. Ct., Feb. 27, 1998).

19. 28 U.S.C.S. §1738(c).

20. 798 N.E.2d 941 (2003).

21. *Id.* at 955-956 (internal citations omitted).

22. *Id.* at 966.

23. *Id.* at 969.

24. 570 U.S. 744 (2013).

25. *Id.* at 827.

26. *Id.* at 772.

27. Bostic v. Schaefer, 730 F.3d 352, 367 & 377 (2014); *cert. denied*, 138 S. Ct. 308 (2014).

28. Geiger v. Kitzhaber, United States District Court for the District of Oregon, Case No. 6:13-cv-01834-MC, 12 (2014).

29. *Obergefell*, 135 S. Ct. at 2594.

30. *Id.*

31. *Id.* at 2959.

32. *Id.* at 2596.

33. *Id.* at 2599-2601.

34. *Id.* at 2602.

35. *Id.* at 2604.

36. Peter Nicholas, Backdating Marriage, 105 Calif. L. Rev. 395, 400 (2017). The discussion here focuses on the retroactivity of the *Obergefell* decision, but the same issue of retroactivity could potentially arise under state law in those jurisdictions that had previously invalidated the ban on marriages between same-sex partners.

37. Lee-Ford Tritt, Moving Forward by Looking Back: The Retroactive Application of *Obergefell*, 2016 Wis. L. Rev. 873, 891.

38. *Id.* at 893-905.

39. Ranolls v. Dewling, 223 F. Supp. 3d 613, 624 (2016).

40. *Obergefell*, 135 S. Ct. at 638-639. Dissenting opinion of Chief Justice Roberts, joined by Justices Scalia and Thomas.

41. Craig v. Masterpiece Cakeshop, 370 P.3d 272 (Colo. Ct. App. 2015). This case ended up before the Supreme Court, which ruled for the bakery on very narrow grounds that have little precedential value. *See* Masterpiece Cakeshop, Ltd. v. Colorado Civil Rights Commission, 138 S. Ct. 1719 (2018).

42. Brush & Nib Studio, LC v. City of Phoenix, CA-CV16-0602, 25 (2018).

43. State of Washington v. Arlene's Flowers, 389 P.3d 543, 566 (Wash. 2017).

44. Following its decision in *Masterpiece Cakeshop*, see *supra* note 41, the Supreme Court vacated the Washington Supreme Court's decision in State of Washington v. Arlene's Flowers in favor of the two men, and remanded the case back to the court for further consideration in light of its ruling in *Masterpiece Cakeshop*.

45. http://www.ncsl.org/research/human-services/state-laws-regarding-marriages-between-first-cousi.aspx (accessed Nov. 2, 2015).

46. Robin L. Bennett et al., Genetic Counseling and Screening of Consanguineous Couples and Their Offspring: Recommendations of the National Society of Genetic Counselors, 11 J. Genetic Counseling 97 (2002).

47. Carolyn Bratt, Is Oedipus Free to Marry?, 18 Fam. L.Q. 267, 288-289 (1984) (citations omitted).

48. Teri Dobbins Baxter, Child Marriage as Constitutional Violation, 19 Nev. L.J. 40, 47 (2018). *See also* Lisa V. Martin, Restraining Forced Marriage, 18 Nev. L.J. 919 (2018).

49. Tahirih Justice Ctr., Falling Through the Cracks 4 (2017), http://www.tahirih.org/wpcontent/uploads/2017/08/TahirihChildMarriageReport-1.pdf   [https://perma.cc/63WN-YC9E], 3.

50. Baxter, *supra* note 48, at 49, quoting Ashley Belanger, Child Marriage and Religion in the United States, Teen Vogue (Sept. 7, 2017 8:00 AM), https://www.teenvogue.com/story/child-marriage-and-religion-in-the-united-states.

51. *Id.* at 50-52.

52. For further detail, *see id.* at 77-80.

53. Parks v. Lee, York County Family Court 2016-DR-45-1061 (2016).

54. As a way of alleviating some of the hardships imposed on same-sex couples prior to the advent of marital equality, some states and municipalities created domestic partnership or civil union registries, which typically offered limited relationship rights and

recognition to registered couples. Going a step beyond this, some states offered equal benefits to couples in a civil union, minus, of course, the status recognition of marriage.

55. 18 Cal. 3d 660, 557 P.2d 106, 134 Cal. Rptr. 815 (1976).

56. *Marvin*, 557 P.2d at 122.

57. The state of Illinois remains an outlier in this regard. *See* Stefanie L. Ferrari, Cohabitation in Illinois: The Need for Legislative Intervention, 93 Chi.-Kent L. Rev. 561 (2018).

58. Some couples do enter into formal cohabitation agreements in order to structure their post-dissolution rights and obligations. Some couples also execute a variety of additional legal documents, such as wills and durable powers of attorney, in order to create rights between them similar to those that the law grants to married couples.

59. Margaret M. Mahoney, Forces Shaping the Law of Cohabitation for Opposite Sex Couples, 7 J.L. Fam. Stud. 135, 161 (2005). Cohabitation is treated as a formal legal status in few states. As with marriage, then, rights and obligations flow from the existence of the relationship itself, thus eliminating the need to prove the existence of an agreement.

60. Mark Ellman, Unmarried Partners and the Legacy of Marvin v. Marvin: "Contract Thinking" Was *Marvin*'s, 76 Notre Dame L. Rev. 1365 (2001).

61. American Law Institute, Principles of the Law of Family Dissolution: Analysis and Recommendations (2002), §6.03 (1). The Principles provide detailed guidelines for "identifying those nonmarital relationships which bear a sufficient resemblance to marriage to justify and require similar post-relationship obligations between the parties," whom the Institute refers to as "domestic partners." Ellman, *supra* note 60, at 1378-1379.

62. In addition to Ellman, *see* Nancy D. Polikoff, Making Marriage Matter Less: The ALI Domestic Partner Principles Are One Step in the Right Direction, 2004 U. Chi. Legal F. 353; Marsha Garrison, Is Consent Necessary? An Evaluation of the Emerging Law of Cohabitation Obligation, 52 UCLA L. Rev. 815 (2005).

63. Section 18-3 defines places of public accommodation as:

> [A]ll public places of entertainment, amusement or recreation, all public places where food or beverages are sold, public places operated for the lodging of transients or for the benefit, use or accommodation of those seeking health or recreation and all establishments offering their services, facilities or goods to or soliciting patronage from the members of the general public. Any dwelling, any private club or any place which is in its nature distinctly private is not a place of public accommodation.

Chapter Two

Premarital and Postmarital Agreements

In Chapter 1, we saw that the trend has been away from state regulation of marriage, toward a legal model that emphasizes individual choice. With this increased emphasis on private ordering, **premarital agreements** have gained in both legal and social acceptance. More recently, **postmarital agreements** have also become somewhat more common. These arrangements allow couples to control the terms of their dissolution in the event the marriage ends in divorce.[1] Accordingly, these agreements are often particularly attractive to wealthy individuals who are entering into a marriage with substantial income and assets. They may also be attractive to individuals who have children from a previous relationship, as they allow a parent to protect assets intended for his or her children from claims of the new spouse in the event of a divorce.

Premarital agreements have become an increasingly important dimension of the private ordering of marriage; however, they have not been accepted without controversy and some judicial ambivalence. Accordingly, as discussed in this chapter, in many states premarital contracts are reviewed more carefully than ordinary contracts. The standard of review may be higher, and certain types of provisions, particularly those involving children, are likely to be unenforceable even if the parties knowingly and voluntarily agreed to the terms, although the trend is clearly in favor of treating them like other agreements.

The Traditional Approach to Premarital Agreements

Until the early 1970s, premarital agreements made in contemplation of a possible divorce were generally considered **void as against public policy**. Although courts no longer disfavor such agreements, the public policy concerns that historically led states to withhold recognition from premarital agreements continue to retain some force today, and those concerns inform the debate over whether the agreements should be treated like "ordinary" contracts or whether, because of their unique nature, they should occupy a special place in the law. These concerns have also shaped the development of the rules and standards governing the enforceability of premarital agreements. Historically, the most significant fear was that premarital agreements would encourage divorce because the party who stood to benefit from the agreement would have less incentive to remain in the marriage when things got rocky. According to this way of thinking, a wealthy man whose wife had waived her right to support would be more inclined to walk away from a troubled marriage than a man who knew he would be burdened with alimony payments, thus undermining the state's interest in preserving marriage as a fundamental social unit.

A related fear was that the enforcement of premarital contracts would lead to the post-divorce impoverishment of women. In opinion after opinion, judges expressed the concern that women would be pushed into signing agreements by financially secure and sophisticated men, and they would give up future rights they did not know they possessed. As discussed below, this protective impulse has shaped much of the present law regarding enforceability.

Nonrecognition of premarital agreements was also a logical extension of the principle that spouses lacked the authority to alter the terms of the marital relationship because defining the rights and obligations of spouses was a public, rather than a private, matter. Accordingly, since, a husband could not legally shed his duty of support during the marriage, it was considered unfair to allow him to contract out of this obligation in the event of divorce.

Another powerful apprehension was that if couples entering into a marriage were allowed to contract with one another, marriage would be reduced to a commercial enterprise. The vision of couples participating in protracted financial negotiations in contemplation of a possible divorce was an uncomfortable one that suggested the world of family was no different from the world of commerce and that spouses were more like business associates than intimate companions.

Consideration

To many, the infusion of contractual ordering into a realm of life thought to be based on ties of mutual affection and commitment would radically alter the meaning of family and make spouses more like business associates than intimate companions. Do you agree?

The Growing Acceptance of Premarital Agreements

In 1970, the Florida Supreme Court, in the landmark case of Posner v. Posner,[2] held that premarital agreements made in contemplation of divorce are not per se invalid, and other states soon followed suit. This trend corresponded with changing notions about marriage and divorce. As individuals acquired greater legal freedom to structure the terms of their marriage, it was a logical development that they be permitted to structure the terms of marital dissolution. The acceptance of no-fault divorce, which eliminated many of the traditional barriers to marital dissolution, also contributed to the acceptance of premarital agreements. With the increased acceptability and availability of divorce, the argument that premarital agreements would facilitate marital dissolution no longer carried the same weight that it had when divorces were more difficult to obtain. (See Chapter 4 for more detail on "no-fault" divorce reform.) In fact, some argue that premarital agreements actually encourage marriage because they allow individuals who might otherwise be wary of getting married, based on a fear of what they might lose upon dissolution, to control the terms of any future divorce.

Another key factor underlying the acceptance of premarital agreements was the changing status of women. Today, courts no longer assume, as they once did, that women are so financially unsophisticated that they will not be able to comprehend the significance of these agreements and will be taken advantage of by prospective husbands. In a related vein, the financial dependence of married women is no longer presumed. Thus, the protective impulse behind nonrecognition is now seen as outdated— a relic of the time when women were regarded as lacking legal capacity and in need of the paternalistic protection of the law, as explained by the Pennsylvania Supreme Court in the case of Simeone v. Simeone:[3]

> Such decisions rested upon a belief that spouses are of unequal status and that women are not knowledgeable enough to understand the nature of contracts they enter. Society has advanced, however, to the point where women are no longer regarded as the "weaker" party in marriage . . . nor is there viability in the presumption that women are uninformed, uneducated, and readily subjected to unfair advantage in marital agreements . . . paternalistic presumptions and protectors that arose to shelter women . . . have, appropriately, been discarded.

Concerns have been voiced, however, that these assumptions of equality mask the fact that in most heterosexual marriages women continue to be the economically subordinate partner, and that enforcement of premarital agreements may reinforce the post-divorce economic disparity between husbands and wives.[4]

■
  ## Legal Requirements

Threshold Considerations

Premarital agreements are contracts. Accordingly, to be enforceable, they must, at a minimum, satisfy certain threshold requirements generally applicable to all contracts. However, as discussed below, unlike with most other contracts, satisfying these requirements may not be enough to make a premarital agreement enforceable. These threshold requirements are:

1. There must be an offer and an acceptance of the offer.
2. The contract must be supported by **consideration**. Consideration is the bargained-for exchange of something of value—here, the mutual promise of marriage.
3. The parties must have the capacity to enter into a contract.
4. The subject matter of the agreement cannot be illegal.

Additionally, in most jurisdictions, premarital contracts come within the **statute of frauds**, which is a rule specifying that certain types of contracts must be in writing in order to be enforceable. Most likely, the agreement will also need to be signed by both parties, and the signatures may need to be both witnessed and notarized.

The Fairness Requirement

As a general rule, our legal system emphasizes **freedom of contract**—the right of each individual to freely structure his or her affairs. A corollary of this principle is that once parties have entered into a contract, they are entitled to rely upon it, and courts will protect the expectancies that arise from the terms of the agreement. Without proof of conduct that rises to the level of fraud, misrepresentation, duress, or the like, courts typically will not refuse to enforce a contract because it is more favorable to one party. Unless these more serious kinds of concerns can be established, considerations of fairness with respect to either the process by which the contract was negotiated (such as where a party felt rushed into signing it) or the resulting terms (such as where a person agrees to pay more for a painting than it is worth) are essentially irrelevant. Thus, as a general rule, adherence to the freedom-of-contract principle means that an individual cannot avoid contractual obligations because he or she realizes that the deal is unfair or more favorable to the other side. The primary exception to this rule is the doctrine of **unconscionability**, which allows a court to inquire into issues of fairness in outrageous situations; for this doctrine to apply, there usually must be gross overreaching by a party who is in a vastly superior bargaining position.

However, when a dispute involves a premarital contract, courts typically review the agreement for evidence of unfairness in either the process of negotiating the agreement, referred to as **procedural fairness**, or in the resulting terms, referred to as **substantive fairness**. This hands-on approach, as distinct from the traditional hands-off approach to contract review, flows from a number of considerations. First, by entering into a premarital contract, parties are substituting their own terms for state laws that determine rights of support and property distribution between divorcing spouses. In effect, these agreements create private law in an area long considered to be under the exclusive authority of the state because of its special interest in the marriage. Thus, the subject matter of premarital agreements is quite different from that of more ordinary contracts, such as those governing the purchase and sale of real estate.

Second, parties to a typical contract stand at "arm's-length" distance from one another—they are generally not intimately connected and each party can be assumed to be acting in his or her own self-interest. In contrast, parties to a premarital agreement are in an intimate relationship, or what the courts refer to as a "confidential relationship," and are thought to be more vulnerable to being unduly influenced by the other. This risk is compounded by the fact that the parties often are negotiating from positions of unequal bargaining power. Premarital agreements are usually proposed by the prospective spouse with greater wealth who stands to gain more from avoiding state divorce laws, and the other party may feel that she or he has no choice but to sign or face the cancellation of the wedding. Closely related, at least in the early days of recognition, were lingering concerns about the inability of prospective brides to comprehend the details of the financial terms being proposed by her future husband, particularly where differences in wealth were pronounced.

Third, the performance of contractual obligations usually begins within a reasonably short and clearly defined time period after the contract is executed. In contrast, with premarital contracts, the time of performance is uncertain or may never come to be since the triggering event is divorce. Performance of the terms could thus come several years or even several decades after execution of the contract. With the passage of time, unforeseen events may intervene that would make performance of the original terms unfair.

Finally, perhaps this heightened standard of review reflects a continued uneasiness about the contractualization of family life, rooted in a sense that the domestic realm should remain distinct from the commercial realm, courts may be reluctant to fully import legal standards developed in the realm of impersonal dealings into the realm of intimate relationships.

Requirements of Procedural Fairness

Although the clear trend is in favor of treating premarital contracts more like ordinary agreements with a corresponding emphasis upon individual autonomy and choice, most courts still look to see if the parties treated each other fairly when negotiating the terms of the agreement. If a court determines that in the course of negotiating the agreement one party did not treat the other fairly, such as by not fully disclosing assets, it may invalidate the agreement.[5]

The requirement of full and fair disclosure is usually the most important consideration, and the general rule is that both parties have an affirmative duty to make full disclosure even where this information is not requested by the other. Although the standard for determining what constitutes adequate disclosure varies from state to state, more than a mere recitation of numbers is necessary. Thus, for example, a party may be required to determine the value of his or her property and to disclose assets that he or she is entitled to receive in the future. If disclosure is not adequate, entry into the agreement is not considered voluntary, as a party cannot freely relinquish assets or income without knowing their correct value or even that they existed.

In some states, a limited exception to the disclosure requirement may be made where one party has actual and specific knowledge of the other potential spouse's assets. However, a general familiarity with the other's financial reputation is unlikely to justify the failure to disclose.

In preparing premarital agreements, even if not specifically required by state law, most attorneys will prepare a full schedule of their client's income and assets, which is attached to the agreement as an exhibit (see Exhibit 2.1). Frequently, paralegals will be asked to assist in this process. Great care must be taken to obtain complete and accurate information, as this may determine the subsequent enforceability of the agreement. Often a client is given a written questionnaire to complete regarding his or her income and assets. On the next page is a sample list of the information a client might be asked to provide.

In evaluating procedural fairness, some courts also consider factors such as whether the party challenging the agreement understood its provisions at the time of signing, whether she or he was made aware of the legal rights being waived (e.g., to spousal support) by entry into the agreement, and whether she or he had the opportunity to review the agreement with an independent attorney. Most jurisdictions require only that a party has the opportunity to review the agreement with an attorney; actual consultation is not required. The primary objective is to prevent one partner from presenting the other with an agreement for the first time at the rehearsal dinner and telling her or him that it must be signed if the wedding is to proceed as planned. As with the requirement of financial disclosure, these elements also relate to whether entry into the agreement was free and voluntary.

SAMPLE QUESTIONS FOR COMPILING SCHEDULE OF ASSETS

1. Do you own any real estate or have an interest in any realty? If yes, please provide a detailed list, including location of the real estate, nature of your interest, purchase date, purchase amount and amount of your down payment, current fair market value, and the amount of your equity in the real estate.
2. Please provide an itemized list of all household furnishings and effects owned by you, including the fair market value of each item.
3. Please provide an itemized list of all artwork owned by you, including the fair market value of each item.
4. Please provide an itemized list of all collections owned by you, including but not limited to collection items such as stamps, coins, cards, antiques, rare books, guns, and records. Include the fair market value of each collection.
5. Please provide an itemized list of all jewelry owned by you, including the fair market value of each item.
6. Please provide a detailed list of all stocks, bonds, retirement accounts, pension plans, and profit-sharing plans, including the nature of your interest, identifying information for each item, and the current value of your interest in each.
7. Please provide a detailed list of all other assets owned by you that are not set out above, together with the fair market value of each asset.

Exhibit 2.1 Schedule of Assets for Sandra Lope

	Fair Market Value	Encumbrance	Net Value
Real Estate			
Location: 16 Armand Road			
Recorded at: Norfolk County,			
Registry of Deeds;			
Book No. 814, Page No. 9	$240,000	$170,000	$70,000

Exhibit 2.1   Continued

	Fair Market Value	Encumbrance	Net Value
Personal Property			
Household Furnishings:			
Complete set of bedroom, living room, dining room, and kitchen furniture	$3,800	$0	$3,800
Other Household Items (list all worth more than $100):			
Tiffany lamp	$600	$0	$600
Indoor gym equipment	$1,500	$0	$1,500
Computer	$2,500	$0	$2,500
Kitchen appliances (including refrigerator and microwave)	$1,100	$0	$1,100
Antique phonograph	$1,200	$0	$1,200
Collections:			
Rare jazz records	$3,500	$0	$3,500
Jewelry (list all worth more than $100):			
Antique diamond ring	$1,200	$0	$1,200
Rolex watch	$1,400	$0	$1,400
Automobiles:			
2001 VW Bug	$16,000	$4,000	$12,000
Bank Accounts:			
Savings account, Union Federal Bank, account no. 1743	$4,000	—	—
Individual Retirement Account, Union Federal Bank, account no. 97363	$12,000	—	—
Stocks and Bonds:			
80 shares of General Utility Stock	$800	—	—

Note: This sample Schedule of Assets is for one party only. In actuality, each party would complete one.

In jurisdictions where freedom of contract is emphasized over considerations of procedural fairness, courts may not be concerned with the above considerations. Returning to the *Simeone* decision, which embodies a freedom of contract over a fairness approach, the court stated:

> Absent fraud, misrepresentation, or duress, spouses should be bound by the terms of their agreements. Contracting parties are normally bound by their agreements, without regard to whether the terms thereof were read and fully understood. . . . Based upon these principles, the terms of the present prenuptial agreement must be regarded as binding, without regard to whether the terms were fully understood by appellant. *Ignorantia non excusat.* Accordingly, we find no merit in a contention raised by appellant that the agreement should be declared void on the ground that she did not consult with independent legal counsel. To impose a *per se* requirement that parties entering a prenuptial agreement must obtain independent legal counsel would be contrary to traditional principles of contract law, and would constitute a paternalistic and unwarranted interference with the parties' freedom to enter contracts.[6]

Some courts use a somewhat flexible approach to evaluating formation fairness. They may be stricter if the parties do not stand on equal footing, such as where one partner is much wealthier or better educated than the other. However, if they stand on relatively equal footing with respect to income, assets, and education, the court may be less concerned with procedural irregularities. Also, as discussed below, if the outcome is fair, courts may be less concerned with procedural irregularities.

Requirements of Substantive Fairness

In addition to reviewing whether the process of contract formation was fair, courts in most jurisdictions will also review the actual terms of the agreement to see if they are fair. However, the *Simeone* decision is illustrative of the growing emphasis on considerations of contractual freedom over contractual fairness. In *Simeone*, the Pennsylvania high court not only limited the scope of review for procedural fairness to considerations of adequate disclosure but also held that the terms of an agreement should not be reviewed to determine if they are fair:

> The reasonableness of a prenuptial bargain is not a proper subject for judicial review. . . . By invoking inquiries into reasonableness, . . . the functioning and reliability of prenuptial agreements is severely undermined. Parties would not have entered into such agreements, and

indeed may not have entered into their marriages, if they did not expect the agreements to be strictly enforced.[7]

Fairness can be measured as it existed at the time the contract was executed, or as it exists at the time of performance, or both. Again, this kind of review is a substantial departure from the usual contract law approach that gives individuals "freedom" to make bad deals. Subject to the limited unconscionability exception, a person cannot avoid an ordinary contract because he or she subsequently realizes that it is unfair or one-sided.

At Formation.   In jurisdictions where the terms of a premarital agreement are reviewed for fairness, a court would first evaluate them in light of the circumstances as they existed at the time the contract was executed. For example, looking back to the time of contract formation, the waiver of alimony by a two-career couple not intending to have children appears equitable, whereas a waiver by a woman planning to stay home and raise a large family would not. At this phase of the review, events taking place after execution are not considered.

States differ in the standards they use to determine if the terms were fair at the time of execution. Some will not enforce provisions that are "unreasonable," such as a waiver of support by a spouse with a good job but with a much lower earning potential than his or her partner, although something more than a mere inequality of result is generally required. Other states will strike only clauses that are unconscionable or so unfair that they "shock the conscience." In a few jurisdictions, alimony waivers are considered per se unfair and will not be enforced, although this is a minority approach.

At Performance.   In addition to determining if the terms were fair at the time the contract was executed, in some states courts are also able to review them to see if they are also fair at the time of divorce. This is sometimes referred to as the **second glance doctrine** or second look doctrine. Here, traditional freedom of contract principles are clearly subordinated in favor of protecting an economically vulnerable spouse. By way of example, let us return to our two-career couple who did not plan to have children and included an alimony waiver in their prenuptial agreement. Assuming this was fair at the time of execution, if they then changed their minds and decided to have children, the waiver might be deemed unfair at the time of performance if one parent had cut back on employment to care for them. At second glance, terms that appeared fair at the time of contract formation would now work a hardship because of changed circumstances. In some states, however, courts will only take into account a change in circumstances that was unforeseeable at the time the agreement was executed. Under this approach, the onset of a disease after the parties married might well warrant the non-enforcement of a spousal support waiver due to the unforeseeability of this occurrence, whereas a spouse's decline in health from a disease that she or he had at the time of marriage would most likely not warrant such a waiver, unless it could be established that the decline was not foreseeable.

Many courts, however, consider this too great an interference with rights of contractual freedom, adhering to the view that once parties have made an agreement that is fair at the time of execution, they are entitled to rely on it. So viewed, the only proper role of the court is to protect legitimate expectations arising from the agreement.

Courts will usually take a second glance only at support-related clauses, and they tend to employ a very high standard of review in order to strike a balance between avoiding hardship and honoring contractual expectations. At this stage, many courts will invalidate only a term waiving or limiting support rights where enforcement would leave a party unable to meet basic needs or would force him or her onto public assistance. Other courts are less strict and will invalidate a clause if enforcement would result in a substantial reduction in a party's standard of living, even if poverty is not threatened.

The Interdependence of Procedural and Substantive Fairness

Although the above discussion treats the requirements of procedural and substantive fairness as independent variables, many courts regard them as interdependent. Accordingly, where the substantive terms are fair, a court may choose to overlook procedural deficiencies; for example, financial disclosure will not be insisted on as a pure formality. Likewise, if the result is clearly unfair, a court may presume that the procedure was inherently flawed and proceed to review the agreement with particular care.

Consideration

Do you think that premarital agreements should be treated as ordinary contracts with the traditional emphasis on individual contractual freedom, or do you think courts should scrutinize them more carefully to make sure both spouses' interests are protected?

Common Types of Provisions

In light of the above history, it is not surprising that even in more liberal jurisdictions, courts may be reluctant to accept certain types of provisions.

Moreover, as discussed below, with respect to clauses involving children, traditional family law principles also factor into the general rule of non-enforceability. Although the discussion is far from exhaustive, we now consider kinds of provisions that many couples include in their premarital agreements.[8]

Property

Perhaps the most common and generally least controversial type of pre-marital provisions are those that address how the property that the parties accumulated over the marriage is to be allocated in the event of divorce. In effect, these provisions allow a couple to opt out of the legal rules that would otherwise control the disposition of their property (see Chapter 8).

Most significant here is a determination of which assets will be regarded as separate, and thus unreachable by the other spouse in the event of a divorce, and what is to be considered marital property that is subject to distribution under applicable state rules. The ability to insulate property from the potential divorce claims of a spouse can be particularly important to an individual who already has children, as it enables him or her to preserve and eventually bequeath the intended assets to them.

Many patterns are possible here. Parties might simply seek to ensure that assets they come into the marriage with will continue to be defined as their sole and separate property, regardless of how they might otherwise be classified at the time of divorce under state law. Parties might also seek to classify all assets purchased during the marriage as the separate property of the acquiring spouse, free from any claims of the other, or they might set out a schema for determining which assets are to be considered separate and which are to be considered marital that differs from the classification pattern under state law.

Spousal Support

Courts have typically been more wary of provisions in which one or both spouses waive their right to spousal support. Of particular concern is that a spouse might find herself unable to make ends meet, and thus end up on public assistance. Accordingly, some courts will not enforce alimony waivers, often based on the view that they are "void as against public policy," although this traditional approach is now a distinctly minority position.

In the majority of states that now permit parties to waive spousal support rights, many have addressed concerns about potential post-divorce impoverishment through rules governing the review process. Thus, as discussed above, many require that the terms of the waiver be closely examined to ensure that they are fair, even if such a substantive review is not required for the property provisions. Some also mandate a second glance (see above) to ensure that even if fair at the time of enactment, the waiver is still fair at the time of divorce. In addition to, or in lieu of, substantive fairness requirements, some states also employ heightened procedural fairness requirements to ensure that a support waiver is truly free and voluntary.

Child Custody and Child Support

Despite the clear trend in favor of allowing spouses to structure in advance the consequences of divorce, this trend stops when it comes to provisions regarding children. Reflecting long-standing family law principles, this general proscription on the enforceability of child-related provisions is unlikely to change.

With respect to premarital efforts to determine custodial arrangements in the event of divorce, courts are in accord that spouses cannot determine in advance what would be in the "best interest" of their future offspring were they to eventually divorce (see Chapter 5). Although, as we have been discussing, parties can opt out of other rules (such as those governing the distribution of assets) through private ordering, the state retains a duty to ensure that custodial arrangements are carefully tailored to promote the well-being of children at the time of divorce.

Similarly, courts will not enforce provisions intended to modify or eliminate either party's child support obligations. Mandated by state law, the right to support runs to the child, not to the custodial parent, and thus cannot be waived or limited by a "third party."

▪ Postmarital Contracts

Although still less common than premarital agreements, a growing number of couples are now entering into postmarital contracts in order to determine the financial aspects of dissolution in the event their marriage ends in divorce. A couple might also choose to enter into a postmarital agreement in order to modify the terms of an agreement they entered into prior to their marriage based on a change in circumstances arising during the course of their marriage.

Many states now recognize the validity of these agreements, although, as discussed below, their enforceability may be governed by stricter standards than those governing premarital agreements. However, a few states have determined, either by statute or judicial decision, that they are not enforceable, while others have not yet addressed the issue.

Some commentators have suggested two primary reasons that might make postmarital contracts a more attractive option than contracts of the prenuptial variety. First, because the parties are already married, the dreaded last-minute situation where one party presents the other with an agreement at the rehearsal dinner and says "sign or the wedding is off" is avoided, thus potentially making them less coercive. Second, and perhaps more importantly, the actual circumstances of a couple's life together may be clearer as their life together unfolds, thus enabling them to more carefully tailor an agreement to their actual, as distinct from their projected, needs. For example, as one commentator puts it, if it turns out that "a couple's first child has autism, the wife may choose to forgo a career opportunity to care for her child. A postnuptial contract would allow her to tailor her rights upon divorce to ensure that her sacrifice is borne equally by both parents," in a way that would not have been possible prior to the marriage on account of this unforeseen circumstance.[9]

However, many courts that have considered the issue have instead concluded that postmarital contracts should be held to a higher standard of review than premarital agreements. Of particular concern is that potential for coercion may be greater in the context of an ongoing marriage than it is prior to the wedding as one spouse may threaten divorce if the other refuses to sign an agreement that is presented unilaterally at a rocky moment in the relationship.[10] For example, in a 2010 case of first impression, the Massachusetts high court, although rejecting the wife's claim that "marital agreements . . . should be declared void against public policy because they are 'innately coercive,'" concluded that "a marital agreement stands on a different footing from a premarital agreement" because "parties have greater freedom to reject an unsatisfactory . . . contract" before they have embarked on married life.[11] However, once married, a party may feel coerced into signing an agreement in order to save "a long, existing family relationship to which she [or he] has committed her [or his] best years"[12] while knowing that the failure to give in to a spouse's unilateral demand would result in "'the destruction of a family and the stigma of a failed marriage.'"

Chapter Summary

Until the 1970s, premarital agreements made in contemplation of divorce were generally considered void as against public policy in large part because they were thought to encourage divorce. Nonrecognition was also thought necessary to protect women from being taken advantage of by financially savvy prospective spouses as well as from post-divorce impoverishment. However, influenced by the growing acceptance of no-fault divorce and the changing socioeconomic status of women, the majority of jurisdictions now recognize these agreements. Although less common, many states now also recognize postmarital agreements.

Although now generally accepted, many courts still treat premarital and postmarital agreements differently from ordinary contracts and in the event of a dispute emphasize fairness over strict adherence to freedom of contract principles. A near-universal rule is that for a premarital agreement to be enforceable, the parties must have entered into it freely and with full knowledge of the other spouse's financial circumstances. Beyond this, courts may review other procedural elements as well, such as whether the parties understood the terms of the agreement at the time of execution. Some courts will also look to see if the terms of the agreement were fair at the time of execution, and some will also take a "second glance" to determine if the terms are fair at the time of enforcement. However, the clear trend is to treat premarital agreements more like ordinary contracts, resulting in a growing emphasis on contractual freedom over contractual fairness.

Key Terms

Premarital Agreements	Freedom of Contract
Postmarital Agreements	Unconscionability
Void as Against Public Policy	Procedural Fairness
Consideration	Substantive Fairness
Statute of Frauds	Second Glance Doctrine

Review Questions

1. What is a premarital contract?
2. Why would someone enter into one?
3. Why were premarital contracts made in contemplation of divorce once considered void as against public policy?
4. Why did courts gradually come to accept these agreements?
5. In what ways are premarital contracts treated differently from ordinary contracts?
6. Why are they treated differently?
7. What will a court look to in determining procedural fairness?

8. What will a court look to in determining substantive fairness?
9. How are the two concepts interrelated?
10. What direction are courts moving in with respect to reviewing premarital contracts? What considerations underlie this shift?
11. What kinds of provisions do couples typically include in a prenuptial agreement?
12. What is the general approach that courts take with respect to each type of provision?
13. What are postnuptial contracts? How do they differ from premarital agreements?

Discussion Questions

1. In the event of a dispute over the enforcement of a premarital contract, do you think the agreement should be treated like an ordinary contract or do you think a court should review it for unfairness? Identify arguments that support both positions. Additionally, in developing the arguments in favor of the fairness approach, discuss how "fair" is fair—should the courts look only at procedural fairness? Or should they also consider substantive fairness at the time of execution? At the time of execution and performance? Some combination as determined by the circumstances?
2. If you were planning to get married, would you want to enter into a premarital contract? Why or why not? Are there any factors that would influence your decision? For example, what if you were wealthy or already had children? How would you feel if the person you were intending to marry insisted on entry into a premarital agreement? Again, would it make a difference if your spouse had children? Was very wealthy? Had other "concrete" reasons for his or her insistence on an agreement? In formulating your answer, think about the economic as well as emotional issues.
3. Do you think premarital agreements denigrate the meaning of marriage by making it more like a commercial transaction?
4. Do you think postmarital contracts avoid some of the problems associated with premarital contracts? Do they present other potential difficulties?

Assignments

1. Determine if premarital agreements are recognized in your state. If they are, determine the following:

- What is required for premarital agreements to be enforceable? For example, what kind of disclosure is required?
- What is the applicable standard of review? Are they treated like ordinary contracts?
- Do courts consider procedural fairness? Substantive fairness?
- Will courts take a "second glance" at any of the terms to see if they are fair at the time of execution? How is the concept of fairness defined?

(Note: If premarital agreements are not recognized in your jurisdiction, find a recent case that sets out the rationale for nonrecognition and explain the reasoning of the court.)

2. Assume that you are a paralegal working in a small law firm. A new, wealthy client has come to the office because he wants a premarital agreement drafted. His prospective wife, although not wealthy, has a well-paying job. He is 36, and she is 35. It is a first marriage for both of them. They do not plan to have children.

   The attorney you work for has asked you to draft a letter to the client. In the letter you are to explain how the law in your jurisdiction treats premarital agreements* and what steps need to be taken to best ensure that the agreement will be enforced. You should also inform the client about the kinds of provisions that he should consider including in the agreement.

   (*Note: If you are in a nonrecognizing jurisdiction, then assume you are in a state that is very concerned about fairness and follows the second glance approach.)

3. Assume you are a clerk working for a justice in your state's highest court. The court will soon be reviewing a case involving a dispute in which a wife is seeking to set aside a premarital agreement on the following two grounds. First, when she signed the agreement, she did not understand that she was giving up her right to alimony. Second, she believes that the alimony waiver is unfair given that her husband is extremely wealthy, and she has become disabled over the course of the marriage. She says the waiver was unfair at the time of execution and is even more so now at the time of performance.

   The justice you work for knows the trend is to treat premarital agreements more like ordinary contracts, and she wonders if it is time for your state to join this trend. She would like you to write her a short memo in which you set out some of the pros and cons of adopting this approach.

Cases for Analysis

The following case is one of the first to hold that premarital agreements entered into to structure rights upon divorce are not void as a matter of public policy. Key to the decision is a recognition of the changing nature of marriage and the increased social acceptance of divorce.

POSNER v. POSNER
233 So. 2d 381 (Fla. 1970)

ROBERTS, Justice.

This cause is before the court on rehearing, . . . the wife having appealed from those portions of the decree awarding a divorce to the husband and the sum of $600 per month as alimony to the wife pursuant to the terms of an antenuptial agreement between the parties.

The three appellate judges . . . each took a different position respecting the antenuptial agreement concerning alimony. Their respective views were (1) that the parties may validly agree upon alimony in an antenuptial agreement but that the trial court is not bound by their agreement; (2) that such an agreement is void as against public policy; and (3) that an antenuptial agreement respecting alimony is entitled to the same consideration and should be just as binding as an antenuptial agreement settling the property rights of the wife in her husband's estate upon his death. . . .

At the outset we must recognize that there is a vast difference between a contract made in the market place and one relating to the institution of marriage.

It has long been the rule in a majority of the courts of this country and in this State that contracts intended to facilitate or promote the procurement of a divorce will be declared illegal as contrary to public policy. . . . The reason for the rule lies in the nature of the marriage contract and the interest of the State therein.

. . . We have, of course, changed by statute the common-law rule respecting the indissolubility of a marriage . . .; but the concept of marriage as a social institution that is the foundation of the family and of society remains unchanged. . . . Since marriage is of vital interest to society and the state, it has frequently been said that in every divorce suit the state is a third party whose interests take precedence over the private interests of the spouses. . . .

The state's interest in the preservation of the marriage is the basis for the rule that . . . an antenuptial agreement by which a prospective wife waives or limits her right to alimony or to the property of her husband in the event of a divorce or separation, regardless of who is at fault, has been in some states held to be invalid. . . . The reason that such an agreement is said to "facilitate or promote the procurement of a divorce" was stated in Crouch v. Crouch, *supra*, as follows:

> "Such contract could induce a mercenary husband to inflict on his wife any wrong he might desire with the knowledge his pecuniary liability would be limited. In other words, a husband could through abuse and ill treatment of

his wife force her to bring an action for divorce and thereby buy a divorce
for a small fee less than he would otherwise have to pay.". . .

There can be no doubt that the institution of marriage is the foundation of the familial and social structure of our Nation and, as such, continues to be of vital interest to the State; but we cannot blind ourselves to the
fact that the concept of the "sanctity" of a marriage—as being practically
indissoluble, once entered into—held by our ancestors only a few generations ago, has been greatly eroded in the last several decades. . . .

With divorce such a commonplace fact of life, it is fair to assume that
many prospective marriage partners whose property and familial situation
is such as to generate a valid antenuptial agreement settling their property rights upon the death of either, might want to consider and discuss
also—and agree upon, if possible—the disposition of their property and
the alimony rights of the wife in the event their marriage, despite their best
efforts, should fail. . . .

We know of no community or society in which the public policy that
condemned a husband and wife to a lifetime of misery as an alternative
to the opprobrium of divorce still exists. And a tendency to recognize this
change in public policy and to give effect to the antenuptial agreements of
the parties relating to divorce is clearly discernible. . . .

We have given careful consideration to the question of whether the
change in public policy towards divorce requires a change in the rule
respecting antenuptial agreements settling alimony and property rights of
the parties upon divorce and have concluded that such agreements should
no longer be held to be void ab initio as "contrary to public policy." If such
an agreement is valid . . . and if, in addition, it is made to appear that the
divorce was prosecuted in good faith, on proper grounds, so that, under
the rules applicable to postnuptial alimony and property settlement agreements referred to above, it could not be said to facilitate or promote the
procurement of a divorce, then it should be held valid as to conditions
existing at the time the agreement was made. . . .

QUESTIONS

1. According to the court, why have premarital agreements that set out the
   rights of spouses in the event of divorce generally been considered void
   as against public policy?
2. In thinking about whether to allow premarital agreements, how is the
   court influenced by the changing nature of marriage and divorce?
3. Does the court hold that all premarital agreements are valid? What may
   an agreement not do?

In the following case, the Supreme Court of Pennsylvania takes a "hard-line" approach to premarital agreements. In treating them more like ordinary contracts, the court moves away from the dominant view that premarital agreements should be reviewed under a stricter standard than those applicable to contracts entered into in the business realm.

SIMEONE v. SIMEONE
525 Pa. 392, 581 A.2d 162 (1990)

FLAHERTY, Justice.

At issue in this appeal is the validity of a prenuptial agreement executed between the appellant, Catherine E. Walsh Simeone, and the appellee, Frederick A. Simeone. At the time of their marriage, in 1975, appellant was a twenty-three year old nurse and appellee was a thirty-nine year old neurosurgeon. Appellee had an income of approximately $90,000 per year, and appellant was unemployed. Appellee also had assets worth approximately $300,000. On the eve of the parties' wedding, appellee's attorney presented appellant with a prenuptial agreement to be signed. Appellant, without the benefit of counsel, signed the agreement. Appellee's attorney had not advised appellant regarding any legal rights that the agreement surrendered. The parties are in disagreement as to whether appellant knew in advance of that date that such an agreement would be presented for signature. Appellant denies having had such knowledge and claims to have signed under adverse circumstances, which, she contends, provide a basis for declaring it void.

The agreement limited appellant to support payments of $200 per week in the event of separation or divorce, subject to a maximum total payment of $25,000. The parties separated in 1982, and, in 1984, divorce proceedings were commenced. Between 1982 and 1984 appellee made payments which satisfied the $25,000 limit. In 1985, appellant filed a claim for alimony pendente lite. A master's report upheld the validity of the prenuptial agreement and denied this claim. . . .

We granted allowance of appeal because uncertainty was expressed by the Superior Court regarding the meaning of our plurality decision in Estate of Geyer, 516 Pa. 492, 533 A.2d 423 (1987) (Opinion Announcing Judgment of the Court). The Superior Court viewed *Geyer* as permitting a prenuptial agreement to be upheld if it either made a reasonable provision for the spouse or was entered after a full and fair disclosure of the general financial positions of the parties and the statutory rights being relinquished. Appellant contends that this interpretation of *Geyer* is in error insofar as it requires disclosure of statutory rights only in cases where there has not been made a reasonable provision for the spouse. . . .

There is no longer validity in the implicit presumption that supplied the basis for *Geyer* and similar earlier decisions. Such decisions rested upon a belief that spouses are of unequal status and that women are not knowledgeable enough to understand the nature of contracts that they enter. Society has advanced, however, to the point where women are no longer regarded as the "weaker" party in marriage, or in society generally. Indeed, the stereotype that women serve as homemakers while men work as breadwinners is no longer viable. Quite often today both spouses are income earners. Nor is there viability in the presumption that women are uninformed, uneducated, and readily subjected to unfair advantage in marital agreements. Indeed, women nowadays quite often have substantial education, financial awareness, income, and assets.

Accordingly, the law has advanced to recognize the equal status of men and women in our society. . . . Paternalistic presumptions and protections that arose to shelter women from the inferiorities and incapacities which they were perceived as having in earlier times have, appropriately, been discarded. . . . It would be inconsistent, therefore, to perpetuate the standards governing prenuptial agreements that were described in *Geyer* and similar decisions, as these reflected a paternalistic approach that is now insupportable.

Further, *Geyer* and its predecessors embodied substantial departures from traditional rules of contract law, to the extent that they allowed consideration of the knowledge of the contracting parties and reasonableness of their bargain as factors governing whether to uphold an agreement. Traditional principles of contract law provide perfectly adequate remedies where contracts are procured through fraud, misrepresentation, or duress.

. . . Prenuptial agreements are contracts, and, as such, should be evaluated under the same criteria as are applicable to other types of contracts. . . . Absent fraud, misrepresentation, or duress, spouses should be bound by the terms of their agreements.

Contracting parties are normally bound by their agreements, without regard to whether the terms thereof were read and fully understood and irrespective of whether the agreements embodied reasonable or good bargains. . . . Based upon these principles, the terms of the present prenuptial agreement must be regarded as binding, without regard to whether the terms were fully understood by appellant. *Ignorantia non excusat*.

Accordingly, we find no merit in a contention raised by appellant that the agreement should be declared void on the ground that she did not consult with independent legal counsel. To impose a per se requirement that parties entering a prenuptial agreement must obtain independent legal counsel would be contrary to traditional principles of contract law, and would constitute a paternalistic and unwarranted interference with the parties' freedom to enter contracts.

Further, the reasonableness of a prenuptial bargain is not a proper subject for judicial review. . . .

By invoking inquiries into reasonableness, however, the functioning and reliability of prenuptial agreements is severely undermined. Parties would not have entered such agreements, and, indeed, might not have entered their marriages, if they did not expect their agreements to be strictly enforced. If parties viewed an agreement as reasonable at the time of its inception, as evidenced by their having signed the agreement, they should be foreclosed from later trying to evade its terms by asserting that it was not in fact reasonable. . . .

Further, everyone who enters a long-term agreement knows that circumstances can change during its term, so that what initially appeared desirable might prove to be an unfavorable bargain. Such are the risks that contracting parties routinely assume. Certainly, the possibilities of illness, birth of children, reliance upon a spouse, career change, financial gain or loss, and numerous other events that can occur in the course of a marriage cannot be regarded as unforeseeable. If parties choose not to address such matters in their prenuptial agreements, they must be regarded as having contracted to bear the risk of events that alter the value of their bargains.

We are reluctant to interfere with the power of persons contemplating marriage to agree upon, and to act in reliance upon, what they regard as an acceptable distribution scheme for their property. A court should not ignore the parties' expressed intent by proceeding to determine whether a prenuptial agreement was, in the court's view, reasonable at the time of its inception or the time of divorce. . . .

In discarding the approach of *Geyer* that permitted examination of the reasonableness of prenuptial agreements and allowed inquiries into whether parties had attained informed understandings of the rights they were surrendering, we do not depart from the longstanding principle that a full and fair disclosure of the financial positions of the parties is required. Absent this disclosure, a material misrepresentation in the inducement for entering a prenuptial agreement may be asserted. *Hillegass*, 431 Pa. at 152-53, 244 A.2d at 676-77. Parties to these agreements do not quite deal at arm's length, but rather at the time the contract is entered into stand in a relation of mutual confidence and trust that calls for disclosure of their financial resources. *Id.*, 431 Pa. at 149, 244 A.2d at 675.

McDermott, Justice, dissenting.

I dissent. . . . I am in full agreement with the majority's observation that "women nowadays quite often have substantial education, financial awareness, income, and assets." . . . However, the plurality decision I authored in Estate of Geyer, 516 Pa. 492, 533 A.2d 423 (1987), as well as the Dissenting Opinion I offer today, have little to do with the equality of the sexes, but everything to do with the solemnity of the matrimonial union. I am not willing to believe that our society views marriage as a mere contract for hire. . . . In this Commonwealth, we have long declared our interest in the stability of marriage and in the stability of the family unit. Our courts must seek to protect, and not to undermine, those institutions and interests which are vital to our society. . . .

. . . Thus, while I acknowledge the longstanding rule of law that pre-nuptial agreements are presumptively valid and binding upon the parties, I am unwilling to go as far as the majority to protect the right to contract at the expense of the institution of marriage. Were a contract of marriage, the most intimate relationship between two people, not the surrender of freedom, an offering of self in love, sacrifice, hope for better or for worse, the begetting of children and the offer of effort, labor, precious time and care for the safety and prosperity of their union, then the majority would find me among them.

In my view, one seeking to avoid the operation of an executed pre-nuptial agreement must first establish, by clear and convincing evidence, that a full and fair disclosure of the worth of the intended spouse was not made at the time of the execution of the agreement. . . . In addition to a full and fair disclosure of the general financial pictures of the parties, I would find a pre-nuptial agreement voidable where it is established that the parties were not aware, at the time of contracting, of existing statutory rights which they were relinquishing upon the signing of the agreement. . . . It is here, with a finding of full and fair disclosure, that the majority would end its analysis of the validity of a pre-nuptial agreement. I would not. An analysis of the fairness and equity of a pre-nuptial agreement has long been an important part of the law of this state. . . . I am not willing to depart from this history, which would continue to serve our public policy.

At the time of dissolution of the marriage, a spouse should be able to avoid the operation of a pre-nuptial agreement upon clear and convincing proof that, despite the existence of full and fair disclosure at the time of the execution of the agreement, the agreement is nevertheless so inequitable and unfair that it should not be enforced in a court of this state. . . .

It is also apparent that, although a pre-nuptial agreement is quite valid when drafted, the passage of time accompanied by the intervening events of a marriage may render the terms of the agreement completely unfair and inequitable. While parties to a pre-nuptial agreement may indeed foresee, generally, the events which may come to pass during their marriage, one spouse should not be made to suffer for failing to foresee all of the surrounding circumstances which may attend the dissolution of the marriage. Although it should not be the role of the courts to void pre-nuptial agreements merely because one spouse may receive a better result in an action under the Divorce Code to recover alimony or equitable distribution, it should be the role of the courts to guard against the enforcement of pre-nuptial agreements where such enforcement will bring about only inequity and hardship. It borders on cruelty to accept that after years of living together, yielding their separate opportunities in life to each other, that two individuals emerge the same as the day they began their marriage.

At the time of the dissolution of marriage, what are the circumstances which would serve to invalidate a pre-nuptial agreement? This is a question that should only be answered on a case-by-case basis. However, it is not unrealistic to imagine that in a given situation, one spouse, although trained in the workforce at the time of marriage, may, over many years, have become economically dependent upon the other spouse. In reliance upon the permanence of marriage and in order to provide a stable home for a family, a spouse may choose, even at the suggestion of the other spouse, not to work during the marriage. As a result, at the point of dissolution of the marriage, the spouse's employability has diminished to such an extent that to enforce the support provisions of the pre-nuptial agreement will cause the spouse to become a public charge, or will provide a standard of living far below that which was enjoyed before and during marriage. In such a situation, a court may properly decide to render void all or some of the provisions of the pre-nuptial agreement. . . .

The majority is concerned that parties will routinely challenge the validity of their pre-nuptial agreements. Given the paramount importance of marriage and family in our society, and the serious consequences that may accompany the dissolution of a marriage, we should not choose to close the doors of our courts merely to gain a measure of judicial economy. . . .

QUESTIONS

1. According to the lower court's reading of the precedent case of *Estate of Geyer*, when will a premarital agreement be upheld?
2. What does the Pennsylvania Supreme Court see as the underlying presumption of the *Geyer* decision?
3. Why does the court think this presumption is no longer valid?
4. How does this lead the court to rethink the rules regarding the enforceability of prenuptial agreements?
5. According to the decision, will a party's lack of understanding of the terms of a premarital agreement invalidate the agreement? What about a party's failure to consult with legal counsel? Why does the court take the position that it does?
6. What position does the court take regarding the reasonableness of the agreement at the time of execution? At the time of enforcement? Explain the court's position.
7. What is the court's position with respect to whether full and fair disclosure is required?

8. What position does the dissent take with respect to considerations of reasonableness at the time of execution? At the time of enforcement? Why does the dissent reject the majority approach?

In the following case, the court addresses the issue of whether post-marital agreements are enforceable. Determining that public policy supports their enforceability, it then considers the standards to be used for determining their validity.

BEDRICK v. BEDRICK
300 Conn. 691, 17 A.3d 17 (2011)

McLachlan, J.

This appeal involves a dissolution of marriage action in which the defendant, Bruce L. Bedrick, seeks to enforce a postnuptial agreement. Today we are presented for the first time with the issue of whether a post-nuptial agreement is valid and enforceable in Connecticut.

The defendant appeals from the trial court's judgment in favor of the plaintiff, Deborah Bedrick. The defendant claims that the trial court improperly relied upon principles of fairness and equity in concluding that the postnuptial agreement was unenforceable and, instead, should have applied only ordinary principles of contract law. We conclude that post-nuptial agreements are valid and enforceable and generally must comply with contract principles. We also conclude, however, that the terms of such agreements must be both fair and equitable at the time of execution and not unconscionable at the time of dissolution. Because the terms of the present agreement were unconscionable at the time of dissolution, we affirm the judgment of the trial court. . . .

In August 2007, the plaintiff initiated this action, seeking dissolution of the parties' marriage, permanent alimony, an equitable distribution of the parties' real and personal property and other relief. The defendant filed a cross complaint, seeking to enforce a postnuptial agreement that the parties executed on December 10, 1977, and modified by way of handwritten addenda on five subsequent occasions, most recently on May 18, 1989.

The agreement provides that in the event of dissolution, neither party will pay alimony. Instead, the plaintiff will receive a cash settlement in an amount to be "reviewed from time to time." The May 18, 1989 addendum to the agreement provides for a cash settlement of $75,000. The agreement further provides that the plaintiff will waive her interests in the defendant's car wash business, and that the plaintiff will not be held liable for the defendant's personal and business loans.

In its memorandum of decision, the trial court stated that, although "[t]here is scant case law addressing the enforcement of postnuptial agreements in Connecticut . . . it is clear that a court may not enforce a postnuptial agreement if it is not fair and equitable. . . . [C]ourts have refused to enforce postnuptial agreements for lack of consideration, failure to disclose financial information, or an improper purpose." Concluding that the agreement was not fair and equitable, the trial court declined to enforce it. The court found that the value of the parties' combined assets was approximately $927,123, and ordered, inter alia, the defendant to pay lump sum alimony in the amount of $392,372 to the plaintiff. The defendant filed a motion to reargue claiming that the court should have applied principles of contract law in determining the enforceability of the agreement.

Following reargument, the trial court issued a second written decision, again declining to enforce the postnuptial agreement, and noting that the Connecticut appellate courts have not yet addressed the issue of the validity of such agreements. The court further declined to apply Connecticut's law governing prenuptial agreements, reasoning that, unlike a prenuptial agreement, a postnuptial agreement is "inherently coercive" because one spouse typically enters into it in order to preserve the marriage, while the other is primarily motivated by financial concerns.

The trial court additionally determined that, even if postnuptial agreements were valid and enforceable under Connecticut law, the present agreement did not comply with ordinary contract principles because it lacked adequate consideration. The court explained that, because past consideration cannot support the imposition of a new obligation, continuation of the marriage itself cannot constitute sufficient consideration to support a postnuptial agreement. Moreover, the trial court emphasized that the plaintiff did not knowingly waive her marital rights because she neither received a sworn financial affidavit from the defendant nor retained independent legal counsel to review the agreement.

The trial court also opined that enforcement of the agreement would have been unjust and was "not . . . a fair and equitable distribution of the parties' assets" because the financial circumstances of the parties had changed dramatically since the agreement was last modified in 1989. Since 1989, the parties had had a child together and the defendant's car wash business had both prospered and deteriorated. This appeal followed.

The defendant contends that the trial court improperly applied equitable principles in determining whether the postnuptial agreement was enforceable and, instead, should have applied only principles of contract law. Specifically, the defendant cites Crews v. Crews, 295 Conn. 153, 167, 989 A.2d 1060 (2010), in which we stated that "equitable considerations codified in our statutes . . . have no bearing on whether [a prenuptial] agreement should be enforced. . . . In other words, whether . . . [a] court . . . thinks the agreement was a good bargain for the plaintiff does not enter into the analysis of the issue." (Internal quotation marks omitted.) . . .

We begin our analysis of postnuptial agreements by considering the public policies served by the recognition of agreements regarding the dissolution of marriage, including prenuptial, postnuptial, and separation agreements.

Historically, we have stated that "[t]he state does not favor divorces. . . . Its [public] policy is to maintain the family relation[ship] as a life status." (Citation omitted.) McCarthy v. Santangelo, 137 Conn. 410, 412, 78 A.2d 240 (1951). Accordingly, prenuptial agreements were generally held to violate public policy because they promoted, facilitated or provided an incentive for separation or divorce. McHugh v. McHugh, 181 Conn. 482, 488-89, 436 A.2d 8 (1980). Similarly, a separation agreement is not necessarily contrary to public policy unless it is made to facilitate divorce or is concealed from the court. . . .

Postnuptial agreements may . . . encourage the private resolution of family issues. In particular, they may allow couples to eliminate a source of emotional turmoil—usually, financial uncertainty—and focus instead on resolving other aspects of the marriage that may be problematic. By alleviating anxiety over uncertainty in the determination of legal rights and obligations upon dissolution, postnuptial agreements do not encourage or facilitate dissolution; in fact, they harmonize with our public policy favoring enduring marriages. . . .

Postnuptial agreements are consistent with public policy; they realistically acknowledge the high incidence of divorce and its effect upon our population. We recognize "the reality of the increasing rate of divorce and remarriage." Heuer v. Heuer, 152 N.J. 226, 235, 704 A.2d 913 (1998). . . . "[B]oth the realities of our society and policy reasons favor judicial recognition of prenuptial agreements. Rather than inducing divorce, such agreements simply acknowledge its ordinariness. With divorce as likely an outcome of marriage as permanence, we see no logical or compelling reason why public policy should not allow two mature adults to handle their own financial affairs. . . . The reasoning that once found them contrary to public policy has no place in today's matrimonial law." (Internal quotation marks omitted.) Brooks v. Brooks, 733 P.2d 1044 1050-51 (Alaska 1987). Postnuptial agreements are no different than prenuptial agreements in this regard.

Having determined that postnuptial agreements are consistent with public policy, we now must consider what standards govern their enforcement. . . . To aid in our analysis of the enforceability of postnuptial agreements, we review our law on the enforceability of prenuptial agreements. Two different sets of principles govern decisions as to the enforceability of a prenuptial agreement; the date of the execution of the agreement determines which set of principles controls. . . .

[T]he Connecticut Premarital Agreement Act [applicable to agreements entered into after October 1, 1995] provides that a prenuptial agreement is unenforceable when: (1) the challenger did not enter the agreement voluntarily; (2) the agreement [was] unconscionable when executed or enforced; (3) the challenger did not receive "a fair and reasonable disclosure of the amount, character and value of property, financial obligations and income of the other party" before execution of the agreement; or (4) the challenger did not have "a reasonable opportunity to consult with independent counsel." General Statutes §§46b-36g. . . .

[T]he party seeking to challenge the enforceability of the [prenuptial] contract bears a heavy burden. . . . [W]here the economic status of [the] parties has changed dramatically between the date of the agreement and the dissolution, literal enforcement of the agreement may work injustice. Absent such unusual circumstances, however, [prenuptial] agreements freely and fairly entered into will be honored and enforced by the courts as written. . . .

Although we view postnuptial agreements as encouraging the private resolution of family issues, we also recognize that spouses do not contract under the same conditions as either prospective spouses or spouses who have determined to dissolve their marriage. The Supreme Judicial Court of Massachusetts has noted that a postnuptial "agreement stands on a different footing from both a [prenuptial agreement] and a separation agreement. Before marriage, the parties have greater freedom to reject an unsatisfactory [prenuptial] contract. . . ."

The Appellate Division of the New Jersey Superior Court has also recognized this "contextual difference" and has noted that a wife "face[s] a more difficult choice than [a] bride who is presented with a demand for a prenuptial agreement. The cost to [a wife is] . . . the destruction of a family and the stigma of a failed marriage." Pacelli v. Pacelli, 319 N.J. Super. 185, 190, 725 A.2d 56 (App. Div.), cert. denied, 161 N.J. 147, 735 A.2d 572 (1999). A spouse who bargains a settlement agreement, on the other hand, "recogniz[es] that the marriage is over, can look to his or her economic rights; the relationship is adversarial." Id., 191. Thus, a spouse enters a postnuptial agreement under different conditions than a party entering either a prenuptial or a separation agreement. . . .

Other state courts have not only observed that spouses contract under different conditions; they have also observed that postnuptial agreements "should not be treated as mere 'business deals.'" Stoner v. Stoner, 572 Pa. 665, 672-73, 819 A.2d 529 (2003). They recognize that, just like prospective spouses, "parties to these agreements do not quite deal at arm's length, but rather at the time the contract is entered into stand in a relation of mutual confidence and trust. . . ." (Internal quotation marks omitted.) Id., 673. . . .

Because of the nature of the marital relationship, the spouses to a postnuptial agreement may not be as cautious in contracting with one another as they would be with prospective spouses, and they are certainly less cautious than they would be with an ordinary contracting party. With lessened caution comes greater potential for one spouse to take advantage of the other. This leads us to conclude that postnuptial agreements require stricter scrutiny than prenuptial agreements. In applying special scrutiny, a court may enforce a postnuptial agreement only if it complies with applicable contract principles, and the terms of the agreement are both fair and equitable at the time of execution and not unconscionable at the time of dissolution. . . .

We further hold that the terms of a postnuptial agreement are fair and equitable at the time of execution if the agreement is made voluntarily, and without any undue influence, fraud, coercion, duress or similar defect. Moreover, each spouse must be given full, fair and reasonable disclosure of the amount, character and value of property, both jointly and separately held, and all of the financial obligations and income of the other spouse. This mandatory disclosure requirement is a result of the deeply personal marital relationship. . . .

[I]n determining whether a particular postnuptial agreement is fair and equitable at the time of execution, a court should consider the totality of the circumstances surrounding execution. A court may consider various factors, including "the nature and complexity of the agreement's terms, the extent of and disparity in assets brought to the marriage by each spouse, the parties' respective age, sophistication, education, employment, experience, prior marriages, or other traits potentially affecting the ability to read and understand an agreement's provisions, and the amount of time available to each spouse to reflect upon the agreement after first seeing its specific terms . . . [and] access to independent counsel prior to consenting to the contract terms." Annot., 53 A.L.R.4th 92-93, §§2 [a] (1987). . . .

With regard to the determination of whether a postnuptial agreement is unconscionable at the time of dissolution, "[i]t is well established that [t]he question of unconscionability is a matter of law to be decided by the court based on all the facts and circumstances of the case." (Internal quotation marks omitted.) Crews v. Crews, supra, 295 Conn. 163. . . .

Unfairness or inequality alone does not render a postnuptial agreement unconscionable; spouses may agree on an unequal distribution of assets at dissolution. . . . Instead, the question of whether enforcement of an agreement would be unconscionable is analogous to determining whether enforcement of an agreement would work an injustice. . . . Marriage, by its very nature, is subject to unforeseeable developments, and no agreement can possibly anticipate all future events. Unforeseen changes in the relationship, such as having a child, loss of employment or moving to another state, may render enforcement of the agreement unconscionable.

II

Now that we have set forth the applicable legal standards for postnuptial agreements, we turn to the present case and address the question of whether the trial court properly concluded that the parties' postnuptial agreement should not be enforced. . . .

Although the value of the parties combined assets is $927,123, the last addendum to the agreement, dated May 18, 1989, provides that the plaintiff will receive a cash settlement of only $75,000. This addendum was written prior to the initial success of the car wash business in the early 1990s, the birth of the parties' son in 1991, when the parties were forty-one years old, and the subsequent deterioration of the business in the 2000s. At the time of trial, the parties were both fifty-seven years old. Neither had a college degree. The defendant had been steadily employed by the car wash business since 1973. The plaintiff had worked for that business for thirty-five years, providing administrative and bookkeeping support, and since approximately 2001, when the business began to deteriorate, the plaintiff had managed all business operations excluding maintenance. In 2004, the plaintiff also had worked outside of the business in order to provide the family with additional income. Since approximately 2007, when the plaintiff stopped working for the business, the defendant had not been able to complete administrative or bookkeeping tasks, and had not filed taxes. . . .

[W]e previously have determined that the question of whether enforcement of a prenuptial agreement would be unconscionable is analogous to determining whether enforcement would work an injustice. . . . The facts and circumstances of the present case clearly support the findings of the trial court that, as a matter of law, enforcement of the agreement would be unconscionable. We therefore do not need to remand this case to the trial court because its findings satisfy the test for enforceability, which we articulate today. Accordingly, we hold that the trial court properly concluded that the agreement was unenforceable.

QUESTIONS

1. Why does the court conclude that postmarital agreements should be enforceable?
2. What does the court say about the difference between postmarital agreements as compared to both premarital and separation agreements?

3. Why does the court ultimately conclude that postmarital agreements require "stricter scrutiny" than premarital agreements?
4. What standard of review does the court adopt?
5. Why does the court conclude that the agreement between the parties is not enforceable?

Endnotes

1. This chapter will use the term "premarital agreement" or "premarital contract." Synonymous terms are "prenuptial agreement" and "antenuptial agreement." Note that the focus in this chapter is on premarital agreements, which are made in contemplation of divorce, not death. Agreements that spell out rights upon the death of one or both spouses generally have been accepted by the courts because there are no countervailing policy considerations.

2. 233 So. 2d 381 (Fla. 1970).

3. 525 Pa. 392, 581 A.2d 162 (1990).

4. *Id.* at 166.

5. For a detailed discussion of cases between 2000 and 2007 involving issues of procedural fairness, *see* Judith T. Younger, Lovers' Contracts in the Courts: Forsaking the Minimum Decencies, 13 Wm. & Mary J. Women & L. 349 (2007).

6. *Simeone*, 581 A.2d at 167-168. The Uniform Premarital Agreements Act (UPAA), which was approved by the National Conference of Commissioners of Uniform State Laws in 1983, and has since been adopted in about half of the states, also has contributed to this trend. Although not going as far as the *Simeone* decision, the UPAA clearly favors enforceability of premarital agreements and limits. Regarding the UPAA, *see* Elizabeth Barker Brandt, The Uniform Premarital Agreements Act and the Reality of Premarital Agreements in Idaho, 33 Idaho L. Rev. 539 (1997).

7. *Simeone*, 581 A.2d at 167. Under the UPAA, the standard of review for substantive unfairness is unconscionability.

8. For further detail on other types of provisions, *see* Jonathan E. Fields, Forbidden Provisions in Prenuptial Agreements: Legal and Practical Considerations for the Matrimonial Lawyer, 21 J. Am. Acad. Matrimonial Law 413 (2008).

9. Sean Hannon Williams, Postnuptial Agreements, 2007 Wis. L. Rev. 827, 828.

10. *See id.* at 838-845 for a discussion of some of these cases.

11. Ansin v. Craven-Ansin, 457 Mass. 283, 929 N.E.2d 955, 962 (2010). The court also concluded that postmarital contracts are different than separation contracts executed at the time of divorce because these are "negotiated when a marriage has failed." *Id.* at 963.

12. *Id.* at 962, quoting C.P. Kindregan Jr. and M.L. Inker, Family Law and Practice §50:15 (3d ed. 2002).

Chapter Three

Domestic Violence

All states have enacted laws that enable victims of **domestic violence** (also referred to as **domestic abuse** or **intimate partner violence**) to obtain civil orders of protection from abuse. These laws came about largely as a result of a women's movement that focused public attention on the extent and seriousness of violence directed toward women by their male partners. Insisting that partner violence was not simply a private matter, activists successfully campaigned for laws that would allow victims to seek legal protection from abuse.

These laws are the focus of this chapter. To put them into context, we first briefly examine the historical approach of the law to spousal abuse. This history reveals a tradition of support for a husband's right of physical authority over his wife; however, it also reveals challenges to the social acceptance of a male's physical dominance over his spouse. We also take a brief look at some statistics documenting the pervasiveness of intimate partner violence and its continued disproportionate impact on women.[1]

The Traditional Approach

Roman law required that "married women . . . conform themselves entirely to the temper of their husbands and the husbands to rule their wives as necessary and inseparable possessions."[2] A husband could beat his wife to make her obey him. If a married woman drank, committed adultery, or engaged in other conduct that threatened his honor, her husband could beat her to death without inquiry or punishment, although some limits eventually were placed on a husband's right to administer unduly violent and "unjustifiable" beatings. Charged with the responsibility of maintaining domestic order, a husband with an "unruly" wife was considered derelict in his obligations.

The right of a husband to use physical force against his wife was carried forward into English common law. Here, as the legal head of the household, a husband could physically discipline his wife to command her obedience both for its own sake and because he was legally responsible for her misconduct. He was directed to use the same moderation in physically chastising his wife as he would use when disciplining his apprentices or children.

In the United States, acceptance of the doctrine of marital unity (see Chapter 1) implied acceptance of a husband's right of "moderate chastisement"—although, as we will see, this was not without challenge. In the early days of the nation, a husband, as head of the household, was generally thought entitled to use the degree of force necessary to make his wife obey. Wives who disobeyed or displayed bad tempers were blamed for causing the violent reaction in their husbands through their disregard for his authority. This traditional understanding is captured by the following passage from an 1862 decision from North Carolina, in which the court denies the wife's divorce petition because she did not explain the circumstances giving rise to the blows administered by her husband, thus failing to prove they were not her fault:

> [W]e are of the opinion that it was necessary to state the circumstances under which the blow with the horse-whip, and the blows with the switch were given; for instance, what . . . had she done, or said to induce such violence on the part of the husband? . . .
>
> The wife must be subject to the husband. Every man must govern his household, and if by reason of an unruly temper, or an unbridled tongue, the wife persistently treats her husband with disrespect, and he submits to it, he . . . loses the respect of the other members of his family, without which he cannot expect to govern them. . . . It follows that the law gives the husband power to use such a degree of force as is necessary to make the wife behave herself and know her place. . . . [S]o that there are circumstances under which a husband may strike his wife with a horse-whip or may strike her several times with a switch, so hard as to leave marks on her person, and these acts do not furnish sufficient grounds for divorce.[3]

The court here appears to draw a distinction between "justifiable" and unjustifiable beatings, thus indicating that the law did not grant husbands unlimited authority over their wives. Beatings that were "unprovoked" by the wife, or involved more force than necessary to secure her obedience, might furnish grounds for a divorce on the basis of cruelty or possibly subject a husband to criminal prosecution.

Early Reform Impulses

As we saw above, there is a long history of support for a husband's right to command the obedience of his wife through the use of physical force. However, starting with the Puritans, there were some early efforts aimed at altering this traditional allocation of authority.[4]

In 1641, the Puritans passed the first law in the Western world to expressly prohibit wife beating; a few years later, this law was amended to also prohibit husband beating. For the Puritans, who hoped to establish a religious community in the New World, violence between family members was a sin that lowered the standing of the community before God. Neighbors were encouraged to watch over each other's households and report instances of abuse to the minister. Ministers preached against the evils of wife abuse, and serious cases could be brought before the church court, which sought to disgrace the sinner. The goal of this intervention was reconciliation and family preservation. Protection of the victims was not a primary concern, and where necessary to uphold their authority, husbands remained entitled to use physical force against a spouse.[5]

In the early 1800s, the temperance movement, which sought to ban the sale and consumption of alcohol, became the first reform movement to draw attention to domestic cruelty. Linking violence to excess alcohol use, women temperance reformers focused on the threat they believed male drinking posed to the well-being of women and children. Through speeches and literature, they vividly depicted images of women and children being terrorized by men who had been converted into "brutes" by liquor. Although highly critical of this male behavior, temperance reformers did not seek to protect or empower women, as these approaches would have been considered too radical. Instead, they called on women to use their moral influence to reform their husbands. They emphasized the womanly duty of self-sacrifice for the benefit of their families.

In the mid-1800s, the women's rights movement also sought to publicize the plight of abused women. However, unlike the temperance reformers, these activists did not focus on the moral obligation of women to reform men; instead, they sought to lessen women's dependence on their husbands by seeking reform of marriage laws that subordinated women and of divorce laws so as to make divorce easier in cases of violence. Seen as unwomanly radicals, these activists were accused of seeking to destroy the family. Their efforts to change the law were regarded as subversive of the moral order and met with little success.

After the Civil War, there was another attempt to address the issue of wife abuse. Members of the legal establishment, including judges and prosecutors, campaigned to bring back the whipping post to punish wife beaters, and between 1882 and 1905, three states actually passed such laws. However, the protection of abused wives was not the real focus of this effort; rather, it was part of a broader campaign to control individuals, notably newly freed slaves and immigrants, who were considered by many in the ruling elite to be a threat to the social order. This campaign came to an end at the turn of the century when Progressive Era reformers shifted the focus away from punishment toward seeking to understand and eliminate the root causes of criminal activity.[6]

As a result, the issue of domestic violence moved off the national agenda as a matter of pressing social concern. Newly established family courts were entrusted with the responsibility of resolving the problem within the confines of each family unit. Abuse complaints were handled by the family court's social service department. The goal of intervention was reconciliation. Once again, women were charged with responsibility for ending the violence, and they were frequently counseled on how to improve their homemaking skills in order to gain their husbands' respect.[7]

This focus on resolving domestic violence within the family context was reinforced by the emerging field of psychiatry, which sought to explain domestic violence as a function of interpersonal dynamics. Seen as rooted in the realm of psychological functioning, a mental health approach to domestic violence was emphasized over any kind of legal response. This remained the prevailing approach until the late 1960s, when domestic violence again emerged as a social problem that called for a public rather than a privatized solution.[8]

Present Legal Approach to Domestic Violence

During the 1960s, the women's rights movement again focused public attention on the issue of domestic violence. Reformers challenged the prevailing understanding that intimate violence was a private matter expressive of the interpersonal personal functioning of an individual couple and instead located its roots in the history of male authority over women in the domestic realm. As part of a broader effort to reallocate this historical imbalance of power, legal reform efforts focused on the enactment of **abuse prevention laws**.

Now in effect in all states, these laws enable victims of domestic violence to obtain **protective orders** through a simplified court procedure. More recently, these state efforts have been strengthened by the federal Violence Against Women Act (VAWA). After taking a close look at the protections available under abuse prevention laws and the general process for obtaining protective orders, we will consider some of VAWA's key provisions.

Before turning to the law, it is important to recognize that intimate partner violence remains a serious problem, accounting for 21 percent of all violent crime.[9] Although overall rates have declined significantly since the 1990s, it is hard to pinpoint what this drop in domestic abuse actually means with regard to changing norms in intimate relationships, as the "overall pattern and size of the decline were similar to the decline in the overall violent crime rate."[10] What remains unchanged is the gendered pattern of violence, with women constituting the clear majority of victims of both nonfatal and fatal acts of domestic violence.

Obtaining Civil Orders of Protection Under Abuse

Prevention Laws

To understand generally how abuse protection laws work, it is helpful to consider a number of basic questions. These questions can also be used to analyze the provisions of an individual state's law. They include the following:

- What kinds of relationships qualify for a protective order?
- What kind of harms entitles a victim to obtain a protective order?
- What kinds of protection are available?
- What is the process for obtaining an order?
- How is the order enforced?

These questions will guide our discussion, but keep in mind that the precise answers vary from state to state.

Qualifying Relationships

Abuse prevention laws are intended to provide protection to persons who are being abused by someone with whom they have an intimate, family, or family-like relationship. When parties are in a more distant relationship, such as that of neighbor or co-worker, protection cannot usually be obtained through an abuse prevention law, although other remedies, such as a criminal action, may be available. In addition, a number of states now have harassment laws that permit an individual who is being harassed to seek a civil **harassment order** without the requirement of a special qualifying relationship.

The statutes in some states are fairly comprehensive and allow someone to seek protection from abuse by a range of persons with whom they have a "special" relationship. An inclusive statute might permit someone to seek protection from:

- a spouse or former spouse;
- a cohabiting partner or former cohabiting partner (but some statutes frame this category more broadly to include all household members even if there is no family or intimate relationship);
- the parent of a child in common;
- family members related by blood and possibly by marriage;
- a dating or an intimate partner (a topic discussed below).

Many statutes are not this inclusive, and impose specific eligibility qualifications on certain categories of individuals. For example, although all statutes include spouses and most, if not all, include former spouses, some exclude spouses who are in the process of getting a divorce or a legal separation. (Note that similar relief may be provided through comparable provisions in the applicable divorce or separation statute.) And although virtually all statutes cover unmarried cohabiting partners, some exclude former cohabiting partners. This is an unfortunate omission because research shows that battered women are at increased risk of abuse when they leave a relationship. Some cohabitation provisions specify that a couple must live together in a spousal-like relationship, which historically has been used to deny coverage to victims in a same-sex relationship, and many provisions exclude other householders unless they are family members.

Many states now permit an individual to seek protection from a person with whom he or she has had a child, even if they do not have any kind of ongoing relationship. These are often referred to as "child in common" provisions. In states that have such a provision, an issue that has come up is whether a woman can seek protection while she is pregnant but has not yet given birth. In recognition of the fact that where there is a history of violence, a pregnant woman may be at high risk of abuse, some "child in common" provisions expressly extend coverage to pregnant women. Where the statute is silent, case law is divided. Some courts have held that battered pregnant women come within the purpose and intent of the "child in common" provision, while other courts have denied coverage based on a narrow reading of the statutory language holding that birth is a condition precedent to eligibility.[11]

In addition to the above relationships, some states permit an individual who is assisting a victim of violence to seek an order of protection for him- or herself. In effect, this person is regarded as being in a "special" relationship with the abuser based on the connection with the victim, as this connection may place him or her in direct risk of harm. Other states have extended their laws to cover the threat posed by persons connected to the victim through a current or past relationship. For example, Texas allows a party to obtain a protective order against a person who was previously married to or in a dating relationship with the victim's current spouse or dating partner. While in Oklahoma, abuse victims may seek a restraining order against "present spouses of ex-spouses."[12]

In addition, a few jurisdictions also allow an employer to seek an order of protection against a party who is abusing or threatening an employee in order to protect both the intended target and other personnel from harm. However well intentioned, important concerns have been raised about these kinds of measures. Most significant is the concern that an employer-initiated order may place an intended victim at greater risk of harm, particularly if "the employer acted without her knowledge or acquiescence," as it can potentially make her "more vulnerable at home if she does not have her own protective order in place [as] a workplace restraining order would be limited to protecting the target at the workplace."[13] Compounding this concern is the fact that in seeking an order, an employer is not required to assess whether taking unilateral action without the consent of the targeted employee will increase the risk of personal harm, particularly if she does not have her own order of protection.

Going beyond these narrowly crafted third-party provisions, a few states have eliminated the relationship requirement altogether. However, the available protections may be more limited if the parties are not in a "qualifying" type of relationship. Other states have instead enacted a separate and distinct protective law that does not require proof of a special relationship. For example, in 2010, Massachusetts enacted a harassment prevention law that allows a party to seek a restraining order against any person, including a complete stranger, for protection from physical abuse or harassment.[14]

As states have sought to determine which relationships should qualify for protection, some tension has existed around the inclusion of dating relationships and same-sex couples, which, of course, can be overlapping categories. Accordingly, we take a brief look at some of the issues particular to these two categories of relationship.

Dating Relationships

At first, abuse prevention laws did not address dating violence, which was not considered to be a serious or common problem. However, it became increasingly apparent that intimate partner abuse is not limited to marital

or cohabiting relationships and also occurs within the context of dating relationships. Research reveals that women are at greatest risk of being abused
when they are between the ages of 16 and 24 and that approximately one
in three to one in five young women in high school have been physically
and/or sexually abused by someone they were dating. Compounding the
seriousness of the problem, young women who are in abusive dating relationships are at particular risk for other serious health problems, including
eating disorders, drug and alcohol abuse, and suicidality.[15]

Presently, the majority of states have amended their abuse protection
laws to include individuals in dating or engagement relationships. Some
statutes refer simply to dating relationships, while others impose specific
definitional requirements. For example, in Massachusetts, one of the first
states to include dating relationships in its abuse protection law, an individual must first establish the existence of a "substantial dating or engagement relationship." In evaluating substantiality, a judge is to consider the
duration and type of the relationship and the frequency of the parties' interaction. If the relationship has ended, the judge must consider how much
time has elapsed since termination.[16] Some statutes impose very specific
qualifying requirements. For example, some define a "dating relationship"
as one that is sexually intimate, thus potentially excluding relationships
at an early stage of development or those between young teens. Others
require that one or both parties be adults, thus again excluding teens, while
others require the parties to be in a heterosexual dating relationship, which
excludes same-sex dating couples.

These kinds of limitations are in response to concerns that some have
raised—that including dating partners would open the floodgates to petitions by persons who are simply friends or acquaintances and therefore
outside the intended scope of abuse prevention laws. Writing this distinction into law, New York's recently enacted Expanded Access to Family
Court Act, which enables persons who "are or have been in an intimate
relationship" to seek a restraining order, makes clear that "neither a
casual acquaintance nor ordinary fraternization between two individuals
in business or social contexts shall be deemed to constitute an 'intimate
relationship.'"[17]

Experts in the field have raised a number of concerns about these
limitations. First, they exclude some potential victims of dating violence,
such as teens, who might need the protection offered by a restraining order.
Second, some of the qualifying conditions—such as that the relationship
be substantial or that the parties be sexually intimate—give judges considerable discretion in deciding if a petitioner qualifies for protection. If the
judge's standard is not met, the petitioner may be in even greater danger
because she has brought the perpetrator into court but then leaves without
a protective order in place. Third, requiring proof that the relationship has

reached a certain level of intimacy or has lasted for a certain time period means that abuse cannot be addressed early on in the relationship and, since violence often escalates in frequency and severity over time, a victim of dating violence may have to wait until there is a risk of serious injury before being eligible for protection. Further, experts generally agree that the earlier the intervention in a violent relationship, the more likely it is to succeed.

Teen Dating Relationships.   Teen dating violence raises some particular concerns. Looking outside of the law for a moment, one concern is that although it is often difficult for any victim of domestic violence to disclose their situation to others (see "Working with Victims of Domestic Violence" box), disclosure can be especially difficult for teens who are struggling to establish their autonomy and adult sense of self. In addition, if there is violence at home, a teen may assume that such treatment is the norm. Another complicating factor is that if abuse is disclosed, adults may discount the potential seriousness of the situation based on the view that romantic relationships between teenagers are not very serious and can easily be ended.[18]

Teens also face legal barriers that adults usually do not have to contend with. First, if a statute excludes dating relationships altogether or limits them to adult dating relationships, most teens will not be able to obtain a protective order unless they are in another qualifying relationship, such as where they are seeking protection from a family member or the father of a "child in common." Second, if there is a "sexual intimacy" requirement, it is possible that a teen dating relationship will not qualify. Moreover, even if a teen is sexually active within the meaning of the statute, she may be more reluctant than an adult would be to share this with a judge. This is particularly likely to be true if a parent has accompanied her to court. This leads us to a third limitation: Many statutes do not permit a minor to seek a protective order on his or her own, but require that it be filed on the minor's behalf by a parent or other responsible adult. Alternatively, a statute might permit a minor to file for a protective order on his or her own, but then require the court to notify the minor's parents that the he or she has done so. Although the involvement of a parent or other caring adult can provide a minor with much-needed support, these adult involvement requirements may deter some teens from seeking help due to a sense of shame or the need to keep their dating relationship a secret. Finally, some statutes do not permit a party to obtain an order of protection from an abuser who is under the age of 18, thus significantly limiting the availability of protection to teens who are in peer dating relationships.[19]

It is important to note that, in addition to facing age-based obstacles to obtaining relief, teens who are in an abusive dating relationship with a same-sex partner may well face another separate set of barriers based on their sexual orientation. As we are about to see, in some states, same-sex couples remain outside the bounds of the abuse prevention law.

Same-Sex Couples

Intimate partner violence is not limited to heterosexual couples; however, the law has been slower to respond to victims who experience violence within the context of same-sex relationships. In large part, this reflects the legal system's historic reluctance to take same-sex relationships seriously. Additional complicating factors have included concerns within the gay and lesbian community that disclosure of abuse within same-sex relationships would exacerbate existing negative stereotypes, and an apprehension that judges would not respond to these cases with the seriousness and sensitivity that they merit. Although these concerns have clearly diminished over time, particularly now that marriage equality is the law of the land, they nonetheless retain some force today.

Abuse prevention laws have traditionally taken three basic approaches toward same-sex couples. Historically, a minority of statutes expressly limited the availability of protections to "opposite-sex couples," although today this is mainly a relic of the past. Moreover, under *Obergefell*, it is hard to imagine how any such remaining limitations could pass constitutional muster. At the other end of the continuum, a few statutes expressly extended protections to same-sex couples, thus formally equalizing the treatment of same-sex and heterosexual relationships in advance of the *Obergefell* decision. In most states, however, the abuse prevention law does not either expressly include or expressly exclude same-sex couples. Accordingly, where an abuse victim can demonstrate that he or she is in a qualifying relationship, there should be absolutely no doubt about the law's applicability. That being said, it does not necessarily mean that same-sex couples are *treated* equally. For example, one study showed that dual arrests are much higher in same-sex domestic violence cases as compared to those involving heterosexual couples. As a result, the victim does not receive the legal protection that she or he is entitled to under the law.[20]

Covered Conduct

What types of abusive behavior trigger eligibility for protection? There is not as much variability here as there is with respect to who is entitled to seek protection, but some statutes are more comprehensive than others and include types of conduct, such as the malicious destruction of property, that is usually not covered by abuse prevention laws. The following discussion focuses on the kinds of behaviors that are covered in most states.

Most often petitioners are seeking protection from physical abuse, and all states authorize the issuance of protective orders in this situation. Protection usually can also be sought for *attempted physical harm*, such as where someone throws a rock at someone but misses.

Most statutes also cover *threatened physical harm*. Generally, a petitioner must show that he or she was placed in fear of imminent bodily harm—the definition of criminal assault. However, as a practical matter, some judges are reluctant to issue orders for threats of harm in the absence of a history of physical abuse. This reluctance can put a victim at great risk because threats often escalate into violence; for instance, research indicates that up to 50 percent of battered women who are murdered by their partners had previously been threatened with death.[21] Some states also authorize relief for *emotional* or *verbal abuse,* which does not involve threats of physical harm, although these provisions are not common. Courts tend to interpret these provisions narrowly, and may, for instance, grant relief only where there has been a prior history of abuse or where an intent to harm can be inferred from accompanying conduct. An order may also be based on **stalking** (see section below entitled "Supplementing the Enforcement Process: Criminal Anti-Stalking Laws") either as a distinct behavior or as tied to some other category of recognized harm, such as threatened physical harm.

Orders also may be granted based on *harassment* or *interference with an individual's liberty,* although most states do not recognize these as separate qualifying behaviors, but subsume them into another category of harm such as threatened physical harm. Harassment has been defined to include a range of conduct, such as preventing a person from leaving a room, pulling the telephone out of the wall or cutting the wires, or slashing the tires of someone's car. Based on an understanding of domestic violence as an expression of power, some commentators have pushed for an expanded recognition of these types of harms in order to fully account for the complex array of strategies that abusers use to gain control over a partner's or former partner's life.[22]

Many statutes also expressly authorize the granting of protective orders based on sexual assault. In states where sexual assault is not specifically mentioned, judges are likely to include this conduct in their working definition of physical abuse. *Sexual assault* is generally understood to involve coercing someone to engage in sexual relations against her or his will through force, threats of force, or, possibly, duress, such as where someone says, "If you do not have sex with me you'll never see your children again." In such cases, the consent is negated by the coercion.

As discussed in Chapter 1, the issue of forced child marriages has been receiving growing attention in the United States. To date, according to one comprehensive study on the subject, only the state of Texas currently has adopted an express provision permitting "the issuance of a protection order upon a finding that a family or household member engaged in acts or omissions forcing or coercing a child to enter into a marriage.'"[23] As the author of this study details, it may be possible for a victim of a forced marriage to pigeonhole her request for protection into another category of harm that exists alongside of coercion, such as physical or sexual abuse. However, these types of qualifying conduct may not necessarily be present. Rather, coercion may occur through "emotional, psychological, and financial means . . . such as threatening to harm or kill themselves, isolation, social ostracization; declaring the ruin of a family's reputation; and threatening to withhold financial support, kick the individual out of the house, or have the individual deported."[24]

In addition to running into obstacles regarding the qualifying conduct, a party seeking to avoid being coerced into a marriage by way of a protective order may also encounter obstacles when it comes to meeting the qualifying relationship requirement. One concern is that many states prevent minors from seeking protective orders without the consent of one or both parents — accordingly, this option may be foreclosed to her if it is her parents who are seeking to compel her to marry. She may also be out of luck vis-à-vis her intended spouse if she is not actually in a qualifying dating relationship with him, as only a handful of states specifically permit protection from an engagement partner in a situation that does not rise to the level of a dating relationship as defined by statute.[25] However, given the increased attention the issue of forced child marriages is currently receiving, it will not be surprising if other states begin to consider amending their laws along the lines of the Texas provision.

Available Remedies

Most abuse prevention laws authorize a fairly broad range of specific remedies, including a "catchall" provision that allows a judge to tailor the remedy to the circumstances of the case before him or her. In this section, we look at the generally available remedies.

Before doing so, however, a brief word is in order about a supplemental approach that has slowly been gaining traction in some states: turning to tort law as a way of obtaining compensation for injuries caused by domestic violence beyond what may be awarded under a state's abuse prevention law. In this regard, the ability to seek compensation for emotional pain and suffering may be of particular relevance. Highlighting this trend, according to one report, "the majority of interspousal tort actions involve domestic violence."[26]

A number of traditional tort actions are potentially available to domestic violence victims, depending, of course, on the circumstances of the case. These include assault and battery, false imprisonment, and the intentional infliction of emotional distress. In addition, a few states now recognize domestic violence as a distinct form of tortious conduct. This approach often provides a more generous statute of limitations than is typically available in tort actions, which can be particularly beneficial to domestic violence victims who, due to the fear of reprisal, may well delay the initiation of legal proceedings beyond the usual time limits.[27]

Refraining from Further Abuse

Judges in all states can enjoin the abusive party from engaging in conduct that places the victim at risk of harm. This is often expressed as a requirement that the abuser refrain from committing any further acts of abuse as defined by the applicable abuse prevention law. This provision is commonly referred to as a **restraining order**. By itself, a restraining order does not usually prohibit contact between the parties; it simply prohibits abusive behavior.

Vacate and Stay-Away Orders

In most, if not all, states, a judge can issue a **vacate order**, which requires a batterer to vacate the victim's home. In many instances, removal of the perpetrator is an important step in securing the safety of the abused party, but in other cases, this remedy is worth little because they are left living in a place that is known to the abuser. Thus, despite the fact that the law may require the perpetrator to depart the premises, safety concerns may force the victim to vacate the shared premises. The issuance of a vacate order does not affect the vacated party's title to the property.

When the parties do not live together, a judge can issue a **stay-away order**, which requires the abuser to stay away from the victim's home. This stay-away order can be supplemented by language that further requires the abuser to stay away from other places such as the victim's place of work, her parents' house, and her neighborhood. Stay-away provisions can also be used to supplement a vacate order.

No-Contact Orders

Most abuse prevention laws expressly authorize a judge to issue a **no-contact order**. Where not expressly authorized, a no-contact order can issue under a law's "catch-all" provision. When drafted with care and specificity, no-contact orders can greatly enlarge the scope of available protection because they can be used to prohibit the abusive party from seeking any contact with the victim through any means or in any place. No-contact orders also can be drafted to prevent individuals who are acting on the abuser's behalf from contacting the victim.

Custody and Visitation

Most abuse prevention laws authorize judges to include temporary custody awards of minor children in a protective order. In some states, custody can be awarded only to the person seeking relief, while others employ a rebuttable presumption against awarding custody to the perpetrator of violence.

Some statutes permit a judge to fashion a temporary visitation order; however, recognizing that visitation often carries with it a serious risk of continued abuse, judges frequently impose specific conditions to help ensure the safety of the victim as well as the children, and in some states this is statutorily required. Accordingly, supervised visitation may be ordered, or the parties may be required to drop off and pick up the children at the home of a third party or other neutral location, such as a police station or a social service agency. Such arrangements may need to be made through an intermediary. By so structuring visitation, the need for contact between the parties is minimized, which, in turn, reduces the risk of continued abuse. Despite the availability of these preventive measures, some judges are reluctant to interfere with a parent's visitation rights and hesitate to impose restrictions except in the most egregious circumstances.

It is important to be aware that these custody and visitation orders are temporary in nature and may be superseded by orders entered in a subsequent divorce, custody, or separation proceeding. Moreover, if such an action is pending at the time a protective order is sought, the judge in the abuse action may be required to defer to this proceeding in matters of custody and visitation. If you are assisting someone who is seeking a restraining order, it is important to be aware of how the various statutory provisions governing custody and visitation interact in your jurisdiction. The interactive patterns are often complex and can result in conflicting orders that must be properly prioritized so the controlling order can be determined. The failure to do this can leave a client unprotected and at risk of violating a court order that has been superseded by a subsequent one.

Protection of Pets

A number of studies have documented a substantial rate of co-occurrence between domestic violence and cruelty to animals. In some instances, harm or threatened harm to a pet may be a deliberate strategy for the purpose of controlling or intimidating a victim. Here, "the harm caused to the animal is not an end in itself; rather, it is committed solely or primarily because the suffering of the animal inflicts 'psychological trauma' upon the ultimate victim."[28] Supplementing this body of work, there has also been a growing awareness of the fact that a victim of intimate partner violence may be reluctant to leave an abusive relationship based on fears for the safety of their pets they may be forced to leave behind.[29]

Responding to these realities, a rapidly growing number of jurisdictions have amended their abuse protection laws to provide for the safety and well-being of household pets. Typically, these laws include provisions within the remedies section of the law for the protection of pets and for the preservation of the relationship between the pet and the domestic violence victim. These types of measures enable a judge to order a defendant to stay away from and to refrain from abusing or injuring a pet, and/or to grant the exclusive care, custody, and possession of the pet to the petitioner.[30]

Support and Monetary Compensation

Most states authorize the inclusion of a temporary child support and/or a temporary spousal support award in a protective order. However, even where allowed, some judges are reluctant to make support awards, perhaps believing that financial matters are best addressed in a divorce proceeding. The failure to provide financial support, whether through a statutory exclusion or a judicial omission, can compromise a battered woman's safety. If she is unable to provide for herself and her children, she may feel that she has no choice but to return to the abuser.

Distinct from support, most statutes enable a judge to order the abuser to compensate the victim for any financial loss suffered due to the abuse. Compensation might include out-of-pocket medical expenses, the repair or replacement of damaged property, lost wages, and moving costs. However, frequently fearful that the court action will provoke retaliation, many victims are reluctant to request relief not directly related to securing their safety and the safety of their children.

Treatment/Counseling

In most states, a judge can order an abuser to participate in a treatment or counseling program that works specifically with batterers. **Batterer intervention programs**, as they are generally referred to, generally target men who abuse female intimate partners, but some now provide services to women who abuse their male partners and to gay men and lesbians. A growing number of states have adopted mandatory guidelines that batterer intervention programs must follow. These guidelines allow for state oversight of the quality and effectiveness of the program. Guidelines often relate to matters such as staff qualifications, intake and discharge procedures, and the intervention approach.

Unlike the above-discussed remedies, a judge may only have the authority to order a party into a batterer intervention program after a violation of the protective order has occurred. However, a judge may be able to *recommend* that an abuser seek help as part of the initial order. Where intervention is ordered rather than just recommended, the abuser's attendance is monitored, often by having the program send periodic reports back to the judge; if sessions are missed, the judge can impose sanctions.

Most experts in the field are at best cautiously optimistic about whether batterer intervention programs are effective in changing behavior. It appears that they may have a "small but significant" effect when part of a coordinated community anti-violence effort, rather than being relied on as the singular solution to domestic abuse. Research also indicates that intervention may be more effective with some men, for instance those without a significant mental disorder or substance abuse problem, than with others. One concern in this regard is that victims are often lulled into a false sense of security when they learn that the person who abuses them has enrolled in a batterer intervention program, as they assume that this will end the violence. To guard against this, most programs have some means for communicating with the partners of participants. Some send out a cautionary brochure explaining that intervention often does not result in changed behavior, and many programs will contact the partner of a participant if they have cause to believe that she is at risk of harm.

Electronic Monitoring

A relatively new remedy that a number of states have adopted is to permit the **electronic monitoring** of domestic violence perpetrators. Although a recent development in this context, "[e]lectronic monitoring has been used for decades to track convicted sex offenders who have been deemed a high risk."[31] As a general rule, electronic monitoring cannot be ordered at the *ex parte* stage (discussed below) based on due process fairness requirements. While at least one state allows it to be ordered at the second hearing stage when the "permanent" order is entered and there is a substantial risk of continued violence, other states will not order electronic monitoring unless a protective order has actually been violated.[32]

Generally, where ordered, a party wears a GPS tracking device that notifies law enforcement when he or she enters into an **"exclusion zone"** as set out in the protective order. These zones can include a party's home, place of work, as well as other frequently visited locations. The unauthorized entry into an exclusion zone typically results in arrest. This technology also allows the victim to be notified if the abuser enters an exclusion zone; however, not all law enforcement agencies utilize devices that include this critical feature. Another limitation is that these devices do not alert law enforcement if the perpetrator approaches the victim outside of an established exclusion zone.[33]

Relinquishment of Firearms

The use of a firearm significantly increases the chance of a violent death. Current research shows that "the presence of guns in the homes is associated with a 3-fold increased homicide risk within the home."[34] More specifically, and of direct relevance to this chapter: "[t]he risk connected to gun ownership increases to 8-fold when the offender is an intimate partner or relative of the victim and is 20 times higher when previous domestic violence exists."[35]

Given these potentially deadly consequences, many abuse prevention laws now include gun (and other weapon) possession provisions that restrict an abuser's access to firearms and ammunition. In some states, the entry of a protective order based on specific criteria, such as, the abuser poses a credible threat to the safety of the petitioner, results in a mandatory prohibition on the possession of a firearm. More commonly, however, a judge is given the discretion to enter in an order prohibiting the abuser from possessing a firearm. Additionally, some abuse prevention laws allow a judge to revoke the abuser's license to carry a firearm for the duration of the protective order.

Supplementing these state law provisions, in 1994, based on a recognition of the increased risk of lethality when domestic violence involves firearms, Congress, in addition to passing the Violence Against Women Act (discussed below), amended the Federal Gun Control Act of 1968 to criminalize the possession of a firearm or ammunition by a party who is already subject to a qualifying restraining order.[36] In 1996, Congress further amended the Gun Control Act by approving the "Domestic Violence Offender Gun Ban." Frequently referred to as the Lautenberg Amendment, after its Senate sponsor, this provision makes it illegal for a party who has been convicted of a misdemeanor crime of domestic violence to purchase or possess a firearm.[37] Unlike the 1994 Act, which provides limited exceptions to the possession ban for certain governmental employees, such as police officers and military personnel who are required to carry a weapon as part of their official duties, the Lautenberg Amendment does not contain any such exceptions. Accordingly, much to the chagrin of many gun rights advocates, it effectively disqualifies "people with domestic violence misdemeanor convictions from doing law enforcement or military work that requires carrying a gun."[38]

However, this federal law does contain a number of crucial gaps. For example, it does not apply to convicted stalkers, and it contains what is often referred to as the "boyfriend exception" — meaning that it does not cover dating relationships unless the parties cohabited or have a child in common.[39] A number of states have enacted measures to close the various loopholes in the federal law. For example, in the wake of the recent school shooting in Parkland, Florida, Oregon passed a law that eliminates the "boyfriend exception" by subjecting dating partners to the same restrictions on gun purchases and ownership as others who have committed domestic violence offenses. According to one study, these state measures have resulted in a 19 percent decrease in the risk of homicides by intimate partners.[40] At present, measures have also been introduced that likewise seek to plug the holes in the federal law. For example, in 2014, Senator Amy Klobuchar (D-MN) introduced legislation that would both eliminate the "boyfriend exception" and prevent stalkers from purchasing or possessing a firearm.

Statutory Obligations of Police Officers

Although not technically a form of relief, it should be pointed out that most abuse prevention laws impose specific obligations on police officers to assist victims of domestic violence. An officer may be required to provide a victim with information about obtaining an order, to arrange or provide transportation to a hospital or shelter, to remain on the scene until the threat of immediate danger has passed, and to assist the victim to collect his or her belongings. In some states, the police may be able to seize a batterer's weapons where they have cause to believe that continued possession exposes the victim to the risk of serious injury. As discussed below in the section entitled "Enforcement of Protective Orders," the police also have a role in serving and enforcing protective orders.

Court Procedure: Obtaining Protective Orders

Due to the urgent nature of domestic violence cases, the court process for obtaining protective orders is simpler and quicker than it is in most other kinds of cases. Filing a petition does not require a lawyer. Many petitioners successfully obtain orders on their own, but it can be helpful to have an advocate present. Unanticipated issues can arise in the course of a hearing, particularly if minor children are involved, that an advocate can help sort out. It can also be very frightening and possibly dangerous for a victim to face an abuser in court, especially where the perpetrator has threatened to take revenge if a court action is filed. An advocate can provide much needed support and help ensure that the victim is not pressured into abandoning the action. It should be noted that the scope of what an advocate is permitted to do varies from state to state and sometimes from judge to judge within an individual state.

This section provides a general step-by-step overview of the process for obtaining a protective order. Of course, the particulars vary from state to state, and local rules should always be consulted.

The court process for obtaining a protective order usually takes place in two distinct stages. First, the person seeking protection (the petitioner) goes to the appropriate court and files a complaint for protection from abuse (Exhibit 3.2). Many jurisdictions also require a supporting affidavit. As part of the filing process, most states allow the petitioner to request that his or her address be kept confidential. The case is generally heard right away on an *ex parte* basis, which means that notice is not given to the other side. If the petitioner shows an imminent risk of danger or that there will be an imminent risk once the other side knows the action has been filed,

Exhibit 3.1   Outline of the Steps for Obtaining a Protective Order

1. The party seeking the order files a complaint with a supporting affidavit. A filing fee is usually not required.
2. In most cases, the complaint is heard on an *ex parte* basis.
3. A temporary protective order is issued. Depending on the jurisdiction, the date for the second hearing may be set at this time.
4. Service is made on the defendant.
5. At the second hearing, the original order may be extended, modified, or vacated. If extended, a date for its expiration is usually established.
6. Prior to the expiration of the protective order, the plaintiff may return to court to seek an extension.

Exhibit 3.2   Request for Protective Order

| **DV-100** | **Request for Domestic Violence Restraining Order** | Clerk stamps date here when form is filed. |

You must also complete Form CLETS-001, Confidential CLETS Information, and give it to the clerk when you file this Request.

(1) Name of Person Asking for Protection:

_____ Age: _____

Your lawyer in this case *(if you have one):*

Name: _____ State Bar No.: _____

Firm Name: _____

Address *(If you have a lawyer for this case, give your lawyer's information. If you do not have a lawyer and want to keep your home address private, give a different mailing address instead. You do not have to give your telephone, fax, or e-mail.):*

Address: _____

City: _____ State: _____ Zip: _____

Telephone: _____ Fax: _____

E-Mail Address: _____

Fill in court name and street address:

Superior Court of California, County of

Court fills in case number when form is filed.

Case Number:

(2) Name of Person You Want Protection From:

_____

Description of person you want protection from:

Sex: ☐ M ☐ F   Height: _____ Weight: _____ Hair Color: _____ Eye Color: _____

Race: _____ Age: _____ Date of Birth: _____

Address *(if known):* _____

City: _____ State: _____ Zip: _____

(3) Do you want an order to protect family or household members?   ☐ Yes ☐ No

If yes, list them:

Full name	Sex	Age	Lives with you?	Relationship to you
_____	____	____	☐ Yes ☐ No	_____
_____	____	____	☐ Yes ☐ No	_____
_____	____	____	☐ Yes ☐ No	_____

☐ *Check here if you need more space. Attach a sheet of paper and write "DV-100, Protected People" for a title.*

(4) What is your relationship to the person in ② ? *(Check all that apply):*

a. ☐ We are now married or registered domestic partners.
b. ☐ We used to be married or registered domestic partners.
c. ☐ We live together.
d. ☐ We used to live together.

If you do not have one of these relationships, the court may not be able to consider your request. Read Form DV-500-INFO for help.

e. ☐ We are related by blood, marriage, or adoption *(specify relationship):* _____
f. ☐ We are dating or used to date, or we are or used to be engaged to be married.
g. ☐ We are the parents together of a child or children under 18:

Child's Name: _____ Date of Birth: _____
Child's Name: _____ Date of Birth: _____
Child's Name: _____ Date of Birth: _____

☐ *Check here if you need more space. Attach a sheet of paper and write "DV-100, Additional Children" for a title.*

h. ☐ We have signed a Voluntary Declaration of Paternity for our child or children. *(Attach a copy if you have one).*

This is not a Court Order.

Judicial Council of California, www.courts.ca.gov
Revised July 1, 2016, Mandatory Form
Family Code, § 6200 et seq.   **Request for Domestic Violence Restraining Order**
(Domestic Violence Prevention)   DV-100, Page 1 of 6 →

Exhibit 3.2   Continued

Case Number:

⑤ Other Restraining Orders and Court Cases

a. Are there any restraining/protective orders currently in place OR that have expired in the last six months (emergency protective orders, criminal, juvenile, family)?

☐ No   ☐ Yes *(date of order):*   and *(expiration date):*   *(Attach a copy if you have one).*

b. Have you or any other person named in ③ been involved in another court case with the person in ②?

☐ No   ☐ Yes *If yes, check each kind of case and indicate where and when each was filed:*

Kind of Case	County or Tribe Where Filed	Year Filed	Case Number *(if known)*
☐ Divorce, Nullity, Legal Separation			
☐ Civil Harassment			
☐ Domestic Violence			
☐ Criminal			
☐ Juvenile, Dependency, Guardianship			
☐ Child Support			
☐ Parentage, Paternity			
☐ Other *(specify):*			

☐ *Check here if you need more space. Attach a sheet of paper and write "DV-100, Other Court Cases" for a title.*

Check the orders you want. ☑

⑥ ☐ Personal Conduct Orders

I ask the court to order the person in ② not to do the following things to me or anyone listed in ③:

a. ☐ Harass, attack, strike, threaten, assault (sexually or otherwise), hit, follow, stalk, molest, destroy personal property, disturb the peace, keep under surveillance, impersonate (on the Internet, electronically or otherwise), or block movements

b. ☐ Contact, either directly or indirectly, in any way, including but not limited to, by telephone, mail or e-mail or other electronic means

The person in ② will be ordered not to take any action to get the addresses or locations of any protected person unless the court finds good cause not to make the order.

⑦ ☐ Stay-Away Order

a. I ask the court to order the person in ② to stay at least _____ yards away from *(check all that apply):*

☐ Me   ☐ My school
☐ My home   ☐ Each person listed in ③
☐ My job or workplace   ☐ The child(ren)'s school or child care
☐ My vehicle   ☐ Other *(specify):* _____

b. If the person listed in ② is ordered to stay away from all the places listed above, will he or she still be able to get to his or her home, school, job, workplace, or vehicle?   ☐ Yes ☐ No *(If no, explain):*

_____

⑧ ☐ Move-Out Order

(If the person in ② lives with you and you want that person to stay away from your home, you must ask for this move-out order.)

I ask the court to order the person in ② to move out from and not return to *(address):*

_____

I have the right to live at the above address because (explain):

_____

This is not a Court Order.

Exhibit 3.2   Continued

Case Number:

---

⑨ Guns or Other Firearms or Ammunition

I believe the person in ② owns or possesses guns, firearms, or ammunition. ☐ Yes   ☐ No ☐ I don't know
If the judge approves the order, the person in ② will be ordered not to own, possess, purchase, or receive a firearm or ammunition. The person will be ordered to sell to, or store with, a licensed gun dealer, or turn in to law enforcement, any guns or firearms that he or she owns or possesses.

⑩ ☐ Record Unlawful Communications

I ask for the right to record communications made to me by the person in ② that violate the judge's orders.

⑪ ☐ Care of Animals

I ask for the sole possession, care, and control of the animals listed below. I ask the court to order the person in ② to stay at least _____ yards away from and not take, sell, transfer, encumber, conceal, molest, attack, strike, threaten, harm, or otherwise dispose of the following animals:

_____

_____

I ask for the animals to be with me because:

_____

_____

⑫ ☐ Child Custody and Visitation

a. ☐ I do not have a child custody or visitation order and I want one.

b. ☐ I have a child custody or visitation order and I want it changed.

If you ask for orders, you must fill out and attach Form DV-105, Request for Child Custody and Visitation Orders.

You and the other parent may tell the court that you want to be legal parents of the children (use Form DV-180, Agreement and Judgment of Parentage).

⑬ ☐ Child Support *(Check all that apply):*

a. ☐ I do not have a child support order and I want one.

b. ☐ I have a child support order and I want it changed.

c. ☐ I now receive or have applied for TANF, Welfare, CalWORKS, or Medi-Cal.

If you ask for child support orders, you must fill out and attach form FL-150, Income and Expense Declaration or Form FL-155, Financial Statement (Simplified).

⑭ ☐ Property Control

I ask the court to give *only* me temporary use, possession, and control of the property listed here:

_____

_____

⑮ ☐ Debt Payment

I ask the court to order the person in ② to make these payments while the order is in effect:

☐ *Check here if you need more space. Attach a sheet of paper and write "DV-100, Debt Payment" for a title.*

Pay to: _____   For: _____   Amount: $ _____   Due date: _____

⑯ ☐ Property Restraint

I am married to or have a registered domestic partnership with the person in ② . I ask the judge to order that the person in ② not borrow against, sell, hide, or get rid of or destroy any possessions or property, except in the usual course of business or for necessities of life. I also ask the judge to order the person in ② to notify me of any new or big expenses and to explain them to the court.

⑰ ☐ Spousal Support

I am married to or have a registered domestic partnership with the person in ② and no spousal support order exists. I ask the court to order the person in ② to pay spousal support. *(You must complete, file, and serve Form FL-150, Income and Expense Declaration, before your hearing).*

This is not a Court Order.

Exhibit 3.2   Continued

Case Number:

(18) ☐ **Rights to Mobile Device and Wireless Phone Account**

   a. ☐ **Property control of mobile device and wireless phone account**
   I ask the court to give **only** me temporary use, possession, and control of the following mobile devices:
   _____ and the wireless phone account for the
   following wireless phone numbers because the account currently belongs to the person in **(2)** :
   (including area code): _____   ☐ my number   ☐ number of child in my care
   (including area code): _____   ☐ my number   ☐ number of child in my care
   (including area code): _____   ☐ my number   ☐ number of child in my care
   ☐ *Check here if you need more space. Attach a sheet of paper and write "DV-100, Rights to Mobile Device*
      and Wireless Phone Account" for a title.

   b. ☐ **Debt Payment**
   I ask the court to order the person in **(2)** to make the payments for the wireless phone accounts listed in 18a
   because: _____
   Name of the wireless service provider is: _____   Amount: $ _____   Due Date: _____
   If you are requesting this order, you must complete, file, and serve Form FL-150, Income and Expense
   Declaration, before your hearing.

   c. ☐ **Transfer of Wireless Phone Account**
   I ask the court to order the wireless service provider to transfer the billing responsibility and rights to the
   wireless phone numbers listed in 18a to me because the account currently belongs to the person in **(2)** .
   If the judge makes this order, you will be financially responsible for these accounts, including monthly service
   fees and costs of any mobile devices connected to these phone numbers. You may be responsible for other fees.
   You must contact the wireless service provider to find out what fees you will be responsible for and whether you
   are eligible for an account.

(19) ☐ **Insurance**
   I ask the court to order the person in **(2)** NOT to cash, borrow against, cancel, transfer, dispose of, or change the
   beneficiaries of any insurance or coverage held for the benefit of me or the person in **(2)**, or our child(ren), for
   whom support may be ordered, or both.

(20) ☐ **Lawyer's Fees and Costs**
   I ask that the person in **(2)** pay some or all of my lawyer's fees and costs.
   You must complete, file, and serve form FL-150, Income and Expense Declaration, before your hearing.

(21) ☐ **Payments for Costs and Services**
   I ask the court to order the person in **(2)** to pay the following:
   You can ask for lost earnings or your costs for services caused directly by the person in **(2)** *(damaged property,*
   medical care, counseling, temporary housing, etc.). You must bring proof of these expenses to your hearing.
   Pay to: _____   For: _____   Amount: $ _____
   Pay to: _____   For: _____   Amount: $ _____

(22) ☐ **Batterer Intervention Program**
   I ask the court to order the person listed in **(2)** to go to a 52-week batterer intervention program and show proof
   of completion to the court.

(23) ☐ **Other Orders**
   What other orders are you asking for? _____
   _____
   _____
   _____

   ☐ *Check here if you need more space. Attach a sheet of paper and write "DV-100, Other Orders" for a title.*

This is not a Court Order.

Exhibit 3.2   Continued

Case Number:

(24) ☐ **Time for Service (Notice)**

*The papers must be personally served on the person in **(2)** at least five days before the hearing, unless the court orders a shorter time for service. If you want there to be fewer than five days between service and the hearing, explain why below. For help, read <u>Form DV-200-INFO</u>, "What Is Proof of Personal Service"?*

_____

_____

(25) **No Fee to Serve (Notify) Restrained Person**

If you want the sheriff or marshal to serve (notify) the restrained person about the orders for free, ask the court clerk what you need to do.

(26) **Court Hearing**

The court will schedule a hearing on your request. If the judge does not make the orders effective right away ("temporary restraining orders"), the judge may still make the orders after the hearing. If the judge does not make the orders effective right away, you can ask the court to cancel the hearing. Read <u>form DV-112</u>, *Waiver of Hearing on Denied Request for Temporary Restraining Order,* for more information.

(27) **Describe Abuse**

Describe how the person in **(2)** abused you. Abuse means to intentionally or recklessly cause or attempt to cause bodily injury to you; or to place you or another person in reasonable fear of imminent serious bodily injury; or to harass, attack, strike, threaten, assault (sexually or otherwise), hit, follow, stalk, molest, keep you under surveillance, impersonate (on the Internet, electronically or otherwise), batter, telephone, or contact you; or to disturb your peace; or to destroy your personal property. (For a complete definition, see Fam. Code, §§ 6203, 6320.)

a. Date of most recent abuse: _____

  1. Who was there? _____

  2. Describe how the person in **(2)** abused you or your child(ren):

  _____

  _____

  _____

  _____

  _____

  ☐ *Check here if you need more space. Attach a sheet of paper and write "DV-100, Recent Abuse" for a title.*

  3. Did the person in **(2)** use or threaten to use a gun or any other weapon? ☐ No ☐ Yes *(If yes, describe):*

  _____

  _____

  4. Describe any injuries: _____

  _____

  _____

  5. Did the police come? ☐ No ☐ Yes
     If yes, did they give you or the person in **(2)** an Emergency Protective Order? ☐ Yes ☐ No ☐ I don't know
     Attach a copy if you have one.
     The order protects ☐ you or ☐ the person in **(2)**

This is not a Court Order.

Exhibit 3.2 Continued

Case Number:

㉗ Describe Abuse (continued)

Has the person in ② abused you (or your child(ren)) other times?

    b. Date of abuse: _____

       1. Who was there? _____

       2. Describe how the person in ② abused you or your child(ren):

           _____

           _____

           _____

           _____

          ☐ *Check here if you need more space. Attach a sheet of paper and write "DV-100, Recent Abuse" for a title.*

       3. Did the person in② use or threaten to use a gun or any other weapon? ☐ No ☐ Yes *(If yes, describe):*

           _____

       4. Describe any injuries: _____

           _____

       5. Did the police come? ☐ No ☐ Yes

          If yes, did they give you or the person in ② an Emergency Protective Order?

          ☐ Yes ☐ No ☐ I don't know *Attach a copy if you have one.*

          The order protects ☐ you or ☐ the person in ②

          If the person in ② abused you other times, check here ☐ and use Form DV-101, Description of Abuse or describe any previous abuse on an attached sheet of paper and write "DV-100, Previous Abuse" for a title.

㉘ Other Persons to Be Protected

The persons listed in item ③ need an order for protection because *(describe):* _____

_____

_____

_____

_____

_____

_____

㉙ Number of pages attached to this form, if any: _____

I declare under penalty of perjury under the laws of the State of California that the information above is true and correct.

Date: _____

_____   ▶ _____

Type or print your name   *Sign your name*

Date: _____

_____   ▶ _____

Lawyer's name, if you have one   *Lawyer's signature*

This is not a Court Order.

For your protection and privacy, please press the Clear This Form button after you have printed the form.   **Print this form**   **Save this form**   **Clear this form** the judge can issue a **temporary order** without notice to the other side. Some statutes limit the relief that is available at this stage to restraining and eviction orders and postpone consideration of matters such as custody, support, and counseling until the second hearing. Some judges limit the relief they will grant at this stage even if not so restricted by the applicable statute, which concerns many advocates.

Because abuse frequently takes place on weekends or in the evening when courts are closed, most states have a procedure in place for obtaining after-hour emergency orders. An emergency judge might be available on a 24-hour on-call basis, or an official, such as a magistrate, might be empowered to issue after-hour orders. These orders generally are good only until the next business day.

Service must be made on the other side (the respondent). This is usually accomplished by a police officer or a sheriff. As a general rule, service must be made in hand, although statutes often permit alternative means of service under specified circumstances, such as allowing the papers to be left at the last and usual address when attempts at personal service have failed. As a general rule, the *ex parte* orders are not considered to be in effect until service has been made. In addition to being given a copy of the complaint and any *ex parte* orders, the respondent must be informed of the right to be heard in court. In some states, a second hearing date is set at the *ex parte* hearing, usually for somewhere between 10 to 20 days later, and the initial orders are only good until then. In other states, the second hearing date is not set by the court but must be requested by the responding party, who has a right to be heard promptly. Here, the *ex parte* orders remain in effect until the second hearing is held; if a hearing is not requested, they remain in effect until a judicially selected or a statutory expiration date is reached.

The next stage is the second hearing at which both parties are given the opportunity to present their version of what took place. After hearing the evidence, the judge can either extend or decline to extend the original orders for an additional period of time. The judge can also address any matters that may have been left unresolved at the *ex parte* stage, such as support. Most states allow orders to be extended for up to at least one year, although, as noted above, the trend is in favor of longer extension periods, and a few states do not impose any mandatory durational limits. (For an example of an abuse prevention order, see Exhibit 3.3.) Most states allow the petitioner to return to court to seek an extension before the orders issued at the second hearing expire. An extension generally can be granted based on a credible fear of renewed harm—acts of violence do not need to have been committed while the order was in effect.

Although the practice has drawn considerable criticism and has been prohibited in a number of jurisdictions, some judges are inclined to grant **mutual orders of protection** at the second hearing whereby each party is ordered to refrain from harming the other, despite the fact that only one

Exhibit 3.3   Abuse Prevention Order

DV-110	**Temporary Restraining Order**

Clerk stamps date here when form is filed.

Person in ① must complete items ①, ②, and ③ only.

① Name of Protected Person: _____

Your lawyer in this case *(if you have one):*
Name: _____ State Bar No.: _____
Firm Name: _____
Address *(If you have a lawyer for this case, give your lawyer's information. If you do not have a lawyer and want to keep your home address private, give a different mailing address instead. You do not have to give your telephone, fax, or e-mail.):*
Address: _____
City: _____ State: _____ Zip: _____
Telephone: _____ Fax: _____
E-mail Address: _____

Fill in court name and street address:

Superior Court of California, County of

② Name of Restrained Person: _____

Description of restrained person:

Court fills in case number when form is filed.

Case Number:

Sex: ☐ M ☐ F   Height: _____   Weight: _____   Hair Color: _____   Eye Color: _____
Race: _____ Age: _____ Date of Birth: _____
Address *(if known):* _____
City: _____ State: _____ Zip: _____
Relationship to protected person: _____

③ ☐ Additional Protected Persons

In addition to the person named in ①, the following persons are protected by temporary orders as indicated in items ⑥ and ⑦ *(family or household members):*

Full name	Relationship to person in ①	Sex	Age
_____	_____	_____	_____
_____	_____	_____	_____

☐ *Check here if there are additional protected persons. List them on an attached sheet of paper and write, "DV-110, Additional Protected Persons" as a title.*

The court will complete the rest of this form.

④ Court Hearing

This order expires at the end of the hearing stated below:

Hearing Date: _____ Time: _____ ☐ a.m. ☐ p.m.

This is a Court Order.

Judicial Council of California, www.courts.ca.gov
Revised July 1, 2016, Mandatory Form
Family Code, § 6200 et seq.
Approved by DOJ

Temporary Restraining Order
(CLETS—TRO)
(Domestic Violence Prevention)

DV-110, Page 1 of 6

→

Exhibit 3.3   Continued

Case Number:

---

(5) ☐ **Criminal Protective Order**

    a. ☐ A criminal protective order on form CR-160, *Criminal Protective Order—Domestic Violence,* is in effect.
        Case Number: _____ County: _____ Expiration Date: _____

    b. ☐ No information has been provided to the judge about a criminal protective order.

To the person in ❷

The court has granted the temporary orders checked below. If you do not obey these orders, you can be arrested and charged with a crime. You may be sent to jail for up to one year, pay a fine of up to $1,000, or both.

(6) **Personal Conduct Orders** ☐ Not requested ☐ Denied until the hearing ☐ Granted as follows:

    a. You must **not** do the following things to the person in ① and ☐ persons in ③ :

        ☐ Harass, attack, strike, threaten, assault *(sexually or otherwise),* hit, follow, stalk, molest, destroy personal property, disturb the peace, keep under surveillance, impersonate *(on the Internet, electronically or otherwise),* or block movements

        ☐ Contact, either directly or indirectly, in any way, including but not limited to, by telephone, mail, e-mail or other electronic means

        ☐ Take any action, directly or through others, to obtain the addresses or locations of the persons in ① *and* ③. *(If this item is not checked, the court has found good cause not to make this order.)*

    b. Peaceful written contact through a lawyer or process server or another person for service of <u>Form DV-120</u> *(Response to Request for Domestic Violence Restraining Order)* or other legal papers related to a court case is allowed and does not violate this order.

    c. ☐ Exceptions: Brief and peaceful contact with the person in ①, and peaceful contact with children in ③, as required for court-ordered visitation of children, is allowed unless a criminal protective order says otherwise.

(7) **Stay-Away Order** ☐ Not requested ☐ Denied until the hearing ☐ Granted as follows:

    a. You **must** stay at least *(specify):* _____ yards away from *(check all that apply):*

        ☐ The person in ①   ☐ School of person in ①
        ☐ Home of person in ①   ☐ The persons in ③
        ☐ The job or workplace of person in ① ☐ The child(ren)'s school or child care
        ☐ Vehicle of person in ①   ☐ Other *(specify):* _____

    b. ☐ Exceptions: Brief and peaceful contact with the person in ①, and peaceful contact with children in ③, as required for court-ordered visitation of children, is allowed unless a criminal protective order says otherwise.

(8) **Move-Out Order** ☐ Not requested ☐ Denied until the hearing ☐ Granted as follows:

You must take only personal clothing and belongings needed until the hearing and move out immediately from *(address):* _____

This is a Court Order.

Exhibit 3.3   Continued

Case Number:

(9) No Guns or Other Firearms or Ammunition

a. You cannot own, possess, have, buy or try to buy, receive or try to receive, or in any other way get guns, other firearms, or ammunition.

b. You must:
  - Sell to, or store with, a licensed gun dealer, or turn in to a law enforcement agency, any guns or other firearms within your immediate possession or control. Do so within 24 hours of being served with this order.
  - Within 48 hours of receiving this order, file with the court a receipt that proves guns have been turned in, stored, or sold. (You may use Form DV-800, *Proof of Firearms Turned In, Sold, or Stored,* for the receipt.) Bring a court filed copy to the hearing.

c. ☐ The court has received information that you own or possess a firearm.

(10) Record Unlawful Communications

☐ **Not requested**   ☐ **Denied until the hearing**   ☐ **Granted as follows:**

The person in (1) can record communications made by you that violate the judge's orders.

(11) Care of Animals   ☐ **Not requested**   ☐ **Denied until the hearing**   ☐ **Granted as follows:**

The person in (1) is given the sole possession, care, and control of the animals listed below. The person in (2) must stay at least _____ yards away from and not take, sell, transfer, encumber, conceal, molest, attack, strike, threaten, harm, or otherwise dispose of the following animals:

_____

_____

(12) Child Custody and Visitation ☐ **Not requested**   ☐ **Denied until the hearing**   ☐ **Granted as follows:**

Child custody and visitation are ordered on the attached form DV-140, *Child Custody and Visitation Order* or *(specify other form):* _____ . The parent with temporary custody of the child must not remove the child from California unless the court allows it after a noticed hearing (Fam. Code, § 3063).

(13) Child Support

Not ordered now but may be ordered after a noticed hearing.

(14) Property Control ☐ **Not requested**   ☐ **Denied until the hearing**   ☐ **Granted as follows:**

Until the hearing, *only* the person in (1) can use, control, and possess the following property:

_____

(15) Debt Payment ☐ **Not requested**   ☐ **Denied until the hearing**   ☐ **Granted as follows:**

The person in (2) must make these payments until this order ends:

Pay to: _____   For: _____   Amount: $ _____   Due date: _____

Pay to: _____   For: _____   Amount: $ _____   Due date: _____

(16) Property Restraint   ☐ **Not requested**   ☐ **Denied until the hearing**   ☐ **Granted as follows:**

If the people in (1) and (2) are married to each other or are registered domestic partners, ☐ the person in (1) ☐ the person in (2)   must not transfer, borrow against, sell, hide, or get rid of or destroy any property, including animals, except in the usual course of business or for necessities of life. In addition, each person must notify the other of any new or big expenses and explain them to the court. *(The person in (2) cannot contact the person in (1) if the court has made a "no contact" order.)*

Peaceful written contact through a lawyer or a process server or other person for service of legal papers related to a court case is allowed and does not violate this order.

This is a Court Order.

Exhibit 3.3   Continued

Case Number:

(17) Spousal Support

Not ordered now but may be ordered after a noticed hearing.

(18) Rights to Mobile Device and Wireless Phone Account

    a. Property control of mobile device and wireless phone account

      ☐ Not requested ☐ Denied until the hearing ☐ Granted as follows:

      Until the hearing, only the person in ① can use, control, and possess the following property:

      Mobile device *(describe)* _____ and account *(phone number):* _____

      Mobile device *(describe)* _____ and account *(phone number):* _____

      Mobile device *(describe)* _____ and account *(phone number):* _____

      ☐ *Check here if you need more space. Attach a sheet of paper and write "DV-110 Rights to Mobile Device and Wireless Phone Account" as a title.*

    b. Debt Payment ☐ Not requested ☐ Denied until the hearing ☐ Granted as follows:

      The person in ② must make these payments until this order ends:

      Pay to *(wireless service provider):* _____ Amount: $_____ Due date: _____

    c. Transfer of Wireless Phone Account

      Not ordered now but may be ordered after a noticed hearing.

(19) Insurance

☐ The person in ① ☐ the person in ② is ordered NOT to cash, borrow against, cancel, transfer, dispose of, or change the beneficiaries of any insurance or coverage held for the benefit of the parties, or their child(ren), if any, for whom support may be ordered, or both.

(20) Lawyer's Fees and Costs

Not ordered now but may be ordered after a noticed hearing.

(21) Payments for Costs and Services

Not ordered now but may be ordered after a noticed hearing.

(22) Batterer Intervention Program

Not ordered now but may be ordered after a noticed hearing.

(23) Other Orders ☐ **Not requested** ☐ **Denied until the hearing** ☐ **Granted as follows:**

_____

_____

_____

_____

_____

_____

☐ *Check here if there are additional orders. List them on an attached sheet of paper and write "DV-110, Other Orders" as a title.*

(24) No Fee to Serve (Notify) Restrained Person

If the sheriff serves this order, he or she will do so for free.

Date: _____   _____

                                            Judge (or Judicial Officer)

This is a Court Order.

Exhibit 3.3   Continued

Case Number:

Warnings and Notices to the Restrained Person in ❷

If You Do Not Obey This Order, You Can Be Arrested And Charged With a Crime.

- If you do not obey this order, you can go to jail or prison and/or pay a fine.
- It is a felony to take or hide a child in violation of this order.
- If you travel to another state or to tribal lands or make the protected person do so, with the intention of disobeying this order, you can be charged with a federal crime.

You Cannot Have Guns, Firearms, And/Or Ammunition.

 You cannot own, have, possess, buy or try to buy, receive or try to receive, or otherwise get guns, other firearms, and/or ammunition while the order is in effect. If you do, you can go to jail and pay a $1,000 fine. You must sell to or store with a licensed gun dealer or turn in to a law enforcement agency any guns or other firearms that you have or control. The judge will ask you for proof that you did so. If you do not obey this order, you can be charged with a crime. Federal law says you cannot have guns or ammunition while the order is in effect.

Service of Order by Mail

If the judge makes a restraining order at the hearing, which has the same orders as in this form, you will get a copy of that order by mail at your last known address, which is written in ②. If this address is incorrect, or to find out if the orders were made permanent, contact the court.

Child Custody, Visitation, and Support

- **Child custody and visitation:** If you do not go to the hearing, the judge can make custody and visitation orders for your children without hearing from you.
- **Child support:** The judge can order child support based on the income of both parents. The judge can also have that support taken directly from a parent's paycheck. Child support can be a lot of money, and usually you have to pay until the child is age 18. File and serve a *Financial Statement (Simplified)* (form FL-155) or an *Income and Expense Declaration* (form FL-150) if you want the judge to have information about your finances. Otherwise, the court may make support orders without hearing from you.
- **Spousal support:** File and serve an *Income and Expense Declaration* (form FL-150) so the judge will have information about your finances. Otherwise, the court may make support orders without hearing from you.

Instructions for Law Enforcement

This order is effective when made. It is enforceable by any law enforcement agency that has received the order, is shown a copy of the order, or has verified its existence on the California Law Enforcement Telecommunications System (CLETS). If the law enforcement agency has not received proof of service on the restrained person, and the restrained person was not present at the court hearing, the agency shall advise the restrained person of the terms of the order and then shall enforce it. Violations of this order are subject to criminal penalties.

Arrest Required if Order Is Violated

If an officer has probable cause to believe that the restrained person had notice of the order and has disobeyed the order, the officer must arrest the restrained person. (Pen. Code, §§ 836(c)(1), 13701(b).) A violation of the order may be a violation of Penal Code section 166 or 273.6.

This is a Court Order.

Temporary Restraining Order
(CLETS—TRO)
(Domestic Violence Prevention)

Exhibit 3.3 Continued

Case Number:

If the Protected Person Contacts the Restrained Person

Even if the protected person invites or consents to contact with the restrained person, the orders remain in effect and must be enforced. The protected person cannot be arrested for inviting or consenting to contact with the restrained person. The orders can be changed only by another court order. (Pen. Code, §13710(b).)

Conflicting Orders–Priorities for Enforcement

If more than one restraining order has been issued protecting the protected person from the restrained person, the orders must be enforced according to the following priorities (see Pen. Code, § 136.2, and Fam. Code, §§ 6383(h), 6405(b)):

1. *EPO:* If one of the orders is an *Emergency Protective Order* (form EPO-001), and it is more restrictive than other restraining or protective orders, it has precedence in enforcement over all other orders.

2. *No-Contact Order:* If there is no EPO, a no-contact order that is included in a restraining or protective order has precedence in enforcement over any other restraining or protective order.

3. *Criminal Order:* If none of the orders includes a no-contact order, a domestic violence protective order issued in a criminal case takes precedence in enforcement over any conflicting civil court order. Any nonconflicting terms of the civil restraining order remain in effect and enforceable.

4. *Family, Juvenile, or Civil Order:* If more than one family, juvenile, or other civil restraining or protective order has been issued, the one that was issued last must be enforced.

Child Custody and Visitation

• The custody and visitation orders are on form DV-140, items ③ and ④ They are sometimes also written on additional pages or referenced in DV-140 or other orders that are not part of the restraining order.

• **Forms DV-100 and DV-105 are not orders. Do not enforce them.**

Certificate of Compliance With VAWA

This temporary protective order meets all "full faith and credit" requirements of the Violence Against Women Act, 18 U.S.C. § 2265 (1994) (VAWA), upon notice of the restrained person. This court has jurisdiction over the parties and the subject matter; the restrained person has been or will be afforded notice and a timely opportunity to be heard as provided by the laws of this jurisdiction. **This order is valid and entitled to enforcement in each jurisdiction throughout the 50 states of the United States, the District of Columbia, all tribal lands, and all U.S. territories, commonwealths, and possessions and shall be enforced as if it were an order of that jurisdiction.**

(Clerk will fill out this part.)

—Clerk's Certificate—

Clerk's Certificate
[seal]

I certify that this *Temporary Restraining Order* is a true and correct copy of the original on file in the court.

Date: _____   Clerk, by _____ , Deputy

This is a Court Order.

Temporary Restraining Order
(CLETS—TRO)
(Domestic Violence Prevention)

For your protection and privacy, please press the Clear This Form button after you have printed the form.

[Print this form] [Save this form]   [Clear this form] party has requested relief. By suggesting that both persons are responsible for the violence, mutual orders fail to hold abusers accountable for their behavior. They can also create enforcement problems for police responding to a call for assistance because each party can claim that he or she is the protected one and that the other should be arrested. Additionally, a mutual order can adversely impact the petitioner in a subsequent custody or visitation dispute in which the court is directed to consider the existence of prior protective orders when making an award because both parties will appear to be equally responsible for the violence. (See the discussion later in this chapter regarding VAWA and mutual restraining orders.)

Where the responding party fails to appear at the second hearing, many courts will continue the order based on the evidence presented by the petitioner, and in some states this result is mandated by statute. In other states, a bench warrant may be issued to secure the respondent's appearance. In some states, if the petitioner fails to appear, the action may be automatically dismissed. Advocates for battered women have raised serious concerns about this approach because a victim's failure to appear at the second hearing may be the result of fear or intimidation, rather than the result of a voluntary decision not to proceed.

Enforcement of Protective Orders

If protective orders are to be worth more than the paper they are written on, effective enforcement is essential. Accordingly, although the orders themselves are civil in nature, violations can be prosecuted in the criminal justice system. Importantly, in most states, the act of violating an order is, in and of itself, a separate and independent crime. This is particularly valuable in situations where the violating behavior may not itself be an independent crime, such as where a party continually telephones the petitioner in violation of a no-contact order. However, most acts committed in violation of a protective order are themselves crimes (e.g., trespass, assault, battery, and false imprisonment), and a party can thus be prosecuted for any specific criminal acts as well as for violating the order.

Until fairly recently, the criminal justice system did not take domestic abuse cases as seriously as other criminal matters, seeing them primarily as private family matters. Police officers were frequently reluctant to make arrests, and prosecutors often used their discretion to drop cases, especially if the victim was at all ambivalent about proceeding, without first inquiring whether the reluctance stemmed from fear or coercion. Advocates for battered women began to press for change, demanding that intimate assaults be taken as seriously as other kinds of violence and not treated as inconsequential private spats.

Responding to these concerns, most states have adopted mandatory arrest policies that require police officers to arrest a suspect, without having to first obtain a warrant, whenever there is probable cause to believe an act of domestic violence has occurred, regardless of whether the officer witnessed the incident or not. By requiring arrest, these laws are intended to remove police discretion.

However, greatly disappointing domestic violence advocates, in 2005, in the case of Gonzales v. Castle Rock, the U.S. Supreme Court held that a victim does not have a constitutionally protected right to police enforcement of a restraining order. In this case, Ms. Gonzales sued the local police department after they ignored her calls that her husband had taken the couple's three daughters in violation of a restraining order. Tragically, he ended up murdering the three girls. Although the police ignored Colorado's mandatory arrest law, the Court concluded that Ms. Gonzales did not have a recognized "property" interest in the restraining order because, despite the "seemingly mandatory legislative command," police apparently maintained some discretion over the arrest decision.

It should be noted that the Supreme Court's ruling was not the end of the matter. Following her loss at the nation's highest court, Jessica Lenahan (formerly Jessica Gonzalez) became the first domestic violence survivor from the United States to bring her case before the Inter-American Court on Human Rights (IACHR).

In a landmark 2011 ruling, the IACHR held that the failure of the government to protect Jessica and her children constituted a violation of their human rights. In addition to recommending that Ms. Lenahan and her family receive "full reparations" for their loss, the IACHR also recommended that the United States "adopt multifaceted legislation at the federal and state levels, or to reform existing legislation making mandatory the enforcement of protection orders and other precautionary measures to protect women [and children in the context of domestic violence] from imminent acts of violence, and to create effective implementation mechanisms."[41]

This decision has had an important ripple effect as it has increasingly been invoked by local jurisdictions as a "basis for declaring freedom from domestic violence as a human right."[42] Tracking this approach, in 2014, President Obama issued two proclamations — one on the twentieth anniversary of the Violence Against Women Act (see below) and the other during National Domestic Violence Awareness Week — in which he similarly affirmed that it is a "basic human right to be free from violence and abuse."[43]

Similarly, many states have adopted mandatory prosecution (or no-drop) policies that enable a prosecutor to pursue a domestic violence case even if the victim does not want to proceed. Some states maintain what is often referred to as a "soft-drop" approach, which means that there is no consequence to the victim if she chooses not to cooperate with the prosecution. In contrast, in states with a "hard-drop" approach, a victim may face contempt proceedings if she opts not to testify against her abuser.

Although the adoption of mandatory arrest and prosecution policies clearly signifies that domestic violence is being taken more seriously by the criminal justice system, this approach is nonetheless quite controversial. Supporters of a mandatory approach worry that the traumatic effects of abuse and the fear of reprisal can compromise the ability of victims to make appropriate decisions that maximize their well-being. They further worry that the "ongoing humiliation and assaults of personhood may encourage women to believe that they are partially responsible for their partner's violence which may compromise their ability to judge their own best interests."[44] So viewed, the benefit of a mandatory approach is that it permits the state to intervene in situations where a victim might not act in accordance with her own safety needs.

On the other hand, many advocates for battered women believe that mandatory policies deprive victims of the right to make decisions for themselves based upon a personal and individualized assessment of their own needs and safety concerns. Critics worry that divesting a woman of decisional authority will "perpetuate the disempowerment of the victim by sending a message that she is too helpless to survive without the controlling direction of a stronger person."[45] Another concern is that mandatory policies may actually endanger the people they were intended to protect, as anger over an arrest and prosecution may prompt an abuser to seek revenge against a victim, who, had she been given a choice, might have decided that it was too risky to seek the assistance of the criminal justice system.[46]

It should also be noted that in addition to these measures, a few states have enacted mandatory reporting laws that require health care professionals to report suspected cases of domestic violence to law enforcement. Although these are intended to advance the state's interest in protecting victims of abuse, like the other mandatory policies, these measures have likewise come under considerable criticism. Of particular concern is that again they take control away from victims of abuse. Additionally, the fear is that an abuser might seek to prevent an injured party from seeking medical care out of fear that he or she will be reported to the authorities.

Supplementing the Enforcement Process: Criminal Anti-Stalking Laws

In 1990, California enacted the nation's first anti-stalking law following the murder of actress Rebecca Schaeffer, the star of a popular sitcom—*My*

Sister Sam—by a fan who had pursued her for over two years. Since then, all states have enacted criminal anti-stalking laws, and in 2006, Congress enacted the Interstate Stalking Punishment and Prevention Act, which makes it a federal crime to travel across state lines for the purpose of stalking someone.[47] As discussed in greater detail below, these laws punish a range of threatening behaviors and can be an important additional source of protection for victims of intimate partner violence. Moreover, since stalking laws do not contain a "special relationship" requirement, they can also be used to fill important gaps in coverage in situations that fall outside the scope of abuse prevention laws.

As indicated by the rapid proliferation of these laws, stalking has come to be recognized as a serious problem that potentially effects upwards of 3 million people a year. Reinforcing the seriousness of the problem, studies indicate a "strong link between stalking and emotionally abusive and controlling behavior," and between "stalking and lethal forms of partner violence against women." Most victims are stalked by someone they know—most commonly a former intimate partner. The majority of stalking victims are female, and the majority of perpetrators are male, although this pattern is far from absolute.[48] It should also be noted that although it was a celebrity murder that focused public attention on the dangers of stalking, about 85 percent of stalking victims are "ordinary" people with no "celebrity or public status."[49]

Although the precise contours vary from state to state, stalking is generally defined as harassing or threatening behavior that an individual engages in on a repeated and often escalating basis, which causes the victim to fear for his or her safety. It can include a variety of unwanted behaviors, such as following or spying on someone, repeatedly showing up uninvited at a person's home or work, making repeated phone calls, and repeatedly waiting in places for the victim (see the discussion below regarding cyberstalking). Recognizing that behavior which may seem fairly innocent at the start frequently escalates in both frequency and severity, and may result in serious physical harm or even death if not stopped, most statutes provide for the escalation of penalties for repeat violations. Additionally, in many states, the initial act of what is considered "aggravated" stalking, such as stalking in violation of a protective order and/or while armed with a weapon, will result in an enhanced penalty.

Despite these common threads, state laws vary quite a bit. For example, some jurisdictions require proof of a credible threat of bodily harm, while others treat the stalking itself as criminal behavior. By way of example, imagine a situation where every day when she leaves work, a woman's former boyfriend is standing at the exit staring at her. He then follows her a few blocks before vanishing into the crowd. On weekends, he is often waiting at the corner of her street and again follows her a few blocks. In states that require a "credible threat of bodily" harm, this may not be considered stalking. In contrast, where a "credible threat of bodily" harm is not a formal element of the crime, this behavior is likely to constitute stalking; in effect, the threat is implicit in this persistent course of conduct.

Some statutes also require proof that the stalker intended to induce fear in his victim. However, because it can be difficult to prove what a person's specific intent was, many states have made stalking a "general intent" crime. This means that intent to cause harm does not need to be established, only that the defendant intentionally engaged in a prohibited act.[50]

Cyberstalking

When stalking laws were first enacted in the 1990s, "few could have foreseen the current widespread use of e-mail, the Internet, chat rooms, websites, (GPS) cell phones, and tiny hand-held video and digital cameras to stalk."[51] Also unanticipated was that social networking sites, such as Facebook and MySpace, would provide stalkers with an easy way to track and monitor the whereabouts of their intended victims based upon updating posts designed to keep family and friends abreast of current activities, or that spyware could be remotely installed on someone's computer as a way to gain access to "all of the victim's computer activities, including passwords to e-mail and social networking sites."[52] Today, however, what is commonly referred to as "**cyberstalking**" is a significant problem that the law has only begun to catch up with. Like "offline" stalkers, most "online" stalkers "are motivated by a desire to control their victims,"[53] and they use a wide range of techniques to accomplish this, for instance:

> [a] cyberstalker may send repeated, threatening, or harassing messages by the simple push of a button. More sophisticated cyberstalkers use programs to send messages at regular or random intervals without being physically present at the computer terminal. . . . In addition, a cyberstalker can dupe other Internet users into harassing or threatening a victim by, for example, posting a victim's name, telephone number, or e-mail addresses on a bulletin board or chat room.[54]

Although, like "offline" stalking, cyberstalking may place a victim in fear of his or her life, and may lead to actual physical violence, law enforcement officials do not always take cyberstalking as seriously because it does not involve direct contact. Accordingly, the advice to a victim may simply be to turn off the computer. This advice, however, clearly fails to account for the potential seriousness of the offender's actions, and the devastating impact they can have on a victim.

This lack of a serious response also fails to account for the fact that the cloak of anonymity offered by electronic means of communication may embolden a stalker who realizes that his true identity may be very hard to track down. As explained by the Department of Justice in a report to Congress:

> Anonymity is a great advantage for the cyberstalker. Unknown to his victim, the perpetrator could be in another State, around the corner, or in the next cubicle at work. The perpetrator could be a former friend or lover, a total stranger met in a chat room, or simply a teenager playing a practical joke. A victim's inability to identify the source of the harassment or threats can be particularly ominous, and the view of anonymity might encourage the perpetrator to continue these acts.[55]

Although the technology has clearly outpaced the law, the law is beginning to catch up. A number of states have either enacted specific cyberstalking laws, or amended their existing stalking laws to specifically include cyberstalking. In addition, the above-discussed Interstate Stalking Law makes it a federal crime to use an "interactive computer service . . . to engage in a course of conduct that causes serious emotional distress" or that places a person in "reasonable fear of the death of, or serious injury to" himself or herself, an immediate family member, or his/her spouse or intimate partner.[56] However, these laws may not be comprehensive, and may, for example, focus mainly on electronic communication and not include other technologies, such as video cameras and global positioning systems, that a stalker may use to track a victim's whereabouts. Moreover, regardless of the categories of coverage, if drafted with specificity, statutes may simply fail to keep abreast of the ever-increasing array of technologies that a stalker uses to harass or threaten a victim. In other states, existing definitions of stalking may be broad enough to encompass at least some types of cyberstalking, whereas in other states, cyberstalking may fall outside the definitional boundaries of the applicable law. This is clearly an area of law that is rapidly developing as states continue to grapple with complex issues raised by the recent explosion in technologies.[57]

Specialized Domestic Violence Courts

As we have seen, intimate partner violence is a pervasive and multidimensional problem, and, in contrast to other types of family law matters, abuse prevention cases are both civil and criminal in nature. Adding to the complexity and potential fragmentation of the legal response, families may also be involved in separate proceedings, such as a divorce or custody action, in which domestic violence is a central consideration. The various court actions are rarely coordinated despite their overlapping issues.

This lack of coordination is inefficient, and it can result in conflicting or inconsistent orders. But research points to a more serious consequence: that this "disjointed approach . . . has proven ineffective at stopping violence and protecting victims from repeated violence."[58] Even more chilling is the fact that violence may actually escalate after a victim has sought legal protection from abuse, and many domestic homicide victims had obtained a protective order prior to their death.[59]

Responding to this grim reality, many jurisdictions across the country have established specialized **domestic violence courts** to solve the problems inherent in the traditionally fragmented approach to domestic violence cases. Although the models vary, most use a carefully coordinated approach in the handling of the civil and criminal components of these actions at its core. As one commentator observes:

> [B]y making domestic violence cases a top priority, many of these specialized court programs are able to "afford the victim a supportive and rapid procedural response to her complaint." Through the use of trained court personnel and cooperating victim advocates, these specialized domestic violence courts are able to inform a victim about the court process, both in criminal and in civil protection order cases. This assistance in negotiating the legal system is particularly helpful for pro se civil litigants who, without such help, may have previously been at risk of failing to recognize available remedies or social services available to them in the community.[60]

Another important advantage is that civil and criminal jurisdiction may be combined in a single court thus enabling the court to both issue protective orders and prosecute criminal violations. Other innovations include the use of specially trained domestic violence clerks who can help victims navigate the court system, and, in some jurisdictions, the assignment of the case to a single judge who assumes responsibility for all of the related legal matters.

The Federal Response to Domestic Violence: The Violence Against Women Act

In 1994, Congress enacted the **Violence Against Women Act (VAWA)**[61] as part of a national effort to combat intimate partner violence against women. In addition to establishing federal protections and remedies for abuse victims, VAWA provides grants to states to enable them to better meet the needs of domestic violence victims, by, for example: training police officers, supporting community anti-violence initiatives, providing victims with legal advocacy services, and assisting victims with immigration matters.

VAWA must be reauthorized every five years. This has occurred regularly since the law's inception and, as discussed below, its scope has been gradually expanded. However, as this current edition of the book goes to press, the current reauthorization bill, which was due to be approved in 2018, is currently stalled in the Senate due to the opposition of some lawmakers to proposed expanded protections for domestic violence victims.

Perhaps most controversial are measures that seek to tighten the gun own-ership rules for individuals convicted of domestic violence offenses. As has been widely reported in the press, the NRA has actively lobbied against these measures, which has contributed to the stalemate over the reautho-rization of VAWA.

Although a comprehensive examination of VAWA is well beyond the scope of this text, we begin by looking at some of the Act's key provisions. We then take a brief look at some of the changes introduced by the most recent reauthorization of the Act.

Select Provisions of VAWA

This section highlights some of VAWA's key provisions. However, as noted above, please keep in mind that this discussion is not intended to be com-prehensive in nature.[62]

The Criminalization of Interstate Domestic Violence.   Under VAWA, it is a federal crime to cross a state line to violate a protective order. It is also a crime to cross a state line in order to injure, intimidate, or stalk an inti-mate partner. Under VAWA III, cyberstalking is now a federal crime, as is stalking through surveillance and by the use of devices such as Global Positioning Systems and interactive computer systems.

By making these acts federal crimes, VAWA makes it easier to prose-cute abusers who pursue their partners across state lines.

The Extension of Full Faith and Credit to Abuse Prevention Orders.   VAWA fills a significant enforcement gap by requiring states to give full faith and credit to protective orders from other states that meet the basic requirements of the Act—including the court that has jurisdiction over the parties and provides the defendant with reasonable notice and an opportunity to be heard—and to enforce these orders as if they were issued by a court in that state. Prior to VAWA, states often did not recog-nize protective orders from other states and required domestic violence victims who had left their home states to obtain new orders. VAWA III makes it clear that states must now also give full faith and credit to custody, visitation, and support provisions that are included in protective orders.

Protections for Battered Immigrant Women.   VAWA recognizes that bat-tered immigrant women are a vulnerable population. The fear of depor-tation or the dependence on a spouse for obtaining lawful permanent resident status may prevent immigrant women from seeking protection from or filing criminal charges against an abuser. VAWA therefore per-mits a battered immigrant to self-petition for lawful permanent resident status, which frees her from reliance on an abusive spouse to obtain this status. Pursuant to more recent amendments, now battered immigrant women also are entitled to expanded opportunities to petition for relief from deportation proceedings. However, at the present moment, undocumented victims of violence may be particularly reluctant to seek the protections they are entitled to given the increased threat of deportation under the current administration.[63]

If you are assisting a battered woman who is an immigrant, a variety of other protections may be available to her under VAWA and other related laws. Knowledge of these laws and of immigration law (which is a complex and highly specialized field) is essential for anyone working with immigrant women to ensure that their rights are fully protected and that no action is taken that jeopardizes their immigration status. Family law practitioners would be well advised to consult with an immigration expert in these situations.

The Violence Against Women Reauthorization Act of 2013

As noted above, VAWA has been reauthorized and expanded several times since 1994, with the most recent reauthorization Act being signed into law in 2013. As discussed here, among other provisions, VAWA 2013 fills two historic gaps in the Act as follows.

First, in recognition of the fact that American Indian and Alaska Native women suffer from a higher rate of intimate partner violence than any other population of women, the previous reauthorization of VAWA increased funding for, and improved the delivery of services to, Native American women. However, a continued problem was that tribal courts lacked criminal jurisdiction over non-Indian perpetrators of domestic and dating violence, even if the acts were committed on Indian lands. VAWA 2013 addressed this problem by recognizing the inherent sovereignty of tribes to exercise "special domestic violence criminal jurisdiction" over both Native and non-Native Americans. Accordingly, tribes can now criminally enforce civil orders of protection and prosecute perpetrators of domestic and dating violence whether they are Native American or not. The Act further clarifies the authority of tribal courts to issue and enforce civil orders of protection against non-Native Americans as well as Native Americans.[64]

Second, VAWA 2013 includes a strong antidiscrimination provision that bars any program or activity that receives VAWA funds from discriminating against any person seeking access to assistance or services on the basis of gender or sexual orientation. This provision also ensures that the term "victim" as used in the Act includes someone who has been injured by a same-sex intimate partner.[65] VAWA also recognizes LGBT persons as an "underserved population," thus making organizations that work with victims of same-sex intimate partner violence eligible for grants designed to expand and improve the delivery of protective services to the LGBT community.[66]

Working with Victims of Domestic Violence

Although there is no easy formula for how to work with victims of partner violence, the following considerations will contribute to effective and supportive interactions with clients who have been abused:

- Victims often feel a tremendous sense of shame and may be reluctant to acknowledge the violence in their lives. Listen carefully for clues that may suggest an abusive relationship—for example, a woman who says, "Well, I don't get out much; my husband doesn't approve of my friends." Inquire further in a sensitive manner. You might, for example, respond to such statements with the following questions: "Why doesn't your husband approve of your friends?" and "What might happen if you went out with someone he doesn't approve of?" With a client who is not quite ready to open up, these questions work more effectively than do more direct questions such as "So, is your husband abusive?"

- Trust the client's assessment of the danger; too often, professionals minimize the potential risks that victims face.

- Depending on the allocation of responsibilities in your office, you or the attorney for whom you work should fully inform clients about the abuse prevention laws in your state. If your office does not assist clients in obtaining protective orders, then provide referrals.

- Understand that it can be very difficult for persons to extricate themselves from an abusive relationship. For example, a client may have no money and be unable to find housing that she can afford. She may fear greater harm if she leaves. She may fear community or family disapproval, or she may worry about taking the children away from their father. It is not your job to criticize her for failing to leave or take action. She should know that your services are available if and when she does decide to leave or seek a court order.

- Make certain you have information available regarding local shelters, hotline numbers, and battered women's support groups. These are invaluable resources. Many shelters, hospitals, and police departments have developed materials on "safety plans" that help domestic violence victims think through how best to extricate themselves from a dangerous situation. You should also make these available.

■ If you are assisting an abuse victim who is an immigrant to this country, you should be aware that certain protections may be available under the federal Violence Against Women Act. In this situation, it may be appropriate for the client to also meet with an immigration law specialist (see the discussion above on VAWA).

Chapter Summary

Domestic violence is a serious problem among intimate partners, including those who are in dating relationships. All states have abuse prevention laws that enable domestic violence victims to obtain civil orders of protection. In some states, the statutes are broad and cover most intimate and family relationships; in other states, the scope of coverage is narrower, and many individuals—for example, someone being abused by a dating partner or a former cohabiting partner—may not be able to obtain protection. Protection can be obtained from a wide range of abusive behaviors, including physical abuse, attempted physical abuse, sexual assaults, and threats of harm and harassment. Many types of relief can be included in a protective order, such as ordering the respondent to refrain from further acts of abuse, to vacate the premises, to avoid any contact with the petitioner, and to relinquish any firearms. In most jurisdictions, the courts can also make temporary support and custody awards. A recent trend is to include provisions for the protection of pets.

A protective order is usually obtained in two stages. First, the petitioner appears before the court in an *ex parte* proceeding at which time temporary relief may be ordered. The other party is then served with the orders and informed of the right to be heard. At the second hearing, each party is given the opportunity to present their version of events. The judge may either extend or decline to extend the *ex parte* order. Specialized domestic violence courts that provide integrated legal and social services are a recent innovation designed to eliminate the disjointed approach to domestic abuse cases.

Effective enforcement procedures are essential to ensure the safety of abuse victims, and much effort has been devoted to increasing the responsiveness of the criminal justice system, including the adoption of mandatory arrest and prosecution policies. These policies are quite controversial. Some experts believe that the policies play a critical role in enhancing victim safety, while others believe that they disempower victims and put them at risk of retaliatory violence. In many states, the violation of a protection order is an independent crime. All states now have anti-stalking laws that criminalize qualifying harassing or threatening behavior, and many now also treat cyberstalking, which is a rapidly growing problem, as a crime.

At the federal level, VAWA has increased protections for domestic violence victims by criminalizing interstate acts of violence and requiring states to give full faith and credit to protective orders. The Act also provides relief to battered immigrants, such as by allowing them to self-petition for lawful permanent resident status, thus avoiding reliance on the batterer and expanding anti-deportation protections.

Key Terms

Domestic Violence

Domestic Abuse

Intimate Partner Violence

Abuse Prevention Laws

Protective Order

Harassment Order

Stalking

Restraining Order

Vacate Order

Stay-Away Order

No-Contact Order

Batterer Intervention Program

Electronic Monitoring

Exclusion Zone

Ex Parte

Temporary Order

Mutual Orders of Protection

Cyberstalking

Domestic Violence Courts

Violence Against Women
    Act (VAWA)

Review Questions

1. Why was a husband in ancient Rome permitted to beat his wife?
2. What did English common law and early U.S. law say about wife abuse?
3. What was the attitude of the Puritans toward domestic violence?
4. What did the temperance reformers see as the cause of wife abuse? How did they propose to solve the problem?
5. How did women's rights activists view the problem? How did their proposed solutions differ from those of the temperance reformers?
6. What was the post–Civil War approach to combating domestic violence?
7. In brief, what is a civil order of protection?
8. What kinds of relationships would qualify for a protective order in an inclusive state?
9. What kinds of qualifications might a statute place on someone who is in a dating relationship? What problems might these qualifications pose?
10. What kinds of abusive behavior are covered by most abuse prevention laws?
11. What barriers might a minor face in seeking a protective order in the context of a coerced marriage?

12. In what ways might an abuse protection order provide for the safety of a pet?
13. What kinds of relief are generally available under an abuse prevention law?
14. How does electronic monitoring work?
15. Why are gun relinquishment orders important to the safety of victims? What protections are provided by federal law? What gaps exist?
16. What kinds of obligations do police officers have toward victims of domestic violence under an abuse prevention law?
17. Explain the two-step process for obtaining a protective order.
18. How are protective orders enforced?
19. What has been the traditional attitude of the criminal justice system toward domestic abuse cases?
20. How has this changed? What new approaches have been adopted?
21. Why are mandatory arrest and prosecution policies controversial?
22. What is stalking?
23. What is cyberstalking?
24. What is the nature and function of specialized domestic violence courts?
25. What are some of the key provisions of VAWA?

Discussion Questions

1. Many people wonder why battered women do not simply walk away from a relationship after the first incident of abuse. Why do you think this might not be an easy step for someone to take?
2. What do you see as the explanation for the prevalence of domestic violence? Do you think it is an expression of anger or stress, or do you believe it says something about power relationships between men and women?
3. Do you think someone who is in a dating relationship should be allowed to seek protection under abuse prevention laws?
4. Do you think that mandatory arrest and prosecution policies make sense? Why or why not?

Assignments

1. Find the abuse prevention act for your state and determine the following:
   - Which court(s) are these cases heard in?
   - Who can petition the court for relief?
   - Are dating partners eligible? If so, are there any qualifications?
   - What kinds of protection are available?

2. Using the abuse prevention act located for assignment 1, trace the court procedure from start to finish. Make sure you include all relevant timeframes.

3. Assume that you are doing an internship as a legal advocate at a local battered women's shelter. They have asked you to develop a brochure that sets out the basic elements of your state's abuse prevention law and explains the court process so women coming to the shelter will know what their legal rights are. The key here is to make sure the brochure is complete, accurate, and comprehensible to the layperson.

4. A number of women are presently serving time for killing their batterers. A controversial question is whether, as part of their defense cases, expert testimony can be admitted regarding the "battered women's syndrome." Assume you are a trial judge who has been asked to rule on the admissibility of such evidence. Research and then write a legal memorandum setting out your conclusion.

5. Assume that you are a legislative aide in a state that is considering adopting a mandatory arrest and prosecution law. In an advisory memo, evaluate the arguments in favor of and against such an approach, and then develop a persuasive position in which you argue in favor of or against such a law.

Cases for Analysis

This rather straightforward case focuses on the kinds of considerations that courts take into account in determining if circumstances permit the modification or termination of a permanent order — in this regard, it should be noted that not all states issue permanent orders, as is the case here.

FOWLER v. FOWLER
2019 Wash. App. LEXIS 348 (2019)

Maxa, C.J.

James Fowler appeals the trial court's denial of his motion to terminate the permanent protection order his former wife Marta Fowler obtained against him in 2003.

RCW 26.50.130(1) authorizes a trial court to terminate an existing permanent protection order in certain situations. *RCW 26.50.130(3)(a)* states that the court may not terminate a permanent protection order "unless the respondent proves by a preponderance of the evidence that there has been a substantial change in circumstances such that the respondent is not likely to resume acts of domestic violence against the petitioner . . . if the order is terminated." *RCW 26.50.130(3)(c)* provides an unweighted list of nine factors the court may consider in determining whether there has been a substantial change in circumstances.

We hold that the trial court did not abuse its discretion in determining . . . that James had not proved a substantial change in circumstances such that he was unlikely to resume acts of domestic violence. . . .

Accordingly, we affirm the trial court's order denying James's motion to terminate the permanent protection order. . . .

FACTS

In December 1996, James assaulted his then wife Marta in their home when their children were six and three years old. Marta obtained a one-year protection order and filed for legal separation. Following this incident, James received domestic violence treatment and counseling. He also began taking medication for mental health issues. The parties' marriage was dissolved in 1999. The dissolution decree restrained both James and Marta from going to each other's homes or work places. . . .

In November 2002, Marta sought a protection order against James on behalf of herself and their two minor children. Marta alleged in her petition that James had acted angrily and aggressively toward their then 12-year-old son and his friends while the boys were staying at James's residence for a sleepover. James denied these allegations and claimed that, while he was upset with the boys for misbehaving, his behavior toward them was not abusive. The court entered an ex parte domestic violence order of protection, clarifying that James was allowed to attend the children's public events and that he could have visitation with the children on Thanksgiving Day if the parties' son was willing.

In July 2003, Marta requested the entry of a permanent restraining order against James. Her declaration alleged that James had continued to stalk and harass her, noted the fact that James had recently purchased a home half a mile away from hers, and referenced James's mental illness diagnosis. In August, the parties reached an agreed domestic violence order of protection. This order covered both Marta and the two minor children and prohibited James from coming within 1,500 feet of their residence, workplace, or school. The order permanently restrained James from coming near or having any contact with Marta.

In February 2006, James came to their son's school, which was a violation of the 2003 permanent protection order. He explained that he had gone to pick up his son, who was ill, because Marta was out of town. James was charged with violation of the protection order, but the charges later were dropped. The permanent protection order then was amended to allow James to go to their son's school and to pick up their son from school if

Marta was unavailable. In February 2007, the trial court modified the permanent protection order regarding the children, leaving the order in effect for Marta only.

In June 2017, the parties agreed to modify the permanent protection order again to allow James to attend college graduation ceremonies for the parties' daughter, which Marta also was attending. Later in June, James moved for termination of the 2003 permanent protection order. He argued that in the 14 years since entry of the order, the parties had continued to live less than a mile from each other without incident, their children were now both adults, and that he was happily remarried without any criminal convictions or substance abuse issues. He claimed that Marta had shown in several ways that she was not fearful of him. He asked the court to consider that there will be future events involving the children and memorial services for mutual friends that both he and Marta would want to attend. . . .

Marta opposed termination of the permanent protection order, filing a declaration describing the 1996 assault and stating that James had persisted in attempting to communicate with her over the years despite the protection order. She stated, "I am fully convinced that without this permanent protection order, the respondent would appear on my doorstep uninvited, look through my windows, or find other excuses to speak with me when he sees me around the neighborhood." . . .

A hearing on James's motion was held in July 2017 before a superior court commissioner. The commissioner entered an order denying James's motion to terminate the protection order. The commissioner concluded that James had not met his burden of showing that there had been a substantial change in circumstances such that he was not likely to resume acts of domestic violence against Marta.

James filed a motion to revise the commissioner's order. A hearing on this motion was held before the trial court. James argued that he had taken complete responsibility for the 1996 domestic violence incident and had obtained treatment for his bipolar disorder as well as domestic violence treatment. . . . Marta countered that no documentation existed to prove James had completed state-certified domestic violence treatment since the permanent protection order was entered. She argued that James had not taken responsibility for the domestic violence because he blamed her for the incidents in their history, suggested that her anger was her only reason for resisting termination of the order, and that James appeared to be eager to reenter her life. . . .

ANALYSIS

A.   TERMINATION OF PERMANENT PROTECTION ORDERS

The legislature has expressed a clear public policy to protect domestic violence victims. . . . [A] court has authority to enter a protection order restraining a respondent from having any contact with a domestic violence victim.

Such a protection order can be made permanent where "the court finds that the respondent is likely to resume acts of domestic violence against the petitioner or the petitioner's . . . minor children when the order expires."

. . . [T]he court may not terminate a permanent protection order on the respondent's motion unless he or she "proves by a preponderance of the evidence that there has been a substantial change in circumstances such that the respondent is not likely to resume acts of domestic violence against the petitioner . . . if the order is terminated." In response to the motion, the protected party is not required to establish "that he or she has a current reasonable fear of imminent harm by the respondent." . . .

For purposes of determining whether there has been a "substantial change in circumstances," the trial court must consider "only factors which address whether the respondent is likely to commit future acts of domestic violence against the petitioner." *RCW 26.50.130(3)(b)*. The trial court may consider, in no particular order of importance, these unweighted factors:

(i)   Whether the respondent has committed or threatened domestic violence, sexual assault, stalking, or other violent acts since the protection order was entered;

(ii)   Whether the respondent has violated the terms of the protection order, and the time that has passed since the entry of the order;

(iii)   Whether the respondent has exhibited suicidal ideation or attempts since the protection order was entered;

(iv)   Whether the respondent has been convicted of criminal activity since the protection order was entered;

(v)   Whether the respondent has either acknowledged responsibility for the acts of domestic violence that resulted in entry of the protection order or successfully completed domestic violence perpetrator treatment or counseling since the protection order was entered;

(vi)   Whether the respondent has a continuing involvement with drug or alcohol abuse, if such abuse was a factor in the protection order;

(vii)   Whether the petitioner consents to terminating the protection order, provided that consent is given voluntarily and knowingly;

(viii) Whether the respondent or petitioner has relocated to an area more distant from the other party, giving due consideration to the fact that acts of domestic violence may be committed from any distance;

(ix)   Other factors relating to a substantial change in circumstances.

The trial court may not base its determination solely on the passage of time without a violation of the permanent protection order. . . .

Finally, the court may decline to terminate a protection order even if there has been a substantial change in circumstances if the court "finds that the acts of domestic violence that resulted in the issuance of the protection order were of such severity that the order should not be terminated."

B.   SUBSTANTIAL CHANGE IN CIRCUMSTANCES

James argues that . . . factors demonstrate[] a substantial change in circumstances such that he no longer poses a threat of committing domestic violence against Marta, and that the trial court abused its discretion by finding otherwise We disagree.

. . . James argues that the trial court improperly considered the 2006 violation of the permanent protection order as a factor weighing against termination of the order because the violation was only a technicality and the charges were dropped. Based on the trial court's oral findings of fact, it does not appear that great weight was attributed to this factor. However, the court was within its discretion to consider this violation. . . .

The trial court found that James eventually took responsibility but that he had "not completed domestic violence perpetrator treatment or counseling since the [permanent protection order] was entered." . . .

James also argues that his domestic violence treatment following the 1996 incident should have weighed in his favor. Although James presented evidence to indicate that he had undergone some psychotherapy in the past, the letter he provided from his former psychiatrist did not specify the dates of treatment or the issues discussed.

He also notes that the permanent protection order did not expressly require him to seek out domestic violence treatment, and so the lack of records showing that he had undergone this treatment since the order's entry in 2003 should not weigh against him.

However, . . . at the court may consider whether the respondent has "successfully completed domestic violence perpetrator treatment or counseling since the protection order was entered." The statute does not state that the protection order must require the respondent to obtain treatment for the factor to be considered. Here, the court considered the evidence and concluded it was insufficient to find James had completed treatment since the 2003 permanent protection order was entered. The court was within its discretion to consider this fact.

James argues that Marta's lack of consent to terminate the order is relevant only to the extent that it relates to his likelihood to engage in future acts of domestic violence. He claims that her lack of consent does not reflect a risk of recidivism. . . .

Marta presented a number of reasons why she was unwilling to consent to termination of the permanent protection order. She cited the parties' contentious divorce, the 2002 incident at their son's sleepover, James's 2003 move into her neighborhood, the 2014 letter from a neighbor asking her to drop the protection order against James, James's initial reluctance to accept full responsibility for the domestic violence in their past, and the lack of clear records indicating James had undergone domestic violence treatment.

These reasons gave the trial court ample evidence to consider whether her lack of consent to terminate the order was significant to its analysis. The court was within its discretion to consider Marta's lack of consent. . . .

James argues that the trial court should have considered his decision in 2003 to purchase a home in Marta's neighborhood as a point in favor of terminating the permanent protection order rather than a reason to keep it in place. He contends that because the parties have lived in the same neighborhood for many years without incident, this factor weighs against the likelihood of recidivism.

Marta argued at the hearing that James was "right down the road . . . [t]he proximity is incredibly close. There's still ongoing contact, at least indirectly." . . . She argued that a neighbor's letter asking her to drop the permanent protection order against James so he could attend functions at the neighbor's home had caused her to be concerned about James's influence in the neighborhood. The trial court did not abuse its discretion in finding that James's close proximity to Marta weighed against finding that he was less likely to resume acts of domestic violence against her. . . .

Marta argues that the trial court found it especially significant that James agreed in 2003 to make the protection order permanent, because James could have argued at that time that a shorter duration was more appropriate. James responds that the court improperly considered his agreement to enter the permanent protection order as a factor weighing against termination, and that his willingness to cooperate with Marta is not the behavior of someone likely to reoffend.

We affirm the trial court's order denying James's motion to terminate the permanent protection order, but we decline to award Marta her attorney fees on appeal.

QUESTIONS

1. According to the court, under what circumstances may a permanent order of protection be terminated?
2. What are the statutory factors that a court may take into account when making this decision?
3. As determined in this case, what place does the simple passage of time play in deciding if a termination is warranted?
4. Why did the court decide that the husband had not met his burden of proof so as to warrant a termination of the order?

Although the clear tread is in favor of expanding the category of persons who are entitled to protection under state abuse prevention laws, in the below case, the court concludes that co-residents of a residential program for adults with developmental disabilities are not "household members" within the meaning of the law.

SILVA v. CARMEL
468 Mass. 18, 7 N.E.3d 1096 (2014)

IRELAND, C.J.

The defendant appeals from an abuse prevention order issued against her pursuant to G.L. c. 209A by a District Court judge based on events that occurred in a residential program under the auspices of the Department of Developmental Services. Because we conclude that individuals who share a common diagnosis or status, rather than marriage, blood, or other relationships that are enumerated in G.L. c. 209A, §1, and who live together in a State-licensed residential facility, do not qualify as "household members" within the meaning of G.L. c. 209A, §1, we vacate the order against the defendant.

Facts and procedure. The defendant and the victim are intellectually disabled adults who receive services from the Department of Developmental Services (department) in a residential program operated by a third party, Riverside Community Care, with funding from the department. Both individuals have legal guardians, family members in each case, who have been appointed by judges in the Probate and Family Court. The parties do not dispute the following facts that resulted in the complaint for an abuse prevention order: On May 22, 2012, the defendant went upstairs to the hallway outside the victim's bedroom and, during an ensuing altercation, pushed the victim into the bathroom. As a result of being pushed, the victim suffered injuries to her head, neck, and back when she fell backward into a bathtub.

The next day, the plaintiff filed her application for an abuse prevention order on behalf of the victim, which included information that the defendant and the victim are not related but live in the same household, and a description of events that had occurred the previous day. A District Court judge granted an ex parte abuse prevention order pursuant to G.L. c. 209A against the defendant on May 23, 2012. At a hearing to extend the order on June 5, 2012, the judge heard testimony from the guardians of the two women. The plaintiff testified that the victim had experienced multiple physical attacks by the defendant over the prior two years in the house where they lived, including one incident where the defendant had cornered and bitten the victim. The plaintiff provided medical documentation showing that the victim's seizures and anxiety have increased as a result of the situation, and stated that the victim, fearful of leaving her room, "has no life" because of her concerns about being attacked. . . .

The judge determined that, because the defendant and the victim lived "in the same household," the District Court had jurisdiction. The judge extended the initial abuse prevention order against the defendant for one year. The defendant appealed, and we transferred the case from the Appeals Court on own motion.

The defendant asserts, in essence, that residents in a State-governed facility are not eligible for the protections provided by G.L. c. 209A, because receiving services through a residential program run by a governmental agency does not constitute "residing together in the same household" for the purposes of the statute. We agree.

Discussion. We recognize that the central issue of this case involves the serious and important matter of the safety of individuals with intellectual disabilities under State care, and respect the legitimate concerns of the victim's guardian for the safety of her daughter. Nonetheless, we conclude that the relationship between the defendant and the victim, in the circumstances here, is not the type of relationship contemplated by the statute.

General Laws c. 209A protects individuals suffering from abuse by "family or household members." G.L. c. 209A, §1. The statute defines "[f]amily or household members" as

> "persons who: (a) are or were married to one another; (b) are or were residing together in [***] the same household; (c) are or were related by blood or marriage; (d) hav[e] a child in common regardless of whether they have ever married or lived together; or (e) are or have been in a substantive dating or engagement relationship."

Id. At issue is the scope of the phrase "residing together in the same household."

It is undisputed that the individuals here lived in the same residential program at the time of the issuance of the abuse prevention order. The plaintiff points to several ways that this facility functions like a family household, such as through shared living spaces and house rules. The fact that the defendant and victim were in contact in these shared residential spaces, she argues, makes them household members. In its amicus brief submitted on behalf of the plaintiff, Community Legal Aid (CLA) asserts that the department's closures of larger facilities in order to create "home-like residential programs" support an interpretation of G.L. c. 209A that includes individuals residing in department facilities as household members. CLA contends, make clear that its residential programs are homes and the inhabitants are "residing in the same household."

It is true that Massachusetts courts have recognized changes in traditional family structures and households for the purposes of G.L. c. 209A and have allowed individuals in various types of familial relationships to seek protection from abuse from family or household members. . . . Here, however, outside of the fact that the two individuals lived in the same facility, there is no evidence that there was a socially interdependent relationship between the two. The defendant and the victim were not voluntarily living together. They were assigned to the residence by a government agency that is mandated to give individuals in its care the "opportunity to live and receive services or supports in the least restrictive and most typical setting possible" They consequently lack the " 'family-like' connection" that falls under the protection of G.L. c. 209A. . . . The connection between these two individuals, and the reason they resided in the same facility, was solely their individualized service plans that had been established by the department.

Interpreting the definition of "household" in G.L. c. 209A to include individuals living in facilities run by the State, as the plaintiff urges, not only would potentially interfere with certain of the department's requirements to create and implement individual service plans in accordance with client needs, but also, in this case, would fail to comport with the language of the statute. . . . Accordingly, the phrase "residing together in the same household" in G.L. c. 209A, §1, must be interpreted in the context of the statute's other definitions of "[f]amily or household members," which include people who are or have been married, have children together, are related by blood, or have been in a substantive dating or engagement relationship. The two individuals here are not family members, are not in a family-like relationship with each other, did not marry or have a child, and were not involved in a significant dating or engagement relationship. . . . They lived together because of a State agency's decision to house them in the same residential facility in order to receive services related to their disabilities. . . .

Our conclusion is in accord with the statute's purpose, to prevent violence in the family setting. . . . Our conclusion is supported by the fact that the Legislature presumably enacted G.L. c. 258E, which "allow[s] individuals to obtain civil restraining orders against persons who are not family or household members," to close the gap left by G.L. c. 209A.

Conclusion. We remand to the District Court for entry of an order to vacate the abuse prevention order against the defendant.

So ordered.

QUESTIONS

1. What statutory provision did the plaintiff rely on in seeking an order of protection against the defendant?

2. What arguments did the plaintiff rely on in seeking to persuade the court that she was within the terms of this provision?
3. Identify the reasons the court provided in support of its conclusion that the plaintiff was not covered by the law.

This case provides a chilling description of stalking, which includes the use of the Internet to track down the victim who had moved in order to escape her stalker.

HUCH v. MARRS
858 So. 2d 1202, 2003 Fla. Dist. Ct. App. LEXIS 17084 (2003)

GERSTEN, J.

Alan Thomas Huch ("Huch"), appeals the trial court's order granting the appellee, Susan Sareena Marrs' ("Marrs") petition for an injunction against repeat violence. We affirm.

In 1988, Huch met Marrs at her workplace in Texas, where they maintained a platonic friendship until 1993. During this time, Huch tried to win Marrs' affection with expensive gifts. Marrs ended the friendship after Huch became possessive, told others that she was his girlfriend, and threatened to cause trouble between Marrs and her boyfriend.

Huch however, continued to "crack on." Huch ignored Marrs' express wishes to be left alone. He sent Marrs flowers several times a week and even posed as a delivery man to get past security at Marrs' home and work. Huch also showed up uninvited at social gatherings that Marrs attended. After Huch started peering through Marrs' windows at home, she reported him to the Dallas police.

Huch's harassment continued and became so overwhelming, that Marrs moved to Florida in 2001 in an attempt to flee from Huch. In July of 2002, Huch found Marrs through the internet and showed up at her residence in Miami. Huch again posed as a flower delivery man to get past security. Fearing for her safety, Marrs called the police.

Huch admitted to the police that he had obsessive feelings for Marrs. She was understandably scared that Huch was constantly watching her and had followed her half-way across the country. Marrs believed that Huch was delusional, that his obsessive behavior was increasing, and that his behavior had the potential to escalate.

In July of 2002, Marrs filed a petition for injunction against Huch pursuant to section 784.046, Florida Statutes (2001). After a hearing, the trial court entered an injunction for protection against repeat violence based on a finding of stalking. Huch then filed this appeal challenging the sufficiency of the evidence. We conclude the evidence was sufficient to support the entry of an injunction against repeat violence, and affirm.

Stalking is a series of actions that, when taken individually, may be perfectly legal. However, these actions constitute illegal behavior when they are not consensual and intimidate or scare a victim. U.S. Dept. of Justice, Domestic Violence and Stalking, The Second Annual Report to Congress Under the Violence Against Women Act (1997). An injunction for protection from repeat violence hopefully prevents this type of unconsented harassment from escalating. This is particularly important because stalking and obsessive/possessive behaviors are indicators of high victim risk. . . .

Not only are injunctions designed to prevent more serious physical injuries from occurring, they also provide stalking victims relief from emotional distress. . . . See Predick v. O'Connor, 260 Wis. 2d 323, 660 N.W.2d 1, 2003 WI App 46 (Wis. Ct. App. 2003) (stalking victims often suffer long-term emotional injuries at the hands of their stalkers and many experience depression, anxiety, obsessive-compulsive behaviors and even symptoms of post-traumatic stress disorder). All fifty states and the District of Columbia now have stalking statutes.

Florida's "repeat violence statute," provides that a trial court may issue an injunction when a respondent commits two incidents of violence or an incident of stalking directed against the petitioner or the petitioner's immediate family. Section 784.046(1)(b), Florida Statutes (2001).

Stalking is further defined by section 784.048, Florida Statutes (2001), as any person who willfully, maliciously and repeatedly follows or harasses another person. "Harass" means to engage in a course of conduct directed at a specific person that causes substantial emotional distress in such person and serves no legitimate purpose. "Course of conduct" is defined as a pattern of conduct composed of a series of acts over a period of time, however short, evidencing a continuity of purpose. . . .

The purpose of the stalking statute is to criminalize unlawful conduct that falls short of assault or battery. . . . The stalking and repeat violence statutes are designed to protect victims, by ensuring that they do not have to be injured or threatened with death before they could stop a stalker's harassment.

In the present case, Huch repeatedly showed up uninvited to Marrs' home, workplace and social activities, and followed her from Texas to Florida. Huch knew that Marrs did not want him to contact her and yet, he used underhanded methods to gain access to her. We find these activities show a continuing, ongoing act that caused emotional distress to Marrs and served no legitimate purpose. See Pallas v. State, 636 So. 2d 1358 (Fla. 3d DCA 1994) (telephone calls numbering fifty times in one day falls within the definition of harassment); Garza v. State, 736 N.E.2d 323

(Ind. Ct. App. 2000) (defendant's actions including repeated and unwelcome flowers, notes and phone calls were sufficient to support conviction of stalking); State v. Collins, 580 N.W.2d 36 (Minn. Ct. App. 1998) (sending two letters was acting "repeatedly," for purposes of harassment statute). We agree with the trial court's conclusion that sufficient evidence existed to establish that Huch stalked Marrs.

The seriousness of the crime of stalking cannot be overstated. The National Violence Against Women Survey, the first national survey conducted on the issue of stalking, found that over eight million women, approximately one in every twelve, have been stalked at some point in their lives. Joseph C. Mershman, *The Dark Side of the Web: Cyberstalking and the Need for Contemporary Legislation*, 24 Harv. Women's L.J. 255, 258 (2001). Although some acts of stalking may appear benign, these acts are often a prelude to violence against the victims including assault, rape and murder. We commend the trial court for recognizing the seriousness of Huch's actions and entering the injunction.

Affirmed.

QUESTIONS

1. What was the nature of the stalking in this case?
2. How does Florida define stalking and cyberstalking?
3. According to the court, what impact can stalking have upon the victim?

Endnotes

1. Please note that although much of the language in this chapter is cast in gender-neutral terms, gender-specific terminology is also used because most perpetrators of intimate partner violence are male and most victims are women.

2. R. Emerson Dobash and Russell Dobash, Violence Against Wives 35 (1979) (citing Not in God's Image: Women in History (Julia O'Faolain and Lauro Martines eds., 1974)).

3. Joyner v. Joyner, 59 N.C. 324, 325 (1862).

4. This section draws heavily on Elizabeth Pleck, Domestic Tyranny: The Making of American Social Policy Against Domestic Violence from Colonial Times to the Present (1987).

5. *Id.* at 17-31.

6. *Id.* at 108-121.

7. *Id.* at 125-126, 138-142.

8. *Id.* at 145-150.

9. Jennifer L. Truman and Rachel E. Morgan, Nonfatal Domestic Violence, 2003-2012 (2014), U.S. Department of Justice, Office of Justice Programs, Bureau of Justice Statistics, www.bjs.gov/content/pub/pdf/ndv0312.pdf (accessed Nov. 18, 2015).

10. *Id.*

11. Catherine F. Klein and Leslye E. Orloff, Providing Legal Protection for Battered Women: An Analysis of State Statutes and Case Law, 21 Hofstra L. Rev. 801, 825-829 (1993).

12. These provisions can be found respectively at: Texas Stat. Ann., Tit. 4, §71.0021(1) (B) (2012) and Okla. Stat. Ann. Tit. 22, §60.1 (2012). *See also* Kellie K. Player, Expanding Protective Order Coverage, 43 St. Mary's L.J. 579 (2012).

13. Nina W. Tarr, Employment and Economic Security for Victims of Domestic Abuse, 16 Rev. L. & Soc. Just. 371, 374-375 (2007). *See also* Michael D. Moberly, The Workplace Injunction: An Emerging But Imperfect Weapon in the Fight Against Domestic Violence, 26 Am. U. J. Gender Soc. Poly. & L. 831 (2018).

Regarding possible avenues of workplace relief under federal and state employment laws for victims of domestic Violence, *see* Cameron M. Brown Britt, Invisible Inequality and Economic Empowerment: Domestic Violence Discrimination, and the Creation of a New Protected Class, 2 Bus. & Entrepreneurship & Tax L. Rev. 451 (2018).

14. Mass. Gen. Laws ch. 258E.

15. *See* Devon M. Largo, Refining the Meaning and Application of "Dating Relationship" Language in Domestic Violence Statutes, 60 Vand. L. Rev. 939, 954 (2007).

16. Mass. Gen. Laws Ann. ch. 209A, §1.

17. Ch. 326, sec. 7, §812(1) 2008 N.Y. laws 326 (codified as amended at N.Y. Fam. Ct. Act §812(1)(e).

18. Christine N. Carlson, Violence Against Women: Invisible Victims: Holding the Educational System Liable for Teen Dating Violence at School, 26 Harv. Women's L.J. 351, 360 (2003).

19. For further detail, *see* Lisa Vollendork Martin, What's Love Got to Do with It: Securing Access to Justice for Teens, 61 Cath. U. L. Rev. 457 (2012).

20. Alexandra Masri, Equal Rights, Unequal Protection: Institutional Failures in Protecting and Advocating for Victims of Same-Sex Domestic Violence in Post-Marriage Equality Era, 27 Tul. J.L. & Sexuality 75, 84-85 (2018).

21. Klein and Orloff, *supra* note 11, at 859.

22. *See* Margaret E. Johnson, Redefining Harm, Reimagining Remedies, and Reclaiming Domestic Violence Law, 42 U.C. Davis L. Rev. 1107 (2009).

23. Lisa V. Martin, Restraining Forced Marriages, 18 Nev. L.J. 919, 949 (2018), quoting Tex. Fam. Code. Ann. §§71.004, 261.001(1)(M) (West 2017).

24. *Id.* at 945.

25. *Id.* at 944-947.

26. Sarah Lorraine Solon, Tenth Annual Review of Gender and Sexuality Law, Criminal Law Chapter: Domestic Violence, 10 Geo. J. Gender & L. 369, 422 (2009). This trend has been aided by the fact that almost all states have abrogated the doctrine of interspousal immunity that historically barred suits between spouses.

27. For detail, *see id.* at 420-423.

28. Vivek Upadhya, The Abuse of Animals as a Method of Domestic Violence: The Need for Criminalization, 63 Emory L.J. 1163, 1174 (2014); Carol J. Adams, *Woman-Battering and Harm to Animals, in* Animals and Women: Feminist Theoretical Explorations 55, 59 (Carol J. Adams and Josephine Donovan eds., 1995). *See also* Margreta Velluci, Restraining the (Real) Beast: Protective Orders and Other Statutory Enactments to Protect the Animal Victims of Domestic Violence in Rhode Island, 16 Roger Williams U. L. Rev. 224 (2011).

29. Upadhya, *supra* note 28, at 1182-1184.

30. For details on current state laws, *see* Rebecca F. Wisch, Domestic Violence and Pets: List of States That Include Pets in Protection Orders, https://www.animallaw.info/article/domestic-violence-and-pets-list-states-include-pets-protection-orders (accessed Nov. 29, 2015).

31. Nicole Allaband, Using Electronic Monitoring to Enhance Protection Offered by Civil Protection Orders in Cases Involving Domestic Violence: A New Technology Offers New Protection, 24 Rich. J.L. & Tech. 3, 16 (2018).

32. For further detail about specific state requirements, *see id.* at 19-22.

33. *Id.* at 25.

34. Center for Gun Policy and Research, Johns Hopkins Bloomberg School of Public Health, Fact Sheet: Intimate Partner Violence and Firearms. http://www.jhsph.edu/research/centers-and-institutes/johns-hopkins-center-for-gun-policy-and-research/publications/IPV_Guns.pdf (accessed Dec. 3, 2015).

35. *Id.*

36. This law is codified at 18 U.S.C. §922 (g)(8). This provision contains an exception for certain government employees, such as police officers and military personnel, who are required to carry a weapon as part of their official duties.

37. This law is codified at 18 U.S.C. §924(g)(9). For further detail, *see* Lisa D. May, The Backfiring of the Domestic Violence Firearm Bans, 14 Colum. J. Gender & L. 1 (2005); Deborah Epstein, Margaret E. Bell, and Lisa A. Goodman, Transforming Aggressive Prosecution Policies: Prioritizing Victims' Long-Term Safety in the Prosecution of Domestic Violence Cases, 11 Am. U. J. Gender Soc. Poly. & L. 465 (2003); and Darren Mitchell and Susan B. Carbon, Firearms and Domestic Violence: A Primer for Judges, 39 Court Rev. 32 (2002).

38. Allen Rostron, Protecting Gun Rights and Improving Gun Control After District of Columbia v. Heller, 13 Lewis & Clark L. Rev. 383, 406 (2009). Questions have been raised about the continued validity of the Lautenberg Amendment following the Supreme Court's decision in District of Columbia v. Heller, 554 U.S. 570 (2008), in which the Court held that the Second Amendment provides some protection to an individual's right to bear arms for nonmilitary purposes. *See id.* for detail.

39. Giffords Law Center, Domestic Violence and Firearms, https://lawcenter.giffords.org/gun-laws/policy-areas/who-can-have-a-gun/domestic-violence-firearms/ (accessed Mar. 12, 2019).

40. *Id.*

41. Jessica Lenahan (Gonzalez) v. United States, Report No. 80/11 (2011), p. 53. For further developments in the matter, *see* https://www.aclu.org/womens-rights/us-fails-adequately-comply-domestic-violence-recommendations-issued-inter-american-com (accessed Nov. 29, 2015).

42. http://web.law.columbia.edu/human-rights-institute/inter-american-human-rights-system/jessica-gonzales-v-us (accessed Apr. 11, 2016).

43. http://www.lawschool.cornell.edu/womenandjustice/DV-Resolutions.cfm (accessed Apr. 11, 2016).

44. Donna Coker, Criminal Control and Feminist Law Reform in Domestic Violence Law: A Critical Review, 4 Buff. L. Rev. 801, 823-826 (2001).

45. Erin L. Han, Mandatory Arrest and No-Drop Policies: Victim Empowerment in Domestic Violence Cases, 23 B.C. Third World L.J. 159, 176 (2003).

46. *See, e.g.*, Deborah Epstein, Margaret E. Bell, and Lisa A. Goodman, Transforming Aggressive Prosecution Policies: Prioritizing Victims' Long-Term Safety in the Prosecution of Domestic Violence Cases, 11 Am. U. J. Gender Soc. Poly. & L. 465 (2003).

47. 18 U.S.C.S. §2261A(1) (2012). For a compilation of federal and state stalking laws, *see* http://www.victimsofcrime.org/our-programs/stalking-resource-center (accessed July 26, 2012).

48. Katrina Baum, Shannan Catalano, and Kristina Rose, Bureau of Justice Statistics, U.S. Department of Justice, Office of Justice Programs, National Crime Victimization survey, Stalking Victimization in the United States (2009). The link to this report can be found at http://bjs.ojp.usdoj.gov/index.cfm?ty=pbdetail&iid=1211 (accessed July 26, 2012).

49. Naomi Harlin Goodmo, Cyberstalking, A New Crime: Evaluating the Effectiveness of Current State and Federal Laws, 72 Mo. L. Rev. 125, 129 (2007).

50. Strengthening Anti-Stalking Statutes, Legal Series Bulletin #1. http://www.ncjrs.gov/App/Publications/alphaList.aspx?alpha=S (accessed July 25, 2012).

51. Stalking Technology Outpaces State Laws, The National Center for Victims of Crime, http://www.ncvc.org/src (accessed Dec. 1, 2009).

52. *See* Laurie L. Baughman, Friend Request or Foe? Confirming the Misuses of Internet and Social Networking Sites by Domestic Violence Perpetrators, 19 Widener L.J. 933, 942-943 (2010).

53. U.S. Department of Justice, Office of Justice Programs, Violence Against Women Office, Stalking and Domestic Violence, Report to Congress, p. 2 (2001), available online at http://www.ncjrs.gov/pdffiles1/ojp/186157.pdf (accessed Dec. 8, 2009).

54. *Id.*

55. *Id.* at 2-3. *See also* Ashley N.B. Beagle, Modern Stalking Laws: A Survey of State Anti-Stalking Statutes Considering Modern Mediums and Constitutional Challenges, 14 Chap. L. Rev. 457 (2011) and Baughman, Friend Request or Foe, *supra* note 52.

56. 18 U.S.C.S. §2261A(2)(b) (2012).

57. For a discussion of some of the First Amendment concerns raised by these laws, *see* Timothy L. Allsup, United States v. Cassidy: The Federal Interstate Stalking Statute and Freedom of Speech, 13 N.C. J.L. & Tech. (Online) 227 (2012), and Sarah Jameson, Cyberharassment: Striking a Balance Between Free Speech and Privacy, 17 CommLaw Conspectus 231 (2008).

58. Judge Lowell D. Castleton, Bruce J. Castleton, Melissa M. Bonney, and Amber M. Moe, Ada County Family Violence Court: Shaping the Means to Better the Result, 39 Family L.Q. 27, 31 (2005).

59. Betsy Tsai, The Trend Toward Specialized Domestic Violence Courts: Improvements on an Effective Innovation, 68 Fordham L. Rev. 1285, 1292 (2000).

60. Jennifer Thompson, Who's Afraid of Judicial Activism? Reconceptualizing a Traditional Paradigm in the Context of Specialized Domestic Violence Courts, 56 Me. L. Rev. 407, 428 (2004), citing Tsai, *supra* note 59, at 1298.

61. Violence Against Women Act, Pub. L. No. 103-322, 108 Stat. 1902 (1994).

62. A good starting point for further information on the Act as a whole is the Department of Justice's Office on Violence Against Women at http://www.justice.gov/ovw.

63. Kate Segal, Immigration Orders Undermine Violence Against Women Act Protections, The Hill, Mar. 13, 2017, https://thehill.com/blogs/pundits-blog/immigration/323756-new-immigration-orders-a-double-threat-for-immigrant-women.

64. *See* Introduction to the Violence Against Women Act, http://www.tribal-institute.org/lists/title_ix.htm#SDVCJ (accessed Nov. 5, 2015); Shefali Singh, Closing the Gap: Providing Protection for Native American Women Through the Special Domestic Violence Criminal Jurisdiction Provisions of VAWA, 28 Colum. J. Gender & L. 197 (2014).

65. Violence Against Women Reauthorization Act of 2013, P.L. 113-4.

66. *Id.*

Chapter Four

The Law of Divorce, Annulment, and Legal Separation

Put simply, **divorce** is the legal dissolution of a marital relationship. Marriage creates a legal bond; divorce severs it. For the divorcing couple, however, divorce is not this simple; the process is multidimensional, with profound emotional, spiritual, economic, and legal consequences. Lives are profoundly reshaped—often in unanticipated ways. For some, divorce brings tremendous relief and a welcome opportunity to build a better life; for others, it brings loneliness or new relationships that recycle the difficulties of the past.[1]

This chapter focuses on the substantive law of divorce. As you read the chapter and as you work with people going through a divorce, it is important to be aware that the applicable legal principles are not mere abstractions but touch the core of people's lives. Accordingly, divorce law should not be thought of in isolation from its human context. (For a discussion on working with emotionally distraught clients, see Chapter 10 on the divorce process.)

Historical Overview

During the final quarter of the last century, this country underwent a divorce "revolution." Starting with California in 1970, all states adopted some form of no-fault divorce law. Now an integral part of our legal landscape, many people today take the availability of no-fault divorce for granted. However, the no-fault principle is a radically new concept. To understand the significance of this change, we begin with a historical overview of divorce law. We start in premodern England, as our present system is rooted in the English experience.

Religious Underpinnings

Marriage as an Indissoluble Bond

Throughout history, many societies practiced divorce by mutual consent of the parties. This was true in what was to become England and much of western Europe until sometime into the tenth or eleventh centuries when marriage came under the authority of the Catholic Church. As the Church gained influence, a cohesive theology emerged; a systematic body of canon law, including laws regulating marriage, was developed.[2] According to the teachings of the Church, marriage was a sacrament. It conferred grace on a couple and was a spiritual instrument of salvation. The relationship between a husband and a wife was thought to mirror the loving bond between Christ and His Church. Like the bond between Christ and His Church, the marital bond between a husband and wife was considered to be **indissoluble**.

Since it was a sacrament, marriage was placed under the exclusive authority of the Church. Divorce was strictly prohibited, but an individual could petition the ecclesiastical courts for an **annulment** or a legal separation (also known as a *divorce a mensa et thoro*—a divorce from board and bed). Neither of these procedures ran afoul of the doctrine of indissolubility. As discussed later in this chapter, an annulment is essentially a statement that due to existing impediments no valid marriage was ever created, and a divorce from board and bed allowed an innocent spouse to live apart from her or his sinful spouse without dissolving the marital bond.

The Protestant Reformation

In the early 1500s, the Protestant Reformation challenged many of the Catholic Church's teachings, including those related to marriage. According to Reformation thinkers, marriage was not a sacrament—it was of this world and carried no promise of spiritual redemption. Having divested marriage of its holy and redemptive status, the Protestants accepted the necessity of divorce in cases involving grievous marital sins committed in violation of Christian principles.[3]

The English Experience

Influenced by the Reformation, many western European nations became Protestant. Divorce was permitted, and both marriage and divorce came under the control of civil rather than religious authorities. However, in England, the pattern was different. Although King Henry VIII broke with the Catholic Church in 1534 and established the Church of England, the Catholic view of marriage as a sacrament was retained. As a result, divorce was not permitted, and marriage remained under Church control until 1857—far later than the rest of western Europe. By way of historical interest, it should be noted that King Henry's decision to break from the Church was at least in part motivated by the fact that the Pope refused to annul his marriage to Catherine of Aragon when she failed to provide him with a son.

The American Experience

Divorce in the Colonies

Divorce generally was accepted much earlier in this country than it was in England due mainly to the influence of Protestantism. During the colonial period, the availability of divorce varied from region to region. In the New England colonies, divorce was available from the start, although in some areas, only the legislature had the authority to dissolve a marriage. Here, the colonists, mainly Pilgrims and Puritans, although profoundly religious, believed that marriage was a civil concern. For them, the family unit was the foundation on which their pious commonwealth was based. Because these two domains were so closely intertwined, family instability was thought to threaten the stability of the community. Accordingly, if a spouse maltreated his or her partner, and reconciliation was impossible, the New England colonists believed it was important for the innocent spouse to be released from the marriage so he or she could move on to form a new functional family unit. The guilty spouse was usually prohibited from remarrying and creating another dysfunctional family that would again threaten the well-being of the community.[4] In contrast, divorce was unheard of in most of the southern colonies. Here, the teachings of the Church of England held sway, and marriage was regarded as indissoluble, although, as in England, both annulments and divorces from board and bed were permitted. The middle colonies appear to have occupied a middle position between New England, where divorce was well established, and the South, where it was prohibited.

In no region of the country did slaves have formal access to divorce, mainly because the colonists refused to honor the validity of marriages between enslaved persons. Though their practices were not formally recognized, slaves created their own marriage rituals, and historians have located records indicating that some African American churches granted divorces to married slaves. Additionally, although again outside the formal bounds of the law, some plantation owners may have recognized and regulated marriage and divorce among their slaves.

The Rising Tide

Following the colonies' independence from England, two trends became apparent. The divorce rate began to rise rapidly, and many states, including the once-recalcitrant southern states, amended their laws to add new divorce grounds, making divorce somewhat easier to obtain.

A number of factors contributed to this loosening of laws and attitudes. For one, revolutionary ferment found its way into the domestic sphere. Leaders such as Thomas Jefferson transposed arguments about individual rights to liberty and happiness from the struggle against England to the marital context. Divorce was needed to oust spousal tyrants and ensure that women were not trapped in domestic regimes that denied them their humanity. Thus, themes that fueled the revolution contributed to an acceptance of divorce.[5] This connection between divorce and the emancipation of women would be picked up by women's rights reformers in the next century.

Changing expectations about the marital relationship also contributed to a greater acceptance of divorce. With industrialization, production moved out of the home, and the family no longer stood at the center of economic activity. The significance of marriage as an economic arrangement diminished, and spouses increasingly looked to each other for love and companionship. As spouses came to expect more from one another, the risk of disappointment also increased, as marriage did not always provide the parties with what they were looking for. As a result, there was an increased acceptance of divorce as a necessary safety valve for spouses who were trapped in failed marriages.[6]

Despite these changes, divorce was still understood in very narrow terms. Rooted in the Puritan belief in marital wrong as sinful conduct, divorce required serious **marital fault** and only an **innocent spouse** was entitled to a divorce. Divorce was understood as a remedy for the innocent spouse and a punishment for the guilty one. It was not regarded as a right, but as an evil made necessary by the realities of human existence.[7]

Nonetheless, the rising divorce rates and the expansion of divorce grounds, which in a few states went as far as permitting divorce whenever "just and reasonable," evoked a storm of outrage by those who feared that these trends signaled the moral disintegration of both family and society. The debate raged, and in 1885, the National Divorce Reform League, later renamed the National League for the Protection of the Family, was established to limit the spread of divorce and restore moral order.

By the turn of the twentieth century, anti-divorce activists could claim some success. They helped slow the move toward more expansive divorce grounds and secured the repeal of some liberalized divorce laws.[8] For the most part, until the no-fault divorce reform movement of the 1970s, divorce remained firmly linked—at least officially—to grievous marital wrongdoing (but see the discussion of collusive divorce later in this chapter). By retaining the link to fault, divorce law supported the permanency of marriage through limiting the permissible grounds for marital exits while also acknowledging the reality of spousal cruelty and marital failure.

Fault Divorce: Common Grounds and Defenses

In the wake of no-fault divorce reform, **fault divorce** tumbled from its place of preeminence. Some states abolished fault-based divorce altogether and now have only no-fault grounds; in other states, no-fault grounds were added to existing fault grounds, and fault divorce remains an option. The following discussion focuses on three of the most commonly available fault grounds and the primary defenses to charges of marital misconduct. As always, you need to check the specifics of your state's laws because other statutory options may be available. (See Chapters 7 and 8 for a discussion of the role that fault plays in determining spousal awards and the division of property.)

Divorce Grounds

Adultery

Historically, adultery has been regarded as the most serious marital wrong and has been the most widely accepted ground for divorce. **Adultery** is generally defined as an act of sexual intercourse by a married person with someone other than his or her spouse. In the past, the law did not treat a husband's extramarital relations as seriously as a wife's transgressions.

In many states, a woman could not obtain a divorce for adultery unless she could also establish aggravating circumstances, such as cruelty, or that her husband had engaged in a course of adulterous conduct, whereas a man had to show only that his wife had committed a single adulterous act. Although no longer legally true today, some experts believe that social attitudes have not necessarily changed, and that many people continue to regard adultery by a woman, especially if she is a mother, as a greater wrong than when committed by a man.

Because there are usually no eyewitnesses, a claim of adultery, when disputed, is generally established by circumstantial evidence. A party must show that his or her spouse had both the opportunity and the disposition or inclination to commit adultery. Relevant evidence might include love letters, public displays of affection, and frequent visits to a home or hotel or the introduction of venereal disease into the marriage.

Recently, several courts have addressed the question of whether "adultery" is limited to acts of vaginal intercourse between a man and a woman, or whether it also encompasses other types of sexual acts, whether engaged in by heterosexual or same-sex parties. Most courts that have considered this issue have concluded that adultery is not limited to heterosexual vaginal intercourse. As one court explained: "We view appellant's definition of adultery as unduly narrow and overly dependent upon the term sexual intercourse. . . . [E]xplicit extra-marital sexual activity constitutes adultery regardless of whether it is of a homosexual or heterosexual character."[9]

This question was also addressed in a 2015 Opinion Letter by the Attorney General of Maryland in response to an inquiry as to whether "the term 'adultery' under Maryland law includes a spouse's extramarital infidelity with a person of the same sex."[10] Determining that the term "sexual intercourse" as used in the Maryland adultery statute was incapable of a precise definition, the Attorney General turned to the purpose of the statute for "additional guidance" in ascertaining its applicable scope.[11] Asserting that same-sex infidelity " 'damages the foundations of marriage' in the same way as do all extramarital affairs,"[12] he concluded that in the wake of the Supreme Court's decision in Obergefell v. Hodges,[13] making marriage equality the law of the land, ". . . it makes little sense to say that same-sex infidelity does not constitute a breach of the marriage vow."[14]

However, not all who have considered this issue have reached this result. For example, in 2003, the New Hampshire Supreme Court reached the opposite conclusion. Relying on both the dictionary meaning of *adultery* and nineteenth-century case law, the court held that the "concept of adultery was premised upon a specific act. To include in that concept other acts of a sexual nature, whether between heterosexuals or homosexuals, would change beyond recognition this well-established ground for divorce."[15]

The dissenting justices argued that the majority was closing its eyes to "the sexual realities of our world" and that a more realistic definition of adultery would include all "extra-marital intimate sexual activity with another, regardless of the specific intimate sexual acts performed, the marital status, or the gender of the third party."[16]

Of course, the future validity of this approach is called into question by the *Obergefell* decision. Arguably, if it is now unconstitutional to deny marital rights to same-sex couples, it should follow that it is likewise unconstitutional to treat their sexual conduct differently from the sexual conduct of married heterosexual couples, as this would downgrade the meaning and place of intimacy within same-sex marriages.

Desertion/Abandonment

Desertion (or abandonment) has long been accepted as an appropriate ground for divorce. Prior to no-fault divorce, desertion was particularly important in states that did not recognize cruelty or construed it narrowly (see below). As a general rule, desertion requires a departure from the marital residence. Some courts have held that the refusal to have a sexual relationship with one's spouse satisfies the separation requirement even if the parties remain in the marital home; however, withdrawal from other aspects of the marital relationship is unlikely to be considered desertion.

In most jurisdictions, a spouse must prove the following elements to establish desertion:

1. there has been a voluntary separation;
2. for the statutory period;
3. with the intent not to return;
4. without consent; and
5. without justification.

For the separation to qualify, the departing spouse must leave of his or her own will. An involuntary departure, such as where a person is drafted, jailed, or committed to a mental hospital, is not desertion. The separation must exist continuously for the statutory time period. Interruptions by, for example, a good-faith offer of reconciliation or even a single act of sexual intercourse may stop the time from running. As a general rule, the calculation of time begins again if there is a second departure—the time periods cannot be added together.

It is not desertion if the "stay-at-home" spouse consents to the departure because desertion by its very nature is a nonconsensual act. If the departure is justified, such as where a spouse flees physical abuse, it is also not classified as desertion. In fact, the spouse who has caused the departure through his or her misconduct may be considered as the deserting spouse based on the doctrine of **constructive desertion**, which imputes the act of desertion to the spouse responsible for the other's departure.[17]

Cruelty

In most states, **cruelty** was not initially included as a ground for divorce, but by the late 1800s, most divorce statutes had been amended to add it as a ground. It soon became the most commonly used. Statutes employ a variety of terms such as "extreme cruelty," "cruel and inhuman treatment," and "indignities," but the meaning is generally the same. Initially, borrowing from ecclesiastical law, cruelty was narrowly defined to include only repeated acts of severe physical abuse that inflicted bodily harm. The concept has gradually expanded and in most states it now includes acts of mental as well as physical cruelty, although some jurisdictions require that the mental cruelty result in some kind of physical symptoms. Proof that the symptoms abated or improved after the parties separated may also be required. The thinking here is that by requiring "objective" evidence of physical impairment, trivial or false claims of cruelty will be weeded out. However, many courts accept fairly general and unsubstantiated statements about loss of sleep, changes in appetite, and increased anxiety as proof of physical impairment.[18]

Defenses

When marital fault is alleged, the defendant-spouse can raise legal defenses to absolve him- or herself of marital wrongdoing. If successful, the divorce cannot be granted on the basis of the alleged fault. However, because most divorce actions are ultimately settled, these defenses are of little practical significance. Moreover, because of the availability of no-fault divorce, when cases are contested, the dispute almost always involves matters of custody, support, and the like, rather than the grounds for the divorce itself. Nonetheless, some familiarity with the major defenses is important, as a defendant-spouse may need to raise a defense in responding to a fault complaint. (See Chapter 10 on the divorce process.)

Connivance

The essence of the defense of **connivance** is consent. This defense has primarily been used in adultery cases in which the defendant-spouse seeks to prove the party seeking the divorce consented to the adultery, such as by helping to arrange the liaison. In some states, a more passive course of action, such as a spouse's not actively seeking to prevent a known affair, constitutes connivance.

Condonation

The essence of the defense of **condonation** is forgiveness. If a spouse forgives his or her partner's marital misconduct, this misconduct can no longer be the basis of a divorce action; condonation restores the marital innocence of the erring spouse. In some states, if a spouse reengages in wrongful activity, the condonation may be canceled and the original divorce grounds revived.

States differ as to what constitutes forgiveness. In some states, engaging in sexual relations after the plaintiff has learned of the misconduct is by itself condonation; here, the plaintiff's state of mind is irrelevant. In other states, the plaintiff's state of mind is key; the plaintiff must actually forgive the defendant—forgiveness will not be inferred from resumed intimacy.

Recrimination

The defense of **recrimination** has been subject to much criticism and has been abolished in many jurisdictions. Here, a defendant-spouse, rather than seeking to defeat a divorce by minimizing the wrongfulness of his or her conduct, seeks to defeat it by showing that the plaintiff-spouse, rather than being an innocent victim, is also guilty of marital wrongdoing. When mutual wrongdoing is established, neither spouse is entitled to a divorce, and the couple must remain married even though each has treated the other badly. Although seemingly illogical, this defense is rooted in the view of divorce as a remedy for the innocent; accordingly, when both spouses are guilty of marital transgressions, neither qualifies as the innocent victim entitled to relief. In some states the harshness of this result has been modified by the doctrine of **comparative rectitude**, which allows a court to grant a divorce if the plaintiff-spouse's wrongdoing is adjudged to be less serious than the defendant's.

Collusion

Collusion involves an agreement by a couple to obtain a divorce and the deliberate crafting of a case for presentation to the court. Collusion can occur in several ways. The parties could agree that one spouse would actually commit a marital wrong, such as adultery, in order to provide grounds for divorce (this would also be considered connivance). More than likely, the parties would agree to fabricate a marital wrong, exaggerate the extent of their discontent with one another, or fail to present a valid defense. This ground runs counter to the basic assumptions of the fault system, which conceptualizes divorce as an adversarial process. The reality is that although collusion is generally classified as a defense, it is unlikely to be raised by either party because it would prevent the granting of the divorce that the parties were attempting to set up.

No-Fault Divorce

During the 1960s, fault divorce came under increasing attack, and in 1970, California became the first state to enact a **no-fault divorce** law. By 1985, no-fault divorce was available in most states; however, it would not be until 2010, when New York became the last state to enact a no-fault statute, that this option would be available to divorcing couples in all states. As part of this effort to move away from the adversarial model of the past, many states also began to use the word *dissolution* instead of divorce, thus signaling a new emphasis on the state of the marriage rather than the conduct of the parties.[19]

The Underpinnings of Reform

During the 1960s, there was a groundswell of support for divorce reform. Critics of the fault system argued that it was outmoded and ineffectual and that the time had come to give couples the option of divorcing without having to prove marital wrongdoing. The following discussion sets out some of their major criticisms.

Reformers pointed to the practice of collusion as an indication that something was not working with the fault model. In a collusive divorce, spouses who wanted out of their marriage would agree to divorce and then carefully stage the process. In most cases, the defendant would simply fail to appear at the divorce hearing, and the trial court would accept the plaintiff's pro forma recitation about fault. In other cases, fault evidence was manufactured; most commonly, acts of adultery were staged. Some lawyers even helped in the process by providing the paramour, most often the office secretary, to pose for the adulterous photographs. It has been suggested that judges may have been aware of the collusive nature of many divorce actions, but chose to ignore it.

According to historians, the practice of collusion began at the end of World War I and became increasingly frequent over the course of the following decades. It thus appears that although the law on the books was strict in terms of fault requirements, for much of the twentieth century, the reality was quite different, as couples were successfully exiting marriages in the absence of proven fault.[20] Reformers hoped that the introduction of no-fault divorce would bring the law into conformity with actual practice and end the hypocrisy of collusive divorce.

Another powerful criticism was that in noncollusive cases, the focus on fault increased the anger and hostility between the parties, especially since financial awards were often influenced by considerations of fault. The legal system was blamed for heightening antagonism by forcing couples into an adversarial posture, thus destroying any hope of reconciliation and making reasoned custody negotiations impossible. Reformers hoped that by eliminating fault, the process would become less adversarial and thus less destructive to the parties and their children.

Fault divorce was further criticized as being out of keeping with the contemporary understanding of marital relationships. Reformers argued that the messy reality of people's marriages did not conform to the fault model, which naively assumed that all marital breakups involved a good spouse and a bad spouse and that this determination could be made simply by identifying who had committed the marital wrong. To reformers, it had become apparent that the named ground was often a symptom of marital distress rather than the actual cause of the breakup. For example, an affair, rather than being the singular "bad" act that brought a marriage to an end, might instead be a response to a complete withdrawal of affection on the part of the other spouse, thus making it unfair to characterize the affair as the only marital transgression.

In light of rising divorce rates, it was also clear to reformers that strict divorce laws were not forcing couples to resolve their difficulties and remain together in furtherance of the state's interest in marital permanency. Moreover, in keeping with the trend toward greater individual autonomy and privacy within the domestic realm, reformers argued that the right of an unhappy spouse to leave a marriage should not be subordinated to the state's interest in family preservation. Rather than being forced into legal pigeonholes in accordance with the state's view of what kinds of wrongs justified marital departures, reformers believed that an unhappy spouse should have greater control over when and why to leave a marriage. In effect, divorce began to be seen as more of a right than a strictly controlled remedy for a spouse aggrieved by marital wrongdoing.

In seeking to shift the balance from the historic interest of the state in family preservation toward the right of an unhappy spouse to leave a failed marriage, some reformers were influenced by the women's rights movement, which insisted that women be seen as autonomous, self-defining individuals, rather than primarily as dependent members of family units. In short, opening up the divorce process would more readily enable women to exit marriages that they felt trapped in or that otherwise threatened their physical or mental well-being in keeping with the growing emphasis on the needs and aspirations of individual spouses within a marriage, as distinct from the traditional weight accorded the enduring social importance of the marital unit.

No-Fault Laws

Beginning with California in 1970, no-fault reform swept the country. Within 15 years, the legal landscape had been radically altered. When California reformed its law, it essentially opted to abolish all fault grounds and replace them with a single no-fault standard. A significant number of states followed California's lead and now have only no-fault grounds. A majority of states, however, chose to maintain their existing fault grounds and add no-fault provisions, thus creating a dual system of divorce.

No-Fault Grounds

There are two primary no-fault grounds: **marital breakdown** and **living separate and apart**, with the former being the most common. A few states have combined these grounds and require proof of both a marital breakdown and a separation. Although both grounds will be discussed below in greater detail, keep in mind that many states have unique requirements, making familiarity with the laws of your jurisdiction essential.

Marital Breakdown.   Marital breakdown is the principal no-fault ground. Statutes use a variety of terms to express this essential concept—such as **irreconcilable differences** or the "irretrievable" or "irremediable breakdown" of the marriage. Whichever term is used, the emphasis is on the failed state of the marital relationship rather than on the conduct of the spouses.

At least in theory, the judge at the divorce hearing is supposed to conduct a searching inquiry into whether the marriage is in fact broken and beyond hope of repair. (See Chapter 10 on the divorce process.) Factors relevant to this determination include the following:

- the degree to which the parties are unable to relate to one another;
- the extent of any differences between them;
- prior efforts to resolve their marital difficulties; and
- whether there is any hope of reconciliation.

Many states specifically bar evidence of fault; in other states such evidence is not considered relevant, except perhaps to help establish the extent of the breakdown.

No-fault hearings were not intended to be mere rubber stamps of the parties' decision, and judges in most states have considerable discretion to decide whether or not a marriage is truly over. In fact, some reformers hoped to give judges more freedom to deny a divorce if they believed there was any hope of reconciliation than they had under the fault system, where proof of fault mandated the granting of the divorce. Accordingly, in some states, a judge can stay the proceedings until the parties have sought counseling if the judge is not convinced that the marriage is over.

In reality, however, it appears that searching inquiries into whether a marriage is really over are rare. Couples are generally taken at their word that the marriage is beyond repair, and a few states have eliminated the requirement of a hearing if there are no collateral issues to resolve.

Many states do not require both parties to agree that the marriage is over before a no-fault divorce can be granted. This raises the possibility that a spouse could seek to block the divorce by expressing his or her continued love and belief that the marriage was still intact or not beyond repair; but most judges will grant a divorce in this situation on the basis that a viable partnership does not exist where each spouse has such a radically different view of the relationship. When faced with this situation, a judge, where allowed to do so, might stay the proceedings and order the couple into counseling.

Living Separate and Apart.   The other major no-fault ground is that the parties have lived separate and apart for a statutory period of time. Time periods range from about 18 months to three years, with most falling somewhere in between. The underlying assumption is that the separation itself is proof of marital breakdown, and judicial inquiry into the relationship's demise is not required. The term "separate and apart" has generally been construed to require separate residences, but some courts have granted a divorce when a couple remained under the same roof but had essentially ceased all interaction for the requisite time period.

Some courts impose an intent requirement and will not qualify the separation even if it lasts for the statutory period unless the parties intended for it to be a permanent one. Thus, if a separation begins as a temporary one, the statutory period will not start to run unless and until the parties decide to make the separation permanent. Some states also require that the separation be voluntary on the part of both parties. Accordingly, if the parties are living apart because of desertion, flight from abuse, or over the objection of one spouse, the separation is not voluntary and will not qualify the parties for a divorce. Similarly, a separation caused by involuntary circumstances such as the draft, hospitalization, or incarceration would not be a valid ground for divorce. Also, when one spouse is mentally incompetent, a separation initiated by the other spouse will not generally be regarded as voluntary if the non-initiating spouse lacks the ability to comprehend what is going on and to give his or her consent. In a few states, the separation need be voluntary only on the part of one spouse.

Where voluntariness is required, a separation that begins involuntarily can be converted into a voluntary one if the parties agree they wish to live apart. The running of the statutory period is calculated from the time the parties reached this agreement rather than from the time of the initial separation. Many jurisdictions, however, do not impose a voluntariness requirement; accordingly, virtually any separation for the statutory time period can ripen into a divorce action.

The Divorce Counterrevolution

No-fault divorce has come under increasing criticism from a variety of individuals and groups who believe it is undermining the institution of marriage. In 1996, in an effort to strengthen marriage, State Representative Jesse Dahlman of Michigan introduced one of the nation's first comprehensive divorce reform bills. Asserting that no-fault divorce is tantamount to "legalized desertion,"[21] she proposed eliminating "unilateral" no-fault divorce by requiring proof of fault if one spouse objected to the divorce.

Since then, a variety of divorce-reform proposals have been introduced in states across the country with the common goal of making a no-fault divorce more difficult to obtain. Also, in 2000, a grassroots national "Marriage Movement" was born for the purpose of "renewing a marriage culture."[22] As we will see, many view this trend with concern. They fear that those seeking to limit the availability of no-fault divorce aim to turn back the hands of time by re-imposing outdated notions of marriage on contemporary couples. They question both the analysis of the harms of no-fault divorce as well as the proposed solutions.[23]

The Debate over No-Fault Divorce

Critics of No-Fault Divorce. Critics contend that no-fault divorce has contributed to a "divorce culture" that emphasizes the pursuit of individual happiness and fulfillment over commitment to one's spouse and children. According to this view, rather than accepting that all marriages have their ebbs and flows and that it takes effort to sustain intimacy, no-fault divorce encourages spouses to walk out the door in pursuit of their own goals. No-fault divorce is thus blamed for cheapening the meaning of connection and permanence with its seductive promise of an easy way out. As one activist puts it: "No-fault divorce does not expand everyone's personal choice. It empowers the spouse who wishes to leave. . . . The spouse who chooses divorce has a liberating sense of mastery. . . . Being divorced, however, . . . reinforces exactly the opposite sense of life."[24]

Critics further contend that children are the primary victims of this trend toward loosened marital ties. They point to both the economic and psychological dislocation that often follows divorce, and criticize parents for placing their own needs over the needs of their children. Although generally not opposed to divorce that is truly fault-based, they criticize adults whom they see as placing their own need for fulfillment over their children's need for stability and sustained connections.

Supporters of No-Fault Divorce.   Many others, however, challenge the view that no-fault divorce is responsible for altering our understanding of marital commitment. Pointing to the widespread practice of collusive divorce during the fault era, they argue that no-fault divorce responded to rather than initiated changes that had already taken place in society's understanding of marriage. Supporting this view, no-fault supporters point out that divorce rates began to rise before no-fault reform owing to a number of factors, including increased social acceptance of divorce, the Vietnam War (studies consistently show that divorce rates increase during times of war), the women's rights movement, and changing economic conditions.[25] Accordingly, supporters argue that eliminating no-fault divorce is a misguided strategy that will not accomplish its intended goal of significantly reducing the rate of divorce.

Another concern of no-fault supporters is that eliminating no-fault divorce will recreate many of the problems of the past such as the practice of collusive divorce, trapping women in abusive marriages.

Focusing on domestic violence victims, one study concluded that no-fault divorce has led to a "striking decline" in female domestic violence rates and "a decline in females murdered by their intimates."[26] The authors suggest that this is due both to the increased availability of divorce and to the fact that "the switch to a unilateral divorce regime redistributes power in a marriage, giving power to the person who wants out, and reducing the power previously held by the partner interested in preserving the marriage."[27]

Interestingly, Barbara Defoe Whitehead, a self-described critic of contemporary divorce practices,[28] also raises concerns about the impact the elimination of no-fault would have on battered women:

> Some marriages will be preserved that probably should end, including those that involve physical abuse and violence. Unfortunately, fault is likely to be most successful in deterring socially isolated and timorous women, often battered wives, from seeking divorce. It would be a cruel irony indeed if a pro-marriage policy unintentionally became a pro-bad-marriage policy.[29]

Whitehead also points to another possible unintended consequence of reform—that restricting the availability of no-fault divorce may deter people from marrying in the first place. She argues that based on life experience and cultural messages about the high rates of marital failure, young adults are already apprehensive about marital commitments. If they then hear how hard it is to get divorced they may "interpret legal restrictions on divorce as yet another reason to avoid marriage."[30] Thus, Whitehead argues that the current reform effort may backfire and may "further undermine and weaken the commitment to marriage, the very institution it intends to save. Worse, it sends a glum and dispiriting message to a generation already deeply pessimistic about the chances for a lasting marriage."[31]

Supporters of no-fault divorce are also concerned about the well-being of children. They recognize the impact that divorce can have on children but focus on the harms of growing up in a household that is rife with conflict. Again challenging the critics' understanding of causality, they point out that many of the emotional and psychological harms that are attributed to divorce may be due to long-standing problems in the family. Accordingly, efforts to compel parents to remain together may exacerbate rather than alleviate childhood distress. Moreover, no-fault supporters point out that the impact of divorce can be mitigated by carefully structured custody and visitation plans to account for the needs of the children and by support awards that are sufficient to offset the potential economic disruption of divorce.

Legal Reforms

Based on concerns about no-fault divorce, reform measures that aim to make marital dissolution more difficult have been introduced in many states. By increasing the barriers to divorce, it is hoped that spouses will be more inclined to work out their differences, rather than opting for no-fault's promise of an "easy" escape from commitment. These measures have met with some success, but they have also been resisted based on the kinds of concerns discussed above, such as that they will entrap spouses in destructive marriages and discourage people from marrying in the first place. Another important concern is the potential intrusiveness of these measures, as they limit the ability of individuals to decide when a marriage is in fact over. Framed slightly differently, the concern is that these proposals seek to limit choice in furtherance of an idealized notion of marital life that may bear little connection to a couple's daily reality.

Not surprisingly, many of these reforms target no-fault divorce. Some measures propose eliminating no-fault as a ground for divorce altogether; others seek to limit its availability to couples who do not have minor children, and still others seek to impose lengthy waiting periods. Another approach is to require **mutual consent**, thus eliminating the option of "unilateral" no-fault divorce. Accordingly, absent fault, both parties must agree to the divorce—one spouse cannot terminate the marriage over the objection of the other. Based on the view that the state has a legitimate interest in keeping spouses together for the benefit of their offspring, mutual consent provisions are often tied to the presence of minor children. Of concern to opponents is that if one spouse refuses to consent, a divorce cannot be granted until a couple's youngest child turns 18, thus keeping embattled spouses locked together in an unhappy union.[32]

A more recent idea that has been proposed in a few states is to designate the party who is opposed to the divorce the "Responsible Spouse," and then provide him or her with leverage in the fight to save the marriage by way of a disproportionate share of the marital assets and parenting time (unless the party opposing the marriage is guilty of marital fault). Under this model, "[a]n unhappy mate could [still] file for divorce, but he/she would pay a price of less child custody and fewer assets."[33]

Two other reform measures focus on strengthening marriage as a way to reduce the divorce rate. These include **premarital counseling** requirements and the controversial concept of **covenant marriage**, which, as discussed below, is currently available as an option in three states.

Premarital Counseling

Seeking to prevent divorce by strengthening marriage at the front end, a handful of states have passed laws to encourage couples to participate in premarital counseling. By way of an incentive, participants are typically offered a discount on the marriage license fee. Another possible approach is to set a longer waiting period for the issuance of a marriage license, which can then be waived for couples who have gone through premarital counseling.

Although research on the effectiveness of this approach is limited, some studies suggest that participation in premarital counseling may help to weed out poorly matched couples before they actually tie the knot, and it may also improve the communication skills of those who do marry, although the impact on the actual divorce rate is, as of yet, unclear.[34]

Moreover, because premarital counseling laws are far less restrictive of individual autonomy and choice than other divorce reform measures, they have generated less opposition from those who do not believe the state should seek to compel unhappy couples to remain together for the benefit of their children or for the good of society.

Covenant Marriage

In 1997, the state of Louisiana passed the nation's first **covenant marriage** law. Since then, although covenant marriage bills have been considered in many states, only Arizona and Arkansas have followed Louisiana's lead and enacted such a measure into law. Moreover, few couples within these states have availed themselves of this option. To some, the failure of covenant marriage to take hold points to the inherent limitations of a two-tiered approach to marriage, while others argue that it reflects the corrosive effect of our anti-marriage culture.[35] Either way, this controversial innovation merits careful consideration because it remains an important option in the campaign to "restore the institution of marriage" by offering, to "those who belong to a religious community or those who adhere to a traditional morality, a safe haven from the post-modern dominant culture."[36]

Covenant marriage laws give couples who are contemplating marriage a choice—they can either opt for "regular" marriage or choose to enter into a "covenant" marriage. Designed to counter what some regard as the destructive effects of no-fault divorce, covenant marriage seeks to sanctify the marriage bond by stressing the interests of the marriage itself over those of the individual partners.[37] Over the years, commentators have raised the concern that the term "covenant marriage" suggests the use of state law to infuse biblical values into a civil relationship. As an article by Katherine Shaw Spaht, who drafted the original Louisiana law, makes clear, this association is no accident. Rather, as she explains, the appropriation of the term "covenant" in "covenant marriage" was chosen to communicate the understanding that "legal marriage represents a serious commitment and mutual faithfulness, albeit an imperfect reflection of God's love and eternal faithfulness," and that entry into this more exalted union "is closer to the Christian conception of marriage than a 'standard' marriage."[38]

The following language from Louisiana's statute captures the essence of what covenant marriage entails:

> A covenant marriage is a marriage entered into by one male and one female who understand and agree that the marriage between them is a lifelong relationship. Parties to a covenant marriage have received counseling emphasizing the nature and purposes of marriage and the responsibilities thereto. Only when there has been a complete and total

breach of the marital covenant commitment may the non-breaching party seek a declaration that the marriage is no longer recognized.[39]

Drawing on this language and thus using Louisiana's law as the prototype, we now consider some of the defining features that distinguish covenant marriage from "regular" marriage.

First, prospective spouses must take some initial steps in order to enter into a covenant marriage. They must undergo premarital counseling and then sign a Declaration of Intent attesting that they have satisfied the counseling requirement and that they understand that marriage is a life-long commitment. They also must disclose to one another any information that could negatively affect their ability to enter into the marriage and must attest to the fact of full disclosure. Second, embodied in the Declaration of Intent is the obligation to take all reasonable steps, including marital counseling, to keep their marriage together. Third, and perhaps the key distinguishing factor, is that the prospective spouses in a covenant marriage agree in advance that they will not seek a no-fault divorce. By eliminating this option, they commit themselves to divorcing only if there has been a complete breach of the marital commitment, which occurs as essentially defined along traditional fault lines or if the spouses have lived separate and apart for two years.

Proponents hope that entering into a covenant marriage will cause couples to take their marital commitments more seriously. They hope that the counseling requirements and the limits on divorce will reinvigorate marriage by requiring spouses to work hard at their relationships, thus counteracting the seductiveness of easy divorce and restoring the primacy of marital commitment. Counterpoising covenant marriage to the contemporary vision of marriage, Spaht, a leading proponent of this marital approach, explains that "covenant spouses defer to marriage, an abstraction representing a third party to the marriage itself, rather than view marriage as a loose union of two radically autonomous selves. . . ."[40]

Many serious concerns, however, have been raised about covenant marriage. As mentioned above, one concern is that it infuses a biblical conception of marriage into state law, thus breaching the required boundary between church and state. In a related vein, although proponents such as Spaht herald the subordination of individual interests to the marital enterprise, critics worry that this very subordination will reinvigorate the long-standing tradition of *female* subordination within marriage, thus disrupting the modern trend toward greater spousal equality.

Also of concern is that it is impossible to predict the future, and committing one's self in advance to a particular course of action may work to a spouse's detriment. Thus, for example, if a husband turns out to be abusive, by entering into a covenant marriage, a woman has committed herself to participating in counseling with him, when the best and safest course of action may be for her to disengage from the relationship as quickly as possible. Moreover, once having committed to what some have dubbed "super-marriage," the psychological consequences of disentanglement are likely to be greater, thus making it more difficult for an at-risk spouse to extricate herself from this "lifelong" commitment.

Critics also point to the element of coercion. If one spouse wishes to enter into a covenant marriage and the other does not, the commitment of the recalcitrant spouse may be questioned, thus compelling him or her to choose covenant marriage rather than run the risk of no marriage at all. Lastly, critics have also raised concerns about the costs associated with counseling and about the inefficacy of counseling when parties are acting out of legal compulsion rather than genuine desire to work on their problems.

The Law of Annulment

Marriages can also be "terminated" by the granting of an annulment. Although annulments are rare, it is nonetheless important to have a basic understanding of the law in this area. A client who comes to your office may want an annulment for religious reasons, or a client may be confused about the law, believing, for example, that an annulment is the only way to end a short-term or unconsummated marriage.

As you read this section, keep in mind that we are speaking only about the civil annulment process. A number of religious bodies also grant annulments in accordance with their own internal principles and procedures.

Distinguished from Divorce

An annulment is a retroactive declaration that no valid marriage ever existed between the parties. The modern annulment action emerged out of ecclesiastical practice. Unlike divorce, the procedure was consistent with the religious belief in the indissolubility of the marital relationship because an annulment establishes that the parties were never validly married.

Divorce is premised on the existence of a valid marriage. It operates to dissolve the legal bond between spouses based on problems that arose during the course of the marriage. It operates prospectively to terminate the bond from the date of the divorce forward. In contrast, an annulment works retrospectively to invalidate the marital bond based on a defect that existed at the time the marriage was celebrated; it is a statement that because of this defect, the marriage was flawed from its inception. Accordingly, an annulment cannot be granted for a problem that arises after a marriage is celebrated because a valid marriage would have been established, and annulment speaks to marital invalidity. Thus, although common, it is technically incorrect to speak of an annulment as terminating a marriage because it is a declaration that the parties were never in fact married.

Grounds

Grounds for annulment vary from state to state. Most of the grounds can be grouped into two categories: (1) those involving the lack of capacity or intent, and (2) those involving breaches of state marital restriction laws.

This distinction has important practical significance. Some defects make a marriage **void** from its inception, while others make it **voidable**. In general, a marriage contracted in violation of state marital laws is considered void from its inception (however, see below regarding marital age restrictions). This means that a decree of annulment is not required to invalidate the marriage—the marriage is regarded as having never taken place. However, a party may prefer to obtain a decree of annulment in order to eliminate any confusion about his or her marital status.

In contrast, a marriage premised on the **lack of capacity** or intent is generally considered voidable rather than void. A voidable marriage is considered valid until and unless it is invalidated by a decree of annulment. As a general rule, the annulment petition can be filed only by the "innocent" spouse—the one not responsible for the defect. The annulment may be denied if the spouse seeking the annulment knew about the defect at the time of celebration or ratified the marriage by cohabitation after learning of it. Prior knowledge and ratification are not defenses if the marriage is void.

Void Marriages

An annulment can be granted if a marriage is contracted in violation of a marital restriction law. Specific grounds include bigamy, incest, and being under the age of capacity (see the section entitled "Marital Age" in Chapter 1). Incestuous and bigamous marriages are void and cannot be ratified by cohabitation or consent. In contrast, a marriage that is contracted when one or both parties were under age is generally voidable, and continued cohabitation beyond the age of consent will ratify the marriage.

Voidable Marriages

An annulment may also be granted if one party lacked the capacity or the intent to contract a real marriage due to fraud, duress, mental incapacity, insanity, and, possibly, incurable impotence. Of these, considerations of fraud probably come up the most. To warrant an annulment, the fraud must go to the "essentials" of the marriage. This concept has traditionally been limited to the sexual and procreative aspects of marriage, such as concealing a pregnancy by another man, misrepresenting an intent to consummate the marriage, or misrepresenting an intent to have children where no such intent exists. Some jurisdictions have expanded the concept of fraud to include other critical aspects of the marital relationship, such as religious beliefs—for example, where one party pretends to be deeply religious in order to entice the other into marriage.

A spouse may be able to defeat an annulment action by showing that the other spouse has ratified the marriage. For instance, using the example about religious misrepresentation, if the deceived partner remains in the marriage after learning about the deception, she or he will probably be deemed to have ratified the marriage and would not be entitled to an annulment. Similarly, a court might find that the passage of years has mitigated the impact of the defect because the parties would have had the time to establish an independent relationship.

Consequences of an Annulment Decree

As a matter of logic, if an annulment decree undoes a marriage back to the date of celebration, then any children born to the couple would be "illegitimate"; additionally, no marital rights to support or property would accrue. Although this was the common law approach, this is no longer the case in most states.

Children

In keeping with the modern legal approach to children of unmarried parents (see Chapter 12), children of an annulled marriage are no longer considered "illegitimate." Accordingly, the law treats these children similarly to children of divorcing parents when it comes to custody, visitation, and support determinations.

Spousal Support and the Division of Property

Because alleviating financial hardship is considered important enough to outweigh the risk that a party will have been required to support someone eventually determined not to be his or her spouse, many courts will award temporary support during the pendency of an annulment action. However, regardless of need, support will not usually be awarded to a spouse who is denying the validity of the marriage because these are regarded as mutually inconsistent claims. A number of states have enacted statutes allowing an award of permanent alimony in cases of need following an annulment, but some permit an award only if this spouse entered into the marriage with a good-faith belief in its validity. In authorizing support, these statutes eschew reliance on legal formalities and recognize that the declaration of invalidity does not mitigate the financial needs of an economically dependent partner. In the absence of express statutory authorization, a court might make an alimony-like award, such as it might do in a cohabitation case. With respect to property, many statutes expressly authorize the court to make a distribution of accumulated assets much as it would do in a divorce case (see Chapter 9).

Revival

Following an annulment, difficult questions may arise regarding the nature of third-party obligations when such obligations turn on the recipient's marital status. Using a hypothetical, two situations will be briefly discussed.

Let's assume that the marriage of Juan and Maria ended in divorce and that Juan was to pay support until such time as Maria remarried. Now assume that Maria remarries and Juan stops paying alimony based on the fact of her remarriage. What happens if Maria's second marriage is subsequently annulled? Because annulment effectively cancels out the second marriage, Maria could logically argue that there was no remarriage and that Juan's support obligation is subject to **revival**. Moreover, she could claim that he owes her money back to the date he stopped paying. Most courts would reject Maria's claim for support on the basis that Juan had a right to rely on the marriage as it appeared, as distinct from its technical, legal status, and his support obligation would not be revived.

However, when benefits such as Social Security are involved, courts are much more likely to revive payments upon an annulment. For example, if before her second marriage, Juan had died, and Maria was receiving Social Security benefits, these payments would cease upon her remarriage; but if this second marriage were annulled, most courts would revive the payments because the payor does not rely on the remarriage in the same way as a former spouse would when planning for the future.

Legal Separation

The third remedy for an unhappy marriage is a **legal separation**, also known as a "judicial separation," a "limited divorce," and, historically speaking, a "*divorce a mensa et thoro*" (a divorce from board and bed).

The Nature of the Action

A legal separation is a judicial decree formally permitting or, perhaps more accurately, requiring, spouses to live apart. In some states a separation can be granted for an unlimited period of time; in others, there are durational limits. Grounds are generally similar to those found in fault-based divorce laws, although some statutes simply give a judge the discretion to decide if sufficient cause for a separation exists. The no-fault concept has not permeated this action, perhaps because, unlike with a divorce, a couple can always agree to separate without a court decree.

A legal separation does not terminate the marital relationship. Accordingly, it does not free the parties to remarry. As part of its decree, a court can determine custody and award both child and spousal support. In some states, a division of property also may be ordered; in others, the distribution of property is prohibited unless and until the parties actually divorce. One might wonder why an unhappy spouse would file for a legal separation rather than for a divorce. One reason might be religious beliefs that do not permit divorce because the marital bond is considered indissoluble but would allow a separation because this does not dissolve the marriage. A variety of personal and emotional reasons also might influence the decision to seek a separation rather than a divorce. An individual wishing to live apart from his or her spouse may not be ready to file for divorce but might need the protection of court orders (if, for example, he or she fears the other spouse might disappear with the children) or the financial support that the court could award. A spouse also might hope to send a wake-up call to his or her partner.

A number of states provide for the conversion of a separation into a divorce after the passage of a specified period of time. Where conversion is not allowed, filing for a separation and then filing for divorce (should a divorce eventually be desired) entails a significant duplication of efforts; therefore, a client's reasons for wanting to start with a legal separation rather than initiating divorce proceedings should be carefully explored. For instance, if the client knows that the marriage is over but isn't quite ready emotionally to implement the decision, it is worth exploring whether it makes sense to wait to initiate legal proceedings until he or she is ready to proceed with the divorce.

Distinguished from an Action for Separate Maintenance

Upon separation, a party might file a complaint for **separate maintenance**. Although similar to an action for a legal separation, the essence of a complaint for separate maintenance is a claim for support. Thus, the focus is on the plaintiff's need for support, rather than on the reason for the parties' separation. The decree usually does not involve findings on the reason for separation nor does it specifically authorize the parties to live apart, although reconciliation generally terminates the support obligation. Also, in most states the court cannot order a division of property or determine custody as part of a separate maintenance action.

Chapter Summary

Divorce is a legal action that dissolves the marital bond. Our divorce laws are rooted in the Protestant concept of marital sin. Historically, divorce law was premised on marital fault, and a divorce could be granted only to an innocent spouse based on marital wrongdoing. Many couples, however, evaded the law's strictness through the practice of collusive divorce. Beginning in the 1960s, concerns about collusion and the adversarial nature of the fault system led to no-fault reform. Some states eliminated fault grounds altogether and enacted pure no-fault systems. Others added no-fault grounds as an option. The principal no-fault grounds are marital breakdown and living separate and apart for a statutorily prescribed time period.

No-fault laws have been the subject of considerable debate, and there has been a recent backlash against them. Many proposals have been suggested to make divorce more difficult to obtain, especially when a married couple has children. Covenant marriage is a key example of such an effort. A couple entering into a covenant marriage must seek premarital and predivorce counseling and waive the right to seek a no-fault divorce. However, concerns have been voiced about these efforts, including that they blur the line between church and state and may entrap spouses in marriages that are abusive or otherwise destructive.

An annulment is a declaration that no valid marriage ever existed between the parties due to an impediment that was present at the time of celebration. Annulments are usually based on a lack of capacity or intent, or a violation of a marital restriction law. Some defects, such as a prior existing marriage, render a marriage void from its inception, while others, such as the lack of capacity, make a marriage voidable.

A legal separation is a decree that the parties have good cause for living apart. It does not terminate the marital relationship, and the parties cannot remarry. It is distinguishable from an action for separate maintenance, which focuses on support rather than on the reason for the underlying separation.

Key Terms

Divorce	No-Fault Divorce
Indissoluble	Marital Breakdown
Annulment	Living Separate and Apart
Marital Fault	Irreconcilable Differences
Innocent Spouse	Mutual Consent
Fault Divorce	Premarital Counseling
Adultery	Covenant Marriage
Desertion	Void
Constructive Desertion	Voidable
Cruelty	Lack of Capacity
Connivance	Revival
Condonation	Legal Separation
Recrimination	*Divorce a Mensa et Thoro*
Comparative Rectitude	Separate Maintenance
Collusion	

Review Questions

1. What were the Catholic Church's views on marriage?
2. What remedies were available from the ecclesiastical courts for an unhappy marriage?

3. How did the Protestant view of marriage differ from the Catholic Church's? What impact did this have on divorce law?
4. In what way was England different from the other Protestant countries?
5. How did the Puritans view divorce?
6. Explain the relevance of guilt and innocence in a fault-based divorce system.
7. What are the key fault grounds? What are the requirements for each one?
8. What views do courts hold on the question of whether adultery can be defined to include extramarital same-sex relationships?
9. What are the key divorce defenses? What is the essence of each one?
10. What criticism did the no-fault reformers level at fault-based divorce?
11. What is the difference between a pure no-fault system and a dual system?
12. Explain the no-fault ground of marital breakdown.
13. What kind of judicial inquiry is usually conducted in these hearings? How does this differ from the vision of some reformers?
14. Explain the no-fault ground of living separate and apart.
15. What concerns have been raised about the availability of no-fault divorce? What reform measures have been proposed?
16. What concerns have supporters of no-fault divorce raised about present efforts to reform/eliminate no-fault divorce?
17. What is covenant marriage? What do supporters hope to accomplish?
18. What are some of the major criticisms of covenant marriage?
19. What is an annulment, and how does it differ from a divorce?
20. What is the difference between a void marriage and one that is voidable?
21. What is a legal separation? How does an action for separate maintenance differ from a legal separation?

Discussion Questions

1. Many people believe that no-fault divorce makes divorce too easy and has caused people to lose respect for the institution of marriage. Do you think this is true? Why or why not? If so, what do you think should be done? Do you think covenant marriage is a good response to these concerns?
2. With no-fault divorce, a spouse usually can obtain a divorce because he or she no longer loves the other spouse. Should this be permitted over the objection of a spouse who claims to still be madly in love and committed to working out the relationship? What should the court do in this situation? Should the presence of children change the picture?
3. Apart from the needs of children, do you think the state has a legitimate interest in encouraging marital permanency through its divorce laws?

If so, how should the state's interest be balanced with the interests and needs of the parties to a marriage?

Assignments

1. Locate your state's divorce law and determine the following:
   - Are fault grounds still used, or is your state a "pure" no-fault jurisdiction?
   - If yes, what grounds are available? What defenses are available?
   - What no-fault ground(s) is (are) available in your state?
   - What must a party show to qualify for a no-fault divorce?

   Having reviewed the statute, identify and describe any recent changes that are designed to slow down the divorce process (such as waiting periods or counseling requirements) or limit divorce options (such as limiting no-fault divorce to couples without children).

2. A client has come to the office where you work as a paralegal. She is unhappy in her marriage but does not know what she wants to do. The attorney you work for has asked you to draft a letter explaining her legal options. At this point, you do not have all the facts, but, based on a brief interview, you know the following:
   - She thinks that her husband never loved her and that he married her solely to make his family happy.
   - They have been married for three years, during which time, based on his wishes, they have lived totally separate lives, although they have had sexual intercourse on occasion.

   In your letter you should explain the general differences between divorce, annulment, and legal separation and discuss the specific requirements of the laws in your state.

3. Assume you are a legislative aide in a state that is considering enacting a covenant marriage law along the lines of Louisiana's law. The senator you work for has asked you to prepare a "briefing" memo in which you explain the basic requirements of covenant marriage and set out the arguments in favor of and against such a law.

4. Assume you are a law clerk for a family court judge who has recently taken a divorce case under advisement because it raises a new issue of law. The wife filed for divorce on the grounds of adultery because her husband has engaged in an intimate relationship with another man. The husband denies this is adultery, asserting that the concept only covers heterosexual intercourse. The judge has asked you to locate cases from other jurisdictions that have addressed this issue and write an interoffice memorandum in which you first analyze the case law and then set out your thoughts as to how she should rule in this matter.

Cases for Analysis

In the following case, an appeals court takes the unusual step of addressing *sua sponte* whether the divorce decree should be voided due to the mental incompetence of the spouses — an issue that the trial court failed to take into account in issuing its decree. Of concern also is that the divorce was litigated by their adult children through attorneys for each parent, rather than by court-appointed guardians.

BERRY v. BERRY
197 A.3d 788 (Pa. Super. Ct. 2018)

KUNSELMAN, J.:

In this difficult matter, the octogenarian Appellant, Janice Berry ("Wife"), appeals the equitable distribution of the marital estate she shared with the nonagenarian Appellee, Charles Berry ("Husband"). At the time of the trial, the record indicates that Husband and Wife were married for 66 years and both suffered from dementia; the divorce was litigated through their respective lawyers by their adult children who operated under respective powers of attorney. Neither party appeared for the trial. Their adult children were the only witnesses. At the conclusion of the proceedings, the trial court issued a divorce decree and an equitable distribution award. Wife appealed.

On appeal, Wife, represented by new counsel, only challenges the equitable distribution award. . . . We do not reach the merits of this claim, however. Instead, we address *sua sponte* the mental capacity of both parties, which was questioned throughout the divorce litigation, but ignored by the trial court. . . .

The factual overture is this: The parties, who wed on October 14, 1950, entered the final stages of their lives when divorce litigation commenced. After 63 years of marriage, Wife filed a divorce complaint in August 2013. . . .

Daughter said Wife filed for divorce to protect her assets; the letter alleged that the parties' sons, including Husband's power of attorney, Jerry Berry ("Son"), were "moving money from one account to another and opening new joint accounts with their names included." The record indicates this sum was $25,000. Husband evidently became abusive, and the court awarded Wife exclusive possession of the marital home; Husband then went to live with one of his sons before ultimately moving into an assisted living facility. Daughter further alleged that Wife regretted filing for divorce, and instead wished she would have had the sons charged with elder abuse.

The litigation had lingered for years....

The court learned that Husband was too frail to leave his assisted living facility in Virginia to attend the hearing. The court permitted him to be available by phone, but his counsel indicated that telephonic participation would be similarly impossible because Husband was too hard of hearing. Neither Husband nor Wife was present, in person or by phone, at the hearing, which was finally held on July 5, 2017, nearly three years after it was originally scheduled. Only the children appeared under their respective powers of attorney. Significantly, the record reveals no documentation of Son's power of attorney for Husband. Thus, it seems the court proceeded with the divorce litigation with Son acting as attorney-in-fact for Husband, without any written proof of his authority to do so. . . .

The attorneys then addressed stipulations and proceeded with the rest of the hearing. The court divided the parties' assets equally. At the time of the hearing, Husband was 91 years old and lived in an assisted living center near one of the parties' sons in Virginia. . . .

In its opinion and order, the trial court stated that there was no testimony about Wife's health problems. However, our review of the record revealed . . . another letter, dated September 30, 2016, also submitted by Daughter, detailing Wife's own battle with dementia. . . . Dr. Turner indicated that Wife is his dementia patient. . . .

Before we can address the merits of the question raised on appeal, we must address the glaring issue of the parties' competency. . . .

Under the circumstances described above, we cannot ignore the grave questions of whether the Husband was competent enough to bring a proper divorce action and whether Wife was competent enough to defend it. We find the trial court erred by not conducting such proceedings to ascertain these answers, wrongly professing that it was the job of the orphans' court. . . .

Here, we likewise have a duty to protect the parties' rights under such similar, irregular circumstances. In the instant matter, not only were allegations of the parties' dementia made throughout the litigation, but the issue was also placed front and center at the start of the hearing. Incompetency allegations were made once more in each party's post-trial memorandum.

Having determined that our duty to protect the rights of incompetents takes precedence over the usual rules of appellate procedure, we now address the questions of the parties' competency and their children's authority to proceed on their behalf, as powers of attorney, in the divorce and equitable distribution action.

Across the United States, the majority rule is that no incompetent person may initiate a divorce. . . .

[I]t is also settled Pennsylvania law that an adjudged incompetent may prosecute a civil action for divorce *only* by means of a guardian or guardian *ad litem*, and, thus, a divorce decree which was obtained without the assistance of a court appointed guardian or guardian *ad litem* is void.

Moreover, Pennsylvania defines an "incompetent" as a person who, because of infirmities, is unable to manage property *or* lacks the capacity to make reasonable decisions concerning his person. . . .

[O]ur determination [is] that the trial court erred when it proceeded with a hearing and entered an order without first ascertaining the competency of parties.

We have never decided whether a power of attorney can prosecute, maintain or defend a divorce action on behalf of the principal, even when the terms of power of attorney authorize litigation generally. And so we have not decided what happens when that power of attorney is an adult child of one of, or here, both of the parties. . . .

We can reasonably infer that the trial court believed powers of attorney were sufficient to act on behalf of the parties in this matter. . . .

We conclude that Pennsylvania law does not allow an incompetent to bring a divorce action without the court confirming whether the incompetent retains the mental capacity to make reasonable decisions concerning his person, his understanding of the nature of a divorce action, and his desire to maintain this action. We further hold that a power of attorney cannot prosecute, nor defend, a divorce action on behalf of an incompetent principal. . . .

The penultimate question we must decide is whether the trial court erred by not resolving the competency of both parties after the issue was raised, when no prior incompetency adjudication was made as to either of them. Our precedent similarly makes clear that the court erred when it proceeded with the hearing before determining the competency of the parties.

Here, Daughter's October 2016 letter — complete with attached doctor's note — outlined Wife's alleged mental deficiencies. This letter is identified in the record as Wife's "Petition to Set Aside Post-Nuptial Agreement." At that juncture, Wife's counsel and the court were both under an obligation to trigger proceedings to ascertain Wife's competency. Daughter's June 29, 2017 letter, filed a week before the trial, was similarly sufficient to put a halt to the proceedings to determine Husband's competency. Husband's condition was explicitly discussed at trial. Although we are not privy to what happened behind the scenes, we can deduce that the competency question loomed in the background for some time, as evidenced by the trial court's stated, albeit misguided, belief "*throughout this proceeding* that the power of attorney issue is an orphans' court issue, not a divorce issue." The court's decision to proceed with the trial without first ascertaining the parties' competency was erroneous.

Moreover, the court, at the conclusion of the trial, ordered the parties to submit post-trial memoranda of law. Husband's counsel, Attorney

Young, *admitted* in her pre-trial memorandum that Husband was "frail and *demented* and in otherwise poor health." Wife's counsel, Attorney Klingus, similarly stated that the parties "both suffer dementia-related illness.". . .

Upon each allegation that one of these parties was not competent to proceed, the trial court should have continued the proceedings to immediately resolve that question. While the attorneys also mistakenly represented to the court that they had the ability to litigate the divorce through the children's respective powers of attorney, we are stunned that the hearing was even conducted in the parties' absence. . . .

Because the competency of Husband had been reasonably called into question, and because he had not been appointed a guardian *ad litem*, we conclude that decree is void. Because neither parties' competency had been established, we conclude that the trial court's equitable distribution was premature. . . .

QUESTIONS

1. What does it mean for an appeals court to consider an issue on a *sua sponte* basis?
2. Why did the court take this unusual step in the case?
3. What did the court decide about the divorce decree?
4. What was the basis for its decision?

The following case addresses the issue of whether sexual relations between two women comes within the definition of adultery as used in the New Hampshire divorce statute.

IN THE MATTER OF BLANCHFLOWER
150 N.H. 226, 834 A.2d 1010 (2003)

NADEAU, J.   •
. . . The record supports the following facts. The petitioner filed for divorce from the respondent on grounds of irreconcilable differences. He subsequently moved to amend the petition to assert the fault ground of adultery under RSA [Revised Statutes Annotated] 458:7, II. Specifically, the petitioner alleged that the respondent has been involved in a "continuing adulterous affair" with the co-respondent, a woman. . . . The co-respondent sought to dismiss the amended petition, contending that a homosexual relationship between two people, one of whom is married, does not constitute adultery. . . .

Before addressing the merits, we note this appeal is not about the status of homosexual relationships in our society or the formal recognition of homosexual unions. The narrow question before us is whether a homosexual sexual relationship between a married person and another constitutes adultery within the meaning of RSA 458:7 . . . II.

RSA 458:7 provides, in part: "A divorce from the bonds of matrimony shall be decreed in favor of the innocent party for any of the following causes:

. . . II. Adultery of either party." The statute does not define adultery. Id. Accordingly, we must discern its meaning according to our rules of statutory construction.

The plain and ordinary meaning of adultery is "voluntary sexual intercourse between a married man and someone other than his wife or between a married woman and someone other than her husband." Webster's Third New International Dictionary 30 (unabridged ed. 1961). Although the definition does not specifically state that the "someone" with whom one commits adultery must be of the opposite gender, it does require sexual intercourse.

The plain and ordinary meaning of sexual intercourse is "sexual connection esp. between humans: COITUS, COPULATION." Webster's Third New International Dictionary 2082. . . .

We note that the current criminal adultery statute still requires sexual intercourse. . . . Based upon the foregoing, we conclude that adultery under RSA 458:7, II does not include homosexual relationships.

We reject the petitioner's argument that an interpretation of adultery that excludes homosexual conduct subjects homosexuals and heterosexuals to unequal treatment, "contrary to New Hampshire's public policy of equality and prohibition of discrimination based on sex and sexual orientation." Homosexuals and heterosexuals engaging in the same acts are treated the same because our interpretation of the term "adultery" excludes all non-coital sex acts, whether between persons of the same or opposite gender. The only distinction is that persons of the same gender cannot, by definition, engage in the one act that constitutes adultery under the statute.

The petitioner also argues that "public policy would be well served by applying the same law to a cheating spouse, whether the promiscuous spouse chooses a paramour of the same sex or the opposite sex." This argument is tied to the premise, as argued by the petitioner, that "the purpose underlying [the adultery] fault ground is based upon the fundamental concept of marital loyalty and public policy's disfavor of one spouse's violation of the marriage contract with another." We have not, however, seen any such purpose expressed by the legislature. As noted above, the concept of adultery was premised upon a specific act. To include in that concept other acts of a sexual nature, whether between heterosexuals or homosexuals, would change beyond recognition this well-established ground for divorce and likely lead to countless new marital cases alleging adultery, for strategic purposes. . . .

The dissent defines adultery not as a specific act of intercourse, but as "extramarital intimate sexual activity with another." This standard would permit a hundred different judges and masters to decide just what individual acts are so sexually intimate as to meet the definition. The dilemma faced by Justice Stewart and his fellow justices applying their personal standards to the issue of pornography in movies demonstrates the value of a clear objective definition of adultery in marital cases. See Jacobellis v. Ohio, 378 U.S. 184, 12 L. Ed. 2d 793, 84 S. Ct. 1676 (1964).

We are also unpersuaded by the dissent's contention that "it is improbable that the legislature intended to require an innocent spouse in a divorce action to prove the specific intimate sexual acts in which the guilty spouse engaged.". . . [T]he dissent notes that adultery usually has no eyewitnesses and therefore "ordinarily must be proved by circumstantial evidence." While this is true, it does not support the dissent's point. For over a hundred and fifty years judges, lawyers and clients have understood that adultery meant intercourse as we have defined it. It is an act determined not by the subjective test of an individual justice but by an objective determination based upon the facts. What must be proved to establish adultery and what evidence may be used to prove it are separate issues. Adultery cases have always required proof of the specific sexual act engaged in, namely, sexual intercourse. That circumstantial evidence may be used to establish the act does not negate or undermine the requirement of proof that the act actually occurred. . . .

Brock, C.J., and Broderick, J., dissenting . . .

We respectfully dissent because we believe that the majority's narrow construction of the word "adultery" contravenes the legislature's intended purpose in sanctioning fault-based divorce for the protection of the injured spouse. . . .

To strictly adhere to the primary definition of adultery in the 1961 edition of Webster's Third New International Dictionary and a corollary definition of sexual intercourse, which on its face does not require coitus, is to avert one's eyes from the sexual realities of our world. . . .

New Hampshire permits both fault-based and no-fault divorces. . . . The purpose of permitting fault-based divorces is to provide some measure of relief to an innocent spouse for the offending conduct of a guilty spouse. . . . We should therefore view the purpose and fabric of our divorce law in a meaningful context, as the legislature presumably intended, and not so narrow our focus as to undermine its public goals.

From the perspective of the injured spouse, the very party fault-based divorce law is designed to protect, "an extramarital relationship . . . is just as devastating . . . irrespective of the specific sexual act performed by the promiscuous spouse or the sex of the new paramour." S.B. v. S.J.B., 258 N.J. Super. 151, 609 A.2d 124, 126 (N.J. Super. Ct. Ch. Div. 1992). . . . Indeed, to some, a homosexual betrayal may be more devastating. Accordingly, consistent with the overall purpose of New Hampshire's fault-based divorce law, we would interpret the word "adultery" in RSA 458:7, II to mean a spouse's extramarital intimate sexual activity with another, regardless of the specific intimate sexual acts performed, the marital status, or the gender of the third party. . . .

Defining the word "adultery" to include intimate extramarital homosexual sexual activity by a spouse is consonant . . . with the decisions of other courts that have considered this issue. . . .

The majority suggests that to define "adultery" so as to include intimate extramarital homosexual sexual activity by a spouse is to propose a test so vague as to be unworkable. Apparently, a similar test has been adopted in . . . three jurisdictions. . . . Further, while such a definition is more inclusive than one reliant solely upon heterosexual sexual intercourse, we do not believe that "intimate extramarital sexual activity" either requires a more explicit description or would be subject to such a widely varying judicial view. . . .

QUESTIONS

1. According to the court, why did the wife's conduct not come within the meaning of the term "adultery"? What did the court look to in reaching its decision?
2. Why did the dissent disagree with the majority's conclusion?

In this era of no-fault divorce, parties typically do not go to trial over the existence of grounds for divorce. In the following case, however, the court faced the somewhat unusual question of whether the husband's lack of good faith was sufficient to defeat his condonation defense.

LAWRENCE v. LAWRENCE
2006 Miss. App. LEXIS 633 (2006)

GRIFFIS, J., for the Court.

April and Andy were married on May 16, 1998. They had two children. Noah Andrew was born on July 19, 1999. Emma Katherine was born on July 30, 2000. . . .

In the spring of 2003, April and Andy separated for approximately a week. When Andy returned to the marital home, April confronted him about rumors of an affair. At first, Andy denied the affair, but later admitted the affair and begged forgiveness. On April 17, 2003, April filed her initial complaint for divorce on the grounds of adultery or, in the alternative, irreconcilable differences. April and Andy, even though the complaint for divorce was filed, continued to reside together and were not legally separated. Affidavits from April and Andy indicate that Andy admitted his affair, which occurred in 2002. They attempted to reconcile, but April's complaint for divorce was never dismissed.

In the fall of 2003, April began to ask Andy to leave the marital residence, and the divorce proceedings were resumed. They continued to reside in the same household.

In December of 2003, April met Brian Sellers. The following May, April moved from the marital home into a rental home in Caledonia.

In June of 2004, the chancellor entered a temporary order that granted April custody of the two minor children and ordered Andy to pay child support. For several months prior to the temporary order, Andy did not deposit his paycheck into the couple's joint bank account and did not provide any financial support for the children.

On August 4, 2004, Andy filed a motion for summary judgment. He claimed that he was entitled to judgment on the claim of adultery because April condoned his affair. The result was that Andy's adultery could no longer support the grounds for divorce pled in April's complaint for divorce.

ANALYSIS

April argued that condonation was conditional on Andy's continued good behavior. In Wood v. Wood, 495 So. 2d 503, 505 (Miss. 1986), the supreme court held:

> The defense of condonation is recognized in our law. Stribling v. Stribling, 215 So. 2d 869, 870 (Miss. 1968); Starr v. Starr, 206 Miss. 1, 39 So. 2d 520, 523 (1949). Condonation is the forgiveness of a marital wrong on the part of the wronged party. Condonation may be expressed or implied. . . .
>
> The mere resumption of residence does not constitute a condonation of past marital sins and does not act as a bar . . . to a divorce being granted. Compare Miss. Code Ann. §93-5-4 (1972). Condonation, even if a true condonation exists, is conditioned on the offending spouse's continued good behavior. If the offending party does not mend his or her ways and resumes the prior course of conduct, there is a revival of the grounds for divorce. Manning v. Manning, 160 Miss. 318, 321, 133 So. 673, 674 (1931).
>
> In practical effect, condonation places the offending spouse on a form of temporary probation. Any subsequent conduct within a reasonable time after resumption of cohabitation which evidences an intent not to perform

the conditions of the condonation in good faith, may be sufficient to avoid the defense of condonation. . . .

In her response to the motion for partial summary judgment, April offered her affidavit where she testified about her belief that Andy resumed the marital relationship "merely as a ploy to defeat the grounds of adultery" and that he "has continued to have an affair."

We conclude that April's affidavit presented a genuine issue of material fact and Andy was not entitled to a judgment as a matter of law. In *Wood*, the supreme court held that:

> [a]ny subsequent conduct within a reasonable time after resumption of cohabitation which evidences an intent not to perform the conditions of the condonation in good faith, may be sufficient to avoid the defense of condonation, even though the conduct so complained of in and of itself may not be grounds for divorce.

Wood, 495 So. 2d at 505. Based on this language, Andy's intent in the resumption of the marital relationship is indeed an issue to be determined by the chancellor. Simply engaging in the act of sex does not seal the defense of condonation. Thus, April's personal belief that Andy resumed the marital relationship "merely as a ploy to defeat the grounds of adultery" presents a genuine issue of material fact in dispute that does not entitle Andy to a judgment as a matter of law on his defense of condonation.

Accordingly, we reverse the chancellor's entry of a partial summary judgment, and we remand for further proceedings consistent therewith. . . .

QUESTIONS

1. What does the court mean when it says that "condonation places the offending spouse on a form of temporary probation"?
2. Why did the court reverse the chancellor's grant of partial summary judgment and remand the case? On remand, what must the chancellor take into account?

Endnotes

1. *See* Judith S. Wallerstein and Sandra Blakeslee, Second Chances—Men, Women, and Children a Decade After Divorce: Who Wins, Who Loses—and Why (1989).

2. Mary E. O'Connell, Alimony After No-Fault: A Practice in Search of a Theory, 23 New Eng. L. Rev. 437, 444-447 (1988).

3. *See* John Witte, Jr., The Reformation of Marriage Law in Martin Luther's Germany: Its Significance Then and Now, 4 J.L. & Religion 295 (Summer 1986).

4. Glenda Riley, Divorce: An American Tradition 9-15 (1991).

5. Norma Basch, Framing American Divorce: From the Revolutionary Generation to the Victorians 19-30 (1999).

6. Riley, *supra* note 4, at 53-84.

7. O'Connell, *supra* note 2, at 454-455.

8. Riley, *supra* note 4, at 108-112.

9. RGM v. DGM, 410 S.E.2d 564, 566-567 (S.C. 1991).

10. Whether Same-Sex Marital Infidelity Can Qualify as Adultery for Purposes of Family Provisions Governing Divorce, 100 Op. Att'y 105 (2015).

11. *See id.* at 112.

12. *Id.* at 114, citing Schadegg v. Schadegg, Civ. No. 159529, slip op. at 2-3 Mont. Cnty. Cir. Ct. August 15 (1997).

13. 135 S. Ct. 2584 (2015).

14. 100 Op. Att'y, *supra* note 10, at 114.

15. In the Matter of Blanchflower, 150 N.H. 226, 230, 834 A.2d 1010, 1013 (2003).

16. *Id.* at 1014 (dissenting opinion of Justices Brock and Broderick, citing S.B. v. S.J.B., 609 A.2d 124, 126 (N.J. Super. Ct. Ch. Div. 1992)). For further discussion, *see* Peter Nicolas, The Lavender Letter: Applying the Laws of Adultery to Same-Sex Couples and Same-Sex Conduct, 63 Fla. L. Rev. 97 (2011).

17. Homer H. Clark, Jr., The Law of Domestic Relations in the United States 503-506 (Hornbook Series, student ed., 1988).

18. *Id.* at 506-509.

19. It is worth noting that, before 1970, some states had amended their laws to permit divorce without proof of fault where either party had lived separate and apart for a certain period of time or where there had been an irremediable breakdown of the marriage. These earlier efforts are not generally regarded as a significant departure from the fault model because the changes were grafted piecemeal onto old laws, and considerations of fault continued to play a major role in decisions about spousal support and the division of assets.

20. *See* Lawrence M. Friedman, Rights of Passage: Divorce Laws in Historical Perspective, 63 Or. L. Rev. 649 (1984).

21. Katherine Shaw Spaht, Revolution and Counter-Revolution: The Future of Marriage in the Law, 49 Loy. L. Rev. 1, 49 (2003) citing Representative Dalman as quoted in 1997 Mich. Legis. Serv. 5217 (West 1997).

22. "The Marriage Movement: A Statement of Principles," 2000, Center for Marriage and Families at the Institute for American Values. http://center.americanvalues.org.

It should be noted that in 2015, this Statement was updated and renamed "Marriage Opportunity: The Moment for National Action" in an effort to unite liberals and conservatives around the cause of strengthening the institution of marriage based on the convergence of interests. As explained, conservatives need to embrace the reality that "gay marriage is here to stay," while liberals should recognize and be concerned about the fact that "aspirations to family formation are being stymied by wage stagnation and disappointing job prospects among working-class and less educated men. . . ." "Marriage Opportunity: The Moment for National Action," http://americanvalues.org/catalog/pdfs/Marriage-Opportunity.pdf, 1, 6 (accessed May, 2019).

23. Much has been written on both sides of the divorce reform debate, including the following works: Kimberly Diane White, Covenant Marriage: An Unnecessary Second Attempt at Fault-Based Divorce, 61 Ala. L. Rev. 869 (2010); Peter Nash Swisher, Marriage and Some Troubling Issues with No-Fault Divorce, 17 Regent U. L. Rev. 243 (2004/2005); Nicholas H. Wolfinger, The Next Blessings of No-Fault Divorce, 4 Whittier J. Child & Fam. Advoc. 407 (2005); Katherine Shaw Spaht, A Proposal: Legal Re-Regulation of the Content of Marriage, 18 Notre Dame J.L. Ethics & Pub. Poly. 243 (2004); Justin Wolfers and Betsey Stevenson, Bargaining in the Shadow of the Law: Divorce Laws and Family Distress 19 (Stanford Law and Economics Olin Working Paper No. 273; Stanford Law School, Public Law Working Paper No. 73, December 2003), http://www.nber.org/papers/w10175.pdf; Allen M. Parkman, Reforming Divorce Reform, 41 Santa Clara L. Rev. 379 (2001); James Hubie DiFonzo, Customized Marriage, 75 Ind. L. Rev. 875 (2000); Robert M. Gordon, Note, The Limits of Limits on Divorce, 107 Yale L.J. 1435 (1998).

24. Maggie Gallagher and Barbara Defoe Whitehead, End No-Fault Divorce?, First Things: The Journal of Religion and Public Life, August/September (1997) http://www.firstthings.com/article/2008/09/001-end-no-fault-divorce-4 (accessed Oct. 7, 2012).

25. Donna S. Hershkowitz and Drew R. Liebert, The Direction of Divorce Reform in California: From Fault to No-Fault . . . and Back Again?, Counsel Assembly Judiciary Committee, California State Legislature, http://www.assembly.ca.gov (click on Committee Directory, and then click on Committee on Judiciary, and then click on Hearing Reports). *See also* Stephen Bahr, Social Science Research on Family Dissolution: What It Shows and How It Might Be of Interest to Family Law Reformers, 4 J.L. Fam. Stud. 5, 8 (2002).

26. Wolfers and Stevenson, *supra* note 23, at 19. The authors of this study also found that the introduction of no-fault divorce led to a significant decline in female suicides; no such correlation was found for males.

27. *Id*. at 2.

28. Gallagher and Whitehead, *supra* note 24, at 6.

29. *Id*. at 5.

30. *Id*. at 6.

31. *Id*.

32. *See* Lynne Marie Kohm, On Mutual Consent to Divorce: A Debate with Two Sides to the Story, 8 Appalachian J.L. 32 (2008).

33. http://www.marriagesavers.org (accessed Dec. 17, 2015).

34. For a discussion of this research, *see* Alan J. Hawkins, Will Legislation to Encourage Premarital Education Strengthen Marriage and Reduce Divorce?, 9 J.L. Fam. Stud. 79 (2007).

35. *See, e.g.,* Nathan Bracken, Foundational Marriage: A Counteroffer to Covenant Marriage in Utah, 7 J.L. Fam. Stud. 427 (2005); and Katherine Shaw Spaht, Covenant Marriage Seven Years Later: Its as Yet Unfulfilled Promise, 65 La. L. Rev. 605, 628 (2005).

36. Katherine Shaw Spaht, The Last One Hundred Years: The Incredible Retreat of Law from the Regulation of Marriage, 63 La. L. Rev. 243, 261 (2003).

37. Spaht, Revolution and Counter-Revolution, *supra* note 21, at 53-54.

38. Katherine Shaw Spaht, *Mulieris Dignitatem*: The Vocation of Wife and Mother in a Legal Covenant Marriage, 8 Ave Maria L. Rev. 365, 367 (2010). As Spaht also discusses in her article, unique to the Louisiana law are provisions that "communicate to married couples who have chosen a more binding commitment than other couples the kind of behavior that is expected of them," including the imposition of greater familial obligations upon "the covenant wife who becomes a mother"—an identity that "finds a fuller expression in the law of covenant marriage." *Id*. at 366-367.

39. La. Rev. Stat. §9:272 (2004).

40. Spaht, Covenant Marriage Seven Years Later, *supra* note 36, at 629.

Chapter Five

Child Custody

In cases involving child **custody** and **visitation** disputes between divorcing parents, judges face the daunting task of allocating rights and responsibilities between two parents based upon the "best interest" of the child standard.[1] This is a child-centered approach that gives a judge flexibility to tailor a result that is geared toward meeting the specific needs of the children in any given family. On the flip side, the flexibility of the standard means that outcomes can be unpredictable and possibly subjective, thus infusing the process with a sense of indeterminacy.

Following an historical overview of the law of custody, this chapter focuses on the myriad dimensions of the best interest standard, including critiques of it and proposed alternatives. We also consider what happens when a "third party—namely a grandparent or stepparent—seeks ongoing contact with a child over the objection of a legal parent, as the best interest standard assumes that parties stand in equal legal relationship to the child in question, which is not the case in the third-party context.

Before proceeding, a word is in order regarding custody disputes in divorce cases between same-sex parents. Assuming that both spouses are the legal parents of the children in question, as with heterosexual parents, the case would be resolved based on the children's best interest. However, it is critical to recognize that even in a post-*Obergefell* world, the rights of many gay men and lesbians in relationship to the children they are co-parenting are far from certain. If only one partner is regarded as the legal parent, the other partner will most likely be relegated to a disadvantageous third-party status. We take up the issue of how one achieves recognition as a legal parent in Chapters 11 and 13.

■ Evolving Legal Standards

Paternal Preference

Our custody laws have roots in the Roman doctrine of *patria potestas*, which gave fathers the right of absolute control over their children. So complete was this authority that until the fourth century, fathers were entitled to sell their children or have them put to death. Although never vesting fathers with this degree of control over their children's lives, our early laws continued this legal tradition of paternal rights.

The colonial family was hierarchical in nature, and each member had a defined place in its internal structure. The husband/father was the "governor" of the household, and his wife and children occupied well-defined subordinate positions, subject to his unquestioned authority and control. A father had complete command over the education, training, and discipline of his children. He also owned his children's labor—a valuable right in an agrarian society where the world of work and home were essentially one and the same.

In turn, a father was charged with the responsibility of supporting his children and preparing them, particularly his sons, for passage into the world. In sharp contrast, mothers had no legal authority. As explained by William Blackstone, a mother was "entitled to no power, but only reverence and respect."[2]

During this time, custodial rights were understood in property terms: "Custody law held children to be dependent, subordinate beings, assets of estates in which fathers had a vested right."[3] During his lifetime, a father could assign the care and custody of his children to a third party regardless of the wishes of the children's mother, and he could do the same upon his death through his will. Upon family dissolution, the **paternal preference** rule gave fathers a near-absolute right to custody.

Courts and commentators advanced various theories to explain the undisputed legal supremacy of fathers. Their status was said to be divinely ordained or rooted in immutable laws of nature. As explained by one court:

> We are informed by the first elementary books we read, that the authority of the father is superior to that of the mother. It is the doctrine of all civilized nations. It is according to the revealed law and the law of nature, and it prevails even with the wandering savage who has received none of the lights of civilization.[4]

The lack of maternal rights can also be understood as a logical extension of the common law status of married women. How could a married woman, who herself was regarded as incapable of managing her own affairs and in need of male protection, be entrusted with responsibility and control over her children? In the eyes of the law, she was little more than a child herself.

Shift to Maternal Custody

In the late eighteenth century, the patriarchal family structure began to break down as the nation moved from an agrarian to an industrial society. As production moved from the family farm into the factory, the world of work became increasingly identified with men, and the world of home with women. Home was now seen as a sanctuary from the burdens of the harsh world in which women's gentle influence could flourish. Children, who had been seen both as economically valuable assets and as needing a father's stern corrective influence, began to be seen more as innocent beings in need of protection and nurture, and mothers replaced fathers as "the most powerful agent in developing a child's character."[5]

Gradually, the favored legal status of fathers gave way to a clear maternal preference. By the end of the nineteenth century, the common law doctrine of paternal rights had been displaced by the **tender years presumption**, which embodied the belief that children, particularly young children, belonged with their mothers. This shift enhanced the status of married women and curtailed male authority over the domestic realm. It also gave legal meaning to the mother-child bond, entitling women to more than "reverence and respect."

This presumption was expressly incorporated into some statutes, while others authorized the court to award custody to either parent, sometimes specifying that the controlling factor should be in the best interest of the child. However, through judicial decisions, the term **"best interest"** became virtually synonymous with maternal custody, at least with respect to young children, unless the mother was deemed unfit. In some jurisdictions, a preference for paternal custody continued where older children, particularly boys, were involved, as it was thought that the father could better prepare them for life beyond the home. Once established, maternal custody became the unquestioned norm until the latter part of the twentieth century.

The Modern Best Interest Test

By the 1970s, as fixed notions about proper roles for men and women began to break down, the tender years presumption lost favor. By 1990, virtually all states had eliminated the explicit use of the tender years presumption in favor of a gender-neutral best interest standard. Formally uncoupled from gender determinants, the best interest of the child standard is supposed to ensure that each case is resolved on its own merits, with neither parent being given an advantage based on assumptions about gender.

If parents reach an agreement regarding custody and visitation, a judge will review the terms at the divorce hearing (see Chapter 10) to determine whether they promote the best interest of the children. In most states, the judge conducting this review is not required to defer to the wishes of the parents as embodied in their agreement; rather, the agreement is simply viewed as expressive of their preferences and is only one of many factors in the assessment of best interest. Based, however, on the belief that parents are in a better position than the court to know what is best for their children, some states have begun to give more weight to their custodial preferences, by, for example, adopting a presumption that, without clear evidence to the contrary, the agreed-upon terms are in the best interest of the children.

Formulating the Test

The best interest test requires an analysis of a child's needs and an assessment of which parent can best meet those needs. It is intended to be a flexible, child-centered approach that allows a judge to take a child's individual circumstances into account when making a custody determination. The inherent flexibility of this approach allows for an individualized consideration of all relevant factors. On the flip side, the best interest standard has been criticized for being too vague and indeterminate, which means that judges have room to import their personal views into custody determinations, making results unpredictable and possibly idiosyncratic.

Some states have attempted to address this concern by adopting guidelines enumerating specific factors that a judge must consider in making a custody decision. The Michigan statute is a good example of this multifaceted approach. In determining custody, a judge must consider and enter findings of fact on each of the following:

> "[B]est interests of the child" means the sum total of the following factors to be considered, evaluated, and determined by the court:
> a. The love, affection, and other emotional ties existing between the parties and the child.
> b. The capacity and disposition of the parties involved to give the child love, affection, and guidance and to continue the education and raising of the child in his or her religion or creed, if any.
> c. The capacity and disposition of the parties involved to provide the child with food, clothing, medical care or other remedial care

recognized and permitted under the laws of this state in place of medical care, and other material needs.

d. The length of time the child has lived in a stable, satisfactory environment, and the desirability of maintaining continuity.

e. The permanence, as a family unit, of the existing or proposed custodial home or homes.

f. The moral fitness of the parties involved.

g. The mental and physical health of the parties involved.

h. The home, school, and community record of the child.

i. The reasonable preference of the child, if the court considers the child to be of sufficient age to express preference.

j. The willingness and ability of each of the parties to facilitate and encourage a close and continuing parent-child relationship between the child and the other parent or the child and the parents.

k. Domestic violence, regardless of whether the violence was directed against or witnessed by the child.

l. Any other factor considered by the court to be relevant to a particular child custody dispute.[6]

Although these statutes generally require a judge to consider each enumerated factor, they typically do not require judges to prioritize them or give them equal weight. Accordingly, a judge generally has the discretion to assign the weight to each factor that he or she believes it merits based on either the circumstances of the case or individual beliefs about what considerations are most important. For example, one judge might regard the preference of the child as the primary consideration, while another might attach little weight to it. Moreover, the factors do not lend themselves to precise definitions. For example, what does the term "satisfactory environment" mean? One judge might emphasize the emotional environment of a parent's home, while another might consider more tangible qualities, such as dwelling size. In short, although these statutes set out the framework within which custody determinations are to be made, judges nonetheless retain considerable decisional discretion based on the weight and meaning they assign to the individual statutory factors.

Applying the Test

In this section we will look more closely at some of the factors that judges tend to emphasize in custody determinations. These include:

- the parent-child bond;
- past caretaking;
- time availability;
- stability of environment;

- preference of the child; and
- domestic violence.

The Parent-Child Bond.   Important to any custody determination is the attempt to evaluate the strength and integrity of the bond that each parent has with his or her children. In some cases, such as where one parent is abusive or disengaged from the family, this task is easy. However, given that most parents have a deep attachment to their children, this assessment can be difficult and may require a multifaceted approach in which a judge weighs a variety of considerations, such as (1) the amount of time each parent spends with the children, (2) the quality and the appropriateness of the interactions, (3) the degree of emotional engagement, and (4) whom the child relies on for emotional and other kinds of essential support.

Past Caretaking.   Past caretaking has always been an important consideration in custody determinations. Responding to concerns about the vagueness of the best interest standards, some states now give greater weight to considerations of the caretaking role of each parent during the marriage, and favor the **primary caretaker**. Some states have accomplished this by statute, while others leave it to judicial discretion.[7] (See also the discussion of the primary caretaker presumption and the American Law Institute's approximation rule in the section entitled "Critique of and Alternative Approaches to the Best Interest Standard.")

A number of distinct, mutually supportive rationales support reliance on past caretaking as a critical factor in the decisional matrix. First, there is general agreement among experts that a child usually develops the strongest psychological bond with the parent who has been most involved with his or her daily care (i.e., the primary caretaker) and that preservation of this relationship is essential to a child's healthy development. This attachment theory "suggests that a strong, caring parent-child dyad leads to a strong secure attachment [and an emotionally secure child]. This same theory posits that if the care provided is unsupportive or unpredictable, then insecurity is manifested."[8] However, some commentators worry that the attachment theory is too simplistic and does not fully account for the complexity of human relations.

Predictability is another major reason that past caretaking has become an increasingly important consideration in custody determinations. Predictability is important for two distinct reasons. First is the belief that reliance on past caretaking will reduce some of the inherent uncertainty about how a child will be cared for following a divorce. A parent's prior commitment to providing primary care is seen as a reasonably reliable predictor of how he or she will respond to the child's needs in the future, whereas determining how a parent who has not been intimately involved with caretaking will respond is far more speculative. Accordingly, reliance on past caretaking patterns provides a protective buffer for children, carrying forward familiar rhythms and interactions.

Second, this predictability enables couples to enter into custody negotiations with a clearer sense of what they would be likely to gain or lose by going to court. According to some experts, this consideration may be particularly important for women as some studies have shown that mothers are likely to give up some economic benefits in order to secure custody of their children. If results were more predictable, going to court would be less of a risk, and there would be less need to sacrifice financial entitlements for custodial security. (See the discussion of the primary caretaker presumption later in this chapter.[9])

Lastly, reliance on past caretaking accords with the overall trend in favor of the private ordering of family relationships. By looking to the arrangements that the parties agreed on for the care of their children, greater weight is being given to what they believe (or, perhaps, more accurately, believed) makes sense for their family rather than to what a judge believes is best.

Time Availability.   The time that a parent has available to devote to his or her children is another important consideration. This is a sensible concern that tends to favor the parent with a less demanding work schedule, who has more flexibility to respond to the needs—both routine and unanticipated—of the children. It is likely that this parent is the one who has provided most of the past caretaking and thus has a primary attachment to the children.

Stability of Environment.   Children generally have a need for stability and continuity in the wake of divorce's dislocation. Accordingly, judges often give considerable weight to a parent's ability to maintain a stable home environment. The emphasis on stability may lead a judge to look with disfavor on a parent who has moved around a lot. This can be problematic where the frequency of moves is attributable to the economic strain occasioned by the marital breakup. In order to avoid penalizing a parent in this situation, it is important for judges to consider a number of factors, including intangible ones such as continuity of care, when assessing the stability of a child's environment.

Preference of the Child.   Given that the undisputed focus of a best interest inquiry is the child, an important consideration is how much weight should be given to a child's stated preference. This is a difficult question that has generated considerable controversy.

Historically, the custodial preferences of children carried little, if any, weight. This disregard of children's views reflected the traditional understanding of children as lacking an independent legal identity. As we have seen, children traditionally were defined by their dependent and subordinate status within the family unit, and they had no separate voice with which to express a preference. This understanding of children has changed over time. Children, especially as they reach their teen years, are now regarded as distinct legal persons with some degree of autonomy and say about their lives, including post-divorce custodial arrangements.

Today, all states allow for consideration of a child's wishes. Generally, there are no fixed rules about minimum qualifying ages, and many states require that a child's wishes be seriously considered once she or he reaches a certain age, usually 12 or 14. A few states give a child over the age of 14 the right to choose the parent with whom he or she wishes to live, and his or her choice will be disregarded only if that parent is deemed unfit. Even where not specified by statute or judicial decision, most lawyers believe there is no point in litigating a case where a child over the age of 14 has a clear preference, as a court will almost always respect his or her wishes.

Although chronological age is an important factor in determining whether a child's views will be elicited, and if elicited, what weight they will be given, it is not the only consideration. A judge might also look to the child's maturity, including his or her decision-making ability, and the articulated reasons for any expressed preference. Family circumstances, such as whether there is a history of violence or whether a child blames one parent for ending the marriage, may also be taken into account in assessing the reliability of the child's views.

The Debate over the Appropriate Role of Children. There are conflicting views about whether children should participate in custody disputes between their parents. The discussion is often framed as if there were only two possible options—that a child either participates in a decision-making capacity or does not do so at all. However, there are other approaches that give children a voice without requiring them to specify which parent they wish to live with. Before considering these options, we review some of the arguments that have been raised on both sides of the involvement debate, keeping in mind that these views generally assume an "all or nothing" approach.

Some experts believe that it is too stressful for children to be brought into a custody dispute. Children often have complex, shifting views regarding the nature of their relationship with each parent and, by being drawn into the conflict, may feel as if the weight of the world has been placed on their shoulders. Given that children often blame themselves for their parents' divorce, the concern is that participation will intensify their distress.

Another concern is that a child's stated preference may be shaped by considerations unrelated to best interest, such as fear of reprisal or worry about upsetting a parent perceived as sensitive. A child may also be subject to the undue influence of a parent or may choose a distant, disapproving parent as a way of winning that parent's love. A child may also identify with the parent who she or he perceives as being more powerful in order to avoid feeling powerless or like a "loser." This is of particular concern in cases involving domestic violence because a child may seek to avoid identification with the victim, who is perceived as weak and vulnerable, in order to enhance his or her own sense of security. This tendency may be more pronounced in boys, especially as they approach adolescence. A child also may be angry at the parent who initiated the divorce and may blame that parent for destroying the family. This anger, which may not be articulated, may influence the child to choose the "innocent" parent in order to get back at the other.

A further consideration is that judges, who usually are not experts in child psychology, will not be able to unearth these complex and often deeply buried motivations and may thus give too much weight to "surface" explanations. Although the use of experts can be helpful, their presence does not necessarily solve the problem. The complexity of a situation may not be fully revealed within the necessary timeframe for making a decision, and experts often reach conflicting conclusions, thus still leaving a judge with the job of sorting through competing understandings of a situation.

On the other hand, experts who believe the child's preference should be seriously considered argue that children are entitled to a say in a proceeding with such significant implications for their lives and that to do otherwise is paternalistic and demonstrates a lack of respect for the ability of children to participate in important decisions. They fear that if a child is not listened to, his or her true needs might never surface, since parents, although professing concern for the child, are often seeking to vindicate their own rights and fulfill their own needs. Custody battles may become a fight for supremacy between the parents, with the child as a shadow player. Parents may thus distort, deliberately or not, the wishes of the child to suit their own position.

Although recognizing the difficulties inherent in sorting through the motivational factors, those who favor eliciting the views of children believe that judges are capable of sifting through layers of meaning. They suggest that understanding the views of a child is no more challenging than sorting through other kinds of conflicting evidence, and that making sense of the entangled strands of a family's situation is the essence of the judicial function in a custody case.

Drawing on social science research, some experts have shifted the focus away from casting children as *decision makers* to focus on the importance of incorporating them as *participants* in the decisional process. According to these studies, children who are excluded from the process "complain about feeling isolated and lonely during the divorce process, and many older youngsters express anger and frustration about being left out."[10] Providing children with a structured mechanism for giving voice to both their feelings and possible arrangements can counteract these feelings, but inclusion must be more than a symbolic gesture. Children are entitled to expect that "both their parents and the professionals involved will listen with respect to their comments. When parents indicate that they do not value and respect their children's thinking, feelings, worries, and needs, it is unlikely to be helpful, and may create cynicism and anger."[11]

There are several different ways to involve children in the proceedings. One approach is for a judge to conduct an in-chamber interview with a child in order to try to ascertain his wishes and assess best interest. Although this approach is statutorily authorized in most states, it has fallen out of favor in recent years. Increasingly common is the use of a third-party professional—such as a guardian ad litem, mental health expert, mediator, or some combination thereof—who can engage the child in a meaningful discussion of what is going on and what the various options might be, without putting him or her in the difficult position of having to choose between parents. Thus, for example, if a shared custody arrangement is on the table, a child could be given a chance to express his or her views, such as that the arrangement involves too many switches between households and that fewer transfers would be less disruptive.[12]

Another option would be the actual appointment of a lawyer for a child who is the subject of a custody dispute. Although many states make some provision for the appointment of counsel in this context, it does not generally occur as a routine matter, despite the view among many divorce professionals that this is best approach to ensuring that the needs of a child are fully taken into account. Where appointed, an attorney may be unclear about his or her role, and "struggle with the very real contradictions between their perceived roles as lawyer, protector, investigator, and surrogate decision maker."[13] Seeking to alleviate this potential role confusion, the American Bar Association's *Standards of Practice for Lawyers Representing Children in Child Custody Cases* (Standards) makes a clear distinction between two types of appointments. As explained, a lawyer can either be appointed as "child's attorney," in which case his or her role is to provide "independent legal representation in a traditional attorney-client relationship, giving the child a strong voice in the proceeding," or as a "best-interest attorney," in which case he or she "independently investigates, assesses and advocates the child's best interest. . . ."[14] Regardless of which approach is followed, the *Standards* make clear that the attorney should avoid acting as a witness but "instead should offer traditional evidence-based legal arguments such as other lawyers make."[15]

Domestic Violence.   Traditionally, courts did not consider inter-spousal violence—as distinct from physical abuse of the child—relevant to the determination of best interest. Spousal abuse was seen as connected to the marital relationship, with little or no spillover effect into the parent-child arena. However, new understandings of the dynamics of abuse have led to important changes in the law, and whether through judicial decision or legislative enactment, courts in most states are now required to take spousal violence into account when making custody determination. This shift reflects the reality that, even if not themselves direct victims of violence, many children are exposed to acts of parental violence, and that the exposure itself may have enduring negative consequences. Accordingly, in contrast to the historic disassociation of spousal abuse from the well-being of children, the contemporary approach embodies the view that "the perpetrator of violence against any family member engages in unacceptable behavior that violates his . . . obligations as a parent."[16]

According to the research, somewhere between 70 and 87 percent of children in homes where domestic abuse is present have witnessed violence against their mothers,[17] with many of these children witnessing up to half of the incidents that take place.[18] This exposure can have a significant adverse impact on children. According to one early study, "[c]hildren who witness violence between their parents . . . are no less victimized than children who are direct victims of abuse. All our findings show that children from violent homes retain searing memories of violence between their parents."[19] Since then, researchers have confirmed that this victimization has serious emotional and developmental implications. Children exposed to domestic violence are at greater risk of engaging in aggressive and destructive "externally" directed behaviors, such as bullying and assaultive conduct. They also suffer from "internally" directed problems, including depression and anxiety, and they may suffer from post-traumatic stress disorder.[20]

Other negative outcomes include cognitive and behavioral delays, which can affect a child's functioning in school and ability to develop friendships. These consequences may vary with age. Thus, for example, babies and very young children may "develop fear of separation or other new fears," while preschool children "who have witnessed domestic violence have been shown to perform less well on tests of verbal intelligence . . . and to be less empathetic and less able to make accurate social inferences than children from nonviolent homes." They are also "more likely to express negative feelings, to play aggressively, to withdraw from others, and to insult or name-call than nonexposed children." Once they reach school age, exposed children "have more academic difficulties than their peers from nonviolent homes and are also compromised in their ability to judge right from wrong."[21]

Another serious concern is that children who are exposed to battering are at greater risk of both becoming abusers and being abused themselves in intimate relationships. According to one study, about one-half of the children who had witnessed violence between their parents experienced violence in their own adult intimate relationships, the boys as abusers and the girls generally as victims.[22]

In addition to directly impacting the well-being of children, partner abuse has other important implications for child custody determinations. First, men who abuse their partners are more likely to abuse their children. According to two observational studies, "fathers who were violent with their partners were also more physically and emotionally aggressive in interactions with their children."[23] There is also a positive correlation between the severity of the partner abuse and the severity of the child abuse.[24] Of additional concern is a potentially heightened risk of sexual abuse, particularly if substance abuse is involved. Second, abusive ex-spouses are particularly likely to use a range of strategies to try and "undermine the victim's parenting role" in order to estrange the children from that parent.[25]

Also highly relevant is the fact that spousal abuse does not necessarily end upon separation and divorce; in fact, "it is well documented that separation can serve as a catalyst for increased violence" and that "escalated abuse by the batterer as a response to actual or perceived separation is so common that experts have coined the phrase 'separation assault' to describe it."[26] As a corollary, in a tactic that is referred to referred to "litigation abuse," which is "the use of the legal system as a tool of coercive control over the victim,"[27] an abuser may seek to use custody proceedings as a vehicle for maintaining his or her authority over the other parent, particularly since family courts typically allow either party to request multiple hearings in order to ensure that the needs of the children are being accounted for.[28]

Today there is a general agreement that an abusive parent's right of access to the children may need to be limited in order to safeguard the well-being of the abused parent. In turn, paying attention to the safety of the custodial parent has multiple implications for the well-being of children. Not only will this vigilance shield children from continuing exposure to violence, and the associated risk of harm, the reduced threat of violence may well enhance the ability of a caretaker parent to focus on the needs of her children.

Accordingly, the custody statutes in virtually all states now require consideration of domestic violence when determining best interest. These statutes generally take one of two approaches. One approach is to include domestic violence as a factor in the best interest calculus, with a few statutes directing that it be given more weight than other considerations. Of course, as with the best interest standard generally, this approach vests considerable discretion in the judge, although the discretion is limited somewhat if she or he must weigh this factor more heavily than other considerations.

The other approach is to create a rebuttable presumption against awarding sole or joint custody to a parent who has been the perpetrator of domestic violence. Although this statutory approach may appear to take domestic violence more seriously than where it is simply included as a factor for consideration, there is considerable variation from jurisdiction to jurisdiction. For example, in some states, the presumption will only be triggered where there has been physical violence or threats of physical violence; accordingly, other kinds of abusive behavior, such as stalking, do not trigger it. Other jurisdictions require that there be more than a single incident of abuse before the presumption is triggered, or even that the perpetrator have been convicted of abuse. The triggering of the presumption can become particularly tricky if it appears that both parents have engaged in violent behavior toward the other. Most likely it will be regarded as non-applicable; however, the state of Louisiana has adopted a "primary aggressor" provision, which requires the court to determine if one parent is more responsible for the abuse, with the other acting primarily in self-defense.[29]

Statutes also vary with respect to what must be shown to rebut the presumption. A party might, for example, be able to rebut the presumption based upon the successful completion of a batterer's treatment program or a drug or alcohol program. However, if the presumption is rebutted, the statute may require that domestic violence be considered as a factor in the best interest calculus.[30]

Factoring Parental Characteristics/Identities into the Best Interest Test

In determining best interest, it is not uncommon for a parent to argue that some aspect of the other parent's lifestyle or life circumstances would have a detrimental impact on the children, and/or to also claim that conversely he or she is better positioned to meet the needs of the children based on his or her own life circumstances. These kinds of arguments raise the question as to what weight, if any, a judge should give to a parent's lifestyle or life circumstances when determining best interest, especially if these considerations place the parent outside what can loosely be referred to as the "mainstream." Are these matters of morality relevant? Is it appropriate for a judge to base decisions on his or her own views about what constitutes a proper environment for a child? Should a judge be allowed to reflect popular community views—for example, that children should be raised by heterosexual parents?

Judges are not supposed to make custody decisions based on their own subjective sense of what is right for a child, or on their assessment of community standards, as these determinations would embody a judge's own personal view of the world, and would result in highly idiosyncratic and unpredictable outcomes. To prevent this kind of subjective decision making, the basic rule is that there must be a direct **nexus** (or connection) between the parental attribute in question and the well-being of the child. This approach is intended to limit judicial discretion and keep the child's needs at the center of the decision-making process.

However, it is worth considering whether it is realistic to think that judges can completely disregard their own views when deciding the cases that come before them. For example, what if a judge believes that interracial or same-sex relationships are inherently immoral and disruptive of the social order—how likely is it that he or she will be truly able to set aside these views and dispassionately consider whether an award of custody to a parent in such a relationship advances the child's best interest?

Considerations of Race and Culture.   In the landmark case of Palmore v. Sidoti,[31] the United States Supreme Court reversed a Florida trial court decision transferring custody of a young girl from her mother to her father because the mother, who was white, married a black man subsequent to the parties' divorce. In transferring custody, the trial court focused on the possibility that the child would suffer from the stigma of living in a racially mixed household, especially once she began school. In reversing the decision, the Supreme Court made clear that social prejudice should not determine custody outcomes and that the equal protection clause prohibits giving effect to personal bias through the medium of custody adjudications. Moreover, the Court made clear that harm to a child cannot be assumed even though racial prejudice may subject him or her to "a variety of pressures and stresses not present if the child were living with parents of the same racial or ethnic origin."[32]

Although unambivalent in condemning custody decisions premised on racial prejudice, the *Palmore* decision has not been interpreted to mean that race is *never* a permissible consideration in custody determinations. For example, in the case of Gambla v. Woodson, an Illinois appeals court held in a custody dispute involving a biracial child, that although it would have been inappropriate for the trial court to have awarded custody to the mother "solely because she is African-American," it was not in error for having taken into account the fact that she could provide Kira with a "breadth of cultural knowledge and experience" that the father could not offer her, and was therefore in a better position to prepare her daughter for existing "as a biracial woman in a society that is sometimes hostile to such individuals."[33] In responding to *Gambla* and the related cases, one commentator raises an interesting cautionary note, writing that "the issue is not whether a parent's ethnic, or cultural background renders him/her better able to meet the emotional needs of a biracial child, but whether a parent is willing and able to expose a child to his/her heritage and culture to ensure that the child learns the skills s/he will need as a racial minority."[34] In short, the author cautions against using a parent's background as an automatic proxy for being the more suitable parent.

Paralleling this result, the custody statutes in a few states expressly identify a child's cultural background as one of the factors that is to be taken into account when assessing which parent is in a better position to meet the child's needs. In addition, in states where culture is not included as an express statutory factor, some courts have woven a consideration of a child's cultural needs into other statutory criteria for assessing best interest. Thus, for example, in evaluating the importance of maintaining a child's ongoing connection with the community in which he or she lives, a court might include a consideration of the extent to which that community offers the child an opportunity to "interact with others who share his or her heritage."[35]

Sexual Activity: Heterosexual. Another important question is what weight, if any, should a judge give to the sexual behavior of a parent seeking custody of a minor child? The majority view is that sexual behavior by itself or the fact that a parent is living with a partner she or he is not married to is not relevant unless a detrimental effect on the child or the parent-child relationship is clearly established. In requiring proof of a nexus between the behavior of the parent and the well-being of the child, harm to the child is not to be presumed from the fact that the parent is engaged in a nonmarital relationship, as this would be tantamount to a moral pronouncement embodying the judge's subjective views rather than an assessment of the parent's actual ability to care for the child. Rather, such conduct is relevant only where detriment can be shown—for example, where sexual activity occurs in front of the children or where the parent leaves the children on their own in order to pursue a relationship.

Judges may respond somewhat differently if a parent is engaged in a series of sexual relationships, particularly if they are of the one-night-stand variety. Uneasiness about this kind of conduct may result in a judge's presuming harm rather than requiring actual proof of a detrimental impact on the child.

Gay and Lesbian Parents. Although the unquestioned majority approach is that a parent's involvement in a heterosexual dating or cohabiting relationship will not impact his or her ability to obtain or maintain custody absent a clear showing that this involvement somehow harms the child, the law's approach has been far more varied when it comes to gay and lesbian parents. For years, the dominant approach was to presume, without requiring proof of harm, that it was bad for a child to be raised by a gay or lesbian parent. This is frequently referred to as the **per se approach**—in which harm is assumed to flow from the parent's conduct without requiring proof of actual detriment.

This approach was premised on a number of concerns. Foremost was the belief that homosexuality is immoral and unnatural and that children must be protected from its influence. A related concern was that children of gay parents were likely to become gay or sexually dysfunctional. The issue of stigma—that a child raised by a gay or lesbian parent will be the object of scorn and derision—was also frequently raised. For example, in the 1995 *Bottoms* case,[36] which involved a grandmother who sought to obtain custody of her grandchild from her lesbian daughter, the Supreme Court of Virginia, although purporting to reject the per se approach, expressed one of the animating fears: "[L]iving daily under conditions stemming from active lesbianism may impose a burden upon a child by reason of the 'social condemnation' attached to such an arrangement, which will inevitably afflict the child's relationship with its 'peers and the community at large.'"[37]

In a twist on the per se approach, some courts instead have focused on a parent's conduct, rather than on his or her sexual orientation itself, and been willing to award custody so long as the parent agreed not to engage in any activity that might reveal his or her orientation, such as any displays of affection in front of the children or participation in any "gay-identified" activities. Of course, one might reasonably ask if this is a distinction without much of a difference given that a parent is being required to suppress his or her identity as a condition of custody.

Although not all jurisdictions have formally repudiated either of these approaches, they are presumptively unconstitutional under *Obergefell*, as they clearly discriminate against gay and lesbian parents. This equality mandate is further bolstered by evidence-based research showing that "the family environments provided by lesbian and gay parents are as likely as those provided by heterosexual parents to foster and promote children's psychological well-being."[38]

Of course, the possibility always exists that a judge in a nexus state will deny custody based on anti-gay sentiment and then mask the true basis of the decision by articulating reasons unrelated to sexual identity. According to the dissenting justice, this is precisely what occurred in McGriff v. McGriff,[39] a 2004 case from Idaho, in which the mother (Shawn) sought to modify a joint custody arrangement because the father (Theron) was now cohabiting with his male partner. Although the majority of the justices on the Idaho Supreme Court accepted the judge magistrate's assertion that he was not transferring sole custody to the mother because of the father's sexual orientation, the dissenting justice vigorously disagreed:

Although it is clear that Shawn's petition is based on Theron's homosexuality, the majority upholds the magistrate's decision, which clearly appears to take Theron's homosexuality into consideration. Immediately after stating that homosexuality did not play a role in its holding, the magistrate stated, "However, [Theron's] decision to openly co-habit with Nick Case, his partner, is a change in circumstances which will generate questions from the girls and their friends regarding their conservative culture and morays [sic] in which the children live."[40]

As further evidence of the pervasive influence of the father's sexual orientation on the custody outcome, the dissenting justice in *McGriff* also noted that the father's visitation rights were contingent upon his domestic arrangements. In a rebuke to the majority, the dissenting justice states that "[i]f Theron's sexual orientation is not a factor, it is disingenuous that Theron may only exercise his visitation rights if he does not live with his male partner. The majority somewhat incredulously states that the limitation has nothing to do with Theron's homosexuality, rather it is a consequence of hang-up phone calls allegedly made by Theron's partner to [the mother]. . . ."[41]

Religion.   The issue of religion usually comes up in custody disputes in one of two ways. A parent may claim that he or she can best meet the religious needs of the child and should therefore be awarded custody. Alternatively, a parent may claim that the religion of the other parent is detrimental to the child or goes against the child's established identity, and should therefore disqualify that parent from custodial consideration. In the first situation, religion is presented as a positive, qualifying factor; in the second, it is presented as a negative, disqualifying one.[42]

In evaluating these claims, a court becomes involved in a delicate and sensitive task, as it must respect the first amendment rights of both parents. This amendment (which is applied to the states through the due process clause of the fourteenth amendment) prevents state interference with an individual's freedom of religion and undue state involvement with religion (e.g., expressing a preference for one religion over another). Absent a compelling interest, a state must remain neutral and uninvolved where religion is concerned.

Where a parent raises religion as a qualifying factor, it cannot be the sole custodial determinant because the judge would be expressing a preference for the religion of one parent over the religion of the other or over the lack of religious involvement. Moreover, the court would be giving preferential weight to religion, saying, in effect, that it is the most important aspect of a child's upbringing.

Must then a court disregard what a parent has to offer by way of religious education and guidance? The generally accepted view is that although a court may not make a value judgment about religion (or the lack thereof) and cannot presume that one parent is better equipped to meet a child's religious needs, it may consider a child's actual religious needs and determine which parent can best meet them. Accordingly, where religion is an established part of a child's life, matching parent to child in this regard is one aspect of determining who can best provide stability and continuity of care. Thus, for example, if a child regularly attends religious services and educational classes, the court might look at which parent has been actively involved with these activities, much as it would evaluate parental involvement in other areas of the child's life. The essential concern is determining which parent will best be able to meet the ongoing needs of the child, without making a value judgment about the kind of religious upbringing a child should have.

Where religion is raised as a disqualifying factor, the parent often belongs to a religion that is considered outside of the mainstream by the parent seeking custody. Typically, the nonmember parent argues that the other's religious beliefs or practices pose a threat of harm to the child's emotional, physical, or psychological well-being. For example, a common concern is that a child will be isolated from his or her peers by restrictions that prohibit certain activities, such as participation in school celebrations, watching television, or associating with nonmembers. The parent seeking custody may also fear that the child will be alienated from him or her if the religion of the other parent espouses that, as a nonbeliever, he or she is evil and will suffer eternal consequences.

Most courts employ a nexus approach in these cases. A parent must show actual harm before the other parent's religious practices are considered relevant. At least in theory, this avoids the risk that a court will make value judgments about a parent's religion. Other courts employ a somewhat less exacting standard and may disqualify a parent if his or her religious beliefs and practices are shown to pose a substantial or reasonable likelihood of harm. Even under this lower standard, however, general assertions about potential isolation or confusion from being raised in a "different" environment should not be given legal effect.

Under the risk of harm standard, a number of cases have dealt with the difficult question of how to evaluate the potential risk when the parent seeking custody belongs to a religion that prohibits certain medical practices, such as blood transfusions. Some courts have held that where there is no evidence of medical need, the risk is too speculative to justify a denial of custody on that ground alone. For example, in the 1995 case of Garrett v. Garrett, the Nebraska Court of Appeals stated with respect to the award of custody to a mother who was a practicing Jehovah's Witness:

> . . . [I]n order for Jeanne's religion to constitute a ground for awarding custody to Larry, we must be able to determine from the record

that the Jehovah's Witness religion as practiced by Jeanne constitutes an immediate and substantial threat to the minor children's temporal well-being.

As evidence of an immediate and substantial threat to the minor children, Larry makes reference to the fact that even in the case of a medical emergency, Jeanne would refuse to consent to any of the children's receiving a blood transfusion. . . .

No evidence was presented showing that any of the minor children were prone to accidents or plagued with any sort of an affliction that might necessitate a blood transfusion in the near future. We cannot decide this case based on some hypothetical future accident or illness which might necessitate such treatment.[43]

On the other hand, some courts have found that such a belief, in and of itself, poses a substantial risk of harm and do not require specific proof that a child is actually in need of a religiously prohibited medical procedure.

Disability/Illness.   In keeping with the nexus approach, the basic rule with regard to considerations of parental illness or disability is that it is not a relevant consideration unless a direct connection between a parent's health condition and harm to the child can be established. Thus, for example, the fact that a parent is taking medication for depression should be irrelevant; however, if a parent is ravaged by depression, and thus unable to care for his or her child, then there may be a demonstrable nexus between the parent's condition and the well-being of the child.

As eloquently expressed by the Supreme Court of California in the case of In re Marriage of Carney, which involved a parent who had become a quadriplegic following an accident: "If a person has a physical handicap it is impermissible for the court simply to rely on that condition as prima facie evidence of the person's unfitness as a parent. . . . [R]ather, in all cases the court must view the handicapped person as an individual and the family as a whole"; moreover, it is a mistake to "assume that the parent's handicap inevitably handicaps the child."[44]

A number of commentators have raised the concern that there is considerable bias against parents with disabilities, who are often presumed to be less able than nondisabled parents to provide loving and competent care for their children, despite a body of research showing that outcomes for children are similar. For example, a common assumption is that a child of an ill or disabled parent will become "parentified," meaning that roles will be reserved and the child will be forced into that of caretaker, even in the absence of any evidence to show this has occurred.[45] As was the case with gay and lesbian parents, it is thus argued that considerable educational work needs to be done to counter biases and misperceptions that may function to deprive parents with serious illness or disabilities of their custodial rights.

Critiques of and Alternative Approaches to the Best Interest Standard

As the above discussion suggests, the best interest standard has been subject to serious criticisms, including that it is gender-biased and that its open-ended nature means that results are often unpredictable and idiosyncratic. In this section, we consider these critiques and look at two possible alternative approaches: the **primary caretaker presumption** and the American Law Institute's (ALI) "approximation" rule, which are designed to offer greater predictability. In turn, it is hoped that greater outcome certainty will de-escalate parental conflict as there is, at least in theory, less room for subjective assessments of who is the "better" parent.

Gender Bias

Although the best interest standard is gender neutral on its face, concerns continue to be raised that judges import gender bias into their custody decisions. Fathers' rights groups argue that fathers are often less valued as parents than mothers and that judges often assume men cannot be primary caretakers. They thus argue that despite gender-neutral laws, the concept of best interest remains linked to beliefs about the natural superiority of maternal nurturing and caretaking abilities.

On the other hand, many women's groups argue that when fathers seek custody, they are often favored by judges, especially when a mother works outside the home, as women are held to a higher parenting standard than men. Accordingly, an employed mother may be regarded as unsatisfied with her role as mother and as being more concerned with gratifying her own needs than caring for her children. Exacerbating this problem, they note that fathers may get "extra credit" for the time they spend with their children, as this contribution is seen as "special"—as being over and above what is expected of them as men. This double standard thus penalizes mothers for time spent away from their children while unduly rewarding fathers for time spent with them.

Lack of Predictability

The other key critique of the best interest standard is its unpredictability. (Note the connection between these two critiques, since it is the lack of clear standards that arguably enables gender bias to influence custody outcomes.) On the positive side, unpredictability is a function of the standard's flexibility, which permits a judge to tailor results to the circumstances of an individual case. This can be very helpful given the complexity and variability of family relationships. On the other hand, as suggested earlier, it also means that judges have considerable room to make decisions that reflect their personal views of what is best for a child.

Consider the following situation. A couple has two children in grade school and live in a middle-class suburb. The father is employed full time and the mother is a stay-at-home parent. Both parents are kind and loving, but the primary attachment is to the mother. Both parents want sole custody. If the father is awarded custody, he will be able to remain in the home and to offer the children the presumed advantages of a middle-class lifestyle, including keeping the children in the school they presently attend. If the mother is awarded custody, she will need to move to a less expensive community where the schools are not as good because, even with child support and possible part-time employment, she will not be able to afford the home they live in.

What is the likely outcome? Does the best interest standard compel one result over the other? The answer is hard to predict because the outcome depends on whether the judge regards continuity of caretaking or continuity of home, school, and community as more important. Given the flexibility of the standard, and the corresponding decisional discretion of judges, either outcome could be justified as serving the children's best interest.

As noted in the earlier discussion about the past caretaking factor, the indeterminacy of the best interest standard has significant implications for the settlement process (see Chapter 10). If the outcome cannot be predicted with some degree of certainty, then it means that custody negotiations are taking place in the absence of a transparent decisional framework, thus making it difficult for the parties to assess what they stand to gain or lose as they consider various proposals. In significant part, this problem has given rise to the formulation of two alternatives standards—the primary caretaker presumption and the ALI's approximation rule—that seek to make custody outcomes more predictable.

The Primary Caretaker Presumption

Emerging out of dissatisfaction with the vagaries of the best interest standard, a number of states have considered adopting a custodial presumption in favor of the parent who has been the primary caretaker. Under this standard, primary caretaking would be the sole determinant of best interest.

In 1981, in the leading case of Garska v. McCoy,[46] the state of West Virginia became the first state to adopt the primary caretaker standard (although it has since moved to the ALI approximation rule). In adopting this standard, the *Garska* court focused on the harm caused to the primary care parent by the unpredictability of the best interest test:

The loss of children is a terrifying specter to concerned and loving parents; however, it is particularly terrifying to the primary caretaker parent, who, by virtue of the caretaking function, was closest to the child before the divorce. . . . Our experience instructs us that uncertainty about the outcome of custody disputes leads to the irresistible temptation to trade the custody of the child in return for lower alimony and child support payment.[47]

In anchoring custody outcomes to a fixed standard, the court was thus seeking to prevent custody from being used as a bargaining weapon to extract economic concessions from the primary caretaker parent in order to ensure a favorable custody result.

This presumption has been praised for its recognition of the undervalued job of parenting and the importance of the bond between children and their primary caregivers. It has also been praised for introducing certainty into the process and protecting the often-vulnerable economic status of primary caretaking parents. However, the presumption has also been criticized. As with past caretaking, some have critiqued the presumption as overly mechanistic and as failing to account for the complexity of parent-child relationships. Fathers' rights groups have attacked the presumption for being gender-biased, asserting that it is a thinly disguised effort to reintroduce the tender years presumption to the detriment of fathers.[48] Others disagree, noting that if a father is the primary caregiver, the presumption will favor him. Moreover, it is noted that although more mothers than fathers might end up with custody under the presumption, this would reflect the actuality of how families allocate caretaking responsibilities rather than generalized assumptions about gender-appropriate roles.

It has also been argued that the presumption can work against women as well. Although a stay-at-home mom, or one who is employed on a very part-time basis, would clearly be identified as the primary caretaker, the concern is that a judge may not recognize that a woman who works full time may nonetheless still be the primary caregiver. The judge may assume that the world of work and home are incompatible, thus rendering invisible a woman's continued domestic and caretaking responsibilities.

Despite the considerable interest and discussion that the primary caretaker presumption has generated, states have not rushed to adopt it. Nonetheless, it has contributed to ongoing discussions and efforts to reformulate the best interest standard, including the ALI's approximation rule.

The American Law Institute's Approximation Rule

In 2002, after more than a decade of research, the prestigious American Law Institute published the *Principles of the Law of Family Dissolution: Analysis and Recommendations* in order to bring "conceptual clarification and improved adaptation to social needs" to the dissolution process.[49] With respect to custody, the Principles recommend shifting from the best interest standard to a more objective "approximation" standard that would allocate custodial responsibilities between divorcing parents in rough proportion to the amount of time each parent spent engaged in caretaking responsibilities during the marriage. In short, the post-divorce parenting arrangement would *approximate* their pre-divorce arrangement. To date, West Virginia (previously the only state to formally adopt a primary caretaker presumption) is the only state to have formally adopted this approach. Accordingly, if parents have been unable to reach an agreement, the court is required to "allocate custodial responsibility so that the proportion of custodial time the child spends with each parent approximates the proportion of time each parent spent performing caretaking functions for the child prior to the parents' separation," unless such an arrangement would be "manifestly harmful to the child."[50]

Proponents of the approximation approach, argue that it injects a strong measure of predictability into what is currently a highly unpredictable process. In turn, this would yield a clearer framework for negotiations and enable parties to make informed decisions about what they are likely to lose or gain by seeking a judicial resolution of the dispute. With the result more predictable, proponents argue that primary caretakers will be less likely to bargain away economic rights in order to secure custody, thus promoting outcomes that are related to the needs of children, rather than to the bargaining positions of the parties. They also argue that this approach would provide children with greater stability and continuity of care because, to the extent it is possible, their parents would continue to play the same role in their lives that they did prior to the divorce. In short, children would be buffered from some of the radical reconfiguring of the parent-child relationship that so often accompanies a divorce.

However, some important concerns have also been raised about the approximation rule. First, some commentators worry that it is too deferential to parents and not sufficiently child-centered. What if, for example, past caretaking arrangements were adopted to meet the need of the parents rather than to provide optimal care for the children? What if other ways of allocating custodial responsibilities would be better for the children? However, reflecting what is believed to be the rule's overly mechanistic approach to determining custody, these kinds of considerations would not be relevant. Another important question is whether it is overly optimistic to assume that arrangements that worked when the parents presumably got along with one another will continue to work in the aftermath of dissolution when parental cooperation and goodwill is apt to be at a minimum. (Note: This concern also applies to the more familiar joint custody context and will be developed further in that section.)

Additionally, as with the primary caretaker presumption, the argument is made that this approach is simply an effort to sneak the tender years presumption back into custody determinations. However, once again, proponents argue that if mothers end up with more custodial time as a result of the approximation rule, this outcome reflects the reality of existing caretaking arrangements that the parties themselves decided upon, rather than suggesting a built-in gender bias in favor of women.[51]

Custody and Visitation Arrangements

Resolution of a custody case becomes even more complex when one takes the variety of custodial and visitation arrangements that are available into account. Traditionally, custody was essentially a unitary concept—one parent, usually the mother, was responsible for raising the child and making all significant decisions affecting the child's life, and the other parent simply visited.

However, beginning in the 1970s, the wisdom of allocating parental roles along such lines was questioned, and joint custody emerged as an approach that would enable children to maintain an ongoing relationship with both parents following a divorce. By 1990, most jurisdictions had amended their custody laws to include joint custody as an option, and some created a presumption that joint custody is in the best interest of the child, although some of these laws have since been repealed. In this section we focus on the actual working out of custody and visitation arrangements.

Physical and Legal Custody Distinguished

For the sake of clarity, the terms physical and legal custody will initially be defined in reference to one parent, but as will become apparent, either can be shared. Also, you should be aware that there has been some move away from the traditional terminology, in part to reflect the current emphasis on cooperative post-divorce parenting. Thus, for example, the ALI Principles use the term "custodial responsibility" instead of physical custody, and the term "decision-making responsibility" for legal custody. Also, physical custody is now sometimes referred to as residential custody.

Physical custody refers to where a child lives. A parent with physical custody maintains a primary residence for the child and is generally responsible for the child's daily care. With physical custody comes the authority to make all of the day-to-day decisions that arise in the course of caring for a child.

Legal custody refers to decision-making authority. Whereas physical custody incorporates the right to make routine decisions, legal custody gives a parent the right to make major decisions affecting the health, welfare, and education of a child, such as whether a child should go to private school or begin mental health counseling. As a general rule, major decisions are distinguished from day-to-day decisions by their importance and their nonrepetitive nature, although, as discussed in the following section, this distinction is often easier to state than to apply.

Sole and Joint Custody Distinguished

The term **sole custody** refers to the vesting of custodial rights in one parent; either legal or physical custody can be sole. With an award of *sole physical custody*, the child lives with one parent and that parent has primary caretaking responsibility. With an award of *sole legal custody*, one parent has the authority to make all of the major decisions affecting the child. Where both custodies are vested in one parent, the other parent will generally have visitation rights without significant parenting responsibilities.

Joint custody refers to the sharing of rights and responsibilities; both legal and physical custody can be allocated on a joint basis. *Joint legal custody* denotes the sharing of decision-making authority, and *joint physical custody* denotes the sharing of the day-to-day responsibility for raising a child.

A Closer Look at Shared Custody Arrangements

Two shared custody arrangements are most likely: A couple may share both physical and legal custody, or one party may have sole physical custody and share legal custody with the other parent. It is also theoretically possible for a couple to share physical custody, with sole legal custody assigned to one parent, but it is hard to envision many situations where a parent who is responsible for the daily care of a child would not want, or would be deemed incapable of, major decision-making authority.

Where parents share legal custody, neither one is supposed to make a major decision affecting the child without the participation and consent of the other parent, absent emergency circumstances. Where parents disagree, no action can be taken until a resolution is reached. This can have serious implications for the well-being of a child, where, for example, parents disagree about whether the child needs to be evaluated by a therapist. Ultimately, these disputes may have to be submitted to a court for resolution.

In situations where one parent has sole physical custody with shared legal custody, the distinction between major and day-to-day decisions can become critical. Some decisions are easy to characterize: Enrollment in a private school, elective surgery, or mental health counseling are clearly major issues. The choice between blue socks or green or whether to attend a friend's birthday party are clearly of the daily variety. But what about ear piercing? Or violin versus tuba lessons? Or a significant change in hairstyle? These decisions are harder to characterize and can lead to tremendous conflict over who has the right to make such decisions.

Where parents share physical custody, both are responsible, though not always equally, for the day-to-day care of the child. Here, many arrangements are possible. A child could spend roughly equal amounts of time with each parent, rotating between the households according to a fixed schedule that allocates time on a daily, weekly, monthly, or even yearly basis. Each parent would maintain a home for the child, who would in effect have two principal places of residence. It is also possible for the sharing to be less equal. A child might have one primary residence but spend a significant amount of time with the other parent, who would remain much more directly and consistently involved in the child's life than the traditional visiting parent.

The Joint Custody Controversy

The joint custody trend began in the 1980s based on a number of considerations. First, a number of studies indicated that fathers tended to drift out of their children's lives following a divorce, causing children to feel a sense of abandonment and rejection. Rather than blaming fathers for not caring about their children, joint custody proponents saw this disengagement as stemming from the awkwardness and insignificance of being cast in a visitor's role and hoped that, given a more meaningful place in their children's lives, fathers would remain more connected to them. Second, an emerging fathers' rights movement was seeking to combat what they perceived as anti-male bias in the family courts, and joint custody became a central demand as a way of wresting custodial control from women. Third, corresponding to the no-fault goal of making divorce a less adversarial process, it was hoped that joint custody would encourage parents to stop fighting over their children and to work out a cooperative arrangement where neither emerged the victor.

Although it has become more commonplace, joint custody remains a contentious issue. Most experts agree that where parents freely choose joint custody and are committed to making it work, it can be a positive arrangement because it gives a child meaningful contact with both parents.

However, making it work can be extremely difficult. Parents need to be able to set aside their anger and disappointment in the other as a spouse and respect him or her as a parent. In short, they must have the ability to distinguish between their spousal and their parenting roles. Reflective of these complexities, with time, many parents who begin their post-separation lives with joint custody find themselves settling into more traditional patterns, with one parent, usually the mother, assuming primary care responsibility of the children.[52]

Even where parents are able to work things out between them, concerns have been raised that joint custody may overburden children, as it requires them to negotiate life in two different households. This can be particularly difficult for some children either because of their temperament or because of their developmental stage.[53] For example, when parents do not live in the same community, adolescents may resent having to be away from their friends and social network on a regular basis.

The far more contentious issue is whether courts should be able to impose joint custody where one parent objects to it. According to fathers' rights proponents, it is essential for courts to have this authority in order to counteract the bias they believe exists against fathers in the divorce courts. They argue that if joint custody were allowed only where it was agreed upon, mothers could routinely defeat the claims of fathers by objecting to joint custody. Fathers' rights groups thus have lobbied for laws that create a presumption in favor of shared custody; the groups also have brought class action lawsuits based on the argument that state laws that do not ensure each parent an equal share of parenting time violate their fundamental right to the care and custody of their children. Although these legal challenges generally have not been successful, with courts finding that the best interest of children trumps a parent's asserted right to equal custodial time, many states have amended their custody laws to include a preference or presumption in favor of joint custody.

However, serious doubts have been raised about the wisdom of giving courts the authority to compel joint custody over the objection of a parent, particularly in high-conflict families. A major concern is that the frequent interaction that joint custody demands may keep alive spousal animosity and conflict and thereby interfere with the parents' ability to disengage from the marriage. Perpetuating spousal animosity is likely to have a spillover effect on the children, who may experience serious mental health issues as a result of continuing exposure to parental anger and arguments.[54] Based on growing evidence that imposing joint custody on recalcitrant and noncooperative parents can have negative effects on children, and that "the bulk of newly divorced spouses cannot remain as positively involved with each other on an everyday basis as joint physical custody requires, [and] that the presumption is causing more litigation to already crowded dockets," states have begun to move away from joint custody presumptions in favor of making joint custody one of the options to consider when determining the best interest of children.[55]

Concerns about joint custody presumptions or preferences are paramount in cases in which there is a history of domestic violence. As many commentators have pointed out, successful shared parenting arrangements require the ability to cooperate and communicate effectively, and these characteristics are likely to be absent in a relationship that was marked by violence. Moreover, the frequency of the interaction demanded by joint custody may keep the victim at risk of continued harm, with a deleterious spillover effect on the children.[56] Recognizing the seriousness of these concerns, most statutes expressly recognize that where there is a history of violence, joint custody is not likely to be in a child's best interest, and these cases are therefore exempted from any statutory preference in favor of joint custody.

Legal Status of the Noncustodial Parent

At the opposite end of the custodial spectrum from a shared physical and legal custody arrangement is one in which both custodies are vested in a single parent, and the other is a **noncustodial parent**. As discussed below, this parent is usually granted visitation rights; however, before considering visitation, it is important to understand this parent's legal status.

Loss of custody in the context of a divorce action does not sever the parent-child relationship; a mother or father who does not have either legal or physical custody of a child is still that child's parent. (The termination of parental rights is covered in Chapter 13.) The retention of one's legal status as a parent has the following important ramifications:

1. Because custodial determinations are not permanent, a noncustodial parent may always seek to modify the existing arrangement and thus may acquire custodial rights at some point in the future; in contrast, a termination of parental rights results in a permanent severance of the parent-child relationship.
2. Noncustodial parents retain a number of important rights. These include visitation rights; the right of access to school, medical, and other records; and the right to make medical decisions in the event of an emergency or the unavailability of the custodial parent.
3. In addition to these rights, a noncustodial parent remains subject to a support obligation.
4. With the legal relationship intact, benefits and statutory rights that depend on the existence of a parent-child relationship will most likely not be lost. For example, if a noncustodial parent dies without a will,

the child will be entitled to a share of the estate under a state's intestacy laws. However, entitlements that depend on proof of actual dependency may be denied.

Thus, although loss of custody may be a devastating event in a mother's or father's life, she or he is still a parent. This may seem like a legal abstraction to a noncustodial parent, who may no longer feel like a parent; however, the legal relationship carries with it a bundle of rights and an ongoing support obligation.

Visitation Rights

The general assumption is that, following a divorce, it is in a child's best interest to have continued contact with both parents. Accordingly, in virtually all cases, a noncustodial parent (referring here to a parent without physical custody) will be granted visitation rights. Because this parent plays a less significant role in the life of a child than the custodial parent does, courts generally use a lower standard for deciding about visitation than they do for deciding about custody. Accordingly, a parent who may not be capable of providing the day-to-day care and nurture that a child needs will, in most cases, be considered capable of spending some meaningful time with the child on a regular basis.

However, as discussed in more detail below, if continued contact is deemed to pose a risk of emotional or physical harm to a child, visitation rights will be denied or subject to limitations.

The Visitation Schedule

As the following discussion makes clear, working out a viable visitation schedule, including determining the appropriate nomenclature, involves the careful consideration of multiple factors.

Amount of Time and Frequency of Visits.   Because there is so much variability in visitation arrangements, it is hard to state with any certainty how much time the "average" visiting parent spends with his or her children. However, the unquestioned trend is to increase visitation time and frequency well beyond the traditional four hours on Sunday afternoon—which gave Dad just enough time to take the kids to the zoo and out for a quick dinner.

Setting aside, for the moment, those cases in which visitation may pose a threat to a child's physical or emotional well-being, visitation rights are now seen as providing the noncustodial parent with the opportunity to remain an integral part of his or her child's life as opposed to simply being the "fun" parent. When the parents live close to one another, the noncustodial parent may be able to see the child on a regular basis, which can provide a sense of continuity and familiarity. The schedule may well include some overnight time and some extended time during school and summer vacations. When the parents do not live near each other, visitation will, of course, be less frequent, and it will be harder for the noncustodial parent to remain connected to the rhythms of a child's daily life. This may be offset somewhat by extended visitation time over the summer and school vacations.

Setting the Parameters.   Visitation arrangements, as set out in a court order, separation agreement, or parenting plan, can be open-ended, spelled out in elaborate detail, or somewhere in between. An open-ended arrangement generally provides for a right of reasonable or liberal visitation and leaves the details up to the parties. This kind of arrangement usually works best if the parties have been separated for a while and have informally worked out and implemented a mutually satisfactory schedule. Because an open-ended agreement requires frequent communication, it is not likely to succeed if the parties are angry and hostile, or have not been successful at working out an informal arrangement. The constant negotiations necessitated by an open-ended schedule may serve to keep the anger between the parties alive longer and prevent them from settling into a reasonably calm visitation pattern, to the clear detriment of the children. A visitation arrangement can be spelled out with great specificity, detailing precisely when each and every visit is to occur and who is responsible for transporting the children to and from the visits. A visitation schedule for summer and school vacations and holidays also may be detailed. Specific guidelines for when a parent may deviate from the schedule may be included as well. (See Chapter 10 for an example of a separation agreement with a very specific visitation schedule.)

A middle-ground approach is to provide a fairly set schedule, with a proviso that this does not represent the full extent of the visiting parent's rights and that he or she may also visit at mutually agreed upon times. This minimizes the negotiations inherent in a completely open-ended arrangement but also builds in a degree of flexibility that may benefit both parents—especially if it is written to accommodate both of their needs.

Parents often do not anticipate how emotionally difficult the visitation process can be for both them and the child, especially around holidays and when a former partner begins to date. Accordingly, at least in the initial period following a divorce, a good argument can be made that most parents do better with a specific visitation plan that minimizes the need for constant negotiations. Frequently, after the initial emotional intensity has dissipated, parents are better able to be more flexible in responding to the needs of the other parent.

The Boundary Between Shared Physical Custody and Sole Custody with Visitation Rights. The formal boundary between sole custody with visitation rights and joint physical custody cannot always be fixed with precision, although some states have set a minimum amount of time that a parent must spend with a child for the arrangement to qualify as shared custody. For example, the following arrangement could, absent specific statutory criteria, be characterized either way: A child lives with his mother during the week and spends every weekend—from Friday at 6:00 P.M. until Sunday evening—with his father. He also has dinner with his father every Wednesday night.

In negotiating an agreement, many attorneys try to avoid these terms because they carry a lot of emotional baggage. For example, if parents have negotiated an arrangement in which the children are to be with the mother 70 percent of the time and with the father 30 percent, the mother may object to calling this shared physical custody because it obscures the fact that she has the children most of the time. On the other hand, the father might object to his time being identified as visitation because this can suggest minimal involvement. Accordingly, alternative terms such as "primary care parent" and "secondary care parent" can be substituted, or the agreement may refer to shared parenting responsibilities with each parent having custody when the children are with him or her, regardless of how the total time is allocated.

When Unrestricted Visitation Is Not in a Child's Best Interest

Despite the priority that the law gives to preserving the relationship between a child and the noncustodial parent, there are situations in which continued contact is considered not to be in a child's best interest, such as where it would place a child at risk of emotional or physical harm. Another possibility is that visitation would be allowed but would be subject to restrictions, such as that visits be supervised by a third party. The parent might also be required to be in therapy and/or attend some kind of parenting class.

Restrictions on visitation may also be imposed where a history of domestic violence places the custodial parent at risk even if the child has not been a direct victim of the abuse. Here, restrictions are generally aimed at limiting contact between the parents, such as that the child is dropped off and picked up at a neutral location (for instance, an agency that provides custody exchange services) at a timed interval so there is no contact between the parents.

Frequently, a parent who has been denied visitation rights or who has restricted visitation will return to court seeking unrestricted access to his or her child. In response, a judge must determine if the child (or the custodial parent) is still at risk of harm. If visits are being allowed for the first time, a judge is likely to impose some restrictions. Judges vary in their approach to requests for the lifting of existing restrictions. Some judges are reluctant to modify restrictions on the ground that the risk of potential harm does not outweigh the potential benefit of allowing visitation to occur in a more natural, unstructured way. Other judges take the view that if a parent has complied with the requirements of the initial restrictions, he or she is entitled to a second chance to reestablish a relationship with his or her child that is not dependent on the involvement of third parties.

Parenting Plans, Parenting Coordinators, and Parent Education Programs

Although, as noted above, the trend has shifted away from joint custody presumptions in favor of making joint custody an option, this shift does not signal a return to the traditional "zoo daddy" model, in which fathers typically had a few hours of fun with their children on Sunday afternoons and an occasional holiday, with no expectation of a sustained and meaningful role in their children's lives. Rather, as we have seen, the preferred approach today is to create a structure that enables both parents to maintain meaningful ties with their children. Although studies indicate that children fare better when they sustain a quality post-dissolution relationship with both parents, the research also makes clear that continued parental conflict and hostility, which can be exacerbated by frequent contact, has a deleterious impact on children. Accordingly, to minimize post-divorce animosity and enhance the ability of parents to coordinate caring for their children, parenting plans and parenting education programs have become increasingly popular legal options.

A growing number of states now require parents to develop and submit a "**parenting plan**" to the court for approval if custody is to be shared, and a few states require the submission of a plan in all cases involving minor children. In other states, judges have the option of requiring the submission of a plan in any case where they deem it appropriate to do so. A parenting plan is a written agreement in which the parents detail how they intend to care for their children following a divorce. Designed to minimize hostility and foster cooperative parenting, parenting plans generally must cover all aspects of child rearing, including how time between the two households is to be divided, how responsibilities are to be allocated, and how decisions are to be made and disputes resolved. Depending on the state, other matters, such as relocation and child support, may also be addressed. In some states, parents may be required to participate in mediation if they cannot agree upon the terms of a plan.

Parenting plans appear to make a good deal of sense where parents wish to share custody. If carefully crafted, they provide parents with a detailed blueprint for how to manage their post-dissolution parenting roles, including how to handle disputes over child-related decisions, and the allocation of time and responsibilities. However, paralleling the criticisms of joint custody with which these plans are often associated, serious concerns have been raised about the appropriateness of requiring parenting plans in cases involving domestic violence or where there is parental hostility. Accordingly, exemptions or special protections have been incorporated into many of these laws to cover situations where the kind of cooperative parenting envisioned by parenting plans is either not safe or not feasible.

Distinct from the court-affiliated parenting education programs discussed below that are now available in a majority of states on either a mandatory or voluntary basis, a more recent innovation, particularly in high-conflict divorces, is the appointment of a parenting coordinator. A number of states have specifically enacted parenting coordinator provisions, while others rely upon "existing statutes that allow for 'mediators' or 'special masters' as a basis for appointing parenting coordinators," and in the absence of any such statutory authority, it is arguable that "the discretion given to judges to fashion orders in the best interest of . . . children, could be extended . . . to order [parents] to cooperate with a parenting coordinator."[57] The majority of parent coordinators are either attorneys or mental health professionals.

Although the scope of their authority varies from state to state, parenting coordinators typically focus on helping parents develop strategies for resolving conflicts that arise around custody in order to help ensure the smooth implementation of their parenting plan without having to resort to litigation. However, as a general rule, they do not have the authority to alter the parameters of the parenting plan or to change the allocation of custodial rights and responsibilities between the parents. In some states, parenting coordinators are able to make certain decisions when the parents are unable to resolve a conflict that arises over a day-to-day parenting issue, but these decisions are generally subject to court review. Parenting coordinators may also have the authority to made recommendations to the court.[58]

A recent article has suggested that in extremely high conflict cases, a parental coordinator team be put in place to help prevent "parental decisions from being hijacked by one parent or the other."[59] The authors suggest that each parent be assigned their own coordinator and then the two would work together "to clean up [the parents'] toxic communications and facilitate a shifting of that parent's role in the negative conflict dynamic."[60] It is also suggested that the team be interdisciplinary in nature. This approach has yet to be evaluated to see if there is any value added, and of course, having two coordinators would increase the cost of divorce; however, it is possible that this approach might reduce post-divorce custody conflicts and multiple return trips to the court, which themselves can be very costly.

A related trend is the enactment of laws setting up parenting education programs for divorcing parents. Depending on the state or the circumstances of the family, these programs may be mandatory or offered on a voluntary basis, and, like parenting plans, they are intended to facilitate the transition to post-divorce parenting. These programs are designed to educate "parents about the potential effects of their behavior and attitudes on their children."[61] The hope is that, once they gain such awareness, parents will modulate negative behaviors so that they can respond more effectively to the needs of their children.

Most court-affiliated parent education programs are of very short duration, lasting somewhere between a total of two and four hours. Based on concerns that have been raised about their limited effectiveness, some experts in the field have begun to suggest that the adoption of a more time-intensive model would better equip parties with the skills and knowledge needed in order to parent more effectively following a divorce.[62] In this regard, it should be noted that online programs are becoming an increasingly popular way for parents to fulfill court-mandated education requirements, and these programs are often somewhat longer than the typical classroom option, and may well take up to 12 hours to complete.[63]

Again, important concerns have been raised about parent education programs where there has been a history of domestic violence; in states where participation is mandatory, judges are usually allowed to waive the attendance requirement for good cause, such as where necessary to protect a party from the risk of abuse. Other options have also been suggested that would enable a victim of domestic violence to attend a parent education class while also protecting her safety, such as by having the parents attend class on different nights or in different locations.[64]

A more recent innovation is for courts to offer educational programs for the children of divorcing parents to help them understand and cope with the changes in their lives. Children are usually grouped according to age, and the curriculum is adapted to the development needs of the targeted age. Although these programs are usually offered on a voluntary basis, they may be required in some jurisdictions. For instance, under local court rules in Kentucky, children in many parts of the state are required to attend the children's component of the state's Divorce Education program. That portion of the overall program is designed to "provide a sense of security, awareness and understanding as a beginning point for children learning to cope with dual parenting in separate households." Children in grades 1-5 attend Kids' Time, and those in grades 6-8 attend Tweens' Time.[65]

INTERVIEW CHECKLIST

Following is a list of the kinds of information you will need to learn about in cases where custody or visitation (or both) may be an issue. As discussed in greater detail in Chapter 10, it often takes a while for a client to feel comfortable enough to speak openly about the intimate details of his or her life. Thus, absent an emergency situation where an immediate custody decision must be made, all of the following information does not need to be obtained at the initial interview. In fact, you are likely to obtain a more accurate and complete picture if you do not push for all this information up front. Accordingly, the checklist below should not mechanistically be converted into a set of interview questions. Also keep in mind that parents, regardless of their particular situations, are likely to be worried and anxious about their future relationship with their children; you need to be sensitive to the volatility of child-related issues. Remember, too, that information about the other parent coming from your client is likely to be different from the information the other parent provides to his or her own attorney.

1. What is the nature of the relationship each parent has with the child?
2. How have responsibilities been allocated between the parents over time? More specifically:
   - Who makes the child-care arrangements?
   - Who transports the child to and from child care or school?
   - Who arranges the child's activities?
   - Who stays home with the child when he or she is sick?
   - Who supervises homework?
   - Who helps the child get off to child care or school in the morning (e.g., getting breakfast, clothing)?
   - Who is responsible for bathing the child and putting her or him to bed?
   - Who makes the child-related purchases?
   - Who attends school meetings (including parent-teacher conferences)?
3. How much time does each parent have available to be with the child?
4. What is each parent's approach to discipline (including any potential concerns about abuse)?
5. What activities does each parent enjoy with the child?
6. How does each parent intend to make post-divorce adjustments in his or her schedule to accommodate the changed family structure?
7. What are each parent's strengths and weaknesses?
8. Does either parent have a history of alcohol or drug abuse?
9. Does either parent have a history of mental health problems?
10. What are the available support systems, such as friends and relatives, of each parent?
11. What are each parent's commitments, in addition to work?

■ Post-Divorce Custody and Visitation Disputes

Following a divorce, disputes often arise regarding custody or visitation arrangements—or both—and a parent may return to court seeking to either enforce or change existing arrangements. The former is accomplished through a **complaint for contempt** and the latter through a **complaint for modification**; as a general rule, a complaint for modification must be based upon an unforeseen change in circumstances that alters the existing arrangement so that it is no longer in the best interest of the child. Courts have continuing jurisdiction over these disputes until children reach the age of majority and are no longer subject to the custodial authority of their parents. Rather than returning to court, parents also may seek to resolve these disputes through mediation or arbitration; in fact, their separation agreement may require them to try and resolve their dispute through one of these methods before they can seek court relief. (For details on the procedural aspects of this paragraph, see Chapter 10.)

These post-divorce actions can be a double-edged sword. On the one hand, in order to make certain that a child is protected from harm and that his or her needs are being met, courts must have the authority to hear and resolve post-divorce disputes. On the other hand, this creates the possibility that parents who are engaged in an acrimonious dispute for control of a child will continuously return to court, claiming that the child is not being cared for properly. Because courts have a duty to ensure that custodial arrangements do not pose a risk of harm to a child, a court must assess the situation, even where it appears that in bringing the action, the parent was motivated by hostility rather than a genuine concern for the child. Below, we consider three common categories of post-divorce disputes, and the emerging debate over "virtual visitation."

Disputes About Custody

Following a divorce, parents often express concern about the custodial arrangements and seek to change them. Thus, for example, in a situation of shared legal custody, it may turn out that the parents cannot make decisions without a protracted struggle, and the parent with physical custody feels this is interfering with his or her ability to meet the needs of the child. Or where parents share physical custody of a child who is now a teenager, the parent who lives in the town where the child attends school may seek sole custody because the teen resents having to spend sustained time away from his or her primary group of friends.

Or a parent may realize that the other parent, who had been sober for an extended time period at the time of the parties' divorce, has relapsed and is again abusing alcohol and is thus not able to care for the child properly.

In the above examples, the desired modifications are based both on a genuine concern for the well-being of the child and on a change in circumstance that makes the existing arrangement unworkable. Of course, the other parent may not see the situation in the same way, and she or he may vehemently oppose the requested change. Some requests for modification, however, are not based on a concern for the child but stem from continued hostility toward the other parent. Thus, for example, a parent may resent the fact that his or her former spouse is cohabiting with a new partner and may seek to have that parent's custodial rights revoked, claiming that the partner is a bad influence on the child. Note that although this is clearly a change in circumstances, there must also be an adverse impact on the child. It is not always easy for the court to sort out what is going on, and modification actions that stem from parental hostility often become bitter and protracted as old antagonisms resurface.

Disputes About Visitation

As with custody, bitter fights may occur around visitation. The visiting parent may assert that the custodial parent refuses to let him or her see the child, while the custodial parent may assert that he or she always gets the child ready and the other parent never shows up. These disputes are difficult to resolve. Often, there is not much a court can do other than admonish the parties to comply with the terms of the visitation arrangement. If, however, the custodial parent is truly interfering with the visiting parent's ability to see the child by, for example, consistently not being at home when the visiting parent is supposed to pick up the child, the visiting parent can bring a contempt action; the ultimate sanction for interference with visitation rights would be a transfer of custody to the other parent. If, on the other hand, the custodial parent has good cause for limiting access, such as where the visiting parent has shown up intoxicated to pick up the child or there is a consistent failure of the visiting parent to adhere to the schedule, the custodial parent may be able to bring a modification action to curtail or restructure the existing arrangement. Unfortunately, there is no real remedy for a custodial parent who wishes to compel the other parent to exercise his or her visitation rights. A parent cannot be forced to visit when he or she chooses not to.

Relocation Disputes

Following a divorce, most states do not permit a custodial parent to move out of state with the child without first obtaining the consent of the other parent or the court. As might be expected, **relocation disputes** are fraught with bitterness. A custodial parent is likely to resent the potential limitation on the ability to seek a better life, especially in light of the fact that a visiting parent can move about freely without having to secure anyone's consent, and the noncustodial parent is likely to resent the potential loss of access to the child.

States take a variety of approaches to relocation cases, but the recent trend has been to favor the right of the custodial parent to relocate with the children. Generally, the parent must show that the move is motivated by good faith—such as by a job opportunity or the desire to move closer to extended family, rather than by a desire to interfere with the rights of the noncustodial parent—and is in the child's best interest.[66]

Under this approach, the concept of best interest is usually broadened to take the needs of the custodial parent into account based on the view that the child and custodial parent are interdependent, and a move that benefits the parent, by, for example, locating him or her closer to extended family, will inure to the benefit of the child. As explained in one of the first cases to adopt this expanded view of best interest:

> The children, after the parents' divorce or separation, belong to a different family unit than they did when the parents lived together. The new family unit consists only of the children and the custodial parent, and what is advantageous to that unit as a whole, to each of its members individually and to the way they relate to each other and function together is obviously in the best interests of the children. It is in the context of what is best for that family unit that the precise nature and terms of visitation and changes in visitation by the noncustodial parent must be considered.[67]

The relationship between the child and the noncustodial parent is certainly not an irrelevant consideration in jurisdictions favoring the custodial parents in relocation disputes. However, given that the primary focus is on the importance of continuity of care within the custodial household and what is needed to make that family function effectively, the fact that visitation will occur on a less regular basis is generally not enough to prevent a move. It may be enough to defeat the move, however, when considered with other factors, such as where the move is not prompted by reasons calculated to benefit the custodial household but by, for example, a desire to change scenery.

States that favor the custodial parent generally approach the issue differently where the parents share physical custody. Here, the child has two distinct post-divorce households, and his or her best interest is not so clearly identified with one parent as it is when one parent has sole custody. In this situation, a court might decide that preserving the status quo is in the child's best interest and deny the relocation request. Another possible approach would be to modify or terminate the existing custody order, and make a de novo determination of the child's best interest, which would incorporate a determination about relocation.

The other approach is to give more weight to the interests of the noncustodial parent in preserving his or her relationship with the child. Accordingly, the custodial parent most likely will be required to prove more than simply good faith and best interest. In terms of his or her motivation for moving, he or she may need to establish that the move is compelled by "extraordinary reasons." In terms of its impact on the child, the parent may need to show that it offers a "real advantage," although the meaning of this term is not entirely clear. At a minimum, the parent may need to prove that the child would gain a tangible benefit that is not available in the home state. Under this approach, courts generally do not take an expanded view of best interest and will thus not assume, without supporting evidence, that changes for the better in the custodial parent's life naturally benefit the child.

Recently, the trend favoring the custodial parent in relocation disputes has been questioned by some commentators who argue that this approach simply assumes that a child's well-being is tied to the custodial parent, and fails to account for the actual experiences of the child. Thus, for example, one recent study suggests that children might be adversely impacted when they move more than an hour's drive from the noncustodial parent, while others suggest that relocation outcomes might vary based upon a complex array of factors, such as the age of the children, how soon the move follows the time of separation, and the nature and frequency of contact the children and the noncustodial parent have before the move.[68] Such research could well influence the future direction of relocation cases.

Virtual Visitation

In 2001, in the case of McCoy v. McCoy, after finding that the custodial mother had a good-faith reason for relocating to California, a New Jersey court concluded that in assessing whether the existing visitation arrangement could be restructured to "accommodate and preserve the relationship that the child had with her father," the trial court had failed to give adequate weight to the mother's "suggested use of the Internet to enhance visitation."[69] Characterizing her proposal as "both creative and innovative," the appeals court concluded that if the "actual" proposed visitation arrangement was inadequate, the judge should have considered this supplemental means of communication. In what is generally considered to be a groundbreaking approach, the court stressed that technology could be used to ensure "continued development" of the child's relationship with her father, while also preserving the mother's right to move.[70]

Today the concept of **virtual visitation**, which refers to the use of "email, instant messaging, webcams, and other internet tools to provide regular contact between a noncustodial parent and his or her child,"[71] is no longer regarded as groundbreaking, and many courts routinely consider the availability of virtual means of communication when deciding relocation cases. Taking this trend a step further, in an effort to enhance the post-divorce relationship between a child and the noncustodial parent, some judges now include virtual visitation provisions in cases that do not involve an out-of-state move.

When fashioning virtual visitation orders, the growing tendency is for courts to be quite specific about what kind of technology is to be used, who is to pay for it, and when and under what conditions it is to take place. In this regard, the most valuable communications tools are generally considered to be those, such as webcams and Skype, that make "real" time communication possible, thus enabling a parent to be present, albeit virtually rather than physically, in his or her child's life. However, as some commentators have noted, not all judges are fully versed in the wide range of available technologies, and their orders may thus not take full advantage of cutting-edge modalities.

In general, courts do not appear to be factoring the possibility of virtual communication into the relocation decision itself as a threshold matter; custodial parents are thus still expected to establish a legally sufficient reason for the proposed move. Accordingly, in *McCoy*, for example, it was only after the mother had shown, to the court's satisfaction, that the move was prompted by the prospect of a better job and a better climate for her daughter who suffered from asthma, that it considered the possibility of using virtual visitation to supplement the father's actual time with his daughter. In short, it does not appear that courts are relying on the availability of virtual visitation to short-circuit the relocation decision itself.

Concerns, however, have been raised that judges may begin to rely on the availability of this technology in making the underlying relocation decision itself. Here, it would not simply be a way to supplement other avenues of communication once an independent decision had been made, but it would be a factor in the decisional matrix, to be weighed along with other considerations, such as the reason for the move and the best interests of the child. This raises profound questions about the nature of human interaction and how meaningful relationships are maintained with people who are not in physical proximity. Must connection occur in person for it to count as meaningful contact? Can one really "interact" virtually? What is lost when technological connections replace physical contact? What does it mean for human relationships when spatial proximity is no longer needed for "real time" communication? These and other related questions will only become more pressing in the coming years as the distance between virtual and actual reality continues to diminish.

Finally, several states have enacted virtual visitation statutes, and a number of other states are considering such measures. Generally speaking, these legislative enactments are aimed at ensuring greater uniformity and consistency within any given jurisdiction with respect to the circumstances under which virtual visitation can be ordered and how such orders are to be structured. Thus, for example, a statute may spell out that virtual visitation orders are meant to supplement in-person contact and not to serve as a substitute for it, which, according to a recent study, is the approach that divorce professionals appear to prefer.[72]

Although the use of virtual visitation can enhance communication between a child and a noncustodial parent, particularly if that parent lives far away, concerns have been raised about the practice above and beyond the previously noted apprehension that a judge might order it in lieu of rather than as a supplement to face-to-face visitation. Not surprisingly, some professionals worry about the potential implications where virtual visitation is used in cases where there is a domestic violence history, because even though the risk of physical injury is reduced, there is still the risk of emotional and verbal abuse.[73] Another critical concern is that the use of "electronic communication may give the abusive ex-spouse the ability to invade the privacy of his or her former spouse."[74] Particularly worrisome is that it may be used to ferret out that parent's whereabouts in situations where safety needs dictate the nondisclosure of location.

Extending beyond the domestic violence context, some professionals caution about the appropriateness of using virtual modes of visitation in high-conflict cases. Of particular concern is that a parent may use it "maliciously, which can further incite conflict," especially given that it is "easy to just hit 'send' and say things that cannot be taken back."[75] Cautions have also been raised about its use in situations of active litigation, with some divorce professionals reporting that electronic communications are "being used as evidence, as a form of manipulation, or in an attempt to use information gained from the technologies to their advantage in court proceedings."[76]

The Custodial and Visitation Rights of Grandparents and Stepparents

Until this point, the focus of this chapter has been on custody and visitation disputes between divorcing parents. In these disputes, the rights of each party, at least in a formal legal sense, are deemed to be equal. Each is entitled to try to establish that an award of custody to him or her would further the best interest of the child. In this section, we turn to a consideration of custody and visitation disputes between parents and "nonparents"—namely grandparents and stepparents.[77]

In light of the fact that parents have a fundamental constitutional right to direct the upbringing of their children, including deciding who will have access to them, in a dispute between a parent and a "nonparent," there is an automatic preference in favor of the parent based on the assumption that he or she is best able to meet the child's needs. Accordingly, as discussed in this section, the basic rule is that a nonparent must establish something more than best interest in order to maintain an ongoing relationship with a child in the face of opposition from a parent.

Grandparents

At common law, grandparents had no legal right of access to their grandchildren. Parents were said to have a moral but not a legal obligation to permit grandparents to see their grandchildren. In essence, this meant that a grandparent's right of access was derivative; he or she had no direct link to the child as the connection flowed through the related parent. This rule was based on a number of considerations, including the right of parents to control the upbringing of their children and the concern that a legal dispute between grandparent and parent would be destructive to the child, particularly if the child blamed him- or herself for the controversy.

This approach began to change in the 1960s, and today all states have statutes that, to varying degrees, modify the common law rule of no access. Some states have enacted specific grandparent visitation statutes, while others include grandparents within a broader third-party visitation statute. The enhanced legal status of grandparents reflects a number of developments. First, with the graying of the population, the organizational and political clout of senior citizens, an important force behind these laws, has increased. Second, as the divorce rate has risen, increased attention has focused on the importance of providing children with continued access to essential relationships in order to help buffer the dislocation of divorce. And closely related is an increased awareness of how important the bond between a grandparent and child can be.[78] These statutes reflect the changing reality of the U.S. family and the often-vital role that nonparents play in the upbringing of children.

In looking at grandparent visitation statutes, it is helpful to ask two questions: (1) Under what circumstances may a grandparent seek visitation rights, and (2) what substantive standard will be used to resolve the dispute? The first question is often characterized as a matter of standing. **Standing** is a jurisdictional concept that requires a person to have a sufficient stake in the outcome of a controversy in order to be allowed to maintain a legal action; if a party lacks standing, his or her action is dismissed. Some state statutes require that there be some kind of family disruption, such as divorce or parental death, in order for a grandparent to have standing. In other states, however, the applicable statute gives grandparents a more general right to seek visitation without specifying the circumstances under which a petition can be filed; however, based on considerations of family privacy, some courts have sought to impose limiting qualifications, such as a prerequisite of family disruption.

Once it is determined that a grandparent has standing to seek visitation rights, the next consideration is the standard to be used for resolving the dispute. Some states have adopted a best interest standard (see, however, the discussion of *Troxel*), although judges generally require proof of something more than simply that the child would enjoy a continued relationship with the grandparent. Other states have adopted a higher burden of proof, most frequently by requiring the grandparent(s) to establish that the denial of visitation rights would harm the child.

As grandparents began turning to the courts to gain access to their grandchildren after contact had been denied or limited by a son or daughter (or by a daughter- or son-in-law), some parents responded by challenging the constitutionality of the grandparent visitation laws, arguing that such laws were an unwarranted intrusion into the realm of family privacy. Initially, courts tended to uphold the validity of the statutes, finding that any intrusion into a fit parent's right to direct the upbringing of his or her children was offset by the benefit to the child of a continued relationship with his or her grandparent. As expressed by the Kentucky Supreme Court in the case of King v. King, these early decisions tended to sentimentalize the grandparent-grandchild relationship:

> While the Constitution . . . does recognize the right to rear children without undue governmental interference, that right is not inviolate. . . .
>
> In an era in which society has seen a general disintegration of the family, it is not unreasonable for the General Assembly to attempt to strengthen familial bonds. . . . There is no reason that a petty dispute between a father and son should be allowed to deprive a grandparent and grandchild of the unique relationship that ordinarily exists between those individuals. . . .

If a grandparent is physically, mentally and morally fit, then a grandchild will ordinarily benefit from contact with the grandparent.... Each benefits from contact with the other. The child can learn respect, a sense of responsibility and love. The grandparent can be invigorated by exposure to youth, can gain an insight into our changing society, and can avoid the loneliness which is so often a part of an aging parent's life. These considerations by the state do not go too far in intruding into the fundamental rights of the parents.[79]

In 1993, however, starting with the decision of Tennessee Supreme Court, in the case of Hawk v. Hawk, courts began to give greater consideration to the rights of parents to decide who should have access to their children:

... Bill and Sue Hawk argue that grandparent visitation is a "compelling state interest" that warrants use of the state's parens patriae power to impose visitation in "best interests of the children." ... We find, however, that without a substantial danger of harm to the child, a court may not constitutionally impose its own subjective notions of the "best interests of the child" when an intact, nuclear family with fit, married parents is involved.

The requirement of harm is the sole protection that parents have against pervasive state interference in the parenting process.

... [I]t is not within the power of a court, ... to make significant decisions concerning the custody of children, merely because it could make a better decision or disposition. The State is parens patriae and always has been, but it has not displaced the parent in right or responsibility....[80]

The court goes on to critique the Kentucky Supreme Court's *King* decision:

[T]he *King* majority engaged in a sentimental reflection on the "special bond" between grandparent and grandchild.... In his dissent, however, Justice Lambert disputed the constitutionality of a statute "which has as its only standard the subjective requirement of 'best interest of the child'" adding that "mere improvement in quality of life is not a compelling state interest and is insufficient to justify invasion of constitutional rights."[81]

In 2000, the U.S. Supreme Court, in the case of Troxel v. Granville, entered the fray. Under consideration in this case was the state of Washington's opened-ended statute that gave "any person" the right to petition the court for visitation rights at "any time" based on the best interest of the child. This case involved an unmarried couple with two children. After the relationship ended, the father moved in with his parents. He saw his children on a regular basis, with the visits often taking place at his parents' home. About two years after the separation, the father committed suicide. The grandparents continued to visit with the children. The mother then decided to limit the visits, and the grandparents sued for increased access to their granddaughters.

The Washington Supreme Court declared the law unconstitutional, stating, "It is not within the province of the state to make significant decisions concerning the custody of children merely because it could make a 'better' decision."[82] The U.S. Supreme Court agreed that the statute was invalid, but it did so on far narrower grounds, finding that it was invalid only *as applied* to the facts of the case before it. Of primary concern to the Court was the "sweeping breadth" of the statute, which effectively allowed a judge to substitute his or her views regarding visitation for the views of a fit parent:

> Once . . . the matter is placed before a judge, a parent's decision that visitation would not be in the child's best interest is accorded no deference. . . . Instead, the Washington statute places the best-interest determination solely in the hands of the judge. Should the judge disagree with the parent's estimation of the child's best interests, the judge's view necessarily prevails. Thus, in practical effect, in the State of Washington a court can disregard and overturn any decision by a fit custodial parent concerning visitation whenever a third party affected by the decision files a visitation petition, based solely on the judge's determination of the child's best interests.[83]

As the Court explained, an exercise of such unfettered judicial discretion is precisely what happened in *Troxel*. The trial court failed to give any real weight to the mother's views, thus disregarding the usual presumption that fit parents act in the best interest of their children. Moreover, the lower court seemed to have presumed that the visitation request should be granted, thus placing "on Granville, the fit custodial parent, the burden of *disproving* that visitation would be in the best interest of her daughters."[84]

It is critical to recognize that in deciding this case, the *Troxel* Court made clear that it was not declaring as a matter of constitutional principle that all third-party visitation laws are an impermissible encroachment on the rights of parents, or that actual harm must be established before allowing visitation over the wishes of a parent. Rather, it held that, at a minimum, some "special weight" must be given to the stated preference of a fit parent. Read broadly, it can be understood to require almost complete deference to parents, so long as they are fit; read more narrowly, it can be understood to place a burden on grandparents to show that something more than the child's best interest, such as proof of actual harm if visitation is cut off, is needed in order to override the wishes of a fit parent.[85] In short, the result is far from definitive, and states thus continue to exhibit considerable variability in their grandparent visitation laws within the broad constitutional parameters established by the Court in *Troxel*.

Stepparents

Traditionally, if a second marriage ends in divorce, a **stepparent** (the spouse of a child's parent) has not been entitled to visitation or custody on the theory that their status derives from the marriage and thus lasts only as long as the marriage does. This result would, of course, be different if the stepparent had adopted the child because adoption creates a permanent parent-child relationship that is not dependent on the continued existence of the marriage. However, compelled by the awareness that stepparents often play a critical role in the lives of children, particularly when the noncustodial parent is uninvolved, the law has begun to give stepparents greater rights upon marital dissolution.

Some states have statutes that specifically allow a stepparent to seek visitation, and possibly also custodial, rights following a divorce. In other states, in the absence of a statute, courts have used a number of theories to extend parental-like rights to stepparents at the time of marital dissolution. For instance, a Michigan court extended parental status based on the concept of **equitable parenthood** and permitted a stepparent to be treated as a parent where:

> (1) the husband and child mutually acknowledge a relationship as father and child, or the mother of the child has cooperated in the development of such a relationship over a time prior to the filing of the complaint for divorce, (2) the husband desires to have the rights afforded to a parent, and (3) the husband is willing to take on the responsibility of paying child support.[86]

Other courts have extended rights to stepparents based on the doctrine of *"in loco parentis."*[87] Here, parental rights (and obligations, such as the duty to pay child support) may be extended to someone who has assumed the role of a parent over an extended period of time through the provision of sustained nurturance and support. To be *in loco parentis*, a stepparent must intend to participate in a child's life as a parent — a casual relationship will not give rise to this status. Although this doctrine has been used to extend a stepparent-child relationship beyond the end of a marriage of the stepparent to the child's parent, a limitation is that the relationship can be terminated at will by the stepparent (or the child), thus bringing the legal bond with its corresponding rights and duties to an end.

In jurisdictions where stepparents can pursue post-dissolution claims, the approach tends to be more liberal where visitation, as distinct from custody, is at issue. Where there is a meaningful connection between a stepparent and child, a court may recognize the importance of continuing this bond beyond the marriage and allow visitation based on a best interest standard. Following *Troxel*, some courts may be inclined to require more than proof of best interest, while others see a distinction between a grandparent and someone who has been in an actual parental role. Where custody is at issue, the traditional preference in favor of biological parents means that considerably more weight will be given to the expressed views of the legal parent. To prevail, a stepparent may need to establish unfitness or the presence of "extraordinary circumstances" that would merit depriving the biological parent of custody.

Chapter Summary

Historically, fathers had an absolute right to the custody of their children. With industrialization, the rights of fathers yielded to the tender years presumption, which assumed that mothers were the best caretakers of young children. Now, virtually all statutes use a best interest of the child standard. In theory, this is a child-centered, gender-neutral approach to resolving custody disputes. Judges are directed to evaluate each case on its individual merits, focusing on the needs of the child rather than the rights of the parents. Where parental conduct or lifestyle is at issue, most jurisdictions employ the nexus approach and require proof of harm. However, this standard has been criticized for its lack of predictability and objective criteria.

Custody has both a legal and a physical component; either may be awarded on a sole or a joint basis. Although there has been an increased focus on shared custody, this approach has been subject to criticism, especially in cases involving a history of domestic violence. A noncustodial parent is presumptively entitled to visitation unless there is a risk of harm to the child. To facilitate post-divorce parenting, there has been an increased focus on parenting plans and parenting education.

Relocation cases can be particularly challenging for the courts to resolve, and although the trend has been in favor of allowing custodial parents to relocate under particularized showings, the needle may slowly be inching back in the other direction. Virtual visitation orders have become an increasingly common way to maintain communication between a child and a distant parent, although it is generally agreed that virtual visits should augment rather than replace in-person ones.

Custody and visitation disputes may involve claims by "third parties"—namely grandparents and stepparents. Where grandparents are concerned, all states have statutorily modified the common law rule of nonaccess and permit visitation under certain circumstances, and a number of states also now recognize post-divorce claims of stepparents seeking to maintain an ongoing relationship with the child of their spouse.

Key Terms

Custody	Joint Custody
Visitation	Noncustodial Parent
Paternal Preference	Parenting Plan
Tender Years Presumption	Complaint for Contempt
Best Interest	Complaint for Modification
Primary Caretaker	Relocation Disputes
Nexus	Virtual Visitation
Per Se Approach	Standing
Primary Caretaker Presumption	Stepparent
Physical Custody	Equitable Parenthood
Legal Custody	*In Loco Parentis*
Sole Custody	

Review Questions

1. What were the rights of fathers at common law?
2. When and why did mothers become the preferred custodial parent?
3. What is the best interest standard?
4. What factors is a judge likely to consider when determining best interest?
5. What criticisms are commonly made about the best interest standard?
6. What are the pros and cons of basing a custody decision on the stated preference of a child?
7. What impact does witnessing spousal abuse have on children? For what other reasons do courts take intra-spousal violence into account when deciding custody?
8. What are the two main approaches that jurisdictions take with respect to domestic violence in the context of a custody dispute?
9. What did the Supreme Court say in *Palmore* about the role of race in custody disputes?
10. Post-*Palmore*, can race and culture ever be taken into account when deciding custody? Explain.
11. Explain the difference between the nexus and the per se harm approaches to resolving custody disputes where parental lifestyle is an issue. Why doesn't the "nexus" standard always ensure that a result is free from bias?
12. How do courts generally approach the issue of religion when it is raised as a positive factor? As a negative factor?
13. What arguments support taking the views of a child into account when making a custody determination? What arguments weigh against it?

14. What concerns have commentators raised where a parent seeking custody has a disability or serious illness?

15. Explain the primary caretaker presumption. How does it respond to the concerns about the best interest standard?

16. Explain the ALI approximation rule. How does it respond to the concerns about the best interest standard?

17. What is the difference between physical and legal custody? Between sole and joint custody?

18. What concerns have been raised about joint custody? Under what circumstances is it most likely to be successful?

19. What is the legal status of a noncustodial parent?

20. Why will courts generally grant visitation rights to a parent who might not be an appropriate custodial parent?

21. What are the general approaches to structuring visitation?

22. What kinds of restrictions might a court impose on a visiting parent?

23. Discuss the intended functions of parenting plans and parent education programs.

24. What role might a parenting coordinator play in a divorce case?

25. What are the two basic approaches that states take with respect to post-divorce relocation disputes?

26. How have courts taken the possibility of "virtual visitation" into account when faced with relocation decisions?

27. What concerns are raised by virtual visitation orders in cases where there has been a history of domestic violence?

28. In what other situations have concerns been raised about virtual visitation?

29. What was the common law status of grandparents in relationship to their grandchildren?

30. What considerations prompted the passage of grandparent visitation statutes?

31. Under what circumstances do most grandparent visitation statutes permit a grandparent to seek visitation rights? Why did the Supreme Court invalidate Washington's grandparent visitation statute?

32. Explain the concept of "standing."

33. What is the traditional legal status of stepparents? How has this begun to change?

Discussion Questions

1. In determining custody, what weight do you think "moral" considerations should have? Do you think it is possible for judges to set aside their own views of morality when making decisions about custody?

2. What role do you think considerations of a child's cultural/racial heritage should play in a custody dispute? What are the potential benefits of giving weight to this factor? What are the potential risks?

3. Do you think that children are entitled to appointed counsel in contested custody cases?

4. Many fathers' rights organizations have argued that unless a court can order joint custody even where one parent is opposed, men will never be treated fairly. What do you think of this position?

5. Assuming a relocation decision is made in good faith, do you think the court should give greater weight to the desire of the custodial parent to move or to the noncustodial parent's wish to maintain the existing visitation arrangement? What factors would you weigh?

6. Would you allow a grandparent to have visitation rights with a grandchild over the objections of the parent(s)? What factors do you think a court should weigh in making these determinations?

Assignments

1. Locate the custody provisions of your state's divorce statute and answer the following questions:
   - Have any specific guidelines for determining best interest been adopted by statute or judicial decision?
   - Based on the guidelines or key court decisions, what factors are to be considered when determining custody?
   - Is domestic violence a factor to be considered? If so, how?
   - Is joint custody a permissible option? If yes, is there a presumption in favor of joint custody? Can it be ordered over the objection of a parent?

2. Assume you are working in a law firm, and the supervising partner has asked for your assistance in a custody relocation dispute in which your firm is representing the father. The father is seeking to prevent his former wife, who is the custodial parent, and children from moving out of state to another state that is about 350 miles away. Assume that the children are ages 5 and 7, that the father visits with them regularly and has a good relationship with both daughters, and that money is not a significant concern. The attorney has asked you to prepare an in-house legal memorandum in which you analyze the relevant statutory section, if any, and controlling case law on this issue.

3. Develop a detailed client intake questionnaire for use in all cases where custody or visitation might be an issue. Think carefully about all of the

information you would want to know about your client and his or her spouse.

4. Assume you are an appeals court judge in Florida and that the *Palmore* case is back before the court. This time, assume that the father returned to court and won custody of his daughter, whom we'll call Carrie, based on the following facts. Carrie is now school-aged and has been subjected to taunting and harassment. This has been very upsetting to Carrie. She has been experiencing difficulty eating and sleeping and cries every morning about having to go to school. The mother has filed an appeal with your court. As a judge, please decide whether the trial court decision should be affirmed or reversed, and write an opinion explaining your decision.

5. The attorney you work for has asked you to prepare the first draft of a parenting plan for a divorce case she is working on. She represents the wife and is concerned that the parties will not be able to effectively carry out the joint custody arrangement that they want. She would like the plan to be as detailed as possible. At a minimum it should cover the allocation of time and responsibilities, how decisions are to be made, and a process for resolving any disputes that come up. Given her concerns, she would like the plan to be drafted with particular care so that it facilitates the intended custodial arrangement. Following are the relevant facts:

   ■ The parties have agreed to share physical and legal custody of their daughter, Melinda, age 4.

   ■ Both parents work full-time, although the mother's schedule is more flexible, and she tends to work shorter hours than the father; however, she travels about once a month.

   ■ The parties want to try to make this arrangement work, but communication is tense and has gotten worse since the father has begun living with his new girlfriend.

   ■ The parties live in the same town.

   ■ The mother worries that the father is too strict and rigid in relationship to Melinda, and the father worries that the mother is too permissive and sets no rules.

   (Note: If the courts in your state have a standard parenting plan form, you should use this form for the assignment.)

Cases for Analysis

This 1996 case is a good example of how courts have begun to pay careful attention to the impact that witnessing domestic violence has on children.

MARY ANN P. v. WILLIAM R.P., JR.
197 W. Va. 1, 475 S.E.2d 1 (1996)

I. FACTS

The parties were married in March of 1985 and two sons were born of the marriage. William Raphael P. III (Billy) was born in May of 1985 and Mark Patrick P. was born in July of 1986. The record reflects that from the beginning the couple had a troubled marriage. The defendant was physically and mentally abusive to the plaintiff throughout their marriage. . . .

The plaintiff received custody of the children as she was determined to be the primary caretaker. The numerous proceedings held before the family law master focused primarily on the defendant's visitation rights which are at issue in this appeal. At the March 3, 1992, hearing before the family law master, the plaintiff detailed the physical and mental abuse that occurred during the marriage. She testified the defendant did not want her to have either of the boys and he urged her to have abortions both times she became pregnant. He showed little interest in the children when they were infants and openly expressed his disappointment that he had boys instead of girls. . . .

The plaintiff also testified the defendant had a violent temper and would yell and curse at her in front of the children. . . . During arguments, the defendant punched and kicked the plaintiff. He threatened her with a knife. He choked her around the neck so hard she had to wear a scarf to hide the bruises. He drug [sic] her across the floor by her hair in front of the children. The plaintiff testified that when the children would witness this abuse they would scream and cry and try to hide. The defendant would hit and kick the children's toys and broke toys in front of the children in fits of rage. The plaintiff testified that "the trauma and crying that these children have seen in their life is unreal."

During one argument, the defendant locked the plaintiff out of the house and kept the children inside. She testified she was afraid for the children's safety and put her fist through a window to enter the house. She severed three nerves in her arm and underwent surgery to correct the damage.

Billy and Mark have severe allergy problems and needed frequent medical treatments for ear infections, allergies, and colds when they were infants. The plaintiff testified the defendant was not sympathetic to the children's medical needs and, on certain occasions, blocked her attempts to get medical attention for the boys because he believed the plaintiff was overreacting to the children's symptoms. The defendant continued to smoke in front of the boys even though it caused them respiratory problems.

Despite the foregoing, the plaintiff maintains she encouraged the children's visitation with their father following the separation. However, she stated he exercised his visitation rights sporadically. . . .

The plaintiff testified Billy and Mark no longer want to have any contact with their father. It upsets them greatly when they have to visit with him. When the defendant comes to the house to visit, the boys frequently run and hide and have to be coaxed to come out to speak with their father. The plaintiff testified the visitations have had a profound effect on Billy. He has nightmares and acts out aggressively toward other children. Billy builds traps and barricades and frequently checks to see the doors and windows are locked because he is afraid the defendant will enter the house.

Several witnesses who accompanied the defendant on supervised visits testified regarding the boys' and the defendant's behavior. While the evidence is somewhat conflicting, it appears the boys do not want to visit their father and behave poorly in his presence. . . . The defendant . . . stated his visitations with the children are not as bad as the plaintiff contends. He testified that the plaintiff interferes with his relationship with his children. . . .

Christina Marie Arco, Ph.D., a psychologist . . ., testified at a hearing held in October of 1994 that she provided therapy for the children. At a hearing held in January of 1995, Dr. Arco testified she was still seeing Billy for therapy. She stated that Billy's anger and aggressiveness are at very high levels. He has fears and anxieties about his father. Billy told Dr. Arco he wished his father were dead so he would not have to worry about him anymore. Dr. Arco testified that any forced visitation with his father would cause serious regression in Billy. She also stated that the negativity the children have about their father is much more motivated by fear, anxiety, and anger than by any negative comments that may have been made by the plaintiff. . . .

After hearing the . . . evidence, the family law master rendered his recommended order. He found:

> "It is clear that . . . plaintiff does not like the defendant, and justifiably so because of the history of physical violence in their marriage, but that there can be no further justification whatsoever of any restriction of defendant's right of visitation with his children." . . .

. . . The family law master stated that, due to the history of domestic violence in the case, for six months the defendant's visitation with the boys would be restricted to the presence of a third person. . . .

The plaintiff filed exceptions to the family law master's recommended decision. . . . After hearing additional evidence on the issue of whether resumption of visitation would be harmful to the children, the circuit court ordered supervised visitation with the defendant until the boys attain an age where enforced visitation would be "meaningless." . . . The circuit court . . . found the record "only partially supports a conclusion that resumed visitation will result in serious psychiatric regression" and that no "high risk of suicide or withdrawal" should occur if visitation resumes. . . .

. . . Our decision to affirm this portion of the circuit court's order, however, is not determinative of the final disposition of this case. . . .

. . . The family law master found the plaintiff suffered from physical and emotional abuse during the marriage, but failed to address the negative consequences such abuse now has on the children's relationship to and visitation with their father. To be clear, we are not speaking of a child's general reluctance to visit with his or her noncustodial parent. What we are dealing with in this case is Mark's and Billy's documented intense fears and anxieties in visiting with their father. . . .

A fair reading of the record reveals that the boys' feelings of animosity toward their father are in large part due to their father's treatment of their mother. During counseling sessions, the boys stated their father was "mean" because he did "awful things" to their mother. The plaintiff testified that during the marriage the boys would scream and cry when she and the defendant would fight. The defendant's physical abuse of the plaintiff was witnessed by the boys, and they were terrified of their father because of this abuse.

The evidence of the negative impact the physical abuse that occurred during the marriage had in regard to the children's well-being was not rebutted. . . .

This Court joins with the majority of jurisdictions in finding that domestic violence evidence should be considered when determining parental fitness and child custody. In Syllabus Point 1, in part, of Henry v. Johnson, 192 W. Va. 82, 450 S.E.2d 779 (1994), we stated:

> "Children are often physically assaulted or witness violence against one of their parents and may suffer deep and lasting emotional harm from victimization and from exposure to family violence; consequently, a family law master should take domestic violence into account[.]"

See W. Va. Code, 48-2A-1(a)(2) (1992) (domestic violence statute states that children "may suffer deep and lasting emotional harm from victimization and from exposure to family violence"). Similarly, in the dissenting opinion in Patricia Ann S. v. James Daniel S., 190 W. Va. 6, 18, 435 S.E.2d 6, 18 (1993), Justice Workman recognized that "spousal abuse has a tremendous impact on children" regardless of whether the children were directly abused. While custody was not at issue in this case, evidence of domestic violence is still relevant in deciding the visitation issue because it appears to be the root cause for why visitation has not been successful. . . .

. . . Based on the foregoing, we agree with the plaintiff that supervised visitation should not immediately resume. . . . The record is clear that forced visitation at this time would be detrimental to the children and futile on the defendant's behalf without professional intervention. In Mary D. v. Watt, 190 W. Va. at 348, 438 S.E.2d at 528, this Court held that a "family law master or circuit court may condition . . . supervised visitation upon the offending parent seeking treatment." On remand, the circuit court should address this issue. The circuit court should also consider whether it would be beneficial for the defendant and the children to attend counseling sessions together to help build a more positive relationship. . . .

In *Mary D.*, Chief Justice McHugh set forth guidelines to help provide children with a safe and secure atmosphere when supervised visitation is exercised. Although Mary D. dealt specifically with supervised visitation following a finding that sexual abuse occurred, we find it just as applicable in this case where the children harbor such strong feelings against their father, whatever the source of such emotional estrangement. It is in everyone's interest to see that supervised visitation goes as smoothly as possible. In Syllabus Point 3 of *Mary D.*, we held:

In *Patricia Ann S.*, 190 W. Va. at 18, 435 S.E.2d at 18, Justice Workman quoted the following excerpt from L. Crites & D. Coker, What Therapists See That Judges May Miss, The Judges' Journal 9, 11-12 (Spring 1988):

> "'Children learn several lessons in witnessing the abuse of one of their parents. First, they learn that such behavior appears to be approved by their most important role models and that the violence toward a loved one is acceptable. Children also fail to grasp the full range of negative consequences for the violent behavior and observe, instead, the short term reinforcements, namely compliance by the victim. Thus, they learn the use of coercive power and violence as a way to influence loved ones without being exposed to other more constructive alternatives.'" In addition to the effect of the destructive modeling, children who grow up in violent homes experience damaging psychological effects. There is substantial documentation that the spouse abuser's violence causes a variety of psychological problems for children. Children raised in a home in which spouse abuse occurs experience the same fear as do battered children. . . . "'Spouse abuse results not only in direct physical and psychological injuries to the children, but, of greatest long-term importance, it breeds a culture of violence in future generations.'"
>
> "Where supervised visitation is ordered pursuant to W. Va. Code, 48-2-15(b)(1) [1991], the best interests of a child include determining that the child is safe from the fear of emotional and psychological trauma which he or she may experience. The person(s) appointed to supervise the visitation should have had some prior contact with the child so that the child is sufficiently familiar with and trusting of that person in order for the child to have secure feelings and so that the visitation is not harmful to his or her emotional well being. Such a determination should be incorporated as a finding of the family law master or circuit court."

QUESTIONS

1. What was the recommendation of the family law master with respect to visitation?
2. Why did the circuit court order supervised visitation?
3. What critique does this court have of the family law master's findings?
4. According to the court, why is evidence of domestic violence relevant in custody and visitation determinations?
5. What was the court's ultimate decision with respect to visitation? What were the remand instructions to the trial court?

This complex custody case addresses many of the topics discussed in this chapter, including application of the best interest test, joint custody presumptions, the relocation of the custodial parent, and virtual visitation.

DANTI v. DANTI
146 Idaho 929, 204 P.3d 1140 (2009)

J. JONES, Justice.

Ed Danti appeals the divorce decree entered between himself and his ex-wife, Michelle Danti, particularly challenging the provisions awarding Michelle sole physical custody of their two children and allowing her to relocate with the children to California.

Ed and Michelle were married in California in 1996. During their marriage, the couple had two daughters — one in 1998 and the other in 2004. At the time of the proceedings in this matter, the children were eight and two years old, respectively.

Ed and Michelle lived in California until 2004. While there, Ed ran a residential remodeling company and Michelle owned and operated her own day care. They decided to move to Meridian, Idaho, in July 2004. Their plan was to stay in Idaho for a few years and then possibly relocate to California. Once the family arrived in Idaho, Ed began his own custom tile business and Michelle stayed at home with the children.

In August 2005, Ed hired a designer, Heather Clark, to assist him with some of his remodeling projects. Approximately one month after Ed hired Heather, he and Michelle began considering divorce. Michelle was unhappy living in Idaho and the couple fought frequently. Although no definitive resolution was reached, the couple decided to temporarily separate. During their period of separation, Ed continued to live in the couple's home.

Shortly after Ed and Michelle decided to separate, Michelle learned from Heather's husband that Ed was likely having an affair with Heather. Michelle confronted Ed with this information and he admitted having an emotional connection to Heather, but denied any sexual relationship. Over time, however, Ed's romantic feelings for Heather grew. When Ed eventually told Michelle of his feelings for Heather, Michelle informed him that she wanted to move back to California but she agreed not to leave until Ed returned from a trip he was taking to California. In return, Ed agreed to allow Michelle to move to California with the children once he arrived back in Idaho. . . .

Once Ed returned from his trip, Michelle decided to move back to California. Thereafter, Michelle and the children returned to California, but continued to have daily conversations with Ed. During the course of those conversations, Ed was able to convince Michelle to come back to Idaho. Michelle agreed to return after Ed promised that he would end both his personal and professional relationships with Heather.

Once Michelle arrived back in Idaho, she began to suspect that Ed was still seeing Heather. By December 2005, it became obvious to Michelle that, despite his promise, Ed was continuing his relationship with Heather. Consequently, Michelle informed Ed that she planned to return to California. Ed then signed another consent letter giving Michelle his permission to permanently move to California with the children. Before Michelle was able to leave, however, Ed broke down and begged her not to go. Once again, he promised Michelle that if she stayed with him he would end his relationship with Heather. Ed's promise persuaded Michelle and the couple decided to return to California together.

While in California, Michelle learned that Ed was still having regular communications with Heather. Michelle confronted Ed about the communications and he admitted that he had been in touch with Heather. After the confrontation, Ed decided to fly back to Idaho. Once here, he continued to try to convince Michelle to reconcile with him by denying any sexual relationship with Heather.

Ed ultimately persuaded Michelle to move back to Idaho. After returning, Michelle observed Heather at one of Ed's jobsites. This angered Michelle, who decided to call Heather and request a meeting. Michelle then went to Heather's house and the two women discussed their relationships with Ed. Perhaps unsurprisingly, Michelle and Heather discovered that Ed had been lying to both of them. In the midst of their conversation, Ed arrived and admitted that he had been sexually intimate with both women. Upon learning this information, Michelle became upset and left Ed at Heather's house. Although Ed went home briefly that night to pack his belongings, he ended up spending the night with Heather.

The next morning Ed went home to apologize to Michelle. After Ed arrived, however, the couple began arguing and Ed "became enraged and grabbed Michelle by the arms, pushing her up against the laundry room door while screaming at her and poking her in the chest with his finger." All of this occurred in front of the couple's youngest daughter. When Michelle was finally able to break free from Ed, she took her daughter and went to the police station. Michelle reported the incident to the police and Ed was charged with domestic battery. A no contact order was issued and Ed subsequently pleaded guilty to the lesser charge of disturbing the peace. After the issuance of the no contact order, Ed moved in with Heather because he could no longer live in the same house as Michelle.

In March 2006, Michelle filed a complaint for divorce against Ed, in which she alleged irreconcilable differences, adultery, and extreme cruelty. A temporary custody order was issued in May 2006, granting Michelle primary physical custody of the children. The order conditioned Ed's visitation with the children on him not living with Heather and on Heather not being present during visitation. It also required Ed to pay Michelle sixty percent of his net income.

Over the next few months, the intensity of the conflict between Michelle and Ed increased. On more than one occasion, the parties filed police reports alleging that the other had committed various crimes. Additionally, the police were called during at least one custody exchange. At several other exchanges, the couple argued in front of their daughters about topics ranging from the children's involvement in extracurricular activities to visitation schedules and missing clothing.

A trial regarding the divorce, child custody, and child support was held on December 15, 2006. After the trial, the court granted Michelle's request for a divorce on the grounds of extreme mental cruelty and adultery. The judge awarded Ed and Michelle joint legal custody of the couple's children, but granted Michelle sole physical custody. As part of the custody arrangement, Michelle would be permitted to move to California with the children and Ed would receive visitation with the girls in Idaho during portions of their winter, spring, and summer breaks. Ed would also be allowed to visit the girls in the Sacramento, California, area once per month and on certain holidays. . . .

Ed now appeals to this Court. He alleges that the court's award of sole physical custody to Michelle was an abuse of discretion because it: (1) violated Idaho's presumption in favor of joint custody; (2) was not in the best interests of the children; (3) was improperly based on Michelle's status as the children's primary caregiver; (4) disregarded Michelle's numerous acts of "secretly and wrongfully" taking the children out of the state; (5) was based on clearly erroneous findings of fact; and (6) was not based upon a custody evaluation performed by a neutral third party. . . .

In Idaho, the children's best interests are of paramount importance when making decisions regarding the children's custody, including decisions relating to where the children will reside. . . . In determining what is in the children's best interests, courts are required to consider all relevant factors. Relevant factors may include, but are not limited to: the parents' wishes for the children's custody; the children's wishes; the interrelationship and interaction between the children and their parents and siblings; the extent the children have adjusted to their school, home, and community; the character and circumstances of the persons involved; the need to promote continuity and stability in the children's lives; and domestic violence. I.C. §32-717(1)(a)-(g). Additionally, unless one parent is a habitual perpetrator of domestic violence, courts are required to apply Idaho's presumption that an award of joint custody is in the children's best interests. . . . An award of joint custody must provide "that physical custody . . . be shared by the parents in such a way as to assure the . . . children [have] frequent and continuing contact with both parents. . . .

[A] court may decline to award joint custody if doing so will serve the children's best interests. . . . The court must, in addition, "state in its decision the reasons for denial of an award of joint custody." I.C. §32-717B(1). These considerations apply where a parent wishes to relocate with his or her child. An award of physical custody to a relocating parent may only be made if he or she proves that the move is in the children's best interests. . . .

The trial court did not abuse its discretion by awarding Michelle sole physical custody of the children.

Several of the section 32-717 factors played only a slight role in the court's analysis. More specifically, the court concluded that the children's wishes, parents' wishes, and domestic violence were of little consequence. In regards to the children's wishes, the youngest child's wishes were unknown and the oldest child had only expressed her desire to live with her mother on one occasion. Accordingly, their wishes were only given slight weight in the court's analysis. The parents' wishes for the children's custody also had little bearing on the court's decision. The court gave due regard to the parents' wishes but, because they were conflicting, concluded that they did not favor awarding custody to one parent over the other. Finally, domestic violence was of little concern to the court because there was no established pattern of violent behavior by either party. Rather, there was only one occasion of reported violence committed by Ed. Because there was no evidence of habitual domestic violence, the court also concluded that the presumption in favor of joint custody applied.

Of more importance to the court was its concern for continuity and stability in the children's lives. The court concluded that this factor favored awarding physical custody to Michelle. It reasoned that in light of the children's young age they "gain security from a stable environment in which their needs are consistently met." Because Michelle had served as the children's primary caregiver their entire lives and was "best able to meet their physical and psychological needs consistently," she would be more likely to further these objectives. At the same time, the children's need for stability weighed against awarding physical custody to Ed because "he inappropriately involved the children directly in his conflict with Michelle by denigrating her character to them."

Ed disputes the trial court's reliance on Michelle's status as the children's primary caregiver in making its custody award. In doing so, he attempts to analogize the facts of this case to the facts in Hopper v. Hopper, 144 Idaho 624, 167 P.3d 761 (2007). In *Hopper*, the trial court awarded a mother temporary custody after she secretly moved to Montana with her son and obtained a fraudulent domestic violence protection order against the father. . . .

Ed's attempt to analogize the facts of this case to those in *Hopper* is unpersuasive. Unlike the domestic violence claim in *Hopper*, Michelle's claim has not subsequently been determined to be false. Although Ed points to facts that, if true, would tend to undermine Michelle's claim, there was also evidence to support the court's conclusion that Ed was violent with Michelle. The court had before it a police report describing the event, Ed's guilty plea, and Michelle's testimony. Moreover, the trial court specifically found Michelle's account of the event that gave rise to the domestic battery charge more credible.

This case is also distinguishable from *Hopper* because Michelle did not secrete the children from Ed. Unlike the mother in *Hopper* who secretly moved with the child to Montana, Michelle moved to California with the children only after informing Ed and, on two occasions, obtaining his written consent. Nonetheless, Ed attempts to characterize Michelle's moves to California with the children as "kidnapping" and "extortion." He argues that Michelle secretly left Idaho and "fled" to California, then refused to return unless he agreed not to divorce her. He maintains that Michelle forced him to sign the letters in which he consented to the moves by threatening to leave with the children while he was out of town.

Ed's arguments regarding Michelle's moves are unconvincing. The fact that Ed signed written consent statements giving Michelle permission to return to California with the couple's daughters undermines his claim that the moves were secret. On the one occasion that Michelle returned to California without obtaining Ed's written consent, he was aware of her plan to move. Moreover, the trial court implicitly found Ed's assertions that the letters were signed under duress to lack credibility. For these reasons, Ed's claim that Michelle repeatedly kidnapped and secreted the children is without merit.

Next, the trial court found that the interrelationship between the children and their parents favored awarding physical custody to Michelle. Although the evidence indicated that the children were close to both parents, digital telephone recordings submitted by the parties revealed that Michelle had a more constructive relationship with the children. The recordings also revealed that Michelle was "more reasonable and solution-oriented than Ed."

Finally, an award of physical custody to Michelle was supported by the court's analysis of the character of the parties involved. In analyzing this factor, the court acknowledged that both Ed and Michelle demonstrated character flaws throughout the proceedings. However, it concluded that, in light of Ed's behavior, Michelle's self-restraint was "fairly remarkable." Digital recordings of conversations and custody exchanges revealed that Ed made several inappropriate comments to the children and to others in their presence. Further, Ed's affair with Heather reflected poorly on his character. Not only did Ed begin a sexual relationship with Heather while still married to Michelle, he tried to rationalize to his eight-year-old daughter the relationship with Heather and the fact that he was having a baby out of wedlock. In the view of the court, this behavior indicated that Ed would not be a positive role model for his daughters. In all, the court concluded that instead of focusing on the needs of the children, Ed "focus[ed] . . . on Ed and what [he] deserve[d] from his children."

After reviewing the magistrate judge's decision, it is clear that the judge did not err in awarding Michelle sole physical custody of the children. Only after analyzing all of the relevant factors and fully explaining the basis for its decision did the court conclude that awarding Michelle sole physical custody was in the children's best interests. Consequently, it concluded that an award of joint physical custody would not be in the children's best interests and, therefore, that the presumption in favor of joint custody had been overcome.

Nevertheless, Ed argues that the court's decision was an abuse of discretion because it disregarded Idaho's joint custody presumption. . . .

Ed's argument that awarding sole physical custody to Michelle violates Idaho's joint custody presumption misconstrues the law. The joint custody presumption is just that—a presumption. Unlike *per se* rules, presumptions may be overcome. *Id.* In this case, the magistrate concluded that the presumption had been overcome by evidence indicating that an award of joint physical custody was not in the children's best interests. Accordingly, Ed's argument that the court abused its discretion by disregarding the joint custody presumption is unconvincing.

Nor did the court abuse its discretion in allowing Michelle to move with the children to California. . . . [T]he court weighed the benefits the children would receive from moving against the benefits [of] having more regular contact with Ed. After doing so, it concluded that the benefits of having more contact with Ed were "far outweighed by other considerations." The court reasoned that living in close proximity to Ed would potentially result in the children living in a perpetual high-conflict environment. Not only would the children be exposed to Ed's and Michelle's arguments, but also to Heather's high-conflict divorce. The only way to avoid exposing the children to numerous dysfunctional relationships would be to allow them to move with their mother to California. Additional benefits the children would receive if allowed to move included: increased emotional support, the opportunity to be around their extended family, increased stability, and "a psychologically healthier environment." Moreover, the children would not experience much disruption from the move since they had spent significant periods of time in California while Michelle and Ed were separated. The couple's oldest daughter had even been enrolled in school there. In light of these considerations, the court determined that it was in the children's best interests to relocate to California with their mother. . . .

Ed contests the trial court's visitation schedule on the grounds that it will be "impossible to maintain over the next 14 years." Ed also disputes the schedule because he is not reimbursed for all of his travel expenses, he does not have visitation on certain holidays and other "special days," and it requires him to leave his new wife and child eighteen times per year. . . .

Ed has failed to show that the trial court's visitation schedule was an abuse of discretion. In establishing the visitation schedule, the court considered the children's best interests, the parties' need for structure, transportation costs, and the convenience of the parties. Based on these considerations, the court awarded Ed extended visitation with the children in Idaho during their breaks from school, visitation in California once per month and during certain holiday weekends, and regular "virtual visitation" through the use of "telephone, Internet, web-cam, and other wireless or wired technologies." Although the court acknowledged that there may be easier and more cost efficient ways to accomplish visitation, it concluded that Michelle and Ed could not "be counted on to cooperate to that extent." Moreover, the court's visitation schedule was necessary to avoid "placing [the] children in limbo at or during exchanges." . . .

Nor did the court abuse its discretion by declining to award Ed visitation during *every* holiday or "special day." Ed was awarded visitation every other Christmas and Thanksgiving. He was also awarded visitation every spring break, Memorial Day weekend, and Fourth of July. In addition to in-person visitation, the schedule allows Ed to call the children once per week and have "virtual visitation" with them twice per week. Because the visitation schedule adequately ensures that the children's relationship with Ed will be fostered, the fact that it did not award Ed visitation on certain holidays and "special days" does not render it an abuse of discretion.

Similarly, the visitation schedule was not an abuse of discretion simply because it requires Ed to spend approximately one weekend per month away from his new wife and son. In issuing the visitation schedule, the trial court could have reasonably concluded that it would be more convenient for Ed to travel to California over the weekend than it would be for the children to travel to Idaho. Additionally, in light of Ed's accusations that the trial court was only concerned with Michelle's best interest, it is paradoxical that he now asks this Court to consider the fairness of requiring him to spend weekends away from his new family in order to visit his daughters in California. Moreover, his complaint about being away from his family in Idaho contradicts his assertion that he should be awarded additional visitation with the children on certain "special days" in California. In sum, Ed has not shown that requiring him to travel to California in order to visit his daughters was an abuse of discretion. . . .

Ed argues that the magistrate's custody award violates his constitutionally protected parental rights. He maintains that, because he was awarded joint legal custody, he should be allowed to take his children out of the Sacramento area during his California visitation. Ed asserts that the restriction limiting his California visitation to the Sacramento area violates his constitutional right to the "care, custody, and control of [his] children" as pronounced by the United States Supreme Court in Troxel v. Granville, 530 U.S. 57, 66, 120 S. Ct. 2054, 147 L. Ed. 2d 49 (2000).

Ed's constitutional argument is unpersuasive. Initially, it mischaracterizes the rights associated with an award of joint legal custody. Ed's award of joint legal custody gave him the right to share in decision-making regarding his children's health, education, and general welfare. . . . It did not give him the right to take the children wherever he pleases during visitation. Moreover, the award did not violate Ed's constitutional right to the custody, care, and control of his children. As we recently held, . . . a child custody decision that implicates a parent's constitutional rights will be upheld so long as the decision was necessary to ensure the child's best interest. . . . Here, the magistrate determined that moving to California with Michelle and having monthly visitation with Ed was in the children's best interests. A custody award implementing that arrangement was therefore necessary to serve the children's best interests. Further, a specific, rigid visitation arrangement was necessary in light of, among other things, the parties' demonstrated inability to work with flexibility. Because the custody award was necessary to ensure the children's best interests, it did not violate Ed's constitutional right to the custody, care, and control of his children.

QUESTIONS

1. Which factors related to best interest did the court rely on in making its custody decision?
2. Explain why the court declined to award joint custody, given the state's joint custody presumption.
3. Why did the court agree to allow Michelle to move out of state with the children?
4. How did the court structure the visitation award?
5. What role does "virtual visitation" play in the decision?

The following case illustrates the complexity of relocation cases. As presented here, the applicable standard for determining if a removal request should be allowed or not turns on whether a sole or a shared custody arrangement is in place.

MILLER v. MILLER
478 Mass. 642, 88 N.E.3d 843 (2018)

The husband, Benjamin H. Miller, appeals from a Probate and Family Court judgment permitting the wife, Joanna Isabella Miller, to remove and relocate the parties' daughter to Germany, the wife's home country. We have previously held that when deciding whether removal should be permitted, the particular criteria depend on whether physical custody of the child is sole or shared. Where the parent seeking removal has sole physical custody, his or her removal petition is analyzed using what has been called the "real advantage" standard of *Yannas v. Frondistou-Yannas, 395 Mass. 704, 481 N.E.2d 1153 (1985)*. Where, however, the parents share physical custody, a parent's removal request is evaluated using the standard articulated in *Mason v. Coleman, 447 Mass. 177, 850 N.E.2d 513 (2006)*, known as the "best interests" standard. In this case, no prior custody order existed to guide the trial judge as to whether the *Yannas* or *Mason* analysis should apply. In such circumstances, we hold that the judge must first perform a functional analysis, which may require a factual inquiry, regarding the parties' respective parenting responsibilities to determine whether it more closely approximates sole or shared custody, and then apply the corresponding standard. We also take this opportunity to emphasize that the best interests of the child is always the paramount consideration in any question involving removal.

We are satisfied that the judge conducted the requisite functional analysis here, and in determining whether removal was in the child's best interests she afforded considerable weight to the benefits the proposed move to Germany would offer the wife, the child's primary caregiver.

The wife, a German citizen, and the husband, a United States citizen, were married in Tanzania in September, 2007. Their only child, a daughter, was born in Uganda in March, 2008. In July, 2011, the family moved to Massachusetts, where the husband's family resides, so that the husband could attend graduate school. The parties did not intend to remain in Massachusetts and planned to leave once the husband received his graduate degree. The wife had grown up in Germany and had never lived in the United States before, and the husband had not resided here in eighteen years.

The husband ultimately did not attend graduate school, however, and the parties first separated in April, 2012. During this separation, which lasted from April to August, the wife moved with the child to Germany, where they resided with the wife's mother and the child attended a German public school. The wife returned to Massachusetts with the child that August in an attempted reconciliation, but the parties separated for the final time in September, 2012. The husband filed for divorce in May, 2013, citing an irretrievable breakdown of the marriage.

Among the relevant facts found by the judge was the determination that the "[w]ife has been [the child]'s primary caregiver since birth" and has continued in that role following the parties' separation. The wife cared for the child when she was an infant and is now the parent who "arranges and attends her medical appointments," "cares for [the child] when she is ill," "purchases the majority of her clothing, and attends all parent-teacher conferences." The judge also found that although the "[h]usband is not seeking sole physical custody of [the child,] and does not propose that he should be her primary caregiver," the husband does participate in certain parenting tasks, and he and the child have a loving relationship.

Following their divorce filings, the parties filed a stipulation in the trial court stating that they "shall share custody" of the child. . . . In practice, however, the husband often travels for work, and when he does he communicates with the child infrequently, and he misses parenting time that he has not sought to make up. The judge also found that "the parties struggle to communicate effectively regarding parenting issues". . . .

Despite their impressive professional credentials, the husband and wife have both struggled financially since they arrived in Massachusetts, and the judge concluded that their current parenting arrangement is "financially untenable." . . .

Prior to trial, the wife was offered a well-paying job in Germany, which the judge found would enable the wife "to support herself and [the child] without child support from [the h]usband." Beyond a livable salary, its benefits include health insurance and "the ability to work from home most of the time." The wife expressed her intention of accepting the position if her requests for custody and removal were granted. In contrast with Massachusetts, where the wife lacks any family or friends, a return to Germany would place the wife among her extended family. This includes the wife's mother, with whom the child is especially close. . . .

Following a three-day trial, the judge concluded that permanently relocating to Germany with the wife was in the child's best interests and granted the wife's requests for physical custody and removal. The judgment granted the husband "parenting time with [the child] during three of the four annual vacations from school in Germany, including six consecutive weeks during each summer vacation," as well as "additional parenting time with [the child] in Germany upon reasonable notice to [the w]ife by agreement." . . .

Discussion. The husband challenges the judge's removal order on two grounds. First, he argues that the judge erred in applying the "real advantage" analysis of *Yannas*, applicable where a parent seeking removal has sole physical custody of his or her child. The husband contends that because the parties shared physical custody of the child, the judge should have applied the "best interests" standard articulated in *Mason*. Second, the husband argues that even if the judge properly employed the *Yannas* standard, she nevertheless abused her discretion in concluding that removal is in the child's best interests. . . .

Removal petitions in the Commonwealth are evaluated under one of two analyses, depending on the physical custody of the child. Where one parent has sole physical custody, a judge must evaluate that parent's request to remove the child under the "real advantage" analysis. . . . Where, on the other hand, the parents share joint physical custody, a judge must apply the "best interests" analysis. . . . "The main distinction" between these analyses "comes down to the weight that should be assigned to the benefits the relocation would provide the parent seeking to move." . . .

Evaluating custody. In deciding the applicable removal standard where there is no custody order the judge must first evaluate the parties' custodial arrangement and determine whether it more closely resembles sole or shared custody. . . .

In determining which manner of custody is present in a given case, the judge typically will look to an existing custody order between the parties. Even where there is such an order, though, the judge is still required to look beyond its characterization of custody (e.g., "the parties shall share physical custody"), in order to examine "the functional responsibilities and involvement of each parent" with their child in practice. . . .

In other cases, such as the instant one, there is no prior custody order to refer to, as a parent's removal request is concurrent with their divorce complaint. Still, the same principles apply; in deciding the appropriate removal standard, the judge must focus on "functional," as opposed to technical, "divisions in caregiving and parenting responsibilities.". . .

As we explained in *Yannas*, where one parent has sole physical custody, the interests of that child are "so interwoven with the well-being of the custodial parent" that "the determination of the child's best interest requires that the interests of the custodial parent be taken into account" (citation omitted). *Yannas* involves a two-part inquiry. First, a judge must examine "whether there is a good reason for the move, a 'real advantage'" to the parent. . . .

Second, if the custodial parent satisfies that threshold inquiry, the judge must then "consider[] collectively" the interests of the custodial parent, the noncustodial parent, and their child, and balance those interests to determine whether removal is in the best interests of the child. Pertinent considerations at this step include "whether the quality of the child's life may be improved by the change (including any improvement flowing from an improvement in the quality of the custodial parent's life), the possible adverse effect of the elimination or curtailment of the child's association with the noncustodial parent, and the extent to which moving or not moving will affect the emotional, physical, or developmental needs of the child." . . .

In *Mason*, we explained that "[w]here physical custody is shared, the 'best interest' calculus pertaining to removal is appreciably different from those situations that involve sole physical custody." Under *Mason*, "[t]he advantage to the moving parent becomes merely a relevant factor in the over-all inquiry of what is in the child's best interests." This is so because with shared custody, "[n]o longer is the fortune of simply one custodial parent so tightly interwoven with that of the child; [here] both parents have equal rights and responsibilities with respect to the child. . . .

The judge concluded that "[a]lthough [the h]usband was involved in caring for [the child] during the marriage, [the w]ife has always been primarily responsible for her physical and emotional care, as well as day-to-day tasks such as feeding, clothing, and bathing." More significantly, in the opinion's section discussing removal, the judge analyzed the issue solely in terms of the two steps of the *Yannas* analysis. . . .

The husband first argues that the judge abused her discretion in applying the "real advantage" analysis under *Yannas*. He maintains that because the parties shared physical custody of the child, the judge should have evaluated the wife's removal petition using the "best interest" standard of *Mason*, which affords less weight to the advantages a move offers the parent seeking removal. In support of his contention of shared physical custody, the husband relies primarily on the stipulated parenting plan the parties filed in the trial court. . . .

The judge clearly considered the stipulation, having detailed its contents both in her recitation of the case's procedural history and in an individual factual finding. Yet the judge also found that the husband travels frequently for work, and when he does he "communicates with [the child] infrequently" and misses allotted parenting time that he has not sought to make up. With respect to the parties' parenting responsibilities, the judge found that the wife has always been the child's primary caregiver. . . . Likewise, although a hallmark of shared custody is the parents' "ability and desire to cooperate amicably and communicate with one another to raise the[ir] child[ ]," the judge found that "the parties struggle to communicate effectively regarding parenting issues, and that [the h]usband often fails to communicate with [the w]ife." . . .

The *Mason* analysis generally applies where "neither parent has a clear majority of custodial responsibility." Although the terms of the parties' stipulation may have approximated shared custody, the judge concluded (in light of the above facts) that, in practice, their custodial arrangement more closely resembled the sole custody of *Yannas*. . . .

Turning to the judge's application of the *Yannas* analysis, the husband does not argue that the first step of *Yannas* is not satisfied — namely, that there is a real advantage to the wife in moving to Germany.

Instead, the husband only challenges the judge's subsequent conclusion, formally the second step of the *Yannas* analysis, that removal is in the child's best interests. The husband contends that the judge abused her discretion in reaching that conclusion because she failed to consider adequately how removal would impact or benefit the child, and failed to consider reasonable alternative visitation arrangements. . . .

With respect to the effect of the move on the child's quality of life and her "emotional, physical, or developmental needs," the judge found that in Germany the child would be attending better schools and would again be treated by her long-time pediatrician. She found further that in Germany the child would "have support from the loving extended family with whom she has had frequent and extensive contact since birth," including her maternal grandmother, with whom the child "is very close." . . .

More significantly, the judge observed that the child's quality of life will be "particularly" improved "through the impact of the improvement in [the w]ife's quality of life." In Massachusetts, the wife could not meet her expenses and lived in poverty. By contrast, the judge found that the wife's well-paying job in Germany would permit her to support herself and the child, while continuing to fulfil her role as the child's primary caregiver, as the position would enable the wife "to work from home most of the time." . . . In addition, the wife has virtually no support network in Massachusetts because she "has few acquaintances" here and "feels lonely and isolated," but in Germany she would reunite with her supportive extended family.

The trial judge concluded that this improvement in the wife's emotional situation would also "benefit [the child] significantly."

Notwithstanding the direct and indirect benefits a move to Germany would offer the child, the judge also found that the child has a "loving relationship" with her father, and recognized that moving to Germany would have a "detrimental effect" on that relationship. . . .

Interests of the noncustodial parent. Last, the judge must consider the interests of the noncustodial parent. This includes assessing "whether reasonable 'alternative visitation arrangements' might achieve ongoing and meaningful contact appropriate to the circumstances."

The judge found that the husband cares for the child deeply, and recognized the "detrimental effect" separation would have on their relationship. She also acknowledged the husband's concerns "regarding his ability to communicate with [the child] on a regular basis given the six-hour time difference between Massachusetts and Germany," as well as the various travel costs the husband would incur during his visitation periods. The judge concluded that, in addition to frequent telephone and Internet contact, aligning the husband's visitation with the child's extended vacation periods will lessen the detrimental effects of their separation, by providing them with lengthier, and hence more meaningful, visits together. . . .

We discern no abuse of discretion with respect to the judge's consideration and balancing of the interests at stake here. The judge recognized that she was faced "with two difficult alternatives." Granting the wife's removal request would have the negative impact of permanently altering the child's relationship with her father, who cares for her deeply. Yet the judge also determined, on the basis of uncontested factual findings, that "allowing the current shared parenting schedule is financially untenable for the parties." Financial struggle — "poverty," as the wife described her current lifestyle — is in the interest of no child. As in *Yannas,* a move to Germany "would be to the advantage of the wife, financially, emotionally, and socially," and would inure to the child's benefit as well.

QUESTIONS

1. What are the two different standards discussed by the court for determining if a parent's relocation request should be granted?
2. What is the logic behind tying the applicable standard to the custody arrangement?
3. Why did the trial court judge disregard the joint custody arrangement set out in the parties' stipulation? What did the reviewing court have to say about this?
4. In rendering its decision, what did the court say about the interests of each party and the child? What weight did it afford to each?

Endnotes

1. For a discussion of custody disputes involving unmarried parents, see Chapter 11; for a discussion of custody issues in the context of abuse and neglect proceedings, see Chapter 12.

2. William Blackstone, Commentaries on the Laws of England 372-373 (19th London ed. 1857).

3. Michael Grossberg, Governing the Hearth: Law and the Family in Nineteenth-Century America 235 (1985). Although rarely mentioned in works discussing the nature of paternal authority, it is important to recognize that fathers who were slaves did not have this kind of authority over their children; slave owners had complete control over the lives of their slaves without regard for their family relationships.

4. Baird v. Baird, 21 N.J. Eq. 384, 393 (1869) (dissent), quoted in Alan Roth, The Tender Years Presumption in Child Custody Disputes, 15 J. Fam. L. 423, 428 (1976-1977).

5. Elizabeth Pleck, Domestic Tyranny: The Making of American Social Policy from Colonial Times to the Present 39 (1987).

6. Mich. Comp. Laws §722.23 (2009).

7. *See* Katherine T. Bartlett, U.S. Custody Law and Trends in the Context of the ALI Principles of the Law of Family Dissolution, 10 Va. J. Soc. Poly. & L. 5, 16-22 (2002).

8. Robert F. Kelly and Shawn L. Ward, Allocating Custodial Responsibilities at Divorce: Social Science Research and the American Law Institute's Approximation Rule, 40 Fam. Ct. Rev. 350, 356, 358 (2002).

9. *See* Margaret F. Bring, Feminism and Child Custody Under Chapter Two of the American Law Institute's Principles of the Law of Family Dissolution, 8 Duke J.L. & Poly. 301, 308-309 (2001).

10. Joan B. Kelly, Psychological and Legal Interventions for Parents and Children in Custody and Access Disputes: Current Research and Practice, 10 Va. J. Soc. Poly. & L. 129, 150 (2003). According to Kelly, these feelings are also attributed to parents' failure to "talk with their children about even the most elementary and relevant aspects of the separation or divorce." *Id. See also* Barbara A. Atwood, Hearing Children's Voices in Custody Litigation: An Empirical Survey and Suggestions of Reform, 45 Ariz. L. Rev. 629 (2003).

11. Kelly, *supra* note 10, at 154.

12. *Id.* at 152-161.

13. American Bar Association, Section of Family Law, Standards of Practice for Lawyers Representing Children in Child Custody Cases 1 (2003).

14. *Id.*

15. *Id.* at 3.

16. Elizabeth Scott, Parental Autonomy and Children's Welfare, 11 Wm. & Mary Bill of Rts. J. 1071, 1093 (2003).

17. N. Zoe Hilton, Battered Women's Concerns About Their Children Witnessing Wife Assault, 7 J. Interspousal Violence 1 (1990); Leigh Goodmark, From Property to Personhood: What the Legal System Should Do for Children in Family Violence Cases, 102 W. Va. L. Rev. 237 (1999). *See also* Amy Levin and Linda G. Mills, Fighting for Child Custody When Domestic Violence Is at Issue: Survey of State Laws, 48 Social Work 463 (2003).

18. Goodmark, *supra* note 17, at 245.

19. Judith S. Wallerstein and Sandra Blakeslee, Second Chances—Men, Women, and Children a Decade After Divorce 113-121 (1989). *See also* Alan J. Tomkins et al., The Plight of Children Who Witness Woman Battering: Psychological Knowledge and Policy Implications, 18 Law & Psychol. Rev. 137 (1994).

20. Hon. Donna J. Hitchens and Patricia Van Horn, Courts Responding to Domestic Violence; The Court's Role in Supporting and Protecting Children Exposed to Domestic Violence, 6 J. Center for Fam. Child. & Cts. 31 (2005). This article contains an excellent

review of the relevant literature. *See also* Peter G. Jaffee et al., Custody Disputes Involving Allegations of Domestic Violence: Toward a Differentiated Approach to Parenting Plans, 46 Fam. Ct. Rev. 500 (2008).

21. Hitchens and Van Horn, *supra* note 20, at 34. As the authors note, not all children who witness parental violence experience these problems (internal citations omitted). For a brief discussion regarding childhood resiliency, *see id.* at 33-34.

22. Wallerstein and Blakeslee, *supra* note 19, at 110-121.

23. Hitchens and Van Horn, *supra* note 20, at 38. To date, the research has focused on the connection between partner abuse committed by men and their treatment of children.

24. Cynthia Grover Hastings, Letting Down Their Guard: What Guardians Ad Litem Should Know About Domestic Violence in Child Custody Disputes, 24 B.C. Third World L.J. 283, 314 (2004).

25. Jaffee et al., *supra* note 20, at 503.

26. Hastings, *supra* note 24, at 301-302.

27. Emmaline Campbell, How Domestic Batterers Use Custody Proceedings in Family Courts to Abuse Victims, and How Family Courts Can Put a Stop to It, 24 UCLA Women's L.J. 41, 53 (2017).

28. *Id.*

29. Nancy K.D. Lemon, Statutes Creating Rebuttable Presumptions Against Custody to Batterers: How Effective Are They?, 28 Wm. Mitchell L. Rev. 601, 616 (2001).

30. *Id.* at 619.

31. Palmore v. Sidoti, 466 U.S. 429 (1984).

32. *Id.* at 433.

33. Gambla v. Woodson, 367 Ill. App. 3d 441, 853 N.E.2d 847, 863, 869-871 (2006), appeal denied by Gambla v. Woodson, 222 Ill. 2d 571, 861 N.E.2d 654, (2006); *cert. denied*, 2007 U.S. LEXIS 10286 (U.S. Oct. 1, 2007).

34. Solangel Maldonado, Bias in the Family: Race, Ethnicity, and Culture in Custody Disputes, 55 Fam. Ct. Rev. 213, 219 (2017). Note that this article provides a detailed discussion of the ways in which the explicit and implicit biases of judges can shape custody outcomes.

35. *See* Cynthia R. Mabry, The Browning of America—Multicultural and Bicultural Families in Conflict—Making Culture a Customary Factor in Child Custody Disputes, 16 Wash. & Lee J. Civil Rts. & Soc. Just. 413, 422 (2010).

36. Bottoms v. Bottoms, 249 Va. 410, 457 S.E.2d 102 (1995).

37. *Id.* at 108 (quoting Roe v. Roe, 228 Va. 772, 778, 324 S.E.2d 691, 694 (1985)).

38. Henny M.W. Boss, Lisette Kuyper, and Nanette K. Gartwell, A Population-Based Comparison of Female and Male Same-Sex Parent and Different-Sex Parent Households, 57 Fam. Process 148 (2018); Serena Lambert, Gay and Lesbian Families: What We Know and Where to Go from Here, 13 The Family Journal: Counseling and Therapy for Couples and Families 43, 49 (2005). For a comprehensive discussion of these studies, *see* Abie Goldberg, Lesbian and Gay Parents and Their Children: Research on the Family Life Cycle (APA 2009). For an alternative perspective on the research, *see* Lynn D. Wardle, Considering the Impacts on Children and Society of "Lesbigay" Parenting, 23 Quinnipiac L. Rev. 541 (2004).

39. McGriff v. McGriff, 140 Idaho 642, 99 P.3d 111 (2004) (dissenting opinion of Justice Kidwell). For a detailed analysis of the *McGriff* case, *see* Susan M. Moss, McGriff v. McGriff: Consideration of a Parent's Sexual Orientation in Child Custody Disputes, 41 Idaho L. Rev. 593 (2005). The author notes that despite the trial court's assertion that it was not basing the decision on the father's homosexuality, a textual review of the decision reveals a "disproportionate judicial focus on it," with 25 separate references to his "lifestyle," "homosexuality," and "sexual orientation." *Id.* at 632.

40. *McGriff*, 99 P.3d at 125.

41. *Id.*

42. This discussion draws on the following articles: Carol Wah, Restrictions on Religious Training and Exposure in Child Custody and Visitation Orders: Do They Protect or Harm the Child?, 45 J. Church & St. 14 (2003); Carol Wah, Religion in Child Custody and Visitation Cases: Presenting the Advantage of Religious Participation, 28 Fam. L.Q. 269 (1994); The Establishment Clause and Religion in Child Custody Disputes: Factoring Religion into the Best Interest Equation, 82 Mich. L. Rev. 1702 (1984); Collin R. Magnum, Exclusive Reliance on Best Interest May Be Unconstitutional: Religion as a Factor in Child Custody Cases, 15 Creighton L. Rev. (1982).

43. Garrett v. Garrett, 527 N.W.2d 213, 221-222 (Neb. Ct. App. 1995).

44. In re Marriage of Carney, 598 P.2d 36, 42 (Cal. Ct. App. 1979).

45. For further detail, *see* Michael Lanci, In the Child's Best Interests? Rethinking Consideration of Physical Disability in Child Custody Cases, 118 Colum. L. Rev. 875 (2018); Nicole Buonocore Porter, Mothers with Disabilities, 43 Berkeley J. Gender L. & Just. 75 (2017).

46. 167 W. Va. 59, 278 S.E.2d 357 (1981).

47. *Id.* at 360.

48. *See* Ronald K. Henry, "Primary Caretaker": Is It a Ruse?, 17 Fam. Advoc. 53 (1994).

49. ALI Press Release, May 15, 2002, http://www.ali.org. The American Law Institute "engages in intensive examination and analysis of legal areas thought to need reform. This type of study generally culminates in a work product containing extensive recommendations or proposals for change in the law," such as the Principles of the Law of Family Dissolution, http://www.ali.org (accessed May 22, 2004).

50. W. Va. Code, §48-9-206 (2012).

51. The following articles discuss the ALI's approximation rule from a variety of perspectives: Richard A. Warshak, Parenting by the Clock: The Best-Interest-of-the-Child Standard, Judicial Discretion, and the American Law Institute's "Approximation Rule," 41 U. Balt. L. Rev. 83 (2011); Katherine T. Bartlett, U.S. Custody Law and Trends in the Context of the ALI Principles of the Law of Family Dissolution, 10 Va. J. Soc. Poly. & L. 5, 17-18 (2002); Margaret Bring, Feminism and Child Custody Under Chapter Two of the American Law Institute's Principles of the Law of Family Dissolution, 8 Duke J. Gender L. & Poly. 301 (2002); Robert F. Kelly and Shawn L. Ward, Allocating Custodial Responsibility at Divorce: Social Science Research and the American Law Institute's Approximation Rule, 40 Fam. Ct. Rev. 350 (2002).

52. *See, e.g.,* Eleanor Maccoby and Robert H. Mnookin, Dividing the Child: Social and Legal Dilemmas of Custody (1992).

53. *See* Judith S. Wallerstein and Sandra Blakeslee, Second Chances — Men, Women and Children a Decade After Divorce 256-273 (1989).

54. For a discussion of some of these concerns, *see* Christy M. Buchanan and Parissa L. Jahromi, The Best Interests of the Child: A Psychological Perspective on Shared Custody Arrangements, 43 Wake Forest L. Rev. 419 (2009). Judith S. Wallerstein and Janet R. Johnston, Children of Divorce, Recent Findings Regarding Long-Term Effects and Recent Studies of Joint and Sole Custody, 11 Pediatrics in Rev. 197 (1990).

55. Margaret F. Bring, Extending Default Rules Beyond Purely Economic Relationships: Penalty Defaults in Family Law: The Case of Child Custody, 33 Fla. St. U. L. Rev. 779, 782 (2006).

56. *See* Dana Harrington Connor, Back to the Drawing Board: Barriers to Joint Decision-Making in Cases Involving Domestic Violence, 18 Duke J. Gender L. & Poly. 223 (2011); D. Lee Khachaturian, Domestic Violence and Shared Parental Responsibility: Dangerous Bedfellows, 44 Wayne L. Rev. 1745 (1999).

57. Marlene Eskind Moses with Beth A. Townsend, Parenting Coordinators: The Good, The Bad and the Ugly, 48 Tenn. B.J. 24, 25 (2012).

58. *See generally id.*, as well as "Understanding the Parenting Coordination Process," http://www.afccnet.org/ResourceCenter/ResourcesforFamilies/ProductID/10 (accessed July 29, 2012).

59. William RJP Brown, Lauren Behrman, and Jeffrey Zimmerman, Duel or Dual: An Interdisciplinary Approach to Parenting Coordination for Uber-Conflicted Parenting Relationships, 50 Fam. Ct. Rev. 345, 347 (2017).

60. *Id.*

61. Joan Kelly, Psychological and Legal Interventions for Parents and Children in Custody and Access Disputes: Current Research and Practice, 10 Va. J. Soc. Poly. & L. 129, 135 (2002). *See also* Susan L. Pollet and Melissa Lombreglia, A Nationwide Survey of Mandatory Parent Education, 46 Fam. Ct. Rev. 375 (2008).

62. *See* Amanda Sigal et al., Do Parent Education Programs Promote Healthy Postdivorce Parenting? Critical Distinctions and a Review of the Evidence, 49 Fam. Ct. Rev. 120 (2011).

63. Jill R. Bowers et al., A Review of Online Divorce Education Programs, 49 Fam. Ct. Rev. 776 (2011).

64. Victoria L. Lutz and Cara E. Grady, Models of Collaboration in Family Law: Domestic Violence and Parent Education: Necessary Measures and Logistics to Maximize the Safety of Victims of Domestic Violence Attending Parent Education Programs, 42 Fam. Ct. Rev. 363 (2004).

65. For a description of Kentucky's Divorce Education programs, *see* http://courts .ky.gov/courts/circuit/familycourt/divorceeducation (accessed Jan. 15, 2007).

66. *See generally* Lucy S. McGough, Starting Over: The Heuristics of Family Relocation Decision Making, 77 St. John's L. Rev. 291 (2003); Charles P. Kindregan, Family Interests in Competition: Relocation and Visitation, 36 Suffolk U. L. Rev. 31 (2002); Edwin J. Terry, Relocation: Moving Forward or Moving Backward? 31 Tex. Tech L. Rev. 983 (2000).

67. D'Onofrio v. D'Onofrio, 144 N.J. Super, 365 A.2d 27, 29-30 (Ch. Div. 1976), *aff'd*, 144 N.J. Super. 352, 365 A.2d 716 (App. Div. 1976).

68. For a discussion of some of this research, *see* Kenneth Waldron, A Review of Social Science Research on Post Divorce Relocation, 19 J. Am. Acad. Matrimonial Law 337 (2005); Eric G. Mart and Rachel M. Bedard, Child Custody and Post-Divorce Relocation in the Light of Braver et al., 31 Ver. B.J. & L. Dig. 47 (2005).

69. McCoy v. McCoy, 336 N.J. Super. 172, 764 A.2d 449, 454 (2001).

70. *Id.*

71. David Welsh, Virtual Parents: How Virtual Visitation Legislation Is Shaping the Future of Custody Law, 11 J. L. Fam. Stud. 215 (2008).

72. Michael Saini and Shely Polak, The Benefits, Drawbacks, and Safety Considerations in Digital Parent-Child Relationships: An Exploratory Survey of the Views of Legal and Mental Health Professionals in Family Law, 56 Fam. Ct. Rev. 597, 602 (2018).

73. *Id.*

74. *See* Jim Mackay, Virtual Parenting, Government Technology (2006), http://www .govtech.com/magazines/gt/Virtual-Parenting.html (accessed December 19, 2015). *See also* David Welsh, *supra* note 71.

75. Saini and Polak, *supra* note 72, at 602-603.

76. *Id.* at 603.

77. It is also possible that a co-parent in a same-sex relationship may be viewed as a nonparent by the law. This situation is taken up in Chapter 11.

78. *See* Patricia S. Fernandez, Grandparent Access: A Model Statute, 6 Yale L. & Poly. Rev. 109 (1988).

79. 828 S.W.2d 630, 632-633 (Ky. 1992).

80. 855 S.W.2d 573, 580-583 (Tenn. 1993) (internal citations omitted).

81. *Id.* at 583.

82. Troxel v. Granville 530 U.S. 57, 64 (citing the Supreme Court of Washington's decision, Smith v. Stillwell-Smith (In re Custody of Smith), 969 P.2d 21, 31 (Wash. 1998)). The difference in the case name results from the Washington court's consolidation of three cases.

83. *Id.* at 58-59.

84. *Id.* at 68 (emphasis in original).

85. For a discussion of post-*Troxel* decisions, *see* Joan Catherine Bohl, That "Thorny" Issue, California Grandparent Visitation Law in the Wake of Troxel v. Granville, 36 Golden Gate U. L. Rev. 121 (2006); Kristine L. Roberts, Troxel v. Granville and the Courts' Reluctance to Declare Grandparent Visitation Statutes Unconstitutional, 41 Fam. Ct. Rev. 14 (2003).

86. Atkinson v. Atkinson, 160 Mich. App. 601, 608-609, 408 N.W.2d 516, 519 (1987).

87. For a discussion of this approach, *see* Bryce Levine, Divorce and the Modern Family: Providing In Loco Parentis Stepparents Standing to Sue for Custody of Their Stepchildren in a Dissolution Proceeding, 25 Hofstra L. Rev. 315 (1996).

Chapter Six

Child Support

As we have seen so far, family law is primarily a matter of state concern. However, this changes when it comes to **child support**, an arena in which the federal government plays an important role.

In the 1970s, the issue of child support came under intense public scrutiny. Studies documented that in almost half of the families with absent fathers, no child support was awarded, and where awarded, amounts were generally inadequate. Highlighting the problem in a dramatic way, one study showed that two-thirds of noncustodial fathers in Denver paid more in monthly car payments than in child support payments.[1] Where orders *were* entered, there was a high rate of noncompliance. Census data consistently showed that slightly less than 50 percent of custodial parents received the full amount of child support they were entitled to, while almost 30 percent received nothing.[2]

Between 1970 and 1981, the number of people in female-headed families living below the poverty level increased significantly, and the term "feminization of poverty" was coined to underscore the fact that households made up of women and children were sliding into poverty. Underlying the concern about poverty was an increased awareness of the difference in post-divorce standards of living between men and women with children. Studies consistently showed that the financial well-being of men improved following a divorce, while that of women and children deteriorated; for instance, one study found a 17 percent increase in standard of living for men compared to a 29 percent decline for women and children.[3]

At the federal level, there was a growing awareness that many women and children were being forced to turn to public assistance, namely, Aid to Families with Dependent Children (AFDC, more commonly referred to as "welfare"), because they were not receiving the child support they were entitled to. The AFDC program began in 1935 through an amendment to the Social Security Act. Its original purpose was to provide financial assistance to widows with minor children to enable them to keep their children with them. However, by the 1970s, the vast majority of families on AFDC required assistance because of paternal nonsupport rather than paternal death. Although a detailed discussion is beyond the scope of this book, it should be noted that in 1996, as part of a sweeping welfare reform act known as the Personal Responsibility and Work Opportunity Reconciliation Act (PRWORA), Congress abolished AFDC and replaced it with Transitional Assistance to Needy Families (TANF).[4]

This sobering picture prompted the federal government to enter the child support field. In 1974, hoping to force absent parents to become financially responsible and thereby reduce federal welfare expenditures, Congress passed the Child Support Enforcement and Establishment of Paternity Act of 1974, which added **Title IV-D** to the Social Security Act.[5] As explained by Margaret Heckler, then Secretary of the U.S. Department of Health and Human Services, in favor of this increased federal role: "Children deserve to be supported by both parents. For the sake of America's children, we must put an end to what has become a national disgrace. Our new federal legislation will help States obtain support orders quickly and pursue them vigorously."[6] This new law required states to develop comprehensive child support programs to help custodial parents obtain and enforce child support awards.

Since 1974, Congress has amended Title IV-D multiple times and passed other child support legislation intended to strengthen the ability of both states and tribes and tribal organizations to establish and collect child support awards in a timely and efficient manner.[7] Before examining this joint federal-state child support system, we begin with a brief historical overview of the parental support duty.

Historical Overview

According to English common law, fathers had a moral but not a legal duty to support their children; mothers had neither. In contrast, in this country, most states adopted the view that even in the absence of a specific statute, fathers owed their children a legal duty of support; mothers had a support duty only to the extent that fathers were unable to fulfill theirs. A father's obligation was enforceable through the common law doctrine of necessaries, which allowed wives and children to pledge a husband's/father's credit to purchase necessaries that he had failed to provide.

Eventually, this paternal duty was embodied in a variety of statutes. Civil liability was imposed through family responsibility or family expense statutes. Family responsibility laws required fathers or other relatives to support their children so they did not become a public burden;

family expense statutes permitted the taking of parental property to satisfy debts incurred in meeting the family's needs. Nonsupport was also made a crime in all states.

■ Administrative Framework for the Establishment and Enforcement of Child Support Orders

The Federal Office of Child Support Enforcement

The Child Support Enforcement and Establishment of Paternity Act of 1974 established the federal Office of Child Support Enforcement (OCSE). The OCSE is located within the Administration for Children and Families (ACF) in the United States Department of Health and Human Services (HHS). OCSE is the national oversight agency with responsibility for helping states to develop, manage, and run their child support programs effectively and in accordance with federal law.[8] More recently, the OCSE inaugurated a Tribal IV-D Program, which provides direct funding to Indian tribes and tribal organizations for the administration of comprehensive tribal IV-D child support programs.

In addition, the OCSE is responsible for operating the Federal Parent Locator Service (FPLS). The FPLS "is an assembly of systems operated by OCSE to assist states in locating noncustodial parents, putative fathers, and custodial parties for the establishment of paternity and child support obligations, as well as the enforcement and modification of orders for child support, custody, and visitation. It also identifies support orders or support cases involving the same parties in different States."[9]

In 2011, then President Barack Obama issued an executive order directing federal agencies to review and update their regulatory programs in order to "improve program flexibility, efficiency, and responsiveness; promote technological programmatic innovation; and update outmoded ways of doing business."[10] In response, the OCSE engaged in a comprehensive review and revision of its regulations, resulting in the 2016 Flexibility, Efficiency, and Modernization in Child Support Enforcement Programs Final Rule (2016 Final Rule),[11] which, as will be discussed, introduced some important changes into the existing national child support system.

At the State Level: The IV-D Agency

The 1974 Act required each state to develop a comprehensive child support program and to designate a single state agency—often referred to as a **IV-D**

agency—to administer the program. IV-D agencies must provide the following five basic services to custodial parents:

- assistance in locating absent parents;
- establishment of child support awards;
- periodic review of awards;
- enforcement of support awards; and
- where necessary, the establishment of paternity.

Before looking at these components of the child support system, we will look at how custodial parents access the services of a IV-D agency. As will become clear, the process differs depending on whether or not the parent is a recipient of public assistance through TANF (Transitional Aid to Needy Families), the federal block grant program that provides time-limited support to poor families.[12]

Eligibility for IV-D Services

A custodial parent who applies for TANF benefits is automatically referred to a IV-D agency for child support services. In order to receive benefits, she must agree to assign her right to child support to the state. She must also agree to cooperate with the state in its effort to obtain support, unless she can establish good cause for noncooperation, such as the fear of abuse.[13] With the assignment, the noncustodial parent's support obligation runs to the state rather than to the custodial parent.

Once support is collected on behalf of a family receiving public assistance, federal law provides the state with several distribution options. A state can keep all of the collected funds in order to reimburse itself (and the federal government) for assistance payments made to the family. It can choose to "pass through" all of the collected funds to the family, or it can pass through a portion of the funds and retain the balance for reimbursement purposes. Although advocates for low-income families have encouraged states to adopt a "family-first" approach and pass through all of the collected support in order to help lift children out of poverty, few states have adopted this approach. Most either retain all of the collected funds, or pass through a limited amount, typically 50 or 100 dollars to the family.[14] If a state does pass through collected funds, it typically disregards this amount when determining the family's continued eligibility for public assistance.

IV-D agencies also must provide child support assistance to families who are not applying for or receiving public assistance. Today, in contrast to the early years of the IV-D program, most of the families who receive child support services are not on public assistance, although many are former welfare recipients.[15] This represents a shift "from an emphasis on recouping federal funds to the current mission of ensuring the support and care of America's children, without regard to receipt of government assistance."[16] A parent in this category must complete an application requesting IV-D services, and may be charged a nominal fee. Because public funds are not involved, the use of a IV-D agency is optional, and there is no assignment of support rights or a cooperation requirement, and all collected support payments go directly to the custodial parent. (Private child support agencies are discussed later in this chapter.)

Locating Absent Parents

A major barrier to obtaining and enforcing child support orders is that many noncustodial parents cannot be located, and some try to conceal their identity to avoid paying child support. To address this problem, the 1974 Act established the Federal Parent Locator Service (FPLS), which is operated by the OCSE, and required each state IV-D agency to establish its own **parent locator service**.

If a custodial parent does not know where the other parent is, he or she can request assistance from the state parent locator service. The locator service will check the records of other state agencies, such as the registry of motor vehicles or department of revenue, to see if it can locate the absent parent; credit-reporting agencies are also an important source of information. The locator service must also search the State Case Registry, a database with information regarding all state support cases, and the State Directory of New Hires, a database containing information submitted by employers containing information about all new hires, to determine if there is a match. If the parent cannot be located within the state, and there is cause to believe the parent is in another state, the parent locator service in the second state must initiate a search as described in this paragraph.

If the parent still cannot be located, the state locator service can ask the FPLS to assist in the search. Requests for federal assistance must come from a IV-D agency; individuals cannot file a direct request for federal assistance. Information needed to track down a parent can be obtained from both internal and external data sources. Internal to the FPLS is the Federal Case Registry of Child Support Orders (FCR), a comprehensive database containing information on all U.S. child support cases, and the National Directory of New Hires, a database including information about all new hires nationwide and persons who have applied for unemployment. Additionally, the FPLS can conduct an external search through the databases of other federal agencies, such as the Internal Revenue Service or the Social Security Administration. (See the section entitled "Enforcing the Child Support Obligation," later in this chapter, for more information on these databases.)

Although the increased focus on the centralization and exchange of information facilitates the child support collection process, it also raises concerns about the privacy rights of individual family members. Of particular concern is the need to "ensure that the databases are secure enough so that abusers are unable to penetrate their safeguards to locate abused women and children."[17] Accordingly, federal law contains multiple safeguards to protect against the unauthorized use or disclosure of confidential information gathered by IV-D agencies. Additional layers of protection are required in cases involving domestic violence, such as the inclusion of a domestic violence indicator or flag on an at-risk individual's file to restrict disclosure of any information that might jeopardize that person's safety.

Child Support Guidelines

To address the problem of inadequate and inconsistent awards, federal law requires each state to adopt **child support guidelines**. The guidelines must provide specific numeric criteria for the computation of support awards, and calculations must result in a presumptively correct support amount. Deviations from the guideline amount are permitted, but only in circumstances where the guideline amount would be unfair based on the circumstances of the particular case. The reason for the deviation must be stated on the record. Some guidelines include specific factors for a decision maker to consider when determining if a deviation is warranted, while other guidelines are general.

Guidelines are controlling with respect to both temporary and "permanent" child support awards.[18] The guidelines also control in cases in which the parents reach agreement on the support amount; to guard against the risk that a parent might bargain away support rights in exchange for something else of value (most commonly, custody), any deviation must be justified to the court or reviewing agency. To assist in the computation of support amounts, most states make available a standard **support worksheet** or an online support calculator to give parties a working estimate of what the support obligation is likely to be.

The 2016 Final Rule aims to ensure that child support amounts accurately reflect the ability of a noncustodial parent to provide support for his or her children. Accordingly, in addition to being based on the noncustodial parent's "earnings and income," child support guidelines must also take into account "other evidence of ability to pay." This puts a higher burden on states to develop a strong factual basis for a support order, and they must take "reasonable steps" to gather the necessary information through "interviews with both parties, parent questionnaires, investigations, case conferencing, appear and disclose procedures, testimony, and electronic data sources."[19] In addition, states must take the basic subsistence needs of the noncustodial parent into account by "incorporating a low-income adjustment, such as a self-support reserve or some other method determined by the state."[20]

Guideline Formulas

Although federal law requires states to adopt child support guidelines, it left the job of developing the actual guidelines up to the states. In developing their guidelines, a majority of states have adopted the income-shares approach, with most of the others using the percentage-of-income approach. A few states use a hybrid approach, which is often referred to as the "Melson formula" after Judge Elwood F. Melson, Jr., of the Delaware Family Court.[21]

Percentage of Income

The percentage-of-income (or fixed percentage) approach sets the support amount as a fixed percentage of the noncustodial parent's income. Usually, the only relevant variable is the number of children in the household, although some states permit consideration of other factors, such as shared custody arrangements. Thus, for example, the support percentage might be set at 25 percent of the noncustodial parent's income for one child; at 30 percent for two children; and at 34 percent for three children.

The advantage of this model is its simplicity. However, by not building in consideration of multiple factors, the results may be inequitable. For example, a custodial parent who is employed part time or at home with young children would get the same amount of support as a custodial parent who is employed at a well-paying job.

Income Shares

The income-shares approach is premised on the assumption that children are entitled to receive the same share of parental income that they would have had the family stayed together. To arrive at the support amount, the income of both parents is combined and a basic support obligation computed. This obligation is then allocated between the parents in proportion to income, with the noncustodial parent paying his or her share in support payments and the custodial parent assumed to be paying his or her share in direct expenditures on the children.

Critics of this approach argue that it falls short in two ways that are particularly applicable in sole custody cases. First, it ignores the fact that following a divorce, the expenses of the custodial parent generally increase because he or she now must pay for services—such as baby-sitting, household cleaning, and repairs—to compensate for losing the contributions the other parent would have made to the household. Second, it discounts the large noneconomic contribution the custodial parent makes to the well-being of the children.

The Melson Formula

Under this approach, a noncustodial parent is first permitted to keep a minimum level of income for his or her essential needs. This is referred to as a self-support reserve. Then, until the basic needs of the children are met, the parent cannot retain income above this minimum level; it must be allocated to child support. Once these needs are provided for, a percentage of the remaining parental income is allocated to increasing the basic support amount, thus enabling the children to benefit from a higher standard of living.

Determining What Income Is Subject to the Child Support Obligation

In developing their guidelines, states, in addition to determining which basic approach to use, also had to decide what income would be subject to the support obligation. This determination entails two distinct considerations: (1) How is income to be defined? And (2) What support base will be used?

Defining Income

Most guidelines define "income" broadly. All states include earned employment income in their definition, although treatment of sporadic income, such as income from occasional odd jobs or overtime, varies. In some states, sporadic income is excluded. In other states, it is averaged over time and added to regular earnings.

Most guidelines also recognize the concept of **imputed** (or **attributed**) **income**. Here, a parent who is voluntarily unemployed or underemployed is treated as if he or she has income commensurate with his or her earning capacity, and support is calculated based on this amount rather than on actual earnings. By attributing income to a parent and setting the support amount accordingly, a parent must find suitable employment or face sanctions for nonsupport. In some states, if a noncustodial parent remarries or cohabits and voluntarily stops working in reliance on the new partner's income, a portion of the household income will be attributed to that parent. In states where the income of the custodial parent is factored into the support equation, income may also be attributed to this parent where he or she is voluntarily under- or unemployed. However, most courts will not impute income if a parent has reduced his or her earnings due to child-related responsibilities, at least not until the child reaches a certain age—commonly age 6.

The ability to attribute income is important in situations where a parent deliberately reduces earnings in order to avoid a support obligation. However, what if a parent has reasons other than the avoidance of support for reducing his or her income? For example, take the situation of an attorney who after years of working in a major firm decides she is burned out and wants to open a small practice with a resulting loss of income. Should she be permitted to drastically reduce support payments? Is this fair to the children? On the other hand, is it fair to force a parent to remain in a particular career track by maintaining a support obligation based on earning potential?

According to the 2016 Final Rule, if income is to be imputed, the amount must be determined on a case-by-case basis in accordance with the particular circumstances of the noncustodial parent to the extent they are known. In short, states may not "use a standard amount in lieu of fact-gathering."[22]

Some states, either through guidelines or judicial decision, also permit income to be imputed to assets a party owns, such as jewelry or antiques, even if they are not income earning. The rationale for such a policy "is to discourage spouses from placing all of their assets into non-income yielding forms and thus shielding all of their assets from consideration in support."[23]

The definition of *income* almost always includes investment earnings, rents, profit shares, dividends, annuities, and governmental benefits, such as Social Security retirement and unemployment insurance benefits. Some states also include the value of non-income producing assets—such as jewelry, antiques, and undeveloped real estate—within the meaning of the term "income."

Setting the Income Base

In addition to defining income, the relevant income base must be determined. Here, states have three basic choices: Support can be calculated based on gross income, adjusted gross income, or net income.

Gross Income Base. A gross income base is used by many states. In this approach, the gross income of the support obligor is used as the base for determining the support amount. The advantage of this approach is its simplicity and the fact that income cannot be manipulated because no deductions are taken before the support amount is calculated. On the other hand, gross income may not be an accurate measure of the income that is actually available to the support obligor.

Adjusted Gross Income Base. Other states use an adjusted gross income base. To arrive at this amount, federal and state tax obligations, including Social Security, are deducted from gross earnings; nonvoluntary payroll withholdings, such as union dues and retirement payments, as well as prior support obligations also are usually deducted. Support is then based on this adjusted amount. Many believe this is the fairest approach, as it is a more accurate measure of the obligor's available income, although it does not permit the same kind of discretionary deductions that are allowable under the net income approach.

Net Income Base. Still other states use a net income base, which allows for further deductions than the adjusted gross income base. Gross income is reduced, for example, by voluntary payroll withholdings and job-related expenses before the support amount is calculated. The drawback of this approach is that it can be manipulated to show a reduced income, thus limiting the support base. On the other hand, it may be the most accurate indicator of actual available income.

Consideration of Specific Factors

Most child support guidelines include a number of factors that are to be taken into account when calculating the support amount. Others fix a basic amount varied only by a limited number of factors, such as the number of children, and then identify factors that will justify a deviation from the presumptive amount. These factors are relevant in determining both the initial amount and whether a modification is warranted. Commonly considered factors include:

- income of the custodial parent;
- income of a new partner;
- income/resources of the child;
- multiple families;
- extraordinary expenses;
- health insurance; and
- custody and visitation arrangements.

Income of the Custodial Parent

With the exception of states using the percentage-of-income approach, most guidelines take the income of the custodial parent into account. Under the income-shares approach, the income of both parents is combined to establish a basic support obligation. This amount is then allocated in proportion to income, and the noncustodial parent contributes his or her share in support payments. Another approach is to base the initial support calculation on the noncustodial parent's income and then reduce it to account for the custodial parent's income. States generally use a percentage reduction formula, rather than a dollar-for-dollar offset, as this could significantly reduce the amount of support available to the children. In some states, the custodial parent's income is disregarded until it reaches a threshold amount, and then only income above this threshold is considered.

Income of a New Partner

If either parent remarries or cohabits with a new partner, the question often arises as to how this partner income should be treated. As a general rule, this person has no direct support obligation to the children. Accordingly, few, if any, guidelines require inclusion of this income, and some specifically exclude it from consideration. However, because it may free up parental income, some states permit consideration of partner income as a basis for deviating from the presumptive guideline amount.

Income/Resources of the Child

Situations may arise where a minor child has independent resources; for example, he or she may receive governmental benefits, have income from a part-time job, or be the beneficiary of a trust or an inheritance. Most states do not build this into their support formulas or treat this as income to the custodial parent. Again, however, this income may be considered in determining if a deviation from guidelines is appropriate.

Multiple Families

Almost 75 percent of people who are divorced remarry, and many then have children with their new spouses.[24] Cases involving multiple families raise difficult questions about how (often scarce) resources can be fairly allocated between two households.

A thorny question is whether a noncustodial parent should be allowed to reduce support to his or her first family upon establishing a new household, especially if he or she has additional children with this new partner. The traditional guideline approach puts "first families first" and does not permit reductions based on obligations to a subsequent family. The children from the first family are said to have a preexisting, hence superior, claim to the income, which the parent should have considered before starting a second family. However, based on the recognition that this approach may shortchange the children in the second family, who have no control over their place in the birth order, some states do permit support adjustments to account for obligations to subsequently born children. In some of these jurisdictions, the presence of subsequent children can be used as a "shield" to defend against a request for an upward modification but not as a "sword" to request a downward modification.

Given the high failure rate of second marriages, another difficult issue is how support payments to a second family are to be calculated if this relationship also dissolves. If a parent is already paying child support under a court order to a prior family, most guidelines permit him or her to deduct this amount from income before the support order for the second family is calculated. This arguably favors the first family, as the income base available to them is larger; however, it is generally thought fair to protect this family's standard of living from fluctuations based on changes in the noncustodial parent's life over which the family has no control.[25]

Extraordinary Expenses

Guidelines are generally based on the assumption that the custodial parent is responsible for the ordinary costs of raising a child. A trickier question is whether she or he is also responsible for extraordinary expenses, or whether these should be dealt with separately. The term "**extraordinary expense**" has been defined as "any large, discrete, legitimate child-rearing expense that varies greatly from family to family or from child to child," as distinct from "ordinary expenses," which tend to be "relatively small, predictable, and fairly consistent in families of the same size and income level."[26] This issue most often arises with respect to medical, child-care, and educational expenses; as far as medical expenses are concerned, some guidelines specify that unreimbursed medical expenses in excess of an identified dollar amount per occurrence or calendar year are considered extraordinary expenses, while other guidelines identify the qualifying kinds of expenditures.

States use a number of approaches when dealing with extraordinary expenses, and within a particular state, the approach may vary depending on the category of expense. One common approach is to treat extraordinary expenses as an "add-on" to the basic support amount. The expense is prorated between the parents based on their income, and the noncustodial parent's share is added to the support amount. Another possibility is to permit deviations from the guideline amount to account for extraordinary expenses. For example, a judge might be permitted to increase the basic support amount if the custodial parent were faced with significant medical bills. This deviation would most likely be temporary in nature, and the guideline amount would be reinstated once the custodial parent was no longer facing these expenditures.

Health Insurance

Under federal law, state child support guidelines must address how parents will provide for the health care needs of their children. Seeking greater flexibility, the 2016 Final Rule makes clear that this obligation may be satisfied either through the provision of health insurance coverage or the payment of reasonable medical expenses. Moreover, states may not distinguish between private and publicly funded health care plans in determining if this obligation has been met — both qualify for purposes of fulfilling a parent's medical support obligation.

Strengthening this mandate, all child support orders obtained through a state IV-D agency must include a medical support provision, and the agency must petition the court or administrative authority to include health care coverage in the support order if it is available through one or both parents. If ordered, an employer-sponsored group health plan must provide coverage to the children named by the court (or a qualified administrative agency) in what is known as a **qualified medical child support order** (QMCSO).[27]

With respect to the cost of coverage, some state guidelines allow the noncustodial parent to deduct the amount of the premium that is attributable to family coverage from gross income before calculating the support amount. Correspondingly, if the custodial parent is providing the insurance, a portion of the premium amount may be added to the basic support obligation. Another approach is to prorate the cost of the insurance between the parents based on their proportion of the total income, and then add the obligor's share to the support payments. Still other state guidelines consider the provision of health insurance as a ground for deviating from the presumptive support amount.

Custody and Visitation Arrangements

Support guidelines are generally based on the assumption that one parent has physical custody and the other has visitation rights, and visitation-related expenditures do not usually impact the support calculation. However, guidelines may permit adjustments to account for situations where a parent either spends a significant amount of time with a child or, conversely, hardly sees the child at all. Some guidelines spell out what time allocation will trigger a support reduction, such as where the child spends more than a specified percentage of time or more than a certain number of overnights with the noncustodial parent, while other guidelines leave it to the decision maker to decide when a reduction is warranted. The amount of the reduction is usually left to the decision maker, although limits may be placed on his or her discretion. Some judges take a cautious approach to these reductions based on the recognition that increased visitation does not necessarily result in substantial savings in child-related expenditures, as the custodial parent usually remains responsible for them. Although less frequently addressed by guidelines, nonvisitation also may be the basis for an upward revision of support, as the custodial parent is assuming responsibility for visitation-associated expenses that the guidelines implicitly allocated to the noncustodial parent.

Turning to custodial arrangements, it is often assumed that joint physical custody and split custody (where at least one child lives with each parent) will cancel the support obligation because both parents are providing for the children on an equal basis. This assumption, however, is not accurate.

First, although an arrangement may be identified as joint custody, the time allocation between the two households may not be equal. Second, even where it is equal, one parent, typically the primary caregiver during the marriage, often continues to assume greater parenting responsibilities, including making most of the purchases for the child. Thus, although both parents maintain a home for the child, the cost of raising the child is not borne equally. Another concern is that eliminating the support award will put the lower-income parent in a worse financial situation than that parent would have been in had he or she maintained sole custody and received the guideline amount. In this regard, experts note that a disparity in the standard of living between parental households is especially confusing for a child in a joint custody situation, since both residences are the child's home.

Accordingly, although most guidelines permit consideration of these custodial arrangements in determining the support amount, they do not automatically trigger its elimination. One approach that is used is to compute a support obligation for each parent as if he or she had sole custody, offset the amounts, and order the parent with the greater obligation to pay the net amount to the other. Of course, support may be eliminated where parents earn close to the same amount and really share responsibility for raising the children.

Financial Disclosure

As the above discussion makes clear, a proper child support order cannot be calculated unless all relevant information has been disclosed. Accordingly, most, if not all, states require each party to make full financial disclosure to the other, usually by completing and filing a **financial affidavit**. Some also require the filing of supporting documents, such as tax returns and wage stubs. Additionally, in an effort to encourage attorneys to monitor and prevent the filing of fraudulent or inaccurate financial affidavits, some states require the affidavit to be signed by the lawyer as well as by the party submitting it. Exhibit 6.1 is a sample financial affidavit.

Despite their usefulness, affidavits often do not provide a complete financial picture. The form itself may not call for full disclosure. Also, affidavits provide a snapshot of a party's current financial situation but do not give a picture of his or her financial situation over time; for instance, an affidavit probably would not reveal a reduction in income or a transfer of assets or income that took place before the affidavit was completed. In many states that require parties to update affidavits as a divorce proceeds, subsequent changes may be revealed. Accordingly, a party may need to engage in other *discovery*—the process by which a party obtains information from the other side—to gain a more complete picture of the other side's financial situation. This step is critical because the failure to obtain complete and accurate information will result in an inaccurate assessment of a parent's financial situation and thus an incorrect support calculation.

Paralegals often play a critical role in this process. It may be your job to assist the client in completing the financial affidavit. These forms can be confusing. For example, a party who is asked to itemize expenditures on a weekly basis may be inclined to ignore expenditures that are made on a less regular basis, such as for clothing. You can help a client figure out what he or she spends on clothing over the course of a year, accounting for seasonal fluctuations in order to arrive at an average weekly clothing amount.

If formal discovery is required, you may be involved in drafting documents and organizing the responses, including the supporting materials such as tax returns and bank statements that are often requested. You may also be responsible for helping your office's client respond to requests from the other side, which again may require you to sort through and organize financial data. (For more detail on discovery, see Chapter 10.)

Exhibit 6.1   Financial Disclosure Affidavit

**IN THE CIRCUIT COURT OF THE NINETEENTH JUDICIAL CIRCUIT
LAKE COUNTY, ILLINOIS**

IN RE: The ☐ Marriage of: ☐ Custody of: ☐ Support of:

)
)
)
_____)
                       Petitioner)
        and   )   No. _____
)
_____)
                      Respondent)

FINANCIAL AFFIDAVIT 11.02

Affiant, _____, having been duly sworn, upon oath, states

that the information contained herein is true and correct as of _____, 20_____

Name:	Telephone No: (847)
Address:	Petitioner Date of Birth: _____ (mmddyyyy)
	Respondent Date of Birth: _____ (mmddyyyy)
Date of Marriage: _____ (mmddyyyy)	Date of Dissolution of Marriage: (if applicable) _____ (mmddyyyy)

Minor and/or Dependent Children of this Marriage:

Name	Date of Birth (mmddyyyy)	Currently Living With

(Attach additional page(s) as needed)

Current Employer:	Address:
Self Employment:	Address:
Other Employment:	Address:

☐ Check if unemployed

Number of Paychecks per year: *(Please Check box)* ☐ 12   ☐ 24   ☐ 26   ☐ 52   ☐ Other _____

Number of Exemptions claimed: _____

Number of Dependents claimed: _____

Gross Income from all sources last year: _____

Gross income from all sources this year through _____: $ _____
                                                        Date

171-12 FD33 (R01/06)

Exhibit 6.1   Continued

STATEMENT OF INCOME
Gross Monthly Income

Salary/Wages/Base Pay	$	
Overtime/Commission	$	
Bonus	$	
Draw	$	
Pension and Retirement Benefits	$	
Annuity	$	
Interest income	$	
Dividend income	$	
Trust income	$	
Social Security	$	
Unemployment benefits	$	
Disability payment	$	
Worker's Compensation	$	
Public Aid/Food Stamps	$	
Investment income	$	
Rental income	$	
Business income (including non-taxable distributions)	$	
Partnership income	$	
Royalty income	$	
Fellowship/stipends	$	
Other income (specify): _____	$	
TOTAL GROSS MONTHLY INCOME:	$	$

Additional Cash Flow (Monthly)

Spousal support received (specify)	$	
☐ Pursuant to a prior judgment or order in another case	$	
☐ Pursuant to a prior judgment or order in this case	$	
☐ Voluntarily paid in this case	$	
Child Support received (specify)	$	
☐ Pursuant to a prior judgment or order in another case	$	
☐ Pursuant to a prior judgment or order in this case	$	
☐ Voluntarily paid in this case	$	
Total additional cash flow:	$	$

Required Monthly Deductions

Federal Tax (based on _____ exemptions)	$	
State Tax (based on _____ exemptions)	$	
FICA (or Social Security equivalent)	$	
Medicare Tax	$	
Mandatory retirement contributions required by law or as condition of employment	$	
Union Dues (Name of Union: _____)	$	
Health/hospitalization Premiums	$	
Prior obligation(s) of support actually paid pursuant to Court order	$	
Other (specify):	$	
TOTAL REQUIRED DEDUCTIONS FROM INCOME:	$	$
NET MONTHLY INCOME:	$	$

Exhibit 6.1   Continued

STATEMENT OF MONTHLY LIVING EXPENSES

1. Household

a. Mortgage or rent (specify):	$	
b. Home equity loan payment	$	
c. Real estate taxes, assessments	$	
d. Homeowners or renters insurance	$	
e. Heat/fuel	$	
f. Electricity	$	
g. Telephone (include long distance)	$	
h. Water and Sewer	$	
i. Refuse removal	$	
j. Laundry/dry cleaning	$	
k. Maid/cleaning service	$	
l. Furniture and appliance repair/replacement	$	
m. Lawn and garden care/snow removal	$	
n. Food (groceries, household supplies, etc.)	$	
o. Liquor, beer, wine, etc.	$	
p. Other (specify):	$	
SUBTOTAL HOUSEHOLD EXPENSES:	$	$

2. Transportation

a. Fuel	$	
b. Repairs/maintenance	$	
c. Insurance/license/city stickers	$	
d. Payments/replacement	$	
e. Other (specify):	$	
SUBTOTAL TRANSPORTATION EXPENSES:	$	$

3. Personal

a. Clothing	$	
b. Grooming	$	
c. Medical (after insurance proceeds/reimbursement)		
(1) Doctor	$	
(2) Dentist	$	
(3) Optical	$	
(4) Medication	$	
d. Insurance		
(1) Life – Term/Whole (**specify**)	$	
(2) Medical/Hospitalization	$	
(3) Dental/Optical	$	
e. Other (specify)	$	
SUBTOTAL PERSONAL EXPENSES:	$	$

4. Miscellaneous:

a. Clubs/social obligations/entertainment	$	
b. Newspapers, magazines, books	$	
c. Gifts	$	
d. Donations, church or religious affiliations	$	
e. Vacations	$	
f. Other (specify)	$	
SUBTOTAL MISCELLANEOUS EXPENSES	$	$

Exhibit 6.1   Continued

5. Expenses of Minor and/or Dependent Children of this Marriage:

a. Clothing	$
b. Grooming	$
c. Education	
(1) Tuition	$
(2) Books/Fees	$
(3) Lunches	$
(4) Transportation	$
(5) Medication	$
d. Medical (after insurance proceeds/reimbursement)	
(1) Doctor	$
(2) Dentist	$
(3) Optical	$
(4) Medication	$
e. Allowance	$
f. Child care/After-school care	$
g. Sitters	$
h. Lesson and supplies	$
i. Clubs/Summer Camps	$
j. Vacation	$
k. Entertainment	$
l. Other (specify)	$

SUBTOTAL CHILDREN'S EXPENSES:	$	$
TOTAL MONTHLY LIVING EXPENSES:	$	$

STATEMENT OF LIABILITIES

CREDITOR'S NAME	PAYMENT FOR	BALANCE DUE	MONTHLY PAYMENT
		$	$
		$	$
		$	$
		$	$
		$	$
		$	$
		$	$
		$	$
		$	$
		$	$
		$	$
		$	$
		$	$
		$	$
		$	$
		$	$
		$	$
		$	$
		$	$
		$	$
TOTAL LIABILITIES		$	

TOTAL MONTHLY DEBT SERVICE	$

(Attach additional page(s) as needed)

Exhibit 6.1   Continued

STATEMENT OF ASSETS   Valuation Date: _____ **(mmddyyyy)**

Marital Residence and Other Real Estate:	Market Value	Debt
1. Marital Residence at:	$	$
2.	$	$
3.	$	$
4.	$	$
TOTAL REAL ESTATE	$	$

Cars & Other Personal Property:	Market Value	Debt
1.	$	$
2.	$	$
3.	$	$
4.	$	$
5.	$	$
6.	$	$
TOTAL CARS & OTHER PERSONAL PROPERTY	$	$

Businesses:	Market Value	Debt
1. Business Interest -	$	$
2.	$	$
3.	$	$
4.	$	$
5.	$	$
6.	$	$
TOTAL BUSINESSES	$	$

Financial Assets (Cash or Cash Equivalents):	Market Value	
1. Savings or interest-bearing accounts	$	
2. Checking Accounts	$	
3. Certificates of Deposit	$	
4. Money Market Accounts	$	
5. Cash	$	
6. Other (specify):	$	
7. Other (specify):	$	
TOTAL CASH OR CASH EQUIVALENTS:	$	$

Retirement & Deferred Compensation:	Market Value	
1. Retirement:	$	
2.	$	
3.	$	
4.	$	
TOTAL RETIREMENT & DEFERRED COMPENSATION	$	$

Investment Accounts and Securities:	Market Value	
1. Stocks	$	
2. Bonds	$	
3. Tax exempt securities	$	
4. Other (specify):	$	
5. Other (specify):	$	
6. Other (specify):	$	
TOTAL INVESTMENT ACCOUNTS AND SECURITIES	$	$

Exhibit 6.1   Continued

RECAP OF INCOME AND EXPENSES:

Net Monthly Income (+)	$
Total Monthly Living Expenses (-)	$
Less Monthly Debt Service (-)	$
Total Income Available per Month (=)	$

STATEMENT OF HEALTH INSURANCE COVERAGE

Currently effective health insurance coverage? ☐ Yes   ☐ No

Name of insurance carrier: _____

Policy of Group No.: _____

Type of insurance: ☐ Medical   ☐ Dental   ☐ Optical

Deductible: Per individual: $_____   Per family: $_____

Persons covered: ☐ Self   ☐ Spouse   ☐ Dependents

Type of policy: ☐ HMO   ☐ PPO   ☐ Full indemnity

Provided by: ☐ Employer   ☐ Private Policy   ☐ Other Group

Monthly costs: ☐ Paid by Employer   ☐ Paid by employee:

$	for dependents
$	for self

VERIFICATION

The foregoing Financial Affidavit has been carefully read by the undersigned who states under oath, under penalties as provided by law pursuant to 735 ILCS 5/109, that this affidavit includes all of his/her income and expenses, he/she has knowledge of the matters stated and he/she certifies that the statements set forth in this Affidavit are true and correct, except as to matters specifically stated to be on information and belief, and as to such matters the undersigned certifies as aforesaid that he/she believes same to be true.

_____   _____
Signature of Petitioner   Signature of Respondent

_____   _____
Typed or Printed Name of Petitioner   Typed or Printed Name of Respondent

Date signed: _____   Date signed: _____

Enforcing the Child Support Obligation

In addition to addressing the problem of inadequate and inconsistent awards, federal child support laws also address the endemic problem of nonpayment by support obligors, which has resulted in a national support arrearage totaling more than a billion dollars. Seeking to rectify this, an elaborate network of interconnected databases has been created for the collection and exchange of child support–related information (discussed earlier in this chapter in the section entitled "Locating Absent Parents").[28]

Federal law requires states to adopt specific support enforcement methods. Going beyond these requirements, many states have adopted additional enforcement mechanisms such as lottery-winning intercepts or the use of the "Denver boot," "a steel, fifty-pound clamp that is attached to an automobile tire, effectively immobilizing the vehicle by preventing it from being driven until the offender responds to the legal system," which in this context would mean satisfaction of the support debt.[29] Supplementing support collection efforts at the state level, the Federal Office of Child Support Enforcement administers a "federal offset program."

After considering key enforcement mechanisms, we turn to the enforcement process in interstate cases, followed by a discussion about the continued availability of traditional state law remedies for the enforcement of child support orders. We conclude this section with look at the contested entry of private collection agencies into the child support arena.

Support Enforcement at the State Level

Income Withholding

Under federal law, all child support orders must include a **wage** (or income) **withholding** provision that enables support payments to be directly deducted from a noncustodial parent's paycheck, in much the way taxes are withheld. Income also can be withheld from other forms of periodic payments, such as those received from a pension plan or government benefits. Where benefits are concerned, the general rule is that they must be a form of remuneration for employment, such as Social Security or unemployment insurance benefits; needs-based benefits, such as Supplemental Security Income (SSI) payments, are not subject to withholding.[30] This is unquestionably one of the most effective means of ensuring that support is paid.

All child support orders must include a wage withholding provision that is to take place immediately, which means that a party does not have to wait for an **arrearage**—an overdue or unpaid amount—to accrue before the withholding goes into effect. There are only two exceptions to the immediate withholding requirement: (1) when good cause to suspend it is established, and (2) when the parties enter into a written agreement providing for an alternative arrangement.[31]

If the withholding is suspended, it must take effect once an arrearage equal to the support payable for a month has accrued. The noncustodial parent is entitled to notice that withholding is to commence. He or she may challenge the effectuation of the withholding, but may raise only mistakes of fact, such as a miscalculation of the arrearage. The validity of the underlying order cannot be challenged.

Employers are responsible for withholding the designated amount. An employer who fails to withhold child support will be responsible for the amount of support that should have been withheld. Also, fines can be levied against an employer who takes adverse action against an employee because of the withholding.

One problem has been that withholding does not keep up with a parent's job changes if the parent does not provide the information necessary to effectuate the withholding with his or her new employer. The new data-matching process addresses this problem. Information in the State or National Directory of New Hires can be matched with information in the Federal or State Case Registry, which enables the state to contact the new employer and direct it to begin withholding wages in accordance with the existing support order.

Liens

Under federal law, states must now have a law that creates a **lien** against the personal and real property of the noncustodial parent in the amount of unpaid support. A lien is a nonpossessory interest in property, that operates as a cloud against title, and would prevent the noncustodial parent from selling, transferring, or borrowing against the property until the arrearage is paid.

The following passage from the Office of Child Support Enforcement's manual, *Essentials for Attorneys in Child Support Enforcement*, provides an excellent description of how liens operate:

> A lien is often referred to as a "slumbering" interest that allows the noncustodial parent to retain possession of the property, but which prevents transfer of clear title of affected property either directly (by prohibiting the recording agency from issuing a new title or deed) or indirectly (by providing that all subsequent interests in the property will be subject to the lien). The latter method is most common. It works because subsequent potential purchasers and lenders receive notice of the . . . lien . . . [and] reacts to this . . . by requiring the noncustodial

parent to satisfy the lien, or to obtain a release from the custodial parent, before proceeding with the transfer or loan.[32]

Under federal law, the lien must arise as a matter of law, which means that it happens automatically, without any required action on the part of the custodial parent. However, under state law, the custodial parent may need to take certain steps to "perfect" the lien, such as recording a copy of the support order in the appropriate office or registry of public records, in order for it to have priority over other liens.

Credit Reporting

Under federal law, IV-D agencies must report to **credit-reporting** agencies the name of any parent whose support arrearage has reached a specific dollar amount. Before the report is made, the parent must be given notice and an opportunity to correct any inaccurate information. Although reporting does not result in an immediate transfer of income to the custodial parent, it is hoped that the threat of a negative credit report will serve as an inducement to support obligors who might otherwise be tempted to avoid paying child support.

Licenses

Federal law also requires states to adopt procedures by which they can withhold, suspend, or restrict an individual's professional or occupational license, driver's license, or recreational/sporting licenses due to the nonpayment of support. As with credit reporting, these sanctions do not directly transfer money to the custodial parent. Rather, it is hoped that the threat of losing or having restrictions placed on one's license will operate as a strong deterrent to the nonpayment of support.

The Federal Offset Program

The Federal Offset Program assists state to enforce child support obligations through a variety of remedies including the Federal Tax Refund Offset and the Passport Denial Program.[33] These are administered by OCSE in tandem with other federal (and state child support) agencies.

Federal Tax Offset

Acting in tandem with the two federal agencies, the Internal Revenue Service (IRS) and the Financial Management Service (a bureau of the

United States Department of the Treasury), the OCSE can intercept a federal tax refund owed to a noncustodial parent and use the funds to pay a past-due child support obligation. This remedy is available only in cases that are being handled through a state IV-D agency. In other words, a custodial parent acting on his or her own cannot request that delinquent support payments be collected through a tax intercept.

The noncustodial parent is entitled to receive a pre-offset notice that explains the process, including how to challenge the offset. Available arguments are limited. The parent can argue that no support is owed, that the arrearage calculation is incorrect, or that the refund is owed to his or her new spouse and therefore is not subject to the intercept, but the validity of the underlying order itself cannot be challenged.

The Passport Denial Program

Following certification by a state that a noncustodial parent owes at least $2,500 in back child support, the OCSE can submit that parent's name to the Department of State (DOS), which will then refuse to issue him or her a passport. If the parent already has a passport, DOS will revoke it or otherwise restrict its use. A parent is not automatically released from the Passport Denial Program when the support arrearage drops below $2,500, as it is up to each state to determine the terms of release, with some requiring that the full arrearage be paid first. As with the tax intercept, this process can be initiated only by a state IV-D agency.

Interstate Cases

A significant number of child support cases involve parents who live in different states. These cases have been the bane of the child support system. The process of obtaining and enforcing support orders across state lines has been notoriously difficult due to the lack of coordination between states, the lack of access to information, and the low priority given to these cases.[34] To improve this system, the IV-D agency in each state must have a Central Registry that coordinates interstate cases. States also are required to give interstate cases the same priority that they give to cases involving their own residents. Moreover, as discussed here, the Uniform Interstate Family Support Act (UIFSA) and the Full Faith and Credit for Child Support Orders Act (FFCCSOA) are intended to address the ongoing enforcement problems raised by the potential for multiple and conflicting support orders in multistate cases.

The Uniform Interstate Family Support Act

In 1992, the National Conference of Commissioners on Uniform State Laws (NCCUL) adopted the Uniform Interstate Family Support Act (UIFSA) to replace earlier uniform acts that had failed to satisfactorily solve the problems of multiple and conflicting support orders. Subsequently, in 1996, the Personal Responsibility and Work Opportunity Reconciliation Act (known colloquially as the "welfare reform" law) required states to adopt and implement UIFSA by 1998 in order to remain eligible for federal child support funds. In 2000, the child support community asked the National Conference of Commissioners on Uniform State Laws (NCCUSL) to review UIFSA, and in 2001, the NCCUSL approved a number of important amendments, including for example, that the Act's long-arm provisions apply only to the establishment and not to the modification of support order. To date, states have not been required to adopt these amendments, although many have done so. Accordingly, although UIFSA's "basic principles have remained constant," it is important to be aware that there is some variability between states depending upon whether or they have adopted the 2001 amendments or not.[35]

The primary purpose of UIFSA is to avoid the proliferation of competing orders in interstate cases with the resulting confusion regarding validity and enforceability. Accordingly, its "most revolutionary concept is its 'one-order' system," which effectively means that "once a support order is entered, that order controls the child support obligation regardless of whether the parents or child later moves to another state."[36] This then becomes the *Controlling Order* that must be honored by other states.

In order to facilitate the ability of a custodial parent to obtain support in his or her home state, UIFSA contains a very broad long-arm jurisdiction provision for the assertion of personal jurisdiction over the support obligor when it comes to the initial order. This order can then be enforced directly in the state where the noncustodial parent is located. Enforcement can be done directly through the sending of the wage withholding to the employer who must then withhold wages as directed, unless it is contested by the obligor based on the narrowly permitted ground of "mistake of fact." Although these orders are frequently sent by the child support agency on behalf of the custodial parent, this is not required, and a parent or someone acting on his or her behalf, such as an attorney or private collection agency (discussed below), can also send the order.

The order can also be enforced by the appropriate court in the obligor's home state. This process is initiated by the registration of the order with the court. Importantly, "the registered order continues to be the order of the issuing State."[37] Accordingly, the "role of the responding state is limited to enforcing that order except in the very limited circumstances where modification is permitted."[38]

Also very important to the creation and stability of a "one-order" system, the issuing state retains continuing exclusive jurisdiction to modify the order so long as either parent or the child remains in that state, or, if they have all moved, the parties consent to the continued jurisdiction of this state.[39] By vesting continuing authority in the original home state, UIFSA avoids the potential confusion of multiple orders. Only when all parties have left the issuing state, and have not consented to its continued jurisdiction, will modification jurisdiction shift to a new state. Thereafter, "the party petitioning for jurisdiction must be a nonresident of the responding State and must submit himself or herself to the forum state, which must have personal jurisdiction over the defendant."[40] The prefatory comments explain the rather puzzling "nonresident" rule as follows: "A colloquial short-hand summary of the principle is that ordinarily the movant for modification of a child support order must 'play an away game.'"[41]

Although our focus is on interstate as distinct from international support cases, it should be noted that in 2007, the United States became a signatory of the Hague Convention on the Enforcement of Child Support and Other Forms of Family Maintenance (Convention). The aim of the Convention was to establish for the first time "uniform, simple, inexpensive procedures for the processing of international support cases."[42] Subsequently, in 2008, the National Conference of Commissioners on Uniform State Laws amended UIFSA for the purpose of integrating select provisions of the Convention into state law. Congress thereafter approved legislation requiring all states to adopt the 2008 amendments to UIFSA as a condition of receiving continued federal support for their child support programs, which all states have since done. As a result of this compliance, the United States has now formally ratified the Convention.[43]

The Full Faith and Credit for Child Support Orders Act

Reinforcing UIFSA's "one-order" system, the federal Full Faith and Credit for Child Support Orders Act (FFCCSOA) requires states to give "full faith and credit" to properly issued orders from other states.[44] FFCCSOA is intended to be consistent with UIFA with regard to which order is controlling in the event of multiple orders. It also tracks UIFSA's modification rules based on the same concept of continuing exclusive jurisdiction in the home state until such time as both parties and the child have moved away, or the parties consent to continued jurisdiction.[45]

Enforcement Under State Law Procedures

In addition to the remedies discussed above, a support award can also be enforced through traditional state remedies, such as a **criminal nonsupport** or a **contempt proceeding**. These remedies can be pursued by an individual or by a IV-D agency on behalf of a custodial parent who is receiving its services.

Criminal Nonsupport

Most, if not all, states make the failure to support minor children a crime. Generally, nonsupport is classified as a misdemeanor. As in all criminal proceedings, the goal is punishment of the offender and vindication of the public interest. However, most states will suspend the sentence if the defendant agrees to pay support, which accomplishes the civil goal of providing support to the children. If the payment is not made following the suspension, the sentence will be reimposed.

For a conviction, the failure to support must be willful. The state has the burden of proving willfulness by establishing that the defendant had the ability to provide support and deliberately failed to do so. Some states also require proof that the nonsupport left the children in "destitute or necessitous" circumstances. In these states, support from the custodial parent or a third party that keeps the children out of poverty may bar a conviction. The defendant is entitled to the procedural protections that apply in all criminal cases, including the privilege against self-incrimination. This may make proof of ability to pay difficult because the defendant cannot be forced to testify or to disclose adverse information through discovery.

For these reasons, criminal nonsupport actions generally are not the remedy of choice. However, they can be useful where the failure to pay support is flagrant or where the obligor is self-employed, thus precluding wage withholding. The willful failure to pay a past-due support obligation on behalf of a child in another state is now a federal crime. In addition, under the Deadbeat Parents Punishment Act of 1998, it is a felony to travel interstate (or internationally) in order to avoid an unpaid support order that meets specified durational and amount requirements.[46]

Contempt

A contempt action can be brought where an obligor fails to comply with a court order of support. Contempt actions can be either civil or criminal in nature. A contempt action is usually not the remedy of choice, but it can be a useful supplemental remedy, especially where a parent is self-employed and thus not amenable to a wage withholding. However, as developed below, the use of civil contempt for nonpayment of child support has recently come under considerable criticism for its disproportionate impact on low-income support obligors.

Criminal Contempt. A criminal contempt proceeding is punitive in nature and if a jail sentence is imposed, it is for the purpose of punishing the support obligor for disobeying the court's order rather than, as in the case of a civil contempt proceeding, to secure compliance with the order. Accordingly, present ability to pay is not typically a required element; instead, the state must prove that the obligor had the ability to pay at the time of noncompliance. As this is a criminal proceeding, the support obligor is generally entitled to the procedural protections available to other criminal defendants, including the right to appointed counsel.

Civil Contempt.   The purpose of a civil contempt proceeding is to secure compliance with a support order, and a jail sentence may be imposed for this purpose. Given this remedial objective, a civil contempt order must contain what is known as a "purge" clause, which allows the support obligor to be released from jail by purging the contempt, usually by satisfying the terms of the underlying order. Accordingly, it is often said that in the context of a civil contempt proceeding a party holds the key to his or her own release.

But what if the noncustodial parent is poor, and thus does not actually hold the key to the jail cell? In the 2011 case of Turner v. Rogers,[47] the Supreme Court faced the question of whether a parent in this situation was entitled to appointed counsel as in a criminal contempt case. Although the Court concluded that there is no automatic right to appointed counsel in a civil contempt proceeding (although many states do provide for one), it did hold that states must provide sufficient procedural protections so as to minimize the risk of a wrongful incarceration. Of critical importance, a defendant's "ability to pay" must be a central consideration to ensure that there is "an actual and present ability to comply with the purge order,"[48] and the parent must be informed that this is the primary focus of the inquiry.

The 2016 Final Rule looks to *Turner* to ensure that civil contempt hearings meet minimal due process requirements, and child support agencies must accordingly screen cases to determine if a civil contempt action is the appropriate remedial step under the circumstances. The paramount consideration here is whether the noncustodial parent has the "actual and present ability to pay or comply with the support order."[49] By taking this into account, states can help to ensure that "low-income parents are not incarcerated unconstitutionally because they are poor and unable to comply with orders that do not reflect their ability to pay."[50] In keeping with *Turner*, defendants must be given notice that their ability to pay is the central focus of the civil contempt hearing. States are also encouraged to adopt other procedural safeguards to ensure that the due process rights of noncustodial parents are respected.[51]

Enforcement by Private Child Support Collection Agencies

Over the course of the past 10 or 15 years, a new player has entered the child support enforcement field to help custodial parents collect child support that is owed to them—the for-profit child support collection agency. Such an agency promises to fill the existing gap in enforcement services that IV-D agencies seem unable to meet. Many in the child support field argue that this is an idea whose time has come—that we need to face the reality that despite considerable progress, IV-D agencies are not able to handle the high volume of existing support cases. Proponents of this approach have asserted that this "troubling situation is not likely to change, no matter how effectively the state Title IV-D agencies use the vast information and enforcement resources available to them. The amounts of obligated, but uncollected support will continue to mount at a rate beyond the ability of the program ever to collect."[52]

Some have further argued that if we are to solve the current support crises, these private agencies (as well as the private bar) need enhanced power and increased resources. To this end, a variety of legislative proposals have been introduced that would give these private entities access to the databases, the parent locator resources, and the enforcement tools, such as tax refund intercepts, of the IV-D agencies.

Yet many in the field are wary of these agencies and do not want to encourage their proliferation or their access to governmental databases and enforcement tools. Serious concerns have been raised about some of these agencies' business practices, particularly the fees they charge, which can be as high as 50 percent of the collected support, thus diverting funds intended for the support of children. Moreover, these fees often are demanded even if the money is ultimately collected and disbursed by the IV-D agencies.[53] Other criticized practices include contracts that are almost impossible to cancel, harassment of the support obligor, threats of arrest without proper authority, and the collection of fees from current, rather than past, support as required.[54]

Other concerns focus on the risks of providing access to governmental databases and enforcement tools. It is argued that access to information may lead to breaches of privacy or to the potential misuse of highly confidential information and that increasing the tools at the disposal of these agencies may exacerbate existing questionable trade practices.

Again, this raises particular concerns about the safety of domestic violence victims.

Modification and Adjustment of Support Awards

Once a child support amount has been established, subsequent events may occur that warrant a change in the amount. Where this occurs, a parent may seek a **modification** of the support order. Additionally, states must implement a **review and adjustment procedure** for all support cases enforced through the IV-D agency.

Modification Based on Changed Circumstances

Child support orders are not generally considered final judgments and are subject to modification. However, modification actions are not designed to give parents a second bite at the apple; that is, issues that have already been determined are not supposed to be relitigated.

In a "traditional" modification action, the petitioner must show that there has been a **change in circumstances** that justifies an upward or downward revision of the support amount. Most, if not all, states also require that the change was not foreseeable at the time the order was entered. Circumventing this rule, some states have traditionally refused to treat incarceration as a change in circumstances that would permit a downward adjustment in child support — in some of these jurisdictions, the disqualification is framed in terms of a parent's "voluntary unemployment." However, in recognition of the hardship that an accrual of arrearages can impose upon a noncustodial parent upon reentry into the community, under the 2016 Final Rule, states may no longer treat incarceration as a legal bar to modification.

Support amounts agreed on by the parties in a separation agreement are subject to modification, as the right to adequate support belongs to the child and cannot be bargained away by a parent. However, some courts give considerable weight to the parties' agreement and impose a greater burden on the petitioner to prove that a modification is warranted.

Either party can seek a modification. Typically, a custodial parent who is seeking an upward revision looks to changes such as increased needs of the child, an increase in the other parent's income, remarriage of the noncustodial parent, or a decrease in his or her own income. Typically, a noncustodial parent who is seeking a downward revision looks to changes such as a decrease in his or her own income, responsibility for a second family, an increase in the custodial parent's income, remarriage of the custodial parent, or employment of the child.

A contentious question is whether a noncustodial parent can seek a reduction in support payments if the custodial parent is interfering with his or her visitation rights. The majority view is that visitation and support issues are independent variables and should not be linked. Exceptions to this policy of nonlinkage may occur in extreme situations—for example, where a parent falsifies employment information to avoid paying support or a custodial parent hides a child to prevent visitation from taking place.

The fact that support orders can be modified has historically caused considerable confusion in the interstate arena because states have readily modified orders of other states, resulting in multiple and potentially conflicting orders. However, FFCCSOA addresses this problem by vesting exclusive and continuing jurisdiction over the order in the issuing state so long as the child or any other party continues to reside there; as long as this condition is met, other states are precluded from modifying the order.

The Review and Adjustment Procedure

In addition to modifications based on changed circumstances, parents have a right under federal law to have their support orders reviewed every three years (or earlier if a state elects a shorter review cycle). Where the state's child support guidelines or changes in the cost of living justify a modification, a support order will be adjusted either upward or downward to account for the changes. Moreover, under the 2016 Final Rule, processes are now in place for the initiation of the review and adjustment process when a noncustodial parent will be incarcerated for more than 180 days.

Duration of the Parental Support Obligation

In general, a parent has an obligation to support his or her child until the child reaches 18—the age of majority. In certain situations, however, the support obligation may be terminated before majority or extended beyond it. These durational issues are generally controlled by state law.

Termination of Support Prior to Majority

Support can be terminated prior to majority only under very limited circumstances, such as emancipation of the minor, death of the parent paying support, or the termination of parental rights. A custodial parent does not generally have the authority to agree to a termination of support because, again, the right of support belongs to the child not to the parent.

Emancipation

Emancipation extinguishes the reciprocal rights and obligations that exist between a parent and child and releases the child from the authority and control of his or her parents. Many states recognize a common law doctrine of emancipation under which certain acts, most notably marriage and entry into the armed services, are regarded as creating a status that is incompatible with parental control and thus serve to emancipate the minor. In some states, a child who is living on his or her own and is self-supporting may also be considered emancipated. Some states have a statutory emancipation procedure that permits a child, or possibly a parent, to file a court petition seeking a declaration of emancipation.

Once a child is emancipated, the support obligation will in all likelihood terminate because the child is now considered able to care for himself or herself. However, where emancipation occurs through a court proceeding, a court might decide to only partially emancipate a minor, such as for the limited purpose of consenting to medical procedures, and continue the support obligation.

Parental Death

At common law, the death of a parent terminated the support obligation. This responsibility did not pass to the decedent's estate, but the estate was liable for arrearages that had accrued prior to death. Many states now have statutes that authorize a court to hold the parent's estate responsible for continued support payments unless the parties otherwise agreed in a separation agreement.

In the absence of a specific statute or separation agreement, many judges believe that they lack the authority to order post-death support, as this would upset the estate plan of the decedent who has a legal right to disinherit his or her children. According to this view, ordering such support would give greater rights to children of divorced parents compared to children of still-married parents. Other judges take a different view of the matter and may continue support following the death of the noncustodial parent. These judges give greater weight to providing for children than to protecting the stability of estate plans and the expectations of beneficiaries. This approach also recognizes that a noncustodial parent may be more likely to disinherit his or her children, thus creating a greater need for a remedy.

Adoption/Termination of Parental Rights

Where parental rights are extinguished through adoption or an involuntary termination proceeding, the parental support obligation is likewise extinguished. The only issue is identifying *when* the obligation ceases. The general rule is that this occurs upon the actual cessation of the parent-child relationship rather than upon the consent to the adoption.

Extension of Support Beyond Majority

Before looking at the specific exceptions that have been carved out to the otherwise firm rule that child support terminates upon majority, it is worth considering a recent novel call by family law expert Sally Goldfarb for a new legal remedy known as "'expanded post-majority child support,'" which would be modeled after "state statutes and case law that permit child support awards for adults who are in college."[55] This proposal is grounded in the recognition that in "stark contrast to family patterns that prevailed during the middle of the twentieth century," the transition from adolescence to adulthood is currently considerably more protracted than it had been, which has resulted in the greater financial dependence of young adults on their parents.[56]

According to Goldfarb, expanded post-majority child support would also address what she refers to as "troubling patterns of inequality."[57] The first inequity that she is concerned with is that young adults whose "parents are divorced, separated or never married receive less support than those whose parents are married to each other." The second is that "divorced, separated, or never married mothers bear a heavier burden of support for adult children than divorced, separated, or never married fathers."[58] The author also recognizes that the rectification of a third form of inequality, namely the fact that "adult children of affluent parents receive more support than their less privileged counterparts," would require a far more robust public response than simply the adoption of this proposed new approach to child support.[59]

The Adult Student

With the age of majority now set at 18 in most states, the question often arises as to whether an adult child has a right to continued support if he or she is still in high school or wishes to attend college. Most, if not all, states provide for the continuation of support until a child completes high school, even if he or she turns 18 prior to graduation. In short, emancipation for child support purposes is deemed to be the later of these two occurrences.

However, the picture is far less clear when it comes to post-minority support for a child who wishes to attend college.

The question as to whether a parent can be required to pay child support or to contribute to the educational expenses of an adult child has become increasingly pressing given that in today's advanced economy, a college degree (or other type of post-secondary education) is generally regarded as necessary to ensure some measure of financial autonomy and stability. Of particular concern in this regard is the fact that children of divorced parents are significantly less likely than children of still-married parents to receive financial help from one or both parents for college.[60] Capturing this imbalance, one commentator writes that

> parents of intact families achieve extraordinary wealth transfer by providing higher education for their children. This transfer exists almost entirely outside of the traditional child support system. As a result, the equality principle on which child support is based fails to accommodate children of non-intact families in receiving higher education.[61]

To remedy this inequity, the author suggests that the federal child support laws should be amended to require "states, when establishing their guidelines, to provide for some level of post-secondary support absent any agreement between the parents."[62] However, this proposal raises the counter equity argument noted below that doing so would impose a *formal* duty on divorced parents that is not likewise imposed on parents who are married.

As for the approaches that states do take, a sizable minority of jurisdictions have enacted statutory provisions that permit a judge to order the continuation of child support up to a certain post-minority age, typically 21 or 22, if the child is a full-time student or regularly attending school. In some of these states, in addition to or in lieu of child support, a parent can be ordered to pay a share of the child's educational expenses. Where both types of payments are ordered, the child support amount is typically adjusted downward to account for the parent's contribution to the costs of the child's education.[63] Even if not expressly authorized by statute, most states will enforce an agreement between parents that obligates one or both of them to provide child support for a post-minority child who is attending college.

In the absence of a specific statute, courts generally take one of two approaches to the award of support for post-minority students. Many judges believe it is not fair to require divorced parents to pay for their children's college education, since, had the family remained together, the parents would have been free to decide whether or not to contribute to their children's college education, and the children would have no legal claim to such support.

Other courts take the position that education is a basic parental obligation and will order support in appropriate cases. These courts often point out that had the parents remained together, it can be assumed that they would have made a reasonable effort to finance their children's education and that divorce should not work as a deprivation. They are also aware that if support is not ordered, the financial burden will most likely fall on the custodial parent.

In deciding whether to order support so a child may attend college, courts generally look at a number of factors, including the reasonable expectations of the child, academic interest and ability, and the parents' financial status. Courts may also try to determine whether the family would have provided a college education had the parents remained together. Unfortunately, these factors may work against a young person who is not from a middle-class family, as a judge may decide that a college education is not necessary or within reasonable expectations.

Mental and Physical Disabilities

With a handful of exceptions, all states permit courts to continue support beyond age 18 where an adult child is mentally or physically disabled and is incapable of self-support. Effectively, whether based on the common law or a statute, the underlying rationale for this approach is that where a disability renders a child "unable to support oneself, this prevents the child from becoming emancipated; accordingly, 'the presumption of emancipation upon reaching majority is inapplicable.'"[64]

However, in many jurisdictions, a significant limiting factor is that the disability must have begun while the child in question was a minor. Accordingly, if a child becomes disabled after reaching adulthood, parents cannot be required to pay child support even if their child is not able to be self-supporting.

Tax Implications of Child Support Awards

There are two basic tax questions to consider with regard to the payment of child support:

- How are payments to be treated for tax purposes?
- What is the relationship between paying support and claiming the dependency exemption for the children?

The basic rule is that child support payments are not considered income to the custodial parent and are not subject to taxation. Because payments are not includible in the recipient's income, the noncustodial parent is not entitled to deduct the amount of the payments from his or her income. In effect, payment of child support is a tax-neutral event.

The custodial parent is entitled to claim the children as dependents for federal tax purposes. That parent is also entitled to all other child-related tax benefits, including, for example, the child and dependent care credit. However, because the noncustodial parent is usually in a higher tax bracket, the dependency exemption may be worth more to this parent. Accordingly, as part of divorce negotiations, parties often negotiate over who will take the **dependency exemption**. If the custodial parent agrees that the noncustodial parent can claim the children, the custodial parent must effectuate this arrangement by signing a written release. The release can be made permanent or for a temporary period. Parties may also agree to alternate years for claiming the exemption or to each claim the exemption for a different child.

It is important to be aware that the custodial parent who relinquishes the dependency exemption may also be deemed to have relinquished other child-related tax benefits. The rules in this regard are somewhat variable based mainly upon the year of divorce. Accordingly, if your office is representing a custodial parent who is considering releasing the dependency exemption to the other spouse, careful attention must be paid to these rules so as to avoid the unintended result of your client giving up more than was bargained for.[65]

Chapter Summary

In 1974, Congress enacted the Child Support Enforcement and Establishment of Paternity Act, marking the entrance of the federal government into the child support arena. States must now have a comprehensive child support program in effect, which is administered by a single entity, known as a IV-D agency. Child support awards must be based on guidelines that use numeric criteria to arrive at a presumptive amount; deviations are permitted under limited circumstances. States must also have an array of enforcement mechanisms in place to help with the collection of child support. The most important of these is income withholding. To aid in the establishment and enforcement of child support, federal law has mandated the creation of an extensive interconnected set of databases, which permit the collection, sharing, and matching of information regarding child support cases.

Interstate cases have been the bane of the child support system. To address this situation, all states must now have a central registry for the coordination of interstate cases. Furthermore, all states have adopted UIFSA, which, by continuing modification jurisdiction in the issuing state for as long as a parent or child remains there, eliminates the problem of conflicting orders. Under FFCCSOA, all states must give full faith and credit to child support orders of other states.

A parent's support obligation generally lasts until a child reaches the age of majority (18) but, under limited circumstances, it can be terminated earlier or extended beyond this point. Support orders can be modified based on a change in circumstances; they are also subject to a periodic review and adjustment process.

Child support payments are not considered income to the recipient— nor are they deductible by the payor. Unless released, the dependency exemption belongs to the custodial parent. The release of this exemption may result in the release of other child-related tax benefits.

Key Terms

Child Support	Wage Withholding
Title IV-D	Arrearage
IV-D Agency	Lien
Parent Locator Service	Credit Reporting
Child Support Guidelines	Criminal Nonsupport
Support Worksheet	Contempt Proceeding
Imputed/Attributed Income	Modification
Extraordinary Expense	Review and Adjustment Procedure
Qualified Medical Child Support Order (QMCSO)	Change in Circumstances
	Emancipation
Financial Affidavit	Dependency Exemption

Review Questions

1. Why did the federal government decide to enter the child support field?
2. When was the federal Office of Child Support Enforcement established, and what is its function?
3. What is a IV-D agency, and what is its role in the child support field?
4. What must a custodial parent do when applying for public assistance? What is the nature of the parent's relationship with the IV-D system?
5. How does a custodial parent who is not on public assistance access the services of a IV-D agency?
6. What is a parent locator service?
7. Explain how child support guidelines work, making sure that you include an explanation of the concept of deviation.
8. What new obligations does the 2016 Final Rule place on child support agencies?

9. Identify and explain the various guideline approaches.
10. How do states generally define income?
11. What is meant by imputed or attributed income, and when is this concept used?
12. Explain the terms "gross income," "adjusted gross income," and "net income" in the child support context.
13. How do guidelines typically treat income of the custodial parent's new partner?
14. How do guidelines treat the income of a child?
15. Where a parent is ordered to pay support for a second family, how is his or her prior support order usually accounted for?
16. How do guidelines treat the situation where an obligor wants to pay less to his first family because he now has a second family with minor children?
17. Explain the concept of extraordinary expenses and how states treat them when determining support.
18. When might visitation arrangements trigger an adjustment in support?
19. Why do courts generally not terminate support where parents have joint custody? What approaches do courts take in these situations?
20. What kinds of databases exist at state and federal levels, and what roles do they play in the child support system? What concerns have been raised about them?
21. Explain how income withholding works. When can an income withholding be bypassed?
22. What is a lien, and what role does it have in the child support context?
23. What is the concept of a tax refund intercept?
24. What is the function of the central registry in an interstate case?
25. What is the overall purpose of UIFSA? What are its key provisions?
26. What does FFCCSOA require?
27. What role do private support collection agencies seek to fill? What arguments have been raised in favor of and against such an approach?
28. What is the goal of a criminal nonsupport case? How is the civil goal of supporting children accomplished?
29. Explain the difference between criminal and civil contempt.
30. What did the Supreme Court have to say about civil contempt proceedings in the case of Turner v. Rogers?
31. Explain the two ways in which support orders can be changed.
32. What is the relationship between support and visitation?
33. What circumstances might trigger a termination of support prior to majority?
34. What circumstances might permit a continuation of support after majority?

35. What approaches do states take with respect to post-minority support for children who are attending school?
36. As a general matter, what tax impact does child support have?
37. Who is entitled to the dependency exemption? How can the other parent become entitled to it?

Discussion Questions

1. Despite all the developments discussed in this chapter, serious concerns still exist regarding the inadequacy of support payments and noncompliance with support orders. Why do you think child support continues to be such a social problem? Given what you have learned about divorce, what dynamics do you think might be at work?
2. Let's take a hypothetical case: A couple divorces when their child is three years old. Mom has custody, and Dad moves out of state. For the first few years, Dad sees the child regularly, but now he has remarried and his visits are infrequent. He is now happy and actively participating in the raising of his two new children.

   He wishes to reduce support to his first child because he feels resentful about providing for a child he has no relationship with and money is tight in his new household. Do you think he should be permitted to do this? What do you base your opinion on? Does your answer change if Mom has interfered with his visits without good reason? Does your answer change if Mom left him because he was abusive? Should these kinds of issues influence support determinations?
3. Here's another hypothetical: Two parents divorce. Dad has custody of the two children, ages 2 and 4. He works half time. Mom is a corporate executive and hates her work. She earns a good salary and pays enough child support so that Dad and the children are reasonably comfortable. It is important to Dad that the children not be in full-time day care. Mom decides to leave her job and pursue her lifelong dream of being a freelance writer. Assume that Mom is acting in good faith; in other words, she is not making this job change for the purpose of avoiding child support. Do you think the court should impute income to her based on her earning capacity and use this figure for the calculation of support? How do you balance the equities in this situation? What factors would you weigh?
4. Should judges be able to order divorced parents to contribute to their children's college education?
5. Do you think private support collection agencies are a good idea? Do you think they benefit or harm children?

Assignments

1. Obtain a copy of your state's child support guidelines and answer the following questions:
   a. What approach is used?
   b. How is income of the custodial parent treated?
   c. How is income of the child treated?
   d. What happens when the obligor has a prior family? A subsequent family?
   e. How are extraordinary expenses treated?
   f. What other factors influence the amount?
2. Obtain a copy of the child support worksheet that is used in your state to calculate support awards. Using the worksheet and consulting the guidelines where necessary, calculate a support award based on the following facts:
   a. Mom has custody of the two children, ages 4 and 9.
   b. Her gross income is $22,000; her adjusted gross income is $18,700.
   c. She has yearly child-care expenses of $8,000.
   d. Dad's gross income is $46,000; his adjusted gross income is $39,000.
   e. He spends what would be considered a typical amount of time visiting with his children.
   f. Dad maintains a family health insurance policy that covers the children; the cost of this policy to him is $380 per month and the cost of maintaining an individual policy would be $190 per month.
   g. The nine-year old child has severe learning disabilities, which require the hiring of special tutors; the monthly cost of this is $225.
   h. Neither parent has other children.
3. Develop a client intake questionnaire for use in cases where support is an issue. Make sure you consult the guidelines so that all relevant considerations are accounted for.
4. Assume that a client in your office is seeking a divorce from her husband, who left the state five years ago. Since that time, she has had no contact with him, but she does know where he is living. Locate UIFSA as adopted by your state and determine whether your state can exercise personal jurisdiction over him for purposes of entering a child support order. Now, do the same but with the following change. Assume that the client and her husband never lived together in your state but that she moved here following their separation. However, the husband makes periodic visits to see the child. Under this set of facts, can your state obtain personal jurisdiction over him? Explain your answer.

Cases for Analysis

In this child support case, the South Carolina Supreme Court takes the unusual step of reversing a decision it had issued only two years prior in which it held that ordering a divorced noncustodial parent to pay college expenses violated the equal protection clause.

McLEOD v. STARNES
396 S.C. 647, 723 S.E.2d 198 (2012)

Justice HEARN.

Less than two years ago, this Court decided *Webb v. Sowell*, 387 S.C. 328, 692 S.E.2d 543 (2010), which held that ordering a non-custodial parent to pay college expenses violates equal protection, thus overruling thirty years of precedent flowing from *Risinger v. Risinger*, 273 S.C. 36, 253 S.E.2d 652 (1979). We granted permission in this case to argue against precedent . . . so that we could revisit our holding in *Webb*. Today, we hold that *Webb* was wrongly decided and remand this matter for reconsideration in light of the law as it existed prior to *Webb*.

FACTUAL/PROCEDURAL BACKGROUND

Kristi McLeod (Mother) and Robert Starnes (Father) divorced in 1993 following five years of marriage. Mother received custody of their two minor children, and Father was required to pay child support. . . .

In August 2006, the parties' older child, Collin, reached the age of majority and enrolled as a student at Newberry College. . . . To help take advantage of this opportunity, he sought all scholarships, loans, and grants that he could. Father wholly supported Collin's decision to attend Newberry. Indeed, Father wrote an e-mail in March 2006 agreeing to repay all of Collin's student loans upon graduation. He even co-signed a promissory note for Collin's student loans. Furthermore, in an August 2006 letter, Father agreed to pick up "odd expenses from [Collin]'s education" and told Collin to call him whenever he "needs a little help." Interestingly, Father took it upon himself in that same letter to unilaterally decrease his weekly child support from $175 to $100. Mother later acquiesced in this reduction, apparently in consideration of Father's assurances that he would support Collin while he was in college. However, Father did not uphold his end of the bargain, nor did he regularly pay the percentage of his bonus as required.

Mother brought the instant action in March 2007 seeking an award of college expenses. . . . Father counterclaimed, asking that the court terminate: (1) his child support for Collin because he had attained the age of majority and graduated from high school. . . . He also denied that he should be required to pay any college expenses for Collin. A temporary order was filed in June 2007 that . . . ordered Father to contribute $400 per month towards Collin's college expenses. . . .

The final hearing was not conducted until March and July 2009. The court dismissed Mother's claim for college expenses on the ground that it violated the Equal Protection Clause of the United States Constitution. . . .

I.   COLLEGE EXPENSES

Mother argues the family court erred in finding that an order requiring Father to pay college expenses for Collin violates equal protection. We agree.

In *Webb*, we held that requiring a parent to contribute toward an adult child's college expenses violated the Equal Protection Clause. . . . We are not unmindful of the imprimatur of correctness which stare decisis lends to that decision. However, stare decisis is not an inexorable command. . . .

. . . "Stare decisis should be used to foster stability and certainty in the law, but[] not to perpetuate error." *Fitzer v. Greater Greenville S.C. Young Men's Christian Ass'n*, 277 S.C. 1, 4, 282 S.E.2d 230, 231 (1981), *superseded by statute on other grounds*, S.C. Code Ann. §33-55-200, *et seq.* (2006). . . .

We are at the first practical moment to reexamine *Webb*, a "single precedent case" concerning a constitutional question because it is the first and only case in this State finding an equal protection violation in these circumstances. We now believe *Webb* reversed the burden imposed on parties operating under rational basis review for equal protection challenges and should therefore be overruled.

In *Webb*, we were asked to determine whether requiring a non-custodial parent to pay college expenses was a violation of equal protection. . . . Absent an allegation that the classification resulting in different treatment is suspect, a classification will survive an equal protection challenge so long as it rests on some rational basis. If we can discern any rational basis to support the classification, regardless of whether that basis was the original motivation for it, the classification will withstand constitutional scrutiny. . . .

In *Webb*, the majority viewed the classification created by *Risinger* for equal protection purposes as those parents subject to a child support order at the time the child is emancipated. . . . Without any elaboration, the majority concluded that there is no rational basis for treating parents subject to such an order different than those not subject to one with respect to the payment of college expenses. Upon further reflection, we now believe that we abandoned our long-held rational basis rule that the party challenging a classification must prove there is no conceivable basis upon which it can rest and inverted the burden of proof. . . .

This State has a strong interest in the outcome of disputes where the welfare of our young citizens is at stake. As can hardly be contested, the State also has a strong interest in ensuring that our youth are educated such that they can become more productive members of our society. It is entirely possible "that most parents who remain married to each other support their children through college years. On the other hand, even well-intentioned parents, when deprived of the custody of their children, sometimes react by refusing to support them as they would if the family unit had been preserved." *In re Marriage of Vrban*, 293 N.W.2d 198, 202 (Iowa 1980). Therefore, it may very well be that *Risinger* sought to alleviate this harm by "minimiz[ing] any economic and educational disadvantages to children of divorced parents." *Kujawinski v. Kujawinski*, 71 Ill. 2d 563, 376 N.E.2d 1382, 1390, 17 Ill. Dec. 801 (Ill. 1978). . . . There is no absolute right to a college education, and section 63-3-530(A)(17), as interpreted by *Risinger* and its progeny, does not impose a moral obligation on all divorced parents with children. Instead, the factors identified by *Risinger* and expounded upon in later cases seek to identify those children whose parents would *otherwise* have paid for their college education, but for the divorce, and provide them with that benefit.

We accordingly hold that requiring a parent to pay, as an incident of child support, for post-secondary education under the appropriate and limited circumstances outlined by *Risinger* is rationally related to the State's interest. While it is certainly true that not all married couples send their children to college, that does not detract from the State's interest in having college-educated citizens and attempting to alleviate the potential disadvantages placed upon children of divorced parents. Although the decision to send a child to college may be a personal one, it is not one we wish to foreclose to a child simply because his parents are divorced. It is of no moment that not every married parent sends his children to college or that not every divorced parent refuses to do so. The tenets of rational basis review under equal protection do not require such exacting precision in the decision to create a classification and its effect.

Indeed, Father's refusal to contribute towards Collin's college expenses under the facts of this case proves the very ill which *Risinger* attempted to alleviate, for Father articulated no defensible reason for his refusal other than the shield erected by *Webb*. What other reason could there be for a father with more than adequate means and a son who truly desires to attend college to skirt the obligation the father almost certainly would have assumed had he not divorced the child's mother? Had Father and Mother remained married, we believe Father undoubtedly would have contributed towards Collin's education. Collin has therefore fallen victim to the precise harm that prompted the courts . . . to hold that a non-custodial parent could be ordered to contribute towards a child's college education. Thus, this case amply demonstrates what we failed to recognize in *Webb*: sometimes the acrimony of marital litigation impacts a parent's normal sense of obligation towards his or her children. While this is a harsh and unfortunate reality, it is a reality nonetheless that *Risinger* sought to address. . . .

We now hold *Risinger* does not violate the Equal Protection Clause because there is a rational basis to support any disparate treatment *Risinger* and its progeny created. In fact, the case before us particularly demonstrates the need for a rule permitting an award of college expenses in certain circumstances in order to ensure children of divorce have the benefit of the college education they would have received had their parents remained together. Accordingly, we reverse the order of the family court and remand this matter for a determination of whether and in what amount Father is required to contribute to Collin's college education under the law as it existed prior to *Webb*.

QUESTIONS

1. Why did the *Webb* court conclude that it was unconstitutional to require noncustodial parents to contribute to their children's college expenses?
2. What interests of the state did the court take into account in reaching its decision?
3. What did the court have to say about noncustodial parents when it comes to helping their children with college expenses? What did the court say about this father in particular?
4. What exactly did the court rule with regard to the circumstances under which it may be appropriate to order a parent to help with his or her child's college expenses?

———

In this "high income" case, the Pennsylvania high court ordered the custodial parent to pay child support to the noncustodial parent based on the significant disparity in their incomes. The decision provides an interesting discussion of the relationship between support and child custody, particularly when one takes the views of the dissent into account.

COLONNA v. COLONNA
581 Pa. 1, 855 A.2d 648 (2004)

Justice NEWMAN.

Appellant Mary M. Colonna (Mother) and Appellee Robert J. Colonna (Father) were married in 1983 and separated in 1996. . . . At the time of separation, the parties agreed to a temporary order of shared legal and physical custody, pursuant to which the children lived three and one-half days per week with each parent. They later amended the agreement to provide that the children would alternate between parental homes on a weekly basis. . . .

On November 19, 1997, the trial court ordered Father to pay . . . child support and to provide health insurance for Mother and the children. . . .

By Order dated May 4, 1998, the trial court awarded primary legal and physical custody to Father during the school year, and primary legal and physical custody to Mother during the summer. Mother has partial custody of one or more of the children on Tuesday and Thursday during the school year, and Father has partial custody of one or more of the children on Tuesday and Thursday during the summer. The parties alternate holidays and weekends throughout the year, and each parent has two weeks with the children for summer vacation.

On July 24, 1998, Father sought to terminate child support on the basis that he was now the children's primary custodian. . . .

The master determined that Mother had custody 27% of the year, and Father had custody 73% of the year. She was troubled by the disparities in the parties' income and the fact that Mother has certain fixed expenses incident to her alternating weekend and summer custody. . . .

. . . The Superior Court concluded that for purposes of calculating child support, the custodial parent is the obligee and the non-custodial parent is the obligor. Because the children spend 73% of the time with Father and 27% with Mother, the Superior Court determined that Father, as the obligee, does not owe child support to Mother, who is the obligor. The Superior Court relied upon Pa.R.C.P. 1910.16-1, Explanatory Comment B.2., which provides:

> Each parent is required to contribute a share of the child's reasonable needs proportional to that parent's share of the combined net incomes. The custodial parent makes these contributions entirely through direct expenditures for food, shelter, clothing, transportation and other reasonable needs. In addition to any direct expenditures on the child's behalf, the non-custodial parent makes contributions through periodic support payments.

Accordingly, the Superior Court held that Mother was not entitled to child support. It concluded:

> Where primary physical custody is changed from one parent to the other parent, no valid justification remains for requiring the new custodial parent to continue payments that are intended to be purely for the support, benefit and best interest of the children. Consequently, directing support payments to a non-custodial parent . . . serves no purpose for the children after custody changes and would only confer a personal benefit upon the non-custodial parent if the payments were allowed to continue.

Colonna v. Colonna, 2001 PA Super 368, 788 A.2d 430, 442 (Pa. Super. 2001).

We adamantly disagree with this conclusion. . . . [W]e are troubled by the disparity in the parties' incomes and are concerned that the refusal to consider this as a factor when fashioning a support order may be contrary to the best interests of the children. We must always be mindful of the fact that the support laws work in conjunction with our custody laws. The General Assembly has declared:

> It is the public policy of this Commonwealth, when in the best interest of the child, to assure a reasonable and continuing contact of the child with both parents after a separation or dissolution of the marriage and a sharing of the rights and responsibilities of child rearing by both parents. . . .

23 Pa. [Cons. Stat.] §5301.

Where the parent who does not have primary custody has a less significant income than the custodial parent, it is likely that he or she will not be able to provide an environment that resembles the one in which the children are accustomed to living with the custodial parent. While a downward adjustment in lifestyle is a frequent consequence of divorce that affects both adults and children, we would be remiss in failing to ignore the reality of what happens when children are required to live vastly different lives depending upon which parent has custody on any given day. To expect that quality of the contact between the non-custodial parent and the children will not be negatively impacted by that parent's comparative penury vis-a-vis the custodial parent is not realistic. Issuing a support order that allows such a situation to exist clearly is not in the best interests of the children.

Therefore, where the incomes of the parents differ significantly, we believe that it is an abuse of discretion for the trial court to fail to consider whether deviating from the support guidelines is appropriate, even in cases where the result would be to order child support for a parent who is not the primary custodial parent. . . .

In a case such as the instant matter, the trial court should inquire whether the non-custodial parent has sufficient assets to provide the children with appropriate housing and amenities during his or her period of partial custody. We specifically note that the term "appropriate" does not mean equal to the environment the children enjoy while in the custodial parent's care, nor does it mean "merely adequate." The determination of appropriateness is left to the discretion of the trial court, upon consideration of all relevant circumstances.

Mr. Chief Justice CAPPY, dissenting.

Because I believe that a custodial parent should not be obligated to pay child support to a non-custodial parent, I must respectfully dissent.

. . . I find the majority's approach disquieting because I believe it transforms a child support action into a quasi-equitable distribution action. In my view, the majority's new rule is not so much addressing whether the needs of the children are being met . . . but rather is focused on augmenting the wealth of the non-custodial parent. While such a focus may be proper in an equitable distribution matter, it has no place in a child support action. A child support action should not be used to jerry-rig a new balance between the respective financial positions of the spouses. . . .

[M]ost importantly, I am not in accord with the majority's foundational premise concerning the relationships between parents and children. The majority appears to be of the belief that if there is a disparity in income, the parent-child relationship will perforce be corrupted by the wealthier parent's desire to "buy the affection of the children. . . ." Majority slip op at 7 n.5. . . . The majority believes we should capitulate to what it perceives to be a social reality, and redistribute the wealth so that the affections of the child will not be alienated due to a parent's inability to provide the child with material advantages comparable to those provided by the wealthier parent.

I am disturbed by this approach. First, I can find no basis in the law for the proposition that a non-custodial spouse must be enabled, via payments from the custodial parent, to provide material advantages and entertain her children in the same lavish fashion as may the custodial parent. This simply has not been the law of this Commonwealth.

Furthermore, I am disturbed by the philosophy underpinning this rule. Unlike the apparent view of the majority, I do not believe that the health of any given parent-child relationship is measured by a parent's ability to provide a surfeit of expensive possessions or experiences for her child. Rather, the parent-child relationship thrives, or withers, based on the availability of intangibles such as love, attention, and affection. While it may be true that we live in a highly materialistic culture, does this fact stand in contradiction to the timeless realities of parenting? Or, to put it colloquially, can money buy love? I think not. And, more importantly, I balk at this court's implication that not only are a child's affections for sale, but also that our judiciary should be in the business of fostering the market for such a "commodity." For the foregoing reasons, I respectfully dissent.

Mr. Justice Castille joins this dissenting opinion.

QUESTIONS

1. What is the parties' custodial arrangement?
2. Why does the court reference the custody statute given that this is a support case?

3. How does the court justify the support award?
4. What reasons does the dissent give for objecting to the decision?
5. What philosophical concerns does the dissent raise?

In the following case, the court addresses the question of whether a child support order should be modified or terminated when a parent is incarcerated, which here was because the father had sexually assaulted his daughter. The opinion is thoughtful and clear and is instructive on the issue of modification/termination in general.

YERKES v. YERKES
573 Pa. 294, 824 A.2d 1169 (2003)

Justice NIGRO. The question presented in this case is whether incarceration, standing alone, is a "material and substantial change in circumstances" that provides sufficient grounds for modification or termination of a child support order. We hold that it is not.

Appellant Keith A. Yerkes ("Father") and Appellee Lydia A. Yerkes ("Mother") were married in November 1978 and separated in August 1992. During their marriage, the parties had two children: Amy, born in January 1983, and Richard, born in August 1988. Immediately following the parties' separation, Mother sought child support from Father. The parties eventually reached an agreement for support in November 1992.

In 1994, Father was arrested for sexually assaulting Amy, who was eleven years old at the time. He was ultimately convicted of aggravated indecent assault and has been incarcerated for that crime since August 1994. Father . . . will be released by August 2004.

In May 1997, Father petitioned the trial court for modification or termination of the November 1992 support order. . . .

The thrust of Father's argument is that his support obligation should be modified or terminated because he is unable to pay due to his imprisonment and the inadequate wage he earns. . . .

To give effect to the requirement of reasonable financial support, the Pennsylvania Rules of Civil Procedure provide a comprehensive set of guidelines for the appropriate amount of child support to be contributed by each parent. See generally Pa. R.C.P. No. 1910.16-1 to 1910.16-7. . . .

This Court has never directly addressed whether incarceration, standing alone, is a "material and substantial change in circumstances" that provides sufficient grounds for modification or termination of a child support order. A review of cases from other jurisdictions, however, reveals a wealth of case law that can be loosely categorized into three groups, each of which represents a different approach to assessing the effect of incarceration on support obligations. The first approach, dubbed the "no justification" rule, generally deems criminal incarceration as insufficient to justify elimination or reduction of an open obligation to pay child support. See *Thurmond*, 962 P.2d at 1068-70; *Halliwell*, 741 A.2d at 644. The second approach, known as the "complete justification" rule, generally deems incarceration for criminal conduct as sufficient to justify elimination or reduction of an existing child support obligation. See *Thurmond*, 962 P.2d at 1070-71; *Halliwell*, 741 A.2d at 644-45. Finally, the third approach is the "one factor" rule, which generally requires the trial court to simply consider the fact of criminal incarceration along with other factors in determining whether to eliminate or reduce an open obligation to pay child support. See *Thurmond*, 962 P.2d at 1071-72; *Halliwell*, 741 A.2d at 645.

The fundamental disagreement between those courts applying a "no justification" rule and those adopting one of the other two rules hinges on whether relief should ever be granted to incarcerated parents. It appears that each court's ultimate conclusion on this issue is driven by three underlying considerations: (1) whether allowing relief to an incarcerated parent serves the best interests of the child, (2) whether relief is in accord with fairness principles, and (3) whether it is appropriate to treat incarceration in the same manner as voluntary unemployment.

With regard to the first consideration, i.e., whether relief serves the best interests of the child, courts invoking the "no justification" rule often maintain that it is in the best interests of the child for the support order to remain intact because of the possibility of future reimbursement. . . . On the other hand, those jurisdictions that reject the "no justification" rule often counter that such an approach to the best interests principle is unrealistic:

> [Under the "no justification" rule,] the child support judgment will not be paid during the time that the parent is incarcerated, and therefore the judgment will simply accrue with interest. Such a situation provides little or no benefit to anyone. The children do not receive the benefit of the proceeds during the time they require the funds, and the parent is simply confronted with a large, nondischargeable judgment upon release from prison, at a time when the prospect of paying a large judgment with interest is extremely unlikely. At current interest rates the judgment will double every 6 or 7 years. How this can be in the children's best interest is difficult . . . to imagine.

Pierce, 412 N.W.2d at 293 (quoting Ohler v. Ohler, 220 Neb. 272, 369 N.W.2d 615, 618-19 (Neb. 1985) (Krivosha, C.J., dissenting)). . . .

Having considered the arguments on both sides of this issue, we conclude that the best interests of the child are better served by the "no justification" rule than by a rule that would allow suspension of the support obligation during an obligor's incarceration. As the Appellate Division of the Superior Court of New Jersey has cogently explained:

> We perceive two possible scenarios. In the first, the obligor is incarcerated and the support obligation is not suspended. Payments go into arrears. Upon release, the obligor cannot pay both current support and arrears, so only the current support is paid. In the second scenario, the obligor is incarcerated and the obligation is suspended during incarceration. Upon release, the obligor resumes paying the pre-incarceration support obligation. . . .
>
> In both situations, the child receives no support during the obligor's incarceration, and in both, the child begins to receive support upon the obligor's release. . . . [T]he scenario-one child suffers during the obligor's incarceration, but there is a possibility of compensation at some point in the future. The scenario-two child also suffers during the obligor's incarceration, but there is no realistic chance that the substantial arrearage will ever be fully paid. . . .
>
> Thus, scenario two works to the benefit of the obligor, while scenario one works to the benefit of the child, at least theoretically. The scenario-two child essentially takes on a burden because the obligor has been relieved temporarily of the parental duty of support.
>
> The question is which scenario is worse. Clearly, it is scenario two, in which the child has no real hope of ever seeing the missed support payments to which (s)he is entitled. . . .

Halliwell, 741 A.2d at 645-46 (footnote omitted). We agree with the New Jersey court that, although none of the three rules will provide short-term relief to the child, the "no justification" rule at least provides for the possibility that the obligor will repay the support owed to the child. . . .

With regard to the second consideration, i.e., which approach is most "fair," proponents of the "no justification" rule often reason that fairness principles dictate that an obligor should not benefit from criminal conduct or be allowed to use it as a means to escape child support obligations. . . . These courts often opine that because the needs of the children have not changed, their needs must prevail over the difficulties of the incarcerated parent. . . . On the other hand, those rejecting the "no justification" rule argue that fairness weighs in favor of the obligor because, without relief, the obligor parent would be saddled with an onerous burden upon release from prison. . . .

On balance, we believe that fairness principles also weigh in favor of the "no justification" rule, primarily because affording relief to the incarcerated parent would effectively subordinate child support payments to the parent's other financial obligations. . . . As such, we simply cannot justify relieving incarcerated parents of their child support obligations when they are not relieved of their other financial obligations. . . .

Finally, with regard to the third consideration, . . . courts following the "no justification" rule often liken obligors who are sent to prison for criminal conduct to those who voluntarily assume lower paying jobs or leave their jobs. . . . As the Supreme Court of Montana stated:

> . . . We see no reason to offer criminals a reprieve from their child support obligations when we would not do the same for an obligor who voluntarily walks away from his job. Unlike the obligor who is unemployed or faced with a reduction in pay through no fault of his own, the incarcerated person has control over his actions and should be held to the consequences. . . . [An obligor] should not be able to escape his financial obligation to his children simply because his misdeeds have placed him behind bars. The meter should continue to run.

Mooney, 848 P.2d at 1023 (citation omitted). . . . On the other hand, the Supreme Court of Alaska has rejected the analogy to voluntary unemployment:

> Although incarceration is often a foreseeable consequence of criminal misconduct and all criminal acts are in some sense voluntary, non-custodial parents who engage in criminal misconduct seldom desire the enforced unemployment that accompanies incarceration; nor can they alter their situation; and, in stark contrast to parents who consciously choose to remain unemployed, jailed parents rarely have any actual job prospects or potential income. Equating incarceration to voluntary unemployment would require us to ignore these significant, real-life distinctions.

Bendixen, 962 P.2d at 173. . . .

[W]e agree with the courts favoring the "no justification" rule that it is appropriate to analogize incarceration to voluntary unemployment. . . .

[I]t is foreseeable that criminal conduct can lead to incarceration, a reduction in income occasioned by criminal incarceration is clearly within the control of the obligor. Thus, we conclude that an incarcerated obligor, though in somewhat different circumstances from a voluntarily unemployed obligor, has control over his or her circumstances. . . .

In sum, we conclude that the "no justification" rule best serves the interests of the child and is in harmony with fairness principles and the child support laws of Pennsylvania. . . . In this case, Father was incarcerated for sexually assaulting his daughter. His sole argument in support of his petition for modification or termination of his child support obligation was that his incarceration made him unable to pay. Thus, Father cannot obtain relief from his child support obligations. . . .

QUESTIONS

1. What are the three approaches that jurisdictions take with respect to whether incarceration justifies relief from a child support obligation?
2. What approach does the court adopt?

3. What considerations underlie this approach?
4. As reviewed here, what views do other courts take with respect to these considerations?
5. At the end of the decision, the court notes that the result is "particularly appropriate" given that the father's incarceration stems from his sexual assault of his daughter—how significant do you think this factor is? Do you think the result would have been the same if the incarceration was for a reason unrelated to his family? Will this be a distinguishing factor in the future?

Endnotes

1. *See* Lucy Yee, What Really Happens in Child Support Cases: An Empirical Study of Establishment and Enforcement of Child Support Orders in the Denver District Court, 57 Denv. L.J. 21 (1979).

2. Joseph I. Lieberman, Child Support in America: Practical Advice for Negotiating and Collecting a Fair Settlement 11 (1988).

3. *Id*. at 14.

4. Pub. L. No. 104-193 (1996).

5. Pub. L. No. 93-647 (1974) (codified as amended at 42 U.S.C. §§651-662).

6. U.S. Dept. of Health and Human Services, Child Support: An Agenda for Action (1984).

7. No systematic attempt will be made to match developments with a particular legislative enactment. For your reference, some of the more significant amendments to date include the Child Support Enforcement Amendments of 1984, Pub. L. No. 98-378, 98 Stat. 1305 (42 U.S.C. §667); the Family Support Act of 1988, Pub. L. No. 100-485, 102 Stat. 2343 (codified in scattered sections of 42 U.S.C.); the Child Support Recovery Act of 1992, Pub. L. No. 102-521, 106 Stat. 3403 (codified as amended at 18 U.S.C. §228 and scattered sections of 42 U.S.C.); The Personal Responsibility and Work Opportunity Reconciliation Act of 1996, Pub. L. No. 104-193, 110 Stat. 105 (42 U.S.C. §§601 et seq.); and the Deficit Reduction Act of 2005, Pub. L. No. 109-171, 120 Stat. 4.

It should also be noted that this chapter does not address the complex issue of *who* may be liable for child support in the context of "nontraditional" family structures. This issue is touched on in Chapter 11. For further information, the following articles are a good starting point: Leslie Joan Harris, The Basis for Legal Parentage and the Clash Between Custody and Child Support, 42 Ind. L. Rev. 611 (2009); Laura W. Morgan, Child Support Fifty Years Later, 42 Fam. L.Q. 365 (2008); Katherine K. Baker, Bionormativity and the Construction of Parenthood, 42 Ga. L. Rev. 649 (2008); M. Scott Serfozo, Sperm Donor Child Support Obligations: How Courts and Legislatures Should Weigh the Interests of Donor, Donee, and Child, 77 U. Cin. L. Rev. 715 (2008); Jennifer L. Rosato, Children of Same-Sex Parents Deserve the Security Blanket of the Parentage Presumption, 44 Fam. Ct. Rev. 74 (2006); Sara R. David, Turning Parental Rights into Parental Obligations—Holding Same-Sex, Non-Biological Parents Responsible for Child Support, 31 New Eng. L. Rev. 921 (2005).

8. A state that does not comply with federal law risks losing a percentage of its federal funding for the administration of its child support program.

9. http://www.acf.hhs.gov/programs/cse/newhire/library/brochures/fpls/fpls.htm.

10. Office of Child Support Enforcement, Division of Policy and Training, Flexibility, Efficiency, and Modernization in Child Support Enforcement Programs: Final Rule.

11. Resource guides can be found at https://www.acf.hhs.gov/css/resource/final-rule-resources.

12. As noted above, in 1996 Congress replaced AFDC with the Transitional Aid to Needy Families program. Designed, at least in theory, to move people off of public assistance, among other differences, TANF includes a lifetime cap on the number of months that a person may receive benefits. For further discussion, *see generally* the relevant publications on the Center for Law and Social Policy's website: http://www.clasp.org (accessed Nov. 14, 2012).

13. For a detailed discussion of safety concerns raised by the child support collection process, *see* Ali Stieglitz and Amy Johnson, Final Report: Making Child Support Safe: Coordinating Child Support and Public Assistance Agencies in Their Response to Domestic Violence (2001), available at http://www.acf.hhs.gov/programs/cse/pubs/reports/mpr8548300/index.html; and Susan Notar and Vicki Turetsky, Models for Safe Child Support Enforcement, 8 Am. U. J. Gender Soc. Poly & L. 657 (2000).

14. For further detail, including a discussion of how collected support is to be allocated once a family is no longer receiving TANF benefits, *see* Paul Legler and Vicki Turestsky, More Child Support Dollars to Kids: Using New State Flexibility in Child Support Pass-Through and Distribution Rules to Benefit Government and Families (2006), Center for Law and Social Policy, http://www.clasp.org/admin/site/publications/files/0305.pdf. Regarding each state's approach, *see* Michelle Vinson and Vicki Turetsky, State Child Support Pass-Through Policies, http://www.clasp.org/admin/site/publications/files/PassThroughFinal061209.pdf (accessed Jan. 19, 2010).

Please note that a detailed discussion about the complex relationship between the child support and the public assistance systems is beyond the scope of this text. If you are working with clients who are applying for or receiving public assistance, you must become familiar with the interplay between them. This is particularly important if your client is a victim of domestic violence, as the initiation of a child support action can trigger or escalate abuse or possibly lead to the disclosure of a victim's whereabouts. It may also trigger a retaliatory custody or visitation action. The above-referenced Center for Law and Social Policy website is an excellent place to start your inquiry.

15. Vicki Turetsky, What If All the Money Came Home? Welfare Cost Recovery in the Child Support Program, 43 Fam. Ct. Rev. 402 (2005).

16. Office of Child Support Enforcement, Essentials for Attorneys in Child Support Enforcement, ch. 3 (3d ed. 2002) (*Essentials*), http://www.acf.hhs.gov/programs/cse/pubs/2002/reports/essentials (accessed Jan. 22, 2010).

17. Notar and Turetsky, *supra* note 13, at 698.

18. The word "permanent" does not mean forever, as support awards are modifiable. Rather, the term "permanent support" is used to distinguish awards that are entered at the time of divorce from those that are entered during the pendency of the case and are thus interim in nature.

19. Office of Child Support Enforcement, Division of Policy and Training, Flexibility, Efficiency, and Modernization in Child Support Enforcement Programs: Final Rule, https://www.acf.hhs.gov/sites/default/files/programs/css/ocse_final_rule_presentation.pdf.

20. *Id.*

21. *See* http://www.ncsl.org/research/human-services/guideline-models-by-state.aspx (accessed Dec. 23, 2015).

22. Office of Child Support Enforcement, Division of Policy and Training, Final Rule, Training, Flexibility, Efficiency, and Modernization in Child Support Enforcement Programs, Guidelines, https://www.acf.hhs.gov/sites/default/files/programs/css/fem_final_rule_guidelines.pdf.

23. Laura W. Morgan, Imputing Income to Non-Income and Low-Income Earning Assets, 17 Am. J. Fam. L. 191 (2004).

24. *Essentials, supra* note 16, ch. 9. Although questions about multiple families usually arise in the course of a modification proceeding, the topic will be discussed here in keeping with the organizational format of many guidelines. For an excellent discussion on this topic, *see* Marianne Takas, U.S. Dept. of Health and Human Services, The Treatment of Multiple Family Cases Under State Child Support Guidelines (1991).

25. For further discussion, *see* Adrienne Jennings Lockie, Multiple Families, Multiple Goals, Multiple Failures: The Need for "Limited Equalization" as a Theory of Child Support, 32 Harv. J.L. & Gender 109 (2009).

26. Sally F. Goldfarb, Child Support Guidelines: A Model for Fair Allocation of Child Care, Medical and Educational Expenses, 21 Fam. L.Q. 325, 331 (1987).

27. For details, *see* Compliance Guide for Qualified Medical Child Support Orders, http://www.acf.hhs.gov/programs/cse/pubs/2003/guides/dept_labor_qmcso.html (accessed Jan. 19, 2010).

28. Office of Child Support Enforcement FY 2006 Annual Report to Congress, http://www.acf.hhs.gov/programs/cse/pubs/2009/reports/annual_report (accessed Jan. 19, 2010).

29. Drew A. Swank, Das Boot! A National Survey of Booting Programs' Impact on Child Support Compliance, 4 J.L. Fam. Stud. 265, 268 (2002).

30. *Essentials, supra* note 16, ch. 10.

31. Revised Program Instructions for Immediate Wage Withholding (1994) http://www.acf.hhs.gov/programs/css/resource/instructions-immediate-wage-withholding-orders-issued-not-being-enforced (accessed Dec. 21, 2015).

32. *Id.* at p. 9.

33. The other two remedies include an Administrative Offset, which allows designated federal payments other than tax refunds to be offset, and the Multistate Financial Institution Data Match, which authorizes the federal OCSE to obtain and transfer the account information of delinquent parents to state child support agencies for enforcement purposes. *See* Overview of the Federal Offset Program (2014), http://www.acf.hhs.gov/programs/css/resource/overview-of-the-federal-offset-program#admin-offset (accessed Dec. 21, 2015).

34. Interstate Child Support Remedies (Margaret Campbell Haynes with Diane G. Dodson eds., 1989).

35. John J. Sampson and Barry J. Brooks, Uniform Interstate Family Support Act (2001) With Prefatory Notes (With Still More Annotations), 36 Fam. L.Q. 329, 339 (2002).

36. TEMPO, 2001 Revisions to Uniform Family Support Act (2001), http://www.acf.hhs.gov/programs/css/resource/2001-revisions-to-the-uniform-interstate-family-support-act-uifsa (accessed Dec. 26, 2015).

37. Sampson and Brooks, *supra* note 35, at 345.

38. *Id.*

39. This consent exception was added by the 2001 amendments.

40. Sampson and Brooks, *supra* note 35, at 345.

41. *Id.*

42. White House Press Release, Statement by NSC Spokesperson Ned Price on the Hague Convention on International Recovery of Child Support and Other Forms of Family Maintenance (Aug. 30, 2016), https://obamawhitehouse.archives.gov/the-press-office/2016/08/30/statement-nsc-spokesperson-ned-price-hague-convention-international.

43. For detail, *see* https://www.acf.hhs.gov/css/resource/us-ratification-of-hague-child-support-convention, and the related links.

44. FFCCSOA can be found at 28 U.S.C. §1738B (2001).

45. However, as discussed in Steven K. Berenson, Home Court Advantage Revisited: Interstate Modification of Child Support Orders Under UIFSA and FFCCSOA, 45 Gonz. L. Rev. 479 (2009/2010), a potential for conflict between the two Acts in light of the fact that "FFCCSOA permits a party to seek modification in their 'home court,' provided the court has personal jurisdiction over the non-moving party," while UIFSA requires this party to bring the action in the home state of the other party. *Id.* at 485.

46. Child Support Recovery Act, as amended by "Deadbeat Parents Act," Pub. L. No. 105-187 §2, 112 Stat. 618 (1998) (codified at 118 U.S.C. §228).

47. 564 U.S. 431 (2011).

48. Turner v. Rogers Guidance, Action Transmittal 12-01, June 18, 2012, https://www.acf.hhs.gov/resource/turner-v-rogers-guidance.

49. Office of Child Support Enforcement, Division of Policy and Training, Final Rule: Training, Flexibility, Efficiency, and Modernization in Child Support Enforcement Programs, Civil Contempt — Ensuring Noncustodial Parents Have the Ability to Pay

https://www.acf.hhs.gov/sites/default/files/programs/css/fem_final_rule_civil_contempt.pdf.

50. *Id.*

51. For further detail, *see* Turner v. Rogers Guidance, *supra* note 48.

52. Laura W. Morgan, Private Attorney Access to Child Support Enforcement Tools: Recommendations of the Interstate Commission, 16 Am. J. Fam. L. 169 (2002).

53. Drew A. Swank, Note from the Field: Child Support, Private Enforcement Companies, and the Law, 2002 Army Law 57, 58.

54. *Id.*

55. Sally F. Goldfarb, Who Pays for the "Boomerang Generation"? A Legal Perspective on Financial Support for Young Adults, 37 Harv. J.L. & Gender 45, 49 (2014).

56. *Id.* at 50 and 50-68.

57. *Id.* at 48.

58. *Id.* at 48-49.

59. *Id.* at 49.

60. Monica Hof Wallace, A Federal Referendum: Extending Child Support for Higher Education, 58 Kan. L. Rev. 665 (2010).

61. *Id.* at 667.

62. *Id.* at 686.

63. These determinations can be quite complex and variable. For a detailed discussion, *see* Madeline Marzno-Lesnevish and Scott Adam Laterra, Child Support and College: What Is the Correct Result?, 23 J. Am. Acad. Matrimonial Law. 335 (2009).

64. Kathryn Burns, Post-Majority Child Support for Children with Disabilities, 51 Fam. Ct. Rev. 502, 504 (2013), quoting Riggs v. Riggs, 353 S.C. 230, 235 (2003).

65. Given this variability, these rules are not detailed here. The following article is a good place to start: Thomas M. Spade, Structuring Tax Dependency Post-Divorce for Noncustodial Parents, 51 Fam. L.Q. 241 (2017).

Chapter Seven

Spousal Support

At the time of divorce, one spouse may be required to provide financial support to the other. This support, traditionally known as **alimony**, from the Latin *alimonia*, meaning nourishment or sustenance, is now also commonly referred to as maintenance or **spousal support**. As we will see, no-fault divorce reform triggered a major restructuring of the traditional support model that was closely linked to marital fault and grounded in a vision of permanent female economic dependence.

Historical Overview

English Roots: Alimony and Fault

Our spousal support laws are rooted in the English ecclesiastical practice of awarding alimony as part of a divorce from board and bed, which, as discussed in Chapter 4, enabled a couple to live apart without severing the marital bond. Alimony was considered an extension of the husband's marital duty to support his wife, who upon marriage lost most of her property rights and control over her earnings. Alimony was awarded only to "innocent" wives; if a wife was the "guilty" party, the right was lost. The amount of the support award was influenced by the degree of the husband's fault as well as by the value of the property that he had acquired from the wife during the marriage.

In continuing the practice of awarding alimony, most U.S. jurisdictions followed the rule of limiting it to innocent wives, although some seem to have abandoned this rule based on considerations of economic necessity. Courts continued to speak of alimony as a substitute for the husband's duty of support, although some questioned the logic of extending a marital duty when the relationship giving rise to it had been dissolved.[1] In any event, the practice was most likely continued based on economic reality—most married women simply did not have the means to support themselves.

In awarding alimony, courts came to explain it in terms of the role it played in a fault-based divorce system. It became the measure of damages paid to an injured wife to compensate her for the loss occasioned by her wrongdoing husband, much like damages in a tort or breach of contract action. Without alimony, a guilty husband would be benefiting from his wrongdoing—a result at odds with the prevailing view of divorce as a remedy for the grievously wronged. Thus, although compelled by economic necessity, alimony was cast as a punishment for wrongdoing and inextricably linked to fault.[2]

Alimony on the Eve of the No-Fault Reform Era

As discussed in Chapter 4, our thinking about divorce was radically reshaped in the 1970s in the wake of no-fault reform. Because alimony was bound up with considerations of fault, this reform triggered a transformation in the nature of the spousal support obligation. Before looking at this shift, we briefly consider key characteristics of the support obligation as it existed on the eve of no-fault divorce reform:

1. Although alimony was still linked to determinations of fault, this link had become weaker as the fault premise undergirding our divorce system was increasingly being called into question. Accordingly, the idea of alimony as a form of damages was beginning to lose hold.[3]
2. The concept of alimony was highly gendered. In most states, alimony could not be awarded to husbands, as women had no duty to support their husbands. Alimony, by its very nature, was understood as a male responsibility.
3. Alimony awards were "permanent" and incorporated an assumption of continued female economic dependence.

As the underlying fault rationale for alimony was called into question, some courts began to speak disparagingly of women who sought support. In the words of one judge, alimony had ensured a "perpetual state of indolence" and had the potential to convert a "host of physically and mentally competent young women into an army of alimony drones who neither toil nor spin and become a drain on society and a menace to themselves."[4] This fear appears to have been unfounded, however, as the average alimony award was modest; for instance, in 1968, the median award was $98 per month, nowhere near the amount needed to secure a life of indolence.[5]

Impact of No-Fault Reform

With no-fault reform, the traditional legal framing of divorce as a necessary evil justifiable only in cases of grievous marital wrongdoing gave way to a greater acceptance of divorce as a solution for unhappy marriages. The elimination of fault as an essential precondition for the granting of a divorce led many in the field to reconceptualize marriage as a partnership which, as in the business world, is terminable by either party based on dissatisfaction with the undertaking. In keeping with the partnership model, the desirability of allowing each partner to make a **clean break** from the marriage was emphasized, and, as with the dissolution of a business relationship, continuing obligations deriving from the failed marital relationship were henceforth to be kept to a minimum. As discussed in this chapter, the declining role of fault and the corresponding emergence of the partnership model of marriage prompted a profound reconceptualization of the traditional support model.

Property Division as the Primary Distributive Event

With no-fault reform, many states began to emphasize property division as the preferred way to adjust the post-divorce economic rights of the parties. As the division of property is a final, unmodifiable event (see Chapter 8), it was thought to more closely correspond with the emerging partnership model of marriage than did an award of spousal support. As in a business, the assets of the failed enterprise would be distributed, leaving the former partners free to pursue other endeavors unencumbered by the past. Alimony, embodying notions of continued obligation, was to be deemphasized and awarded only in exceptional cases. Underlying the emphasis on property division was an often-unstated assumption that the divorcing spouses should be equally capable of achieving **economic self-sufficiency** regardless of any differences in their labor market participation during the marriage. (Note: As discussed in Chapter 8, the partnership model also incorporates a contemporary understanding of marriage as a joint enterprise in which the whole enterprise benefits from the individual contribution of each spouse, thus creating an entitlement to a share of accumulated assets at the time of divorce.)

Shifting the Focus from Moral to Economic Considerations

As discussed, prior to no-fault reform, alimony awards were linked to marital conduct. The court looked back into the marriage and used alimony as a way to compensate an innocent wife for past harms. With the uncoupling of alimony from fault, alimony awards have been re-anchored to economic considerations and, in a blame-free manner, are supposed to respond to financial needs arising out of the marital relationship. However, as discussed below, a recurring concern raised by many judges, practitioners, and scholars alike is the lack of a clear conceptual framework within which support awards are to be determined, thus leading to a lack of consistency and predictability. Nonetheless, in keeping with the clean-break approach, the overall emphasis has been to move away from the idea of a continuing obligation even where need or financial inequality exists.

Degendering the Support Obligation

The support obligation has also been uncoupled from its origins as a male-only responsibility. The Supreme Court has held that gender-specific alimony laws are unconstitutional because they carry the "inherent risk of reinforcing stereotypes about the 'proper place' of women and their need for special protection."[6] In theory, spousal support is now a gender-neutral concept and is no longer premised on an assumption that married women, as a class, are financially dependent and incapable of self-support. In practice, however, few men (at least in heterosexual unions) meet the economic criteria for a support award.

Shifting from an Assumption of Female Economic Dependence to an Assumption of Economic Self-Sufficiency

Following no-fault reform, the idea of permanent alimony awards fell out of favor. Seen as embodying outmoded assumptions regarding female economic dependence and requiring ongoing entanglement, a clear trend developed in favor of short-term support awards intended to help a spouse acquire the skills needed to become self-supporting. (See the discussion of rehabilitative alimony below.) In sharp contrast to the past, this shift embodied the assumption that all married women, regardless of the role they played during the marriage, should be self-supporting either at the time of divorce or following a brief transitional period. It thus corresponded with both the changing role of women and the partnership model of marriage, which minimizes the ongoing responsibility of a former spouse.

Critique of the "Clean-Break" Approach

The clean-break approach has an appealing simplicity. At least in theory, as with former business partners, each spouse exits the failed enterprise with a share of the accumulated assets ready to build a new life free from financial entanglements from the failed enterprise. However, despite this surface appeal, the clean-break approach has been subject to significant criticism, particularly by feminist scholars and practitioners who argue that its failure to account for the gendered reality of family life economically disadvantages many women.[7]

To begin with, some have argued that the analogy itself is flawed because it is based on a distortion of what actually occurs in the business realm: The decision to dissolve even an ongoing business concern, so the argument goes, does not bring all mutual obligations between partners to a screeching halt. Rather, following the actual dissolution of a partnership, such as when a partner leaves a law firm, there may be a protracted period in which the partners wind up their affairs. During this time, the partners "continue to be linked by mutual obligations and continue to share a fiduciary relationship," and no matter how "'strained' the relationships between the partners may actually be, the UPA (Uniform Partner Act) views the process of winding up as a 'cooperative'" venture.[8]

Of primary concern, critics of the clean-break model argue that its gender-neutral approach masks the fact that many women in heterosexual marriages continue to do the bulk of the domestic labor, particularly where there are children. For example, according to one study, even when a husband and wife are employed full time, "a mother still does 40 percent more child care and about 30 percent more housework than the father."[9] Accordingly, to accommodate these domestic responsibilities, in many marriages, women are more likely than their husbands to "sacrifice professional goals in order to focus on the family" and to "restrict their work hours, find work close to home, give up opportunities for advancement, and suffer decreased earnings."[10] Although, of course, this dynamic is certainly not the case in all households.

In turn, this marital division of labor is likely to have significant economic implications that exist far beyond the end of the marital relationship, as a woman in this situation will likely leave the marriage with a **diminished earning capacity** due to the workplace accommodations she made, such as passing up promotions, or working shorter hours, in order to accommodate domestic responsibilities. In contrast, a husband who has been far less encumbered by household and child-related responsibilities is likely to exit the marriage with an **enhanced earning capacity** due to the fact that he has not had to juggle work and family obligations to the same extent as his spouse. Consequently, the reality is that "women and children generally end up poorer after divorce than men";[11] for instance, according to the 2009 United States Census, "nearly twice the amount of divorced women than divorced men had incomes in the past twelve month below the poverty level."[12]

Accordingly, critics of the clean-break approach argue that its underlying assumption that a division of assets will permit both parties to begin life anew with an equal capacity for economic self-sufficiency is erroneous as it ignores the far-reaching economic consequences of this marital history. By failing to recognize and account for the impact that these kinds of domestic arrangements, which certainly may have worked well for a couple during their marriage, have on the relative economic positions of divorced spouses, the clean-break approach assumes an equality that may well not exist to the disadvantage of divorcing women. Compounding this problem, critics also note that this approach mistakenly assumes that all divorcing couples have accumulated sufficient assets over the course of their marriage to ensure the post-divorce economic security of both spouses—a reality that is simply not the case in many, if not most, marriages.[13]

Closely related is the concern that the clean-break approach ignores the fact that a majority of divorcing couples have minor children who will continue to have needs following the divorce. The approach thus assumes a level of disengagement that does not correspond with the reality of the continued involvement that comes with having children in common. Further, the economic disparity between divorcing spouses is likely to be even more pronounced in households with children, as parenthood often has a significant impact on the wage gap between male and female workers.

Following from this, critics argue that alimony needs to be reformulated to eliminate the disadvantage that flows from this marital allocation of work and family responsibilities; since the economic consequences of marriage continue beyond its duration, critics argue, so must the financial obligations. Although the proposals vary, a common thread is that, at least for a period of time following a divorce, earnings be subject to some kind of pooling requirement so that the primary wage earner does not disproportionately gain from the marital allocation of labor. Critics have suggested several specific proposals: that income be treated as a form of marital property, which, like the accumulated assets, would be subject to the claims of the partnership based on an assumption of joint contribution to the marital enterprise as a whole; that income be distributed to ensure that each household enjoys an equal standard of living; that the husband be required to buy out the wife's interest in his enhanced earning capacity; and that income be shared to "reflect the returns flowing from efforts made while the joint marital venture was operational."[14]

Some of these concerns, coupled with concerns about the lack of theoretical coherence as to the underlying purposes of spousal support and the lack of predictability in awards, have begun to influence lawmakers. As developed below, a variety of support reforms are again being considered, including the use of alimony guidelines, and a number of courts have shown a renewed commitment to permanent support awards.

Consideration

Do you think alimony should be used as a vehicle for adjusting economic inequalities rising out of a division of labor during marriage to ensure that the spouse with lower earnings is not disadvantaged by his or her marital role?

Support Determinations

Whether adopted by statute or by judicial decision, most states now use a multifactored approach to determine if spousal support should be awarded in a specific case, and if so, the amount to be awarded. Although, much as in custody cases, judges are required to consider all of the enumerated factors, they also usually have the discretion to give each factor the weight they believe it merits in light of the particular circumstances of the case. Again, as with custody, this gives judges the flexibility to consider the unique circumstances of a divorcing couple's situation, but it also makes it difficult to predict the circumstances under which alimony will be awarded. In this section, we first look at the kinds of factors that courts weigh in deciding about spousal support. Reflecting the concerns about the unpredictability and uncertainty of this approach, we look at some of the reform proposals that are currently being considered, followed by a discussion of the basic ways that support awards can be structured.

Factors to Be Considered

In most states, judges are required to consider a variety of factors when deciding if a spouse should be provided with support. These factors often include the following:

- financial need;
- earning potential;
- age;
- duration of the marriage;
- physical and mental health;

- income and financial resources;
- the marital standard of living; and
- contribution to the marriage.

Additionally, although greatly diminished in importance and eliminated from consideration in many jurisdictions, some states still include marital fault as one of the factors that must be considered. Where it is identified as a factor to be considered, marital wrongdoing is generally balanced against other factors, such as need. Also, even in states where marital fault in the traditional sense of the word is not identified as a factor, economic fault may be a permissible consideration. Thus, for example, in assessing the husband's need for support, the court might give weight to the fact that the wife had squandered the family fortune on her lover, thus placing the husband in an economically vulnerable position.

Additionally, a handful of states specifically identify domestic violence as a factor to be taken into account in the support calculus. Although considerations of fault may play a role here, its inclusion also importantly reflects the economic reality that "surviving abuse pushes women into poverty due to health complications, homelessness, and unemployment."[15] Conversely, in some states, a documented history of abuse may prevent the perpetrator from being awarded support. For example, in California, a domestic violence conviction within the five years prior to a divorce creates a rebuttable presumption against an award of support to the convicted spouse.

It should also be noted that "contribution to the marriage" is not limited to financial considerations but is generally intended to account for a spouse's nonmonetary contributions to a marriage in the domestic realm. This allows for the recognition that a spouse may have a diminished capacity for self-support because of a primary commitment to the home and/or child rearing.

The general rule is that a judge must consider all of the enumerated factors but can assign them whatever weight he or she believes is appropriate in light of the circumstances of each case. This provides a consistent framework for evaluating cases, while giving a judge the freedom to attach different weights to different combinations of factors based on a couple's particular situation. However, in most jurisdictions, financial need is typically considered to be the most important factor in the support calculus, and judges may view other considerations through the prism of financial need. Thus, for example, a spouse's need may be deemed more acute due to advanced age or ill health, as these factors tend to build off of one another in a cumulative manner.

To get a clearer picture of how this works, let's look at how a judge might weigh different factors based on the individual circumstances of a case. For example, in a case involving a disabled spouse, a judge might give significant weight to considerations of health and need and little or no weight to the fact that the spouses were married only for a short period of time. However, in another short-term marriage case, the same judge might give considerable weight to this factor and decide that the brevity of the relationship precludes a support order. In yet another short-term marriage situation where one party—let's say a husband in his early 60s—gave up a good job to move across the country to join his new spouse and has been unable to find work, the same judge might again discount duration in favor of the combined weight of need, age, earning potential, and, possibly, contribution, with respect to the sacrifice he made so the couple could be together.

Searching for Greater Certainty: Alimony Guidelines and the American Law Institute's Compensatory Principle

As indicated by the above discussion, an important advantage of the flexibility that is built into this multifactorial approach is that judges can make individualized determinations that fit the facts of each case, rather than having to squeeze everyone into a one-size-fits-all support package. As we have seen, in determining if alimony is to be awarded, the duration of the marriage might be a critical consideration in one case and an insignificant one in another.

However, the flexibility of this approach is also problematic, and has been the source of much critical commentary. At the heart of these concerns is that the support calculus is permeated with a lack of consistency and predictability. According to one study, this uncertainty may dissuade economically dependent spouses from even seeking support based on the "reluctance to expend money on litigation costs without the likelihood of any beneficial result."[16] Moreover, as we saw in the child custody context, the lack of certainty can make it very difficult for parties to negotiate a settlement. Without a coherent framework, it is difficult to assess the value of a negotiated exchange if one does not know what one is giving up or gaining in the exchange process.

On a more abstract level is the concern that when courts weigh these factors, they do so in the absence of a clear theoretical rationale for the award of spousal support. Thus, each factor is weighed separately without a clear understanding of how each one fits into a conceptual whole—that the essential purpose of spousal support cannot be stated with clarity because the factors point in multiple directions.[17] Thus, for instance, the fault factor looks backward into the marriage and preserves the historical association between support and punishment, while other factors, such as need, direct a judge to look ahead into the future. Still other factors, such as contribution, suggest a compensatory purpose, and some, such as earning capacity, may reflect multiple impulses—a judge might be inclined to look to the future to determine if a spouse will be capable of self-support and/or back into the marriage to determine if there has been a diminution of earning capacity due to the assumption of domestic responsibilities. As one judge wryly put it: "Modern spousal support encompasses at least . . . five separate and distinct functions. Yet we treat them as one. In short, we are calling every animal in the zoo a cat, and in doing so, we lose our ability to apply rational criteria to decision-making."[18]

This brief discussion reveals a theme that weaves through the family law field as a whole, namely, the abiding tension between the need for discretion and flexibility on the one hand, and the desirability of predictability and coherence on the other. Given, as we have seen, that the law of spousal support is clearly tilted in favor of a flexible, individualized approach, proposed reforms generally seek to incorporate greater predictability and coherence into the support determination process. We now look briefly at two such proposals.

Spousal Support Guidelines

When it comes to child support, the tension between flexibility and predictability has clearly been resolved in favor of predictable outcomes. As we have seen, in accordance with the federal mandate, all states have adopted detailed child support guidelines and employ specific numeric criteria for the computation of support awards that lead to predictable amounts. Accordingly, from the outset of a divorce, spouses can envisage with reasonable accuracy what the support amount is likely to be.

Seeking this same kind of predictability, some family law experts have recommended a similar approach to spousal support. The use of clear guidelines and numeric criteria would, they argue, remove the guesswork from the process and allow parties to negotiate their differences based on a clear understanding of what a court is likely to do. To this end, a few states and a number of counties have recently adopted a guidelines approach to spousal support awards, and this may be a slowly growing trend.[19]

However, where adopted, spousal support guidelines do not necessarily provide the same degree of certainty that is typically provided by child support guidelines. Perhaps the most obvious reason for this difference is that in the child support context, the underlying obligation is assumed; accordingly, guidelines do not need to focus on the question of whether the support should be awarded in the first place. Instead, as required by federal law, they can simply be structured to provide a computational framework that yields a "presumptively correct support amount."[20]

In contrast, as we have seen, there is not a parallel entitlement to spousal support; accordingly, in any given case, the issue is typically not simply *how much* support is due, but *whether* it is due at all, and if so, for how long and for what purpose is it to be paid. As a result, it is clearly more difficult to develop spousal support guidelines that readily yield a "presumptively correct support amount" as these multiple determinations often shade into one another. (See Chapter 6.)

In addition to this complexity, in some jurisdictions, guidelines are only used for the purpose of determining temporary spousal support awards, and they thus do not control the ultimate outcome, which remains indeterminate. Furthermore, guidelines may be developed for the purpose of providing parties with a starting point for negotiations, rather than being structured to provide a presumptively correct support amount, which once again leads to less predictability than is the case with regard to child support.[21]

ALI's Compensatory Principle

Another proposed approach has been to provide a clear doctrinal rationale for spousal support awards beyond simply the articulation of financial "need." To this end, seeking to clearly link the necessity for support to the actual economic consequences of the marital relationship, the ALI's *Principles of the Law of Family Dissolution* urges a compensatory focus that seeks to allocate the "financial losses that arise at the dissolution of a marriage according to equitable principles that are consistent and predictable in application."[22] Central to this shift is the recognition that, especially in long-term marriages, there often is a "loss in living standard experienced at dissolution by the spouse who has less wealth or earning capacity."[23]

As articulated in the principles, loss is directly related to a spouse's contribution to the marriage, and thus rather than suggesting dependency, as support so often does, this reframes support as a necessary and coherent response to the prior allocation of marital roles and responsibilities. As one commentator put it: "In the paradigm shift that this approach follows, there is an implicit recognition of 'entitlement' rather than 'charity.' Payments are made because they are earned rather than pled for. 'Need' is more clearly defined as being an outcome of loss, rather than a reason in and of itself."[24]

Different Approaches to Structuring Spousal Support

As developed in this section, support can be structured in a variety of ways to accomplish different objectives. Each approach has its own rules regarding the modification and termination of the support award.

Permanent Alimony

"Permanent" alimony is probably what most people think of when they think of alimony, but since no-fault reform it has been somewhat eclipsed by rehabilitative support (discussed below). The primary purpose of **permanent alimony** is to provide financial assistance to the spouse in an economically weaker position. It is payable in regular intervals on an ongoing basis.

INTERVIEW CHECKLIST

In any case where spousal support is an issue, you will need to obtain the following kinds of information about both parties. It is unlikely that you will be able to obtain all of the necessary information about your client's spouse from an interview; discovery will probably be needed to complete the picture. (See Chapter 10.)

1. Obtain complete employment histories for each job held during the marriage and for a reasonable time before it, including the following information:
   - job titles
   - promotions
   - salaries
   - hours worked
   - general responsibilities
2. Obtain the educational histories of each spouse, including any specific career training.
3. Ask about the parties' career goals, including any educational plans.
4. Get explanations of any gaps in the parties' employment histories—especially those stemming from child rearing or other domestic responsibilities.
5. Ascertain factors that may affect the parties' employment potential, such as:
   - earning capacity
   - general market outlook for each spouse's career/job
   - health considerations that may impact future employment
6. Obtain a picture of the ways in which each spouse has contributed to the marriage. Focus on both financial and nonfinancial contributions.

Permanent alimony can also serve a compensatory purpose. A spouse (almost always the wife) who restricts her participation in the paid labor force to care for her family experiences a loss of earning capacity over the course of the marriage. At the same time, the earning capacity of her spouse is enhanced, as he is freed up to focus on his labor market participation. Although this may be a mutually beneficial arrangement during the marriage, upon divorce the spouses stand on very different footing—in effect, there has been a transfer in earning ability from one spouse to the other. Alimony payments may be used to offset this result and compensate a spouse for the **opportunity cost** of having invested a significant portion of her time in the domestic realm to the detriment of her earning ability. Unlike that of rehabilitative support, the goal of permanent alimony is not to help a spouse achieve economic self-sufficiency, and there is no duty to use the money for this purpose. Accordingly, a defining aspect of a permanent support award is that it is not subject to a fixed time limitation but is continuous.

Although permanent alimony is not subject to durational limits, *permanent* does not necessarily mean forever. The term is used to distinguish support awarded at the time of divorce from support awarded during the pendency of the divorce action—known as **alimony pendente lite**, or **temporary alimony**—which is intended to assist a spouse during this interim period. Thus, although not subject to pre-established durational limits, permanent alimony is subject to reduction or termination based on a **change in circumstances**, with the near universal rule being that remarriage of the recipient spouse or the death of either one terminates the obligation. (See the section entitled "Post-Divorce Modification and Termination of Support," below.)

Lump-Sum Support

Although not a frequently used option, many states authorize the award of a **lump-sum support** payment, sometimes referred to as **alimony in gross**. Unlike permanent alimony, this involves the payment of a sum certain. It is generally paid in a single installment, although it can also be made payable in periodic installments until the full amount of the order is reached. Once ordered, most states agree that the recipient acquires a vested right to the entire amount, thus making it nonmodifiable based on a change in circumstances, including remarriage of the recipient. This remains true even where the lump sum is payable in installments. If the payor dies before the full amount is paid, the balance is chargeable to his or her estate; likewise, if the recipient dies before receiving payment in full, the balance due can be collected by his or her estate. Accordingly, along the lines of the old adage "a bird in the hand is worth two in the bush," a recipient may prefer to accept a potentially smaller but definite lump-sum payment instead of running the risk that periodic payments will not always be made.

Rehabilitative Support

As noted above, following no-fault reform, **rehabilitative support**, often called **transitional support**, became the preferred approach in many jurisdictions. Rehabilitative support is awarded on a time-limited basis for the purpose of enabling an economically dependent spouse to obtain the education or training necessary to become financially self-sufficient.

To establish the durational limit, a court will try to predict how long it will take for a spouse to become self-sufficient and then set this as the date for the expiration of the obligation; in some states, maximum time limits are set by statute. In some states, courts may retain jurisdiction and extend the time limit if a spouse can show that despite a good-faith effort he or she has not been able to achieve the degree of self-sufficiency contemplated at the time of the award. Many jurisdictions, however, do not permit extensions even where a spouse is not yet self-sufficient despite a good-faith effort. Here, rather than focusing on the economic situation of the spouse seeking to achieve self-sufficiency, the courts prioritize the expectancy interest of the payor spouse and his or her wish to plan for the future unencumbered by unexpected obligations from a previous marriage.

Although there is general agreement that the goal of rehabilitative support is self-sufficiency, there is disagreement about what this means. A few states take a bare-bones approach and consider a person self-sufficient if, at the end of the rehabilitative period, he or she is not dependent on public assistance. Other courts, particularly in situations involving a long-term marriage, define self-sufficiency by reference to the marital standard of living. Here, the goal is met when a spouse is able to obtain employment that would enable him or her to approximate the prior marital standard of living.

Rehabilitative support took hold quickly during the period of no-fault reform, as it represented a break from the traditional alimony model that was associated with outmoded assumptions about fault and the economic incapacity of divorced women. Its underlying objectives were commendable and consistent with the new approach to restructuring family obligations following divorce. Rehabilitative support sets out to accomplish the following goals:

- to enable previously economically dependent spouses to develop their earning potential and realize true independence;
- to enable spouses to make a clean break and begin life anew on equal footing in keeping with the partnership view of marriage; and
- to release spouses from ongoing financial obligations derived from a failed relationship.

Beginning in the mid-1980s, however, a countertrend emerged. Appellate judges began to set aside rehabilitative awards, denouncing them as an abuse of judicial discretion. One judge went so far as to label them a "male-oriented, sexist approach."[25] These reversals have generally come in cases of long-term marriages where a woman has forgone labor market participation or has moved in and out of the workplace based on the needs of her family. According to the courts, the goal of economic self-sufficiency is illusory in these situations because a woman who has been family-centered will not be able to recapture her lost earning potential, and a rehabilitative award would leave the spouses with a gross disparity in earning capacity—a result that undervalues her contribution to the marriage.

Accordingly, trial courts have become a bit more circumspect, particularly in cases involving long-term marriages where responsibilities have been allocated along traditional gender lines. Rather than assuming that a rehabilitative award is appropriate, a court might instead place a burden on the party seeking to limit support to show how the other spouse will be able to achieve meaningful financial independence within the proposed timeframes. This may require evidence about available educational programs and labor market conditions in the spouse's area of interest that indicate a likelihood of employment at a decent wage.

The Backlash Against "Permanent" Spousal Support Awards

Although, as noted above, some judges have begun to back away from awarding transitional support in cases involving long-term marriages where one spouse has primarily put her efforts into the domestic realm, there has also been somewhat of a counter-push against the award of "permanent" alimony, which is beginning to find its way into law. In large measure, this momentum for reform reflects the efforts of divorced men and their new spouses, many of whom are members of what are known as "second wives clubs." In support of their position, these reformers argue that it is unfair to keep men tethered to their former wives via support payments—payments that some second wives assert they are forced to underwrite through their own earnings. It is sometimes also argued that alimony reform will help to empower first wives by encouraging them to become "self-supporting," rather than continuing to depend upon a man for economic support.[26]

Responding to this push, a number of states have amended their spousal support laws to put limits on permanent support awards, such as by restricting them to marriages over a certain duration. Relatedly, some states have adopted or are considering adopting retirement termination provisions, which either incorporate a presumption that support payments terminate upon the obligor's retirement or treat this as a change in circumstances, which would typically permit a downward adjustment or termination of payments.

Some have greeted this trend with considerable concern based on the hardships that it may impose on "first wives," particularly if minor children are in the picture. Critically in this regard, it is noted that the most significant gender pay gap is between married women and married men with children, due in large part to the continued unequal allocation of household responsibilities. For example, one study found that even when both spouses in a heterosexual marriage work full time, "'the mother does 40 percent more child care and about 30 percent more housework than the father.'"[27] To accommodate their domestic obligations, married women may accordingly "restrict their work hours, find work close to home, give up opportunities for advancement, and suffer decreased earnings"; as a result, they "rarely maintain the momentum in their careers that their husbands can."[28]

Building on this, it is further noted that the financial impact of divorce is not gender neutral. For example, according to one study, in the first year after divorce, women lost approximately 40 percent of their pre-divorce income, while men gained approximately 5 percent of their pre-divorce income; moreover, although women showed some recovery in subsequent years, their poverty risk remained above 25 percent even several years after divorce. In contrast, the poverty risk for men "remained unchanged across the divorce process."[29] Looked at another way, according to census data, 30.4 percent of custodial mothers and their children live in poverty, compared to 18.8 percent of custodial fathers and their children.[30] Accordingly, critics of this new reform trend argue that spousal support awards remain a critical tool in adjusting post-divorce economic inequalities.

The Professional Degree Cases

Although the permanent, lump-sum, and rehabilitative approaches to spousal support are relatively easy to characterize, there has been considerable confusion regarding what to do in cases where one spouse supports the other through a professional degree program, thus greatly increasing the degreed spouse's future earning capacity, but the marriage ends before these gains are realized. In this section we consider the various options.

The Degree as Property

One option is to treat the degree as marital property and subject it to division along with the other marital assets. However, the overwhelming majority of jurisdictions have rejected this approach, deciding that a degree, or the enhanced earning capacity it represents, does not fit within the meaning of the term "property." In deciding against this approach, courts have focused on the difficulty of valuing a degree, as this would require speculation about the course someone's career will take.[31] They have also focused on other characteristics that distinguish a degree from other forms of property such as that acquisition of a degree requires substantial personal effort and sacrifice; that it lacks an objective value in the open market; and that it is personal to the holder and cannot be sold, transferred, or left to future generations. (See Chapter 8 for property-related concepts.)

Spousal Support Options

Although generally declining to treat the degree or the enhanced earnings it represents as marital property, courts may consider it when determining the appropriateness and amount of support. One approach is to fashion a reimbursement alimony award; another is to consider the non-degree-holding spouse's contribution as a relevant factor in the support calculus.

Reimbursement Alimony.   The Supreme Court of New Jersey is generally credited with developing the concept of **reimbursement alimony** in the 1982 case of Mahoney v. Mahoney, in which the husband left the marriage soon after earning an advanced degree with the wife's dedicated support:

> In this case, the supporting spouse made financial contributions towards her husband's professional education with the expectation that both parties would enjoy material benefits flowing from the professional license or degree. It is therefore patently unfair that the supporting spouse be denied the mutually anticipated benefit while the supported spouse keeps not only the degree, but also all of the financial and material rewards flowing from it. . . .
>
> . . . Also, the wife has presumably made personal financial sacrifices, resulting in a reduced or lowered standard of living. Additionally, her husband, by pursuing preparations for a future career, has forgone gainful employment and financial contributions to the marriage. . . . She has postponed, as it were, present consumption and a higher standard of living, for the future prospect of greater support and material benefits. . . . The unredressed sacrifices . . . coupled with the unfairness attendant upon the defeat of the supporting spouse's shared expectation of future advantages, further justify a remedial award.[32]

In fashioning the award, the court held that the supporting spouse was entitled to be reimbursed for all financial contributions made to the training of the other spouse, including "household expenses, educational costs, school travel expenses and any other contribution used by the supported spouse in obtaining his or her degree or license."[33]

Many jurisdictions have followed New Jersey's lead and will reimburse a spouse for contributions to the other's education, recognizing that the supporting spouse made significant sacrifices based on the reasonable expectation that he or she would share in the future gain represented by the degree. Through reimbursement, courts can adjust this imbalance by returning the contribution to the spouse who will not participate in the anticipated benefits because of divorce.

Consistent with their focus on dashed expectations, courts have generally disallowed reimbursement where the marriage continued for a reasonable period of time after the degree was obtained on the theory that the supporting spouse would have realized his or her expectation during the marriage. Moreover, unlike where the divorce follows on the heels of the degree, there is likely to have been an accumulation of assets that can be divided.

Some courts have broadened the concept of reimbursement alimony beyond simply providing recompense for actual expenditures to include "lost opportunity costs," such as forgone income while the degree-holding spouse was enrolled in school and possibly also for forgone educational opportunities. Alternatively, some courts have instead provided rehabilitative support so the non-degree-holding spouse could also obtain further education.

An important critique of the reimbursement approach is that it only repays a spouse's initial investment in the career of the other and does not provide the spouse with any return on the investment through giving him or her a share of the increased earnings attributable to the enhanced earning capacity. Simply put: "[T]his approach treats the supporting spouse as a lender, not as an investor in the asset."[34]

The Degree as a Relevant Factor.   A number of courts have declined to embrace the concept of reimbursement. Instead, they prefer to consider the degree as one of the factors that must be weighed in determining if support should be awarded. This is a flexible approach enabling courts to emphasize different considerations. Thus, one court might give greater weight to the contribution and sacrifice of the supporting spouse, while another might focus on the enhanced earning capacity of the degree-holding spouse relative to the stagnant or possibly even diminished earning capacity of the supporting spouse.

■ Medical Insurance

The issue of continued medical coverage frequently arises with considerable urgency at the time of divorce because one spouse, typically the primary wage earner, may have a group policy through his or her employer that provides family coverage. Many states now have laws that authorize the court to order a spouse to continue to provide health insurance coverage for his or her former spouse, at least during the time that a support order is in effect.

In addition, although there is no federal law comparable to state statutory provisions requiring the continued provision of health insurance, divorced spouses may be entitled to post-divorce coverage under COBRA (short for the Consolidated Omnibus Budget Reconciliation Act), which was passed by Congress in 1986. Under COBRA, employers with more than 20 employees must provide the spouse of a divorcing employee with a temporary extension of group health coverage if a timely request is made. However, the covered spouse is responsible for the entire amount of the premium since COBRA does not hold the employer or the employed spouse responsible for the cost of the continued coverage.[35]

Post-Divorce Modification and Termination of Support

The General Concept

Following a divorce, as with custody or child support, either party may seek to revise the spousal support amount by filing a complaint for **modification**. Some states have enacted specific modification statutes that set out the basic requirements for these post-divorce actions, while in others the requirements have been established by judicial decisions. In either event, the basic principles discussed below are fairly stable; however, as always, the precise procedural and substantive details vary from state to state.

This action is usually filed in the court that entered the original support order, which has continuing jurisdiction over the matter. If a support order is not entered at the time of divorce, a court may lose jurisdiction; accordingly, to protect against this, some courts will order payment of a nominal support amount, such as a dollar per month. This preserves its jurisdiction should the need for support arise in the future. The complaint for modification must be based on a change in circumstances that makes the original order unfair. States use different yardsticks to measure unfairness. Some employ a strict unconscionability standard, while others employ a more relaxed standard. Again, the general rule is that the change must have been unforeseeable. Accordingly, a future job change that was known about at the time of the original order cannot generally be the basis for a modification, as this should have been accounted for in the original order. Similarly, most jurisdictions will not base a modification upon inflation or cost-of-living increases in the obligor's salary, as these events are foreseeable and could have been addressed.

In addition to being unforeseeable, courts may require that the change be involuntary. Accordingly, an obligor who seeks to reduce payments because she has left the corporate world to become an artist will probably not be successful. Likewise, a support recipient who relocates to a luxury apartment complex and then seeks an upward revision based on the increased rent is not likely to succeed.

Modifiability and Termination of "Permanent" Support

Remarriage, cohabitation, and a change in financial circumstances are the most common reasons for a modification action. Each is discussed below.

Remarriage

In most states, the statutory rule is that an award of "permanent" support automatically terminates upon the remarriage of the recipient spouse. In some of these jurisdictions, termination occurs immediately upon remarriage without the need for any kind of court action, while in others the support obligor must file a modification petition, which almost certainly will be granted. The principle underlying the termination rule is that the recipient's new spouse has a support obligation, and a person is not entitled to be supported by both a spouse and a former spouse at the same time.

The basic rule—that remarriage terminates the spousal support obligation—has also been firmly established by judicial decision in states that do not have a statutory termination provision through judicial decision. Although some of these jurisdictions follow the automatic termination approach, others are more flexible. A few treat remarriage as simply a factor to be considered in determining whether a change in circumstances justifies a modification, although the more common approach is to presume termination, absent a showing of extraordinary circumstances. The concept of "extraordinary" is typically defined narrowly, and the burden of proof is placed upon the alimony recipient, rather than, as is usually the case, on the person seeking the modification.

This termination rule raises difficult questions about what should happen if a spouse who is receiving rehabilitative support remarries during the rehabilitative period. From a recipient's perspective, the remarriage may be irrelevant, as he or she is seeking to regain economic independence. However, from the payor's perspective, it may seem unfair to continue paying support in a situation where the former spouse is remarried and now has access to other sources of income. It should thus come as no surprise that jurisdictions approach this issue differently, with some giving greater weight to the recipient's interest in completing the education he or she embarked on, while others are more focused on shifting responsibility to the new spouse.

The general rule is that remarriage by the paying spouse does not entitle him or her to a downward revision of support. Courts generally focus on the voluntary aspect of the act and the inequity to the former spouse. However, remarriage combined with other circumstances, such as the birth of children, may support a downward revision. Conversely, if the payor spouse remarries someone with substantial income or assets, the question may arise as to whether the recipient spouse can rely on this as a change in circumstances warranting an upward adjustment. While it is clear that the recipient has no direct claim on the new spouse's income, some courts may be willing to consider a modification based on the fact that this money may liberate some of the former spouse's income.

Cohabitation

Whereas remarriage almost always terminates alimony, the result is less certain where a recipient cohabits with a new partner because, unlike marriage, cohabitation does not impose a legal duty of support. The majority approach is to focus on whether cohabitation has resulted in an improvement in the recipient's financial situation—and only where it has will support be reduced or terminated. Some states impose an initial threshold requirement: The party seeking to reduce or terminate support must show that the relationship is not merely fleeting but instead rises to a certain level of intensity and commitment. Only when this has been shown will the court consider the cohabiting party's financial situation. A few states employ a rebuttable presumption that cohabitation automatically improves a party's financial situation. This presumption shifts the burden of proof to the cohabiting spouse to show that his or her financial situation has not improved as a result of the relationship.

Change in Financial Circumstances

Parties frequently seek to modify support based on a change in the financial circumstances of one or both of them. As noted above, a court will generally not modify due to foreseeable changes such as an annual cost-of-living salary increase. On the other hand, an increase in salary based on an unexpected promotion may warrant an upward revision of support. However, many jurisdictions will not modify based on this type of event alone and instead also require proof of an increased financial need on the part of the recipient spouse. A mutual change in circumstances is generally required on the theory that the recipient spouse does not have an automatic right to share in this gain as it is unrelated to the marital enterprise. In response, the recipient spouse might argue that she is entitled to a share in this increase to compensate for the fact that the original order did not provide her with adequate income, but it was all that the payor spouse could afford at the time. Here, the modification would serve a compensatory purpose. If the recipient spouse's financial circumstances improve, a downward revision is generally allowed.

Modifiability of Specific Types of Support

Even where a change in circumstances can be established, spousal support awards other than permanent alimony are generally considered nonmodifiable.

Lump-Sum Support

The majority rule is that a lump-sum award is not modifiable or terminable by death or remarriage. The support recipient is deemed to have acquired a vested right to the full amount, even if it is payable in installments.

Rehabilitative Support

The rules regarding modifiability of rehabilitative support are more complex. Because this award is for a designated purpose, most courts—absent extraordinary circumstances—will not modify it for reasons unrelated to the original purpose of the award. For example, whereas a change in circumstance such as a job promotion might warrant an increase in permanent alimony, it would not warrant an increase in rehabilitative support, as this is incidental to the goal of helping the support recipient achieve economic self-sufficiency.

Some courts will not modify a rehabilitative award to extend the durational limit or increase the support amount even where the request is directly related to the goal of achieving economic self-sufficiency. Although this may be fair where the party has not taken reasonable steps to obtain education or training, it can be a harsh result where the person has made a good-faith effort but the original time estimate was inadequate or where she or he has encountered unanticipated obstacles such as illness or the loss of affordable child care.

Reimbursement Alimony

The general rule is that reimbursement alimony is not modifiable or terminable by the death of either party or the remarriage of the recipient spouse. This is a logical result because the award is not based on present financial circumstances but rather is designed to repay a spouse for past expenditures. Accordingly, post-divorce changes in circumstances are irrelevant. However, it is hard to imagine a court refusing to make some adjustment, perhaps in the nature of a temporary suspension of payments, in a case of genuine hardship such as serious illness.

Agreement of the Parties to Prohibit Modification

Sometimes parties include a clause in a separation agreement stating that neither will seek to modify the support award in the future. Such a clause often is insisted upon by the supporting spouse, who wants to limit his or her obligation. Some jurisdictions may refuse to honor such a clause on public policy grounds, especially if enforcement would force a spouse into public assistance. Here, the duty to pay support is regarded as having a public dimension that cannot be abrogated by a private agreement.

■ Enforcement of Support Awards

As is often the case with child support orders, once spousal support has been ordered, the risk of nonpayment is substantial, and the recipient may need to take action to enforce the order.

Contempt

In most states, the primary enforcement mechanism is an action for **contempt**. As with child support, the contempt action can be either civil or criminal in nature (see Chapter 6). Most likely, an obligor will not be found in contempt if the inability to pay existed at the time the support payments were due. A more complicated question, which jurisdictions split on, is whether present inability to pay is a valid defense where the defendant had the ability to pay at the time payments were due.

If a defendant is found to be in civil contempt, the court will order him or her to pay the overdue amount, and a payment schedule is usually established. To compel payment, the court may impose a jail sentence, but, in keeping with the remedial purpose of a civil contempt action, the defendant must be given the opportunity to purge the contempt by paying the arrearage and thus avoid jail. The right to purge oneself of the contempt is ongoing, and the jail sentence is imposed for an indefinite time, terminable upon payment of the arrearage. Where there is a present inability to pay (and this is not considered a valid defense), a jail sentence will generally not be imposed because the obligor does not have the means to purge the contempt. In contrast, a sentence in a criminal contempt case is imposed for a fixed period of time because the purpose is punitive, and the defendant cannot shorten it by purging the contempt.

Other Enforcement Measures

In seeking to enforce a spousal support award, a recipient who also has a child support order in place may be able to obtain enforcement assistance from the state's IV-D agency, and many of the same collection tools, such as wage withholding and tax refund intercepts, are available to secure spousal support payments (see Chapter 6). Additionally, many states, in implementing the enforcement procedures required under federal law for child support, extended their availability to spousal support recipients who choose not to go through the IV-D agency or are not eligible for IV-D agency support because they do not also have a child support order in place.

As with child support, spousal support awards can be enforced across state lines under the Uniform Interstate Family Support Act (UIFSA). However, child support collection is the priority of the interstate system and dominates enforcement efforts.

Bankruptcy and the Support Obligation

Filing for **bankruptcy** provides an individual who is overwhelmed by indebtedness with the opportunity to discharge qualified debts, thus enabling him or her to make a "fresh start." What then happens if the individual seeking to be relieved of his or her debts has existing financial obligations to a spouse or child stemming from a divorce or separation?

Until recently, the Bankruptcy Code prevented the discharge of debts that were in the nature of support payments; however, the Code allowed the discharge of debts that were in the nature of a property settlement, such as payments being made to a former spouse to effectuate the debtor's buyout of the equity in the marital home, subject to a possible hardship exception. However, the Bankruptcy Abuse Prevention and Consumer Protection Act of 2005 eliminated the distinction between debts for support and those in the nature of a property settlement with regard to personal bankruptcy filings. Accordingly, the rule of non-dischargeability has now been extended to most property settlement obligations.[36]

Tax Consequences

Until recently, in contrast to child support payments, under the federal tax code, spousal support payments were treated as taxable income to the recipient and the payor spouse was correspondingly entitled to a deduction from gross income for the amount paid. While this old rule remains in effect with respect to any divorce or separation instrument that was executed prior to December 31, 2018, going forward, alimony payments are no longer includible in the recipient's income nor deductible from the payor's. The new rule may be applied to modifications of pre-2019 support decrees or agreements if the parties mutually consent to this change.[37]

Chapter Summary

Prior to no-fault reform, marriage embodied a clearer notion of permanent commitment and obligation. Upon divorce, if the husband were at fault, the wife had a claim to continued support. After no-fault reform, marriage was often analogized to a partnership, with divorce as the vehicle for making a clean break from the past. In keeping with this partnership model of marriage, property distribution became the preferred approach to adjusting economic rights between spouses. The clean-break approach has been criticized for failing to account for economic disparities between spouses that frequently result from the marital division of labor.

In deciding whether to provide spousal support, judges usually consider multiple factors, with need as a central determinant. In most jurisdictions, fault is no longer a central consideration, and it may not play any role in the support determination; however, marital misconduct continues to operate as a bar to a support award in a few states. This approach promotes flexibility, as judges may assign whatever weight they deem appropriate to individual factors based on the facts of a case; however, such flexibility also contributes to a lack of predictability and coherence. Consequently, a few jurisdictions have implemented numeric guidelines for the computation of amounts, much as in the child support arena, and the ALI recommends shifting to a compensatory focus.

Following no-fault reform, "permanent" alimony fell out of favor, and rehabilitative support, with its emphasis on helping a spouse to become economically self-sufficient, became the preferred approach. However, some courts have reevaluated the appropriateness of rehabilitative support in cases involving long-term marriages where a spouse has little chance of becoming economically self-sufficient. More recently, based mainly on the activism of divorced men in conjunction with their new spouses, who may be members of "second wives clubs," the tide may be again turning away from "permanent" awards based on the view that it is unfair to saddle the former spouse with this ongoing obligation. This trend has been greeted with alarm by those who argue that this unfairly exacerbates the economic inequities of divorce. In addition to permanent and rehabilitative support, courts may award lump-sum alimony. Additionally, in professional degree cases, some courts may award reimbursement alimony.

"Permanent" support awards are subject to modification based on changed circumstances and are terminable upon remarriage, death, and (possibly) cohabitation. Some states permit the modification of a rehabilitative award if, despite a good-faith effort, the recipient has not become self-sufficient. Lump-sum payments are generally not modifiable.

The most common enforcement mechanism for failure to pay spousal support is a contempt action. Other enforcement mechanisms—such as wage withholding—are also now available following the expansion of available procedures in the child support arena.

Support payments are not dischargeable in bankruptcy. Reversing the long-standing rule, with respect to any divorce or separation instrument executed after December 31, 2018, spousal support payments are no longer includible in the income of the recipient spouse nor deductible by the payor spouse.

Key Terms

Alimony	Permanent Alimony
Spousal Support	Opportunity Cost
Clean Break	Alimony Pendente Lite
Economic Self-Sufficiency	Temporary Alimony
Diminished Earning Capacity	Change in Circumstances
Enhanced Earning Capacity	Lump-Sum Support

Alimony in Gross   Modification
Rehabilitative Support   Contempt
Transitional Support   Bankruptcy
Reimbursement Alimony

Review Questions

1. What is the historical origin of our spousal support laws?
2. Historically, what was the relationship between marital fault and alimony?
3. What vision of marriage did the no-fault divorce laws embody?
4. Describe the key way in which the support obligation was reformulated following no-fault reform.
5. What criticisms have been raised regarding the clean-break approach to spousal support awards?
6. What kinds of factors do courts consider when making an alimony determination?
7. What are the advantages of the multifactored approach to support determinations? What are the potential problems?
8. Why have some jurisdictions begun to consider adopting spousal support guidelines?
9. Why is it potentially more complicated to develop spousal support as compared to child support guidelines?
10. What approach to spousal support does the ALI recommend adopting?
11. What is permanent alimony? What functions does it serve? Why is permanent alimony not really permanent?
12. What is lump-sum alimony?
13. What is rehabilitative alimony? What functions does it serve?
14. Why has the tide started to turn against the award of "permanent" alimony? Who have been the primary advocates of this reform?
15. When one spouse earns a professional degree during a marriage, how might this be factored into a spousal support award?
16. What is the basic rule regarding modification of a permanent support award?
17. Why is an increase in the cost of living generally not an appropriate ground for a modification?
18. What are the rules regarding remarriage and the termination of support?
19. What are the rules regarding cohabitation and termination of support?
20. What are the rules regarding modification of lump-sum alimony? Rehabilitative alimony? Reimbursement alimony?

21. In a civil contempt action, what right does a defendant have if a jail sentence is imposed?
22. What is the principal defense in a contempt action?
23. What are the rules regarding the dischargeability of family support obligations in a bankruptcy proceeding?
24. What is the rule as of December 31, 2018, regarding the taxation of spousal support awards?

Discussion Questions

1. If a divorce terminates the marital relationship, should the law recognize any continuing obligations to a former marital partner? Explain your position in detail.
2. If a husband and wife mutually agree that the wife will devote most of her energies to caring for the couple's home and rearing their children, should she be "compensated" for this through a spousal support award if the couple divorces? What kinds of considerations do you think are important here?
3. Despite the gender neutrality of spousal support laws, many people express discomfort at the thought of alimony being awarded to men. Why do you think this is? What is your reaction?
4. Some would argue that we have gone too far in eliminating fault as a consideration in support awards. What role do you think fault should play, if any? Are the arguments different if fault is linked to a spouse's economic status, such as where there is a history of domestic violence, which can depress earnings?

Assignments

1. Locate the statutory provisions that govern the award of spousal support for your state and determine the following:
   - What factors, if any, are enumerated for court consideration?
   - Can marital fault be considered? If yes, under what conditions?
   - Do any of the sections specify what kinds of support can be awarded? If so, identify the available support approaches and describe their statutory features.
2. The lawyer for whom you work has asked you to research and draft an in-house memo regarding the approach that your jurisdiction takes in spousal support cases involving professional degrees.

   In approaching this assignment, you should assume that the attorney, although an expert in family law, has little familiarity with the law in this specific area. Make sure that you find all the relevant cases and analyze them carefully, as the attorney needs this information to prepare for a negotiation session in a pending case. (Note: If your jurisdiction does not have any professional degree cases, rehabilitative alimony cases can be substituted.)

3. The attorney you are working for does not do much family law and has asked you to help her figure out whether her client, Mary Smith, is likely to be awarded spousal support—and if so, what kind and in what amount. At this point, you do not have all the necessary information about the case, but she wants you to provide her with a reasonable range of options. To do this, you should examine the cases in your jurisdiction and write her an in-house memo. Try to identify what additional information will be needed in order to determine what, if anything, the client is likely to receive in spousal support.

   Following are the facts as they are presently known: Mary Smith was married to her husband for eight years. They have two minor children, ages 6 and 8. Ms. Smith is a paralegal with an associate's degree in paralegal studies. She has worked half time since the birth of her first child. She presently earns $18,000 per year. Her husband, David Smith, is the director of personnel at a large company. He earns $140,000 per year. You can assume that Ms. Smith will have primary physical custody of the children.

4. Following a lengthy trial, a client of the office you work for was denied spousal support. The attorney on the case is thinking about filing an appeal and has asked you to provide some initial research assessing whether you think the judge made an error of law. He thinks his client is certainly entitled to rehabilitative support and possibly to permanent support. Here are the facts: Tom (your office's client) and his wife Melanie were married for eight years. Melanie was a corporate executive and worked extremely long hours. The couple has no children. They agreed that because Melanie earned so much money, Tom would not work outside of the home, but would maintain their house, pursue his various interests in the arts and music, and serve as a volunteer for various charitable enterprises. In year three of their marriage, Melanie obtained her Ph.D. in Business Administration; she had begun work on this degree the year before the couple married. Tom has an associate's degree in commercial art, although he has never pursued this line of work. In year five, Tom was diagnosed with multiple sclerosis; so far, the disease has been mild with no impact on his level of functioning.

   After locating the cases that you think are relevant, write an informal in-house memo to the attorney on the case in which you discuss whether you think the client is entitled to support and why. Be sure to discuss and cite all relevant cases.

5. Assume you are a legislative aide to a state representative who is considering introducing a bill that would adopt the ALI's compensatory approach to the award of spousal support. The legislator has asked you to read up on this proposal and to prepare a background memo for him in which you explain the ALI approach, including how it differs from your state's present approach to spousal support, and identify at least two key possible advantages and disadvantages of this new approach.

6. Assume you work for a senator in a state that is considering reforming its spousal support law so as to eliminate the option of "permanent" support except under very limited circumstances. The senator does not know how she should vote on the issue and has asked you to write an in-house memo that sets out the arguments in favor of and against such a measure.

Cases for Analysis

Although, as discussed in this chapter, "permanent" alimony awards have recently come under considerable criticism, the court in the following case opts for what it refers to as "traditional" spousal support even though the marriage did not last the typical 20-year threshold in that state for such an award. Key to the decision is the need of the wife—a consideration that the dissent strongly objects to given the marriage's duration.

IN RE MARRIAGE OF LINE NANG BACCAM
2018 Iowa App. LEXIS 996 (2018)

CARR, Senior Judge.

Line and Khampha met in February 1990. At the time, Line was twenty years old and Khampha was twenty-eight. The two began dating shortly thereafter. Line moved into the home Khampha owned in 2003. Their first child was born in 2004, followed by the birth of a second child in 2006. . . .

In May 2015, Line petitioned to dissolve the marriage. . . .

Pursuant to the parties' agreement, the court granted Line physical care of the children. It also granted the parties joint legal custody of the children. The court ordered Khampha to pay Line $1002.87 per month in child support, $1000.00 per month in spousal support.

Khampha challenges the district court's award of spousal support to Line in the amount of $1000.00 per month until Khampha reaches the age of sixty-seven or remarries. Although the court stated it was "not labeling this support with any of the categories enumerated in previous decisions by our appellate courts," Khampha characterizes the award as traditional spousal support and argues their marriage was of insufficient duration to justify such an award.

In determining whether to award spousal support, the court considers the factors set out in *Iowa Code section 598.21A(1) (2015)*. Because we accord the trial court considerable latitude in determining matters of spousal support, we will disturb such an award only when there has been a failure to do equity.

Our supreme court has observed that, typically, traditional spousal support is awarded in cases involving long-term marriages, noting that "marriages lasting twenty or more years commonly cross the durational threshold and merit serious consideration for traditional spousal support." Although marriages of shorter duration are less likely to result in an award of traditional spousal support, there is no "fixed formula" for determining whether to award traditional spousal support. However, as our supreme court has repeatedly noted, precedent is of little value because the court must determine an award of spousal support on the particular circumstances of each case.

One of the factors cited by the district court cited in determining [if] Line should receive spousal support is the disparity in the parties' incomes. From 2012 to 2016, Khampha earned between $53,455.00 and $59,894.00 per year. In contrast, the district court determined that Line was capable of earning between $22,000.00 and $23,000.00 per year in a clerical position based on her clerical employment at Citibank from 1997 until the company downsized in 2010. After Line left Citibank, she began working as a care provider for her father, earning between $14,655.00 and $14,955.00 per year from 2014 through 2016. Although Khampha focuses on Line's decision to care for her father rather than returning to a job in financial services where she could earn a greater salary, Line testified that her reasons for assuming care of her father were twofold. First, she cited that another care provider would have difficulty communicating with her father, for whom Line has to act as an interpreter during doctor appointments and other tasks. Second, she testified that her position as a care provider is part-time and provides her with flexible working hours, which allows Line to attend to her children's needs outside of school. The second factor becomes especially significant given the needs of the younger child, who has a diagnosis of selective mutism and whose anxiety is so great that it caused her to vomit on almost a daily basis while in preschool. As reported by the child's therapist, the child "has anxiety related to using words outside of specific family members, eating and using the bathroom at school." Although Khampha's attorney attempted to dismiss Line's concerns about caring for her children while working a fulltime job as those of any divorced parent, it is evident from the record that the resources available to other divorced parents with regard to transportation and childcare are not an option here given the younger child's needs.

The decision to award traditional spousal support primarily depends on the need of the spouse receiving the support balanced against the ability of the supporting spouse to pay. . . .

The record shows Line has a need for spousal support and Khampha has the ability to pay it. However, the amount ordered by the district court—$1000.00 per month—leaves Khampha with a shortfall of $473.00 per month and Line with a surplus of $547.00 per month. This is inequitable. We find an equitable award of spousal support to be $460.00 per month.

In sum, the facts of this case warrant an award of traditional spousal support even though the length of the marriage does not cross the "durational threshold" for such awards. The award of traditional spousal support is warranted by Line's need to be available to care for the children, especially the younger child, which reduces Line's ability to reach her actual earning capacity as the district court determined based on her prior earnings at Citibank. The spousal-support award could be the subject of a later modification action if the child's needs abate or the child reaches the age of eighteen and no longer needs any special care from Line. As discussed above, we reduce the amount of the spousal support award to $460.00 per month. . . .

McDONALD, Judge (dissenting).

. . . [O]ur courts have . . . case-by-case, developed workable constructs to guide the provision of spousal support. . . . Our cases have come to recognize three primary forms of spousal support: traditional, rehabilitative, and reimbursement.

Traditional spousal support is inapplicable here. Traditional spousal support allows the recipient spouse to continue to live the lifestyle to which he or she had become accustomed over a lengthy period of time. Generally, only "marriages lasting twenty or more years commonly cross the durational threshold and merit serious consideration for traditional spousal support." This case did not involve a lengthy marriage—the majority determined that the parties were married for only thirteen years. In the absence of a lengthy marriage crossing the durational threshold, an award of traditional spousal support is inappropriate. . . .

Rehabilitative support is also inapplicable here. "Rehabilitative spousal support is 'a way of supporting an economically dependent spouse through a limited period of re-education or retraining following divorce, thereby creating incentive and opportunity for that spouse to become self-supporting.'" In this case, Line does not seek further training or education. Line has chosen to be a fulltime caretaker for her father instead of resuming her career in finance. While it is Line's right to forego more gainful employment to care for her father, her exercise of this right does not create an obligation for Khampa to continue to subsidize Line's choice. Rehabilitative support is inappropriate in this case.

Nor is reimbursement spousal support appropriate under the circumstances of this case. "Reimbursement spousal support allows the spouse receiving the support to share in the other spouse's future earnings in exchange for the receiving spouse's contributions to the source of that income." *Id.* A typical scenario in which the court may grant reimbursement support is when the dissolution occurs shortly after one spouse has obtained a professional degree and license with the financial support of the other. Khampha did not pursue post-secondary education during his marriage to Line. There is no evidence Line made sacrifices in order to allow Khampha to further his career. In fact, Khampha continued to support his family through his job at Firestone when Line took a substantial pay cut and began to care for her father in 2010. Reimbursement spousal support is inapplicable here.

Although none of the generally-recognized forms of spousal support are applicable here, the majority affirms the award of spousal support. . . .

The spousal support in this case is a new form of spousal support— need-based spousal support. The majority asks whether the recipient spouse has a need and whether the other spouse has the ability to pay. If the answer to both questions is yes, then support should be awarded. In my view, if one spouse has a financial need, the next question should not be whether the other spouse has the ability to pay. Instead, the next question should be whether the facts and circumstances of the case are such that it would be equitable to require the other spouse to satisfy the need. The answer to that question is derived from looking at the constellation of principles embodied in the traditionally-recognized forms of spousal support. Only if one or more of the generally-recognized categories is applicable, i.e., only if it would be equitable to require spousal support, should we ask the question of whether the other spouse has the ability to satisfy the recipient spouse's need.

Here, there are no generally-recognized categories of spousal support applicable to the case at hand. There are no extraordinary circumstances justifying the departure from the traditional categories of spousal support. It is not equitable to force one spouse to subsidize a former spouse merely because he or she can. This is particularly true where, as here, the recipient spouse is voluntarily underemployed. I would this affirm the judgment of the district court but modify the decree to eliminate any award of spousal support.

QUESTIONS

1. Why did the court decide that spousal support was appropriate in this case?

2. What specific factors did it take into account in fashioning the award?
3. Explain the objections of the dissent to the support award.
4. What would you have decided if you were the judge in this case?

———————————

The following case considers the potential relationship between marital-fault, post-separation conduct, and the spousal support obligation.

S.M.C. v. W.P.C.
2012 Pa. Super. 92, 44 A.3d 1181 (2012)

Opinion by DONOHUE
W.P.C. ("Husband") appeals from the order . . . entered by the hearing officer which, *inter alia*, granted S.M.C. ("Wife") spousal support. . . .

ENTITLEMENT TO SPOUSAL SUPPORT

Husband's first three issues on appeal address the trial court's determination that Wife is entitled to spousal support. He asserts that it was error for the trial court to award spousal support in this case because of her voluntary departure from the marital residence, and her exposure of Husband to indignities by going on a cruise with her friends prior to separation and engaging in an extramarital affair post-separation. . . . He also argues that the trial court erred by excluding evidence of Wife's post-separation affair. . . .

The law pertaining to spousal support in Pennsylvania is clear: "Married persons are liable for the support of each other according to their respective abilities to provide support as provided by law." 23 Pa. C.S.A. §4321(1). A long-recognized exception to the obligation to pay spousal support exists where the recipient spouse conducts him or herself in a manner that would constitute grounds for a fault-based divorce. . . .

Initially, we note that all of Husband's arguments regarding Wife's non-entitlement to spousal support are grounds for a fault-based divorce, *to wit*, indignities and desertion. . . . We begin with Husband's argument that he was subjected to indignities based upon Wife's post-separation extramarital affair. . . . The trial court found that Wife's post-separation conduct was irrelevant for purposes of determining her entitlement to spousal support based upon this Court's decision in Jayne v. Jayne, 443 Pa. Super. 664, 663 A.2d 169 (Pa. Super. 1995), and thus her post-separation relationship with another man was not a basis for denying Wife spousal support.

In *Jayne*, the wife testified that she believed her husband was engaging in an extramarital affair after they separated. . . . Based on this evidence, the hearing master concluded that the wife had presented sufficient evidence to grant a divorce on the ground of indignities. . . .

Because the extramarital affair and protection from abuse proceedings both involved post-separation conduct by the husband, and the record did not support a finding that they shed light upon the behavior of the parties pre-separation, the *Jayne* Court concluded that the evidence should not have been considered by the hearing master. *Id.*

Turning to the case *sub judice*, we agree with the trial court that the holding announced in *Jayne* case precludes the consideration of post-separation conduct in determining whether Wife is entitled to spousal support. Although Husband is correct that the holding does not specifically address spousal support, as we stated above, spousal support can only be denied if the recipient spouse exhibits conduct that would constitute a ground for fault-based divorce. *A fortiori*, if there is no evidence of conduct that would constitute grounds for a fault-based divorce, then a spouse is entitled to support. Because post-separation conduct does not constitute a basis for granting a fault-based divorce without evidence that it sheds light on the pre-separation conduct of the parties, it likewise cannot be a basis for precluding the award of spousal support.

The record does not support a finding that Wife engaged in an extramarital affair prior to separation. Likewise, just as in *Jayne*, the record does not support a finding that Wife's post-separation conduct shed light on her conduct prior to separation. The evidence of Wife's post-separation affair was therefore irrelevant, as it did not constitute a ground for fault-based divorce based on indignities. As such, the hearing officer correctly excluded evidence of Wife's post-separation affair, and the trial court did not abuse its discretion by denying Husband's exceptions on that basis.

Husband also contends that Wife should not have been granted spousal support because she went on a cruise without him, over his objection, which he argues gives rise to a finding of indignities, as he was angry and hurt by her behavior. . . .

There is no specific definition or test as to what constitutes indignities. "Indignities may consist of vulgarity, unmerited reproach, habitual contumely, studied neglect, intentional incivility, manifest disdain, abusive language, malignant ridicule, and every other plain manifestation of settled hate and estrangement." *Hunsinger v. Hunsinger*, 381 Pa. Super. 453, 554 A.2d 89, 91 (Pa. Super. 1989) (quoting *McKrell v. McKrell*, 352 Pa. 173, 180, 42 A.2d 609, 612 (1945)). A single act by a spouse, however, will not give rise to a finding of indignities. Rather, "indignities 'must consist of a course of conduct or continued treatment which renders the condition of the innocent party intolerable and his or her life burdensome . . . a course of conduct as is humiliating, degrading and inconsistent with the position and relation as a spouse.'" *Id.*

Clearly, the act of going on a single vacation with friends despite Husband's protestations does not qualify under the above definition of indignities. Furthermore, Husband's testimony that he was "angry" and "insulted" by Wife going on the cruise is insufficient to show that her travel rendered his condition intolerable or his life burdensome. . . .

Husband further argues that Wife was not entitled to spousal support because she left the marital home without cause and against his wishes, i.e., a claim of desertion. The trial court found that Wife was justified in leaving the marital residence based upon Husband's emotional abuse of Wife.

In order to overcome a claim of desertion, the trial court must find that the departing spouse presented evidence of "an adequate legal cause for leaving." *Clendenning v. Clendenning*, 392 Pa. Super. 33, 572 A.2d 18, 20 (Pa. Super. 1990) (citations omitted). . . .

In *Clendenning*, testimony by a wife regarding her husband's anger, yelling, beating his cane on a table, and demands that she conduct herself in accordance with his wishes was found to be an adequate legal cause for the wife to have left the marital home. . . .

In the case at bar, Wife testified that Husband was "emotionally abusive." She indicated that she attended marriage counseling for three years before leaving in an attempt to save their marriage, but that Husband did not participate. Wife testified that Husband sent her "mean messages" while she was on a cruise with her friends, calling her a "whore" and telling her to "suck his dick," which caused her to be afraid to return to the home. Wife stated that Husband "bullied" her, and that she and E.C. were fearful when they knew Husband was coming home.

Based upon existing precedent, we conclude that there was sufficient evidence for the trial court to conclude that Wife had adequate legal cause to leave the marital home, and that she did not depart "maliciously or casually on a whim or caprice.". . .

QUESTIONS

1. Why was the husband seeking to show that the wife had engaged in behavior that would entitle him to a fault divorce?
2. What impact did the wife's post-separation conduct have on the husband's support obligation?
3. Under what circumstance might this conduct have been given more weight by the court?

The following case focuses on the question of whether a spouse may request the extension of a rehabilitative support award *after* the original order has expired. It also looks at what a spouse must show in order to establish that there has been a change in circumstances that would warrant a modification, and lastly considers the tricky issue of how an income-generating asset should be taken into account for purposes of determining spousal support and the division of marital property.

LOUTTS v. LOUTTS
309 Mich. App. 203, 871 N.W.2d 298 (2015)

The parties are Russian immigrants who were married in 1988 and came to the United States a few years later. They have one adult son. In 2000, plaintiff Georgii Loutts (referred to as George) started QPhotonics, a business that buys, sells, imports, and exports light emitting diodes and laser diodes. Plaintiff has a Ph.D in Materials Science earned in 1990 from General Physics Institute in Moscow, and he worked as a physics professor at Norfolk State University in Virginia until the parties moved to Ann Arbor in 2007.

Defendant has a Ph.D in International Relations, earned in 2004 from Old Dominion University in Norfolk, Virginia, and a Master's degree in Economics from Moscow State University in Moscow. Defendant had earned $14,000 a year as an adjunct professor at Old Dominion, and she was hired as a bookkeeper/accountant for QPhotonics at a salary of $2,000 a month after the parties moved to Ann Arbor. In 2008, near the time plaintiff filed for divorce, defendant was fired from the QPhotonics job.

Plaintiff filed for divorce in December 2008. Following a bench trial, the parties' divorce judgment was entered on March 9, 2010. The trial court ruled that permanent spousal support was not appropriate "because both parties have PhDs, are in good health, and are clearly employable." However, plaintiff was required to pay defendant rehabilitative spousal support in the amount of $1,510 a month for a period of four years. Plaintiff was awarded the marital home, and defendant was ordered to vacate the home before April 1, 2010, which she did. The trial court determined the value of QPhotonics to be $280,000 and awarded the business to plaintiff, and half of its value, $140,000, to defendant. The rest of the property was split approximately equally, and plaintiff was ordered to pay defendant $247,788 as an equalizer. . . .

Following the judgment of divorce, defendant appealed in this Court, which remanded to the trial court. . . .

Nine months after this Court's decision to remand, defendant filed in the trial court a "Motion to Recalculate Spousal Support, Modify Spousal Support, and Extend It. . . ." Defendant argued that her health had deteriorated substantially. Specifically, she alleged that she suffered from bleeding stomach ulcers that led to hospitalization on three occasions, the first occurring in March 2012. Nevertheless, defendant asserted that she continued to look for work. However, she alleged that she was unable to obtain suitable employment because she was overqualified for the few jobs that existed in her geographical area, and because Michigan's declining economy made it nearly impossible to find work. . . .

The trial court stated that rehabilitative spousal support had been ordered at $1,510 a month retroactive to April 23, 2009, and that it terminated on April 23, 2013. Despite defendant's claim that her health problems began before September 2012, the trial court noted that she waited until June 14, 2013, to request modification and extension of her spousal support. The trial court noted that the spousal support terminated before the request to modify and extend was made, despite the fact that the alleged change of circumstance occurred approximately one year before the termination. Accordingly, the trial court held that any request for a modification or extension of spousal support must occur before the termination of the duty to pay. The trial court acknowledged that MCL 552.28 authorizes the modification of alimony on a showing of changed circumstances, but noted that defendant's reading of the rule was unreasonable because it would allow a party to "come back five, ten or even 20 years later to request a modification of spousal support because of a 'change of circumstance.' " Therefore, the trial court denied defendant's request to modify and extend spousal support. The trial court did, however, recalculate the spousal support using $34,000 as defendant's imputed income. This increased defendant's monthly spousal support to $1,790, for a total of $85,920 over four years, which was $13,440 more than the original award. . . .

Defendant contends that there is no requirement that a motion to modify or extend spousal support be made within the initial term of support awarded. The trial court denied defendant's motion to modify and extend spousal support, citing the fact that the support terminated on April 23, 2013, before the request to modify and extend was made. Accordingly, the trial court held that any request to modify or extend spousal support had to be made before the support terminated.

MCL 552.28 creates a statutory right for either party to seek modification of spousal support. It provides:

> On petition of either party, after a judgment for alimony or other allowance for either party or a child, or after a judgment for the appointment of trustees to receive and hold property for the use of either party or a child, and subject to section 17, the court may revise and alter the judgment, respecting the amount or payment of the alimony or allowance, and also respecting the appropriation and payment of the principal and income of the property held in trust, and may make any judgment respecting any of the matters that the court might have made in the original action.

In interpreting MCL 552.28, our Supreme Court in *Rickner v. Frederick*, 459 Mich 371, 379; 590 NW2d 288 (1999), determined that the plain language of the statute did not create a bright-line rule such as the one imposed by the trial court in this case. In *Rickner*, the trial court awarded the plaintiff spousal support and ordered the issue to be automatically reviewed in two years. *Id.* at 372. The judgment of divorce was later modified to state that spousal support would terminate if the plaintiff died, remarried, or cohabitated with a man. *Id.* at 373-374. The trial court cancelled the spousal support and ordered that the file be closed after learning that the plaintiff was cohabitating with a man. *Id.* at 374-375. Almost two years after the file was closed, and three years after spousal support had been cancelled, the plaintiff was no longer cohabitating and moved to reinstate her spousal support. She also claimed that her multiple sclerosis had worsened substantially, and she was unable to work. *Id.* at 375. Expressing its concern in language nearly identical to that employed by the trial court in the present case, the trial court in *Rickner* denied the motion to reinstate spousal support and stated:

> [T]here must come a time where these matters are over with. The alimony has been terminated. To think then that person could come in in five years, ten years, 20 years later and ask again that alimony be reinstated, the Court finds to be a situation that simply would never put matters to rest. One would never know when the othe[r] party might decide that they want to come in and at least file a motion. Maybe they can't meet the criteria, as has been pointed out by counsel, because there are certain criteria, but these matters have to be laid to rest. [*Rickner*, 459 Mich. at 376 (second alteration in original).]

This Court affirmed, but our Supreme Court reversed, stating,

> In this instance, we are faced with a statute that simply provides that "[o]n petition of either party, after a judgment for alimony . . . the court may revise and alter the judgment, respecting the amount or payment of the alimony . . ., and may make any judgment respecting any of the matters that the court might have made in the original action." MCL 552.28. This is a case in which the court originally provided alimony, and thus continuing jurisdiction is plainly provided by the statute.
>
>   This conclusion is buttressed by the absence of a prior Michigan appellate decision holding that the statutory power to modify is extinguished if it is once exercised to eliminate alimony. Further, the statutory power to modify is not dependent on triggering language in the judgment.
>
>   For these reasons, we are persuaded that the proper reading of the statute is that the Legislature intends, in cases in which alimony is initially ordered, that the court retain the power to make necessary modifications in appropriate circumstances. [*Rickner*, 459 Mich. at 378-379 (citations omitted).]

Accordingly, based on *Rickner* and the plain language of MCL 552.28, it was error for the trial court to interpret the law to state that any request to modify or extend spousal support had to be made before the initial support terminated. However, we conclude that this error was harmless because the trial court's two orders implicitly conclude that defendant failed to show a change of circumstances sufficient to warrant modification or extension of the rehabilitative spousal support.

To modify a spousal support award, the moving party must show that there has been a change of circumstances since the judgment of divorce. . . . Defendant argued that her deteriorating health and her inability to find work constituted a change of circumstances. Although the trial court cited in its first order the fact that defendant's motion was untimely, it also noted that it was reviewing all the documents and testimony and had taken the modification of spousal support under advisement. The court further noted that it was very specific in ordering rehabilitative support for four years and denying permanent spousal support. In its second order, the court noted that, at the time the divorce judgment was entered, defendant was clearly employable based on her education and professional experience, and it referred to the expert testimony from the trial regarding defendant's potential job prospects. The trial court's two orders made it clear that, in addition to determining that defendant's motion was untimely, the court was also relying on the reasons initially set forth in the divorce judgment as a basis for limiting its award of support to rehabilitative spousal support for four years.

Further, as the trial court noted in its first order, despite claiming that her ulcers began in March 2012, defendant did not file her motion to modify and extend spousal support until June 2013, which certainly diminished the urgency for further spousal support to address her alleged health issues. Moreover, except for the few times she was hospitalized and prevented from working, defendant never asserted that her alleged medical issues hindered her ability to work. In fact, she stated that despite her ulcers, she continued to look for employment. Defendant's main reason for seeking continued spousal support appears to be her inability to obtain suitable employment because she was overqualified for the jobs available in her geographical area and because Michigan's economy was declining. However, she did not identify any jobs for which she applied and was turned down based on her qualifications. In fact, defendant did not provide evidence to support any of the allegations in her motion to modify and extend spousal support. Thus, the record is clear that defendant did not sustain her burden to show that circumstances had changed since the divorce judgment, and therefore, the trial court did not abuse its discretion by denying her motion to modify and extend spousal support.

Next, defendant argues that the trial court erred by determining that the equities in this case did not warrant using the value of QPhotonics for purposes of both property division and spousal support. The trial court determined that the valuation of QPhotonics could be used for either property division or spousal support, but not both. . . . Because the trial court applied a bright-line rule and did not consider the specific facts and circumstances of the case, this Court directed the trial court on remand to redetermine spousal support by deciding whether the equities in this case warranted using the value of QPhotonics for purposes of both property division and spousal support.

On remand, the trial court thoroughly discussed its decision to use the value of QPhotonics for the purpose of property division, but not spousal support. The trial court relied on plaintiff's expert who stated that "where a business is valued on the present value of the future income to the owner, some of the earnings/profits are considered as payment for labor (reasonable compensation) and the remaining profits (excess compensation) are reduced to present value and multiplied by a factor to yield a business value." The trial court stated, "If this excess compensation is considered in awarding spousal support, then it could be argued that the Court would be awarding the same dollars twice.". . .

QUESTIONS

1. What was the trial court's position with regard to when a motion to modify a spousal support award must be brought?
2. Why did the appeals court reverse the trial court's ruling with regard to when a motion to modify can be brought?
3. What did the court decide with regard to whether or not the wife was entitled to an extension of the support award?
4. Why did the appeals court conclude that the trial court had correctly excluded the value of QPhotonics for the purpose of determining spousal support?

Endnotes

1. *See* Mary O'Connell, Alimony After No-Fault: A Practice in Search of a Theory, 23 New Eng. L. Rev. 437 (1988).

2. *Id.* at 454-455.

3. *Id.* at 482-491.

4. Doyle v. Doyle, 5 Misc. 2d 4, 158 N.Y.S.2d 909, 912 (1957).

5. Lenore J. Weitzman, The Divorce Revolution: The Unexpected Social and Economic Consequences for Women and Children in America 145 (1985).

6. Orr v. Orr, 440 U.S. 268, 288 (1978) (citing United Jewish Orgs. v. Carey, 430 U.S. 144, 173-174 (1977)).

7. *See generally* Alicia Brokars Kelly, Actualizing Intimate Partnership Theory, 50 Fam. Ct. Rev. 258 (2012); Alicia Brokars Kelly, Rehabilitating Partnership Marriage as a Theory of Wealth Distribution at Divorce: In Recognition of a Shared Life, 19 Wis. L.J. 141 (2004); June Carbone, Income Sharing Redefining the Family in Terms of Community, 31 Hous. L. Rev. 359 (1994); Ann L. Estin, Alimony and the Rehabilitation of Family Care, 71 N.C. L. Rev. 721 (1993); Twila L. Perry, Alimony: Race, Privilege, and Dependency in the Search for Theory, 82 Geo. L. Rev. 2481 (1994).

8. *See* Cynthia Lee Starnes, Mothers as Suckers: Pity, Partnership, and Divorce Discourse, 90 Iowa L. Rev. 1513, 1546 (2005).

9. Rachel Biscardi, Dispelling Alimony Myths: The Continuing Need for Alimony and the Alimony Reform Act of 2011, 36 W. New Eng. L. Rev. 1, 7-8 (2014), quoting Division of Labor, Marriage and Family Encyclopedia, http://family.jrank.org/pages/408/Division-LaboroContemporary-Divisions-Labor.html.

10. *Id.* at 8.

11. Jill C. Engle, Promoting the General Welfare: Legal Reform to Lift Women and Children in the United States Out of Poverty, 16 J. Gender Race & Just. 1, 10 (2013).

12. Biscardi, *supra* note 9, at 6.

13. *See* Joan Williams, Is Coverture Dead? Beyond a New Theory of Alimony, 82 Geo. L.J. 2227, 2282-2283 (1994).

14. Robert Kirkman Collins, The Theory of Marital Residues: Applying an Income Adjustment Calculus to the Enigma of Alimony, 24 Harv. Women's L.J. 23, 50 (2001). For a discussion of various reform proposals, *see* Alicia Brokars Kelly, Actualizing Intimate Partnership Theory, 50 Fam. Ct. Rev. 258 (2012); Alicia Brokars Kelly, Rehabilitating Partnership Marriage as a Theory of Wealth Distribution at Divorce: In Recognition of a Shared Life, 19 Wis. L.J. 141 (2004); June Carbone, Income Sharing Redefining the Family in Terms of Community, 31 Hous. L. Rev. 359 (1994); Ann L. Estin, Alimony and the Rehabilitation of Family Care, 71 N.C. L. Rev. 721 (1993); Twila L. Perry, Alimony: Race, Privilege, and Dependency in the Search for Theory, 82 Geo. L. Rev. 2481 (1994); Cynthia Starnes, Divorce and the Displaced Homemaker: A Discourse on Playing with Dolls, Partnership Buyouts, and Dissociation Under No-Fault, 60 U. Chi. L. Rev. 67 (1993); Joan Williams, Is Coverture Dead?, 82 Geo. L. Rev. 2227 (1994).

15. Jill C. Engle, Promoting the General Welfare: Legal Reform to Lift Women and Children in the United States Out of Poverty, 16 J. Gender Race & Just. 1, 15 (2013).

16. Mary Kay Kisthardt, Rethinking Alimony: The AAML's Considerations for Calculating Alimony, Spousal Support or Maintenance, 21 J. Am. Acad. Matrimonial Law 61 (2008).

17. *See* Marie Gordon, Spousal Support Guidelines and the American Experience: Moving Beyond Discretion, 19 Can. J. Fam. L. 247 (2002); June Carbone, The

Futility of Coherence: The ALI's *Principles of the Law of Family Dissolution*, Compensatory Spousal Payments, 43 J.L. & Fam. Stud. 43 (2002).

18. Gordon, *supra* note 17, at 301 (citing Leslie Herndon Spillane, Spousal Support: The Other Ohio Lottery, 24 Ohio N.U. L. Rev. 281, 318-331 (1998)).

19. *See* Marshal S. Willick, A Universal Approach to Alimony: How Alimony Should Be Calculated and Why, 27 J. Am. Acad. Matrimonial Law 153 (2014/2015); Charles P. Kindegran, Reforming Alimony: Massachusetts Reconsiders Postdivorce Spousal Support, 46 Suffolk U. L. Rev. 13 (2013). For concerns regarding approach, *see* Biscardi, *supra* note 9.

20. However, as we saw in Chapter 6, when it comes to the matter of post-minority support for children who are in school, questions may in fact be raised about the existence of the underlying obligation itself.

21. For a discussion of some of these issues, *see* Kisthardt, *supra* note 16, and Judith G. McMullen, What Social Science and Popular Culture Tell Us About Women, Guilt, and Spousal Support After Divorce, 19 Duke J. Gender L. & Poly. 41 (2011).

22. Geoffrey C. Hazard, Jr., Forward to the Principles of the Law of Family Dissolution: Analysis and Recommendations, at §5.02 cmt. a (proposed final draft 1997), cited in Carbone, *supra* note 17, at 64-65.

23. Carbone, *supra* note 17, at 65 (citing §5.05 of the Principles of the Law of Family Dissolution).

24. Gordon, *supra* note 17, at 269.

25. Avirett v. Avirett, 187 N.J. Super. 380, 383, 454 A.2d 917, 919 (Ch. Div. 1982) (overruled on other grounds). For discussion of this trend, *see* Joan M. Krauskopf, Rehabilitative Alimony: Uses and Abuses of Limited Duration Alimony, 21 Fam. L.Q. 579 (1988).

26. Biscardi, *supra* note 9, at 3.

27. *Id.* at 8, quoting Melissa A. Milkie, Sara B. Raley, and Suzanne M. Bianchi, Taking on the Second Shift: Time Allocations and Time Pressures of U.S. Parents with Preschoolers, 88 Social Forces 487, 487-517 (2009)).

28. *Id.* at 8-9.

29. Thomas Leopold, Gender Differences in the Consequences of Divorce: A Study of Multiple Outcomes, 55 Demographics 769, 785 (2018). It should be noted that data for this study comes from Germany, but studies in the United States show a significant gendered gap in post-divorce standards of living. For example, one study showed that on average, the women experienced a 27 percent decline in their post-divorce standard of living, while men on average experienced a 10 percent increase. Biscardi, *supra* note 9, at 7.

30. Jennifer Wolf, The Single Parent Statistics Based on Census Data, https://www .verywellfamily.com/single-parent-census-data-2997668 (2018).

31. It is worth noting that despite the reluctance of the family courts to engage in this kind of valuation, it is done routinely in personal injury cases when deciding how much to award a plaintiff for lost future earnings.

32. Mahoney v. Mahoney, 91 N.J. 488, 453 A.2d 527, 534-535 (1982).

33. 453 A.2d at 534.

34. *See* Alicia Brokars Kelly, The Marital Partnership Pretense and Career Assets: The Ascendancy of Self over the Marital Community, 81 B.U. L. Rev. 59, 107 (2001).

35. COBRA, Pub. L. No. 99-272, 100 Stat. 82 (29 U.S.C. §§1161 et seq.) (1986). For additional detail, *see* Elizabeth L. Bennett and John W. Goldsborough, Guaranteeing Medical Insurance Coverage After Separation and Divorce, 28 Fam. L.Q. 305 (1994).

36. This is intended as a brief, simple introduction to the relationship between support obligations and bankruptcy law. However, this area of the law is quite complex. For

further detail, *see* Tiffany S. Franc and Jeff Nesson, Bankruptcy Considerations in Family Law Practice, 46 Md. B.J. 24 (Feb. 2013); Daniel A. Austin, For Debtor or Worse: Discharge of Marital Debt Obligations Under the Federal Bankruptcy Abuse Prevention and Consumer Protection Act of 2005, 51 Wayne L. Rev. 1369 (2005).

    37. For a discussion of some of the pre-2019 tax rules, *see* Joanne Ross Wilder, Divorce and Taxes: Fifty Years of Changes, 24 J. Am. Acad. Matrimonial Law. 489 (2012); Stacia Gawronski, Spousal Support Under the Federal Tax Code, 20 J. Contemp. L. Issues 63 (2011/2012).

Chapter Eight

Division of Marital Property

This chapter focuses on the division of **marital property** at divorce. Since no-fault reform, the trend has been to treat the division of property as the primary economic event between divorcing spouses. The rationale for this development is that a division of property, as distinct from an award of alimony, is more in keeping with the modern partnership view of marriage, which seeks to allow both spouses to make a clean break from the past, unencumbered by the failed relationship. In theory, the partnership is fully dissolved after the distribution, leaving the parties free to reconstruct their lives without ongoing financial obligations or entanglements.

Accordingly, in some jurisdictions, spousal support is now an option only where the court determines there is insufficient property to provide for the needs of both spouses. However, as discussed in the previous chapter, this approach has drawn increasing criticism for failing to recognize that a division of property may not account for the fact that spouses may exit from a marriage with very different earning capacities based, at least in part, on the marital allocation of work and family commitments.

Historic Overview of the Two Marital Property Systems

Although the differences have become less pronounced over time, two marital property systems exist in this country. In this section, we compare the common law and community property approaches to marital property.

The Common Law Approach

As discussed in Chapter 1, the common law vision of the marital relationship assumed the loss of a wife's legal identity. The approach to marital property rights in these jurisdictions flowed directly from this understanding of marriage. Accordingly, property rights were vested in the husband, with the limited exception of the wife's realty, which he merely controlled.

Even as married women gradually acquired property rights through the passage of the Married Women's Property Acts, the concept of community property (see below) did not take hold. Instead, traditional common law property concepts, which extolled the virtues of individual rights, were simply extended to married women.[1] Property was his or hers based on who supplied the purchase funds—which in reality meant that the assets were effectively his.

Historically, common law states divided property at divorce according to **title**, which meant that the spouse who owned an asset was entitled to it. Mitigating the potential harshness of this approach, a number of courts developed the **special equity** rule, under which a spouse who had made a financial contribution to property titled in the name of the other could be granted an equitable interest in the asset, thus entitling her or him to a share at divorce. Some courts expanded this rule to provide rights based on the nonfinancial contributions of a homemaker spouse. Begun as an exception, this rule helped pave the way for the shift from a title-based approach to the division of marital property to the equitable distribution rules now in effect in all common law states.

The Community Property Approach

Rather than looking to English common law principles when devising rules regarding marital property rights, eight states, based on patterns of colonial influence and territorial acquisition, looked to Spanish or French civil law and adopted their community property approach. These states are Arizona, California, Idaho, Louisiana, Nevada, New Mexico, Texas, and Washington.[2]

In contrast to the common law approach, civil law states did not consider the husband and wife to be a single person. Instead, marriage was viewed as a partnership, and each spouse was presumed to act for the benefit of the marital unit as a whole rather than for his or her own good. Accordingly, the contributions of the parties to the marriage, including those of a homemaker spouse, were recognized by giving each spouse an immediate, vested interest in the accumulated assets (subject to the exception for "separate property" discussed below), although husbands had the right of exclusive management and control over community assets. Upon divorce, this community property was divided equally between the spouses.

The Two Marital Property Systems Today

Although historically quite distinct, the differences between the two marital property systems are largely a relic of the past. We begin this section with a discussion of the community property approach to the division of marital assets, since, as discussed, in moving from title to equity as the basis for distributing assets upon divorce, the common law states have borrowed heavily from the community property approach.

As indicated above, the community property states have long viewed marriage as a partnership, and the contributions of each spouse, financial or otherwise, are correspondingly regarded as contributing to the welfare of the marital community as a whole. Accordingly, unless falling into the definition of separate property as discussed in the section entitled "Defining Marital and Separate Property," below, assets that are acquired during the marriage belong equally to both spouses, without regard to title or the source of purchase funds. This **community** (or marital) **property** is then subject to division at the time of divorce. Although most community property states historically divided community property on an equal basis, many now use an equitable division standard, which (as developed later in this chapter) allows a court to make an unequal distribution based on considerations of fairness.[3]

Similarly, most debts that are incurred during the marriage are regarded as "community debts," and are likewise allocated between the spouses upon divorce without regard for who incurred it. However, tracking the distinction between marital and separate property discussed below, a debt that is incurred by one spouse for his or her own benefit rather than for the benefit of the marriage may be characterized as separate—which is not always an easy determination to make.

Property that is not acquired through the expenditure of marital efforts or funds is considered separate property and belongs to the acquiring spouse rather than to the community. Neither spouse acquires rights in the other's separate property because it stands apart from the marital enterprise. Typically, separate property includes assets brought into the marriage, gifts and inheritances acquired by one spouse during the marriage, and property acquired in exchange for separate property. At divorce, each spouse takes his or her separate property, although in a few states, courts may have limited authority to transfer separate property in cases of extreme hardship. The distinction between separate and community property is easy to state; however, in practice, navigating the boundaries between the two can be difficult (see the section entitled "Classification of Property," below).

No-fault divorce also helped to usher in changes in the rules of property distribution in common law states; and they all now divide marital property according to **equitable distribution** principles rather than title. Influenced by the sharing principles long recognized in community property states, the equitable distribution approach acknowledges that the accumulation of marital assets derives from the efforts of both spouses. Accordingly, at divorce, a spouse's nonfinancial contributions to the well-being of a household will give rise to an enforceable property interest in accumulated assets.

Following the community property approach, the majority of equitable distribution jurisdictions classify property at divorce as either marital or separate. This is often referred to as the **dual property** approach because a formal distinction is made between the two categories of assets. The distributive authority of the courts is restricted to the marital estate, although a few states have created a limited exception to this rule and permit distribution of separate property in cases of hardship. The classifying principle is essentially the same as in the community property states. Property acquired during the marriage through the efforts of either spouse or the expenditure of marital funds is considered marital because it derives from the contribution each is credited with making to the partnership. **Separate property** is that which is unrelated to this joint undertaking and generally includes property owned prior to marriage, gifts, inheritances, and property acquired in exchange for separate property.

In contrast to the dual property approach, a minority of states have adopted what is known as an **"all-property"** approach. Here, no formal distinction is made between separate and marital property, and courts are empowered to distribute all assets, regardless of when and how they were acquired. This is sometimes referred to as the "hotchpot of assets" approach. It should be noted, however, that the informal practice among attorneys in all-property states when negotiating a settlement may be to disregard property that would be considered separate in a community or dual property state, or to allocate it separately from the balance of the marital estate in order to give greater weight to its "separate" identity.

When it comes to debts, they similarly "belong" to the spouse who incurred them during the marriage. At the time of divorce, in contrast to historic practices, many common law jurisdictions now allocate responsibility for the debts between the spouses in accordance with the applicable equitable distribution principles; however, in the absence of a statute that expressly vests a court with this authority, some judges may regard this as a discretionary rather than an obligatory judicial function.[4]

With the adoption of equitable distribution laws, the difference between common law and community property states has become less pronounced, although the all-property approach is exclusively identified with common law states. Accordingly, this chapter will focus on general legal concepts and will not distinguish between the two approaches unless relevant; however, you should bear in mind that regardless of which approach is followed, each state has its own rules and standards.

Before proceeding, however, one essential difference should be noted. In community property states, the ownership interest of each spouse attaches at the time of property acquisition. Consequently, co-ownership rights come into being during the marriage; at the time of divorce, the court is dividing property that is already jointly owned by the spouses. In contrast, in common law states, each spouse holds the property acquired during the marriage as his or her own, and the ownership interest of the non-acquiring spouse does not attach until the time of divorce. As a result, when property is divided, a spouse may resent that something that "belongs" to him or her is being taken away and given to the other spouse as a consequence of the divorce rather than recognizing that the accumulated assets represent the cumulative efforts of both parties.

The Property Distribution Process

The process of dividing property between divorcing spouses can be broken down into four steps:

1. *Defining property.* A preliminary issue in some cases is whether a particular asset falls within the definition of the term "property"; if it falls outside the definition, the asset is not subject to distribution.
2. *Classification.* Except in all-property states, property must be classified as either marital or separate.[5]
3. *Valuation.* The value of each asset must be determined.
4. *Distribution.* The assets must be allocated in accordance with the applicable legal standard.

Before we look at these four steps, a few general points should be considered. First, in many cases, especially where the parties have few assets, the division of property is relatively simple, and couples often figure this out themselves without involving their attorneys or applying formal legal principles. A couple may simply divide their belongings based on need or preference. Of course, an attorney should ensure that a client understands that without a more formal process, there is no way of knowing whether the client is getting the share of assets that he or she may legally be entitled to.

Second, when couples do fight about property, the fight is often rooted in the emotional undertow of divorce. An object may be treasured for its sentimental meaning or it may have tremendous symbolic importance for one or both parties. For example, if your client is fighting fiercely for the old brown sofa, it may have become the symbolic locus of his or her anger and he or she may not really care about the sofa itself. Alternatively, the client may believe it is worth fighting for based on its sentimental worth—perhaps it was the couple's first purchase, thus standing as a reminder of happier times. If you are involved in helping to resolve a property dispute, it is important to be aware of these potential dynamics so you can help a client sort out what is going on; that way needless time, money, and emotional energy is not spent pursuing an object for the wrong reason.

Third, when a property dispute does involve legal considerations, such as classification or valuation, the governing rules are often complex and variable; for example, there are multiple approaches to valuing a closely held corporation, which differ from the multiple approaches to valuing pension plans or commodity futures. Expert witnesses are often required to resolve the complex legal and accounting issues.

Defining Property

Most cases do not involve definitional questions. During the marriage, couples accumulate items such as furniture, jewelry, cars, and household goods, which are so clearly property that this definitional step is bypassed without any thought to the matter. However, there are times when it is not clear whether a particular item, such as the goodwill of a professional practice or an unvested pension, is in fact property.

Since the enactment of equitable distribution laws and increased emphasis on the division of property, these definitional questions have assumed increasing importance, and this is an ever developing and expanding area of the law. When working on a case, you must carefully consider all possible property interests. This means there is much room for creative legal thinking. Who knows? Given the right opportunity, you may "discover" a new form of property!

The Tangible/Intangible Distinction

Traditionally, property was defined as a tangible item over which an individual could exercise absolute dominion and control. **Tangible property** is easy to identify, as it is what we normally think of as property—it has a physical presence and can be touched, seen, and transferred from one person to another.

Over time, the definition of property has expanded. Moving beyond physical presence, property is now usually described in relational terms as the "bundle of rights" a person has in something. In essence the concept has been "dephysicalized,"[6] and thus, **intangible assets**—assets that lack a physical presence and cannot be ascertained by the senses—may well come within the concept of property. Intangible assets often involve the right to something, such as the future right to participate in a pension plan or, as evidenced by a stock certificate, the right to participate in the management of a corporation and receive a proportional share of earnings.

Common examples of intangible assets include the goodwill of a business, a legal claim, stocks, bonds, and pension plans.

Few property distribution statutes provide a definition of the term "property," so courts have had to struggle with the concept. Some jurisdictions are expansive and consider a broad array of intangibles to be property. Other jurisdictions are more restrictive and tend to exclude intangibles that lack traditional property attributes. Accordingly, if an intangible asset cannot easily be transferred to another person, is difficult to value, and cannot be owned jointly, a court in a restrictive jurisdiction is likely to determine that it is not property. Thus, for example, in comparing a professional degree (see Chapter 7) with a car, one can see how such a court might refuse to consider it property. Unlike the car, the degree cannot be transferred or left to someone as an inheritance, its worth is much harder to determine, and it cannot be jointly owned. Underlying these distinctions—and potentially significant to the courts—is that many of these intangibles, such as a degree or goodwill, seem personally connected to the efforts of the holder.

Most definitional battles focus on whether or not an intangible interest should be treated as property. The outcome can have significant consequences for the economic future of the divorcing spouses because intangibles, such as a pension or the goodwill of a business, may be very valuable. Before looking at these definitional disputes more closely, however, we turn to a question that has recently received considerable attention: At the time of divorce, how should disputes over the family pet be resolved? Should a pet be treated as an item of property or as a member of the household?

Divorce and the Family Pet

More like a possession (such as a chair) or more like a child? Courts have increasingly been confronted with this issue as a growing number of divorce cases involve a dispute over the future of a beloved family pet. This uptick has been attributed to a number of related factors. One consideration is the developing cultural awareness of the important role that pets can play in human's lives. This recognition is supported by research indicating the beneficial impact that a relationship with a loved animal can have on a person's well-being, for example, by helping to calm someone with an anxiety disorder, or to ease the loneliness that typically accompanies the death of a partner.[7] Another consideration is that as more couples choose not to have children, pets are likely to play a more important role in their lives, and conflicts over them may thus well take on added weight as a relationship ends.

However, as it presently stands, based on established legal doctrine, pets are generally considered to be the "personal property" of their "owners." Accordingly, upon divorce the determination of a pet's future is controlled by property distribution principles. Thus, for example, a court might award a dog to a spouse who came into a marriage with the pet based on the classification principle that the dog is a separate asset, rather than to the spouse who had been the pet's primary caretaker over the course of the marriage. In effect, this "pet as property" approach means that the fate of the family dog or cat will be resolved by reference to the same principles that govern the distribution of the household furniture or a couple's automobiles.

Over the past 15 or so years, this approach has increasingly been challenged by a number of legal scholars, animal rights activists, and litigants seeking to maintain their post-dissolution relationship with a pet, who have argued that pets should be moved out of the property category and treated more as family members. Embodying this shift, there has been a parallel effort to revise the language used to characterize these relationships by substituting the term "guardian" for "owner" and "companion animal" for "pet" in order to honor the fact that animals are sentient and emotional beings and that "these relationships are of a deep and enduring nature"; moreover, the term "guardian" also "connotes a greater sense of responsibility." This shift in nomenclature has been incorporated into some municipal ordinances.[8]

Correspondingly, advocates of this recharacterization of pets from property to family member argue that conflicts between divorcing spouses over a pet should be treated as akin to a custody dispute rather than as a disagreement over the allocation of marital assets, and that a standard akin to the "best interest of the companion animal" should be employed to determine custody and visitation rights. This standard would recognize that unlike a chair, animals are living beings who are both loyal and loving and like children, are dependent upon adults to provide for their basic needs. Moreover, as with a child, the loss of relationship cannot be redressed by providing a spouse with an offsetting asset to compensate him or her for the deprivation caused by award of the pet to the other spouse.

However, courts and legislatures have not generally been receptive to these arguments, and pets generally continue to be treated as property in the marital dissolution context. For example, in a 1995 Florida divorce case, the appeals court concluded that the trial court had erred in awarding custody of the couple's dog to the husband with visitation rights to the wife because under Florida law a dog is personal property and "[t]here is no authority which provides for a trial court to grant custody or visitation pertaining to personal property."[9] As a policy matter, the court further stated: "Determinations as to custody and visitation lead to continuing enforcement and supervision problems (as evidenced by the proceedings in the instant case). Our courts are overwhelmed with the supervision of custody, visitation, and support matters related to the protection of our children. We cannot undertake the same responsibility as to animals."[10]

Taking this a step further, a court in Pennsylvania refused to enforce an agreement between a divorcing couple regarding the allocation of custodial and visitation rights stating:

> In seeking "shared custody" and a "visitation" arrangement, Appellant appears to treat Barney, a dog, as a child. Despite the status owners bestow on their pets, Pennsylvania law considers dogs to be personal property. . . . Appellant, however, overlooks the fact that any terms set forth in the Agreement are void to the extent that they attempt to award custodial visitation with or shared custody of personal property. . . . As the trial court aptly noted, Appellant is seeking an arrangement analogous, in law, to a visitation schedule for a table or a lamp.[11]

Similarly, in the 2014 case of Hamet v. Baker, the Supreme Court of Vermont affirmed the trial court's conclusion that it lacked the authority to "impose an enforceable visitation order for the dog" on the grounds that "an order of property division is final and not subject to modification" and that in contrast to "enforcement of other kinds of property division orders, enforcement of a family companion animal would require the power of modification, since the animal's well-being . . . could be a substantial factor in the analysis."[12]

Although courts have continued to resist treating disputes between divorcing spouses over a family pet as akin to a child custody dispute, animal lovers can take heart in the fact that some judges have quietly begun to pay attention to the post-dissolution needs of family pets within the "pet as property" paradigm. Accordingly, in the above-referenced case of Hamet v. Baker, although firm in its view that "pet animals are property" and thus subject to the rules of equitable distribution, the Vermont high court made equally clear that they are "a special category of property" due to the fact that they "are alive and form emotional attachments with their owners that run in both directions."[13]

An unpublished 2011 Virginia divorce case also provides an excellent example of this hybrid approach. At trial, although each party introduced relevant evidence under the state's equitable distribution law to estab-lish his or her superior claim to the dog, which included a dispute over whether the dog should be classified as a marital asset, or, as argued by the wife, a separate asset based upon the assertion that the dog had been a gift to her from her husband, they also testified to the fact that "they loved the dog and they considered her to be a family member," and each "presented evidence that they had a strong bond with the dog."[14]

Following the court's decision to award the dog to the wife under the equitable distribution statute, with an offsetting financial award to the hus-band so he could acquire a dog "of like kind," the husband filed an appeal arguing that the court had erred by failing to "consider that the dog is not an inanimate object, but rather a living sentient being," and by refusing to use the "best interest standard." Although the appeals court rejected the husband's argument that the dispute should have been resolved by reference to a best interest rather than an equitable distribution standard, it approvingly pointed out that in making its allocation decision, the trial court "noted that a dog has a unique 'intrinsic value' because the parties care for the dog and have a 'significant interest' in the dog," and that it did "not in any way want to minimize the significance of a pet in a person's life." Accordingly, the lower court had properly taken into account "the unique circumstances presented by determining the equitable distribution of the dog," and made sure she would be provided with a "stable and car-ing environment."[15]

Clearly, the kinds of considerations that these two court took into account would not be relevant when deciding which party was entitled to, say, a lamp or sofa. Arguably, this suggests that at least some judges may be increasingly willing to smuggle considerations of a pet's best interest into the equitable distribution analysis.

Unvested Pensions, Accrued Leave Time, and Professional Goodwill: Are They Property?

In this section, we look at three intangible assets that have posed defini-tional difficulties for the courts—unvested pensions; accrued vacation and sick leave time; and professional goodwill. These assets have been selected because they raise recurring issues that are central to the definitional pro-cess. Before proceeding, it should be noted that sometimes the question we are considering here—whether an intangible asset is property or not—is framed as an inquiry into whether the asset should be considered a sepa-rate rather than a marital asset because of its special characteristics, such as that it is personal to the holder, and nontransferable. Regardless of which approach is used, the relevant considerations are quite similar—for example, professional goodwill (discussed below) may be deemed not property because it is personal to the holder, or it may be deemed separate property for the same reason.

Unvested Pensions.   **Pensions** are an important job-related benefit. They are a form of deferred compensation: An employee earns the right to the benefit in the present, but realization of the benefit is deferred until retirement or some other future date after the employee has left his or her job. Some pension plans are funded solely by employer contributions; others are funded solely by employee contributions; and some are funded by a combination of employer and employee contributions.

An individual's interest in his or her pension is either vested or unvested.[16] When rights are vested, an employee does not forfeit retirement benefits when he or she leaves the place of employment prior to retirement. Vesting usually occurs after an employee has worked for an employer for a specified number of years. In contrast, if an employee who is not vested leaves the job, he or she forfeits the retirement benefits. The right to retirement benefits is thus contingent on continued employment through the vesting period.

The clear trend is to recognize both vested and unvested pensions as a property interest. However, there has been considerable debate over unvested pensions, and some jurisdictions continue to regard them as an expectancy interest rather than as a form of property because the right to benefits is contingent upon continued employment through the vesting period, which may or may not take place. In general, an expectancy is not considered a form of property because of its uncertain, conditional nature.

Other jurisdictions give greater weight to a spouse's interest in an unvested pension because, although presently uncertain, the right to benefits will become legally enforceable upon the happening of a future contingency—fulfillment of the time requirement. This greater certainty serves to distinguish an interest in an unvested pension from a true expectancy, such as the hope of being named a beneficiary in a will, which is completely speculative, and supports treating unvested pensions as property.

In defining unvested pensions as property, many jurisdictions have been influenced by equitable considerations. A pension is often a couple's most valuable asset, and exclusion based on a technical distinction would downgrade the contribution of a homemaker spouse to the marital enterprise because, although both partners contributed to the marriage, only the employed spouse would enjoy retirement benefits. Another fairness consideration is that the right, although contingent, is acquired during the marriage. (See the discussion regarding distribution of pensions later in this chapter.)

Accrued Vacation and Sick Leave Time.   Many employers permit their employees to accumulate unused sick and vacation time. Upon retirement, an employee may be paid the value of this accrued time. The question has arisen in a number of cases as to whether this accrued time is a marital asset, capable of valuation and division upon divorce. Although the courts that have considered this issue are divided, the majority approach is toward inclusion.

In seeking to determine whether accrued leave time is an asset, many courts have framed it as a question of whether this time is an alternative form of wages and thus not property, or more akin to deferred compensation, such as a pension, and thus includible as property. In addressing this question in a decision from 2000, the Kentucky Court of Appeals concluded that "since it replaces wages on days when the worker does not work, it really is only an alternative form of wages," and is thus "less tangible, more difficult to value, and more personal than pension and retirement benefits," and therefore should not be classified as property.[17]

In direct contrast, the Colorado Supreme Court recently held that where a spouse has "an enforceable right to be paid for accrued vacation or sick leave, as established by an employment agreement or policy" this accrued leave is a property interest.[18] In reaching this conclusion, the Court rejected the above view that accrued leave is "'really only an alternative form of wages' intended to 'replace[] wages on the days when the worker does not work'"[19] in favor of characterizing it as "compensation earned for services already performed" in situations where "the employee has an enforceable right to receive payment for such leave," thus making it akin to "other forms of 'deferred' compensation, such as a pension benefit or stock options granted in exchange for past or present services."[20]

Goodwill of a Professional Practice.   **Goodwill** is an intangible asset that is most commonly identified with commercial businesses. It can be defined generally as a business's good reputation in the community that generates the expectation of continued future patronage. Put another way, it is the value of a business that is in excess of the combined value of a business' net assets. Because it can readily be valued and transferred for consideration if the business is sold, there is little question that the goodwill of a business is an intangible property interest that is subject to distribution upon divorce.[21]

There is less agreement, however, where the goodwill of a professional practice is involved.[22] A minority of jurisdictions do not regard the goodwill of a professional practice as property. Underlying this exclusion is the belief that the goodwill attaches to the individual professionals in the practice rather than to the practice itself. So attached, **professional goodwill** is both nontransferable and hard to value; moreover, even if a value could be assigned, it would be too tied to the vagaries of the individual's career path to have real meaning. Thus lacking these essential attributes of property—transferability and amenability to valuation—this minority of jurisdictions regards professional goodwill more like future earning capacity, which can be considered in calculating child support, rather than as a marital asset. At the other end of the spectrum, a number of jurisdictions take the view that professional goodwill attaches to the practice itself rather than to the individual partners, and thus it is fully included in the marital estate.

Most states, however, take an in-between position and seek to distinguish between "enterprise" and "personal" goodwill. Here, goodwill that is attributable to the reputation of an individual is not considered property because, as noted above, it cannot be readily valued or transferred, whereas goodwill that is attributable to the reputation of the business itself is considered part of the marital estate and subject to division at the time of divorce. As with unvested pensions, some courts that treat personal professional goodwill as an intangible asset may also be influenced by the fact that the goodwill, although securing future benefits, is built up during the marriage, thus making exclusion unfair.

And What About the Virtual World?

Before turning to a consideration of the classification of property, a word is in order regarding **virtual assets**, and whether or not they should be treated like other forms of intangible property for purposes of divorce. When speaking of virtual assets, it can be helpful to think of them as falling into one of two broad categories; however, please note that this categorization is not intended to be all-encompassing, but rather is simply aimed at giving you a working sense of what is at issue here. To this end, it can be helpful to think of one category as being comprised of items such as URLs, websites, social networking accounts, blogs, and e-mail accounts, and the other being comprised of virtual environments, which have been defined as "three dimensional virtual versions of the real world . . . [in which] virtual objects change hands for real money."[23] Notably, as a result of this "crossover," these virtual spaces have "value in real dollars."[24]

Although to date there is little in the way of guidance from the courts as to whether or not virtual property qualifies as property for purposes of equitable distribution,[25] commentators generally agree that our virtual belongings should be "regulated and protected like real world property."[26] In a classic article on the subject, author Joshua Fairfield argues that this parallel treatment is warranted based on the fact that "virtual property shares three legally relevant characteristics with real world property"—namely, it is "rivalrous," meaning that "if one person owns and controls [it] another does not"; "persistent," meaning that "unlike the software on your computer, [it does] not go away"; and "interconnected," meaning that "[o]ther people can interact with [it]."[27] Fairfield offers the example of a pen to buttress his argument. As he explains:

> If I hold a pen, I have it and you don't. Rivalrousness. If I put the pen down and leave the room, it is still there. That is persistence. And finally, you can all interact with the pen—with my permission, you can experience it. That is interconnectivity. Why is code trying so hard to mimic these properties? Rivalrousness gives me the ability to invest in my property without fear that other people may take what I have built. Persistence protects my investment by ensuring that it lasts. Interconnectivity increases the value of the property due to network effects — not least of which is the fact that other people's experience of my resource may be such that it becomes desirable, and hence marketable, to them.[28]

Although Fairfield was not focused on the treatment of virtual assets in the divorce context, his theory of indistinguishability has been very influential among commentators who have staked out a position in favor of inclusivity.[29] At present, it remains to be seen how the courts and legislatures will handle this issue, but certainly the unquestionable trend in favor of an inclusive concept of property strongly suggests that in the years to come, more couples will be having to resolve disputes over the allocation, valuation, and distribution of their virtual assets.

Classification of Property

The classification of property as marital or separate is a crucial step in both common law dual property and community property states because it determines the pool of assets that is subject to division. (Although, in a few states, courts can reach even separate property in cases of hardship.) In theory, classification is not relevant in all-property states; however, in practice, classification principles may influence how attorneys and possibly judges approach the distribution of property.

Defining Marital and Separate Property

In most states, marital and separate property are defined in relationship to one another: One is what the other is not. Frequently, a statute will define marital property as all property acquired during the marriage, except for that which is considered separate. Separate property is then specifically defined, and almost always includes property owned at the time of marriage, gifts, inheritances, and items received in exchange for separate property. Some statutes also identify specific assets, such as appreciation on separate property, unvested pensions, and professional licenses, as coming within the definition of separate property. Again, the rationale underlying the distinction between marital and separate property is that marital accumulations derive from the overall contribution of both spouses to the marriage, regardless of which spouse actually paid for any particular item, whereas separate assets do not derive from the marital efforts of either spouse and thus stand apart from the marriage. However, as discussed later in the chapter in the section entitled "Transmutation," the initial characterization of an asset may change over time. Classification also can be influenced by presumptions, and in most states it is presumed that all property owned by the spouse at the time of divorce is marital. This places the burden of proof on the party who is claiming that a particular asset is separate property, and he or she must produce sufficient evidence to rebut the presumption, or the asset will be considered marital and subject to division.

The Significance of Timing

A central characteristic of marital property is that it is acquired during the marriage. As a general rule, **premarital acquisitions**, property that a spouse comes into the marriage with, remain his or her separate property. This distinction usually is straightforward, but a few situations require elaboration.

Determining the Time of Acquisition. If a person purchases an asset, such as a car, before getting married and then makes payments on it after the marriage, is the car a premarital or a marital acquisition? One approach known as the **inception of title rule** fixes the time of acquisition at the time of initial purchase because this is when title or the right to title is obtained. Once set, the characterization cannot be changed, and postmarital contributions have no impact on the classification. Here, property is a unitary concept and value cannot be apportioned between the marital and the separate estates, although the nonowner spouse might be entitled to some reimbursement for his or her contribution.

Most jurisdictions have rejected this approach as too formalistic and incompatible with sharing principles because it focuses on title to the exclusion of contribution. The preferred approach in determining the time of acquisition is the **source of funds rule**. Here, acquisition is seen as a dynamic process that unfolds over time as payment is made; one might say that each payment effectuates a partial acquisition. Accordingly, an asset can be both marital and separate, and its value apportioned between the two estates in proportion to contribution.

A brief example will demonstrate the difference between these approaches. Let's say that in 2001, Nekeisha purchases an oil painting for $12,000. She pays $8,000 in cash and takes out a loan to pay the balance.

One month later, she marries Victor, and payments on the loan are made from their newly established joint checking account. In year three, the loan is paid off. Unfortunately, in year four, the couple divorces.

Under the inception of title rule, the entire value of the painting would be the separate property of Nekeisha because she acquired title or the right to title before the marriage, although Victor may be entitled to reimbursement. Under the source of funds rule, the value of the painting would be apportioned between Nekeisha's separate estate and the marital estate in the amounts of $8,000 and $4,000, respectively, thus adding to the total worth of marital assets. (Note that this example assumed the painting did not increase in value during the marriage. Appreciation raises other issues, which are discussed later in this chapter.)

Property Acquired in Contemplation of Marriage or During Cohabitation.   Usually there is no doubt that property owned by a person at the time of marriage is separate. However, sometimes purchases may be made in contemplation of marriage. In this situation, some jurisdictions have stretched statutory categories and will treat this property as marital based on the parties' intent to use it as such. Here, intent displaces the timing of acquisition as the controlling factor.

A related question is how property acquired during a period of premarital cohabitation will be treated. Most courts will not consider assets acquired during a period of cohabitation as marital based on a reluctance to treat cohabitation as the legal equivalent of marriage. However, if, while cohabiting, property is purchased in contemplation of marriage, it might come within the above rule and be treated as marital based on the parties' intent rather than on the fact of cohabitation. For example, in 2014, the Hawaii Supreme Court recognized that a cohabiting couple may establish a "premarital economic partnership," which then allows their premarital contributions to be taken into account when dividing property upon divorce. The establishment of such a partnership requires the following four elements: The parties have "(1) cohabited; (2) intended there to be a premarital economic partnership; (3) devoted their energies and financial resources for one another; and (4) subsequently marry."[30]

Same-Sex Couples. As discussed in Chapter 1, courts around the country are grappling with the question as to whether *Obergefell* should be applied retroactively so as to backdate the inception of a same-sex couple's marriage to an earlier point in their relationship, such as to when they would have married had they been permitted to do so.[31] Clearly, this raises difficult questions in terms of fixing the date for determining which assets come within the marital estate and which remain the separate property of each individual spouse. To date, this issue remains unresolved as part of the wider uncertainty regarding the extent to which jurisdictions are willing give retroactive effect to *Obergefell* — although, as noted in Chapter 1, the trend does seem to be in favor of applying the decision backwards in time in order to achieve the goal of true marital equality.

Fixing a Cutoff Point for Marital Acquisitions.   Timing questions that can influence classification also arise at the other end of the relationship—specifically, at what point in the dissolution process will acquired assets no longer be considered marital? Strictly speaking, a husband and wife remain legally married until a final decree of divorce is entered; thus, property that is acquired up until this moment in time are technically marital. However, motivated by practical and policy considerations, most jurisdictions use an earlier cutoff point after which time property that is acquired is no longer considered marital despite the continuation of the legal relationship.

To signal the effective end of the marital partnership, most state statutes fix the cutoff point at the date of legal separation, the initiation of a permanent separation, or the filing of a dissolution action, although a few states leave it to the discretion of the judge. Although utilizing different moments in time, each of these approaches reflects the underlying view that once spouses have gone their separate ways, the theoretical justification for pooling based on mutual contribution and effort no longer exists. It should be noted that practical problems can arise where the cutoff point is the date of permanent separation. Frequently, a separation that is intended to be permanent is followed by a series of contacts, some or all of which may rise to the level of reconciliation. This makes it difficult to fix the date of separation, particularly if the spouses disagree about the meaning and impact of these post-separation contacts, which makes it difficult to classify property accumulated during these intervals of parting and coming together.

Looking Beyond Definitions: The Complexities of Classification

Although the distinction between marital and separate property is easy to state, applying it can be difficult. This section discusses some situations that present difficult classification issues.

Gifts. As a general matter, a **gift** is a voluntary transfer of property made with donative intent, meaning that the gift-giver (donor) simply wishes to give the recipient something without requiring anything in exchange. For a gift to be effective, the transfer must be complete—the donor must fully relinquish all vestiges of ownership and control.

In the divorce context, a gift is generally classified as separate property, as it is not acquired through the effort of either spouse. Sometimes, however, a transfer that appears to be a gift is really not, such as when the donor, rather than being motivated by donative intent, is providing compensation for past or future services. Community property jurisdictions have long distinguished between gifts made with true donative intent and those that are really a form of compensation, treating the latter as marital property because the acquisition is tied to the recipient's efforts. This distinction is now also made in some common law dual property jurisdictions.

For example, assume that Bob and Karen are married. One day Karen's great-aunt Ernestine gives her a beautiful oil painting that is worth a lot of money. At first glance, classification appears obvious: The painting is a gift to Karen and is thus her separate property. However, what happens if the next time Bob and Karen visit Ernestine, she mentions that she gave the painting to Karen as a way of thanking her for taking such good care of her during her last illness? Now, arguably, if the couple were to divorce, Bob could argue that the painting should be classified as marital property because it was not given to Karen as a gift but as a form of compensation and thus was acquired through the expenditure of marital efforts.

What if instead of being from a third party, the gift is from one spouse to another? Should these be treated in the same manner? What if the gift was purchased from marital funds—should the source of contribution or the nature of the exchange control the classification?

In some states, interspousal gifts have been exempted from the general characterization of gifts as separate property by either statute or judicial decision, with some of these states limiting the exclusion to gifts that were purchased with marital funds. The underlying rationale here is that unlike third-party gifts, interspousal gifts derive from partnership efforts. In contrast, other jurisdictions focus on the gift aspect of the transaction, rather than on the source of funds. These courts treat completed interspousal gifts in the same manner as third-party gifts, even where purchased with marital funds.

Damage Awards.   Damage awards, such as those from personal injury cases, as well as disability or workers' compensation benefits, often trigger difficult classification questions (which in some jurisdictions may instead be framed as definitional questions). By way of illustration, this discussion will focus on personal injury awards.

If an injury occurs during the marriage, a minority of jurisdiction employ what is known as the *mechanistic approach,* which classifies the entire personal injury award as marital. Conceptually, this is similar to the inception-of-title rule as the timing of the entitlement to the award controls its classification. Courts that follow this rule, often do so because "personal injury proceeds are not included in the statutory definitions of separate property or the exceptions to marital property."[32]

In contrast, most states now employ the *analytical approach* according to which an award is divided into component parts and allocated between the separate and marital estates in accordance with general classification principles.[33] Accordingly, most states will classify the portion of the award attributable to lost wages and medical expenses as marital property because it compensates for economic loss incurred during the marriage. The portion of the award attributable to the pain and suffering of the injured spouse is then classified as separate property because it is so intimately connected to the injured spouse that it is deemed to exist apart from the marriage. If the award also compensates the injured person for future economic losses, this portion of the award usually would be classified as separate because the other spouse has no recognized interest in these future rights.[34]

Appreciation of Separate Property.   Difficult classification issues can arise in situations where separate property has increased in value over the course of the marriage. One approach is to tie the classification of the **appreciation** to the classification of the underlying asset. This means that if the asset is characterized as separate, any appreciation in value—even if it occurred during the marriage—will also be classified as separate. This approach is similar to the previously discussed inception of title rule that fixes ownership at the time of acquisition.

Let's return to Nekeisha and the oil painting she purchased for $12,000 one month before her marriage to Victor. If the painting increased in value during the marriage, under this approach the entire increase would be classified as separate based on the classification of the underlying asset. Note that any reimbursement due Victor would not capture the value of this increase.

As with the inception of title rule, most jurisdictions have rejected this approach as too rigid and not in keeping with contemporary sharing principles. The preferred approach is to classify appreciation based on the reason for the increase. If the increase is unrelated to spousal efforts and is due to causes such as inflation or market conditions, it is usually considered the separate property of the spouse who owns the asset. This kind of increase is often referred to as *passive appreciation.* If instead the gain is due to the investment of marital funds or efforts, it is usually considered marital. This kind of increase is often referred to as *active appreciation.* If the gain is attributable to both passive and active forces, it can be apportioned between the separate and marital estates.[35]

Property Received in Exchange for Separate Property.   What happens if a spouse exchanges or sells separate property during the marriage? Most jurisdictions treat property that is received in exchange for separate property as separate: The exchange is regarded as an alteration in the form of the asset, which leaves its underlying separate nature intact.

Generally, based on the presumption that all property owned at the time of divorce is marital, the party seeking to segregate an asset from the marital estate has the burden of proving its separate identity. Where exchanged property is involved, segregation requires **tracing** the asset directly back to a separate source. Tracing can be simple, such as where one painting has been exchanged for another, or it can be complex, such as where there have been successive exchanges or where funds from an account containing separate and marital funds have been used. If the tracing fails, and the separate identity of the asset cannot be established, it will be treated as marital. As discussed below, this result is transmutation by commingling.[36]

The Nature of the Asset.   Classification difficulties also may be triggered by specific types of property. As noted above, these inquiries are sometimes framed as definitional questions and sometimes as classification ones. Personal injury awards are a good example of an interest that poses difficult classification issues as well as presenting an underlying definitional question. Similar issues are raised when other damages awards, such as disability or workers' compensation benefits, are involved.[37]

Assuming, for the sake of discussion, that we are in a jurisdiction that considers a personal injury award to be property, the traditional approach was to classify the entire award as marital if it was acquired during the marriage. However, this is now a minority approach, and the clear classification trend is to divide the award into component parts and allocate them between the separate and marital estates in accordance with general classification principles. Using this approach, most states will classify the portion of the award attributable to lost wages and medical expenses as marital property because it compensates for economic loss incurred during the marriage.[38] The portion of the award attributable to the pain and suffering of the injured spouse is then classified as separate property because it is so intimately connected to the injured spouse that it is deemed to exist apart from the marriage. If the award also compensates the injured person for future economic losses, this portion of the award usually would be classified as separate because the other spouse has no recognized interest in these future rights.

Transmutation

Our final classification topic is transmutation. **Transmutation** refers to a post-acquisition change in an asset's classification from separate to marital or from marital to separate, although almost all transmutation cases involve the reclassification of separate assets.[39] Transmutation can occur in four ways: (1) by agreement, (2) by joint titling, (3) by commingling, and (4) by use.

Transmutation by Agreement. The simplest way that transmutation can occur is where the parties agree to recharacterize property. Statutes in many community property states and a few common law jurisdictions specifically authorize this result, although the term "transmutation" is usually not used. In the absence of express authority, most courts will uphold an agreement between spouses to recharacterize property. The agreement may need to be in writing and conform to whatever requirements the particular jurisdiction imposes on marital agreements.

Transmutation by Joint Titling. Property may be transmuted if a spouse places separate property or property purchased with separate funds in joint name—for example, where one spouse purchases a car with inherited funds and then takes title in both names. In most jurisdictions, joint titling triggers a rebuttable presumption that the separate asset has transmuted into a marital one because the titling demonstrates an intent to bestow a benefit on the marital estate. To rebut the presumption, a spouse may be able to show that the intent of joint titling was not to confer a benefit upon the marital estate but instead was done for estate planning purposes or to satisfy the requirements of a lender or because of pressure from his or her spouse. If the presumption is rebutted, the property will not transmute but rather will retain its original characterization as separate property.

Transmutation by Commingling. The most common way for property to transmute is by commingling. When separate property has been mixed with marital property, it will be treated as marital unless the party wishing to segregate the asset can establish its separate identity. Here the failure of a party to keep assets separate may be regarded as evidence of an intent to benefit the marital estate. The party wishing to claim an asset as separate must be able to "uncommingle" the mass of property. As with exchanged property, this is done by tracing. If the separate identity of the asset cannot be established with sufficient certainty, the tracing fails and the property is deemed to have transmuted by commingling.

Transmutation by Use. A few jurisdictions allow transmutation by use. For example, if a spouse permits the other to use his or her separately owned car on a regular basis, this use could transmute the car into a marital asset. This approach has been both praised for promoting sharing principles and criticized as an encroachment on individual property rights that effectively punishes a spouse for his or her generosity.[40] Depending on the situation, the same result might also be accomplished by reference to the commingling doctrine.

Valuation

Before property can be divided between spouses, marital assets need to be valued. Valuation involves determining the worth of the assets so that an appropriate distribution can be effectuated. Where an equitable (distinct from an equal) distribution standard is used, separate assets also may need to be valued, as the value and nature of this estate may influence the allocation of marital property. For example, if one spouse has considerable separate assets, it may be fair to give the other spouse a greater share of the marital estate (see the section entitled "Distribution," later in this chapter).

As a practical matter where property issues are resolved by agreement rather than at trial, parties often divide up their belongings without having them valued, as **valuation** can be both expensive and time consuming. Of course, this means that there is no real way of knowing whether the settlement is fair, especially if potentially valuable assets are involved. In this situation, attorneys usually include a provision in the separation agreement in which the parties acknowledge that they have knowingly and willingly dispensed with a valuation and have divided their property without full knowledge of its worth.

When property issues are resolved at trial, it can be a reversible error for the court to divide property without first determining value. Although valuation may be framed as the court's responsibility, in many jurisdictions, a party who fails to present evidence of value is deemed to have waived his or her right of appeal on this issue.

Valuation Methods

Few statutes specify how assets should be valued, and a wide range of approaches are generally acceptable. When a trial court is presented with competing valuation methods, it has relative freedom to select among the approaches or to combine them to arrive at its own value.

A common valuation approach is to determine an asset's fair market value. **Fair market value** is generally described as the price a willing buyer would pay to a willing seller where neither party is under any compulsion to buy or sell. Establishing this price requires detailed knowledge of the asset as well as the specific market conditions that would influence transferability. Although common, the fair market value approach is far from universal and would not be appropriate where, for example, a closely held corporation or a pension is involved, as neither has a readily determinable market value.[41]

The Role of Experts

The valuation of assets is generally outside the expertise of lawyers and requires the use of experts. As a general rule, there is no such thing as an all-purpose valuation expert. Instead, an expert must be carefully selected based on his or her specialized knowledge. For example, an accountant may be the most appropriate person to value a professional corporation but would not be the best choice where a rare stamp collection is involved; this would require the services of a rare stamp appraiser. Where real estate is involved, a real estate broker or appraiser would be appropriate, but if the present value of a pension needs to be determined, the services of an actuary would be required as this entails an assessment of how future risks impact the value of the employee spouse's interest.

Clearly, in any single case, the valuation process may require more than one expert. This can greatly increase the time and expense of a divorce proceeding and can significantly disadvantage the spouse with less income, who may lose the battle of the experts. To address this problem, some courts, upon request, may order one spouse to pay the costs of the other's experts or may appoint its own expert and order one party to pay all or most of the costs. The expense and time involved in hiring experts may encourage couples to settle rather than litigate; alternatively, it may encourage the financially more secure spouse to litigate vigorously in order to outdo the other.

Time of Valuation

An important valuation issue is when value should be determined. Possible dates include time of (1) separation, (2) trial, or (3) entry of the decree of dissolution. Traditionally, most jurisdictions selected a single valuation time and used it in all cases. However, the trend is toward greater flexibility, with a preference for determining value as close to the date of distribution as possible. However, most courts will readily depart from this approach where required by considerations of fairness. For example, if after separation one party dissipates assets, the court may use the date of separation for valuation purposes. This date might also be used if an asset has appreciated in value based on the post-separation efforts of one spouse.

Distribution

After property has been classified as marital or separate and valued, the actual distribution must be effectuated. This final step is the focus of this section.

The Standard for Division: Equal or Equitable?

When dividing property, the majority of states use an *equitable distribution standard,* which directs courts to divide the property in a manner that is described as fair, just, or equitable. A minority of states, made up mainly of community property jurisdictions, use an *equal distribution standard.* These courts must divide marital property equally between the spouses— although a few states permit deviations based on equitable considerations, such as where one spouse has no other resources and is otherwise likely to end up on public assistance. A few states use a *hybrid approach.* Here, property is to be divided equitably, but there is a rebuttable presumption that equitable is in fact equal. Accordingly, a party seeking a greater share of the assets would have the burden of proving why this is fair under the particular circumstances.

With the exception of the hybrid states, appellate courts in jurisdictions using an equitable distribution standard have generally made clear that it is inappropriate for trial courts to rely on fixed formulas or presumptions. However, it is generally acceptable for a court to use a 50-50 split as its starting point, as long as this does not result in an overly mechanistic approach to the allocation of assets. Nonetheless, as a practical matter, some judges and lawyers seem to assume that equitable means equal, thus implicitly placing a burden on the party seeking a greater share of the assets to justify why this division is appropriate.

A frequent concern raised by commentators who have examined the economic impact of divorce on women is that a division that appears equal or equitable on its face may have a very different value to each spouse based on differences in earning capacity, as the spouse with higher earnings can more readily replace items that were lost in the distribution.[42] This problem may be exacerbated if the low-earning spouse also has custody of the children, as the custodial parent often has increased household needs. Moreover, as we have seen, these considerations are often linked, because a spouse with greater domestic responsibilities frequently has a diminished earning capacity. One suggested solution is for courts to look beyond ensuring that the distribution appears equitable or equal solely at the time of divorce, and to assess the relative impact of the distribution on each spouse over time in light of earning potential and domestic arrangements as well. When this suggests a diverging value, the allocation could be adjusted to ensure greater fairness over time.

Consideration of Specific Factors

Most states with an equitable distribution standard have a statute that enumerates the factors that must be considered in determining how property is to be allocated. Some statutes are general in their approach, while others are detailed. Frequently, the factors that must be considered are the same as those that must be considered in making a spousal support award.

The following section from the New Jersey statute is a good example of a fairly detailed approach to what must be taken into account when determining the distribution of property:

> In making an equitable distribution of property, the court shall consider, but not be limited to, the following factors:
> a. The duration of the marriage or civil union;
> b. The age and physical and emotional health of the parties;
> c. The income or property brought to the marriage or civil union by each party;
> d. The standard of living established during the marriage or civil union;
> e. Any written agreement made by the parties before or during the marriage or civil union concerning an arrangement of property distribution;
> f. The economic circumstances of each party at the time the division of property becomes effective;
> g. The income and earning capacity of each party, including educational background, training, employment skills, work experience, length of absence from the job market, custodial responsibilities for children, and the time and expense necessary to acquire sufficient education or training to enable the party to become self-supporting at a standard of living reasonably comparable to that enjoyed during the marriage or civil union;
> h. The contribution by each party to the education, training or earning power of the other;
> i. The contribution of each party to the acquisition, dissipation, preservation, depreciation or appreciation in the amount or value of the

marital property, or the property acquired during the civil union as well as the contribution of a party as a homemaker;

j. The tax consequences of the proposed distribution to each party;

k. The present value of the property;

l. The need of a parent who has physical custody of a child to own or occupy the marital residence or residence shared by the partners in a civil union couple and to use or own the household effects;

m. The debts and liabilities of the parties;

n. The need for creation, now or in the future, of a trust fund to secure reasonably foreseeable medical or educational costs for a spouse, partner in a civil union couple or children;

o. The extent to which a party deferred achieving their career goals; and

p. Any other factors which the court may deem relevant.[43]

As we have seen in other contexts, most statutes set out the factors that must be considered in dividing property, but do not require that equal weight be given to each one. Accordingly, judges are free to weigh the factors as deemed appropriate in light of the circumstances of the individual case. This approach maximizes the flexibility and discretion of the court and is generally considered to be consistent with the goal of achieving a fair result, but, as we have seen, the potential downside of this flexibility is that it can lead to inconsistent results.

In some jurisdictions, judges must make detailed findings of fact showing the consideration given each statutory factor. In others, a more general statement in support of the result is acceptable. In states using an equal distribution standard or presumption, findings of fact are usually required only when the judge departs from the norm and makes an unequal distribution.

Effectuating the Distribution

There are many ways that property can be divided between the parties. The simplest and most common way to distribute property is for each spouse to take possession of a designated portion of the assets. For example, the wife might get the living room furniture and the husband the dining room furniture; the wife the computer and the husband the stereo; each might get one-half of the linens, the towels, the kitchen items, and so on until everything is distributed.

If a couple has a significant asset—such as a business, a valuable collection, or (as discussed in greater detail next) a house or pension—with no other comparable assets, a number of options are possible. Probably the simplest alternative is to award one spouse the major asset and give the other a greater share of the remaining assets. However, this may not always be feasible because the remaining property is often not of sufficient offsetting value. Another option is for the asset to be sold and the proceeds divided. Or one spouse could retain the asset and buy out the other's marital interest in it. Where a buyout occurs, a lump-sum payment (where feasible) is generally preferable to installment payments because it provides a clean break and minimizes the risk of nonperformance.

The Marital Residence.   Many property disputes center on the marital residence, most likely due to the convergence of financial, emotional, and practical considerations. In the event of a dispute, a court may consider the desirability of enabling the children to remain in their home because this provides them with some stability at a time of tremendous change. In fact, some property distribution statutes expressly include this as a factor for judicial consideration. (See, e.g., list item 1 of the New Jersey statute shown above.) Dispositional options for the marital residence include the following:

1. Sell the house and divide the proceeds.
2. One spouse keeps the house, buying out the other spouse or exchanging offsetting assets.
3. Keep the house in joint name, with one spouse having the right of exclusive use and occupancy until a future dispositional date.

If neither spouse wishes to retain the house, it can be sold and the proceeds divided equally or in accordance with the overall distribution formula. In some cases, a sale may be the ultimate result because no other option is feasible.

If the parties agree in principle that one spouse can retain the house, the question becomes how this can be accomplished. Often the simplest solution is to give the other spouse an asset or assets of roughly equal value; sometimes a pension will be used as the offsetting asset. Frequently, however, there will not be enough resources to do this, since a house is often the most valuable asset a couple owns. Another option is for the acquiring spouse to buy out the interest of the other spouse. To do this, the acquiring spouse usually takes out a home equity loan or refinances the existing loan. Again, this may not be feasible because he or she may not qualify for the loan or have the ability to make the loan payments.

If neither of the above options is feasible, another possibility is to keep the property in joint name and give one spouse the right of exclusive use and occupancy until a designated time in the future, such as the emancipation of the youngest child or the remarriage of the occupying spouse. Upon the earliest of these to occur, the occupying spouse would be required to effectuate a buyout of the other spouse's interest or to sell the house and allocate the proceeds according to a preexisting formula. The non-occupying spouse is often given the right of first refusal.

The advantage of this approach is that it enables a spouse to remain in the home, which may be particularly important where children are involved, without having to either give up a share of other assets or go into debt. But there is also a significant drawback: The property continues to be owned by two people with enough relational difficulties that they cannot live together. For this arrangement to have any hope of working, it is best that all necessary details be spelled out in the court's order or in the parties' separation agreement. It may also be advisable for the court to retain jurisdiction in case problems arise after the divorce. Some of the issues that need to be addressed are the following: Who pays for repairs? Who pays for improvements that increase the value of the house? How are these expenses accounted for upon sale? What if the occupying spouse neglects the house and its value declines? How are sale proceeds to be allocated? How is appreciation accounted for? Even when these details are worked out with care, the emotional risk factor involved in this approach remains a wild card.

Pensions. The distribution of pensions raises complex issues. This section provides a basic overview of the two principal ways pensions can be divided.[44]

The Present Value Approach.   One approach is to determine the present value of the pension and then assign the nonemployee spouse an offsetting share of property. The primary advantage of this approach is that the matter is resolved at the time of divorce and is not left hanging until some future date. However, it also presents some potential disadvantages. First, it is often difficult and costly to determine the present value of a pension plan because it is not payable until some time in the future and a number of contingencies—such as the salary of the employee spouse—can influence its value or affect whether it is payable at all. Second, there may not be enough offsetting property; even where there is, the nonemployee spouse gets the offsetting property immediately, while the employee spouse must wait until a future date to enjoy his or her share of the distribution. Additionally, if the plan is not vested, the employee spouse bears the risk of not receiving a full share of the distribution; however, she or he has some control over this, as a voluntary job change can be postponed until after the pension has vested. Accordingly, this approach is not generally used if a plan is unvested or the employee spouse is years away from retirement.

The "If, As, and When" Approach.   The other approach is to award the nonemployee spouse a share of pension funds "if, as, and when" the employee spouse receives them. Typically, at the time of divorce, the court uses a formula for allocating the future payments between the spouses; however, it is also possible that a court might instead opt to reserve juris-diction over the matter and defer the determination of the nonemployee's share until the pension actually matures, and is thus payable. In determin-ing the percentage amount, most states use a "marital fraction" formula that calculates the nonemployee's share based on the ratio that the years of the marriage bear to the total number of years of employment at the time of distribution.

The primary advantages of this distribution method are that it avoids the need to determine the present value of the plan; an offsetting award is not required; and the risk of nonreceipt is not borne solely by the employee spouse because the nonemployee spouse receives his or her share "if, as, and when" the employee spouse does. If the employee leaves before his or her pension vests, neither spouse gains or loses in a differential fashion. However, a potential disadvantage to the nonemployee spouse is the fact that the other spouse has control over this eventuality and thus has the ability to defeat the interest of the nonemployee spouse. This could give the employee spouse the upper-hand in the event of postmarital disagree-ments, as he or she could threaten to quit work if the other spouse did not capitulate to his or her demands.

Where the pension funds are actually reached, distribution is usually made pursuant to a **Qualified Domestic Relations Order** (QDRO), which is served on the administrator of the pension. A QDRO is a judgment or decree of a state court that enables the nonemployee spouse to receive all or part of the benefits that are payable to the employee spouse. A QDRO must be carefully drafted so it satisfies the legal requirements of the Employee Retirement Income Security Act (ERISA), as modified by the Retirement Equity Act of 1984 (REA), and contains all of the necessary information, such as the formulas used to determine the amounts of payment, how pay-ments are to be made, and when payments will begin and end.[45]

Tax Consequences of a Property Distribution

For federal tax purposes, property transfers between spouses either during a marriage or after a marriage ends, which are incidental to a divorce, are not taxable events.[46] To understand the significance of this rule, it is helpful to step outside the divorce context for a moment. Assume that A purchases a painting for $10,000 and five years later sells it to B for $20,000. Upon the sale, A has realized a gain of $10,000, which is subject to taxation. However, if A were married to B, and this transfer were made during the marriage or incident to a divorce, *A* would not realize any taxable gain even if *A* receives an asset worth $20,000 in exchange for the painting.

Let us now analyze the transfer from *B*'s perspective. Where *A* and *B* are strangers, and *B* purchases the painting for $20,000, *B* acquires what is referred to as a **cost basis** in the painting of $20,000. If *B* subsequently transfers the property, his gain will be computed using this basis as the starting point. Accordingly, if he sells the painting for $35,000, he will realize a gain of $15,000 ($35,000 – $20,000). However, if *A* and *B* are spouses, and the transfer is incident to a divorce, the tax consequences for *B* are quite different. Here, *B* acquires *A*'s basis of $10,000—it is literally carried over from *A* to *B* (as it would be in the case of a gift). Now, if *B* sells the painting for $35,000, he will realize a gain of $25,000 ($35,000 – $10,000).

Clearly, this rule impacts the actual value of a property transfer because the recipient of appreciated property may eventually be accountable for a significant gain. These potential tax consequences must be taken into account when effectuating a division; otherwise, parties may not actually receive the value that they believe they have agreed to.

Chapter Summary

Historically, courts in common law states had limited distributive authority—property followed title. Courts in community property states had much greater authority; marriage was viewed as a partnership, and all property acquired through the expenditure of marital efforts or funds was divisible. Now, title is no longer determinative in common law states. With the passage of equitable distribution laws, these jurisdictions have moved closer to the community property model. Most states, including all community property states, distinguish between separate and marital property, although some permit distribution of all property owned by a couple at the time of divorce. Most of these states employ a rebuttable presumption that all property owned by a couple at the time of divorce is marital.

A division of property entails four critical steps: (1) a determination whether the asset in question is in fact "property"; (2) the classification of property as either marital or separate (this step is not required in all-property states because the courts in these jurisdictions can reach both separate and marital property); (3) the value of each asset must be determined; and (4) the assets must be allocated in accordance with the applicable legal standard, with states employing either an equitable or an equal division rule.

The transfer of property incident to a divorce does not result in a taxable gain or loss to the transferring spouse; however, the recipient acquires a carry-over basis in the transferred asset that may result in a significant gain at the time of a future transfer.

Key Terms

Marital Property

Title

Special Equity

Community Property

Equitable Distribution

Dual Property

Separate Property

All-Property

Tangible Property

Intangible Assets

Pensions

Goodwill

Professional Goodwill

Virtual Assets

Premarital Acquisitions

Inception of Title Rule

Source of Funds Rule

Gift

Appreciation

Tracing

Transmutation

Valuation

Fair Market Value

Qualified Domestic Relations
   Order

Cost Basis

Review Questions

1. Following no-fault reform, why did property distribution become the preferred way to address the economic interests/needs of divorcing spouses?
2. Describe the partnership view of marriage that underlies the community property approach to the division of marital assets.
3. Prior to the passage of equitable distribution laws, how did common law states divide property? What was the special equity rule?
4. When and why did common law states shift to an equitable distribution model?
5. What is a dual property state? What is an all-property state?
6. What is the key difference between community property and common law equitable distribution states?
7. What steps are involved in the division of property?
8. How has the definition of property changed over time?
9. What is the difference between tangible and intangible property?
10. How does the law characterize family pets (a.k.a. "companion animals")? What implications does this have for divorce cases? What new approach have some suggested the law should take?
11. What is the difference between a vested and an unvested pension?
12. Why do some states exclude unvested pensions from their definition of property?
13. Explain why some jurisdictions include professional goodwill in their definition of property and others exclude it.

14. What are common examples of virtual assets?
15. What characteristics do virtual assets share with tangible assets?
16. Why is classification a critical step in dual property and community property states but not in all-property states?
17. How is marital property generally defined?
18. What is generally included within the definition of separate property?
19. Why is it important to determine when property is acquired?
20. How might the *Obergefell* decision be relevant when considering the timing of marital acquisitions?
21. What is the inception of title rule? The source of funds rule?
22. How might property acquired in contemplation of marriage be classified? Why? What about property acquired during premarital cohabitation? Why?
23. What cutoff dates are commonly used for determining when property will no longer be considered marital?
24. What is a gift? When might a gift be classified as marital rather than separate?
25. What is the difference between passive and active appreciation? Why is this difference important with respect to the appreciation of separate property?
26. What happens to the classification of separate property that is exchanged for other property during the marriage?
27. Explain the concept of tracing.
28. How are personal injury awards classified?
29. What is transmutation? Explain the four different ways by which property can transmute.
30. Why is valuation important?
31. What is meant by the term "fair market value"?
32. At what point in the process is property usually valued?
33. What is the difference between an equal and an equitable distribution standard?
34. How do courts decide what is equitable? What factors are generally considered important?
35. What are basic ways a distribution can be effectuated?
36. Describe the dispositional options for the marital residence.
37. What are the two different approaches to distribution of a pension? What are the relative advantages and disadvantages of each approach?
38. What is a QDRO?
39. What are the basic tax consequences of a property distribution?

Discussion Questions

1. Do you think it is appropriate to treat marriage as a partnership? Is this fair to both spouses? Does it imply an equality that may not exist in all marriages? How might this be problematic?

2. Let's assume that Mr. Jones worked hard at a small company to provide for his family. He never particularly enjoyed his work but took his financial obligations to his family seriously. His wife, Ms. Jones, happily stayed home and raised the children and took care of the house.

   Assume that the Joneses are getting divorced after 15 years of marriage. During this time, Mr. Jones contributed to his pension plan at work, and he is fully vested. Should this asset be subject to division? Is it fair to Mr. Jones to divide this employment asset, which is based on his workplace efforts? Explain your position.

3. Some commentators have argued that what is equal or equitable should be determined, at least in part, by looking at future results. Viewed from this perspective, a division that appears equal or fair on its face may reveal itself as less valuable to a more economically vulnerable spouse who cannot readily replace lost assets.

   In dividing property, should the court seek to ensure that the resulting impact of the award is equal or fair, even if this would require making disproportionate allocations?

4. Assume that for most of an eight-year marriage the husband has been very depressed. As a result, he has bounced from job to job with frequent periods of unemployment and has contributed little by way of caring for the house and the children. The wife has held down a steady job and has done most of the home care and child care.

   There is no question that their contributions are grossly unequal. How should this impact the property division? Does it make any difference to the issue if the wife knew about the husband's depression before the marriage? Does it make any difference if, instead of being depressed, the husband was an alcoholic? Drug dependent? Physically ill? Lazy?

5. In the divorce context, do you think the law should treat pets as personal property and distribute them like other assets, or would it be preferable if they were regarded more like children and decisions made based on the best interest of the pet?

6. Assume that a same-sex couple lived together in a state that did not permit them to marry. In the wake of *Obergefell*, do you think their marriage should be backdated to when they began to live together for purposes of determining what property comes within their marital estate? What considerations might be particularly relevant here?

Assignments

1. Locate the property distribution statute for your state and try to answer the following questions based on the statutory language. Note that not all questions will be relevant in all jurisdictions.
   a. Are you in a community property or an equitable jurisdiction state?
   b. Does your state use a dual property or an all-property approach?
   c. How is marital/community property defined? How is separate property defined?
   d. Are there any statutory presumptions?
   e. Is there a cutoff date for the acquisition of marital property?
   f. What factors must a court consider when making a distribution?
2. Review the relevant cases in your jurisdiction to determine what factors the courts seem to think are the most important when allocating property. Write a memo analyzing your findings.
3. Interview an attorney or a paralegal who works in the family law field. Ask him or her about the following:
   ▪ In what proportion is property usually divided between the spouses?
   ▪ Under what circumstances does this vary?
   ▪ What factors do lawyers and judges seem to think are the most important?
   ▪ How are the nonfinancial contributions of spouses with regard to domestic responsibilities viewed? Are they respected as much as financial contributions?
4. The attorney you work for has asked you to draft him a memo setting out the options in the following situation: His client, Ms. Perez, is getting divorced from Mr. Rivera. The parties have two small children, and Ms. Perez will have physical custody. The couple owns a small house. Ms. Perez wishes to remain there while the children are young. In theory, Mr. Rivera has no problem with this, but he's not going to let her do this without receiving what he is entitled to. The house is worth about $150,000, and there is an outstanding mortgage of $120,000. Mr. Rivera has a vested pension plan, but its value has not yet been determined.

   What are all of the possible ways that a settlement could be structured? Set out the advantages and disadvantages of each possible option.

   As part of the memo, the attorney also wants you to draft some preliminary separation agreement language that gives Ms. Perez the right of exclusive use and occupancy of the residence. You should cover as many contingencies as you can.
5. Draft a comprehensive checklist that can be used when working on cases to ensure that all property has been considered.
6. The attorney you work for has asked you to look into how appreciation of premarital property is handled in your state. Her client, Rita Small, came into the marriage with a summer home and a rare stamp

collection. Both assets appreciated in value during the course of the marriage. Although she does not yet have accurate or complete information about the increases in value, you can assume that the increase in the value of the stamp collection is attributable to market forces and the increase in the value of the house is attributable to market forces as well as to improvements that were made by the husband. Write an in-house memo explaining how the appreciation will be classified. Be sure to consider whether your jurisdiction treats passive and active appreciation differently.

7. The judge you work for has asked you to do some research in preparation for a divorce case that includes a dispute over a much-loved family dog. She wants you to do the following:
   a. Determine if there are any statutes in your state that are relevant to determining the legal status of pets.
   b. Determine if there are any cases in your state that would have bearing on this matter—do not limit yourself to divorce cases.
   c. Locate and read at least three articles on the topic, and provide the judge with a summary of the different arguments that are presented in terms of how pets should be treated in a divorce case.

8. The attorney you work for is a bit of a "technophobe" and has very little comprehension of the virtual world. He has recently met with a new client, and the client and her wife apparently have a wide array of what may well be deemed virtual assets. The attorney would like you to write a short factual memo explaining the world of virtual assets to him so he can tackle this brave new arena. Be sure to explain what might be included within the category of virtual assets and why they should potentially be treated as divisible property.

Cases for Analysis

The following case focuses on the question of whether the wife is entitled to an equal share of the husband's inheritance proceeds based on the donative intent of the decedent.

OLESBERG v. OLESBERG
206 Or. App. 496, 136 P.3d 1202 (2006)

ROSENBLUM, J.
Wife appeals from a judgment of dissolution of the parties' 27-year marriage. . . . We . . . conclude that the trial court erred in finding that husband had rebutted the presumption of equal contribution as to the inheritance

and we modify the property division to award wife one-half of the account bearing the inheritance proceeds.

The parties were both 47 years old at the time of trial and in good health. They were married in 1976 and separated in 2001. The parties met in high school and married when husband was in his second year of college in Idaho. While husband completed college, wife worked full time and husband worked part time. In 1978, they moved to Portland so that husband could attend dental school. Wife found a job checking groceries at Safeway and became head checker. Husband's parents helped the parties financially in the early part of their marriage, including payment of tuition and a house down payment. Husband graduated from dental school in 1982 and, in December 1982, the parties jointly purchased a dental practice. For the first few years, the dental practice earned little or no income and wife supported the family with her full-time employment. The dental practice began to turn a profit in 1985 and the parties' income from the practice has increased over the years. Wife worked full time at Safeway until 1985, when their third child was born, at which time she began working three days a week. In 1986, wife quit work to stay home with the children. . . .

From 1987 to 1994, wife managed the household. . . . In 1995, wife took a part-time job, but continued to manage the family's finances and do all the dental practice billing and bookkeeping until 2001, when the parties separated. . . .

After husband's father retired, the parties began sending husband's parents money each month, which the parties considered repayment of college tuition and the house down payment. Additionally, husband's parents had a cabin in Coeur d'Alene, Idaho. To help the parents financially, in 1985, husband and wife—together with husband's sister, Janae, and her husband—purchased the cabin and began making monthly payments on a 10-year contract. Husband's brother did not participate in that transaction. Husband's father passed away in 1996, and husband's mother inherited his estate.

Shortly before the parties separated in 2001, husband's mother died. Her estate consisted of her home, the balance due on the Idaho cabin, and some cash. Husband's sister, Janae, was the personal representative of the estate. She set up an account for each beneficiary—Janae, husband, and their brother Mark—and divided the proceeds of the estate equally among them. The estate forgave $45,000 of indebtedness on the cabin. Husband's inheritance from his mother came to approximately $65,000. Husband kept the money in the same account set up by Janae and has never commingled it with the parties' assets. The balance has grown to $87,000. . . .

The . . . question is whether the trial court erred in failing to award wife an equal share of the account bearing the proceeds of husband's inheritance from his mother. Husband concedes that the inheritance is a marital asset because it was acquired during the marriage and that, like any other gift, it is subject to a rebuttable presumption of equal contribution. ORS 107.105(1)(f); Kunze and Kunze, 337 Ore. 122, 133, 92 P.3d 100 (2004). The presumption is rebutted by evidence that the asset was acquired "free of any contributions from the other spouse." *Kunze*, 337 Ore. at 135.

In *Kunze*, the court held that a finding that the wife "had been the sole object of her aunt's donative intent" overcame the presumption that the husband had contributed equally to the initial acquisition of the inherited asset. 337 Ore. at 143. Since *Kunze*, we held in Tsukamaki and Tsukamaki, 199 Ore. App. 577, 583, 112 P.3d 416 (2005), that, when the marital asset is a gift, one spouse may rebut the presumption of equal contribution by evidence that "the other spouse neither contributed to its acquisition nor was the object of the donative intent." 199 Ore. App. at 583. Thus, the evidence necessary to rebut the presumption of equal contribution in this case is that wife did not contribute to the inheritance and was not the object of husband's mother's donative intent.

Wife contends that she contributed to the acquisition of the inheritance because there is evidence that the inheritance is related in part to funds that wife and husband provided to his parents over the years. We find that husband's inheritance did not bear a direct relationship to past financial support that the parties provided to his parents; rather, it was simply the result of an equal division of the mother's estate among her three children, husband and his two siblings. Thus, we find that wife did not contribute financially to the acquisition of the inheritance.

The remaining question is whether husband established that wife was not an object of his mother's donative intent. The trial court, apparently relying on husband's evidence that the estate was simply divided three ways, found that "there was no donative intent from [husband's mother] to [wife]" and held that husband had rebutted the presumption of equal contribution. Wife contends that the trial court erred, because there is no evidence that husband's mother did not intend for her to benefit from the inheritance.

We agree with wife that to rebut the presumption of equal contribution, it is not sufficient to show simply that the inheritance devolved only to husband and his siblings in equal shares. The fact that the mother's estate was divided three ways among her children does not establish that she had no intention to benefit wife, her daughter-in-law of 25 years. If that evidence were sufficient to overcome the presumption of equal contribution, the presumption would not only be rendered meaningless, but it would also incorrectly place the burden on the nonrecipient spouse to rebut it. See Wilson and Wilson, 155 Ore. App. 512, 516-17, 964 P.2d 1052 (1998) (in determining whether a party has rebutted the presumption, "we consider whether the party seeking to rebut the presumption has produced evidence that his or her spouse was not the object of the donor or devisor's intent and did not otherwise contribute to the acquisition of the gift or inheritance. Mere lack of evidence tending to reinforce the presumption is insufficient." (Citation omitted.)). We conclude that, to defeat the presumption, husband must provide affirmative evidence that wife was not an object of her mother-in-law's donative intent. No such evidence was presented here. Cf. Ahearn and Whittaker, 200 Ore. App. 29, 113 P.3d 439 (2005) (evidence that the husband's parents' gift to the husband was intended to replace property that he had received before the marriage and given without consideration to a sibling established that the husband was sole object of his parents' intent). Thus, we conclude that the presumption of equal contribution was not rebutted.

If the presumption of equal contribution is not rebutted, then, in the absence of other considerations, the appropriate "just and proper" division of that asset is an equal division. *Kunze*, 337 Ore. at 134. We conclude on this record that an equal division of the account bearing the inheritance proceeds is just and proper.

Dissolution judgment modified to award wife . . . an equal share of account bearing proceeds of inheritance; otherwise affirmed.

QUESTIONS

1. Why, under Oregon law, is there no dispute over the fact that the inheritance proceeds are marital rather than separate?
2. Explain the role that the "rebuttable presumption of equal contribution" plays in this case.
3. What evidence does the husband offer to rebut the presumption?
4. What arguments does the wife offer to show equal contribution?
5. What does the court conclude and why?

The following case focuses on classification issues. In deciding if the assets in question are separate or marital, the court focuses on marital effort, the distinction between transmutation and active appreciation, and on the tracing process.

SCHMITZ v. SCHMITZ
88 P.3d 1116 (Alaska 2004)

FABE, Chief Justice.

. . .

II. FACTS AND PROCEEDINGS

A. FACTUAL HISTORY

Michael Schmitz and Christina Schmitz married in Juneau in January 1999. The couple's child, Johnathon, was born in March 1999. While Christina and Michael were married, Christina was Johnathon's primary caregiver. Michael and Christina separated in August 2001.

Michael is a certified public accountant and a partner in the firm of Schmitz & Buck. Michael has owned a fifty percent interest in Schmitz & Buck. . . . In addition to his partnership in Schmitz & Buck, Michael owns a twelve-and-a-half percent share in the Nugget Men's Store. . . . Michael's share in the store was purchased with proceeds from a tort settlement resulting from a car accident. . . .

Michael holds two accounts at First National Bank Alaska. He refers to one account as his "checking" or "regular" account and the second as his "investment" or "business" account. Michael deposited income from his accounting business into both of the accounts. . . .

B. CHARACTERIZATION OF THE COUPLE'S ASSETS AS SEPARATE OR MARITAL

The first step in equitable division of marital property requires the trial court to determine what property is available for distribution; to accomplish this, the trial court must characterize assets as separate or marital property. . . .

1. Michael's Businesses: Schmitz & Buck and the Nugget Men's Store

The trial court found that Michael's separate property, including his interest in the Nugget Men's Store and Schmitz & Buck, remained his separate property because Michael had no intention to transmute the assets from separate to marital. Christina argues that the trial court made two errors in its characterization of the Nugget Men's Store and Schmitz & Buck as separate property. First, she argues that the court erred in applying a transmutation analysis rather than an active appreciation analysis. Second, . . . Christina asserts that Michael spent significant marital time and energy on both. . . . Specifically, Christina argues that Michael worked at Schmitz & Buck seven days a week during tax season . . . and that he worked approximately eleven hours each day during that period. She notes that for the Nugget Men's Store, Michael did the monthly accounting, prepared the monthly financial statements, as well as the business's tax return, and attended the store's annual meeting. . . .

Marital property includes all property acquired during the marriage, "excepting only inherited property and property acquired with separate property which is kept as separate property." We have recognized that a spouse's premarital separate property can become marital through transmutation or active appreciation. Transmutation occurs when a married couple demonstrates an intent, by virtue of their words and actions during marriage, to treat one spouse's separate property as marital property. "Active appreciation occurs when marital funds or marital efforts cause a spouse's separate property to increase in value during the marriage. . . ."

The elements of active appreciation are significantly different from those of transmutation. Transmutation requires intent, as demonstrated through conduct, to change the character of property from separate to marital. To find active appreciation in separate property, the court must make three subsidiary findings: "First, it must find that the separate property in question appreciated during the marriage. Second, it must find that the parties made marital contributions to the property. Finally, the court must find a causal connection between the marital contributions and at least part of the appreciation."

In addressing the question whether the property at issue was separate or marital, the trial court focused only on the theory of transmutation. This focus was overly narrow and should have included an analysis of whether Michael's efforts during the marriage caused the value of his businesses to increase. . . .

As to Schmitz & Buck, Christina proved that Michael spent significant marital time working at the business. . . .

Because the proof of Michael's increased income that Christina was able to present suggests that the business's value may have increased during the marriage, we remand this issue to the superior court, to allow Christina an opportunity to present evidence of the increase in the value of Schmitz & Buck during the marriage.

By contrast, an active appreciation analysis fails on the element of marital contribution when applied to the Nugget Men's Store. The record shows that Michael's involvement with the store was quite limited: He only performed some accounting and tax returns for the store and attended its annual meeting. We cannot say, therefore, that Christina met her burden of proof on the element of marital contribution for the Nugget Men's Store. Accordingly, we affirm the superior court's determination that the Nugget Men's Store is Michael's separate property.

2. The First National Bank Accounts

Christina argues that because Michael deposited money he earned during the marriage into both of his First National Bank accounts, the superior court should have characterized the accounts as marital property. Michael counters that the accounts are comprised in part of his separate property and that commingling of separate and marital funds in the accounts does not transmute the accounts into marital property. He argues that these accounts are his separate property. . . .

Some assets might have been acquired . . . from another asset "through exchange, appreciation, or income." These assets are referred to as secondary property because such an asset requires for its classification the classification of another asset.

To classify secondary assets, courts "must first identify the specific asset from which it was derived (the source asset), and then determine the classification of that asset." This process is referred to as tracing. . . . The process of tracing can . . . be described as a search of sources backward through time until every asset is linked to primary marital or primary separate property. . . .

The party seeking to establish that the property is separate always bears that burden of proof; thus untraceable assets are marital property.

Both parties concede that the bank accounts included both marital and separate property. . . . The record suggests that Michael deposited earnings from his accounting business into his "business" account. The record also suggests that in addition to marital property, Michael also deposited separate property, for example, proceeds from the Nugget Men's Store.

A spouse's separate property does not become untraceable to its separate source merely because it is mixed with marital property in the same secondary asset. However, placing separate property in joint ownership is rebuttable evidence that the owner intended the property to be marital. If evidence is presented that is sufficient to overcome this presumption, tracing can take place.

If, however, the sources can be proved but their respective amounts cannot, the proper ratio cannot be determined. Thus, even when it is known that a mixed secondary asset derived partly from a separate source, if the amount contributed from that source cannot be determined, then the asset cannot be traced and "the unknown amount contributed from the separate source transmutes by commingling and becomes marital property." [W]e remand to the superior court to make findings as to whether the presumption that commingled property is intended to be marital has been rebutted and if so, to make findings recharacterizing the accounts.

QUESTIONS

1. What does the court say the basic distinction is between separate and marital property?
2. Why did the trial court hold that the two businesses remained the separate property of the husband?
3. Why does the court discuss the concepts of appreciation and transmutation—why are they relevant?
4. As discussed by the court, what is the key difference between these two concepts?
5. What does the court conclude with respect to Schmitz & Buck? With respect to Nugget's Men's Store? Why is the result different?
6. What is a "secondary" asset?
7. Explain what the court means by "tracing."
8. What does the court conclude with respect to the bank accounts? Why?

The following case focuses on classification issues. In deciding if the home in question should be classified as marital or separate property, the court looks at a number of factors, including the donative intent of a monetary gift that was used toward the cost of the home and the contribution of each party toward the design and building of the home.

CASTLE v. CASTLE
2018 Miss. App. LEXIS 517 (2018) (en banc)

FAIR, J., for the court:

  After fifteen years of marriage, Mary and Jason Castle separated as a result of Jason's adultery. . . . On appeal, Jason argues that the chancery court erred by classifying a house as a marital asset. The house was intended to serve as the marital home but was still under construction at the time of the separation, and Jason argues that it was his separate property. . . . After review of the record, we find the chancellor acted within his discretion. Thus, we affirm.

FACTS AND PROCEDURAL HISTORY

Mary and Jason married in 1999 in Tuscaloosa, Alabama. At the time, Mary was twenty-three years old, and Jason was twenty-five. During their marriage, the Castles had a son (born in 2001) and two daughters (born in 2002 and 2004).

. . . During the marriage, Mary was a stay-at-home mother and did not work outside the home. The Castles' daughters both have dyslexia and attend regular tutoring outside of school. The daughters also have health issues that require them to see out-of-town doctors. In addition, all three Castle children are involved in extracurricular activities.

Jason began working for his father in the pipeline industry when he was fifteen years old, and he went to work in the industry full-time when he was eighteen years old. In the early years of the parties' marriage, Jason worked for several different pipeline construction companies operating heavy equipment. Eventually he was promoted to foreman. In 2005, Jason began working for his father's company, Progressive Pipeline Inc. (PPI), as a superintendent, and PPI later promoted him to construction manager.

Jason's father, Mike Castle Sr., and two partners formed PPI in 1999. PPI built transmission pipelines throughout the southeastern United States. Eventually, Mike Sr. bought out his two partners.

In 2008, Mike Sr. formed Progressive Pipeline Holdings LLC (PPH), a holding company with seven subsidiaries. Mike Sr. created PPH for estate planning purposes because his three sons could not have afforded to purchase an interest in PPI. At the time it was formed, PPH had little or no book value because it had no significant assets or contracts. Mike Sr. gave Jason . . . a twenty-percent non-voting interest in PPH.

In 2008 and 2009, PPI subcontracted many of its projects to PPH so that PPH could establish a work history, obtain bonding, satisfy state licensing requirements, and develop client relationships. By 2012, PPH had essentially taken over the operations of PPI. Jason worked as a construction manager for PPH.

In 2008, the Castles moved into a four-bedroom, three-bath home in Collinsville. In 2011, Jason and his brother Zachary formed Castle Holdings LLC to acquire 103.5 acres of land near Meridian, where they planned to build homes. Mike Sr. or PPI loaned Castle Holdings approximately $222,525, which covered most or all of the purchase price for the land. Mike Sr. testified that he did not expect his sons to repay the loan and considered the money a gift. . . .

Jason first built a house at 209A Mt. Horeb Road (the 209A house). The 209A house is a two-bedroom, two-bathroom house with approximately 1,800 square feet. Jason and Mary agreed that the 209A house was worth $277,884. At trial, Mary referred to the 209A house as "the barn." She testified that they built the 209A house primarily to store "Jason's toys" and only intended to live in it a short time while they built their "forever home" nearby on the same property. The Castles moved into the 209A house in 2012, at which point they sold their Collinsville home for $365,000.

In May 2014, Zachary signed a warranty deed conveying 56.6 acres of the Castle Holdings property to Jason and Mary as joint tenants with full

rights of survivorship. Jason testified that he did know about the convey-
ance until after Mary filed for the divorce. Zachary did not testify, and
there is no explanation in the record as to why the property was conveyed
from Castle Holdings to Jason and Mary at that time.

The same month that the property was conveyed to them as joint tenants, Mary and Jason began construction of a second home at 209B Mt.
Horeb Road (the 209B house). The 209B house, which was intended to be
the Castles' "forever home," is located only about 600 or 700 feet away
from the 209A house. The 209B house is an 8,237-square-foot, three-story,
five-bedroom, seven-bathroom house with an elevator. Mary and Jason
agreed that the 209B house is worth $1,500,000. Mary referred to the 209B
house as "the castle."

Mary testified that she spent almost two years planning and designing
the 209B house. According to Mary, she "picked out almost every detail of
the whole house," modified some of the floor plan, and "made changes to
[the] layouts of some of the rooms." Mary testified that she spent countless
hours selecting brick, stone, cabinetry, carpet, tile, stains, lighting, hard-
ware, bathroom finishes, and appliances for the home. She also designed
an elaborate staircase in the home.

Mary testified that Jason chose some of the floors, the roof, and an
air conditioner, designed a "safe room" for his guns, and helped design
a bar area in the basement. However, Mary testified that she "did everything else" as far as designing the home. She testified she interacted with
their contractor on an almost daily basis. Jason agreed that Mary helped
to design the house, but he disapproved of many of her choices, which he
considered extravagant. Originally, the account used to pay for construction of the 209B house was a joint account, and Mary wrote most of the
checks for the construction. The account was funded with Jason's distributions from PPH.

In November 2014, Mary discovered that Jason was having an affair.
The Castles separated because of Jason's affair. They briefly reconciled, but
Mary later discovered that Jason had not ended the affair. They separated
again, and in April 2015 Mary filed for divorce on the grounds of adultery
or, in the alternative, irreconcilable differences. . . .

. . . After the couple separated, Jason continued to live in the 209A
house with Mary and the children until December 2015. Jason then moved
into the "castle" at 209B in January 2016. Mary and the children never lived
in that house.

A three-day trial on all remaining issues was held in August 2016.
Jason admitted to the affair during trial.

The chancery court ruled that Jason's interest in PPH was non-marital
property because it was essentially a gift to Jason from Mike Sr. For the same
reasons, the court ruled that distributions from PPH that Jason deposited

in separate bank accounts were Jason's separate property. However, the court found that the 209B house was marital property. The court granted Jason the exclusive use and possession of the 209B house but awarded Mary twenty-five percent of its value in the equitable distribution of the marital estate. . . .

Jason argues that the chancery court erred by classifying the 209B house as a marital asset. . . ..

"[W]hen dealing with property in divorce," the chancery court must first "determine what assets are marital and what assets are nonmarital." Our Supreme Court has "define[d] marital property for the purpose of divorce as being any and all property acquired or accumulated during the marriage." Such assets "are marital assets and are subject to an equitable distribution by the chancellor." *Id.* However, "[p]roperty acquired in a spouse's individual capacity through an inter-vivos gift or inheritance is separate property, even if such property is acquired during the marriage."

"The law presumes that all property acquired or accumulated during marriage is marital property." The party claiming that the asset is separate, nonmarital property has the burden of proof and must overcome the presumption that the asset is marital property. . . .

In this case, the chancery court ruled that Jason failed to rebut the presumption that the 209B house was marital property. On appeal, Jason argues that the 209B house was separate property because it was built on land that was originally purchased by Castle Holdings LLC with money that, in substance, was a gift from Mike Sr. In addition, the construction account was funded by Jason's distributions from PPH, which the chancery court deemed separate property. Finally, Jason emphasizes that the 209B house was not completed until after Mary filed for divorce, so Mary never lived in the home.

It is true that a "gift made to *one spouse* during the marriage remains the separate property of that spouse." However, "[g]ifts may be made to either party to a marriage or to the marital union itself." "Whether a gift was made to one or both spouses is determined by the donor's intent." Deborah H. Bell, *Mississippi Family Law* §6.03[1][a], at 139 (2d ed. 2011). And, "absent clear proof otherwise," gifts to the marital union "are assets of the marital estate."

As discussed above, Jason and Zachary formed an LLC to acquire the property at issue, and the LLC subsequently conveyed the property to Jason and Mary as joint tenants with rights of survivorship. Jason claims that he was unaware that Zachary, acting on behalf of their LLC, conveyed the property to Mary and him. In any event, the formal titling of property is not determinative of its marital or separate character; the chancery court must determine whether, in substance, the property should be treated as marital or separate.

The evidence at trial showed that Jason acquired the property specifically because he and Mary planned to build their marital home on the property. The Castles built the smaller 209A house as a temporary house, and the family lived there for over two years prior to the separation. During that time, they began construction on the much larger 209B house, only 600 or 700 feet away from the 209A house. The Castles never intended for the 209A house to be the permanent marital home and always intended to move into the 209B house as soon as it was finished. Moreover, although Jason complained that Mary spent extravagantly on the design and furnishings of the 209B house, he acknowledged that Mary was extensively involved in the design and construction of the house. There is no dispute that the 209B house would have been the marital home but for Jason's continued infidelity, which led to the breakdown of the marriage and the divorce.

The chancery court found that the land on which the Castles built the 209B home was essentially "a gift from [Mike Sr.] through Castle Holdings[] LLC," and the land was conveyed to Mary and Jason as joint tenants with rights of survivorship in 2014, when the Castles had been married for over fourteen years. The court also found that "Mary and Jason jointly participated in the planning and designing of [the house] as their anticipated marital home." The court acknowledged that the house was constructed using distributions from PPH, which the court deemed Jason's separate property, but the court found that "Mary contributed her time and effort in the construction of the house before construction started and after construction started." On these facts, the court found that "Jason failed to rebut the presumption that the [land and home] are marital property." Therefore, the court found that the 209B house was marital property subject to equitable distribution.

We cannot say that the chancery court clearly or manifestly erred by finding that the 209B house was marital property. To begin with, although Jason emphasizes that the land on which the house was built was essentially a "gift" from Mike Sr., that is not the end of the inquiry. The gift was made three years before the parties separated, and the clear purpose of the gift was to allow Jason *and Mary* to build a new home for their family. Under the circumstances, the chancery court properly treated the gift as a gift to the marital union, not as a gift of separate property to Jason alone. . . .

Moreover, it is clear that the parties *both* contributed time and efforts to the planning, design, and construction of the 209B house. The chancery court found that most or all of the funds used to build the house had been Jason's separate property; however, when Jason contributed those funds toward the construction of the marital home, the funds lost their separate character. . . . The chancery court had discretion to give Jason credit for his monetary contributions to the home, and the court exercised that discretion by awarding Jason seventy-five percent of the value of the home. But the fact that the home was built with separate funds does not automatically make it separate property. . . .

Finally, we agree with the chancery court that it is not dispositive that Mary never moved into the 209B house. Jason and Mary planned to move into the 209B house as their marital home, and Mary and the children lived in the 209A house—only 600 or 700 feet away—throughout the construction of the 209B house. The 209A house is on the same property as the 209B house, and it was only intended to serve as a temporary house for the family. It appears that the Castles planned that the 209A house would have served as a guest house or for storage of "Jason's toys" once the 209B house was complete. There is no dispute that the 209A house is marital property, and we see no reason that the adjacent 209B house should or must be treated differently.

As stated above, we begin with a presumption "that all property acquired during marriage is equitable property." On the facts of this case, we cannot say that the chancery court clearly or manifestly erred by finding that Jason failed to rebut that presumption with respect to the 209B house.

QUESTIONS

1. What intent did the parties have when they began construction of the 209B home?
2. What contributions did each spouse make toward the design and purchase of the home?
3. What did the court say about the donative intent behind the gift of land made by the husband's father?
4. What did the court say about the nature of the separate funds that the husband contributed to the construction of the house?
5. What weight did the court give to the fact that the wife never lived in the house under dispute?

Endnotes

1. *See* Judith T. Younger, Marital Regimes: A Story of Compromise and Demoralization, Together with Criticism and Suggestions for Reform, 67 Cornell L. Rev. 45, 61-64 (1981).

2. Wisconsin also is now generally regarded as a community property state due to statutory changes initiated in 1986.

3. *See* James R. Ratner, Distribution of Marital Assets in Community Property Jurisdictions: Equitable Doesn't Equal Equal, 72 La. L. Rev. 21 (2011).

4. For detail, *see* Margaret M. Mahoney, The Equitable Distribution of Marital Debts, 79 UMKC L. Rev. 445 (2010).

5. For the sake of simplicity, the term "marital property" includes what would be referred to as "community property" in community property jurisdictions.

6. This word, coined by Willard H. DaSilva, conveys wonderfully the shift in the meaning of the word "property." Willard H. DaSilva, *Property Subject to Equitable Distribution*, *in* Valuation and Distribution of Marital Property (John P. McCahey ed., 1985).

7. For a review of some of the research on the benefits of pets, *see* Dana Casciotti, Pets and Health: The Impact of Companion Animals (2014), http://center4research.org/healthy-living-prevention/pets-and-health-the-impact-of-companion-animals (accessed Dec. 27, 2015).

8. Elizabeth Paek, Fido Seeks Full Membership in the Family: Dismantling the Property Classification of Companion Animals by Statute, 25 Haw. L. Rev. 481, 489 (2003); Rebecca Huss, Separation, Custody and Estate Planning Issues Relating to Companion Animals, 74 U. Colo. L. Rev. 181, 198-199 (2003); David Favre, Living Property: A New Status for Animals Within the Legal System, 93 Marq. L. Rev. 1021 (2010); Tabby T. McLain, Adapting the Child's Best Interest Model to Custody Determinations of Companion Animals, 6 J. Animal L. 151 (2010); Christopher D. Seps, Treating Pets as Persons in Tort and Custody Disputes, 2010 U. Ill. L. Rev. 1339.

9. Bennett v. Bennett, 650 So. 2d 109, 111 (Fla. Dist. Ct. App. 1995).

10. *Id.*

11. Desanctis v. Prichard 803 A.2d 230, 233 (Pa. Super. Ct. 2002).

12. Hamet v. Baker, 2014 VT 39, 97 A.3d 461, 465 (2014).

13. *Id.* at 463. In light of the fact that the state's equitable distribution permits the consideration of relevant factors beyond those enumerated in the statute (which, it should be noted, is the case in many jurisdictions) the court concluded that where pets are concerned "the welfare of the animal and the emotional connection between the animal and each spouse" can be taken into account in fashioning an award. *Id.* at 464.

14. Whitmore v. Whitmore, 2011 Va. App. LEXIS 57 (unpublished opinion).

15. *Id.*

16. Note that the concept of vesting applies only to the employer's contribution; an employee is always vested with respect to his or her own contribution.

For a good discussion of pension plans, *see* Mary E. O'Connell, On the Fringe: Rethinking the Link Between Wages and Benefits, 67 Tul. L. Rev. 1421 (1993); Susan J. Prather, Characterization, Valuation, and Distribution of Pensions at Divorce, 15 J. Am. Acad. Matrimonial Law 443 (1998).

17. Bratcher v. Bratcher, 26 S.W.3d 797, 801 (Ky. Ct. App. 2000), citing Thomasian v. Thomasian, 79 Md. App. 188, 556 A.2d 675, 681 (Md. Ct. Spec. App. 1989).

18. Cardona v. Castro, 2014 CO 3, 316 P.3d 626, 628 (2014).

19. *Id.* at 631, citing Thomasian v. Thomasian, 79 Md. App. 188, 566 A.2d 675, 681 (Md. Ct. Spec. App. 1989).

20. *Id.* at 633-634.

21. *See generally* Christopher A. Tiso, Present Positions on Professional Goodwill: More Focus or Simply More Hocus Pocus?, 20 J. Am. Acad. Matrimonial Law 51 (2006).

22. For a discussion about whether "celebrity goodwill" should be treated as an asset that is subject to division in a divorce, *see* Erika Evans, A "Little Ditty About Jack and Diane": Why Jackie's Good Name Should Be Considered Community Property in California Under the Concept of Celebrity Goodwill, 17 Chap. L. Rev. 633 (2014); Paloma Peracchio, The Value of Creative Professionals in the Entertainment Capital of the World: Why "Celebrity Goodwill" Should Be a Divisible Community Property Interest in California Divorces, 28 Loy. L.A. Ent. L. Rev. 1229 (2007/2008).

23. Joshua Fairfield, Virtual Property, 85 B.U. L. Rev. 1017, 1058-1059 (2009).

24. *Id.* at 1059.

25. In this regard, it should be noted that a number of states have enacted laws that treat social networking and e-mail sites as personal probate property for estate purposes, thus potentially allowing survivor access. *See* Lillian Marie Grapper, "Yours, Mine, or Ours?": Ownership and Management of Electronic Communication in Community Property Regimes, 18 Tul. J. Tech. & Intell. Prop. 161, 176-177 (2015).

26. Fairfield, *supra* note 23, at 1048.

27. *Id.* at 1053, and 1049-1055.

28. *Id.* at 1054-1055.

29. *See, e.g.,* Grapper, *supra* note 25, at 173-174, and Sally Brown Richardson, Classifying Virtual Property in Community Property Regimes: Are My Facebook Friends Considered Earnings, Profits, Increases in Value, or Goodwill?, 85 Tul. L. Rev. 717, 747 (2011).

30. Thomas E. Crowley III and Stephanie A. Rezents, Premarital Economic Partnerships and the Division of the Marital Estate in Hawaii Divorces, 22 Haw. B.J. 4 (2018).

31. For a discussion of the difficulties inherent in determining the appropriate back-date, *see* Peter Nichols, Backdating Marriage, 105 Calif. L. Rev. 395, 430-434 (2017).

32. Patrick M. Erne, Personal Injury Awards and Divorce: Pennsylvania Should Adopt the Analytical Approach Through Statute to Promote Fairness and Consistency, 23 Widener L.J. 843, 854 (2014).

33. *Id.*

34. A third method, which is of little practical relevance today, is to treat the entire award as the separate property of the injured spouse. This is referred to as the "unitary" approach.

35. *See generally* Joan M. Krauskopf, Classifying Marital and Separate Property: Combinations and Increase in Value of Separate Property, 89 W. Va. L. Rev. 996, 997 (1987).

36. For a detailed analysis of the complexities of tracing, *see* J. Thomas Oldham, Tracing, Commingling, and Transmutation, 23 Fam. L.Q. 219 (1989).

37. *See* Aloysius A. Leopold, "Loss of Earning Capacity" Benefits in the Community Property Jurisdiction—How Do You Figure?, 30 St. Mary's L.J. 367 (1999).

38. For a review of different approaches to the classification of the loss of earning capacity benefits, *see* Leopold, *id.* at 385-397.

39. For an interesting discussion on this topic, *see* J. Thomas Oldham, Should Separate Property Gradually Become Community Property as a Marriage Continues?, 72 La. L. Rev. 127 (2011).

40. *See* Krauskopf, *supra* note 35, at 1008. For a discussion of some of this and other related considerations in relationship to the marital home, *see* Brett R. Turner, Unlikely Partners: The Marital Home and the Concept of Separate Property, 20 J. Am. Acad. Matrimonial Law 69 (2006). On transmutation generally, *see* Oldham, *supra* note 36, ch. 11.

41. *See generally* Brett R. Turner, Theories and Methods for Valuing Marital Assets, 25 J. Am. Acad. Matrimonial Law 1 (2012). *See also* Sean McKendry, Business Valuations and Divorce: An Analysis of Massachusetts' Approach to the "Double-Dip" Dilemma Compared to New York and New Jersey, 15 Suffolk J. Trial & App. Advoc. 247 (2010).

42. *See* Joan Williams, Do Wives Own Half? Winning for Wives After *Wendt*, 32 Conn. L. Rev. 249 (2000).

43. N.J. Rev. Stat. §2A:34-231.

44. This discussion is very general in nature. It does not address valuation issues, the different kinds of private pensions, or the connection between the two. Nor does it include consideration of Social Security benefits. For further information, *see* Stanley W. Welsh and Frank J. Hargrave, Social Security Benefits at Divorce: Avoiding Federal Preemption to Allow Equitable Division of Property at Divorce, 20 J. Am. Acad. Matrimonial Law 285 (2007); Dylan A. Wilde, Obtaining an Equitable Distribution of Retirement Plans in a Divorce Action, 49 S.D. L. Rev. 141 (2003); Elizabeth Barker Brandt, Valuation, Allocation, and Distribution of Retirement Plans at Divorce: Where Are We?, 35 Fam. L.Q. 237 (2001). The following two articles focus on the timely issue of the distribution of military retirement benefits: Patricia K. Hinshaw, Navigating the Uniformed Services Former Spouses' Protection Act, 19 S.C. Law 32 (2008); and Michael T. Flannery, Military Disability Election and the Distribution of Marital Property upon Divorce, 56 Cath. U. L. Rev. 297 (2007).

45. Prior to the Retirement Equity Act (REA), pension funds could not be reached in a divorce because of ERISA's general anti-assignment rule, prohibiting the transfer of an employee's pension funds to a third party. The rules governing distribution of pension funds are complex and must be followed with great care in order for the QDRO to be effective. *See* Margaret R. Cooper, A Family Practitioner's Guide to Overcoming QDRO Phobia, 8 Del. L. Rev. 213 (2006).

46. I.R.C. §1041. *See generally* James A. Fellows, Tax Issues, 40 Real Est. L.J. 218 (2011); Craig D. Bell, Need-to-Know Divorce Tax Law for Legal Assistance Officers, 177 Mil. L. Rev. 213 (2003).

Chapter Nine

Jurisdiction

This chapter focuses on **jurisdiction**, which, stated broadly, refers to the authority of a court to hear and resolve cases. The question of jurisdiction must be carefully considered before a legal action is commenced because the lack of jurisdiction affects the availability and validity of court orders.

Overview of Subject Matter and Personal Jurisdiction

Before looking at the jurisdictional issues that arise in divorce actions, it is important that you understand the basic concepts of subject matter jurisdiction and personal jurisdiction.

Subject Matter Jurisdiction

Subject matter jurisdiction refers to the authority of a court to hear a particular type of dispute. The subject matter jurisdiction of a court is generally established by statute. Some courts, such as a housing court or a juvenile court, are granted limited subject matter jurisdiction and can hear only certain kinds of cases. Other courts, such as a district court, are granted general subject matter jurisdiction and can hear a wide array of criminal and civil matters. In most states, exclusive subject matter jurisdiction over divorce actions—including all collateral issues such as support, property, and custody—is vested in a specialized court commonly known as the family court or the family and probate court.

In contrast to personal jurisdiction, which a party can voluntarily assent to (see below), parties cannot confer subject matter jurisdiction on a court, and judgment that is rendered by a court that lacks subject matter jurisdiction is void.

Personal Jurisdiction

Personal jurisdiction refers to a court's ability to exercise authority over a defendant. The exercise of jurisdiction must conform to the requirements of the due process clause of the fourteenth amendment, which prohibits a state from "depriving any person of life, liberty or property" without providing fair procedures, such as notice and the opportunity to be heard. The requirement of procedural fairness has also been interpreted to mean that a state may not exercise authority over a defendant who lacks a sufficient relationship with that state. Accordingly, considerations of personal jurisdiction are significant in cases involving parties who live in different states. To ensure that the court has personal jurisdiction over the defendant, the plaintiff can always file the action in the state where the defendant lives, but this is more expensive, time consuming, and inconvenient.

Consistent with the due process clause, states can acquire personal jurisdiction over a defendant based on domicile, minimum contacts, consent, or presence.

1. *Domicile.* States have personal jurisdiction over all persons who are domiciled within its borders. **Domicile** means that the state is someone's permanent home—the place they leave from and return to. It is important to be aware of the distinction between "domicile" and "residence." A person may have several places of residence, such as a college dorm or one's family home, but only one domicile (one's "permanent" home).[1]
2. *Minimum contacts.* A state may exercise personal jurisdiction over a nonresident defendant who has sufficient **minimum contacts** with the state such that it is not unfair to require him or her to return to the state and respond to a lawsuit there.

   To implement this minimum contacts rule, most states have enacted what are known as **long-arm statutes**. These statutes generally specify the kinds of contacts that will give rise to personal jurisdiction and typically include the following contacts: transacting business within the state, owning property within the state, or committing a tortious act within the state. A few states have elected not to enumerate the qualifying contacts but instead employ statutory language to the effect that the state will permit the exercise of jurisdiction to the fullest extent possible under the due process clause.

   A number of states have also enacted special long-arm provisions for use in family law cases. Here, the assertion of jurisdiction is often premised on the fact that the state was the marital domicile for a period of time preceding the filing of the divorce action. Other provisions are framed more broadly and tie the exercise of jurisdiction to the maintenance of an ongoing relationship with a person located in that state or to the payment of support; however, these contacts must be of a sufficient nature to satisfy the fairness requirements of the due process clause. Additionally, all states have enacted the Uniform Interstate Family Support Act (UIFSA), which contains a broad long-arm provision for the assertion of jurisdiction over nonresident defendants in support matters.

3. *Consent.* A nonresident may consent to jurisdiction and thereby agree to submit him- or herself to the authority of the court.
4. *Presence.* A state can exercise personal jurisdiction over a nonresident who is physically present and personally served with a summons within that state.

Jurisdiction and the Divorce Action

Turning to the divorce action, jurisdictional concepts are best understood if examined in relationship to specific aspects of the proceeding, as different considerations come into play at different points in the process. Specifically, we will look at the jurisdictional standards that govern the dissolution of the marital relationship, the award of support, the distribution of property, and the determination of custody.[2]

It thus goes without saying that in the course of your work as a paralegal you must always be attuned to jurisdictional considerations and any relevant time periods within which jurisdiction must be asserted. If you are responsible for interviewing clients, it is essential that you inquire into the location of all parties as this can have critical consequences for your client.

Does the Court Have Jurisdiction to Dissolve the Marriage?

Having just set out the importance of personal jurisdiction over a party in order to exercise authority over him or her, we immediately bump up against the well-worn axiom that for every rule, there is an exception. In this instance, divorce provides the exception because in most, if not all, states, a court can dissolve a marriage even if it does not have personal jurisdiction over the defendant so long as the plaintiff is domiciled in that state.

Thus, when it comes to divorce, it is the plaintiff's relationship with the "forum" state (the state in which the action is filed) that matters. The rationale for this domicile rule is captured by the following passage from a 1942 U.S. Supreme Court decision:

> Each state as a sovereign has a rightful and legitimate concern in the marital status of persons domiciled within its borders. The marriage relation creates problems of large social importance. Protection of off-spring, property interests, and the enforcement of marital responsibilities are but a few of the commanding problems in the field of domestic relations with which the state must deal. Thus it is plain that each state . . . can alter within its own borders the marriage status of the spouse domiciled there, even though the other spouse is absent.[3]

According to this reasoning, a relationship with the defendant is not necessary because states have an overriding interest in the marital status of persons living within their borders.[4]

If a spouse is not actually domiciled in a state, but has gone there for the purpose of obtaining a divorce, the defendant-spouse may be able to attack the validity of the divorce judgment for lack of jurisdiction. This right is generally limited to a spouse who did not receive notice of the action and therefore did not have an opportunity to raise jurisdictional objections during the divorce proceeding.

Before leaving the topic of a court's authority to dissolve a marriage, a brief word about the dissolution of same-sex marriages is in order. Prior to the Supreme Court's decision in Obergefell v. Hodges (see Chapter 1), states that did not permit same-sex marriage or recognize the validity of marriages that were entered into in a sister state, generally refused to allow a same-sex couple to dissolve their union within the jurisdiction based on the view that doing so would implicitly recognize the existence of the underlying marriage in contravention of state law. However, now that marriage equality is the law of the land, so too is divorce equality, and a party who is seeking to dissolve a marriage to a same-sex partner should have equal access to the courts in all 50 states.

Does the Court Have Jurisdiction to Award Support?

As discussed above, jurisdiction to dissolve a marriage is based on domicile; personal jurisdiction over the defendant is not required. However, the jurisdictional rule is different where spousal and child support is involved; a state must have personal jurisdiction over a defendant in order to adjudicate support rights. Accordingly, it is possible that a state would have the authority to dissolve a marriage but lack the authority to enter a support award. This is sometimes referred to as a **divisible divorce**.

This, however, is where long-arm statutes come into play. These statutes permit a state to assert its authority over a nonresident within the fairness requirements of the due process clause, and many states authorize the assertion of long-arm jurisdiction over a nonresident when that state had been the marital domicile of the parties. Often, this is a time-limited option, and personal jurisdiction will continue for only a fixed period of time, perhaps for a year or two, after the individual has left the state. Once this time period has expired, the state loses its ability to assert personal jurisdiction over the defendant unless there are other independent qualifying bases.

In addition to state long-arm statutes, the Uniform Interstate Family Support Act (UIFSA), which was discussed in Chapter 6, also contains a long-arm provision that a state can use to acquire personal jurisdiction over a nonresident defendant in order to establish a spousal or child support order. Under the Act, this state will retain continuing exclusive jurisdiction to modify the order so long as the support obligor, the support obligee, or the child for whose benefit support is being paid continues to live in that state. In addition, in states that have adopted the 2001 amended version of UIFSA, the parties may consent to continued jurisdiction in this state even if everyone has moved out.[5]

UIFSA sets out the following eight grounds for the exercise of personal jurisdiction over a nonresident defendant:

1. The defendant is personally served within the state.
2. The defendant consents to jurisdiction.
3. The defendant at one time resided with the child in the state.
4. The defendant resided in the state at one time and provided "prenatal expenses or support for the child."
5. The child lives in a state as a result of the parent's "acts or directives."
6. The defendant "engaged in sexual intercourse in the state" that may have led to the child's conception.
7. The defendant "asserted paternity in the putative father registry."
8. Where there is any other basis for the state's exercise of jurisdiction.[6]

All of these jurisdictional grounds are available in child support cases, but only grounds one, two, and eight are available for the assertion of personal jurisdiction over a nonresident in spousal support cases.

Does the Court Have Jurisdiction to Divide Property?

The jurisdictional rules regarding property distribution are more complex than they are with respect to support and will be set out as a series of general principles:

1. As a foundational matter, jurisdiction is not premised upon domicile as it is for the divorce itself.

2. If the court has personal jurisdiction over the defendant, it may effectuate a division of all property located within its borders.

3. Even if a court lacks personal jurisdiction over a defendant, it may be able to effectuate a division of property based on its authority over property located within its borders. This is known as **in rem jurisdiction**. As a general rule, to satisfy due process requirements, in rem jurisdiction requires a connection between the underlying cause of action and the claims to the property—a connection that would be satisfied in the divorce context. (Some commentators have questioned the fairness of this rule, and we thus may see a gradual shift to a minimum contacts rule. As always, you should check the status of your state's jurisdictional requirements when it comes to dividing property in a divorce with a nonresident defendant.)

4. Even if it has personal jurisdiction over the defendant, a court cannot directly affect title to property that is located outside the state. However, it may be able to accomplish this result indirectly by ordering the defendant to convey title to the property. In short, based on its authority over the defendant, a court can require him or her to take actions that affect how the property is held, even though the court is unable to affect title directly.

Does the Court Have Jurisdiction to Determine Custody?

Traditionally, most states exercised jurisdiction over child custody matters based on the physical presence of the child within its borders. Although this rule usually meant the court that granted the divorce had jurisdiction over the initial custody determination, it also served to encourage a dissatisfied spouse to remove his or her children to a new state in order to relitigate the issue in hope of a more favorable outcome. In addition to encouraging parental removals, this approach often resulted in conflicting decrees, creating an enforcement nightmare.

In 1968, prompted by this jurisdictional morass, the National Conference of Commissioners on Uniform State Laws (NCCUSL) approved the Uniform Child Custody Jurisdiction Act (UCCJA) in the hope that consistent jurisdictional standards would deter the removal or kidnapping of children, eliminate interstate jurisdictional competition, and prevent states from relitigating custody decisions from other states. All states have since adopted the UCCJA, although some states have modified the uniform provisions. In 1980, in the face of continued parental removals and interstate jurisdictional conflicts, Congress passed the Parental Kidnapping Prevention Act (PKPA)[7] to close some of the gaps left open by the UCCJA. In 1997, in light of ongoing jurisdictional complexities and inconsistencies, the National Conference adopted the Uniform Child Custody Jurisdiction and Enforcement Act (UCCJEA), which revised the UCCJA.[8] As of December

31, 2018, the UCCJEA has been adopted in all states except Massachusetts. Where adopted, it replaces the UCCJA. However, it is important to have an understanding of both Acts, as you may encounter prior cases in your work that were decided under the UCCJA.

This chapter provides you with a basic overview of key jurisdictional rules; however, you should be aware that the Acts contain many other important rules, such as those pertaining to notice and disclosure, that are not addressed here. Moreover, the discussion does not cover the array of differences and potential conflicts between the Acts, nor does it discuss other laws that might come into play in an interstate custody case, such as the full faith and credit provisions of the Violence Against Women Act (VAWA).[9] In light of these complexities, it is very important that when conducting a client interview, you elicit detailed information about the present and past locations of both parties and the children as this can have important jurisdictional implications. Bear in mind that interstate custody cases are among the most complex in the family law field and contain many traps for the unaware.[10]

Jurisdictional Requirements Under the UCCJA and the UCCJEA

In this section, we consider the four jurisdictional bases for **initial custody determinations** under the UCCJA and the UCCJEA: (1) home state, (2) significant connection, (3) emergency, and (4) last resort.[11] An important consideration underlying these Acts is that in contrast to the traditional approach, the mere physical presence of a child in a state is not sufficient to confer jurisdiction; in fact, with the exception of emergency jurisdiction, the physical presence of a child, although preferred, is not an essential prerequisite to a state's assumption of jurisdiction.

Initial Custody Determinations

Home State Jurisdiction.   A state that is or has been the child's home may assert **home state jurisdiction** over a custody dispute. A home state is the state in which a child has lived for six continuous months or, if younger than six months, has lived in from birth. Temporary absences from the state do not stop the running of the clock but are included in the time computation.

A state may exercise jurisdiction if it is the child's home state at the commencement of the custody proceeding or if it was the child's home state within six months prior to the commencement of the proceeding. Once a state acquires "home state" status, it can retain that status for six months after the departure of the child so long as a parent or a parent substitute remains in that state.

Significant Connection Jurisdiction.   A state may exercise **significant connection jurisdiction** in situations where it has a significant connection with the child and at least one contestant, and substantial evidence is available in that state that is relevant to the merits of the custody determination.

Comparing the Relationship Between Home State and Significant Connection Jurisdictions in the UCCJA and the UCCJEA.   Under the UCCJA, "home state" and "significant connection" jurisdictions were the most important jurisdictional bases, and because the Act did not expressly prioritize between them, it was possible for two states to claim jurisdiction at the same time. For example, let's assume that a couple who has lived in state Y separated. Dad then moved to state X with the couple's daughter, who is ten years old, and Mom remained in state Y. Eight months later, Dad files for divorce and requests custody of the child. At this point, home state jurisdiction has shifted from state Y to state X because the child has lived there for the six months prior to the filing of the action. However, because the child had spent most of her life in state Y, under the UCCJA, it could have claimed significant connection jurisdiction. Importantly, however, the UCCJEA closes this loophole (as does PKPA, which is discussed below) by prioritizing home state jurisdiction. Under the UCCJEA, a state may exercise significant connection jurisdiction only where there is no home state, or the home state declines jurisdiction. Thus, in our above example, state Y could not claim significant connection jurisdiction because X is now the home state, unless state X declined to hear the case.

Emergency Jurisdiction.   A state may exercise **emergency jurisdiction** where the child is physically present in the state and has been abandoned or needs emergency protection from abuse or neglect. Although the child must be physically present, the endangerment need not have occurred within that state. Courts are generally cautious when proceeding under this section and will generally assume emergency jurisdiction only in "extraordinary circumstances." Also, most courts will assume emergency jurisdiction only on a temporary basis to stabilize the situation and will then refer the case back to the state with either home state or significant connection jurisdiction.

Comparing Emergency Jurisdiction in the UCCJA and the UCCJEA in Domestic Violence Cases.   The UCCJA was silent about spousal abuse, which thus generally resulted in the refusal of states to grant emergency jurisdiction in situations where a parent had fled to escape abuse in the absence of direct harm to the child, even though (as discussed in Chapter 5) bearing witness to violence can be devastating to children. Under the UCCJEA, however, emergency jurisdiction has been broadened to include situations in which it is necessary in an emergency "to protect the child because the child, or a sibling or parent of the child, is subjected to or threatened with mistreatment or abuse."[12]

Last Resort Jurisdiction.   Last, and in this case least, a state that does not meet the requirements of any other section may assume jurisdiction if no other state has or is willing to do so, and it is in the best interest of the child for it to do so. This **last resort jurisdiction** is subsidiary in nature to the others, and is rarely invoked. An example of when it might be used is where a child has moved around so frequently that no state qualifies as the home state or has a significant connection to the child.

Modification Jurisdiction

Although an important goal of the UCCJA was to limit the ability of states to modify custody determinations of other states to prevent the proliferation of potentially conflicting orders, as with initial determination jurisdiction, it was possible that two states could simultaneously assert **modification jurisdiction**, sometimes referred to as **continuing jurisdiction**, thus resulting in potentially conflicting custody orders. As with the exercise of initial custody jurisdiction, the UCCJEA has closed this loophole (as does PKPA) by providing for continuing, exclusive modification jurisdiction in the initial state (subject to the emergency jurisdiction exception) until one of two determinations are made: (1) the initial state determines that it no longer has jurisdiction because it lacks a significant connection to the case and substantial evidence is no longer available there, or (2) it is established that neither the child nor either parent "presently resides" there.[13]

Even still, however, some confusion remains, as states have interpreted the term "presently resides" in a variety of different ways when determining whether or not a state still has continuing and exclusive modification jurisdiction. In this regard, it should be noted that this is particularly sticky given that, as explained by the Supreme Court of Colorado in the case of Brandt v. Brandt, while

> it is clear from the statute that only a court of the issuing state can decide that it has lost jurisdiction due to an erosion of a 'significant connection' between the child and the state . . . it is equally clear that a court in either the issuing state or any other state may divest the issuing state of jurisdiction by making a determination that the child and both parents do not "presently reside" there.[14]

Thus, for example, the *Brandt* court held that a determination as to whether or not a party still "presently resides" in a state "involves an application of a totality of the circumstances test" with the weighing of factors, such as the "length and reasons for the parents' and the child's absence from the state" and their "intent in departing from the state and returning to it."[15]

According to one commentator who reviewed court decisions from across the country, the opinions "are mostly ad hoc decisions, reflecting nothing of a consensus" on how to determine if a party "presently resides" within a state.[16] As discussed, it is thus possible that a court in one state might conclude that a party "presently resides" in a state based on the fact that she or he continues to own a house there even if she or he now lives elsewhere, while another might conclude that the maintenance of a home within a state does not mean that a party "presently resides" there if she or he is currently living someplace else.[17]

Declining Jurisdiction

In addition to determining when a state may properly assume jurisdiction over a custody dispute, the UCCJEA encourages states to decline jurisdiction under certain circumstances (as in the UCCJA). Based on the doctrine of *forum non conveniens*, states are encouraged to decline jurisdiction if it is an inconvenient forum and another state is in a better position to hear the case. Further, based on the "clean hands" doctrine, states are urged to refuse jurisdiction where the petitioner has engaged in wrongful conduct such as improperly removing a child from the home state. However, a parent who has fled a state with a child for good cause, such as to escape from violence, should not be penalized by this provision. In this regard, the UCCJEA makes clear that as long as the emergency jurisdiction requirements are met, a state may not decline jurisdiction based on the conduct of the petitioner.[18]

Deployed Parents. In 2012, the National Conference of Commissioners on Uniform State Laws approved the Uniform Deployed Parents Custody and Visitation Act (UDPCVA) to address the "wide variability in the ways that states handle child custody and visitation issues that arise when service members are deployed"—a problem that is made more complicated by the fact that these cases often involve two states due to the "mobile nature of military service."[19] In addition to a number of substantive provisions, including, for example, that a parent's past or future deployment should not be taken into account when determining the child's best interest, absent a showing that it has a "material effect" on his or her well-being, the Act seeks to avoid jurisdictional conflicts by declaring that deployment does not alter a service member's residence under the UCCJEA. To date, fewer than half the states have actually adopted the UDPCVA, although many states are currently considering adopting it or similar legislation.[20]

Jurisdictional Requirements of PKPA

As we have seen, the UCCJA did not resolve the problem of interstate jurisdictional conflicts. Accordingly, in 1980, Congress enacted the Parental Kidnapping and Prevention Act (PKPA). PKPA requires states to give full faith and credit to custody decrees of other states if they conform to PKPA's jurisdictional requirements. Thus, states must enforce and cannot modify conforming decrees from other states unless certain conditions (discussed below) are met.

Like the UCCJEA, PKPA has four jurisdictional bases: home state, significant connection, emergency, and last resort. As with the UCCJEA, PKPA prioritizes home state jurisdiction. Accordingly, for a decree to be enforceable under PKPA, it can assume significant connection jurisdiction only if no other state qualifies as the home state; the two are not alternative jurisdictional bases. If a state does assume jurisdiction based on its connection with the case where another state qualifies as the home state, the decree will not be entitled to interstate recognition in other states. PKPA also vests exclusive, continuing jurisdiction in the initial state so long as a parent or the child remains there, and the state has jurisdiction under its own laws. So long as this state has jurisdiction, no other state may modify its decree. Modification jurisdiction shifts only when everyone has moved away from the decree state (or it declines jurisdiction) and another state can satisfy PKPA's jurisdictional requirement.

In sum, the hope is that PKPA (and now also the UCCJEA), by giving priority to the home state and vesting continuing jurisdiction in a single state, will eliminate the final vestiges of interstate competition in the custody arena. However, due to the complex legal and factual nature of these cases, true interstate harmony is unlikely in the foreseeable future.

International Child Abduction

In addition to the complex jurisdictional issues that are raised by custody disputes involving two or more states, the process of globalization with the corresponding increase in transnational migration makes it more likely that disputes over children will be played out globally. Accordingly, in addition to controlling the jurisdictional rules in interstate cases, the UCCJEA is now also applicable to cases involving child custody determinations from other countries. Under the Act, courts are directed to treat a foreign country "as if it were a State of the United States" and are accordingly to recognize and enforce a "child-custody determination made in a foreign country under factual circumstances in substantial compliance with jurisdictional standards" of the

UCCJEA.[21] The only exception to this requirement is if the "child custody law of a foreign country violates fundamental principles of human rights."[22]

On an international level, many countries have been particularly concerned about the importance of establishing common legal standards for the handling of cases in which a parent is charged with the wrongful removal of a child to another country, as the return process has historically been quite haphazard. Accordingly, in 1980, the Hague Conference on Private International Law (the Hague Conference is a global intergovernmental organization whose primary purpose is to work for the "progressive unification" of the rules of private international law)[23] approved a multilateral treaty, known as the Hague Convention on the Civil Aspects of International Child Abduction (Convention). The Convention "seeks to protect children from the harmful effects of abduction and retention across international boundaries by providing a procedure to bring about their prompt return."[24]

Similar to PKPA and the UCCJEA, the Convention seeks to deter parents from removing a child to another jurisdiction with the hope of obtaining a more favorable custody outcome. To this end, for the purpose of determining custody, jurisdictional priority is vested in the country that is a child's "habitual residence"—a concept that is doctrinally similar to that of "home state" jurisdiction. Despite its centrality, the Convention does not define the term "habitual residence," and there is currently a split in the federal circuits over how it is to be determined. Some circuits look at the issue from the perspective of the child. As one court put it, "a child's habitual residence is the place where he or she has been physically present for an amount of time sufficient for acclimatization and which has a 'degree of settled purpose' from the child's perspective."[25] However, other circuits look at the issue from the perspective of the parents and seek to determine what their shared intent was regarding what was to be the child's place of habitual residence.

In brief, if a parent removes a child to another country in violation of the "left-behind" parent's custodial rights, he or she can file a legal action seeking the return of the child.[26] If the court determines that the child was removed from a country that is his or her place of "habitual residence," it can order the prompt return of the child, unless the parent who took the child can justify the removal based upon the limited exceptions provided in the Convention, such as that the "left-behind" parent consented to the removal, or that the child "objects to being returned and has attained an age and degree of maturity at which it is appropriate to take account of its views."[27]

A parent may also seek to avoid having to return the child through proof that "there is a grave risk that his or her return would expose the child to physical or psychological harm or otherwise place the child in an intolerable situation."[28] Most commonly, this provision has been invoked by mothers who have fled domestic violence. Here too there is a split among the circuits as to whether violence directed toward a parent meets the grave risk of harm to the *child* requirement. While some circuits have recognized that proximity or exposure to violence against a parent does pose a serious potential risk to the physical and/or mental well-being of a child so as to meet the grave risk standard, others have found the link to be too attenuated.[29]

It is important to be aware that a hearing held pursuant to the Convention is intended to address the narrow question of whether the removal was wrongful and thus whether the child should be returned home. Under the terms of the Convention, the court making this determination is precluded from deciding the merits of the custody case, unless it determines that the removal was not wrongful, and that the child may remain in that country.

Chapter Summary

Broadly stated, jurisdiction refers to the authority of a court to hear a case and render a binding decree. More specifically, subject matter jurisdiction refers to the authority of a court to hear specific types of cases, while personal jurisdiction refers to a court's authority over a defendant. Personal jurisdiction can be based on domicile, minimum contacts, consent, or physical presence. Long-arm statutes allow states to assert personal jurisdiction over nonresident defendants who have sufficient minimum contacts with the forum state. The assertion of personal jurisdiction must satisfy the fairness requirement of the due process clause.

Jurisdiction to dissolve the marriage is usually based on domicile; personal jurisdiction over the defendant is not required. However, a court cannot order a defendant to pay support if it does not have personal jurisdiction over him or her. Personal jurisdiction may be asserted over a nonresident through the long-arm provisions of UIFSA or state jurisdictional statute. Where property is concerned, a distribution can be effectuated based either on personal jurisdiction over the defendant or on the court's in rem authority over property located within its borders.

Jurisdiction over child custody disputes is determined by the UCCJEA (in all states but Massachusetts) and PKPA. These Acts respond to the earlier "physical presence" rule, which encouraged parental abductions and created enforcement nightmares. These Acts establish four jurisdictional bases for when a state may assert jurisdiction over a custody dispute: home state, significant connection, emergency, and last resort, with priority given to home state jurisdiction. The UCCJEA and PKPA vest continuing exclusive jurisdiction in the home state until certain conditions are met; PKPA also requires states to give full faith and credit to conforming custody decrees from other states. In the global arena, the Hague Convention on the Civil Aspects of International Child Abduction likewise seeks to deter the wrongful removal of children and to ensure their prompt return to their place of "habitual residence," absent extenuating circumstances.

Key Terms

Jurisdiction	Initial Custody Determinations
Subject Matter Jurisdiction	Home State Jurisdiction
Personal Jurisdiction	Significant Connection Jurisdiction
Domicile	Emergency Jurisdiction
Minimum Contacts	Last Resort Jurisdiction
Long-Arm Statutes	Modification Jurisdiction
Divisible Divorce	Continuing Jurisdiction
In Rem Jurisdiction	

Review Questions

1. Broadly defined, what is jurisdiction?
2. What is subject matter jurisdiction?
3. Explain the concept of personal jurisdiction. What are the ways in which a court can obtain personal jurisdiction over a defendant?
4. What is a long-arm statute?
5. What is the jurisdictional basis for dissolving a marriage?
6. What criticisms have been raised about this approach?
7. Explain the jurisdictional role of UIFSA in support cases.
8. What is meant by the term "divisible divorce"?
9. Explain the jurisdictional concepts that are relevant to the distribution of property.
10. Traditionally, what has been the basis for the exercise of jurisdiction over a child custody dispute? What problems did this create?
11. What are the four jurisdictional bases under the UCCJEA and PKPA? Why were these laws enacted?
12. Explain the concept of continuing, exclusive modification jurisdiction under PKPA. When is that jurisdiction lost?
13. Under what circumstances do the UCCJA and the UCCJEA encourage states to decline jurisdiction?
14. Under PKPA, when must a state enforce the decree of another state?
15. Under PKPA, when can a state modify the decree of another state?
16. Under PKPA, at what point does the continuing jurisdiction of the decree state terminate?

17. What would be the result if a new state modified a decree where the decree state had continuing jurisdiction?
18. What is the Hague Convention on the Civil Aspects of International Child Abduction?
19. Pursuant to the Convention, on what grounds can a parent try to justify the removal of a child from his or her place of "habitual residence"?

Discussion Questions

1. PKPA's continuing jurisdiction rule has been criticized as favoring stability over the needs of children because it can vest exclusive jurisdiction in a state that has lost any meaningful relationship with the child. Do you think the Act has gone too far? Should a state with no present connection with a child have modification jurisdiction? How do you accommodate the goals of flexibility and predictability?
2. Do you think the emergency jurisdiction provision of the UCCJEA might encourage parents to flee with children in the absence of a genuine emergency situation in order to try and gain an advantage in a custody dispute? Is there another way to protect the needs of victims of violence?

Assignments

1. Using the appropriate digest, find all the cases from your state that involve an interstate custody dispute. Now choose two of the cases and analyze how the court made its decision. In the course of your analysis, refer back to the UCCJEA (or the UCCJA if in Massachusetts) and make sure that you both understand and discuss all provisions relevant to the court's analysis in each case.
2. Locate UIFSA as adopted by your state. Now, locate any additional long-arm statutes that can be used in support cases in your state. Review the circumstances under which long-arm jurisdiction can be asserted and determine if they add anything to the UIFSA grounds.
3. Assume a client has come to your firm's office seeking a divorce. All you know at this point is that she and her husband and their children have moved frequently over the past five years, and she has recently moved to your state with the children. In preparation for the interview, an attorney in your office has asked you to develop some questions so that all facts bearing on jurisdiction will be covered. In developing the questions, make sure you think about all aspects of the case.

Cases for Analysis

The following case focuses on personal jurisdiction and service of process.

GOODIN v. DEPARTMENT OF HUMAN SERVICES
772 So. 2d 1051 (Miss. 2000)

PRATHER, Chief Justice, for the court:

STATEMENT OF THE CASE

The Mississippi Department of Human Services ("DHS"), on behalf of Diana Goodin-McKay ("McKay"), sought to enforce an Arizona child support order against John T. Goodin ("Goodin") in the Chancery Court of Winston County. The chancellor granted DHS' petition, and Goodin has appealed, asserting the following assignments of error: . . .
. . . The chancery court lacked personal jurisdiction over Goodin. . . .

STATEMENT OF THE FACTS

Goodin and McKay married in Mississippi and later became residents of Arizona where they eventually divorced. Pursuant to the divorce, the Superior Court of Cochise County, Arizona, ordered Goodin to pay $776 in monthly child support for the two unemancipated children born of this marriage.

After the divorce, McKay and the two children returned to Mississippi to live. . . . Goodin also returned to Mississippi. . . .

Goodin, by his own admission, did not pay child support between February 1998 and July 31, 1999. . . . Because Goodin had not paid child support in that period, DHS, on behalf of McKay, sought to enforce the Arizona order in Mississippi, filing a Petition to Enforce and Give Full Faith and Credit to a Foreign Child Support Judgment ("Petition") in the Chancery Court of Winston County, Mississippi.

Following the filing of the Petition, Goodin appeared before Chancellor Edward Prisock, and with the assistance of counsel opposite, objected to the court's jurisdiction over him [and] . . . to service of process. . . . At the hearing, . . . Goodin again objected to the court's jurisdiction, stating that he was a resident of Arizona, not Mississippi. . . . Goodin reiterated his previous position as to service of process, testifying that he had never been personally served, that service had been left with his mother at her home, and that he did not reside with her. . . .

LEGAL ANALYSIS

I.   DID THE CHANCERY COURT POSSESS PERSONAL JURISDICTION OVER GOODIN?

Goodin contends that he is an Arizona resident as he still owns a house and is still a registered voter there and, therefore, is not subject to the jurisdiction of the Winston County Chancery Court. This Court, however, need not consider whether Goodin is a domiciliary as he was properly served process while physically present in Mississippi.

The United States Supreme Court has held that a nonresident of a State is subject to the jurisdiction of that State's courts if properly served process while physically present in that State. Burnham v. Superior Court, 495 U.S. 604, 628, 110 S. Ct. 2105, 2119, 109 L. Ed. 2d 631, 650 (1990). One may properly serve process to a defendant in Mississippi by having the sheriff or his deputy physically deliver a copy of the summons and complaint to the defendant. . . .

[T]his Court finds Goodin personally subject to the jurisdiction of this State's courts under *Burnham*. DHA properly served Goodin a copy of the summons and complaint as is reflected in the "proof of service" form, signed by Winston County Deputy Sheriff Curtis Austin, indicating he personally served process to Goodin in Mississippi. While Goodin maintained at the hearing that he had not been properly served process by DHS, Goodin fails to raise that issue on appeal. The Court has long held that issues not properly raised on appeal are procedurally barred from consideration. . . . Even were Goodin's contention not procedurally barred, this Court finds substantial, credible evidence in the "proof of service" form to support the chancellor's finding that the trial court had jurisdiction over the parties and affirms the trial court's decision. . . .

QUESTIONS

1. What was the Mississippi Department of Human Services seeking to do in this case?
2. Why did Goodin argue that the court lacked personal jurisdiction over him?
3. Why did he argue that service had been improper?
4. How did the court respond to his arguments? According to the court, what was the connection between service and jurisdiction? What case did the court rely on in reaching its result?

The following case focuses on a father's effort to have Maine assume jurisdiction over his parenting petition under the UCCJEA and the Hague

Convention with respect to his 15-month-old daughter, who had resided with her mother in Guatemala since her birth.

SEEKINS v. HAMM
2015 ME 157, 2015 Me. LEXIS 171

SAUFLEY, C.J.

Christopher Seekins and Jennifer Hamm met in Guatemala, and their daughter was born there in August 2013. Although neither Hamm nor the child has ever been to Maine, Seekins filed a parental rights and responsibilities complaint in the Maine District Court. Seekins now appeals from a judgment entered in the District Court . . . that granted Jennifer Hamm's motion to dismiss the complaint based on a determination that Maine lacks jurisdiction pursuant to the Uniform Child Custody Jurisdiction and Enforcement Act (UCCJEA), 19-A M.R.S. §§1731-1783 (2014). We affirm the judgment of dismissal, concluding that the court applied the applicable law properly.

I. BACKGROUND

On November 18, 2014, when the child was approximately fifteen months old, Seekins filed a complaint in Maine to establish parental rights and responsibilities. Hamm retained counsel and moved to dismiss the complaint for lack of jurisdiction. She argued that Maine lacked long-arm jurisdiction over her pursuant to 14 M.R.S. §704-A (2014).

Seekins filed a memorandum in opposition to the motion to dismiss, in which he raised the Convention on the Civil Aspects of International Child Abduction ("Hague Convention") and the federal statute providing remedies for international child abductions that violate the Hague Convention. . . . He also cited to the Uniform Interstate Family Support Act (UIFSA). . . . Hamm filed a response addressing these other sources of law. In Seekins's reply, he additionally raised the federal international parental kidnapping statute, *see* 18 U.S.C.S. §1204 (LEXIS through Pub. L. No. 114-73).

The court held a hearing on Hamm's motion to dismiss in March 2015. Seekins was the only witness. Shortly thereafter, the court entered a written judgment in which it found that Seekins now resides in Maine, that neither Hamm nor the child has ever been to Maine, and that the child has resided in Guatemala with Hamm since her birth. The court dismissed Seekins's complaint because, pursuant to the UCCJEA, the initial child custody determination must be made in the "home state"—which for this child is

Guatemala, not Maine—absent a showing that the home state has declined jurisdiction. *See* 19-A M.R.S. §1745(1). Seekins timely appealed from the judgment. . . .

II.   DISCUSSION

A.   APPLICATION OF THE UCCJEA

With certain exceptions not applicable here, "a court of this State has juris-diction to make an initial child custody determination only if"one of four criteria is met. *See* 19-A M.R.S. §1745(1). Jurisdiction will lie in Maine if (A) Maine "is the home state of the child on the date of the commence-ment of the proceeding or was the home state of the child within 6 months before the commencement of the proceeding and the child is absent from this State but a parent or person acting as a parent continues to live in this State"; (B) no other state has "home state" jurisdiction; (C) any "home state" declined jurisdiction on the basis that Maine is the more appropri-ate forum; or (D) "[n]o court of any other state would have jurisdiction" pursuant to the preceding criteria. *Id.* §1745(1)(A)-(D). Section 1745(1) "is the exclusive jurisdictional basis for making a child custody determination by a court of this State." *Id.* §1745(2). Thus, although the child's physical presence is not necessarily required for the court to make a child custody determination, *id.* §1745(1), (3), at least one of the criteria of section 1745(1) must be met for the court to have jurisdiction.

The "home state" of a child over the age of six months is "the state in which a child lived with a parent or a person acting as a parent for at least 6 consecutive months immediately before the commencement of a child cus-tody proceeding." 19-A M.R.S. §1732(7). "A period of temporary absence of any of the mentioned persons is part of the period." *Id.*

When determining jurisdiction, "[a] court of this State shall treat a foreign country as if it were a state of the United States," unless the child custody laws of that foreign country violate "fundamental principles of human rights," 19-A M.R.S. §1735(1), (3), as provided in article 20 of the Hague Convention, *see* UCCJEA §105 uniform cmt., *included with* 19-A M.R.S.A. §1735 (2012). There is no indication in the record that the child cus-tody laws of Guatemala violate fundamental principles of human rights; indeed, the Hague Convention has been in force between Guatemala and the United States since January 1, 2008. . . .

Although Seekins disputes the *reasons* that neither Hamm nor the child has visited Maine, the child's actual place of residence is not in dispute and is dispositive of jurisdiction. The child was more than six months old when the complaint was filed, and she had lived in Guatemala with her mother for the six consecutive months immediately preceding Seekins's commencement of his parental rights and responsibilities action. *See* 19-A M.R.S. §1732(7). Guatemala—not Maine—is the child's home state based on the child's actual place of residence. *See id.* There is no evidence that Guatemala has declined jurisdiction; thus, the initial proceeding with respect to the child must be pursued there. Because of the lack of subject matter jurisdiction, the court appropriately dismissed the complaint.

B.   INAPPLICABILITY OF OTHER LEGAL AUTHORITIES

During the course of the case, Seekins cited to several additional sources of law in support of his contention that the District Court had jurisdiction to determine parental rights and responsibilities for the child. The federal authorities that Seekins cited do not confer jurisdiction on the Maine District Court and are inapplicable. The Hague Convention is inapplicable because the removal or the retention of a child is wrongful only if "it is in breach of rights of custody attributed to a person . . . under the law of the State *in which the child was habitually resident immediately before the removal or retention,*" Hague Convention art. 3(a), *opened for signature* Oct. 25, 1980, T.I.A.S. No. 11,670, 1343 U.N.T.S. 89, *reprinted in* 51 Fed. Reg. 10494 (Mar. 26, 1986) (emphasis added), and 18 U.S.C.S. §1204, an international parental kidnapping statute, simply does not apply on these facts.

The Maine sources cited by Seekins also fail to establish a basis for jurisdiction. The Uniform Interstate Family Support Act does not govern child custody and contact and does not provide a basis for jurisdiction because the child was not conceived in Maine, the mother was not served in Maine and did not consent to jurisdiction in Maine, and neither the mother nor the child ever resided in Maine. . . . Finally, whether or not Seekins and Hamm originally agreed to bring the child to reside in Maine, that did not occur, and the parties to a court case may not, even by mutual consent or agreement, confer jurisdiction on the court. . . .

III.   CONCLUSION

The District Court considered all of the parties' arguments and the sources of law cited by each party in determining that the UCCJEA governed its determination of jurisdiction in this matter. The UCCJEA applies, and the court properly applied the law. We affirm the resulting judgment dismissing Seekins's complaint.

QUESTIONS

1. What sources of law did the father invoke in seeking to persuade the Maine court that it had child custody jurisdiction?
2. Why did the court reject the father's claim under the UCCJEA? Under the Hague Convention? Under the other sources of law that he cited?
3. Would the result have been different if the parties had agreed to move to Maine, and the mother then changed her mind and remained behind in Guatemala with the child?

Endnotes

1. Although many statutes use the term "residence," virtually all courts have interpreted this to mean domicile.

2. Regarding the requirements of jurisdiction in domestic violence actions, *see* Aaron Edward Brown, What Does the Fox Say: Domestic Violence, Personal Jurisdiction, and the State's Sovereignty in Declaring the Protected Status of Its Citizens, 14 U. St. Thomas L.J. 530 (2018), and Cody J. Jacobs, The Stream of Violence: A New Approach to Domestic Violence Personal Jurisdiction, 64 UCLA L. Rev. 684 (2017).

3. Williams v. North Carolina, 317 U.S. 287, 298-299 (1942).

4. Some commentators have suggested that this domicile rule is out of keeping with the modern jurisdictional emphasis on the relationship of the defendant to the adjudicating state and recommend that a minimum contacts standard be used in divorce cases, as it is in other civil actions. *See* Rhonda Wasserman, Divorce and Domicile: Time to Sever the Note, 39 Wm. & Mary L. Rev. 1 (1997); Rhonda Wasserman, Parents, Partners, and Personal Jurisdiction, 1995 U. Ill. L. Rev. 813; E. Roy Hawkins, The Effect of Schaffer v. Heitner on the Jurisdictional Standard in Ex Parte Divorces, 18 Fam. L.Q. 311 (1984).

5. UIFSA §205 (2001). For a detailed explanation of UIFSA, *see* John J. Sampson and Barry J. Brooks, Uniform Interstate Family Support Act (2001) With Prefatory Notes (With Still More Annotations), 36 Fam. L.Q. 329 (2002).

6. UIFSA §201(1)-(8) (2001). *See* Sampson and Brooks, *supra* note 5, at 357-363, for a detailed commentary on UIFSA's long-arm provisions.

7. 28 U.S.C. §1738A (1994). *See generally* Christine L. Jones, The Parental Kidnapping and Prevention Act: Is There New Hope for a (Limited) Federal Forum, 18 Temp. Pol. & Civ. Rts. L. Rev. 141 (2008); Linda M. DeMelis, Interstate Child Custody and the Parental Kidnapping Prevention Act: The Continuing Search for a National Standard, 45 Hastings L.J. 1329 (1994).

8. The text of the UCCJEA can be found at: http://www.uniformlaws.org/shared/docs/child_custody_jurisdiction/uccjea_final_97.pdf (accessed Dec. 30, 2015). For further details on various aspects of the UCCJEA, *see* Andrea Charlow, There's No Place Like Home: Temporary Absences in the UCCJEA Home State, 28 J. Am. Acad. Matrimonial Law 25 (2015); Kevin Wessel, Home Is Where the Court Is: Determining Residence for Child Custody Matters Under the UCCJEA, 79 U. Chi. L. Rev. 1141, (2012); Deborah Goelman and Darren Mitchell, Look Both Ways Before You Cross State Lines: Using the Uniform Child Custody Jurisdiction and Enforcement Act to Assist Domestic Violence Survivors, 43 Clearinghouse Rev. 346 (2009).

9. For details, on the full faith and credit provisions of VAWA, *see* http://www.bwjp.org/our-work/projects/protection-orders.html (accessed Jan. 30, 2015). You should be aware that other laws come into play if the child who is the subject of the custody dispute is an American Indian or if the conflict involves more than one country (international disputes are briefly discussed at the end of the chapter). In the former situation, reference must also be made to the Indian Child Welfare Act of 1978, 25 U.S.C. §§1901 et seq., the Indian Civil Rights Act of 1968, 25 U.S.C. §§1301 et seq., and the appropriate Tribal Code. For details, *see* http://www.tribal-institute.org/lists/icra.htm (accessed Jan. 30. 2015).

10. Although the focus here is on custody disputes that arise in the context of divorce, the UCCJEA and PKPA apply to custody disputes that arise in a variety of contexts, including abuse and neglect, guardianship, and abuse prevention proceedings.

11. *See* UCCJEA §201. The text of the Act is available at http://www.uniformlaws.org/shared/docs/child_custody_jurisdiction/uccjea_final_97.pdf (accessed Dec. 29, 2015).

12. UCCJEA §204(a). *See* Julie Morley, A Silver Lining in Domestic Turmoil: A Call for Massachusetts to Adopt the UCCJEA's Emergency Jurisdiction Provision, 43 New Eng. L. Rev. 135 (2008).

13. UCCJEA §201.2.

14. Brandt v. Brandt, 2012 CO 3, 268 P.3d 406, 412 (2012).

15. *Id.* at 408.

16. Kevin Wessel, Home Is Where the Court Is: Determining Residence for Child Custody Matters Under the UCCJE, 79 U. Chi. L. Rev. 1141, 1158 (2012).

17. *Id.* at 1155-1158.

18. UCCJEA §208(a).

19. Why States Should Adopt the Uniform Deployed Parents Custody and Visitation Act, http://www.uniformlaws.org/Shared/Docs/Deployed_Parents/UDPCVA%20Why %20States(1).pdf (accessed Dec. 29, 2015).

20. *See generally* Mark E. Sullivan, G. Brentley Tanner, and Ashley L. Oldham, The Deployed Parents Custody and Visitation Act, 27 J. Am. Acad. Matrimonial Law 391 (2015).

21. UCCJEA §105(a) & (b).

22. *Id.* §105(c).

23. https: www.hcch.net/en/about (accessed Mar. 1, 2019).

24. https://www.hcch.net/en/instruments/conventions/specialised-sections/ child-abduction (accessed Dec. 29, 2015). For further detail, *see* Kirkpatrick Townsend & Stockton, LLP and the National Center for Missing & Exploited Children, Litigating International Child Abduction Cases Under the Hague Convention (2012); Noah L. Browne, Relevance and Fairness: Protecting the Rights of Domestic Violence Victims and Left-Behind Fathers Under the Hague Convention on International Child Abduction, 60 Duke L.J. 1193 (2011). For the relationship between the UCCJEA and the Hague Convention, *see* Robert G. Spector, Divorcing the International Family: Memorandum Accommodating the Hague Convention, 63 Okla. L. Rev. 615 (2011).

25. Feder v. Evan-Feder, 63 F.3d 217, 224 (3d Cir. 1995).

26. For details about the process, *see* Robert D. Arenstein, How to Prosecute an International Child Abduction Case Under the Hague Convention, 30 J. Am. Acad. Matrimonial Law 1 (2017).

27. Article 13, Hague Convention on the Civil Aspects of International Child Abduction, http://www.hcch.net.

28. *Id.*

29. *See* Kevin Wayne Puckett, Hague Convention on International Child Abduction: Can Domestic Violence Establish the Grave Risk Defense Under Article 12?, 30 J. Am. Acad. Matrimonial Law 259 (2017).

Chapter Ten

The Divorce Process

In this chapter, we look at how a divorce case makes its way through the legal system. We begin with the initial client interview and move through each successive stage of the process from the filing of the action through postjudgment procedures. As we progress, we look at the role paralegals play in the preparation of a case and at the skills they need. We also look at some important ethical considerations.

The Initial Client Interview

We begin with the initial client interview. At this meeting, detailed information about the client's situation is obtained; of equal importance, the interview establishes the foundation for the office's relationship with the client. One important goal is to develop a sense of mutual trust and purpose between the interviewer and the client.

Good interviews do not just happen; they require sensitivity and skill. Unfortunately, many legal professionals do not give much thought to client interviewing, perhaps because it does not appear to require specialized legal skills and knowledge. However, a poorly conducted interview can have long-term repercussions. A client who leaves a law office feeling disrespected or unheard may not develop the trust and confidence essential to a good working relationship. As a result, he or she may be reluctant to fully disclose all relevant information, particularly if it is of a sensitive or potentially damaging nature.

It is important to be attuned to the role that culture plays in the communication process, as the failure to do so can lead to misunderstandings with potentially serious consequences. In a powerful example of this dynamic, sociolinguist Diane Eades describes how differences in cultural approaches to seeking information played a major role in the conviction of an Australian Aboriginal woman for killing her abusive husband. Using standard interviewing techniques, which are based on the assumption that direct questions are the best way to elicit information, the woman's attorneys had been unsuccessful in eliciting her story, which included a horrific history of violence, from her. As Eades explains, when "Aboriginal people want to find out what they consider to be significant or . . . personal information, they do not use direct questions. . . . People volunteer some of their own information, hinting about what they are trying to find out. Information is sought out as part of a two-way exchange."[1] Moreover, personal information is not generally shared in the absence of a developed, trusting relationship. Called in as a sociolinguistic expert in the appeal, Eades concluded that it would have been extremely difficult for the defendant to share highly personal information in the context of a formal interview with a stranger. This is a dramatic example of the failure of cultural sensitivity, but it is an important reminder of how cultural differences (as well as other differences, including class and educational backgrounds) can lead to communication difficulties between clients and legal professionals.

Another important consideration in conducting effective interviews is understanding the emotional impact of divorce. Clients going through a divorce frequently enter a law office with intense feelings and emotional needs that cannot be ignored. Before we look at the interview process, we briefly consider the emotional framework within which divorce interviews often take place.

The Emotional Context

The breakup of a marriage can wreak emotional havoc in a person's life. Profound feelings of jealousy, anger, hopelessness, and despair are often unleashed. The process of divorce has been described as the emotional opposite of falling in love, generating powerful feelings of hate and rage rather than of intense pleasure.[2] A person going through a divorce may feel as if he or she has failed in a central aspect of life, and thus may be struggling with acute feelings of worthlessness. He or she is likely to go through many emotional stages: "Divorce is best conceptualized as a series of transitional life experiences rather than a single discrete event. Therefore, . . . the impact of divorce on family members will vary with the point in the transition process."[3]

Many of the clients you interview are thus likely to be experiencing overwhelming and constantly shifting emotions. This can make your task difficult, but it is important to remain sensitive to what the client may be going through. If clients are going to trust you, they need to feel that their well-being matters. The failure to acknowledge a client's emotional needs can also interfere with his or her ability to move onto other topics, whereas the acknowledgment of these feelings can facilitate this process.

Providing emotional support is particularly important in the divorce context where, as noted above, individuals often experience a diminished sense of self-worth. Moreover, divorce often disrupts a person's social support system. Friends and family may disapprove of the marital split, feel loyalty to the other spouse, be uncomfortable with the intensity of feeling, or fear that "another person's divorce will illuminate the cracks in their own relationships."[4]

However, as important as providing support is, you also need to be aware of the limitations of your role. Your job is not to help the client analyze or resolve his or her feelings, although the client may on some level expect you to do this. You are not the client's friend or therapist, and you should be careful not to take on these roles. You should be attuned to when a referral to a mental health professional might be appropriate. Before bringing up the possibility of a referral with a client, be sure that you know what the policy of your office is. It may be that this responsibility is entrusted to the supervising attorney.

Conducting the Client Interview

The Role of the Paralegal

In many offices, paralegals are responsible for conducting the initial interview. In other offices, attorneys conduct them, while in others, the two work as a team. Also, within a single office, the practice might vary based on the nature, sensitivity, and complexity of the case. Regardless of who conducts the interview, it is important, if possible, that the client meet both the attorney and paralegal who will be working on the case. This personalizes the process and helps establish rapport and trust.

Ethical Considerations

When working with clients, it is important to be aware of the ethical rules that define the parameters of the professional relationship.[5] Interviews and all other contact must conform to ethical requirements. Accordingly, before focusing on the client interview, we consider the ethical framework within which paralegals operate. We then focus on the rules regarding the unauthorized practice of law and client confidentiality because these bear most directly on the paralegal-client relationship.

The Ethical Framework

All states have a code of ethics that is binding on attorneys. These codes are not directly binding on paralegals, but paralegals are expected to adhere to them, and noncompliance may result in a disciplinary action against the attorney for whom the paralegal works. These codes are promulgated by the highest court in each state, and most are modeled after the American Bar Association's (ABA) Model Rules of Professional Conduct.

The codes contain disciplinary sanctions for ethical violations. The most serious sanction is disbarment. In many states, the code of ethics has been supplemented by statutes that impose civil or criminal penalties for certain unethical acts, such as the unauthorized practice of law.

Many states now have guidelines in place to assist attorneys in working effectively with paralegals, and some states specifically require that "attorneys take affirmative steps to educate legal assistants about the attorney's ethical obligations and to ensure their compliance."[6]

The two major national paralegal organizations, the National Federation of Paralegal Associations and the National Association of Legal Assistants, both have promulgated ethical codes that are binding on paralegals, as have some local and regional paralegal associations. Sanctions, including removal from membership, may be imposed for ethical violations. These codes do not carry the same weight as those for attorneys do, both because they are not court-promulgated and because paralegals are not presently state licensed and thus cannot be barred from practice as can an attorney.[7]

Also relevant when considering standards of conduct is the fact that, like attorneys, paralegals can be sued for malpractice. Although malpractice actions extend well beyond ethical breaches, the failure to conform to expected standards of behavior can play a role in these suits.

Specific Practices

The Unauthorized Practice of Law.   All states limit the practice of law to licensed attorneys, but determining what is meant by the term "practice of law" is not always easy. Certain conduct, such as signing court pleadings, conducting depositions, or representing a client in court, are considered to be the practice of law. But even here, there are some exceptions. For example, some states allow paralegals to appear in court for an attorney on uncontested matters, and many allow paralegals to serve as advocates in domestic violence cases. Paralegals also are allowed to represent clients before many state and federal administrative agencies.[8]

The giving of legal advice is also regarded as the practice of law; however, the definition of this term is imprecise. At a minimum it includes independently advising a client about her or his legal rights, a potential course of action, and the predicting of legal outcomes. Thus, it is clear that advising a client as to what kind of divorce should be filed is the giving of legal advice; but what about explaining basic statutory options such as the difference between a fault and a no-fault divorce? Some would classify this as legal information, which a paralegal could disseminate, while others would classify it as advice. Although a paralegal cannot provide legal advice independently, he or she can serve as a conduit between the attorney and client as long as it is made clear to the client that the advice is from the attorney and not from the paralegal.

Maintaining the appropriate boundaries can be difficult. Clients are often vulnerable and without reliable support, and may implore you to tell them what to do. This can be hard to resist. It is flattering, and you are likely to be moved by the client's situation and want very much to help. But, no matter how difficult, it is important to work within the existing ethical framework and not be pulled into doing more than is appropriate.

Client Confidentiality.   In working with clients, you must always be aware of your ethical responsibility to maintain strict client **confidentiality**. The duty to maintain client confidences is at the heart of the attorney-client relationship and is also binding on paralegals. Without the assurance of confidentiality, a client may be reluctant to provide all of the information that is needed to thoroughly prepare a case, especially if it is of a sensitive, embarrassing, or potentially damaging nature. The client may worry that it will be disclosed to the opposing side or to other third parties. Accordingly, clients should be told at the outset of the interview that their communications with the office are strictly confidential. If you sense a client is struggling with whether to tell you something, it can be helpful to remind him or her that disclosures are confidential.

You should also be aware that there may be limited exceptions to the confidentiality rule, such as where a client discloses that he or she is planning to commit a serious crime or where there is good cause to believe that the client is harming his or her children. Depending on the situation and the state you are in, disclosure may be discretionary or it may be required, such as where a child protective law requires all persons who believe a child is being abused or neglected to file a report with a state's child protective agency (see Chapter 12). A decision to disclose should never be made lightly, as it is a clear exception to the overriding duty to maintain client confidentiality. As a paralegal, you should never act on your own in this regard. You should review the situation with the supervising attorney who may well be the one who is ultimately responsible for the disclosure decision.

Developing Good Listening Skills

The manner in which you listen to clients is vital because it signals whether you are simply going through the motions or are really paying attention to what is being said. If a client senses that you are engaged, he or she is likely to open up more because people are generally more comfortable when they sense their listener is responsive to what they are saying.

Nonverbal Communication.   In thinking about how you listen to someone, it is important to recognize that much is communicated nonverbally. Direct eye contact signals that you are present and engaged. It also enables you to pick up nonverbal clues from the client that might otherwise be missed.

Likewise, your body position is important. Leaning forward toward the client indicates involvement. A somewhat relaxed posture tends to reduce the distance between the interviewer and interviewee. In contrast, leaning back in a chair with legs up on a desk can signal a lack of focused attention and involvement. This position also can be intimidating to a client because it tends to enhance the status of the interviewer.[9]

Active Listening.   Through a technique known as **active listening**, you can let a client know that you are really hearing what is being said. Active listening involves the use of verbal responses that reflect back to the client the informational or emotional content of what has been said.

With respect to the reflection of informational content, you should occasionally repeat back to the client some of the key information he or she has given you. This makes it clear that you have heard what has been said and have not been daydreaming about the upcoming weekend. It also helps ensure the accuracy of your information gathering because it gives the client the opportunity to correct any misunderstandings.

This should not become a mechanical process, and you should not break the flow of the story. A good time to reflect back is when the client has come to a logical break in the narrative. Be careful, however, that you do not begin to sound like a parrot, who is mindlessly repeating back what it has heard.

With respect to the reflection of emotional content, you should occasionally respond to what the client says she or he is going through on an emotional level. This acknowledges that you are aware of the client's emotional needs and that it is acceptable for him or her to express them. Although it may be tempting to share your personal experiences as a way of showing the client that you can understand what he or she is going through, these kinds of disclosures should be avoided. Although it is important to be supportive, you should never lose track of the fact that this is a professional relationship.

To illustrate the technique of active listening, let's assume that you are interviewing a client named Carl Johnson and that you are beginning the narrative phase of the interview. (See the discussion on the narrative phase next.) You have asked him, "Why don't you tell me something about your marriage?" and he has responded as follows:

> Well, my wife and I have been married for 15 years. We met in college—she was my first true love, and has remained my only love during all these years. We have had a few rocky patches. My mother died right after our daughter was born. I became depressed. I had been very close to both my parents and had already lost my dad.
>
> My wife felt I withdrew from her and the baby. I denied it at the time, but in retrospect, I realize she was right. In any event, I thought we had a loving marriage.
>
> Well, a few years ago, my wife seemed more remote. She lost interest in sex and, well, things just seemed different. At first I attributed it to the pressure we were under. My business had gone under, I was looking for work, we had our daughter, my wife was working full time, and I was still struggling with depression.
>
> We were also threatened with foreclosure proceedings, although we were able to save the house by borrowing money from her parents. Since then, they haven't let me forget that if I had been a proper husband, able to hold down a decent job, my family would not have been in that predicament. I also think they blame me for the fact that their daughter works so hard, but they don't understand that she loves her job.
>
> Anyway, I gradually began to get suspicious that something else was going on. My wife began to have more night meetings, a few times when I answered the phone the person at the other end hung up—all the classic signs. For a while she denied that anything was going on, but finally, about a month ago she admitted that she had been seeing someone in her office. I asked her to break it off, but she said she couldn't promise to do that and needed some time to work things out. Well, that was it. I was and still am totally destroyed. It's embarrassing to admit, but she is the only woman I have ever had sex with. As far as I am concerned the marriage is over.

This is probably a logical point to interject briefly. To reflect the emotional content, you might simply say something like: "I can see why you are devastated. This must be a very difficult time for you." You want to avoid statements like, "I know what you are going through, I remember what it was like when my husband walked out on me." This may seem obvious, but, in the intensity of the moment, the temptation to support a client in this manner can be hard to resist.

To reflect the informational content, you might say something like:

> I'd like to take a minute to make sure I understand what you have just told me; please let me know if anything I say is inaccurate.

You and your wife have been married for 15 years, and despite a few rough times, you would characterize your relationship as solid. You have one child.

You've struggled with depression, particularly after the death of your mother. Recently, your wife has acknowledged she is having an affair, and is not sure what she wants to do. As a result, you have decided your marriage is over.

The Interview Itself: A Three-Stage Approach

It is useful to think of the interview as having the following three distinct stages:

1. *Opening stage:* establishes the parameters of the interview and creates an atmosphere of trust
2. *Information-gathering stage:* elicits the client's basic story (narrative phase) and fills in the key details with questions (focused phase)
3. *Wrapping up or disengaging phase:* concludes the interview

This three-stage approach should not be followed mechanistically. Each person you interview is unique, and you need to accommodate a range of expressive styles. Some clients may respond only to focused questions; while others, at least initially, will be so overwhelmed that they will not respond to focused questions. They may need to tell you their story over and over in their own manner and sequence. This human dimension is the great challenge that no book can fully prepare you for.

In the following sections, we will look at each stage of the interview process, using the interview with Mr. Johnson to demonstrate various points. The model presented here assumes that a preprinted form is not being used for anything more than obtaining the basic factual information needed to complete a divorce complaint — such as the place and date of the marriage, the date last lived together, and the names and birthdates of the marital children — although some offices do use forms to obtain comprehensive client information.

Stage 1: Establishing the Parameters and Creating an Atmosphere of Trust.   When a client first comes to a law office, it is important to realize that he or she is probably nervous. Engaging in some preliminary chit-chat can help put a client at ease. For example, you might inquire whether he or she found the office without difficulty, whether it is still snowing, or the like. It is also a nice gesture to offer a cup of coffee or tea.

At the beginning, you should explain who you are and what role you will play. Let's assume that Mr. Johnson has just entered your office. To begin the interview, you might say something like the following:

> Hi, Mr. Johnson, my name is Elaine Chin. I am the family law parale-gal who will be working on your case with Attorney Jane Martin. I am going to be interviewing you today. Afterward, Attorney Martin and I will meet to review the information and begin preparing your case. If Ms. Martin returns from court before we are finished with the inter-view, I will introduce you to her.

You should then inform the client that everything he or she tells you will be held in strict confidence, and explain what will take place during the interview. Following is an example of what this might sound like:

> Mr. Johnson, I am going to begin by asking you some very basic ques-tions so I'm sure to get all the information that is asked for on the court forms. I will use our standard questionnaire for this.
>
> Afterward, I'll ask you to tell me about your situation and what you are thinking about doing at this stage. During the course of the interview, I will take some notes so I'm sure to remember everything you tell me.
>
> Also, you should know that everything you tell me is strictly con-fidential within this office. You do not need to worry that somehow your wife or her attorney will find out about what you tell us.
>
> Once I have a complete picture of your situation, we'll be through for the day. But, before you go, I'll tell you what you can expect and what you need to begin doing, such as collecting necessary papers.
>
> Do you have any questions before we begin?

At this point, the client knows who you are, what to expect, and that communications are confidential. This establishes a solid foundation for the interview itself.

Stage 2: Obtaining Information.   Where possible, it is best to gather infor-mation in two phases. In the first phase, the client should be encouraged to tell his or her story. In the second phase, the interviewer can complete the inquiry by asking focused questions. This is sometimes referred to as a "funneling" process because the questions begin broadly and then gradu-ally become narrower.

Eliciting the Client Narrative.   In the first phase of information gath-ering, the emphasis is on having the client tell his or her story. This is done by asking open-ended questions that elicit a narrative rather than a focused response. In using open-ended questions, the interviewer loses some control over the process because the client shapes the telling of the story. However, this approach respects the fact that it is the client's prob-lem and acknowledges that "the client is an important, essential resource in the information gathering process."[10] Open-ended questions can be either general or topic-specific. By asking topic-specific questions, the interviewer focuses the field of inquiry while still calling for a narrative response.

By way of example, let's return to Mr. Johnson. As set out above, the initial question to him was, "Why don't you tell me something about your marriage?" and in answering, he mentioned he has a child. A logical follow-up question might be, "Why don't you tell me about your child?" This question is topic-specific but is still open-ended because it asks for a narrative response. Let's assume that he gives the following answer:

> Well, Sara is our only child. She's seven and is in the second grade. She's a terrific kid, I know all parents say that, but she really is special. She does real well in school, has a lot of friends, and loves sports.
>
> Lately, though, she seems to be having a bit of a hard time. I've tried to talk to her about it, but sometimes she just doesn't seem to want to talk much to me. My wife says it's because I didn't bond with her as a baby, but I think she's going through something now, maybe with all this marriage stuff. I'm sure it's nothing serious.
>
> Her last report card was real good, but her teacher says that Sara has been kind of withdrawn at school. I am very worried about how she'll react to the divorce. I guess she's kind of a sensitive kid.

As he completes talking about his daughter, you could direct him to other topic areas by asking similar questions, such as, "You mentioned earlier that a few years ago your wife started seeming remote. Why don't you describe this period to me?"

It is during this narrative phase that the technique of active listening is particularly important. If possible, it is best to take a minimum of notes during this phase because note taking can interfere with your ability to remain focused and engaged.

Focusing in: Following up with Closed-Inquiry Questions.   After the narrative phase, you should proceed with more focused questions to elicit more complete information. At this point, you will probably want to take detailed notes. As you shift to the closed-inquiry phase, you gain greater control over the process; however, where possible, your inquiry should be informed by and responsive to what the client tells you.

To begin this phase, you might say something like this to the client:

> Mr. Johnson, you've given me a good picture of your situation. Now, what I would like to do is go back over what you have told me and ask you some specific questions so I am sure my information is complete. Also, I will now be taking notes so I have a good record of what you tell me.

You can then go back over the information in a focused manner. Here is what some follow-up questions to Mr. Johnson about his daughter might sound like:

Q: You used the word "special" in describing your daughter. Why don't you tell me what you mean by that?

A: Well like I said, she does well in school, has a lot of friends, and loves sports. But, I guess beyond that, she is just a very kind and thoughtful child. She seems to have a sensitivity beyond her years. She understands a lot about the world, and really wants to help people.

Q: Does she understand what is happening at home?

A: To some extent. We've told her that Mommy and Daddy don't love each other anymore and that Daddy will be moving to a new home, but that I still love her very much. I don't think she really understands why I've been sleeping in the guest room or why Mommy and Daddy aren't speaking to each other much.

Q: Why don't you tell me more about your relationship with Sara?

A: As I said, I was somewhat depressed when she was first born, and maybe I wasn't really that involved with her care, but I think I've made up for that in the past five or so years. During this time, I've been very involved in her care.

Q: Can you describe your caretaking role?

A: Well, sometimes I bring her to school in the morning, but I usually have to be at the office pretty early and I try to pick her up from her after-school program a few times a week. I share putting her to bed at night, and on weekends I try to do a special activity with her—just the two of us.

Q: How would you characterize the division of child-care responsibilities between you and your wife?

A: Well, I think it's pretty equal. I'm a pretty involved dad—I mean maybe it's not fifty-fifty, but I'm not one of those dads who doesn't even know the names of his child's friends.

Q: At some point, I'll probably want to get more detail on the caretaking arrangements, but let me ask you a few other things first. You mentioned that your daughter has been having a hard time, and hasn't wanted to speak with you about what's going on. Can you elaborate on this?

A: Let me start with our relationship. We've been pretty close. I don't spend as much time with her as I would like, but when we're together we have a lot of fun. Sometimes I get impatient with her and then I feel badly. I guess she usually confides more in her mother; I try not to get jealous, but sometimes I feel left out. I can't express my feelings as well as my wife can—we didn't do any of that in my family, and maybe it's a male thing also—so maybe Sara feels somewhat closer with her mom. But I love my daughter and would do anything for her.

Q: Who does your daughter turn to for comfort when she is sick or doesn't feel well?

A: Both of us, but my wife is usually the one to stay home with her when she is sick. Her job is more flexible than mine is, and when I was self-employed, I couldn't afford to take the time off. Also, sometimes, I think my wife overindulges her, and keeps her home if she just has a sniffle. I don't think it's good to treat kids like babies. With respect to what Sara has been going through, she's been kind of moody and withdrawn. I don't know if it's in response to what has been going on at home, or if it's just one of those things that kids go through.

Q: Have you consulted anyone about this?

A: No—it hasn't seemed like that big a deal. But, maybe with the divorce we should have her talk to someone. I don't really know.

Here, the interviewer is clearly trying to elicit specific information, but the questions flow from the client's answers, and there is a nice sense of give and take. This is not always possible. Where the client is less focused, the interviewer cannot be as responsive and will need to impose more of a structure in order to obtain the necessary information. Also, in reviewing these questions, you should note the constant pattern of moving from broader to narrower questions; this funneling process is also valuable within this closed-inquiry phase.

Stage 3: Wrapping Up the Interview.   Once you have obtained the necessary information, it is time to wrap up the interview. At this point, you need to tell the client what will happen next and explain what he or she needs to do, if anything. You should remind the client to feel free to call you with any questions.

To conclude the interview, you might say something like this:

> Mr. Johnson, I think I have gotten all of the information that I need today. Let me explain what will happen next. I will write up the results of our interview and will go over them with Attorney Martin. She will evaluate your options, and we will then set up a meeting so she can go over things with you in detail. At that time she will also review our office's fee structure and if you wish to proceed she will work out a fee agreement with you.
>
> In the meantime, I am going to give you a financial statement to fill out. I'll give you some written instructions, but feel free to call me if you have any questions. It would be very helpful if you could complete this before our next meeting.
>
> I will call you by the end of the week to set up the next meeting. But please don't hesitate to call me if anything at all comes up before then. You can also call Attorney Martin directly, but it is likely easier to reach me because she is often in court. You should also be aware that as a paralegal, I cannot give you legal advice. I can answer some questions for you, but others I will need to convey to Ms. Martin, and then she can call you back, or I can communicate her response to you.

■ The Divorce Action: Initial Steps and Discovery

In this and subsequent sections, we trace the stages of a divorce case from the drafting of the complaint through postjudgment procedures. This discussion is intended to give you an overview of this process, but it is important to recognize that each state has its own procedural rules. In some states, these rules are found in the code of civil procedure, which applies generally to all civil actions;[11] other states have specialized rules of domestic procedure; and other states use a combination of general and specialized procedural rules. When working on a case, it is essential that the applicable rules be ascertained and followed so that a client's rights are safeguarded.

Please note a couple of points about terminology. First, this chapter uses the terms "complaint," "plaintiff," and "defendant," but other terms such as "petition," "petitioner," and "respondent" (respectively) may be used in some states. Also, in most instances where a phrase such as "the plaintiff files the complaint" or "the defendant must answer in a timely fashion" is used, the task is actually performed by that party's attorney. The language denotes which side is responsible for the task, not the allocation of responsibility between a party and his or her attorney.

The Initial Steps

The following steps in the divorce process will be discussed in this section:

1. Drafting/filing the complaint
2. Service of process
3. Defendant's response

The Complaint

The first official step in the divorce process is the filing of the **complaint** (or **petition**); until the complaint is filed, the court has no authority over the parties. Divorce complaints tend to be fairly straightforward, and, in many states, preprinted forms are available from the court. (See Exhibit 10.1 for an example of a preprinted petition from the state of Connecticut.) Despite this relative simplicity, the complaint is a crucial document that must be drafted with care because it frames the plaintiff's case to both the court and the defendant.

The Functions of a Complaint. Like any other complaint, the divorce complaint serves a number of purposes. It identifies the parties to the action and, through a recitation of the parties' addresses and the length of time that the plaintiff has lived in the state, establishes whether the court is the proper one with respect to both jurisdiction (see Chapter 9) and venue (see below).

The complaint also sets out the facts that underlie the action. At a minimum, these would include the following basic allegations:

- when and where the parties were married;
- the names and birthdates of any children of the marriage;
- the location where the parties last lived together; and
- the date and cause of marital separation.

Beyond this, states vary with respect to how much factual detail is required, but at a minimum, the complaint must include sufficient information to establish the basis for the divorce. For instance, if a plaintiff filed a divorce for cruel and abusive treatment, in some states it would be sufficient to state that the defendant treated him or her in a cruel and abusive manner on a particular occasion or occasions; while in other jurisdictions, greater detail about the acts constituting the cruel and abusive behavior would need to be set out.

The complaint also includes a **request for relief** (sometimes known as a **prayer for relief**), in which the plaintiff sets out the relief he or she is seeking. In addition to asking the court to dissolve the marriage, the plaintiff sets out what she or he is seeking with respect to collateral matters such as custody, support, and the division of property. These are usually stated in general terms; for example, the plaintiff may request a reasonable amount of support or a fair and equitable division of property. However, local rules or customs might call for greater detail. States' rules differ with respect to whether a plaintiff can ask for something at trial that was not requested in the complaint. Some states strictly limit a plaintiff to the relief requested in the complaint, while others are more liberal. To avoid potential problems, many complaints are drafted to include a "catchall" phrase, asking the court to award any and all further relief that is deemed fair and equitable.

Amending the Complaint. After filing, a plaintiff may wish to change something on the complaint. For example, a plaintiff who files a fault divorce may subsequently agree to amend to a no-fault divorce. In most states, a plaintiff is permitted to amend the complaint within a specified time period, such as before the defendant files the answer, without seeking permission from the court or the defendant. After this time, the plaintiff must seek the permission of either the defendant or the court. Most courts are fairly liberal in allowing amendments unless the rights of the defendant would be prejudiced.

Exhibit 10.1   Divorce Complaint

DIVORCE COMPLAINT **(DISSOLUTION OF MARRIAGE)** JD-FM-159 Rev. 10-18 C.G.S. §§ 46b-40, 46b-56c, 46b-84, P.A. 18-14 P.B. § 25-2, et seq.	STATE OF CONNECTICUT **SUPERIOR COURT** www.jud.ct.gov	CROSS COMPLAINT CODE ONLY **CRSCMP**

<table>
<tr><td>
☐ **Complaint:** Complete this form. Attach a completed *Summons* (JD-FM-3), a *Notice of Automatic Court Orders* (JD-FM-158) and a blank *Appearance* (JD-CL-12).
☐ **Amended Complaint**
☐ **Cross Complaint:** Complete this form and attach to the *Answer* (JD-FM-160) unless it is already filed.
</td><td>
ADA NOTICE
The Judicial Branch of the State of Connecticut complies with the Americans with Disabilities Act (ADA). If you need a reasonable accommodation in accordance with the ADA, contact a court clerk or an ADA contact person listed at www.jud.ct.gov/ADA.
</td></tr>
</table>

Judicial District of	At *(Town)*	Return date *(Month, day, year)*	Docket number

Plaintiff's name *(Last, First, Middle Initial)*	Defendant's name *(Last, First, Middle Initial)*

1. Plaintiff's birth name *(If different from above)*	2. Defendant's birth name *(If different from above)*

3. a. Date of marriage	3. b. Date of civil union that merged into marriage by subsequent ceremony or by operation of law	4. Town and State, or Country where marriage took place

5. *("X" all that apply)*

☐ The *("X" one)* ☐ plaintiff ☐ defendant has lived in Connecticut for at least 12 months immediately before the filing of this divorce complaint or before the divorce will become final.

☐ The *("X" one)* ☐ plaintiff ☐ defendant lived in Connecticut at the time of the marriage, moved away, and then returned to Connecticut, planning to live here permanently.

☐ The marriage broke down after the *("X" one)* ☐ plaintiff ☐ defendant moved to Connecticut.

6. A divorce is being sought because: *("X" all that apply)*

☐ This marriage has broken down irretrievably.

☐ Other *(must be reason(s) listed in section 46b-40(c) of the Connecticut General Statutes):*

_____

_____

_____

"X" and complete all that apply for items 6-13. Attach additional sheets if needed.

7. ☐ No children were born to either the plaintiff or defendant after the date of this marriage.

8. ☐ There are no children of this marriage under the age of 23.

9. ☐ The following children are either: (a) the biological and/or adoptive children of both of the parties, or (b) have been born to one of the parties on or after the date of the marriage and are claimed to be children of the marriage. *(List only children who have not yet reached the age of 23.)*

Name of child *(First, Middle Initial, Last)*	Date of birth *(Month, day, year)*

10. ☐ The following children were born on or after the date of the marriage to the *("X" all that apply)* ☐ plaintiff ☐ defendant and are not children of the other party to this marriage. *(List only children who have not yet reached the age of 23.)*

Name of child *(First, Middle Initial, Last)*	Date of birth *(Month, day, year)*

Print Form   *Page 1 of 2*   Reset Form

Exhibit 10.1   Continued

11. If there is a court order regarding custody or support for any child listed above, name the child(ren) below and specify the person or agency awarded custody or ordered to pay support:

Child's name	Name of person or agency awarded custody	Name of person ordered to pay support
Child's name	Name of person or agency awarded custody	Name of person ordered to pay support
Child's name	Name of person or agency awarded custody	Name of person ordered to pay support

12. The *("X" all that apply)*   ☐ plaintiff   ☐ defendant   or any of the child(ren) listed above have received from the State of Connecticut:
   ☐ financial support *("X" one)*   ☐ Yes   ☐ No   ☐ Do not know
   ☐ HUSKY Health Insurance *("X" one)*   ☐ Yes   ☐ No   ☐ Do not know
   If yes, **you must** send a copy of the Summons, Complaint, Notice of Automatic Court Orders and any other documents filed with this Complaint to the Assistant Attorney General, 55 Elm Street, Hartford, CT 06106, and file the Certification of Notice *(JD-FM-175)* with the court clerk.

13. ☐ The *("X" all that apply)*   ☐ plaintiff   ☐ defendant   is pregnant with a child due to be born on _____.
   The other parent of this unborn child is the   ☐ plaintiff or   ☐ defendant   ☐ unknown   *(date)*
                                                    ☐ not the plaintiff   ☐ not the defendant.

14. The *("X" all that apply)*   ☐ plaintiff   ☐ defendant   or any of the child(ren) listed above has received financial support from a city or town in Connecticut. *("X" one)* ☐ Yes *(City or town:_____)*
   ☐ No   ☐ Do not know. If yes, send a copy of the Summons, Complaint, Notice of Automatic Court Orders and any other documents filed with this Complaint to the City Clerk of the town providing assistance and file the Certification of Notice *(JD-FM-175)* with the court clerk.

The Court is asked to order: *("X" all that apply)*

☐ A divorce (dissolution of marriage).

☐ A fair division of property and debts.

☐ Alimony.

☐ Child Support.

☐ An order regarding the post-majority educational support of the child(ren).

☐ Name change to:
   _____

Regarding Parental Decision-making Responsibility:
☐ Sole custody.
☐ Joint legal custody.
☐ A parenting responsibility plan which includes a plan for the parental decision-making regarding the minor child(ren).
                           AND
Regarding Physical Custody:
☐ Primary residence with: _____
☐ Visitation.
☐ A parenting responsibility plan which includes a plan for the schedule of physical care of the minor child(ren).

And anything else the Court deems fair.

Signature	Print name of person signing	Date signed
Address		Juris number *(If applicable)* Telephone *(Area code first)*

If this is an Amended Complaint or a Cross Complaint, you must mail or deliver a copy to anyone who has filed an appearance and you must complete the certification below.

Certification

I certify that a copy of this document was or will immediately be mailed or delivered electronically or non-electronically on (date)_____ to all attorneys and self-represented parties of record and that written consent for electronic delivery was received from all attorneys and self-represented parties of record who received or will immediately be receiving electronic delivery.
Name and address of each party and attorney that copy was or will be mailed or delivered to*

*If necessary, attach additional sheet or sheets with name and address which the copy was or will be mailed or delivered to.

Signed *(Signature of filer)*	Print or type name of person signing	Date signed
▶		
Mailing address *(Number, street, town, state and zip code)*		Telephone number

JD-FM-159 Rev. 10-18   *Page 2 of 2*

[Print Form]   [Reset Form]

Joint Petitions.   In some states, spouses may have the option of filing a **joint petition**, a no-fault petition for divorce jointly. Here, the parties are considered co-petitioners; neither is the plaintiff or the defendant. Joint petitions may entail special procedures or requirements. For example, in Massachusetts, parties who file a joint petition also must file an affidavit of irretrievable breakdown of the marriage, attesting to the fact that the marriage is over. A signed separation agreement also must be filed at this time or shortly thereafter. In California, couples without children who have been married a short time and have few assets may be eligible to file a Joint Petition for Summary Dissolution, which enables them to get divorced without a court hearing. (See Exhibit 10.2 for a sample joint petition and supporting affidavit.)

Filing the Complaint

Once the complaint is drafted, it is filed in the appropriate court together with any other required documents, such as a certified copy of the parties' marriage certificate. Before the complaint and any accompanying documents are accepted for filing, they are usually reviewed by a clerk to ensure that everything is in order. Upon acceptance, the case is assigned a **docket number**, which is then used on all subsequent case documents. In most states, filing can be done either in person or by mail. The advantage of filing in person is that any problems with the paperwork can be taken care of at the time. Also, as this responsibility is frequently delegated to paralegals, it provides a good opportunity to become familiar with the courts and court personnel.

Venue.   **Venue** is a geographical concept that determines the specific court in which an action must be filed. Thus, for example, once it is ascertained that the probate and family court has subject matter jurisdiction over divorce actions, venue rules would tell you which probate and family court the action should be filed in. As a general rule, an action is filed where either the plaintiff or the defendant lives or where the cause of action arose. In divorce cases, other factors, such as where the parties last lived together as spouses, may be relevant to determining venue.

Exhibit 10.2 Joint Petition and Affidavit

Commonwealth of Massachusetts
The Trial Court

_____ **Division**

Probate and Family Court Department

Docket No. _____

JOINT PETITION FOR DIVORCE PURSUANT TO G.L. c. 208, § 1 A

_____ and _____

Petitioner A			Petitioner B		

_____ _____

(Street address)			(Street address)		

(City/Town)	(State)	(Zip)	(City/Town)	(State)	(Zip)

1. Petitioners were lawfully married at _____

on _____ and last lived together at _____

on _____

2. The minor or dependent child(ren) of this marriage is/are:

_____ _____

(Name of child and date of birth)	(Name of child and date of birth)

_____ _____

(Name of child and date of birth)	(Name of child and date of birth)

3. Petitioners certify that no previous action for divorce, annulment or affirmation of marriage, separate support, desertion, living apart for justifiable cause, or custody of child(ren) has been brought by either against the other except: _____

_____

_____

4. On or about _____ , an irretrievable breakdown of the marriage under G.L. c. 208, § 1A occurred and continues to exist.

5. Wherefore, the petitioners request that the Court:

☐ grant a divorce on the ground of irretrievable breakdown

☐ approve the notarized separation agreement executed by the parties

☐ incorporate and merge the agreement executed by the parties

☐ incorporate but not merge said agreement, which shall survive and remain as an independent contract

☐ allow petitioner A to resume the former name of _____

☐ allow petitioner B to resume the former name of _____

☐ _____

Date _____

_____ _____

(Signature of attorney or petitioner A, if pro se)	(Signature of attorney or petitioner B, if pro se)

_____ _____

(Print name)	(Print name)

_____ _____

(Street address)	(Street address)

(City/Town)	(State)	(Zip)	(City/Town)	(State)	(Zip)

Tel. No. _____   Tel. No. _____

B.B.O. # _____   B.B.O. # _____

CJ-D 101A (9/07)   C.G.F

Filing Fees and Fee Waivers.   Most states charge a **filing fee** for the entry of a civil action. Filing fees are imposed to help defray administrative costs and possibly to deter frivolous actions. This fee, together with the related costs of service of process, can impose a serious financial hardship on low-income persons. So that these costs do not impose a barrier to court access, states must allow low-income divorce plaintiffs to seek a waiver of the filing fee. Plaintiffs also may be able to request that the state pay for costs related to the service of process and, less commonly, for those related to discovery (e.g., the hiring of a stenographer for a deposition). Although ensuring access to the court, the waiver of these fees does not, of course, resolve the greater problem of obtaining access to affordable legal representation. (See Exhibit 10.3 for Application for Indigent Status.)

Accompanying Documents.   Other documents may need to be filed with the complaint. The requirements vary from state to state and may vary within a state depending on the nature of the divorce action. For example, as noted above, in Massachusetts, an affidavit of irretrievable breakdown must accompany a joint petition or the petition will not be accepted for filing. The most common requirement is that the complaint be accompanied by a certified copy of the parties' marriage certificate; if the marriage took place in a foreign country, a qualified translation of the certificate may also need to be filed. Also, if there are minor children, an affidavit (or like document) may need to be filed disclosing any prior or pending custody actions involving the children.

Service of Process

After the complaint is filed, it must be served on the defendant so that he or she is provided with notice of the action in accordance with constitutional due process requirements.

The Summons.   Upon the filing of the complaint, the court issues a summons to the plaintiff (see Exhibit 10.4). A **summons** is a document that informs the defendant that he or she has been sued and that the failure to respond within a certain time period may result in a default judgment. The plaintiff is responsible for completing the summons and serving it on the defendant with a copy of the complaint. This is referred to as **service of process**.

Exhibit 10.3   Application for Indigent Status

IN THE CIRCUIT/COUNTY COURT OF THE ---------------- JUDICIAL CIRCUIT
IN AND FOR --------------- COUNTY, FLORIDA

CASE NO._____

_____
Plaintiff/Petitioner or In the Interest Of
vs.

_____
Defendant//Respondent

APPLICATION FOR DETERMINATION OF CIVIL INDIGENT STATUS

Notice to Applicant: If you qualify for civil indigence you must enroll in the clerk's office payment plan and pay a one-time administrative fee of $25.00. This fee shall not be charged for Dependency or Chapter 39 Termination of Parental Rights actions.

1. **I have _____dependents.** *(Include only those persons you list on your U.S. Income tax return.)*
        Are you Married? Yes   No   Does your Spouse Work?...Yes   No   Annual Spouse Income? $_____

2. **I have a net income of $**_____ paid   weekly   every two weeks   semi-monthly   monthly   yearly   other
_____.
(Net income is your total income including salary, wages, bonuses, commissions, allowances, overtime, tips and similar payments, **minus** *deductions required by law and other court-ordered payments such as child support.)*

3. **I have other income** paid   weekly   every two weeks   semi-monthly   monthly   yearly   other _____.
(Circle "Yes" and fill in the amount if you have this kind of income, otherwise circle "No")

Second Job ....Yes $ _____ No	Veterans' benefits...Yes $ _____ No	
Social Security benefits	Workers compensation...Yes $ _____ No	
For you...................................Yes $ _____ No	Income from absent family members ....Yes $ _____ No	
For child(ren) ....Yes $ _____ No	Stocks/bonds..Yes $ _____ No	
Unemployment compensation ....Yes $ _____ No	Rental income...Yes $ _____ No	
Union payments ....Yes $ _____ No	Dividends or interest...Yes $ _____ No	
Retirement/pensions ....Yes $ _____ No	Other kinds of income not on the list.......................Yes $ _____ No	
Trusts ....Yes $ _____ No	Gifts ....Yes $ _____ No	

I understand that I will be required to make payments for fees and costs to the clerk in accordance with §57.082(5), Florida Statutes, as provided by law, <u>although</u> I <u>may</u> <u>agree</u> <u>to</u> <u>pay</u> more <u>if</u> I <u>choose</u> <u>to</u> <u>do</u> <u>so.</u>

4. **I have other assets:** *(Circle "yes" and fill in the value of the property, otherwise circle "No")*

Cash...Yes $ _____ No	Savings account ....Yes $ _____ No	
Bank account(s) ....Yes $ _____ No	Stocks/bonds..Yes $ _____ No	
Certificates of deposit or	Homestead Real Property*.......................................Yes $ _____ No	
money market accounts.........................Yes $ _____ No	Motor Vehicle* ....Yes $ _____ No	
Boats* ....Yes $ _____ No	Non-homestead real property/real estate* ....Yes $ _____ No	

*show loans on these assets in paragraph 5

Check one: I   DO   DO NOT expect to receive more assets in the near future. The asset is_____.

5. **I have total liabilities and debts of $**_____ as follows: Motor Vehicle $_____, Home $_____, Other Real Property $_____, Child Support paid direct $_____, Credit Cards $_____, Medical Bills $_____, Cost of medicines (monthly) $_____,
Other $_____.

6. **I have a private lawyer in this case**............ Yes No

A person who knowingly provides false information to the clerk or the court in seeking a determination of indigent status under s. 57.082, F.S. commits a misdemeanor of the first degree, punishable as provided in s.775.082, F.S. or s. 775.083, F.S. **I attest that the information I have provided on this application is true and accurate to the best of my knowledge.**

Signed this _____ day of _____, 20____.

_____

_____   _____   Signature of Applicant for Indigent Status
Date of Birth   Driver's License or ID Number   Print Full Legal Name _____
                                                                Phone Number: _____

_____
Address, P O Address, Street, City, State, Zip Code

Exhibit 10.3   Continued

CLERK'S DETERMINATION

Based on the information in this Application, I have determined the applicant to be ( ) Indigent ( ) Not Indigent, according to s. 57.082, F.S.

Dated this _____ day of _____, 20 ____.

Clerk of the Circuit Court by _____

This form was completed with the assistance of: _____

Clerk/Deputy Clerk/Other authorized person.

APPLICANTS FOUND NOT TO BE INDIGENT MAY SEEK REVIEW BY A JUDGE BY ASKING FOR A HEARING TIME. THERE IS NO FEE FOR THIS REVIEW.

Sign here if you want the judge to review the clerk's decision _____

Methods of Making Service.   Service must be made in strict accordance with the applicable rules of procedure. Improper service may result in dismissal of the action. Although procedural requirements vary from state to state, making familiarity with local rules critical, some general principles can be identified. In discussing service, it is useful to distinguish between resident and nonresident defendants.

Serving a Resident Defendant.   The most common method of service is by **personal service** of the papers on the defendant or, where allowed, by leaving them at his or her usual place of residence. In the latter situation, most states require that the papers be left with a competent adult. Traditionally, most states have required that personal service be made by a sheriff, a marshal, or other person specially designated to serve process, but the modern trend is to allow personal service to be made by any disinterested person over the age of 18.

Most states also allow service to be made by mail. Here, the summons and complaint are mailed to the defendant, usually by certified mail requesting acknowledgment of receipt. For the service to be considered good, the defendant must sign and return the acknowledgment card, which is returned to the plaintiff by the postal service. This can be a simple and inexpensive way to obtain service, but if the defendant does not acknowledge service, it does not qualify as personal service.

If the defendant is "of parts unknown" or is avoiding service, most states permit service to be made by publication and mailing. Service by this method usually involves two discrete steps. First, the summons is published in a newspaper for a specific number of weeks; second, the plaintiff sends a copy of the summons and complaint to the defendant at his or her last known usual place of residence. Again, this would be sent by certified mail with acknowledgment requested so the plaintiff would know whether it was actually received.

Service by publication and mailing is often referred to as **constructive service** because, unless the defendant signs the acknowledgment card, there is no way of knowing whether he or she received notice of the action. This has potentially serious ramifications because it most likely means that even if the jurisdictional requirements are met, the court will not be able to assert personal jurisdiction over the defendant (see Chapter 9).

Exhibit 10.4   Summons

IN THE CIRCUIT COURT OF THE _____ JUDICIAL CIRCUIT,
IN AND FOR _____ COUNTY, FLORIDA

Case No.: _____
Division: _____

_____,
    Petitioner,

and

_____,
    Respondent.

SUMMONS: PERSONAL SERVICE ON AN INDIVIDUAL

TO/PARA/A: *{enter other party's full legal name}* _____,
{address (including city and state)/location for service} _____.

IMPORTANT

A lawsuit has been filed against you. You have **20 calendar days** after this summons is served on you to file a written response to the attached complaint/petition with the clerk of this circuit court, located at: *{street address}* _____.
A phone call will not protect you. Your written response, including the case number given above and the names of the parties, must be **filed** if you want the Court to hear your side of the case.

If you do not file your written response on time, you may lose the case, and your wages, money, and property may be taken thereafter without further warning from the Court. There are other legal requirements. You may want to call an attorney right away. If you do not know an attorney, you may call an attorney referral service or a legal aid office (listed in the phone book).

If you choose to file a written response yourself, at the same time you file your written response to the Court, you must also serve a copy of your written response on the party serving this summons at:

{Name and address of party serving summons} _____

_____.

If the party serving summons has designated email address(es) for service or is represented by an attorney, you may designate email address(es) for service by or on you. Service must be in accordance with Florida Rule of Judicial Administration 2.516.

Copies of all court documents in this case, including orders, are available at the Clerk of the Circuit Court's office. You may review these documents, upon request.

You must keep the Clerk of the Circuit Court's office notified of your current address. (You may file Designation of Current Mailing and Email Address, Florida Supreme Court Approved Family Law Form

Florida Family Law Rules of Procedure Form 12.910(a), Summons: Personal Service on an Individual (03/17)

Exhibit 10.4   Continued

12.915.) Future papers in this lawsuit will be mailed to the address on record at the clerk's office.

WARNING: Rule 12.285, Florida Family Law Rules of Procedure, requires certain automatic disclosure of documents and information. Failure to comply can result in sanctions, including dismissal or striking of pleadings.

In some states, the plaintiff may be able to avoid the potential difficulties of trying to obtain service on the defendant by arranging for the defendant to accept service of the complaint. If the defendant is cooperative, the plaintiff can simply provide him or her with a copy of the complaint and the original summons, which the defendant signs to acknowledge **acceptance of service**.

If the plaintiff's attorney arranges for the acceptance of service and the defendant is unrepresented, he or she must be careful not to provide the defendant with any legal advice about the divorce and should encourage the defendant to seek representation. Of course, this applies to paralegals as well.

Serving an Out-of-State Defendant.   Most states authorize service to be made on a nonresident by the same methods that are available for serving residents or by any manner authorized by the defendant's home state. There are practical difficulties in serving a nonresident; however, where the state can exercise personal jurisdiction over the defendant, it is important to make the effort to actually serve the defendant because, as mentioned above, it is usually a necessary precondition to the court's ability to exercise personal jurisdiction over the defendant where the jurisdictional requirements of the long-arm statute are otherwise satisfied.

Return of Service.   The person who serves the defendant must certify when, where, and how service was made. This is usually done on the back of the original summons under the caption Proof of Service (see Exhibit 10.5). The summons is then filed in court. This is known as the **return of service**. Depending on the method of service used, additional papers may need to be filed for the return of service to be complete. For example, if service was by publication, the pages from the newspaper usually must be submitted to the court.

The Defendant's Response

Once the defendant is served, he or she is allowed a certain time period within which to file a response to the complaint; this responsive document is the **answer** (see Exhibit 10.6). This response period is usually significantly longer when service is made by publication.

What happens if a defendant fails to respond? In the typical civil action, a defendant who fails to answer in a timely manner is in default. This has two consequences: (1) the plaintiff is relieved of the obligation of providing the defendant with notice about subsequent case proceedings, and (2) the plaintiff may seek to have a judgment entered in his or her favor without a hearing on the merits. This is known as a **default judgment**.

The practice is somewhat different in the divorce context. Because of the importance of the rights at stake, courts tend to be reluctant to consider a divorce defendant in default and will generally not do so where the defendant has made any effort to preserve his or her rights. Even where the defendant has not responded at all, courts may not consider a divorce defendant to be in default. Accordingly, the plaintiff will not be relieved of the obligation of providing the defendant with notice of all related case proceedings and the court will not enter a judgment by default without a hearing.

As a result of the more relaxed rules about defaults in the divorce context, the local practice custom may be to forgo the filing of an answer. However, this failure may serve to preclude the defendant from contesting matters raised by the plaintiff or from seeking certain kinds of relief. Accordingly, given the unpredictable nature of divorce litigation, the better practice is to file an answer in all cases to ensure that a client's rights are safeguarded.

Exhibit 10.5   Proof of Service

INSTRUCTIONS FOR FLORIDA SUPREME COURT APPROVED FAMILY LAW FORM 12.914
CERTIFICATE OF SERVICE (11/15)

When should this form be used?

After a petition or supplemental petition has been properly served (through either **personal service** or **constructive service**), both parties **must** serve copies of all additional documents or papers they **file** with the clerk on the other **party,** or his or her attorney, if he or she has one. Each time you file a document, you must certify that you provided the other party with a copy. Many of the Florida Family Law Forms already have a place above the signature line for this certification. It looks like this:

I certify that a copy of this document was (   ) mailed (   ) faxed and mailed (   ) e-mailed (   ) hand-delivered to the person(s) listed below on *{date}* _____

Other party or his/her attorney:
Name: _____
Address: _____
City, State, Zip: _____
Fax Number: _____
Designated E-mail Address(es):_____
_____

If a form you are filing has a certificate, you do not need to file a separate **Certificate of Service**, Florida Supreme Court Approved Family Law Form 12.914. However, **each time** you file a document that does **not** have a certificate like the one above, you must file a **Certificate of Service**, Florida Supreme Court Approved Family Law Form 12.914, and serve a copy of the document on the other party.

This form should be typed or printed in black ink. After completing this form (giving the name of each form, document, or paper filed), you should sign the form before a **notary public** or **deputy clerk**. You should file the original with the **clerk of the circuit court** in the county where your case was filed and keep a copy for your records.

IMPORTANT INFORMATION REGARDING E-FILING

The Florida Rules of Judicial Administration now require that all petitions, pleadings, and documents be filed electronically except in certain circumstances. **Self-represented litigants may file petitions or other pleadings or documents electronically; however, they are not required to do so.** If you choose to file your pleadings or other documents electronically, you must do so in accordance with Florida Rule of Judicial Administration 2.525, and you must follow the procedures of the judicial circuit in which you file. **The rules and procedures should be carefully read and followed.**

Exhibit 10.5   Continued

What should I do next?

The copy you are providing to the other party must be either mailed, e-mailed, or hand-delivered to the opposing party or his or her attorney on the same day indicated on the certificate of service.   If it is mailed, it must be postmarked on the date indicated in the certificate of service.

IMPORTANT INFORMATION REGARDING E-SERVICE ELECTION

After the initial service of process of the petition or supplemental petition by the Sheriff or certified process server, the Florida Rules of Judicial Administration now require that all documents required or permitted to be served on the other party must be served by electronic mail (e-mail) except in certain circumstances. **You must strictly comply with the format requirements set forth in the Rules of Judicial Administration.** If you elect to participate in electronic service, which means serving or receiving pleadings by electronic mail (e-mail), or through the Florida Courts E-Filing Portal, you **must** review Florida Rule of Judicial Administration 2.516. You may find this rule at www.flcourts.org through the link to the Rules of Judicial Administration provided under either Family Law Forms: Getting Started, or Rules of Court in the A-Z Topical Index.

SELF-REPRESENTED LITIGANTS MAY SERVE DOCUMENTS BY E-MAIL; HOWEVER, THEY ARE NOT REQUIRED TO DO SO. If a self-represented litigant elects to serve and receive documents by e-mail, the procedures must always be followed once the initial election is made.

To serve and receive documents by e-mail, you must designate your e-mail addresses by using the **Designation of Current Mailing and E-mail Address**, Florida Supreme Court Approved Family Law Form 12.915, and you must provide your e-mail address on each form on which your signature appears. Please **CAREFULLY** read the rules and instructions for: **Certificate of Service (General),** Florida Supreme Court Approved Family Law Form 12.914; **Designation of Current Mailing and E-mail Address**, Florida Supreme Court Approved Family Law Form 12.915; and Florida Rule of Judicial Administration 2.516.

Where can I look for more information?

Before proceeding, you should read General Information for Self-Represented Litigants found at the beginning of these forms. For more information, see rule 1.080, Florida Rules of Civil Procedure and rule 12.080, Florida Family Law Rules of Procedure.

Special notes

Remember, a person who is NOT an attorney is called a nonlawyer. If a nonlawyer helps you fill out these forms, that person must give you a copy of **Disclosure from Nonlawyer**, Florida Family Law Rules of Procedure Form 12.900(a), before he or she helps you. A nonlawyer helping you fill out these forms also **must** put his or her name, address, and telephone number on the bottom of the last page of every form he or she helps you complete.

Instructions for Florida Supreme Court Approved Family Law Form 12.914, Certificate of Service (11/15)

Exhibit 10.5   Continued

IN THE CIRCUIT COURT OF THE _____ JUDICIAL CIRCUIT,

IN AND FOR _____ COUNTY, FLORIDA

Case No.: _____

Division: _____

_____,

Petitioner,

and

_____,

Respondent,

CERTIFICATE OF SERVICE

I certify that a copy of *{name of document(s)}* _____

_____

was ( ) mailed ☐ faxed and mailed ☐ e-mailed ☐ hand-delivered to the person listed below on

{date} _____.

Other party or his/her attorney:

Name: _____

Address: _____

City, State, Zip: _____

Fax Number: _____

Designated E-mail Address(es): _____

_____

_____

Signature of Party

Printed Name: _____

Address: _____

City, State, Zip: _____

Fax Number: _____

Designated E-mail Address(es): _____

_____

IF A NONLAWYER HELPED YOU FILL OUT THIS FORM, HE/SHE MUST FILL IN THE BLANKS BELOW:

[fill in all blanks] This form was prepared for the: *{choose only **one**}* ( ) Petitioner ( ) Respondent

This form was completed with the assistance of:

{name of individual} _____,

{name of business} _____,

{address} _____,

{city} _____,{state} _____,{zip code}_____,{telephone number} _____

Florida Supreme Court Approved Family Law Form 12.914, Certificate of Service (11/15)

The Component Parts of an Answer

Admissions/Denials

In the first portion of an answer, the defendant responds to the factual allegations in the complaint by either admitting or denying them. For example, a defendant might deny the validity of the parties' marriage, that a child named on the complaint was in fact born of the marriage, or that the plaintiff is entitled to the requested relief. Denials thus serve to delineate areas of potential controversy. If the defendant lacks knowledge about an allegation, the defendant can state that he or she is without sufficient information to either admit or deny the matter. If the defendant fails to respond to an allegation, it is usually treated as an admission of that fact.

Affirmative Defenses

In an **affirmative defense**, a defendant seeks to establish that the plaintiff is not entitled to prevail even if his or her allegations are established. Thus, for example, a defendant might assert that by continued cohabitation, the plaintiff forgave the defendant's marital trespasses. Since no-fault divorce, however, as discussed in Chapter 4, affirmative defenses are far less significant. Because it is virtually impossible for one spouse to prevent the other from obtaining a divorce, parties are much less likely to fight about the legal significance of marital fault.

Counterclaims

A defendant can also assert claims for relief against the plaintiff in his or her answer by way of a **counterclaim**. Where a counterclaim is asserted, roles are reversed: The defendant functions as a plaintiff, and the plaintiff functions as a defendant and has a right to respond to the counterclaim.

In a divorce case, a defendant might counterclaim for a divorce from the plaintiff and set out the relief he or she is seeking, such as custody of the children or a spousal support award. Depending on local rules, a defendant might also be able to set out claims for relief even if he or she is not actually counterclaiming for divorce.

The Motion to Dismiss.   A defendant may also respond to a complaint by filing a **motion to dismiss** the divorce action. Common grounds for seeking a dismissal are lack of jurisdiction, inadequate service, or improper venue. If the action is dismissed, the defendant does not need to file an answer. If the motion is denied, the defendant will need to answer, although the time period for responding will be extended. Of course, the plaintiff will most likely refile, making sure to correct the error that led to the dismissal.

Exhibit 10.6   Answer

FL-120

PARTY WITHOUT ATTORNEY OR ATTORNEY STATE BAR NUMBER:	FOR COURT USE ONLY
NAME:	
FIRM NAME:	
STREET ADDRESS:	
CITY: STATE: ZIP CODE:	
TELEPHONE NO.: FAX NO.:	
E-MAIL ADDRESS:	
ATTORNEY FOR (name):	

SUPERIOR COURT OF CALIFORNIA, COUNTY OF
   STREET ADDRESS:
   MAILING ADDRESS:
   CITY AND ZIP CODE:
   BRANCH NAME:

PETITIONER:
RESPONDENT:

RESPONSE ☐ **AND REQUEST FOR** ☐ **AMENDED**	CASE NUMBER:
☐ **Dissolution (Divorce) of:** ☐ Marriage ☐ Domestic Partnership	
☐ **Legal Separation of:** ☐ Marriage ☐ Domestic Partnership	
☐ **Nullity of:** ☐ Marriage ☐ Domestic Partnership	

1. **LEGAL RELATIONSHIP** (check all that apply):
   a. ☐ We are married.
   b. ☐ We are domestic partners and our domestic partnership was established in California.
   c. ☐ We are domestic partners and our domestic partnership was NOT established in California.

2. **RESIDENCE REQUIREMENTS** (check all that apply):
   a. ☐ Petitioner ☐ Respondent has been a resident of this state for at least six months and of this county for at least three months immediately preceding the filing of this Petition. (For a divorce, at least one person in the legal relationship described in items 1a and 1c must comply with this requirement.)
   b. ☐ Our domestic partnership was established in California. Neither of us has to be a resident or have a domicile in California to dissolve our partnership here.
   c. ☐ We are the same sex, were married in California, but currently live in a jurisdiction that does not recognize, and will not dissolve, our marriage. This Petition is filed in the county where we married.
        Petitioner lives in (specify):   Respondent lives in (specify):

3. **STATISTICAL FACTS**
   a. ☐ (1) Date of marriage (specify):   (2) Date of separation (specify):
        (3) Time from date of marriage to date of separation (specify):   Years   Months
   b. ☐ (1) Registration date of domestic partnership with the California Secretary of State or other state equivalent (specify below):
        (2) Date of separation (specify):
        (3) Time from date of registration of domestic partnership to date of separation (specify):   Years   Months

4. **MINOR CHILDREN**
   a. ☐ There are no minor children.
   b. ☐ The minor children are:

Child's name	Birthdate	Age	Sex

   (1) ☐ continued on Attachment 4b.   (2) ☐ a child who is not yet born.
   c. If any children were born before the marriage or domestic partnership, the court has the authority to determine those children to be children of the marriage or domestic partnership.
   d. If there are minor children of Petitioner and Respondent, a completed Declaration Under Uniform Child Custody Jurisdiction and Enforcement Act (UCCJEA) (form FL-105) must be attached.
   e. ☐ Petitioner and Respondent signed a voluntary declaration of paternity. A copy ☐ is ☐ is not attached.

Page 1 of 3

Form Adopted for Mandatory Use
Judicial Council of California
FL-120 [Rev. July 1, 2016]

RESPONSE—MARRIAGE/DOMESTIC PARTNERSHIP
(Family Law)

Family Code, § 2020
www.courts.ca.gov

Exhibit 10.6 Continued

FL-120

PETITIONER:	CASE NUMBER:
RESPONDENT:	

Respondent requests that the court make the following orders:

5. **LEGAL GROUNDS** (Family Code sections 2200–2210; 2310–2312)
   a. ☐ **Respondent contends** that the parties never legally married or registered a domestic partnership.
   b. ☐ **Respondent denies** the grounds set forth in item 5 of the petition.
   c. ☐ **Respondent requests**
      (1) ☐ divorce ☐ Legal separation of the marriage or domestic partnership based on
         (a) ☐ irreconcilable differences. (b) ☐ permanent legal incapacity to make decisions.
      (2) ☐ Nullity of void marriage or domestic partnership based on
         (a) ☐ incest. (b) ☐ bigamy.
      (3) ☐ Nullity of voidable marriage or domestic partnership based on
         (a) ☐ respondent's age at time of registration of   (d) ☐ fraud.
             domestic partnership or marriage.
         (b) ☐ prior existing marriage or domestic partnership.   (e) ☐ force.
         (c) ☐ unsound mind.   (f) ☐ physical incapacity.

6. **CHILD CUSTODY AND VISITATION (PARENTING TIME)**

	Petitioner	Respondent	Joint	Other
a. Legal custody of children to	☐	☐	☐	☐
b. Physical custody of children to	☐	☐	☐	☐
c. Child visitation (parenting time) be granted to	☐	☐		☐

    As requested in ☐ form FL-311 ☐ form FL-312 ☐ form FL-341(C)
                ☐ form FL-341(D) ☐ form FL-341(E) ☐ Attachment 6c(1)

7. **CHILD SUPPORT**
   a. If there are minor children born to or adopted by Petitioner and Respondent before or during this marriage or domestic partnership, the court will make orders for the support of the children upon request and submission of financial forms by the requesting party.
   b. An earnings assignment may be issued without further notice.
   c. Any party required to pay support must pay interest on overdue amounts at the "legal" rate, which is currently 10 percent.
   d. ☐ Other (specify):

8. **SPOUSAL OR DOMESTIC PARTNER SUPPORT**
   a. ☐ Spousal or domestic partner support payable to ☐ Petitioner ☐ Respondent
   b. ☐ Terminate (end) the court's ability to award support to ☐ Petitioner ☐ Respondent
   c. ☐ Reserve for future determination the issue of support payable to ☐ Petitioner ☐ Respondent
   d. ☐ Other (specify):

9. **SEPARATE PROPERTY**
   a. ☐ There are no such assets or debts that I know of to be confirmed by the court.
   b. ☐ Confirm as separate property the assets and debts in ☐ Property Declaration (form FL-160). ☐ Attachment 9b.
      ☐ the following list.   Item   Confirm to

Exhibit 10.6 Continued

FL-120

PETITIONER:	CASE NUMBER:
RESPONDENT:	

10. COMMUNITY AND QUASI-COMMUNITY PROPERTY

a. ☐ There are no such assets or debts that I know of to be divided by the court.

b. ☐ Determine rights to community and quasi-community assets and debts. All such assets and debts are listed

☐ in *Property Declaration* (form FL-160). ☐ in Attachment 10b.

☐ as follows *(specify)*:

11. OTHER REQUESTS

a. ☐ Attorney's fees and costs payable by ☐ Petitioner ☐ Respondent

b ☐ Respondent's former name be restored to *(specify)*:

c. ☐ Other *(specify)*:

☐ Continued on Attachment 11c.

I declare under penalty of perjury under the laws of the State of California that the foregoing is true and correct.

Date:

_____
(TYPE OR PRINT NAME)

▶ _____
(SIGNATURE OF RESPONDENT)

Date:

_____
(TYPE OR PRINT NAME)

▶ _____
(SIGNATURE OF ATTORNEY FOR RESPONDENT)

FOR MORE INFORMATION: Read *Legal Steps for a Divorce or Legal Separation* (**form FL-107-INFO**) and visit "Families Change" at **www.familieschange.ca.gov** — an online guide for parents and children going through divorce or separation.

NOTICE: You may redact (black out) social security numbers from any written material filed with the court in this case other than a form used to collect child, spousal or partner support.

NOTICE—CANCELLATION OF RIGHTS: Dissolution or legal separation may automatically cancel the rights of a domestic partner or spouse under the other domestic partner's or spouse's will, trust, retirement plan, power of attorney, pay-on-death bank account, survivorship rights to any property owned in joint tenancy, and any other similar thing. It does not automatically cancel the right of a domestic partner or spouse as beneficiary of the other partner's or spouse's life insurance policy. You should review these matters, as well as any credit cards, other credit accounts, insurance polices, retirement plans, and credit reports, to determine whether they should be changed or whether you should take any other actions. Some changes may require the agreement of your partner or spouse or a court order.

The original response must be filed in the court with proof of service of a copy on Petitioner.

FL-120 [Rev. July 1, 2016] | **RESPONSE—MARRIAGE/DOMESTIC PARTNERSHIP** (Family Law) | Page 3 of 3

For your protection and privacy, please press the Clear This Form button after you have printed the form. | Print this form | Save this form | Clear this form

Discovery

Discovery is a pretrial process for obtaining information from the other side. Most states have modeled their discovery rules after the federal discovery rules contained in the Federal Rules of Civil Procedure, so these rules will serve as the basis for our discussion. Of course, the rules of your state should always be consulted when working on a case.

General Purpose

Discovery serves a number of important purposes, including the following:

1. It facilitates trial preparation because both parties can use the obtained information to help develop their respective cases.
2. It reduces the possibility of surprise during trial, since information is obtained in advance.
3. It enables both sides to assess the relative strengths and weaknesses of the case and can thus facilitate the settlement process.

Despite these benefits, there is a potentially troubling aspect to discovery. Given how open-ended the process is, it is possible for the spouse with greater resources to "out-discover" the other. This can push the spouse with fewer resources into a premature and potentially disadvantageous settlement. It can also result in different levels of trial preparedness. Either outcome may be the result of a well-crafted strategy or simply a byproduct of thorough preparation. Although courts can impose some limitations, they generally will not interfere with discovery absent egregious behavior.

Scope of Discovery

In most states, the permissible scope of discovery is broad. In keeping with the federal standard, discovery can be had of any unprivileged matter that is *relevant* to the case. The information sought does not need to be admissible at trial so long as it is "reasonably calculated to lead to the discovery of admissible evidence."[12] State rules may or may not define what is considered *privileged* and beyond the scope of discovery. In most states, communications between an attorney and client, a doctor and patient, and a priest and penitent are privileged; communications between spouses and between a psychotherapist and patient may also be considered privileged. Additionally, states generally recognize the privilege against self-incrimination. Many states now also recognize a privilege based on rights of privacy; thus certain very personal information may be off limits.

However, the parameters of this privilege are not always clear, and a party may be deemed to have waived it if she or he has put a particular matter in issue.

In the divorce context, an enormous range of information is commonly sought through the discovery process. For instance, where property or support is at issue, discovery will focus on the other party's financial situation. He or she will be asked for detailed information about income, expenditures, assets, and liabilities in accordance with the applicable statutory factors. For example, a stay-at-home spouse might be asked to detail all of the nonfinancial contributions he or she has made to the marriage by way of household and child-care responsibilities. Where conduct is a permissible factor, a spouse might be asked to detail all of his or her "bad acts." Where custody is at issue, a party may be asked to provide detailed information about his or her relationship with the children, including caretaking functions performed. Discovery can also be used to explore potential areas of concern. A party may be asked about whether he or she has ever struck the child or used drugs or alcohol in the child's presence. Pertinent information can also be discovered from other persons with knowledge about the child, such as neighbors, teachers, and therapists.

Discovery Methods

There are five basic methods of discovery:

1. Depositions
2. Interrogatories
3. Request for production of documents and electronically stored information
4. Request for a physical or mental examination
5. Request for admissions

In any given case, a single method may be used, or more than one may be used in combination with one another. Before considering these different methods, it is important to be aware that some cases are completed without any or with only a minimum of discovery. This may be because the case is simple or is uncontested. It also may be because the parties have the information they need in order to proceed. Cost may also be an important consideration, which, as noted earlier, can be particularly problematic if the weight of this concern falls more heavily on one spouse than the other.

Paralegals often play a major role in the discovery process. Thus, the discussion of each method of discovery includes the responsibilities that a paralegal might be asked to assume. Although not the focus of our discussion, keep in mind that paralegals also often play a significant role in coordinating the logistical aspects of discovery, such as arranging deposition dates. Of course, each office is different, and in any workplace you will need to establish exactly what is expected of you. Also, in setting out these responsibilities, it is assumed that the paralegal's work is subject to an attorney's direction and review.

Depositions.   One common method of discovery is the **deposition**. A deposition can be taken of a party or any potential witness, including an expert witness such as a real estate appraiser or a psychiatrist. If the **deponent** is a party, the deposition can be taken upon sending the party a notice naming the date, time, and location of the deposition and listing any documents he or she should bring. If the deponent is a nonparty witness, his or her presence must be secured by a **subpoena**; if the nonparty witness is to bring documents, he or she must be served with a **subpoena duces tecum**, which specifically designates the documents to be produced.

At the deposition, the deponent is placed under oath and is questioned by the attorney taking the deposition. The other attorney is in the role of "defending the deposition" and may also ask questions. Usually these questions are limited to clearing up confusion or eliciting information that the deponent forgot to provide.

A court reporter or certified shorthand reporter is usually present at a deposition. He or she records the proceeding and prepares a verbatim transcript. Due to the cost involved, some states may permit depositions to be audio- or videotaped. Where this is done, all of the procedural requirements must be carefully adhered to so the validity of the deposition is not subject to challenge.

The primary advantages of depositions are their flexibility and spontaneity. Although most attorneys prepare their witnesses in advance, it is virtually impossible to anticipate and prepare for all possible questions. Even when prepared, the witness must answer the questions on his or her own; unlike answering interrogatories, the defending attorney cannot help craft the answers. Additionally, the deponent's answers can be immediately followed up with additional questions, and the attorney conducting the deposition can pursue a line of inquiry to its logical conclusion. This spontaneous interchange can lead to valuable information. An additional benefit is that witness credibility can be assessed and a determination made about how well he or she is likely to do in court.

The primary disadvantages of depositions are that they are expensive and time-consuming. To minimize these burdens, an attorney might choose to wait to do depositions until he or she has established a baseline of information through the use of interrogatories and requests for documents and then use the depositions to focus on matters already determined to be significant.

The Role of the Paralegal

Taking Depositions

If your office is taking the depositions:

- Determine who should be deposed.
- Prepare the notice of intent to take deposition if a party deponent; prepare the summons or the subpoena duces tecum if a nonparty deponent.
- Organize the information that will be useful in preparing the deposition questions, such as financial documents, bank statements already in your possession, and school records.
- Draft the deposition questions.
- Listen carefully at the deposition and take detailed notes. Provide the attorney with possible additional questions that you think will be useful. Also, help to evaluate the witnesses' credibility; be prepared to discuss how well you think each witness will do in court.
- Review any documents that have been brought to the deposition to ensure that the production request has been fully complied with.
- After the depositions, carefully review the transcript of the deposition and prepare a summary in accordance with your office's summary procedure.

If your office is defending the deposition:

- Develop questions that you anticipate the other side will ask and conduct a mock deposition.
- Organize the documents that your witness is asked to bring. If the attorney is objecting to a production request, draft a motion for a protective order.
- At the deposition, listen carefully and suggest questions that the defending attorney might want to ask the deponent to clarify responses or elicit missing information. Also, evaluate the witness's credibility; be prepared to discuss how well you think the witness will do in court.
- Obtain a copy of the deposition transcript and review it with the witness for accuracy. Correct any mistakes in accordance with local rules.
- Prepare a summary of the deposition transcript in accordance with your office's summary procedures.

Interrogatories. Interrogatories are written questions that must be answered in writing within a certain time period, usually 30 days. Unlike depositions, interrogatories can only be served on parties; they cannot be served on nonparty witnesses. Interrogatories are answered under oath, and in many states the respondent has a duty to supplement answers if additional information becomes available.

Many states limit the number of questions that can be asked, although courts usually have the authority to allow additional questions. Attorneys can also agree to allow additional questions, and some have been known to employ creative numbering techniques in an effort to squeeze in as many questions as possible! Some states have developed standard interrogatory forms for use in appropriate circumstances.

In responding to interrogatories, a party must base his or her answers on all available information. Unlike a deposition, a party cannot respond based solely on what he or she knows personally but instead has an obligation to consult resources in his or her custody or control. For example, if a husband is asked about how much money he spent on clothing in the past five years, he would be obligated to review relevant financial records, such as canceled checks and credit card statements, whereas no such obligation would exist if this question were asked during a deposition. As a result of this duty to investigate, interrogatory answers may be more complete than answers given in a deposition; however, this method lacks the spontaneity and flexibility that characterize the deposition process.

When interrogatories are received by an office, the usual approach is to have the client provide the requested information to the legal team, which then drafts the responses. Clearly, although honesty is required, good drafting skills can help to shape the answers in a light most favorable to the client. Even if follow-up interrogatories are generated by the answers, the second round of responses are again subject to scrutiny. There is no opportunity for the open-ended give-and-take that characterizes the deposition process.

The Role of the Paralegal

Interrogatories

If your office is preparing the interrogatories:

- Analyze what information is needed from the other side.
- Draft the interrogatory questions.
- When the answers are returned, review them carefully to determine if all requested information has been provided. If not, discuss strategies and then draft a letter to the other side seeking supplemental information or draft a motion to compel.
- Summarize the responses and determine what information still needs to be obtained.

If your office is responding to the interrogatories:

- Enter the return date on your office's tickler system, and keep track of it.
- Remind the attorney to contact the other side if additional time is needed; if necessary, prepare a motion requesting additional time.
- Determine if any questions are objectionable and should not be answered; if necessary, prepare a motion for a protective order.
- Contact the client immediately and provide him or her with a copy of the interrogatories and instructions for preparing a response.
- Meet with the client, and review the information and relevant documentation.
- Draft answers. When complete, have client come in to review, make appropriate adjustments, and obtain client signature.
- Make sure that if required by state law, the client understands the obligation to supplement answers.

Request for Production of Documents and Electronically Stored Information. As part of the discovery process, a party may seek to review documents in the possession or under the control of the other side. To access the documents, a party serves a **request for production of documents** that details what is to be made available for inspection. The term "document" is usually defined in the request, and liberal, all-encompassing definitions are the norm. The request also specifies the time, place, and manner of production. Commonly, production is made at the office of the requesting attorney. The requesting party then has the right to make copies of the documents that he or she wishes to retain. A party may also enter onto land or other property in the possession or control of the other side for the purpose of inspection, although court permission may be needed for this. This is not done routinely in divorce cases, but could be important where, for example, the value of a professional practice or a closely held corporation is at issue.

In a divorce case, parties often make very liberal use of the production process, especially when seeking financial information. Among other things, a spouse may be asked to produce all of his or her pay stubs, canceled checks, credit card and bank statements, receipts for purchases over a specified amount, and loan payments over a specific time period, which could well be the length of the marriage. Clearly, these requests can be burdensome to the party who must locate the requested documents as well as to the person, most commonly a paralegal, who must review them!

Interesting issues arise when one spouse requests access to books and records from a professional practice. Access to these documents may be necessary for property distribution purposes in order to establish the value and the nature of the spouse's interest in the practice. The request may be objected to, however, where production could compromise confidentiality through disclosure of information about clients, patients, or work associates. In this situation, a judge is likely to order production but structure it in such a way that confidentiality is preserved by, for example, ordering the deletion of names and identifying information.

In addition to requesting documents, discovery can now be had of electronically stored information (ESI), which includes "emails, voice-mails, instant messages, text messages, documents and spreadsheets, file fragments, digital images and video."[13] Although e-discovery has become increasingly important in the digital era, the process requires a certain amount of technological sophistication and may thus present certain stumbling blocks for the unwary practitioner.

For example, documents frequently contain "invisible" information known as "metadata," which is generally defined as "data hidden in documents that is generated during the course of creating and editing such documents. It may include fragments of data from files that were previously deleted, overwritten or worked on simultaneously."[14] Although hidden, this "data about data" is, in fact, retrievable. Accordingly, when an attorney produces electronic files pursuant to a discovery request, he or she may inadvertently be providing the other attorney with confidential or privileged information that he or she is unaware is embedded in the produced materials in potential breach of the duty to maintain client confidentiality. In terms of the ethical obligation of the recipient, a number of states have concluded that the "receiving attorney has an ethical duty not to review the information" in accordance with a "strong public policy . . . against an attorney engaging in conduct that would amount to an unjustified intrusion into the opposing counsel's attorney-client relationship."[15] However, the law is clearly evolving in this arena, and as one commentator suggests, to avoid potential ethical breaches "an attorney should be charged with an active duty to stay current on technological advances in document transmission to best understand the potential risks and best methods of transmitting information to opposing parties."[16]

In a similar vein, the fact that one has deleted a document does not actually mean that it has been erased from the hard drive; accordingly, "the chances are good that unless the user has used software to erase or wipe the hard drive, significant amounts of deleted data or bits and pieces of deleted data will remain," that can be retrieved by forensic software.[17] Accordingly, if access is given to the actual computer, which may be necessary for the purpose of authenticating the requested electronic data, as with metadata, an attorney may likewise inadvertently be providing the opposing counsel with far more information than he or she realizes if unaware that deleted files are not necessarily vanquished from the computer's memory, thus again potentially compromising client confidentiality.

Although the e-discovery process is clearly not without its difficulties, a spouse who seeks to gain access to the other party's electronically stored information outside of the formal discovery process may well find that not only is the evidence inadmissible, but that he or she has committed a crime under federal and state laws that are designed to protect an individual's right of privacy in the digital realm by prohibiting both the interception of electronic communications and unauthorized access to such communications. In the divorce context, the question of what constitutes "unauthorized" use can be particularly murky, given that spouses may both use the same computer. For example, in the case of Byrne v. Byrne, the husband had a laptop from work that he allowed his children to do their homework on. The wife brought the computer to her attorney because she believed it contained important financial information in its memory. Rejecting the husband's claim that her actions were improper, the court likened the memory of a family computer to a file cabinet, and ruled that in the same manner that the wife "would have access to the contents of a file cabinet left in the marital residence . . . she should have access to the contents of the computer."[18] However, the result may well have been different if, for example, the computer had not been characterized by the court as a family computer or if the wife had gained access to password-protected information. It is important to keep in mind that this is a rapidly evolving area of the law, and the legal standards for what constitutes unauthorized access to electronically stored information tends to be both highly fact-sensitive and variable from state to state.

The Role of the Paralegal

Requesting the Production of Documents

If your office is requesting the documents:

- Determine what documents are needed.
- Draft the request with the requisite specificity so you get what is needed without being flooded with extraneous documents.
- When the documents are received, match them against the request to ensure it has been compiled with. If information is missing or objected to, develop a strategy for obtaining it; draft a letter to the other side requesting the information or draft a motion to compel for court.

- Determine what documents are needed and make copies of them. In the event of uncertainty, err on the side of copying more than is needed rather than less.
- Organize and label the documents so they are immediately accessible.

If your office is responding to a request for documents:

- Upon receiving the request for production, immediately contact the client and set up a time to review the request with him or her. Make sure the client understands the time frame.
- Keep track of the production deadline. If it cannot be met, remind the attorney to contact the other side to arrange an extension; if necessary, draft a motion for an extension of time.
- Determine if any of the requests are objectionable.
- When the documents are provided by the client, review them to see if the request has been complied with and if any documents should be held back based on privilege.
- Organize the documents for production, indicating any objections, and note all instances where documents are unavailable.

Comment: Please note that the same basic tasks are applicable in the context of e-discovery; however, given the complexities of the process, the role of the paralegal should be carefully spelled out by the supervising attorney so as to avoid the kinds of problems discussed above or the myriad of other difficulties that can arise when seeking access to or responding to requests for electronically stored information.

Request for a Physical or Mental Examination. If a party's mental or physical condition is at issue, such as in a contested custody case, the other side may make a **request for a physical or mental examination**. Given the inherently invasive nature of this request, court permission usually must be obtained before a party can be required to submit to such an exam. Courts generally will approve such a request upon proof of "good cause."

The Role of the Paralegal

Physical and Mental Examinations

If your office is requesting the examination:

- Draft the motion asking for court permission and, if necessary, draft an accompanying memorandum or affidavit to support the request.
- If in accordance with local practice, develop a short list of proposed examiners for presentation to the court.
- Review the report and, if needed, prepare a summary. If incomplete, prepare a list of possible follow-up questions to ask the examiner.

If your office is responding to the request for an examination:

- If the request is contested, prepare a memorandum or affidavit setting out the grounds for opposition to the request.
- If in accordance with local practice, prepare a short list of proposed examiners for presentation to the court.
- If the request is allowed, help prepare the client for what to expect.
- View the report and, if needed, prepare a summary.

Request for Admissions.   The final discovery device is the **request for admissions**, in which one side asks the other party to admit to specific legal or factual allegations, to the authenticity of documents, or to the qualifications of an expert witness. Thus, for example, the husband might be asked to admit to the fact that he is taking medication for depression, or that he has twice been married and divorced, or that all documents relating to his business are authentic. This is done primarily to simplify the issues for trial because once something has been admitted to, it does not need to be proved. The request for admission thus differs from other discovery devices because it is used to confirm rather than to obtain information.

In responding to a request for admission, a party can either admit or deny an allegation, state that he or she is without sufficient information to admit or deny, or object to the propriety of the request. However, before responding that he or she is without sufficient information, a party has a duty to conduct a limited inquiry into the matter. In most states a party has 30 days in which to reply to a request for admission.

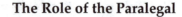

The Role of the Paralegal

Requests for Admissions

If your office is making the request:

- Determine which documents are likely to be introduced at trial and what factual or legal assertions may possibly be reduced to an admission.
- Draft the request for admission.
- Review the response and prepare a summary of what has been admitted to. If the response is incomplete or objections made, draft a letter to the other side or prepare a motion to compel.

If your office is responding to the request:

- Promptly review the document and set up a time to meet with the client. Make sure the client knows about the time limit for responding.
- Keep track of the time limit and remind the attorney to contact the other side if it cannot be complied with; if necessary, draft a motion for an extension of time.
- Carefully prepare a response, making sure that each and every request is properly addressed.[19]

Discovery Difficulties

In most cases, discovery proceeds without too many wrinkles; however, occasionally problems do arise that may require court intervention. Following is a brief discussion about the ways in which the court may be pulled into the discovery process.

Limiting Discovery. A party who believes that discovery has become excessive may seek to limit it by bringing a motion for a protective order. A **protective order** can also be sought when irrelevant or privileged information is requested, but the more common response in this situation is to object to the request. In evaluating the motion, the court looks to determine if the discovery request would produce "annoyance, embarrassment, oppression, or undue burden or expense."[20] If the answer is yes, the court may impose limits even if the information is otherwise discoverable. Courts tend, however, to hold the moving party to a fairly high standard and do not impose limitations lightly.

A party who is concerned about discovery can also file a motion requesting that the court convene a **discovery conference**; in most states, a discovery conference can also be initiated by a judge. At the conference, the court may develop a discovery plan, which typically clarifies the issues for discovery, the methods by which it will proceed, and a time frame for the completion of each phase.

The Motion to Compel and the Imposition of Sanctions.   Where discovery requests are not complied with, attorneys usually try to resolve the matter informally. If this fails, a party can file a **motion to compel**, asking the court to order a response and, possibly, to impose the cost of bringing the motion on the noncomplying party.

Where the motion is allowed, the noncomplying party is then under court order to respond according to the terms and conditions set by the court. Thereafter, the failure to respond will subject this party to sanctions. Possible sanctions include imposing costs, treating certain matters in contention as established, preventing the sanctioned party from introducing certain evidence, and in extreme cases, entering a default judgment or a dismissal of the action. In some jurisdictions, a judge may have the discretion to impose sanctions without having first entered a motion to compel.

The Middle Phase: Moving Toward Resolution or Trial

In addition to discovery, other important events take place between the time of filing of the divorce and the divorce hearing. During this time, the parties generally seek to resolve outstanding issues and protect their respective interests. If matters are resolved, the parties will reduce their agreement to writing and proceed to a relatively simple, uncontested divorce hearing. If matters remain unresolved, they will proceed to trial. This discussion assumes that both parties are participating in the process. If the defendant cannot be located or refuses to participate, an uncontested hearing will eventually be held, but it will be uncontested due to lack of participation—rather than because of agreement.

In this section, we look at what takes place during this middle phase of the divorce process. We begin by looking at court motion practice, followed by a discussion of other dispute resolution mechanisms, specifically negotiation, mediation, and arbitration. We then discuss separation agreements, taking a close look at a sample agreement.

Although this chapter treats each of these topics separately, you should be aware that in the unfolding of an actual divorce case, parties may utilize some or all approaches in various combinations and in various sequences in the process. For example, in one case, a party might first seek temporary orders and then enter into negotiations; in another, the parties might work out an informal interim agreement and then proceed directly to a settlement conference, or they might then turn to the court for temporary orders if an impasse is reached and then resume negotiations. Another couple might reach their final agreement through mediation before the divorce is even filed. In short, there is no prescribed pattern, and the flow of this phase is determined by the circumstances of the individual case.

Motions for Temporary Relief

Overview of Motion Practice

During the pendency of a divorce action, issues may arise that require immediate attention. In this situation, either side can file a motion asking the court to enter an order resolving the matter. Any order entered in response to the motion is temporary and will eventually be superseded by the divorce judgment. The fact that the relief is temporary does not lessen its importance; significant rights may be at stake. Moreover, **temporary orders** frequently shape the final result. As a basic rule, a court's ruling on a motion cannot be appealed because the right of appeal generally attaches to final judgments. However, this rule is not absolute. Thus, for example, a ruling on a motion that would bring a case to an end, such as where a court allows a motion to dismiss, can usually be appealed. Depending on the applicable rules of procedure, appeals may be allowed in other limited situations as well, such as where particularly significant interests are at stake.

Preparation and Service.   Motions are prepared in writing and served on the other party, together with notice as to when and where the motion is to be heard. (For an exception to the advance notice requirements, see the next section, "*Ex Parte* Relief.") Service requirements are usually less formal than at the complaint stage. Most commonly, service is made by the attorney for the moving party either in hand or by mail within the requisite number of days, as determined by the applicable rules of procedure, before the motion is scheduled to be heard.

Frequently, a party will submit an affidavit to the court in support of the motion. An **affidavit** is a first-person, sworn statement that, in this instance, sets out the underlying facts showing why the moving party is entitled to the requested relief. A motion may also be accompanied by a legal memorandum that provides legal support for the moving party's position. The opposing party may also submit an affidavit or a legal memorandum (or both) to show why the requested relief should be denied. In some jurisdictions, either or both of these documents may be required.

Ex Parte Relief.   In certain situations, a party may be harmed if he or she gives the other side advance notice of the motion and hearing date.

For example, let's say that a father is threatening to take the children out of the country and the mother wants to get a court order prohibiting him from doing this. If she gives him advance notice, he might disappear before the hearing takes place. In this situation, the court could hear her motion on an *ex parte* basis, meaning without notice, enter an order, and then provide the father with the opportunity to come to court and present his side of the story. Other examples of when *ex parte* relief may be appropriate include situations where a party is seeking protection from abuse or seeking to prevent a spouse from dissipating marital assets, as again, advance notice could trigger the very result the party is trying to avoid.

Grounded in considerations of procedural fairness, as required by the due process clause, most courts will grant *ex parte* relief only if the moving party can show that giving notice poses a substantial risk of harm. In deciding whether to allow the requested relief, a court must balance the right of an individual to be heard before his or her interests are affected with the need to protect the moving party from the risk of injury or loss. Only where the risk is substantial will it outweigh the procedural rights of the other side. If an order is entered, notice will be provided and the other side will have an opportunity to be heard within a short period of time following the *ex parte* hearing.

Presentation to the Court.   Following service, the motion is presented to the court. The procedure for scheduling motions varies from state to state, and within a state it may vary from court to court. If you are responsible for scheduling a motion, you should always call the particular court to find out how to get the motion heard.

In some states, the hearing on a motion is conducted like a mini-trial. The rules of evidence are in effect, and the parties take the witness stand and give testimony in response to questions by counsel. In most states, however, the presentation is less formal. The parties are not sworn in as witnesses; instead, they stand before the judge with their attorneys, who present and oppose the motion through oral argument. The parties may then be asked some questions by the judge. Here, formal rules of evidence or procedure are not in effect. After hearing the matter, the judge can enter an order on the spot or can take the matter under advisement. A judge is likely to postpone making the decision when the issue is especially complex or controverted. In some states, judges may be able to make decisions based solely on written submissions, thus eliminating the need for a hearing.

Diversion to Court Conciliation or Mediation Services.   In some states, the parties must sit down with a court worker to see if they can resolve matters before the motion can be heard by the judge. Typically, this worker is from the court's family service office or a court-based mediation program. In some states, an exception to the diversion requirement will be made in cases where there is a history of domestic violence. This exception is based on the recognition that it can be unfair and potentially unsafe to require a victim of violence to mediate with an abusive spouse.

If an agreement is reached through this process, it is reduced to writing and presented to the judge for approval. If approved, it becomes the temporary order of the court. If agreement is not reached, the motion is then argued before the judge. In many states, the court worker participates in this court hearing. He or she may report back to the judge on what took place during their session and make recommendations. In other states, the meeting with the court worker is considered confidential, and the worker thus does not participate in the motion session.

While this diversion to a court-based mediation or conciliation program can help couples reach mutually satisfactory agreements, a number of concerns, including the following, have been raised about this process:

1. Especially where they are unrepresented, parties, in locales that do not protect these communications, may not realize that what they tell the court worker is not confidential and will be reported back to the judge.
2. Court workers may pressure the parties to settle, and the failure by a party to agree to a settlement proposal may result in an unfavorable report or recommendation to the court.
3. This process is inappropriate where there has been domestic violence because it requires a victim to sit down, in a spirit of cooperation and conciliation, with someone who has been abusive. In this regard, it should be noted that some diversion programs have a domestic violence exemption.

Specific Divorce Motions

Motion practice in the divorce context is extremely varied. Many motions, such as those for temporary custody or support, are fairly standard, but much creativity can be used to fashion motions to deal with specific problems. For example, let's say that a couple has temporary joint legal custody of their daughter, and the mother has physical custody. The mother gives the daughter a haircut that substantially alters the length and style of her hair. The father objects to her having done this without his consent, and seeks to prevent it from recurring. He could design a motion to address this situation with a caption such as: "Motion to Prevent Wife from Altering Daughter's Hair Without the Husband's Prior Consent." Many attorneys enjoy this creative aspect of family law practice, while it drives others to distraction, particularly when they are on the receiving end of a highly original motion.

Following is a brief description of some of the commonly filed motions, followed by a sample motion and supporting affidavit.

Motion for Temporary Custody and Visitation.   After a divorce is filed, many couples work out an informal, temporary arrangement regarding the children. Where this is not possible, one party will usually file a motion asking the court to award him or her temporary custody. After a hearing, the court will enter an order for custody and visitation, which will then be in effect until the divorce judgment is entered unless problems arise and a change is sought via another motion.

The importance of a temporary arrangement—whether through agreement or by a court order—should not be underestimated. Because courts are reluctant to disrupt children once they are settled into a satisfactory routine, temporary arrangements often ripen into permanent ones. The longer the interim stage, the more likely it is that the parent with temporary custody will end up as the custodial parent.

Temporary custody orders are also important where there is any risk that one parent might flee with the children. If an order is in place, a parent who interferes with the custodial or visitation rights of the other parent can be held in contempt of court. Moreover, a temporary custody order may be a necessary prerequisite to the initiation of parental kidnapping charges in the event a parent disappears with the children. Accordingly, even where parties are able to work things out informally, a temporary custody order may be prudent.

Motion for the Appointment of an Investigator or Evaluator.   Where custody is contested, a party may ask to have someone appointed to perform a custody evaluation or investigation. An investigation is usually done by a guardian ad litem. Typically, a **guardian ad litem** interviews the parents and other involved adults, such as teachers and neighbors, and spends time with the children. He or she may also visit the homes of both parents. The guardian ad litem then files a written report with the court containing his or her recommendations about custodial and visitation arrangements.

In some cases, such as where there are concerns about the mental or emotional well-being of a parent or child, it may make more sense to have an evaluation done by a mental health professional. Here, the evaluation most likely would consist of a series of interviews and observations. Typically, each parent and each child is interviewed separately, and the children are observed alone and with each parent. Again, a written report and recommendations are filed with the court.

In either situation, the parties are entitled to a copy of the report and to an opportunity to question the guardian ad litem or the evaluator in court. This right is important because these reports tend to carry a lot of weight with judges, and parties must be given the chance to question the findings where they disagree with them.

Motion for Temporary Support. During the pendency of a divorce, a party may be in immediate need of child and/or spousal support and unable to wait until a permanent financial arrangement is in place. Accordingly, all states permit an interim award of child support and most permit an interim award of spousal support. Again, because this interim order often ripens into the permanent one, it is vital that all supporting financial documentation be carefully prepared and presented to the court.

Motion for Payment of Fees and Costs. As a general rule, each party is responsible for paying his or her own attorney's fees. However, in most states, a spouse who lacks the resources to secure ongoing representation can ask the court to order the other spouse to pay his or her fees. This request can be made at trial or during the pendency of the action.

In evaluating the request, the court will compare the financial status of both parties. Where there is a significant disparity, the court may award fees. However, there is no right to a fee award, and the decision is generally within the sound discretion of the trial judge. In many states, judges tend to award fees only in cases of extreme hardship.

Motions Relating to the Protection of Assets. A frequent concern during the pendency of a divorce is that a party will dissipate marital assets. To protect against this, the other spouse can seek a variety of protective court orders.

A party can ask the court to issue a restraining order enjoining the other spouse from disposing of or encumbering the assets in question. He or she can also ask the court to attach property, which serves to put the world on notice that the asset is subject to an unresolved claim and makes the asset difficult to sell. The court can also freeze assets that belong to a spouse but are under the control of a third party, such as a bank. Here, the order would command the bank not to allow the spouse to withdraw or transfer funds. These motions need to be drafted with particular care, as they may need to satisfy the technical requirements of nondivorce statutes that govern interests in property.

As mentioned earlier, if a party has a well-grounded fear that upon receiving notice of a motion to protect assets, his or her spouse is likely to dispose of the assets in question, he or she can appear before the court on an *ex parte* basis. If the court agrees that the danger is real, it will secure the asset first and then provide the other side with notice and the opportunity to be heard.

Motion for Protection from Abuse. During the pendency of the divorce, most states allow either party to seek protection from abuse by way of a motion. A spouse can ask that the other party be ordered to leave him or her alone and, if they are still living together, that the abusive spouse be vacated from the marital premises. In most states, this approach is not exclusive; a divorcing spouse may bring a motion within the framework of the divorce, file a separate petition under the state's abuse protection act, or both. However, these approaches may yield different results. The order entered in response to a divorce motion may have less clout than one entered pursuant to the state's abuse prevention law; the former is less likely to be criminally enforceable and it may not enhance the arrest powers of the police (see Chapter 3). Of course, these differences should be assessed before action is taken, so the most appropriate course can be pursued.

Sample Motion and Supporting Affidavit

Exhibit 10.7 is a sample motion for temporary custody with a supporting affidavit. The body of the motion contains the following three parts:

1. The relief desired
2. Supporting reasons
3. A prayer for relief

As a general rule, motions are written in simple, straightforward language so the judge, who in all likelihood has countless motions before him or her, can quickly determine what is being requested.

The Role of the Paralegal

As with discovery, paralegals play an important and varied role in motion practice. Paralegals may be responsible for drafting the necessary court papers—such as the motion, supporting affidavit, and legal memorandum. Drafting the affidavit requires careful interviewing of the affiant to get his or her story, putting it into a cohesive, first-person narrative, and reviewing it with the affiant for accuracy. Preparation of the memorandum requires good research and writing skills, as the appropriate legal authority must be identified and presented in a persuasive manner.

Paralegals can also play a vital role in preparing for the court hearing. Supporting documents such as financial statements may need to be gathered, and clients need to be prepared so they can respond to questions from counsel or the judge. Some attorneys also like to have the paralegal who is working on the case accompany him or her to court. In court, the paralegal can perform a variety of important tasks. For instance, she or he can continue to prepare the client, offer the client emotional support, assist in the preparation of an updated financial statement if requested by the court, or assist the attorney in handling the flow of paperwork. In some jurisdictions, paralegals are allowed to present uncontested motions to the court.

Exhibit 10.7   Motion for Temporary Custody and Supporting Affidavit

STATE OF ANYWHERE

Middlesex County   Family Court,
                                                                        Civil No. 2245

JERRY FREEMAN,
          Plaintiff
v.   PLAINTIFF'S MOTION FOR
                                         TEMPORARY CUSTODY
CARRIE GREEN,
          Defendant

NOW COMES the plaintiff in the above-captioned action and asks that this Honorable Court award him temporary physical and legal custody of the party's minor daughter, Melissa, age seven years old.

In support of his Motion, Plaintiff states as follows, and also incorporates by reference, the attached Affidavit, which more fully sets out the facts in support of his request:

1. That the plaintiff has been the primary caretaker of Melissa for the past three years. Before this time, the parties shared child-care responsibilities on a more or less equal basis.

2. That over the past three years, as a result of depression and increased alcohol consumption, the wife has provided little attention or care to Melissa, and has been emotionally abusive toward her.

3. That the wife moved out of the family home approximately six months ago, and since then has had infrequent and irregular contact with Melissa.

4. That the best interest of Melissa would be served by awarding temporary legal and physical custody to the father so that continuity of care and nurturing is maintained.

WHEREFORE, the Plaintiff requests that this Honorable Court grant this Motion and award him temporary custody of Melissa.

Respectfully Submitted,
Jerry Freeman
By his Attorney

Ellen Jones
Jones & Hernandez
11 Court Street
Freeport, Any State 02167

Exhibit 10.7   Continued

STATE OF ANYWHERE

Middlesex County   Family Court,
                                                                          Civil No. 2245

JERRY FREEMAN,
            Plaintiff

v.   AFFIDAVIT OF PLAINTIFF IN
                                    SUPPORT OF HIS MOTION FOR
                                    TEMPORARY CUSTODY

CARRIE GREEN,
            Defendant

I, Jerry Freeman, do depose and say:

1. I am married to the defendant Carrie Green, and I filed a divorce complaint with this Court on June 18, 2018.

2. We have one child. Her name is Melissa and she was born on March 15, 2011.

3. During the first four years of Melissa's life, my wife and I shared child-care responsibilities, although Carrie was the primary caretaker of Melissa during her first six months. After this time, we both fully participated in all aspects of Melissa's life, including making child-care arrangements for her while we were at work.

4. Three years ago, Carrie lost both of her parents in a tragic accident. As a result, she became depressed and began to drink heavily. She has refused to get any help for either the depression or the drinking.

5. Since then, our family life has been torn apart. Carrie has been unable to hold down a job and has essentially withdrawn from the family. She has been unable to care for Melissa in any predictable manner. For example, she forgot to pick Melissa up from her after-school program on several occasions due to the fact that she was drinking. Needless to say, this was extremely upsetting for Melissa. After this occurred several times, I took over the responsibility for picking up Melissa. I also took her to school, except on those rare occasions when Carrie was able to get out of bed on time to take her.

6. Although she has not been physically abusive, Carrie has become emotionally abusive, especially when she has been drinking. She yells at Melissa for no reason, and also belittles her. But even more upsetting to Melissa has been her mother's withdrawal of love and affection.

7. I feel that I tried desperately to help my wife, but nothing worked, and about six months ago, she moved out.

Exhibit 10.7   Continued

8. During all of this time, I have been the primary caretaker of Melissa in addition to working full-time. I may not be a perfect parent, but I provide her with love and stability. I also am able to take care of all her daily needs.

9. Melissa and I are attempting to rebuild a life. She is in counseling to try to resolve some of her pain and confusion. On a few occasions, in order to help Melissa, the counselor has arranged to have all of us attend a family counseling session. Carrie has failed to attend all but one of these sessions. The one time she showed up, she was intoxicated, and the counselor had to ask her to leave.

10. I fully believe that it is in Melissa's best interest that I be awarded sole custody and I am fully prepared to continue as her primary caretaker.

Signed under pains and penalties of perjury, this 20th day of June 2018.

_____

Jerry Freeman

Alternative Approaches to Dispute Resolution

Ultimately, the overwhelming majority of divorce cases are settled before trial, most commonly through the process of negotiation. In recent years, increasing numbers of divorcing couples also have used two alternative approaches to resolving their differences: mediation and, although far less common, arbitration. In this section, we compare these three dispute resolution approaches. Please note that the discussion is general in nature and does not address the more formal principles and theories of each approach. We also consider two new approaches to the practice of law—the provision of "unbundled" legal services and the collaborative divorce approach.

Negotiation

Through **negotiation**, each attorney acts on behalf of his or her client to see if a settlement can be reached. In contrast to mediation and arbitration, no neutral third party is involved.

Negotiations can take place on the telephone, but it is also common for one side to contact the other at some point in the divorce process to see if a settlement conference can be arranged. This conference can be either two-way, involving just the attorneys, or four-way, involving the attorneys as well as the clients. A four-way conference is generally more productive because the clients can play an active role in initiating and responding to settlement proposals. However, in some situations, such as where there is tremendous animosity between the parties or there is a history of abuse, it may make more sense to have the attorneys meet, at least initially, without the clients present.

Ideally, each attorney will have met with his or her client before the conference to explore what the client wants and where he or she is willing to compromise. The attorney should also help the client to anticipate what the other side is likely to request so he or she can think about possible responses. If this advance work is done, both attorneys will begin the negotiations with a good understanding of their client's positions.

At the conference, ground rules are usually established. An important consideration is whether each issue will be negotiated separately until impasse or agreement or whether everything will be placed on the table at the same time. The advantage of the former approach is that it minimizes the possibility of inappropriate linkage of issues; for example, the husband offering to give the wife sole custody if she drops her request for spousal support. If the parties decide to negotiate each issue separately, any agreement reached on a single issue is usually not considered final until all other issues have been resolved. By conditioning finality of each issue on reaching a comprehensive settlement, the parties do not risk the loss of potential bargaining chips. For example, if the parties agree on a division of property, a spouse could reopen this matter if unable to get what he or she wants with respect to spousal support. Thus, a husband might back away from his agreement to allow a wife to remain in the home if, later in the negotiations, she insists on spousal support.

Once the basic framework is established, one side will open with its offer. This offer rarely represents the party's bottom line because this would leave no room for the give-and-take that characterizes the negotiation process. However, if the proposal is too outrageous, the party may not appear to be negotiating in good faith, which can jeopardize the integrity of the process. When the other side responds, they too will leave room for concessions but again should avoid unreasonable counterproposals.

As the negotiations proceed, it is common for each party to confer privately with his or her attorney. At this time, responses and new proposals can be formulated. These meetings can also serve as valuable cooling-off periods because these conferences tend to get heated.

The negotiating session can conclude in a number of ways. One party may unilaterally declare it over and may even storm out, perhaps because of frustration with the process or as a deliberate "bullying" tactic designed to exact concessions. The parties may also mutually recognize that they can go no further. At this point, they may decide that the case should be marked for trial or that they should reconvene at a future date and give settlement another chance.

If the negotiations end in agreement, one side usually offers to prepare an initial draft of a separation agreement and then send it to the other side for review. This is possible even where the parties have not ironed out all of the details; here, one side offers to see if they can work out the missing details in a mutually satisfactory manner. Although drafting the agreement is time-consuming and potentially more expensive for the client, it is usually advantageous to be the drafter because once something is in writing, it seems to acquire a presumptive validity, and suggesting changes has a bit of an uphill quality to it.

Although paralegals do not, as a rule, participate in the negotiations themselves, they can serve a number of very useful functions at a settlement conference. Because the paralegal is not directly involved in the negotiations, he or she may be able to make observations that the attorney is too engaged to notice, such as subtle shifts in tone of voice or body language that may indicate that the other side is altering its position. An attending paralegal who is able to take in the whole process may also be in a good position to help formulate proposals and counterproposals. Note taking can also make an important contribution; good notes can lay the foundation for a subsequent settlement agreement and are essential if disputes arise over what was agreed on. Before the conference, the paralegal can, of course, play a crucial role in helping to prepare the client for what is often a nerve-wracking experience.

Mediation

Mediation is a nonadversarial approach to dispute resolution. It has become a popular option for divorcing couples who wish to resolve their differences without going to trial. Through mediation, a neutral third party — the mediator — helps couples reach their own agreement. The mediator is not an advocate for either side but rather guides the parties through the process of reaching agreement by helping them to identify important issues, consider options, and structure a realistic settlement.

Divorce mediators come from a range of professional backgrounds,[21] although most are either mental health professionals or attorneys. Mediators may work in interdisciplinary teams. Thus, for example, a social worker and an attorney might work together, as each brings a distinct but complementary body of knowledge and set of skills to the process.

Although there has been a marked increase in the use of mediation as an alternative dispute resolution method, some experts in the field have raised the concern that the field lacks an "articulated theoretical framework" to guide practitioners,[22] and therefore there is a lack of awareness that "very different goals and values among mediators . . . could shape competent performance in fundamentally different ways."[23] In an effort to bring a coherent theoretical framework to the field, some scholars have identified two primary mediation models: the problem-solving model and the transformative model.

According to the *problem-solving model,* the goal of mediation is to arrive at a solution that "solves tangible problems on fair and realistic terms, and good mediator practice is a matter of issue identification, option creation, and effective persuasion to 'close the deal.' "[24] This model is rooted in an "individualist ideology" that presumes that people act in a contained, self-directed way in "pursuit of satisfaction of his or her own separate self interests."[25] Presently, this model is the dominant mediation paradigm.

In contrast, the *transformative model* sees the conflict as "first and foremost a crisis in some human interaction,"[26] as a result of which "the interaction between the parties quickly degenerates and assumes a mutually destructive, alienating, and dehumanizing character."[27] Here, the primary goal of mediation is not problem solving, but changing the interactional patterns between the parties:

> [S]uccess is measured not by settlement per se but by party shifts toward personal strength, interpersonal responsiveness and constructive interaction. . . . The transformative framework is based on and reflects relational ideology, in which human beings are assumed to be fundamentally social—formed in and through their relations with other human beings, essentially connected to others, and motivated by a desire for both personal autonomy and constructive social interaction.[28]

Significantly, the role of the mediator is quite different in each model. In the problem-solving model, the mediator structures the process to help the parties reach a settlement. In the transformative model, the mediator's role is less outcome-oriented and geared more toward empowering the parties to transform their interactional patterns so that they can reengage in a more positive way.[29]

The Mediation Process. Mediation is usually conceptualized as occurring in distinct stages, although the progression is not always linear. Couples often move back and forth between stages as new issues, conflicts, and emotions surface. The following presentation is intended to give you a sense of the stages involved in mediation. Keep in mind that there is no single fixed or correct model and that each mediator develops his or her own style.[30]

Stage One: Building Trust and Establishing Parameters. During the initial session, parties are encouraged to articulate why they have come to mediation and what their expectations, concerns, and goals are. The mediator explains the process, including the nature of his or her role, the responsibilities of the participants, and the applicable ground rules, such as those relating to confidentiality. By the end of this meeting, the parties should have a clear understanding of the process and be able to make an informed decision as to whether they wish to proceed. If the mediation is to continue, a contract to mediate, which sets out the operative framework, is usually signed by the couple and the mediator.

For many mediators, this initial session also serves a screening purpose. As discussed below, some mediators do not believe mediation is appropriate where there has been a history of domestic violence. At this initial meeting, the mediator might ask about abuse or look for clues suggesting a history of abuse. If reasonably certain that abuse has taken place, the mediator might not accept the case. Other mediators, while acknowledging the importance of screening for abuse, would not reject a couple for this reason but instead would set specific ground rules, such as that physical safety is nonnegotiable.

Stage Two: Fact-Finding.   To be effective, mediation requires the voluntary disclosure of all relevant information. Generally, as part of the mediation agreement, parties commit to complete disclosure and to provide copies of documents that would ordinarily be requested in the course of discovery, such as tax returns, bank statements, and asset inventories. Formal discovery is not available in mediation, and the mediator has no authority to compel disclosure. To some, this raises troubling questions about the potential fairness of the process. Of primary concern is the risk that a spouse who has less knowledge of and control over economic resources might unknowingly give up rights to income or assets. Where the mediator knows or suspects that a party is concealing assets, he or she can break off mediation and refuse to resume unless the parties confer with counsel. However, some mediators believe this would be overstepping their bounds, reasoning that the parties assumed this risk when they entered mediation.[31]

Stage Three: Identification/Creation of Options and Alternatives.   After everyone is satisfied that all relevant information has been provided, the mediator helps the parties identify what they see as the various options and assists them in expanding the range of acceptable alternatives. The mediator also seeks to prevent the parties from getting locked into fixed positions before all options have been considered. Thus, a mediator is likely to take an active role in this stage of the process.

Stage Four: Negotiating and Drafting the Agreement.   Once the acceptable options have been identified, the parties are faced with the task of sorting through the possibilities. At this point, the mediator generally steps back so that the parties themselves can reach the agreement, although he or she may play a critical facilitative role.

As the parties seek to reach an agreement, it is not uncommon for one or both of them to ask the mediator whether he or she thinks a certain provision is fair. This raises interesting questions about the mediator's role. Some mediators hold the view that answering such a question would compromise their stance as a neutral third party. Rather than responding, the mediator might direct the party to think about how that option would play out in his or her life and might also suggest that he or she confer with counsel. Other mediators take a more activist stance and will provide the parties with an assessment of what the likely outcome would be if the matter went to court, thus providing them a framework within which to make their decision.

A further potential complication is where the mediator realizes that the agreement is unfair and that one spouse would fare considerably better in court. Here, some mediators simply encourage each party to review the final agreement with an attorney before signing it, reasoning that when the parties agreed to the process they assumed the risk of operating outside formal legal rules. Other mediators take a more active role, especially where the unfavorable result stems from an underlying power imbalance. They might raise pointed questions to push the parties to confront the unfairness of the bargain or strongly urge consultation with counsel during the process rather than waiting until the end.

Consideration

What should the role of the mediator be where there is an imbalance of power between the parties?

Once a settlement is reached, the mediator usually drafts an agreement embodying the parties' understanding. Most, if not all, mediators will strongly encourage each person to review the agreement with his or her lawyer before signing it.[32] The mediated agreement may be redrafted into a formal separation agreement, which includes the standard separation agreement provisions, or it may serve as the document presented to the court for approval at the divorce hearing.

The Controversy: The Appropriateness of Mediation in Cases Involving Domestic Violence.   People working in the family law field have responded to the increased use of divorce mediation with both enthusiasm and trepidation. According to enthusiasts, a primary advantage of mediation is that it stresses cooperation and encourages parties to work out long-term solutions that make sense for them. As a client-centered process, it stresses individual responsibility for decision making, and by not abdicating responsibility to judges or lawyers, participants gain a sense of control over their future. Moreover, it is hoped that by stressing cooperation and communication, mediation will give couples the tools they will need to resolve future disputes, thus promoting greater post-divorce stability and satisfaction.

Despite these potential benefits, many persons who work with battered women, including some mediators, have raised serious concerns about the appropriateness of mediation where violence is a factor.[33] Of primary concern is that mediation emphasizes conciliation and cooperation, which assumes some degree of mutual respect and equality of status within the relationship. Where violence is present, however, there is no equality or mutuality; goals are not achieved through cooperation but rather through coercion and fear. Accordingly, a battered woman may respond based on fear and the overriding desire to remain safe. A further concern is that even a highly skilled mediator will not be able to redress this imbalance of power because it is so deeply embedded in the relationship. The requirement of neutrality, while facilitative in other contexts, will be insufficient to overcome a legacy of fear and lack of mutuality.

Prompted by these concerns, some mediators now attempt to screen out cases with a history of domestic violence as inappropriate for mediation—while others have adopted specific protocols, such as separate interviews, in an effort to ensure a safe process and fair results. However, critics fear that many cases will not be screened out because violence victims often downplay the seriousness of the abuse, and that although well-intentioned, "violence-sensitive" procedures are simply not enough to redress the enduring impact of violence such that a victim can participate in mediation without a sense of fear and disempowerment. However, some suggest that e-mediation—the topic to which we now turn—may be the answer to this longstanding debate in the field.

E-Mediation. The discussion above focuses on face-to-face interactions, which comprise the standard mediation process. However, there is a growing use of **e-mediation** in the family law arena.[34] Originally thought "only suitable for disputes originating in online activity," some research now suggests that it can be a "powerful tool for resolving disputes . . . in which emotional, relational and social issues are at least as important as transactional elements."[35] Reflecting this new reality, e-mediation is "becoming an integral part of effective and affordable divorce mediation services and programs."[36] One distinct advantage of this virtual approach is that it offers a "faster track" to dispute resolution to since it makes "physical meetings, setting up appointments, and wasting valuable time traveling back and forth unnecessary."[37]

Perhaps more importantly than speed and convenience, proponents of e-mediation suggest a number of other advantages that may be particularly beneficial in the divorce context. For example, the fact that the communication is asynchronous "can allow the mediator a more intentional application of the mediator's toolbox" and enables "[p]arties and mediators [to] engage in discussion without the immediate time pressure and other dynamics associated with synchronous, face-to-face conversations."[38] E-mediation also relies heavily on text communication, which some believe can help to "both minimize the effects of 'good talkers' gaining the upper hand or of dominant figures causing others to reduce their participation levels" and temper the highly charged confrontational dynamics that can derail the mediation process.[39]

In addition to the clear safety advantage that is provided by the fact that the parties are not in the same physical space, some suggest that these attributes of e-mediation can be particularly beneficial where there has been a history of violence as they can help to neutralize the power imbalance between the parties. In turn, this may empower an abused spouse to "speak out fully and freely" without fear of being intimidated into silence.[40]

However, a number of concerns have also been raised about the general use of e-mediation that may be particularly applicable in the divorce context. One important consideration is that while distance may offer some benefits, "the lack of warmth, empathy, immediacy, rapport and other attitudes and affects that make face-to-face mediation what it is" are clearly missing from this process.[41] Also potentially problematic is the fact that written messages may easily be misunderstood without the nonverbal cues that typically accompany spoken communication, and once reduced to writing, communications can take on a greater permanence. Of particular concern to domestic violence victims, some also suggest that "it is easier to express oneself aggressively to the computer than to a flesh and blood person" resulting in communication that that is laden with hostile and aggressive remarks.[42]

Arbitration

Long identified with labor, commercial, and international disputes, **arbitration** has not traditionally been used by divorcing couples to reach a settlement agreement. Where utilized in the divorce context, it has typically been pursuant to a clause in a separation agreement in which the parties agree to submit certain post-divorce disputes to arbitration. However, there has been a notable increase in the use of pre-divorce arbitration as an alternative to litigation. Reflecting this trend, a number of states now have specific statutes that govern the use of arbitration in family law cases and address the details of the process as generally described in the following paragraphs.

Arbitration is similar to the judicial process in that the parties present their case to a neutral, third-party decision maker (or panel of decision makers), but the process is considerably more flexible, and the parties retain a greater degree of control than they have in court. A dispute can be submitted to arbitration only if the parties so agree; one side cannot force the other to arbitrate unless specifically required by prior agreement. The arbitrator's authority derives from the parties' agreement; the arbitrator cannot make decisions about matters not directly entrusted to him or her by the parties. Although, as discussed below, an arbitrator's decision is usually entitled to great deference, some courts will not enforce an agreement to submit custody and visitation disputes to arbitration. Other courts have been willing to enforce these agreements, with "the caveat that any decision rendered by the arbitrator is subject to de novo judicial review."[43]

The arbitrator is selected by the parties. Where this is contentious, the attorneys will usually assist in the selection process. In a post-divorce dispute, a selection mechanism may be provided for in the separation agreement. The arbitrator may be a professional working under the auspices of the American Arbitration Association or any other mutually acceptable individual, such as a clergyperson, accountant, therapist, or lawyer. The choice of arbitrator often turns on the nature of the dispute and whether a particular expertise is required.

Arbitration hearings are fairly informal. They are held in a private setting and generally take less time to complete than a trial. In most instances, the arbitrator's decision is binding, subject to very limited rights of court review. As a general rule, there is a presumption in favor of the validity of the arbitral award, and a court will modify or vacate an award only under limited circumstances, such as where there has been fraud or bias, or where the arbitrator exceeded the scope of his or her authority. However, many courts review arbitral decisions more carefully when they are made in the family law context, especially when the rights of children are at stake, and some courts will not enforce provisions relating to custody and visitation. Expressing this perspective, the Supreme Court of Ohio stated, "The process of arbitration, useful when the mundane matter of the amount of support is in issue, is less so when the delicate balancing of the factors composing the best interests of a child is at issue," thus concluding that these decisions must remain with the court.[44]

The Collaborative Divorce Approach

In addition to these three established dispute resolution alternatives, the "collaborative" law approach has also surged in popularity in the divorce context, and a number of states have enacted collaborative law statutes to guide the practice. Determined by the ABA to be an ethical model for the practice of law, a formal opinion of the ABA's Committee on Ethics and Professional Practice provides the following description of the collaborative law process:

> Collaborative law is a type of alternative dispute resolution in which the parties and their lawyers commit to work cooperatively to reach settlement. . . . Participants focus on the interests of both clients, gather sufficient information to insure that decisions are made with full knowledge, develop a full range of options, and then choose options that best meet the needs of the parties. The parties structure a mutually acceptable written resolution of all issues without court involvement. The product of the process is then submitted to the court as a final decree. The structure creates a problem-solving atmosphere with a focus on interest-based negotiation and client empowerment.[45]

As indicated by the above passage, the hallmark of this approach is that the parties and their lawyers commit in advance to settling the case. Reinforcing the centrality of this commitment, the attorneys in a collaborative divorce agree in advance to disqualify themselves from representing their clients in court should the process break down before all issues are fully resolved. Accordingly, if a trial becomes necessary, each party will have to hire a new attorney, which is likely to add both time and cost as the new attorney will need to be brought up to speed on the details of the case.

The **collaborative divorce approach** bears some resemblance to both mediation and negotiation. Like mediation, the focus is on helping the parties work through their differences in a non-confrontational manner. The parties also are encouraged to speak directly to one another in the course of the settlement process. However, in contrast to mediation, no neutral third party guides the process; rather, each spouse is represented by his or her own attorney. Individual representation aligns the collaborative law with the negotiation process that typically accompanies a divorce; however, in contrast, in addition to the emphasis on cooperation, the threat that a party will break off negotiations in favor of litigation if they do not get what they want is considerably less, as the party would have to hire a new lawyer to represent him or her in court. Thus, there is a built-in incentive to settle the case. Collaborative divorce also can be characterized as a type of unbundled legal services (see the discussion that follows), as an attorney is hired for the bounded purpose of settling the case, agreeing in advance not to take the matter to court should the settlement process break down. Another increasingly common characteristic of the collaborative divorce approach is that a team of non-legal professionals, including mental health counselors, divorce coaches, accountants, and parenting coordinators, assist the parties and their attorneys to reach a settlement.

Proponents of this approach stress that the four-way commitment to settlement fosters a creative and engaged problem-solving ethos as distinct from the typically bitter winner-take-all approach of the traditional adversarial model of lawyering. Rather, in a paradigm shift, "no longer is the lawyer putting on blinders as an adversarial advocate. Instead, the collaborative lawyer concentrates on assisting the client and facilitating a settlement that is acceptable to the clients."[46] They also stress the benefit to clients of being at the center of the process. As one commentator explains, in contrast to the "traditional practice of law, where the client's voice is practically not heard and decisions . . . are for the most part those of the attorney," by "actively engag[ing] the parties throughout the process," the collaborative law model makes client "autonomy and self-definition its central motif."[47] Another potential benefit is the emphasis on the development of open and honest channels of communication toward the entwined goals of healing past injuries and building a more stable and cooperative future—a particularly valuable outcome where children are involved.

Not surprisingly, however, the practice also has its detractors. Of particular concern is that the disqualification requirement may potentially put an attorney in breach of the ethical requirement that he or she zealously represent the interests of his or her client, as those interests may well necessitate taking the case to court in the event the settlement process breaks down. Another concern is that rather than being empowering, clients may experience the emphasis on settlement as coercive, since they know that if the process fails, they will need to retain new counsel. Not only is this potentially burdensome in terms of time and money, it can also be daunting to face the prospect of having to develop trust in and rapport with a new lawyer at a time of rupture in the divorce process.

As in the case of mediation, important concerns have been raised about the appropriateness of the collaborative divorce approach in cases involving domestic violence, and many divorce professionals agree that lawyers should screen out these cases.[48] Of particular note, as one commentator writes, in addition to the "emotional and physical safety risks, the process can prevent the at-risk partner from achieving an equitable result and from creating a post-resolution environment where the at-risk party's autonomy is restored" as a result of the coercive control that abusers may assert during the process in order to establish and preserve their dominance over their partners.[49]

Unbundled Legal Services

Although not quite an alternative mode of dispute resolution, an innovative approach to the practice of law that has been gaining popularity in the family law arena also merits attention. In what is referred to as **"unbundled" legal services**, or limited task representation, an attorney agrees to provide a client with limited assistance from a menu of options instead of providing him or her with comprehensive representation. Unbundled services include the giving of legal advice, coaching on how to handle a case, assistance with drafting pleadings (a practice that is also referred to as *ghostwriting*), and perhaps, less typically, representation in court.[50]

Clearly cost-effective, this approach has emerged as a way to provide legal assistance to low- and middle-income litigants who lack the resources to retain a lawyer for full-service representation—and who therefore would otherwise try to navigate the legal system on their own. Of particular note, an increasing number of publicly funded legal services offices that provide representation in civil matters to low-income clients have responded to funding cuts by moving to an unbundled approach as a way to "stretch the scarce attorney resources provided by federal and local governments to improve access to justice."[51] In addition to providing clients who might otherwise be completely on their own with at least some legal assistance, this approach has also been commended for giving individuals greater choice and flexibility by "dissolv[ing] the all-or-nothing model of lawyering and creat[ing] an opportunity to access the expertise of a lawyer only when the client determines that one is needed most"; however, it is important to recognize that the idea of "choice" in this context is essentially illusory as far as low-income clients are concerned, as they are not likely to have a range of options to pick from.[52]

Although this practice model has been praised as an innovative response to the shortage of lawyers for middle-class and low-income clients, and for building greater flexibility into the traditional lawyer-client relationship, some concerns have also been raised about this novel approach to the practice of law. One apprehension is that a client may not fully understand the allocation of responsibilities between himself or herself and the lawyer, particularly if the case turns out to be more complex or contested than originally anticipated, which is not uncommon in the divorce arena. Supporters of the unbundled approach stress that potential confusion can be avoided through the drafting of clear contracts for services; nonetheless, others worry that a party who is confronting the emotional strain of divorce may not have a clear understanding of an agreement for limited assistance, and may therefore may come to expect more from the attorney, especially if the case become more complicated or contested than originally anticipated.

Others have raised broader structural concerns, such as that this approach will institutionalize a two-tiered system of justice—one for the rich and the other for the poor—and that by focusing on the immediate needs of low-income individuals, legal services lawyers will be diverted from engaging in impact litigation aimed at systemic law reform.[53] Responding to these concerns, others stress the exigent nature of responding to "fundamental, urgent needs," and note that without the provision of limited legal services, "[u]nrepresented parties in family law cases may forfeit vital resources such as maintenance and child support, and may have difficulty securing essential protection from domestic violence."[54] To this end, it is urged that additional research be conducted in order to determine "what strategies are most effective and efficient" when it comes to reducing the "justice gap" through the provision of limited legal services to the poor.[55]

Reaching Resolution: The Separation Agreement

As discussed in the above section, divorce cases may proceed along many different pathways, but the vast majority of cases are ultimately settled before trial. Where the parties are able to resolve all outstanding issues, their understanding is embodied in a **separation agreement**. The usual process is for one side to offer to draft an initial agreement, which is then reviewed by the other side. Comments are made, and the agreement usually goes through several revisions before the parties sign it. Once the agreement is executed, the case is considered uncontested, and a simple divorce hearing rather than a trial on the merits can be scheduled. (See the section entitled "The Uncontested Case," later in this chapter.)

Technically, a separation agreement is a contract in which the parties structure their post-divorce rights and responsibilities. However, because of the state's interest in the marital relationship, separation agreements are not treated like ordinary contracts. In most states, they are subject to careful review at the divorce hearing, and a judge can set aside an agreement or any provisions that he or she determines to be unfair or to have been agreed on without adequate disclosure.

Drafting the Agreement

In drafting agreements, most offices rely to some extent on standard forms. For routine clauses, such as those regarding waivers, severability, and the governing law, this usually presents no problem, although each provision should nonetheless be reviewed to make certain it is appropriate in the particular case. (See sample separation agreement below.) Beyond routine clauses, great care must be taken to tailor the separation agreement to the case at hand. Each situation should be carefully reviewed and the agreement drafted with all of the particulars in mind. Unfortunately, this is not always done, and the drafting process can be reduced to a filling in of names and dates on a standardized form. This is unfair to clients because it minimizes the importance of this document that, especially where children are involved, regulates critical aspects of a couple's post-divorce lives for many years into the future.

The Role of the Paralegal

An important part of your work as a paralegal may be to assist in the drafting of separation agreements. Before you begin drafting, it is essential that you have a clear understanding of what has been decided on so the agreement is both complete and accurate. Despite the care with which you approach the task, issues sometimes do not become apparent until the drafting is under way. For example, as you are drafting the visitation provisions, you may realize that in the complexity of the arrangements, the parties neglected to spell out arrangements for the children's birthdays. It can be helpful to the attorney handling the case if you keep track of all possible omissions and bring them to the attorney's attention. It can also be useful for you to draft the missing provisions, but you must make it clear that these are proposed as distinct from agreed-upon provisions.

After the attorney reviews the agreement, he or she may go over it with the client or ask you to do so before mailing it to the other side. Reviewing the agreement with the client ensures that it accurately reflects what your client believes he or she has settled on. In the event your client changes his or her mind about anything—a not infrequent occurrence—it is better to know about it before the agreement is sent to the other side.

If your office is reviewing rather than drafting an agreement, you may be asked to assist in this process. The agreement should be read carefully to make sure that it conforms with what has been decided on. After reviewing it, you should draft a memo to the attorney in charge of the case, setting out any potential discrepancies. Also, during your review, you may notice issues that have not been addressed; these should be noted in your memo, making clear that to the best of your knowledge, these are omissions as distinct from inaccuracies. Most offices will also have the client review the agreement to ensure that it conforms with his or her understanding of what was agreed upon. Again, in the event your client has changed his or her mind about anything, it is always better to know about it before the other side is told that the agreement as drafted looks fine.

Sample Separation Agreement and Comments

The sample separation agreement (Exhibit 10.8), with its explanatory comments, will give you an understanding of how to construct a well-drafted agreement. Keep in mind that this agreement covers one couple's situation; it is not universal in its reach and does not contain all possible provisions.

Exhibit 10.8   Separation Agreement

SEPARATION AGREEMENT BY AND BETWEEN
MARIE SMITH AND DAVID SMITH

This Separation Agreement is entered into this 10th day of May 2018, by David Smith (the "husband" or the "father") and Marie Smith (the "wife" or the "mother"). All of the references to "parties" shall be to the husband and wife.

Statement of Facts

1. The parties were married at Chicago, Illinois, on July 6, 2006 and last lived together at 129 Cherry Lane in Newtowne, State of X, on or about September 15, 2017.
2. Two children were born to the marriage. John was born on October 17, 2010, and Carla was born on May 11, 2008. All of the references to "children" shall be to John and Carla.
3. The husband and wife have separated, they are living apart, and the wife has filed a Complaint for Divorce on the grounds of irretrievable breakdown of the marriage in the Any County Probate and Family Court.

   The husband and wife desire by this Agreement to confirm their separation and to settle between themselves all of the questions pertaining to their respective property and estate rights, spousal support, care and custody of their children, and all other rights and obligations arising from their marital relationship that should be settled in view of the pending Complaint for Divorce.

   NOW THEREFORE, in consideration of the foregoing and of the mutual covenants and agreements hereinafter contained, the parties mutually agree as follows:

Comment:

   These introductory clauses, sometimes referred to as recitals, set out basic factual information about the parties. If the divorce has not been filed at the time the agreement is signed, language should be included to make clear that the subsequent filing of the divorce will not affect the validity of the agreement.

Exhibit 10.8   Continued

Most commonly the parties are referred to as "husband" and "wife." To avoid confusion, it is best not to refer to them as the plaintiff and defendant, since in a future action the designations could be reversed. Some agreements refer to the parties by their first names. This imparts a friendlier, less formal tone, and may not be appropriate in many cases.

The "NOW THEREFORE," clause sets out that the agreement is supported by consideration in that both parties are relinquishing certain rights in exchange for promises from the other.

Article One—Custody and Visitation

A.   Custody

The wife shall have physical custody of the children subject to the husband's right of visitation. Her home shall be their primary residence, and subject to the below exception for when the children are with the husband, the wife shall be responsible for making the day-to-day decisions regarding the children. However, when the children are with their father, he may make the day-to-day decisions necessary in order for him to care for them.

The parties shall have joint legal custody of the children and shall make all major decisions regarding the children together. Major decisions include, but are not limited to, decisions about education, medical care, mental health treatment, camps, and significant after-school activities, such as participation in Little League baseball.

In the event of a medical emergency, either parent may act without obtaining the prior consent of the other parent if consent cannot be secured in a timely fashion. The other parent shall be notified of the emergency at the first possible moment.

Comment:

It is always a good idea to define the custodial terms used in the agreement. If the applicable statute contains a definition, this language can be incorporated into the agreement.

As can be gleaned from the above clause, a fertile ground for post-divorce disputes is whether a certain decision is major or minor. This, of course, is relevant to the allocation of decision-making authority between the parties. One approach to this potential problem is to include a list identifying possible areas of future decision making as either major or minor, but it is virtually impossible to anticipate all contingencies.

Exhibit 10.8   Continued

B. Visitation

The parties agree that the husband may spend time with the children in accordance with the following schedule:

1. The father shall pick both children up from school on Wednesdays and return them to the mother's house by 7:30 P.M. It is understood that he will usually pick them up from their extended day program by 5:00 P.M., but he may pick them up anytime following the end of their regular school day. If the children have homework, he will make sure it is completed before he returns them to the mother's house.

2. So that the father can enjoy separate time with each child, he shall pick up John on Tuesdays, and Carla on Thursdays in accordance with the arrangement described in paragraph 1 above. The inability of one child to visit in a given week due to illness or other commitments will not affect the father's right to spend separate time with the other child. Also, the parties agree to try to arrange another visit to replace the missed one; if this is not practical, the father will forgo the visit for that week.

3. The arrangement described above in paragraphs 1 and 2 shall continue during the summer without alteration, except during designated vacation times, and the father will pick the children up from whatever activity they are enrolled in instead of from school.

4. The arrangement described above in paragraphs 1 and 2 shall be suspended during Christmas, February, and spring vacations. The children will spend February vacation with their father, and he shall be responsible for arranging for child care while he is at work. The children shall remain with their mother for Christmas and spring vacations, but the father agrees to take two days off during each of these weeks, excluding Christmas, New Year's Day, or any other legal holiday that falls during either week, in order to be with the children. These days may be consecutive, and the children can sleep at the father's house on the intervening night.

5. The children will visit with their father every Saturday. On alternate weeks, they may sleep at his house on Saturday night. He will pick them up from their mother's at 9:00 A.M. on Saturday. If it is not an overnight week, he will return them on Saturday at 5:00 P.M. If it is an overnight week, he shall return them by 11:00 A.M. on Sunday.

6. In addition to the above, the parties agree to the following with respect to the summer and holidays:

    (a) Every summer, each parent may spend an uninterrupted two weeks with the children. In selecting vacation weeks, the parties will confer so that vacation schedules can be coordinated with the children's summer activities. Each agrees to provide the other with information about where they will be during this vacation time, and will provide a telephone number and allow the other reasonable telephone access to the children.

Exhibit 10.8   Continued

(b) With respect to holidays, time shall be allocated in accordance with the below schedule. The parties agree that this schedule supersedes the regular visitation schedule.

   (i)   The children shall be with the mother on Mother's Day and her birthday.

   (ii)   The children shall be with the father on Father's Day and his birthday. The children may stay over at the father's house on both of these occasions.

   (iii) The children shall be with the father on the first two nights of Passover and on the first and last nights of Hanukkah. The children may stay over at the father's house on these occasions. The parties further agree that at the request of the father, the children may visit with him on any other major Jewish holiday. However, these will not be overnight visits.

   (iv)   The children shall be with the mother on Christmas Eve and Christmas Day and on Easter.

   (v)   The children shall be with their mother on Halloween. However, the parties agree that the father may come to the mother's home before the children go out trick-or-treating so he can see them in their costumes.

   (vi)   The parties will rotate Thanksgiving Day on a yearly basis. The children shall be with their mother in 2018, their father in 2019, and shall continue to alternate yearly. The parent who does not have the children with him or her on Thanksgiving Day may spend that Friday with them.

   (vii) The parties will rotate spending New Year's Eve and New Year's Day with the children. In 2019, the children shall spend New Year's Eve with their father and New Year's Day with their mother, and shall alternate on a yearly basis.

   (viii) With respect to the children's birthdays, the parties agree that they both shall have the right to spend time with the children on their birthdays. At present, the parties believe they can work out the details on their own. If this does not work, they agree to consult with their attorneys to develop a more structured arrangement.

   (ix)   The parties agree that there will be no special schedule for the rest of the holidays, and the regular schedule will be followed on these occasions.

7. The parties recognize that from time to time something may come up that requires an adjustment in this visitation schedule. For example, the mother occasionally has meetings on Monday evenings; when this occurs, she shall notify the father, and he shall make every effort

Exhibit 10.8 Continued

to arrange his schedule so he can visit with the children on Monday instead of Wednesday. The parties agree they will make every effort to accommodate reasonable requests of the other parent. If such adjustment results in a loss of visitation time by the father, the parties will try to make up this time.

Comment:

This is a very detailed visitation arrangement. Many agreements do not include this level of detail, and some simply provide for the right of reasonable visitation. However, unless the parties get along well, detail can be crucial to the success of visitation arrangements. Parents often underestimate how painful the coordination of custody and visitation arrangements can be, and how easily things can fall apart. A set schedule reduces the amount of negotiation that must take place, and thus reduces the potential for conflict, although, as this agreement does, parties can certainly include language that permits schedule changes based on mutual agreement.

Moreover, even where parents are reasonably friendly, holidays can trigger strong emotional reactions. Without a structure in place, parents may be unable to work out arrangements that permit both of them to spend holiday time with the children. As any family law attorney can attest to, the holiday season is likely to be one of their busiest and most stressful times of year.

Another matter that suggests caution when contemplating an unstructured visitation clause is the new relationship factor. Parents often fail to anticipate how painful it can be when their former spouse begins dating, especially if a relationship becomes serious. At this juncture, even parents who have been flexible and accommodating may find themselves caught up in conflict about arrangements. Mom might be less willing to let the children go to Dad's house when she suspects his new romantic interest is present, and Dad might seek increased time with the children to keep them away from Mom's new romantic interest. In short, parental jealousy and hurt may result in a distortion of previous arrangements.

This agreement makes a clear distinction between physical custody and visitation rights—there is no doubt that the children live with their mother and visit with their father. However, there may be situations where this distinction is blurred. For example, let's assume that at the four-way settlement conference, Mom asks for sole physical custody, and Dad asks for joint physical custody, but, in fact they have similar views about how much time the children should spend with each parent and that the allocation is essentially sole physical custody with liberal visitation rights. But

Exhibit 10.8   Continued

what if Dad objects to being characterized as a visiting parent because it connotes a lack of involvement? Here, creative drafting might save the agreement. Instead of using the terms "sole physical custody" and "visiting parent," Mom could be identified as the primary caretaker parent with her home as the children's primary residence, and Dad could be identified as the secondary care parent. Sometimes when parents are fighting about how they are to be identified, rather than how time is actually to be spent with the children, these kinds of creative compromises can prevent negotiations from collapsing (see Chapter 5).

C.   Parental Cooperation

Each party agrees to foster a feeling of affection between the children and the other party, and each agrees not to do anything to estrange the children from the other party or to hamper the free and natural development of either child's love and respect for the other party. The parties agree not to discuss the other's personal life with the children.

Comment:

Although it is fairly standard to include a parental cooperation clause, these clauses are probably not enforceable. It is unlikely that a court would hold someone in contempt for failing to foster a feeling of affection for the other parent, although a court might alter custody or visitation arrangements if one parent was actively seeking to alienate the children from the other.

D.   Right of Each Parent to Full Medical and School Information

Each parent is entitled access to the health and educational records of the children to the extent permitted by law. Neither parent shall interfere with the other parent's right of access.

Comment:

Language to this effect is pretty standard in most separation agreements. However, when abuse is an issue, access may need to be restricted in order to protect the safety of a spouse or a child. Where a right of access to records is provided by statute, a parent may need some kind of court order in order to limit the rights of the other parent.

Article Two—Child Support

A.   Base Amount and Applicability of the Guidelines

1. The husband shall pay to the wife the sum of $175.00 per week for the support of the children in accordance with the Child Support Guidelines

Exhibit 10.8   Continued

("Guidelines"). The parties agree that the payments shall be by wage assignment, and the husband agrees to promptly notify the court of any changes in his employment and to complete any necessary paperwork so delays will not be occasioned by the change. He shall also maintain group health insurance for the benefit of the children until they reach the age of 23.

2. The parties agree to review the support amount on a yearly basis to determine if it remains in conformity with the Guidelines, and to exchange all documentation necessary for completion of this review no later than ten days before the review date.

   If the amount no longer conforms with the Guidelines, it shall be adjusted so that it is in conformity. If the parties cannot reach agreement, they will consult with their attorneys who shall attempt to reach agreement. Any adjustment shall be reduced to writing as a modification of this agreement, and presented to the court for approval. If the parties acting alone or with the assistance of counsel cannot reach agreement, either party can petition the court for a modification.

   In addition to the above, the parties agree to the following support obligations. In no event shall payments made pursuant to this paragraph affect the husband's weekly support obligation.

   (a) The wife shall be responsible for the first $500.00 of uninsured medical expenses for each child in each calendar year. As used in this paragraph, the term "uninsured medical expenses" shall include, but not be limited to, any deductibles and co-payments, dental expenses, and the cost of mental health therapy, so long as both parties have consented to the particular course of therapeutic treatment. Once this amount is reached, the husband will pay half of the uninsured expenses for that child or both children if the limit is reached for both.

   (b) The parties agree that the children are entitled to a post-secondary education, and that they both will contribute to this education in proportion to their taxable income. The parties further agree that at a minimum their contribution should enable each child to attend a four-year state university, and that contributions should cover the cost of applications and tests, tuition, fees, room and board, and books. The parents' obligation to make educational contributions shall terminate upon the child's reaching his/her 23rd birthday, or upon graduation, whichever occurs first.

3. Upon emancipation of John, the husband's support obligation shall be adjusted downward so it conforms with the guideline amount for one child.

Exhibit 10.8   Continued

Upon emancipation of Carla, the husband's support obligation shall cease, subject to his obligations set out above in paragraph 2(b).

For purposes of this agreement, emancipation shall be defined as:

(a) the child's achieving the age of 18, graduation from high school, or marriage, whichever is later.

Comment:

In addition to establishing the support amount, it is useful to build in a review process tied to the guidelines. Some agreements also contain language defining what constitutes a change in circumstances that would warrant a modification. This can eliminate an area of possible contention, although again, it is virtually impossible to cover all possible contingencies.

Note that with respect to college education, the agreement does not bind the parents to a specific dollar amount. Instead, it provides for proportional contributions and establishes a minimal level of commitment. Often parents are reluctant to commit themselves to paying for college in an agreement. However, without such a commitment, it can be difficult to get the noncustodial parent to contribute, especially if over the years he or she has become less involved with the children, and in many states, the court has no statutory authority to order contribution in the absence of an agreement. Where parents have sufficient income, the option of setting up an educational trust whereby parents are obligated to set aside money on a yearly basis should be explored.

Article Three—Spousal Support

The husband acknowledges that he is fully self-supporting, and he hereby waives any right he may have to seek past, present, or future alimony from the wife.

The wife acknowledges that she is fully self-supporting, and she hereby waives any right she may have to seek past, present, or future alimony from the husband.

Comment:

Here, each spouse is waiving the right to seek alimony from the other. Sometimes, based on the assumption that only the wife might seek alimony, attorneys fail to make these waiver provisions reciprocal, but if the true intent is that neither party shall have a claim, reciprocal waivers are appropriate.

Exhibit 10.8 Continued

It is important to be aware that some judges will not accept a clause calling for a permanent waiver of support rights. Even where such a waiver is accepted, a court might later override it on public policy grounds if support becomes necessary to prevent a former spouse from going on public assistance.

If spousal support is to be paid, the precise nature and extent of the obligation should be spelled out. For example, if the husband is to make rehabilitative alimony payments, the agreement should define the circumstances under which the obligation can be extended, such as where the wife has been unable to complete her course of training due to no fault of her own.

Last, in this case, each party is employed and has health insurance. If one spouse has been covered on the other's plan, language regarding continued coverage should be included, unless other arrangements for coverage have been made.

Article Four—Life Insurance

Until the younger child has reached the age of 23, the husband shall pay for and maintain in full force and effect a life insurance policy on his life having death benefits of no less than $600,000, and he shall name the wife as beneficiary. If the husband dies while the policy is in effect, the wife shall use the funds for the benefit of the children.

Until the younger child has reached the age of 23, the wife shall pay for and maintain in full force and effect a life insurance policy on her life having death benefits of no less than $400,000, and she shall name the husband as beneficiary. If the wife dies while the policy is in effect, the husband shall use the funds for the benefit of the children.

Comment:

It is common to require a support obligor to maintain life insurance for the duration of the support obligation. In the event of death, the insurance would serve as a support replacement. If the custodial parent is also employed, it makes sense to have him or her maintain insurance as well.

In this agreement, the other spouse is named as the beneficiary. This is the simplest way to set things up, but it requires a degree of trust that many parties do not have in one another. Another option is to name the children as direct beneficiaries, but if they are young, this is impractical. Also, where proceeds are left to minors, many states require that management of the funds be placed under court control, which can be inconvenient. Alternatively, the money could be left to the children in trust, with the surviving spouse or a third party named as trustee. This would place

Exhibit 10.8   Continued

the spouse under a formal legal obligation to spend the money on behalf of the children; there is thus greater accountability than if he or she is simply named as the beneficiary with a contractual obligation to use the money for the children.

Article Five—Real Property

1. The parties presently own as tenants by the entirety a house and land located at 129 Cherry Lane, Newtowne ("house").
2. The parties agree that the fair market value of the house is $260,000, as determined by the appraisal done by Best Real Estate Company on April 15, 20018. The parties have placed the house on the market at this price and have listed it with Best Real Estate Company.
3. The parties agree that they will both fully cooperate with all matters related to the sale, including the execution of all necessary documents.
4. Until the house is sold, the wife shall have the right of exclusive use and occupancy and agrees to maintain the house in its present condition. The husband agrees that the wife is entitled to be reimbursed for all expenses related to maintaining the house, including the cost of a weekly cleaning so the house is presentable during this sale period. The wife shall make the monthly mortgage payments to Evergreen Mortgage Company, including principal, interest, and the tax escrow. The husband shall be responsible for paying the water and sewer bills and the homeowner's insurance.
5. Upon sale, after the payment of the mortgage, the broker's commission, and all related costs, the wife shall be reimbursed for all expenditures during the sale period related to maintaining the house; thereafter, sale proceeds shall be divided equally between the parties.
6. If the house is not sold by July 15, 2018, the parties agree to reconsider the asking price. If they cannot agree on a new price, they agree to be bound by the price recommendation of Best Real Estate Company. This process shall be repeated every three months until the house is sold.

Comment:

As discussed in Chapter 8 there are many ways to dispose of real estate in a divorce. Here, the sale option was most likely selected because neither spouse could buy out the interest of the other and there were no significant offsetting assets that could be used to lower the buyout price. Another option would have been to give the wife, as the custodial parent, the right of use and occupancy until some future date, but, as discussed in Chapter 8 the downside of this arrangement is that it keeps the parties enmeshed and frequently leads to unanticipated problems. Here, the parties must continue to interact, but only until the house is sold. If the parties

Exhibit 10.8 Continued

are uncooperative, additional safeguards might be included relative to this time period, such as specifying what happens if the wife does not maintain the property or if a party fails to make a required payment.

Article Six—Personal Property

The parties state that they have divided all of their personal property to their mutual satisfaction. Hereafter, each shall own, have, and enjoy all items of personal property of every kind now or hereafter acquired free of any claim or right of the other with full power to dispose of the same as fully and effectively, in all respects and for all purposes, as if he or she were unmarried.

Comment:

It is generally advisable for the parties to divide their assets before the agreement is executed, as this avoids potential enforcement problems. If this is not feasible, the details of any post-execution transfer should be spelled out.

Article Seven—Debts

1. The wife agrees that she will be solely responsible for payment of the following debts:
   (a) Mastercard (joint account)
       Account number: 66793021
       Amount due: $1,500
   (b) Sears (wife's account)
       Account number: 3390
       Amount due: $479.56
   (c) Evergreen Mortgage Company
       Account number: 73796
       Amount due: $140,000
2. The husband agrees that he will be solely responsible for payment of the following debts:
   (a) American Express (joint account)
       Account number: 440902881
       Amount due: $5,600
   (b) Student Loan Service (husband's student loan)
       Account number: 4490
       Amount due: $4,500
3. Each party represents and warrants to the other that exclusive of the debts identified in this agreement he or she has not incurred any

Exhibit 10.8   Continued

obligations for which the other shall or may be liable. If either party is called upon to pay an obligation that the other is responsible for, the responsible party shall indemnify and hold the other harmless therefrom, including attorney's fees and related expenses. Each, or the estate of each, promises to notify the other if any claim is made against him or her or his or her estate as a result of any debt charge or liability incurred by the other, and to give the other an opportunity to defend against the claim.

Comment:

It is important to recognize that although parties may spell out who is responsible for payment of joint debts, their arrangement is not binding on creditors, as they are not parties to the agreement. Accordingly, notwithstanding the agreement, each party remains obligated to joint creditors. It is extremely important that this be pointed out to clients; otherwise, they may not be getting what they think they agreed to.

As in the above provision, an indemnification clause should always be included whereby each spouse agrees to reimburse the other if called upon to pay a debt allocated to the other. However, this clause may be of limited utility because the nonpayment probably stems from a lack of funds.

Article Eight — General Provisions

General Comment:

In all states, boilerplate provisions such as those that follow are routinely included in agreements. However, they should not be included without review because adjustments may need to be made in individual circumstances.

A.   Separation

The husband and wife shall continue to live apart. Each shall be free from interference, molestation, or restraint by the other. Neither shall seek to force the other to live with him or her, or to otherwise interfere with the other's personal liberty.

Comment:

Despite the language establishing that neither party shall molest or restrain the other, this clause does not take the place of a protective order and should not be relied on as a substitute for one. In most states, it is not placed on record with the police and is not criminally enforceable.

Exhibit 10.8   Continued

B.   General Release

Each party releases and forever discharges the other from all causes of action, claims, rights, or demands whatsoever, at law or in equity, he or she ever had or now has or can hereafter have against the other, by reason of any matter, cause, or thing from the beginning of the world to the date of this Agreement, except any causes of action for divorce and except further that nothing contained in this Article shall release or discharge either party from such party's covenants, promises, agreements, representations, warranties, or other undertakings or obligations as contained in this Agreement.

Comment:

As drafted, this is a very broad release. Each spouse is giving up all rights against the other except for filing for divorce and securing rights pursuant to the agreement. This should be carefully explained to the client, as there may be situations where such a broad waiver is not appropriate.

C.   Waiver of Estate Claim

Except as otherwise provided in this Agreement, each party waives, releases, and relinquishes any and all rights that he or she may now have in the property of the other (such as the right of election, dower, courtesy, and inheritance) and all rights he or she may now have or hereafter acquire under the laws of this state or any other jurisdiction:

   (a) To share, as a result of the marital relationship, in the other party's property or estate upon the latter's death; or
   (b) To act as executor or administrator of the other's estate, or to participate in the administration thereof.

This Agreement shall and does constitute a mutual waiver by the parties of their respective rights of election to take against each other's last will and testament now or hereafter in force under the laws of any jurisdiction.

It is the intention of the parties that their respective estates shall be administered and distributed in all respects as though no marriage had been solemnized between them. The consideration for each party's waiver and release is the other party's reciprocal waiver and release.[56]

Comment:

The primary importance of this clause is to protect each spouse's estate in the event of death before divorce. It serves to shift the statutory consequences of divorce, which is a divestiture of estate rights based on marital status, to the time the agreement is executed.

Exhibit 10.8   Continued

D. Entire Understanding

The husband and wife have incorporated into this Agreement their entire understanding. No oral statement or prior written matter, extrinsic to this Agreement, shall have any force or effect.

Comment:

This relatively simple clause is important because it prevents either party from enforcing any side agreements. For example, let's say that the wife promises the husband that he can have a certain painting in her possession, but this promise is not reflected in the agreement. After execution, the husband cannot enforce this promise because it is not included in this agreement.

E. Voluntary Execution

The husband and wife acknowledge that they are entering into this Agreement freely and voluntarily and that they have each obtained independent legal advice; that they have ascertained all the relevant facts and circumstances; that they understand their legal rights; that each is satisfied that he or she has received full disclosure as to the other's finances, assets, income, expectancies, and other economic matters; and that they clearly understand and assent to all of the provisions of this Agreement.

F. Modification

Any modification of this Agreement shall be in writing and shall be duly signed and acknowledged by each party in the same manner as this Agreement. No oral representation or statement shall constitute an amendment, waiver, or modification of the terms of this agreement.

Comment:

This language requiring that all modifications be in writing precludes either party's establishing new rights based on oral representations.

G. Waiver

A waiver by either party of any provision of this Agreement shall not prevent or stop such party from enforcing such provision in the future. The failure of either party to insist upon the strict performance of any of the terms and provisions of this Agreement by the other party shall not be a waiver or relinquishment of such term or provision; the same shall continue in full force and effect.

Exhibit 10.8   Continued

Comment:

This language should be read in conjunction with paragraph F above. Here, it is made clear that failure to insist on performance of any term will not modify the agreement and is not a waiver of that party's right to subsequently insist on strict performance. For example, if the wife agreed to take a reduced amount of child support for a few weeks because the husband was having financial difficulties, this would not modify the original agreement and at any point she could again insist on full payment.

H.   Consent to Jurisdiction

The parties acknowledge that this Agreement is to be construed and governed by the laws of *State* X. Both parties consent to the continuing jurisdiction of this State in any subsequent action to modify or enforce this Agreement.

Comment:

Generally, the term "continuing jurisdiction" as used here is understood to refer to jurisdiction over the persons of both parties and is not intended to deal with jurisdiction over subsequent custody disputes.

I.   Agreement to Mediate

In the event a dispute arises between the parties concerning any of the terms or provisions of this Agreement, which they are unable to resolve on their own or with the assistance of their attorneys, they agree that before filing any action in court, they will try to resolve the dispute through mediation at the Family Mediation Service or other similar agency. However, nothing in this paragraph shall prevent the wife from going directly to court or pursuing any other legal remedy if the husband defaults on any of his financial obligations under this Agreement.

J.   Severability

If any provision of this Agreement shall be held invalid or unlawful by any court of competent jurisdiction, the remainder of this Agreement shall nevertheless remain valid and enforceable according to its terms.

Comment:

This clause protects the validity of the agreement in the event any provision is found to be invalid or illegal. A clause found to be invalid or illegal would thus be dropped from the agreement without affecting any other clause.

Exhibit 10.8   Continued

K.   Article Headings—No Effect

The headings at the beginning of each article of this Agreement and the titles of the same are included for reference purposes only. They are not terms or conditions of this Agreement.

L.   Execution in Counterpart

This Agreement may be executed in two or more counterparts, each of which shall be deemed as original.

M.   Incorporation and Merger with Spousal Support Exception

At any hearing on the Divorce Complaint, a copy of this Agreement shall be submitted to the court and shall be incorporated and, subject to the below exception, merged into the judgment of divorce and shall not retain any independent legal significance. However, Article Three shall not be merged into the judgment of divorce, but instead shall survive and retain its independent legal significance.

Comment:

At the divorce hearing, the parties' separation agreement is presented to the court for approval. If it is approved, the court incorporates the agreement into the divorce judgment. In effect, through the process of incorporation, the agreement becomes an enforceable order of the court.

Beyond this, the agreement either merges with the court decree and loses any significance as an independent contract, or it survives the incorporation and retains its significance as an independent contract. Whether the agreement merges or survives has important future consequences. If the agreement merges, it ceases to exist as a separate document and is fully modifiable and enforceable as the court's own judgment would be. If the agreement survives, it continues to exist as a contract. This makes modification more difficult because choosing survival over merger usually indicates that the parties intended for the agreement to be permanent. Moreover, if the agreement survives, it is, at least in theory, an independent contract, which may still be enforceable as such.

Frequently, as in the present agreement, some provisions merge and others survive the incorporation. Here, as is commonly done, the spousal support provisions survive, making modification much more difficult.

Signed this 10th day of May 2018.

_____	_____
David Smith	Marie Smith

Exhibit 10.8   Continued

STATE OF X

Then personally appeared the above-named David Smith and acknowledged the foregoing instrument to be his free act and deed for the purposes therein set forth before me.

_____

Notary Public
My Commission Expires: _____

STATE OF X

Then personally appeared the above-named Marie Smith and acknowledged the foregoing instrument to be her free act and deed for the purposes therein set forth before me.

_____

Notary Public
My Commission Expires: _____

The Divorce Hearing

Once the parties have worked out their differences and reduced their agreement to writing, or it has become clear that a settlement is not possible, a **divorce hearing** is requested. Where the parties have reached an agreement, an uncontested hearing is requested; where they have not reached agreement, the request would be for a contested hearing, more commonly referred to as a trial. Most courts retain separate scheduling calendars for contested and uncontested cases. Uncontested hearings are brief and easily scheduled, whereas contested cases usually must be pre-tried, and the trial itself can easily last a week or longer.

The Uncontested Case

In most jurisdictions, the uncontested hearing is a relatively simple matter and may last only for five or ten minutes. The typical hearing occurs in two phases: First is the dissolution phase, and second is the separation agreement review phase. Our focus is on cases that are uncontested because the parties have reached an agreement, but a case can also be uncontested because the defendant fails to appear. In the latter situation, the plaintiff must comply with the requirements of the Soldiers and Sailors Relief Act of 1940, which protects members of the military from default judgments.[57] The plaintiff must attest to the fact that the defendant's nonappearance is not because he or she is serving in the military. If uncertain, the plaintiff may need to determine this before the divorce can proceed.

Dissolving the Marriage

During the marital dissolution phase, the plaintiff must establish that the parties have a validly contracted marriage and that the divorce grounds set forth in the complaint actually exist. Where a joint petition has been filed, either or both of the parties would testify to these matters. Establishing grounds is usually little more than a formality, but the court must be satisfied that the requisite elements are present. Also, keep in mind that "uncontested" is not synonymous with "no-fault." Parties can reach agreement regardless of the underlying grounds; thus, one could have an uncontested divorce that is premised on cruel and abusive treatment. However, once agreement is reached, the plaintiff frequently amends the complaint from fault to no-fault grounds.

Generally, the plaintiff's attorney or the judge will ask the plaintiff a series of questions to elicit the necessary information. Since the case is uncontested, there is no cross-examination. Usually the defendant does not testify; however, in a no-fault case, the judge may ask the defendant if he or she agrees with the plaintiff that the marriage is truly over.

Approving the Separation Agreement

In the second phase of the typical no-fault hearing, the judge reviews the separation agreement. If it is accepted, the judge will approve it for **incorporation** into the divorce judgment, and the agreement will either **survive** or **merge** in accordance with its terms (see article eight, paragraph M of the sample separation agreement).

In some states, the primary focus of the review is on procedural fairness. The judge will inquire into whether the parties entered into the agreement freely and voluntarily and whether they understand it. Even where the focus is on procedural rather than substantive fairness, the judge will usually check to see if the child support amount conforms to the guidelines and, if not, will evaluate whether the deviation is justifiable; some judges will also review spousal support arrangements. In other states, there is an additional focus on substantive fairness, and a judge will scrutinize the agreement in its entirety. In some states, judges will reject a term only if it is unconscionable; in others, judges may reject a term that is unfair or significantly favors one side over the other.

Where the judge believes the agreement is unfair, he or she will usually give the parties a chance to correct the problems and resubmit it for approval. If the necessary changes are minor, they can usually be made on the spot, and the hearing can proceed to completion. However, if the unfairness permeates the agreement, such as where one spouse was forced into signing it, the hearing will probably be suspended until the agreement is reworked or the case recast as a contested one.

Assuming the separation agreement is approved, the judge will enter the **divorce judgment**. The judgment both dissolves the marriage and incorporates the separation agreement, making it an enforceable order of the court. The timing of the entry of judgment varies from state to state. In some states, the judgment enters at the conclusion of the hearing; in others, it does not enter until a certain amount of time has elapsed. In some states, the initial judgment is in the form of a **decree *nisi***. This is an interim judgment, which automatically ripens into a final one unless the parties seek to revoke it. This interim judgment gives the parties a chance to be absolutely certain that they do not wish to reconcile.

The Contested Case

When a divorce case is contested, a trial, rather than a simple hearing, becomes necessary. It is important to keep in mind that when a case is contested, it is almost never because the parties are fighting the divorce grounds; most cases are contested because the parties cannot reach agreement on one or more of the collateral issues, such as support or custody.

The Pretrial Conference

In most jurisdictions, a case cannot proceed to trial until there has been a **pretrial conference** with a judge. This conference generally serves two primary purposes. First, it may be used to explore settlement. In some instances, a judge may actively encourage settlement by indicating the likely outcome if the case were to go to trial. Second, it can be used to simplify matters for trial. The judge can help the parties identify the issues in dispute, and uncontested matters can then be admitted. Additionally, documents can be authenticated and witness lists established.

In preparation for this conference, each party must submit a **pretrial statement**. This document provides the judge with information about the parties and the procedural history of the case. Each party identifies the facts and issues in dispute and his or her position relative to the matters in contention.

The Trial

Throughout this chapter, references have been made to the fact that procedural rules tend to be applied in a more relaxed fashion in the divorce context. However, once a divorce is at the trial stage, this is no longer true; a divorce trial proceeds much like any other civil trial, except it is not tried before a jury. The rules of evidence are in effect, and all testimony and submissions must conform to these rules. Each side has the opportunity to present an opening and a closing statement, introduce evidence, call witnesses, and cross-examine the other side's witnesses, and the entire proceeding is recorded by a court stenographer.[58]

Following the trial, the judge reviews all of the evidence and makes a decision on the merits. The divorce decree is then entered, which both dissolves the marriage and contains the court's order regarding the issues before it. As in uncontested cases, the judgment may enter as a decree *nisi*. In many jurisdictions, the order must contain detailed findings of fact and conclusions of law. These details can be crucial because this order, much like a separation agreement, structures the postmarital relationship between the parties.

Trial Preparation and the Role of the Paralegal

Trials require intensive preparation, and paralegals are often involved in this process.[59] They may be responsible for setting up the **trial notebook**, which is a binder containing everything needed to present the case in court, such as pleadings and motions, witness lists, deposition summaries, and a description of all exhibits. Paralegals may also be responsible for gathering and organizing all potential exhibits and assisting with witness preparation, including preparation of the client. This is an important task, which usually includes the following steps:

1. Reviewing all relevant information with the client to ensure that it is complete and accurate.
2. Reviewing the direct examination questions (the questions that each side asks of its witnesses) with each witness so he or she knows what

to expect at trial. Although witnesses cannot be told what to say, they can be helped with how to present their answers to the court so they are delivered in the most effective or, depending on the circumstances, least damaging manner.
3. Reviewing with the client and other witnesses what the other side is likely to ask of them during cross-examination and explaining how best to respond to these questions, which are usually designed to undermine credibility.

■ Post-Divorce Proceedings

A case is not necessarily over once a judgment has been entered. A party who is dissatisfied with the result can file a post-trial motion for relief or an appeal. Further on down the line, either party can file a modification action (if there has been a change in circumstances) or a contempt action (if the other side has violated an order).

Post-Trial Motions

The two most common post-trial motions are the **motion for a new trial** and a **motion for relief from judgment**, although other motions may be available in some jurisdictions. In permitting these forms of relief, most states have looked to the cognate provisions of the Federal Rules of Civil Procedure and have adopted similar, if not identical, rules.[60]

Motion for a New Trial

After judgment has been entered, the losing party can bring a motion asking the court to set aside the judgment and order a new trial. The essential basis for this motion is that prejudicial errors were made during the course of trial that affected the outcome. The motion is usually presented to the judge who presided over the trial. It must be brought within a short time after entry of judgment, usually within ten days.

Motion for Relief from Judgment

Most states also allow a party to seek relief from judgment for a variety of reasons, including, but not limited to, mistake, inadvertence, excusable neglect, fraud, newly discovered evidence, or for "any other reason justifying relief from judgment."[61] A party usually has longer to file this motion than a motion for a new trial. Under the Federal Rules of Civil Procedure, a party must file the motion within a "reasonable time," which in most instances is not later than a year after judgment was entered. The year time limit does not apply if the underlying reason for the motion falls into the catchall category.

The motion for relief from judgment is generally regarded as a request for extraordinary relief and will be granted only in exceptional circumstances. For example, when a party seeks to set aside a judgment for newly discovered evidence, the party must show that even with due diligence, it could not have been discovered either during the trial or within the period for bringing a motion for a new trial, and that it would likely have led to a different outcome. Where allowed, the court may vacate and modify its judgment, or order a retrial.

Appeals

Overview of Appellate Practice

The losing party can **appeal** from the court's final judgment or that portion of the judgment that is adverse to him or her. The general rule is that a party can appeal only from a final judgment. For appeal purposes, a decree *nisi* is considered the final judgment; if a party waits until the *nisi* decree ripens into a final decree, the appeal is likely to be untimely. Usually, the appeal goes from the trial court to the intermediate **appellate court**, but, in states without an intermediate level court, the appeal goes directly to the state's supreme court. The decision of an intermediate court can usually be appealed to the supreme court.

An appeal is not a retrial. The appellate court reviews what took place at the trial level to determine if any errors were made that might have affected the outcome of the case. This review is based on the record, and new evidence cannot be introduced. In reviewing for errors, the court is primarily concerned with errors of law. Findings of fact cannot be upset unless the court determines that they are unsupported by the evidence. The appeals court cannot substitute its view of what took place for the findings of the trial judge, who actually sees and hears the witnesses and is in the best position to evaluate their credibility.

The appeals court can affirm or reverse the decision of the trial court, or remand the case for a new trial. A remand is likely if additional information is needed, such as if the court improperly excluded evidence or allowed evidence that should have been excluded, as either may have altered the outcome of the case.

Appellate Procedure

Each state has its own rules governing the particulars of appellate procedure. These rules tend to be very detailed and contain multiple time limits that must be met at each step of the process to preserve the right of review. Nonetheless, some basic steps common to most, if not all, states can be identified.

An appeal is commenced by the filing of a notice of appeal. This notice is usually filed in the court that heard the case. After it is commenced, the record on appeal must be prepared. Typically, the appealing party (appellant) is responsible for designating those portions of the trial court materials that he or she wishes to include in the record. In addition to pleadings and documents, the record also includes the transcript of the proceedings or relevant portions of it. The appellant is responsible for contacting the stenographer and making arrangements to have the transcript prepared and filed. If the appellant does not need to have all of the documents or the entire transcript included in the record, the appellant must inform the other side (appellee) what he or she has designated for inclusion, and the appellee then has the right to cross-designate documents or portions of the transcript for inclusion. The actual assembly of the record is done by a trial court clerk. Once it is assembled, the case is docketed with the appeals court.

The parties then submit briefs to the court. The appellant submits the first brief within a certain amount of time after docketing, and the appellee then has a specified number of days after this within which to file his or her brief. The appellant can then file a reply brief responding to the points made in the appellee's brief. After the briefs are submitted, the court can decide the case based on the written submissions alone, or it can schedule oral arguments, which give the attorneys a chance to argue the case before the court. Many states impose strict limits on the time allotted for oral argument.

The Role of the Paralegal

A paralegal may be asked to oversee the appeals process. This is a daunting task that requires making sure each step is taken at the right time and that all rules are complied with. There is very little give here: An omitted detail or a missed deadline can lead to the dismissal of the appeal. Another important role a paralegal can play is in researching and writing the appellate brief. These briefs are painstaking to write. They require fine-tuned analytical skills and must conform to all of the particulars governing the submission of appellate briefs; accordingly, this task is usually assigned only to senior paralegals.

The Complaint for Modification

Modification of judgments has been discussed at various points in this book. Here, some general points are made, and this action is distinguished from other postjudgment procedures.

The basis for a modification action is that circumstances have changed since the entry of the divorce order, making enforcement of certain provisions unfair. A modification is thus different from the postjudgment remedies discussed above because it does not challenge the validity of the order as originally entered; rather, it focuses on subsequent events that have since made it unworkable. Accordingly, a modification action can be filed in a case that was initially settled by the parties.

In principle, a modification is considered a continuation of the original action. In some jurisdictions, it is initiated by the filing of a motion, while in others, a new complaint must be filed and served (see Exhibit 10.9). As with the divorce, a court can enter temporary orders during the pendency of the modification proceeding, and the resulting judgment is itself subject to modification if there is a subsequent change in circumstances. Unlike other postjudgment remedies, there are generally no time limits within which a party may file a modification complaint.

Exhibit 10.9   Motion for Modification

STATE OF INDIANA   )   IN THE_____ _____ COURT
) SS:
COUNTY OF_____   )   CASE NO. _____

IN RE THE_____OF:

_____
Petitioner,

V.

_____
Respondent.

VERIFIED PETITION FOR MODIFICATION OF CHILD SUPPORT

Comes now_____, pro se, and hereby files a Verified Petition for Modification of Child Support, and states as follows:

1.   That parties have_____minor child(ren), namely:

Name	**Date of birth**
_____	_____
_____	_____
_____	_____
_____	_____

2.   _____ is ordered to pay $_____ in current child support effective on_____.

3.   Since that time, there has been a change in circumstances that makes the current order vary more than 20% from what the child support guidelines would indicate should be paid, or so substantial and continuing as to make the terms of the current support order unreasonable for the following reasons:

_____
_____
_____
_____
_____

4.   Child support should be modified to reflect the substantial change in circumstances as

Approved by Coalition for Court Access Best Practices
Group CCA-DC-0219-1004

Exhibit 10.9   Continued

outlined above.

5.   Arrearages are not determined at this time and are reserved for a later date.

6.   _____ requests the Court address the tax exemption assignment.

7.   A hearing should be set to determine if child support should be changed.

WHEREFORE,_____requests that this Court set this matter for hearing, and upon hearing, modify the existing child support as is appropriate, and order all other further relief that is just and proper in the premises.

I affirm under the penalties of perjury that the foregoing representations are true.

_____
Signature

_____
_____
_____

CERTIFICATE OF SERVICE

I hereby certify that I sent a copy of this Petition by first class mail to the opposing attorney, or the opposing party if the opposing party is not represented by an attorney, on _____.

_____
Signature

The Complaint for Contempt

Contempt actions also have been discussed at various points throughout the book; the primary purpose of this section is to contrast this action with other postjudgment remedies.

A contempt action is brought to enforce an existing order where a party is in noncompliance. Like a modification action, a complaint for contempt can be brought following a case that was settled by the parties (see Exhibit 10.10). The action, by seeking enforcement, affirms the ongoing validity of the existing order. It is not uncommon for a defendant in a contempt hearing to argue that as entered, the underlying order is unfair or that circumstances have changed, which makes its current enforcement unfair. Given the range of available corrective procedures, courts are not very sympathetic to these arguments. Most judges will inform a contempt defendant that if he or she wishes to challenge the order, he or she must take the appropriate steps to do so and that, until that time, the plaintiff has a right to rely on the order as it exists.

Exhibit 10.10   Complaint for Contempt

IN THE FAMILY COURT OF _____ **COUNTY, WEST VIRGINIA**

In Re:
The Marriage / Children of: Civil Action No. _____

_____ ,   and   _____ .
Petitioner   Respondent

_____   _____

_____   _____
Address   Address

_____   _____
Daytime phone   Daytime phone

PETITION FOR CONTEMPT

1.   Your name: _____ . List any other name(s) you were known by
          during this case. _____

     Your current address: _____

2.   Name of the person you want the court to hold in contempt: _____
     Address: _____
     Daytime telephone number: _____ Social Security number: _____

3. Your Reasons for Making this Contempt Petition

___**A.**   Failure to Make Payments of Money

     ___ I believe the person I want the court to hold in contempt has failed to make court ordered
     payments of:

     ___ Child support

     ___ Spousal support

     ___ Separate maintenance

     ___ Equitable distribution

     ___ Medical support

     ___ Other (List, and be specific.) _____

You must attach a copy of the order requiring these payments.

List the due dates and amounts for all payments that have not been made.

_____

_____

Exhibit 10.10   Continued

_____

_____

_____

List the total amount due and unpaid on the date you sign this petition: $_____.

__ **B.**   Failure to Obey Court Ordered Parenting Plan

___ I believe the person I want the court to hold in contempt has failed to abide by the terms and conditions of a court ordered Parenting Plan. <u>For each instance you believe the person has failed to abide by the Parenting Plan, you must list the date, and explain</u> *specifically* <u>how the person failed to abide by the plan; and you MUST attach a copy of the Parenting Plan.</u>

_____

_____

_____

_____

_____

_____

__ **C.**   Failure to Obey *Other* Terms, Conditions, or Requirements of a Court Order

___ I believe the person I want the court to hold in contempt has failed to abide by the terms, conditions, or requirements of a court order in some way <u>other than</u> those listed in items A. and B. above. <u>For each instance you believe the person has failed to abide by the terms, conditions, or requirements of an order, you must list the date, and explain</u> *specifically* <u>how the person failed to abide by the order; and you MUST attach a copy of the order.</u>

_____

_____

_____

_____

_____

_____

4.   I have attached to this Petition documents I believe prove the person I have named has failed to obey a court order. The documents I have attached are:

_____

_____

_____

Exhibit 10.10   Continued

For the reasons stated above, I request that the Court issue a Notice of Contempt Hearing / Rule to Show Cause setting a hearing to determine if the person named in this Petition should be held in Contempt of Court.

_____   _____
Your Signature / Petitioner   Date

VERIFICATION of CONTEMPT PETITION

I, _____, after making an oath or affirmation to tell the truth, say that the facts I have stated in this Contempt Petition are true of my personal knowledge; and if I have set forth matters upon information given to me by others, I believe that information to be true.

_____   _____
Signature   Date

This Verification was sworn to or affirmed before me on the ____ day of _____,
200__.

_____
Notary Public / Other Official

My commission expires:_____.

Chapter Summary

Good case preparation begins with a well-organized client interview. At this interview, essential information is obtained and a foundation of trust is established. Active listening and respect for the client's emotional concerns are important in establishing an effective relationship.

The first formal step in a divorce case is the filing of the complaint (or a joint petition). The complaint and summons are then served on the defendant, who must answer within a certain period of time. In theory, failure to respond will result in a default judgment, but most courts are reluctant to default a defendant in a divorce case. Once the case has been initiated, both sides usually engage in the process of discovery, which is used to acquire information about the other side in order to help prepare for trial and/or structure the settlement.

Frequently, during the period between filing and the final hearing, motions for temporary orders will be filed asking the court to provide interim relief. The general rule is that advance notice must be given to the other side; however, *ex parte* relief may be allowed where such notice poses a substantial risk of harm. Notice and an opportunity to be heard must subsequently be provided. Common motions include those for support, custody, the protection of assets, and protection from abuse.

Most parties wish to settle their case and avoid a trial on the merits. The most common approach to dispute resolution is negotiation, where each attorney acts in a representational capacity and seeks to obtain the best possible settlement for his or her client. Another approach, which is growing in popularity, is mediation. Here, a neutral third party assists the parties to reach agreement on their own. A primary advantage of this approach is that it is client-centered; however, concerns have been raised about its appropriateness where there is a history of domestic violence or a significant power imbalance between the parties. Arbitration is another alternative, but it is not used frequently in divorce cases. Here, the dispute is presented to a decision maker who renders a binding decision. The process is more flexible than a court hearing, and the parties retain a greater degree of control.

If all issues are resolved through any of these methods, the parties reduce their understanding to a written separation agreement. This agreement is comprehensive and must be drafted carefully because it governs the post-divorce relationship between the parties. With the execution of the agreement, the case becomes uncontested, and a relatively simple hearing can be scheduled at which the marriage is dissolved and the agreement reviewed and approved by the court.

If the parties cannot reach resolution, the case is contested and a trial on the merits is scheduled. Here, a judge resolves the dispute and enters an order reflecting his or her decision. The losing party can challenge this decision by way of motion or appeal. Further down the line, parties may seek to modify or enforce the existing order by filing a modification or contempt action.

Key Terms

Confidentiality

Active Listening

Complaint/Petition

Request/Prayer for Relief

Joint Petition

Docket Number

Venue

Filing Fee

Summons

Service of Process

Personal Service

Constructive Service

Acceptance of Service

Return of Service

Answer

Default Judgment

Affirmative Defense

Counterclaim

Motion to Dismiss

Discovery

Deposition

Deponent

Subpoena

Subpoena Duces Tecum

Interrogatories

Request for Production of Documents

Request for a Physical or Mental Examination

Request for Admissions

Protective Order

Discovery Conference

Motion to Compel

Temporary Orders

Affidavit

Ex Parte

Guardian ad Litem

Negotiation

Mediation

E-Mediation

Arbitration

Collaborative Divorce

Unbundled Legal Services

Separation Agreement

Divorce Hearing

Incorporation

Survival

Merger

Divorce Judgment

Decree *Nisi*

Pretrial Conference

Pretrial Statement

Trial Notebook

Motion for a New Trial

Motion for Relief from Judgment

Appeal

Appellate Court

Review Questions

1. Why is it important to pay attention to cultural differences when interviewing a client?
2. Why is it important to acknowledge how a client is feeling at the initial interview?
3. What does the term "unauthorized practice of law" mean, and how does it limit your relationship with a client?
4. Why is maintaining client confidentiality so important?
5. What is meant by the term "active listening"?
6. What are the three stages of a client interview?
7. What are the benefits of asking open-ended questions during an interview?
8. What is the funneling process?
9. What purposes are served by the divorce complaint?
10. What are the basic component parts of a divorce complaint?
11. What are the possible consequences of failing to include something in a complaint?
12. What is a joint petition?
13. Explain what is meant by the term "venue."
14. What is a summons?
15. What is meant by the term "service of process"?
16. Why is it important to try to personally serve a defendant?
17. What are the ways in which service can be accomplished?
18. What is "return of service"?
19. What happens if a divorce defendant does not respond to the complaint in a timely fashion? How is this different from other civil actions?
20. What are the component parts of an answer?
21. Why is it generally advisable to file an answer?
22. What is a motion to dismiss? When might a defendant file one?
23. What is the purpose of discovery?
24. Describe the five available discovery procedures.
25. What is "metadata"?
26. What potential "traps for the unwary" need to be kept in mind when responding to a request for electronically stored information?
27. Describe some of the key ways in which paralegals can assist with discovery.
28. What is a protective order, and when may a party seek one?
29. What can a party do when the other side fails to respond to discovery requests?
30. What is a motion? Why would a party file one?
31. When would a party file a motion *ex parte*?
32. What happens to temporary orders once a divorce judgment is entered?
33. Can a temporary order be appealed? Why or why not?

34. What is an affidavit?
35. Describe each of the three dispute resolution approaches, and explain what the key differences are among them.
36. Why do some people argue that mediation is not appropriate in cases where there has been domestic violence?
37. Explain the differences between the two important approaches to mediation: the problem-solving model and the transformative model.
38. Describe the four stages of mediation (using the problem-solving model).
39. What is e-mediation? What possible advantages does it offer over face-to-face mediation? What are its possible limitations?
40. What is a collaborative divorce? How is it similar to and different from other alternative dispute resolution approaches?
41. What concerns have been raised regarding the appropriateness of the collaborative divorce process in cases involving domestic violence?
42. Explain what is meant by the term "unbundled" legal services.
43. What concerns have been raised about the use of unbundled legal services? What considerations support this approach?
44. What is a separation agreement?
45. What are the benefits of spelling out the custody and visitation arrangements?
46. What are the most common ways for real estate to be disposed of?
47. With respect to the allocation of joint debts, why might a spouse be called on to pay a debt allocated to the other party in a separation agreement?
48. What are meant by the terms "incorporation," "merger," and "survival as an independent contract" as used in separation agreements?
49. What takes place at an uncontested hearing?
50. What does a judge look at when reviewing an agreement for procedural fairness? For substantive fairness?
51. How does a trial in a contested case differ from an uncontested hearing?
52. What purpose is served by a pretrial conference?
53. What is a motion for a new trial?
54. What is a motion for relief from judgment?
55. What is the primary focus of an appeals court when reviewing a lower court decision?
56. Outline the steps involved in bringing an appeal.
57. How do modification and contempt actions differ from other postjudgment procedures?

Discussion Questions

1. Assume that you are conducting an initial client interview with a client who is involved in a custody dispute with her husband and that you become fairly certain the client is lying to you. What do you think you should do at this stage of the process? Do you confront the client? Do you ignore your concerns? Are there any techniques you might use for eliciting the truth? Is it your responsibility to elicit the truth?

   Assume that you continue working with this client and, despite your concern, have established a good relationship with her. One day she comes into your office and tells you that she has been lying to you and that she is a drug addict and is frequently high when she is with her children.

   What do you do at this point? In thinking about it, assume that you are the only paralegal in a busy office and that although you could ask to be taken off the case, this would make matters difficult for the supervising attorney.
2. Do you think the discovery process should be as open-ended as it currently is? Why or why not? Are there ways it could be limited without interfering with a party's ability to prepare a case?
3. Is it fair to require one party to pay the other side's attorney where there is a disparity of income? Why or why not?
4. Do you think mediation is appropriate in cases involving domestic violence? What about cases not involving violence, but where there is a significant power imbalance between the spouses?
5. Under which circumstances, if any, do you think that paralegals should be able to provide clients with legal advice?
6. Do you think the provision of unbundled legal services is an effective approach to addressing the country's "justice gap"?

Assignments

1. Draft the custody provisions of a separation agreement in accordance with the following instructions:

   To: Polly Paralegal
   From: Anita Attorney
   Re: Ramirez divorce

   As you know, we represent Ms. Ramirez in her current divorce action. I just completed a round of settlement negotiations, and I would like you to try to draft the custody and visitation provisions of the separation agreement. Following are the things you need to know in order to do this:
   a. The parties have one child, a daughter named Lucinda, age 8.

b. Both parents work outside the home, with the mother working about 35 hours per week and the father working about 50.

c. Both parents have a good relationship with Lucinda, although Mom is clearly the primary care parent.

d. Ms. Ramirez and her husband, Mr. Lewis, cannot stand each other, although they think they can handle joint legal custody.

e. The real issue is physical custody. We have more or less reached agreement as to when each parent will spend time with Lucinda, but we are stuck with how to define the arrangement. Dad is adamant that he not be called the visiting parent, and Mom is adamant that the arrangement not be called joint physical custody.

f. Your job is to try to come up with a creative solution! At this point, just worry about the regular weekly schedule; we will deal with holidays, etc., later.

g. Here are the agreed-on time allocations: (1) Lucinda will stay at Mom's house during the school week, with the exception of Wednesday nights, when Dad will pick her up and she will stay with him. (2) Every other week, Lucinda will stay with Dad from 10:00 A.M. on Saturday until school-time on Monday, and he will take her to school. On the other weekends he will spend Saturdays from 10:00 A.M. until 8:00 P.M. with her.

h. As you can see, Mom has the bulk of time, and there is no doubt in anyone's mind that she will do most of the general parenting stuff, such as schedule doctor's appointments, buy clothes, etc., but it's also clear that Dad has some real time with her. So, good luck with the drafting.

2. This assignment requires you to go to your local family court. Observe at least two different types of court procedures, such as a motion session and part of a trial, and then write a paper detailing what you have observed. In your paper you should do the following:

a. Identify all participants in the proceeding, including court personnel, making sure that you use the correct titles.

b. Identify the nature of the proceeding, such as a motion for temporary support.

c. Identify what each side was trying to accomplish and how they were seeking to do this.

d. Discuss what was most effective and discuss any weaknesses you identified in either side's presentation of their case.

3. With respect to motion practice in your area, determine the following:

a. how motions are served

b. what the time requirements for service are

c. how motions are marked up

d. when, if ever, accompanying affidavits are required

  e. whether parties are ever diverted to some kind of settlement process, and if so, under which circumstances

4. Assume you are working in an office and a divorce client has just fran-
 tically called to inform the attorney handling the case that her husband
 has just threatened to take the kids out of the country so she will never
 receive custody of them. The attorney has asked you to draft an *ex parte*
 motion with a supporting affidavit seeking to prevent the father from
 doing this. Please draft these documents in accordance with the governing standards in your jurisdiction.

5. Your office is representing the husband in a divorce case. The parties
 have three children and are involved in a bitter custody dispute. The
 husband strongly suspects that the wife has begun dating a local drug
 dealer and may have begun using drugs herself. He also worries that she
 is neglecting the children. The children live with their mom but see their
 dad fairly regularly. Their ages are 2, 4, and 5. The mom is not employed
 outside the home. The attorney you work for has asked you to draft a
 set of interrogatories relevant to custody. He wants useful information
 but would like to proceed with tact so things do not blow up. He would
 also like the interrogatories to inquire into the wife's financial situation,
 as child and spousal support are likely to become contested.

6. The attorney you work for has just received a request for the production of electronically stored information (ESI). He is not very computer
 savvy and recognizes that there are potential pitfalls he should be aware
 of. He has asked you to prepare an interoffice memo that explains some
 of the complexities of this process so he does not inadvertently compromise client confidentiality or make other mistakes. You should use
 this text as your starting point, but you should also find two law journal
 articles that go into greater depth regarding some of the potential pitfalls of responding to requests for ESI and incorporate this information
 into your memo.

Endnotes

1. Diane Eades, Lawyer-Client Communication: "I Don't Think the Lawyers Were Communicating with Me": Misunderstanding Cultural Differences in Communicative Style, 52 Emory L.J. 1109, 1118 (2003). This discussion about cultural differences in communication is based on Eades's outstanding article that should be required reading for anyone engaged in client interviewing. It should be pointed out that the defendant's conviction was reversed on appeal, at least in part due to the author's testimony. The article also provides a fascinating description of how the appeal came about.

In addition to the Eades article, *see* the following for thoughtful approaches to the client interview: Robert Dinerstein et al., Connection, Capacity, and Morality in Lawyer-Client Relationships: Dialogues and Commentary, 10 Clinical L. Rev. 755 (2004); V. Pualani Enos and Lois H. Kanter, Problem Solving in Clinical Education: Who's Listening? Introducing Students to Client-Centered, Client-Empowering, and Multidisciplinary Problem-Solving in a Clinical Setting, 9 Clinical L. Rev. 83 (2003); Laurel E. Fletcher and Harvey M. Weinstein, Problem Solving in Clinical Education: When Students Lose Perspective: Clinical Supervision and the Management of Empathy, 9 Clinical L. Rev. 135 (2002).

2. *See* Judith S. Wallerstein and Sandra Blakeslee, Second Chances—Men, Women and Children a Decade After Divorce: Who Wins, Who Loses—and Why 6 (1990).

3. Mavis E. Hetherington and Kathleen A. Camara, *Families in Transition: The Process of Dissolution and Reconstitution*, *in* The Review of Child Development Research 406 (Ross Park ed., 1984).

4. Wallerstein and Blakeslee, *supra* note 2, at 8.

5. This section on ethics draws heavily from Therese A. Cannon's book, Ethics and Professional Responsibility for Legal Assistants (7th ed. 2013). This book is written for both students and working paralegals and is an invaluable guide to legal ethics. For more detail on the topics covered in this section, as well as other ethical considerations, please refer to this book.

6. *Id.* at 28.

7. For more on the regulation and certification of paralegals, you can visit the websites of the two major national paralegal organizations. For the National Association of Legal Assistants, go to http://www.nala.org, and for the National Federation of Paralegal Associations, go to www.paralegals.org (accessed Dec. 30, 2015).

8. In addition to Cannon, *supra* note 5, ch. 3, *see also* Debra Levy Martinelli, Are You Riding a Fine Line? Learn to Identify and Avoid Issues Involving the Unauthorized Practice of Law, 15 Utah B.J. 18 (2002); Marilu Peterson, Do You UPL?, 15 Utah B.J. 44 (2002).

9. *See* Robert M. Bastress and Joseph D. Harbaugh, Interviewing, Counseling, and Negotiating: Skills for Effective Representation (1990).

10. *See* Don Peters, You Can't Always Get What You Want: Organizing Matrimonial Interviews to Get What You Need, 26 Cal. W. L. Rev. 256, 268 (1990).

11. For a good basic book on civil procedure, *see* Joseph W. Glannon, Examples and Explanations: Civil Procedure (5th ed. 2011).

12. Fed. R. Civ. P. 26(b)(1). In addition to the protection of privileged materials, an attorney's work product (e.g., notes) is generally not subject to discovery.

13. Gaetano Ferro, Marcus Lawson, and Sarah Murray, Electronically Stored Information: What Matrimonial Lawyers and Computer Forensics Need to Know, 23 J. Am. Acad. Matrimonial Law. 1, 2 (2010). *See also* Rachel K. Alexander, E-Discovery Practice, Theory and Precedent: Finding the Right Pond, Lure, and Lines Without Going on a Fishing Expedition, 56 S.D. L. Rev. 25 (2011).

14. Mathew Robertson, Why Invisible Electronic Data Is Relevant in Today's Legal Arena, 23 J. Am. Acad. Matrimonial Law. 199, 202 (2011), quoting NYSBA, Formal Op. 782.

15. *Id.* at 208.

16. *Id.* at 209.

17. Ferro et al., *supra* note 13, at 32-35.

18. Byrne v. Byrne, 650 N.Y.S.2d 499, 501 (1996).

19. For more detail, *see* Peggy N. Kerley, Joanne Banker Hames, and Paul Sukys, Civil Litigation, (7th ed. 2014).

20. Byrne v. Byrne, 650 N.Y.S.2d 499, 501 (1996).

21. At present most states do not have formal training and licensing requirements for mediators, although a number of professional organizations have developed practice standards.

22. Dorothy J. Della Noce, Robert A. Baruch Bush, and Joseph P. Folger, Clarifying the Theoretical Underpinnings of Mediation: Implications for Practice and Policy, 3 Pepp. Disp. Resol. L.J. 39, 41 (2002). It should be noted that this article draws from, and builds on, the following work: Robert A. Baruch Bush and Joseph P. Folger, The Promise of Mediation: Responding to Conflict Through Empowerment and Recognition (1994).

23. Della, Bush, and Folger, *supra* note 22 at 47.

24. *Id.* at 50.

25. *Id.*

26. *Id.* at 51.

27. *Id.*

28. *Id.* at 52.

29. *Id.* at 50-52.

30. This discussion of the mediation process is consistent with the "problem-solving" model; it is based in part on the approach set out by Alison Taylor, *A General Theory of Divorce Mediation, in* Divorce Mediation, Theory and Practice (Milne & Folberg eds., 1988).

31. I wish to thank my colleague, Professor David Matz, Professor in the Conflict Resolution, Global Governance and Human Security Department at the University of Massachusetts, Boston, for sharing many of his thoughtful insights into this and other complexities inherent in the mediation process. For a critical look at some of the complexities posed by mediation, *see* Marsha B. Freeman, Divorce Mediation: Sweeping Conflicts Under the Rug, Time to Clean House, 780 U. Det. Mercy L. Rev. 67 (2000).

32. For an interesting argument that this review comes too late in the process to be meaningful, *see* Kevin M. Mazza, Divorce Mediation: Perhaps Not the Remedy It Was Once Considered, 14 Fam. Advoc. 40 (1992).

33. For further discussion of the issues discussed in this section, *see* Dafna Lavi, Till Death Do Us Part?!: Online Mediation as an Answer to Divorce Cases Involving Violence, 16 N.C. J.L. & Tech. 253 (2015); Mary Adkins, Moving Out of the 1990s: An Argument for Updating Protocol on Divorce Mediation in Domestic Abuse Cases, 22 Yale J.L. & Feminism 97, 115 (2010); Lydia Belzer, Domestic Abuse and Divorce Mediation: Suggestions for a Safer Process, 5 Loy. J. Pub. Int. L. 37 (2002); Sarah Krieger, The Dangers of Mediation in Domestic Violence Cases, 8 Cardozo Women's L.J. 235 (2002); Penelope E. Bryan, Killing Us Softly: Divorce Mediation and the Politics of Power, 40 Buff. L. Rev. 441 (1992).

34. This discussion relies heavily on the following two texts: Lavi, *supra* note 33, and Noah Ebner, E-Mediation, p. 375, http://www.mediate.com/pdf/ebner1.pdf (accessed Dec. 31, 2015).

35. Ebner, *supra* note 34, at 375.

36. Lavi, *supra* note 33, at 278.

37. *Id.* at 288.

38. Ebner, *supra* note 34, at 377.

39. *Id.*

40. Lavi, *supra* note 33, at 293-296.

41. Ebner, *supra* note 34, at 378; *see also* Lavi, *supra* note 33, at 296-298.

42. Lavi, *supra* note 33, at 296.

43. Andre R. Imbrogno, Arbitration as an Alternative to Divorce Litigation: Redefining the Judicial Role, 31 Cap. U. L. Rev. 413, 417 (2003). *See also* George K. Walker, Family Law Arbitration: Legislation and Trends, 21 J. Acad. Acad. Matrimonial Law 521 (2008).

44. Kelm v. Kelm, 623 N.E.2d 39, 42 (Ohio 1993). For a discussion of this case as well as others pertaining to arbitration in the divorce context, *see* Imbrogno, *supra* note 43.

45. ABA Committee on Ethics and Professional Responsibility, Formal Opinion 07-447 (2007). Regarding some of the ethical issues presented by the collaborative model, *see* Christopher M. Fairman, Growing Pains: Changes in Collaborative Law and the Challenge of Legal Ethics, 30 Campbell L. Rev. 237 (2008); Larry R. Spain, Collaborative Law: A Critical Reflection on Whether a Collaborative Orientation Can Be Ethically Incorporated into the Practice of Law, 56 Baylor L. Rev. 141 (2004).

46. Susan Saab Fortney, Collaborative Divorce: What Louis Brandeis Might Say About the Promise and Problems, 33 Touro L. Rev. 371, 373 (2017).

47. Dafna Lavi, Can the Leopard Change His Spots?! Reflections on the "Collaborative Law" Revolution and Collaborative Advocacy, 13 Cardozo J. Conflict Resol. 61, 107-108 (2011).

48. Rachel Rebouche, A Case Against Collaboration, 76 Md. L. Rev. 547, 565 (2017).

49. Margaret Drew, Collaboration and Intention: Making the Collaborative Family Law Process Safe(r), 32 Ohio St. J. on Disp. Resol. 373, 382 and 387-393.

50. For further detail, *see* Forrest S. Mosten, Unbundled Services to Enhance Peacemaking for Divorcing Families, 53 Fam. Ct. Rev. 439 (2015); The Changing Face of Legal Practice: Twenty-Six Recommendations for the Baltimore Conference: A National Conference on "Unbundled" Legal Services, 40 Fam. Ct. Rev. 26 (2002); *see also* the American Bar Association's Pro Se/Unbundling Resource Center, http://www.americanbar.org/groups/delivery_legal_services/resources.html (accessed Jan. 1, 2012).

51. Jessica S. Steinberg, In Pursuit of Justice? Case Outcomes and the Delivery of Unbundled Legal Services, 18 Geo. J. on Poverty L. & Poly. 453, 463 (2011).

52. *Id.* at 464.

53. *See, e.g.,* Colleen F. Shanahan, Anna E. Carpenter, and Alyx Mark, Can a Little Representation Be a Dangerous Thing?, 67 Hastings L.J. 1367, 1376 (2016).

54. Deborah L. Rhode, Kevin Eaton, and Anna Porto, Access to Justice Through Limited Legal Assistance, 16 Nw. J. Hum. Rts. 1, 6 (2018).

55. *Id.* at 4 and 17-20.

56. This language is taken from Stephen W. Schlissel, Separation Agreements and Marital Contracts 617-618 (1986).

57. 50 U.S.C. §520.

58. A detailed look at the trial process is beyond the scope of this book and is likely to be covered in other courses.

59. A number of good books discuss the skills that paralegals need to develop if they are to effectively assist with case preparation. For example, *see* Kerley et al., *supra* note 19.

60. Fed. R. Civ. P. 59 & 60(b).

61. Fed. R. Civ. P. 60(b).

Chapter Eleven

Determining Parentage

In Chapter 5 we looked at custody and visitation disputes between heterosexual married couples in the context of divorce where there was no question regarding legal parentage. As discussed, these disputes are generally resolved in accordance with the best interest standard, which recognizes the equal legal standing of each parent. We also considered disputes involving nonparents in which the parties are decidedly not on equal footing due to the long-standing preference given to legal parents. But what happens if the legal status of one potential parent is uncertain due to his or her lack of a marital relationship and/or a biological connection to the child or perhaps his status as a sperm donor? Here, the parental status of this person must be determined before custody or visitation rights can even be considered.

Historically, the legal relationship between parent and child was determined by the marital status of the parents. Simply put, children were considered "legitimate" if born to married parents and "illegitimate" if born to unwed parents. We thus begin this chapter by tracing the evolving status of children born to unmarried (heterosexual) parents. We then consider the constitutional rights of unwed fathers, followed by a discussion of paternity establishment and the relatively new topic of paternity disestablishment. From there, we consider questions of paternity when a child is conceived by donor insemination in the context of heterosexual couples and single women. We then track this issue into the final section of the chapter, which focuses on co-parent rights within the context of same-sex relationships.

■ The Emerging Legal Status of Children of Unmarried (Heterosexual) Parents

Common Law Status: A Child of No One

English common law drew a sharp distinction between children born to married parents and those born to unmarried parents. A child of unmarried parents was considered a "filius nullius"—a child of no one, a bastard. "Bastardy" rules were designed to deter sexual promiscuity, reinforce the institution of marriage, and protect family lineage by ensuring that a father's property, name, and status passed to his legitimate sons in an orderly manner.[1] As a child had no recognizable legal bond with either parent, neither parent had right to custody or a duty of support, although a limited support obligation was imposed by the English Poor Laws, which sought to protect towns from having to maintain these children. Nonetheless, children of unmarried parents often ended up as wards of the parish in which they were born, especially if a parent died, as they had no rights of inheritance.

Some children were saved from the harsh consequences of the bastardy rules by the common law **presumption of paternity**. Based on this presumption, all children born to a married woman were considered offspring of the marriage, even if they were the result of an extramarital relationship. Rebuttal was difficult, and at times could be accomplished only by proof of the husband's impotence or his extended absence from England. Although the presumption of paternity aided children by enfolding them into a family unit, its primary purpose was to shield the family from the taint of immorality. Significantly, this presumption, which remains operative today, allows for the creation of a father-child relationship based upon a legal rule rather than a biological connection.

Early American Reform Efforts

The Roots of Reform

Following the English tradition, our early laws also placed children of unmarried parents outside the connective threads of family relations. As explained by one commentator: "I apprehend this rule to be partly founded in that anxiety which the law everywhere exhibits, to secure domestic tranquility, and partly, in policy, to discourage illicit commerce betwixt the sexes. If a bastard might inherit either to his father or his mother, where they had married, and had a family of children, it might be a real source of domestic uneasiness."[2]

By the beginning of the nineteenth century, attitudes toward these children had begun to soften, resulting in some legal reforms. This shift in views reflected two broader trends. First, as discussed in Chapter 6, attitudes toward children changed as we moved from an agrarian to an early industrial nation. Children were no longer seen as embodiments of original sin in need of harsh corrective measures but as innocent creatures in need of love and nurturance.[3] Second, the post-Revolutionary emphasis on individual rights and responsibilities raised questions about the fairness of the bastardy rules, which stigmatized children based on the conduct of their parents.

Yet we should keep in mind that these legal reforms were not extended to all segments of the U.S. population. For those bound in slavery, family ties continued to be disregarded despite the strength and endurance of the bonds. Slave unions were not accorded legal status, and children continued to be forcibly taken from their parents without regard for the affective ties that linked them together.

Creating Limited Family Rights

A central reform was the extension of legal recognition to the mother-child unit. No longer a child of no one, nonmarital children were now formally recognized as the children of their mothers; as a result, mothers were entitled to custody and obligated to provide support. Mothers were favored over fathers both because, unlike paternal identity, maternal identity was readily established, and because a maternal preference was consistent with the prevailing emphasis on female domesticity and the belief in women's superior nurturing capabilities. Thus, by the middle of the nineteenth century, children were considered "legitimate" in relationship to their mothers regardless of their mothers' marital status, although, as discussed below, states maintained clear legal distinctions between children of married parents and those of unmarried parents.[4]

Legitimation

A second significant reform was the gradual rejection of the harsh common law rule that a child's status was fixed permanently at birth. Beginning with Virginia in 1823, most states amended their laws to allow for **legitimation** where parents married each other after the birth of a child. A few states went further than this and were willing to recognize a father-child relationship based on an acknowledgment of paternity. Although seemingly mild by today's standards, many criticized these innovations for rewarding immorality and destroying the integrity of marriage.[5]

The End of Legal Innovation

For many, these reforms were profoundly disturbing. By focusing on the child as a separate person, they threatened to erode the unity of the marital family in favor of individual recognition and rights. By the end of the nineteenth century, the period of innovation drew to a close, and further change of this magnitude would have to wait until the constitutional challenges of the next century.[6]

Constitutional Developments

Although these nineteenth-century reforms mitigated some of the harsh common law rules, children of unmarried parents remained a distinct legal category of persons. Referred to as "bastards" or "illegitimates," they suffered a variety of legal disabilities, particularly in relationship to their fathers. For example, they were frequently excluded as beneficiaries under statutory benefit programs, such as workers' compensation; they lacked inheritance rights under state intestacy laws; and they were denied standing in wrongful death actions for the loss of a parent. Additionally, unwed fathers had few legal rights in relationship to their children. Beginning in the 1960s, a number of lawsuits were brought challenging this differential treatment of children of unmarried parents and the denial of rights to unwed fathers. In the following sections, we will look at the Supreme Court's response to these challenges.

The Equal Protection Challenge to Differential Treatment

In 1968, in the landmark case of Levy v. Louisiana, the Supreme Court held that the state of Louisiana had violated the **equal protection clause** by denying children the right to recover for the death of their mother under the state's wrongful death law because of their "illegitimate" status. As explained by the Court:

> Legitimacy or illegitimacy of birth has no relation to the nature of the wrong allegedly inflicted on the mother. These children, though illegitimate, were dependent on her; she cared for them and nurtured them; they were indeed hers in the biological and spiritual sense; in her death they suffered wrong in the sense that any dependent would.[7]

The Court thus recognized that the significance of the parent-child relationship does not depend on the marital status of the parents and further that children should not be discriminated against based on parental conduct over which they had no control.

Since *Levy*, the Court has decided a number of cases involving similar equal protection challenges to laws that discriminated against children born to unmarried parents by, for example, denying or limiting their ability to obtain statutory benefits or to inherit under state intestacy laws. Unfortunately, these decisions are not always clear and consistent with one another; nonetheless, some general principles do emerge from them.[8]

First, a court must carefully review any law that classifies children based on the marital status of their parents. Central to this review, the court must evaluate the reason for the statutory classification. If its purpose is to deter nonmarital sexual relations or promote the state's interest in marriage, the classification is invalid because these goals do not justify the discriminatory treatment of children. Children may not be disadvantaged based on circumstances over which they have no control. Moreover, states may not deprive children of benefits based on the assumption that there can be no meaningful parent-child relationship outside the marital family unit.

Second, although a law may not discriminate against children of unmarried parents in order to promote marriage or regulate sexual behavior, all legal distinctions between children of unmarried parents and children of married parents are not necessarily unconstitutional. Most important, if a distinction is carefully drawn for the purpose of preventing fraudulent claims, it is likely to withstand constitutional scrutiny. For example, although a state may not deprive nonmarital children of paternal inheritance rights under its intestacy statute in order to encourage marriage, it probably can condition these rights upon a prior adjudication of paternity in order to prevent fraudulent claims. Thus, a state may be able to exclude a child from receiving a statutory share of benefits where the father-child relationship had not been formally established prior to the father's death.

By limiting the differential legal treatment of children based on the marital status of their parents, the long shadow of the common law has all but been erased. The potential for establishing fully developed legal relationships with both parents now exists. All is not crystal clear, however, and the Supreme Court continues to struggle with the weight and meaning of the father-child bond where it exists outside the marital relationship.

The Legal Status of the Unwed Father

As developed above, the differential treatment of children of unmarried parents is impermissible for the purpose of discouraging nonmarital sexual relations or promoting marriage. Let's look at the issue from a different perspective: What if it is the unwed father rather than the child who is singled out for differential treatment? Should the law treat him in the same manner that it treats an unwed mother or a married father, or does he occupy a distinct legal position in relationship to his child? Are the cases involving the interests of unwed fathers the flip side of the cases involving children, or are different considerations at stake? To consider these questions, we turn to a series of landmark U.S. Supreme Court cases focusing on the rights of unwed fathers. These cases give us a different lens through which to view the unfolding and uncertain legal construction of nonmarital family relations.

Challenging the Exclusion of Unwed Fathers: Stanley v. Illinois.   In 1972, in the case of Stanley v. Illinois,[9] the Supreme Court considered whether it was unconstitutional for a state to presume that all unwed fathers were unfit parents. Peter and Joan Stanley had lived together on an intermittent basis for 18 years. During this time, they had three children. When Joan Stanley died, the state of Illinois initiated a dependency proceeding. The children were declared wards of the state for lack of a surviving parent and placed in the care of a court-appointed guardian. Peter Stanley was not provided with an opportunity to challenge the removal of his children because the state of Illinois presumed that all unwed fathers were unfit to raise their children. In contrast, married parents and unwed mothers could not be deprived of their children without a hearing on the issue of fitness.

Stanley challenged the presumption of unfitness, which effectively severed his tie with his children without inquiry into their actual circumstances, and argued that, like other parents, he too was entitled to a hearing on the question of fitness. Although acknowledging, as argued by the state, that most unwed fathers may in fact be "unsuitable and neglectful" parents, the Court nonetheless agreed with Stanley that he could not be deprived of custody without a hearing. In supporting Stanley's claim, the Court recognized the potential for meaningful relationships between unwed fathers and their children and made it clear that paternal rights do not merit protection only when developed within a marital family unit.

Following *Stanley*, it appeared as if the Court might be moving in the direction of eliminating all distinctions between unwed fathers and other parents. However, the Court did not make clear why it was protecting Stanley's rights. Would a mere biological connection to these children have entitled him to a hearing, or was he entitled because he had both "sired and raised" them?

What Makes an Unwed Father a Father?   After *Stanley*, a number of unwed fathers brought lawsuits challenging state laws that permitted the adoption of nonmarital children based solely on the consent of the mother. Building on *Stanley*, they argued (1) that an unwed father has a constitutionally protected liberty interest in maintaining a parental relationship with his child that cannot be abrogated without his consent absent proof of unfitness; and (2) that differential treatment of unwed fathers and unwed mothers violates the equal protection clause.

In responding to these challenges, the Court answered the question left open in *Stanley*. In the 1983 case of Lehr v. Robertson, the Court clarified that the rights of unwed fathers do not spring into being based solely on the biological link between father and child. According to the Court, the significance of the biological connection is that it provides a father with the unique opportunity to develop a relationship with his offspring. If he grasps that opportunity and assumes some responsibility for the child, he may be entitled to benefits and rights that attach to the parent-child relationship; however, if he fails to grasp this opportunity, he cannot claim a constitutionally protected right to participate in the adoption decision.[10] (Note: We return to the adoption rights of unmarried fathers in Chapter 13.) In short, outside of the marital context, biology alone does not a father make. Instead, a man must act like a father to be legally recognized as one and thus entitled to an equal say regarding adoption. This "biology-plus" approach drew harsh criticism from the dissent, who argued that the biological tie itself merits protection because it is the nature rather than the weight of the interest that is important.

The Court reaffirmed this approach in the 2001 case of Nguyen v. Immigration & Naturalization Service,[11] in which it upheld a gender-based provision in the federal derivative citizenship law, which governs the transmission of U.S. citizenship to children born out of the country where only one parent is a citizen. The challenged provision automatically conferred derivative citizenship on a child if the mother was the citizen parent, but if the father was the citizen parent, he had to first formally establish his paternity and agree in writing to support the child. The Court reasoned that this differential treatment was justifiable because motherhood is established by birth, whereas fatherhood is not. As explained by the Court: "Fathers and mothers are not similarly situated with respect to biological parenthood. . . . Given the proof of motherhood that is inherent in birth itself, it is unremarkable that Congress did not require the same affirmative steps of mothers. . . . In the case of a citizen mother and a child born overseas, the opportunity for a meaningful relationship between citizen parent and child inheres in the very event of birth. . . . [T]he same opportunity does not result from the event of birth, as a matter of biological inevitability, in the case of the unwed father."[12] Again, the dissent was critical of the deployment of this "biology-plus" approach, chastising the majority for relying "on the generalization that mothers are significantly more likely than fathers . . . to develop caring relations with their children"[13] and calling for the use of gender-neutral criteria.

In the 2017 case of Sessions v. Morales-Santana,[14] in an opinion authored by Justice Ginsburg, the Court took a different approach with respect to the residency requirement provision of the derivative citizenship statute. Likewise deploying a clear gender-based distinction, this provision allowed citizen mothers who had lived in the United States for one year prior to a child's birth to transmit citizenship to a child born out of the country, whereas a father was required to have lived in the United States for five years prior to the child's birth. At the outset of the decision, the Court observed that the challenged provision "date[s] from the era when the lawbooks of our Nation were rife with overbroad generalizations about the way that men and women are," including that the "unwed mother is the natural and sole guardian of a nonmarital child."[15] Tying this to the question of citizenship, it explained that this requirement reflected the fear that a "foreign-born child would turn out more 'alien than American in nature,'" and the operative hope was that "a citizen parent with lengthy ties to the United States would counteract the influence of the alien parent."[16] In accordance with a "familiar stereotype," it was assumed that unwed citizen fathers "would care little about, and have scant contact with their nonmarital children," and thus a "prolonged residency prophylactic" was deemed necessary to bolster his capacity to counteract the mother's foreign ways.[17]

Drawing upon a long line of equal protection cases invalidating laws based upon "'overbroad generalizations about the different talents, capacities, or preferences of males and females,'" the Court in *Morales-Santana* held that it was unconstitutional to impose a longer physical presence requirement on unwed fathers based upon stereotypical assumptions that they lack an interest in their children.[18] Although the *Morales-Santana* decision suggests that the Court may review laws that distinguish between unmarried mothers and fathers under a higher level of scrutiny, it is important to recognize that it did not declare all such distinctions invalid. In fact, the Court made it clear that it was not overturning its decision in *Nguyen*, reasoning that the "parental-acknowledgment requirement" at issue in that case was minimal compared to the gender-based "physical-presence" rule at issue in this case.[19]

Accordingly, it is still accurate to say that the legal treatment of unmarried fathers differs from the treatment of unmarried mothers as well as from the treatment of married fathers. Highlighting the intricacy of the law in this area, we turn to the case of Michael H. v. Gerald D., which limits the scope of the biology-plus approach—at least where it bumps up against the presumption of paternity.

The Biology-Plus Approach Confronts the Presumption of Paternity.   The following facts will set the stage for our analysis of the Court's decision in Michael H. v. Gerald D.[20] In 1981, a girl named Victoria was born to a woman named Carol. At the time, Carol was married to Gerald, who was listed as the father on the birth certificate. However, subsequent blood tests showed a 98.7 percent probability that a man named Michael was actually Victoria's father. During Victoria's early years, three men moved in and out of her life. At times, Victoria, Carol, and Gerald made up a household; at other times, Victoria, Carol, and Michael made up a household. (We'll ignore the third man, Scott, who for our purposes is irrelevant, as he did not seek to assert paternal rights.)

To secure his relationship with Victoria, Michael filed a paternity action seeking formal legal recognition as her father. Not surprisingly, Gerald opposed his quest for recognition, arguing that under California law he was Victoria's presumed father based on his marriage to Carol and that Michael lacked standing to assert paternal rights. In response, Michael argued that the presumption was unconstitutional because it deprived him of his interest in maintaining a relationship with his daughter. Drawing on the unwed father cases, Michael argued that since he satisfied both prongs of the *Lehr* test—biological fatherhood plus a developed relationship—he was entitled to recognition as Victoria's father. Having grasped the opportunity afforded him by his biological connection to Victoria, he maintained that California could not bar his assertion of paternal rights based on the marital presumption.

Although there was little doubt that Michael met the biology-plus standard, the Court chose to focus its attention elsewhere. Zooming in on the adulterous relationship between Michael and Carol, the Court determined that the bond between Michael and Victoria was not deserving of recognition because it did not take root within the sanctity of a "unitary family." The Court thus concluded that when faced with a choice between an "adulterous natural father" and a marital father who parents within "the integrity of the traditional family unit," the Constitution does not compel recognition of the "irregular" relationship over one that conforms to traditional standards.[21]

In a biting dissent, it was argued that the unwed father cases had nothing to do with protecting "unitary families" and everything to do with protecting unwed fathers who, like Michael, had developed a relationship with their children. From the dissenter's perspective, the relevant inquiry should have been whether the "relationship under consideration is sufficiently substantial to qualify as a liberty interest under our prior cases," without reference to the constellation of household arrangements.[22] In short, according to the dissent, the goal of protecting the marital unit does not justify overriding the interests of a biological father who seeks to maintain a relationship with his child.

According to the *Michael H.* decision, the federal constitution does not require states to provide unwed fathers with the opportunity to challenge the marital presumption; however, they are not prohibited from doing so. Accordingly, a number of states permit unwed fathers to challenge the presumption and assert their own claim to fatherhood, although many of these states impose a threshold requirement that a father must meet before he can proceed. Typically, he may be required to show that rebuttal of the presumption would be in the child's best interest and/or that he has a substantial relationship with the child. A few states do not impose these limitations and permit a challenge in almost all situations; here, the interests of unwed fathers may be given heightened protection under the state constitution.

Consideration

Do you think unwed fathers should be afforded legal protections based on biology alone, or should more be required?

Establishing Paternity

When parents are unmarried, paternity must be established in order for a man to be recognized as the legal father of a child. The two primary approaches to establishing paternity are **adjudication** and **acknowledgment**. In some instances, as we have seen, it may also be established by presumption, such as when a child is born to a married woman.

In 1973, when Congress entered the child support arena, it also sought to upgrade state procedures for paternity establishment so that more support awards could be established for the benefit of children of unmarried parents. Accordingly, the aptly named Child Support Enforcement and Establishment of Paternity Act (see Chapter 6) directed states to conform their paternity laws to the new federal requirements or risk loss of federal funding. These federal requirements (which have since been strengthened by subsequent federal laws) apply to both the adjudication and the acknowledgment of paternity.

The Adjudication of Paternity

The modern-day paternity action evolved from the colonial-era bastardy proceeding, which was criminal in nature and intended to punish the "fornicator." The goal of punishing sexual misconduct has dropped by the historical wayside, and today, paternity actions (see Exhibit 11.1) are brought to identify a man as the legal father of a child based on his biological connection.

Most paternity actions are initiated by mothers or a IV-D agency (recall from Chapter 6 that in order to receive TANF benefits, a mother must assign her child support rights to the state and cooperate in establishing paternity, unless she can show good cause for noncooperation) so that the child can receive support as well as other potential benefits that flow from an established parent-child relationship. Although far less common, men may also initiate paternity proceedings in order to secure custody and visitation rights. Here, in a historical shift, the father seeks to affirm rather than to deny his paternity. However, as discussed above, if the mother is married to someone else, the presumption of paternity may bar the action, or a man may first have to satisfy a threshold requirement, such as that he has a substantial relationship with the child.

When paternity is contested, states must, under federal law, have procedures in place that require the parties and the child to submit to **genetic testing** if requested by either party. If the case is being handled by the IV-D agency, the agency must pay for the testing; however, it is entitled to recoup the funds from the father if paternity is established. Unlike in years past, when testing required the drawing of blood and was unreliable, DNA-based identity testing today can be done through a cheek swab and can prove or disprove paternity with virtual certainty. Unless an objection is made, the tests must be admissible without foundation testimony or proof of authenticity.

Under federal law, states must have rules in place that create a rebuttable presumption of paternity if the tests indicate that the man is the father of the child within a threshold degree of probability. Once the presumption is triggered, the burden shifts to the man in question to prove nonpaternity by, for example, establishing "nonaccess" or that he is sterile. States also have the option of making the presumption conclusive, in which case it would operate like a court judgment and could be challenged only under very limited circumstances.

Exhibit 11.1   Complaint for Paternity

F.C.A. § § 522, 523, S.S.L. § 111-g
[Note: Nassau County Family Court (NCFC) Information
Sheets containing the Social Security #'s of the parties
and the dependents must be filed with this petition]

Form 5-1
Paternity
10/2012
NCFC 4/2015

FAMILY COURT OF THE STATE OF NEW YORK
COUNTY OF NASSAU
....
In the Matter of a Paternity Proceeding

PETITION for Paternity
(Individual)

Petitioner _____
                   First   M.I.   Last

            -AGAINST-

Respondent _____
                    First   M.I.   Last
....

| FILE # _____ |
| DOCKET # _____ |
| *(Court use only)* |

TO THE FAMILY COURT:

The undersigned petitioner respectfully alleges that:

1.   Check one box only:

        ☐   I am the petitioner and I am the birth mother of the child who is the subject of this petition.
              I am submitting this petition to request an order declaring the respondent to be the father
              of the child.

        ☐   I am the petitioner and I am pregnant with the child who is the subject of this petition. I am
              submitting this petition to request an order declaring the respondent to be the father of the
              child.

        ☐   I am the petitioner and I am the father of the child who is the subject of this petition. I am
              submitting this petition to request an order declaring me to be the father of the child.

        ☐   I am the petitioner and I may be the father of the child who is the subject of this petition.
              I am submitting this petition to request an order determining the paternity of the child.

2a.   Petitioner's Information: **2b.**   Respondent's Information:

Name: _____   Name: _____

Date of Birth: _____ / ____ / _____   Date of Birth: _____ / ____ / _____

*Address: _____   Address: _____

               _____   _____

*** If address is not known to the respondent and you are requesting that your address be kept
confidential from the respondent, print the word CONFIDENTIAL above and print your address
on the NCFC Information Sheet only.**

Exhibit 11.1   Continued

3. The petitioner had sexual intercourse with the above-named respondent during a period of time beginning on or about _____/_____/_____ and ending on or about _____/_____/_____ .

4. a. The ☐ petitioner ☐ respondent gave birth to a ☐ male ☐ female child out of wedlock on [specify date] _____/_____/_____ .

or

b. The ☐ petitioner ☐ respondent is now pregnant with a child who is likely to be born out of wedlock.

5. I am the petitioner and ☐ I am ☐ I am not requesting an order for genetic testing to determine the paternity of the child.

6. At the time the child was conceived, the mother:

☐ was not married (child born out of wedlock),

or

☐ was married to: Name: _____

*Address: _____

_____

* If address is not known to the respondent and you are requesting that the address be kept confidential from the respondent, print the word CONFIDENTIAL above and print the spouses's address on another NCFC Information Sheet only.

7. The name of the person who is or may be the father of the child is _____ .

[check ✔ applicable box(es)]:

a. ☐ He has acknowledged paternity in writing.

b. ☐ He has acknowledged paternity by furnishing support.

c. ☐ He is the petitioner and acknowledges paternity by the filing of this petition.

d. ☐ none of the above.

8. The child's information, specify: Name: _____

Date of Birth: _____/_____/_____

Sex: ☐ Male   ☐ Female

☐ The birth certificate is attached [it must be attached if the petitioner is the mother].

or

☐ The birth certificate is unavailable, because _____ .

Exhibit 11.1   Continued

9a.   Has any other person been named the father of this child by this court or any other court, including a Native American court?

☐ Yes   ☐ No

If yes, specify: Name of Court (include county & state): _____

Docket #: _____

Names on the Case: _____.

9b.   Has any other person signed an acknowledgment of paternity for this child?

☐ Yes, _____ has signed an acknowledgment of paternity.

☐ No

10.   Has there been an application made in any court for the relief herein requested?

☐ Yes   ☐ No

If yes, specify: Name of Court (include county & state): _____

Docket #: _____

Names on the Case: _____.

11.   Does the child live with you?

☐ Yes   ☐ No

If yes, check ✔ one box below.

☐ I have already made an application for child support enforcement services with the Nassau County Department of Social Services Support Collection Unit (SCU); I request that the order of support be payable through the New York State Office of Child Support Enforcement (OCSE).

☐ By filing this petition, I am now making an application for child support enforcement services with SCU. I request that the order of support be payable through OCSE. I understand that I must file additional documentation directly with SCU.

☐ I do not wish to make application for child support services with SCU. I request that the order of support be payable directly to me without involvement from SCU or OCSE or I may not request an order of child support at this time.

12.   Is the child a Native American child subject to the Indian Child Welfare Act of 1978 (25 U.S.C. § § 1901-1963)?   ☐ Yes   ☐ No

Exhibit 11.1   Continued

Pursuant to F.C.A. § 545, upon the entry of an order of filiation, the court shall, upon application of either party, enter an order of support for the subject child.

WHEREFORE, the petitioner requests that this court issue a summons or warrant requiring the respondent to show cause why the court should not enter a declaration of paternity, an order of support and such other and further relief as may be appropriate under the circumstances.

NOTE: (1) A COURT ORDER OF SUPPORT RESULTING FROM A PROCEEDING COMMENCED BY THIS APPLICATION (PETITION) SHALL BE ADJUSTED BY THE APPLICATION OF A COST OF LIVING ADJUSTMENT AT THE DIRECTION OF THE SUPPORT COLLECTION UNIT NO EARLIER THAN TWENTY-FOUR MONTHS AFTER SUCH ORDER IS ISSUED, LAST MODIFIED OR LAST ADJUSTED, UPON THE REQUEST OF ANY PARTY TO THE ORDER OR PURSUANT TO PARAGRAPH (2) BELOW. SUCH COST OF LIVING ADJUSTMENT SHALL BE ON NOTICE TO BOTH PARTIES WHO, IF THEY OBJECT TO THE COST OF LIVING ADJUSTMENT, SHALL HAVE THE RIGHT TO BE HEARD BY THE COURT AND TO PRESENT EVIDENCE WHICH THE COURT WILL CONSIDER IN ADJUSTING THE CHILD SUPPORT ORDER IN ACCORDANCE WITH SECTION FOUR HUNDRED THIRTEEN OF THE FAMILY COURT ACT, KNOWN AS THE CHILD SUPPORT STANDARDS ACT.

(2) A PARTY SEEKING SUPPORT FOR ANY CHILD(REN) RECEIVING FAMILY ASSISTANCE SHALL HAVE A CHILD SUPPORT ORDER REVIEWED AND ADJUSTED AT THE DIRECTION OF THE SUPPORT COLLECTION UNIT NO EARLIER THAN TWENTY-FOUR MONTHS AFTER SUCH ORDER IS ISSUED, LAST MODIFIED OR LAST ADJUSTED BY THE SUPPORT COLLECTION UNIT, WITHOUT FURTHER APPLICATION BY ANY PARTY. ALL PARTIES WILL RECEIVE A COPY OF THE ADJUSTED ORDER.

(3) WHERE ANY PARTY FAILS TO PROVIDE, AND UPDATE UPON ANY CHANGE, THE SUPPORT COLLECTION UNIT WITH A CURRENT ADDRESS, AS REQUIRED BY SECTION FOUR HUNDRED FORTY-THREE OF THE FAMILY COURT ACT, TO WHICH AN ADJUSTED ORDER CAN BE SENT, THE SUPPORT OBLIGATION AMOUNT CONTAINED THEREIN SHALL BECOME DUE AND OWING ON THE DATE THE FIRST PAYMENT IS DUE UNDER THE TERMS OF THE ORDER OF SUPPORT WHICH WAS REVIEWED AND ADJUSTED OCCURRING ON OR AFTER THE EFFECTIVE DATE OF THE ADJUSTED ORDER, REGARDLESS OF WHETHER OR NOT THE PARTY HAS RECEIVED A COPY OF THE ADJUSTED ORDER.

Dated: _____ / _____ / _____

_____
Petitioner [sign name]

_____
Petitioner [print name]

Exhibit 11.1   Continued

....

VERIFICATION

STATE OF   )
                                          :ss.:
COUNTY OF   )

being duly sworn, says that (s)he is the petitioner in the above-named proceeding and that the foregoing petition is true to (his) (her) own knowledge, except as to matters therein stated to be alleged on information and belief and as to those matters (s)he believes it to be true.

_____
Petitioner [sign name before a notary]

Sworn to before me this _____
day of _____ , 20____
_____
Notary Public

Voluntary Acknowledgment of Paternity

Paternity can also be established voluntarily. This approach has gained favor, and under federal law all states must have a simple procedure in place that enables parents to acknowledge paternity by completing a notarized paternity affidavit (Exhibit 11.2). States must offer paternity establishment services at hospitals and at the state agency responsible for maintaining birth records. States may also offer paternity establishment services at other locations where children and parents receive services or care, such as at pediatricians' offices and Head Start programs.

Exhibit 11.2   Voluntary Acknowledgment of Paternity

Illinois Voluntary Acknowledgment of Paternity

PLEASE READ ALL PARTS OF THIS FORM INCLUDING YOUR RIGHTS AND
RESPONSIBILITIES AND INSTRUCTIONS ON THE OTHER SIDE BEFORE
COMPLETING THE FOLLOWING INFORMATION.

File Date for ACU use only

ALL ITEMS MUST BE ANSWERED

Child's Information as shown or will be shown on Birth Certificate   Print all requested information

Child's Name (First)	Middle (if any)	Last (same as on birth certificate)	Suffix (Jr, II, III)
Date of Birth (mm/dd/yy)	Gender ☐ M ☐ F Name of Hospital or Address of Place of Birth		City, County, and State of Birth

Biological Father's Name (first)	Middle (if any)	Last	Suffix (Jr, II, III)
Place of Birth (city, state or foreign country address)		Date of Birth (mm/dd/yy)	SSN/TIN
Address (street address and/or PO box)	City, State, and Zip		Daytime Phone (include area code)

Biological Mother's Name (First)	Middle (if any)	Current Last Name	Maiden Name (before 1st marriage)
Place of Birth (city, state or foreign country address)		Date of Birth (mm/dd/yy)	SSN/TIN
Address (street address and/or PO box)	City, State, and Zip		Daytime Phone (include area code)

Were you married to or in a civil union with a person **other than** the above named father when this child was born or within 300 days before this child was born?   Yes ☐ No ☐
If yes, that person is presumed to be the father (presumed parent) of this child and you are required to provide the presumed parent's name (first/middle/last) _____ . A Denial of Parentage must also be completed by the biological mother and presumed parent to place the biological father's name on this child's birth certificate.

By signing I acknowledge that I have read the rights and responsibilities and instructions on the other side of this form. I have been provided an oral explanation about the VAP and understand my rights and responsibilities created and waived by signing this form.

I UNDERSTAND THAT I CAN REQUEST A GENETIC TEST REGARDING THE CHILD'S PATERNITY. BY SIGNING THIS FORM I GIVE UP MY RIGHT TO A GENETIC TEST.

Each parent must sign and date this form in the presence of a witness age 18 or older. The witness must not be a parent or child named on the VAP.

BIOLOGICAL FATHER: Under the penalties of perjury provided by Section 1-109 of the Illinois Code of Civil Procedure, I certify that my statements in this document are true and correct. I acknowledge that I am the biological father of the above named child and I give my permission to enter my name as the legal father on the birth certificate. I understand that the acknowledgment is the same as a court order for parentage of the child and that a challenge to the acknowledgment is allowed only under limited circumstances and is generally not allowed after 2 years.	BIOLOGICAL MOTHER: Under the penalties of perjury provided by Section 1-109 of the Illinois Code of Civil Procedure, I certify that my statements in this document are true and correct. I am the birth mother of the above named child and I give my permission to enter the biological father's name as the legal father on the birth certificate. I understand that the acknowledgment is the same as a court order for parentage of the child and that a challenge to the acknowledgment is allowed only under limited circumstances and is generally not allowed after 2 years.
Biological Father's Signature _____	Biological Mother's Signature _____
Witness Information	**Witness Information**
Printed Name_____	Printed Name_____
Signature_____	Signature_____
Address_____	Address_____
Phone Number_____	Phone Number _____
Date Parties Signed_____	Date Parties Signed_____

HFS 3416B (R-4-17) To request a certified copy of the VAP go to www.childsupport.illinois.gov and complete and follow instructions on HFS 3416H, Request for a Certified copy of the Voluntary Acknowledgment of Paternity and/or Denial of Parentage.

For Official Use Only_____
        Case #   Docket #   CP RIN   NCP RIN

Before signing the paternity acknowledgment form, a parent must be provided with information regarding the legal consequences of establishing paternity. Some states have developed separate materials for mothers and fathers in recognition of the different concerns that each may have regarding, for example, child support obligations and custody and visitation rights. Although most state materials emphasize the benefits of acknowledging paternity, some address the concerns that victims of violence may have and may recommend against signing if the mother fears for her own safety or the safety of the child.[23] Typically, the parties are told about the availability of genetic testing; such notification is not required, however, thus creating the possibility that the acknowledged father, either knowingly or unknowingly, may not necessarily be the biological father. (See the section entitled "Paternity Disestablishment," below.)

The parties have a set window of time within which to rescind the acknowledgment and thereby disestablish paternity. Thereafter, if the acknowledgment is not rescinded, it operates as a legal finding of paternity and is entitled to full faith and credit in other states. However, a subsequent challenge may be permitted on the limited grounds of fraud, duress, or mistake of fact.

Following the Determination of Paternity

Once paternity is established, the formerly putative father is now the legal father of the child with the rights and responsibilities that this status entails. He can be required to pay child support and can seek court-ordered custody and visitation rights.

If paternity is established in court, a child support order can usually be established at the same time. The fact that the parties are not married should not impact the support amount. As far as custody and visitation are concerned, if the court is one of limited jurisdiction without broad authority over family matters, the father may need to bring a separate action in family court. Moreover, unlike with child support, some states use different substantive standards where unmarried parents of children, as distinct from divorcing parents, are involved. Although the focus remains the best interest of the child, some states employ a rebuttable presumption that it is in the child's best interest to remain with the parent who has been the child's primary caretaker or with whom the child has lived continuously for a certain period of time. This standard often favors the mother, who, especially where parents are unmarried, is likely to be the primary care parent.

Paternity Disestablishment

A controversial issue that courts are deeply divided on is whether a father should be permitted to "disestablish" his paternity—that is, to undo a determination that he is the child's biological father. In large part, the ready availability of reliable genetic testing has prompted this push for biological certainty, even if the quest threatens to disrupt a well-established father-child relationship.

Like joint custody, **paternity disestablishment** is closely identified with the fathers' rights movement, which as noted in Chapter 5, emerged in the 1970s to address a perceived anti-male bias in the family courts. In this context, the ability to disavow fatherhood is seen as necessary to vindicate the rights of men who have been "duped" by women, often with the aid of the legal system. Proponents of "paternity fraud reform" often compare the situation of fathers who learn that they are not a child's biological parent to a criminal who has been wrongly convicted, and argue that "just as DNA evidence has revolutionized criminal laws, it should . . . lead to a revolution in family law . . . in the sense that evidence admissible to 'convict' should also be available to 'exonerate.' "[24] However, "exoneration" in the family law domain does not simply undo a mistake; it also serves to dismantle an established parent-child relationship with potentially devastating emotional consequences for a child. Disestablishment is also likely to have an adverse financial impact on a child, as termination of the legal parent-child relationship typically operates to terminate a man's duty to provide support, which, of course, is often a primary motivating consideration behind the quest to disestablish paternity. Another potentially troubling distinction is that rather than simply seeking to right a wrong, men seeking to disestablish paternity may well be motivated by "anger and a desire to strike back at ex-wives and girlfriends."[25]

Paternity disestablishment cases once again present us with important questions regarding the weight and meaning of fatherhood. Is it a genetic link that makes a man a father? Is it grasping the opportunity presented by a genetic link to develop a relationship with a child, or can fatherhood be achieved in the absence of a biological link by assuming the role of a father in a child's life? How should the competing interests of a father who wishes to disavow his misidentified status be balanced with the needs of the child? As noted in a leading article on the subject, other critical questions include the following:

> At what point should the truth about genetic parentage outweigh the consequences of leaving a child fatherless? Is a child better off knowing his/her genetic heritage or maintaining a relationship with his/her

father and his family that provides both emotional and financial support? Should it matter who brings the action or should the rules be the same for men trying to disestablish paternity, women seeking to oust a father from the child's life, and third parties trying to assert their paternity of a child who already has a legal father?[26]

Broadly speaking, paternity disestablishment cases fall into one of two categories. First, following the establishment of paternity through either a voluntary acknowledgment or a court action, an unmarried father begins to doubt whether he is the biological father and thus seeks to disestablish his paternity. Depending on the state, it may also be possible for the action to be initiated by a mother who seeks to limit or end the involvement of this man in her child's life or by another man who believes that he is the child's biological father. The second category of cases involves an attempt to disestablish the paternity of a man who is the presumed father of a child based on his marriage to the child's mother. The presumed father may seek to disestablish paternity based on doubts about his biological relationship to the child; a man who believes he might be a child's biological father might wish to challenge the paternity of the husband; or the mother herself, often in connection with a pending divorce action, may seek the disestablishment in order to end her husband's formal relationship with the child.

If disestablishment is allowed, a question arises as to what impact this has on the child support obligation. As a general matter, disestablishment ends the father's obligation to pay present and future child support. However, courts have been less willing to forgive support arrearages for a number of reasons, including the hardship that this would impose on children, and that forgiveness would reward the father who had been remiss in making support payments. Likewise, most courts do not permit a father to recoup payments made prior to the disestablishment of paternity, although this is not an absolute rule, and some statutes permit recoupment under carefully delineated circumstances.

States have begun addressing the issue of when to allow paternity disestablishment through both statutory enactments and judicial decisions. For example, some states have passed laws allowing men who have been adjudicated fathers to reopen the court decision to disprove their paternity through the introduction of genetic evidence. In other states, either the mother or the father can seek judicial relief where paternity has been adjudicated or acknowledged. Courts have expressed a dizzying array of opinions on the matter. In part, this reflects differences in underlying fact patterns; however, it also reflects deeply divided views on how the competing interests should be accommodated. We turn now to two paternity disestablishment decisions that weigh the best interest of the child in the decisional calculus very differently.

Considering Best Interest: Conflicting Approaches

In the case of Paternity of Cheryl,[27] the Massachusetts Supreme Judicial Court (SJC) refused to permit an unmarried father to disestablish paternity. Briefly, the facts are as follows. Cheryl was born in 1993. Shortly thereafter, the parents, who were not married, signed a voluntary acknowledgment, which was entered as a court judgment. The father participated in Cheryl's life as a father, and she referred to him as "Daddy." When Cheryl was 6, the state's IV-D agency sought an increase in child support. Five days later, the father raised doubts about his paternity, and genetic tests revealed that he was not the girl's biological father. In rejecting his request to vacate the paternity judgment, the SJC focused on the impact this would have on Cheryl:

> Where a father challenges a paternity judgment, courts have pointed to the special needs of children that must be protected, noting that consideration of what is in a child's best interest will often weigh more heavily than the genetic link between parent and child. . . . [C]hildren benefit psychologically, socially, educationally and in other ways from stable and predictable parental relationships. . . . [W]here a father and child have a substantial parent-child relationship, an attempt to undo a determination of paternity is "potentially devastating to a child who has considered the man to be the father."[28]

In contrast to this child-centered focus, the Court of Appeals of Maryland in Langston v. Riffe concluded that the best interest of the child has no place in a paternity disestablishment action. In this consolidated action, three men were seeking to set aside a paternity judgment based on new evidence indicating in each case that another man might be the child's biological father. At issue was whether, in seeking reconsideration of a paternity judgment, the fathers had an automatic statutory right to blood or genetic testing as they would at the time of paternity establishment or, as argued by the state on behalf of the mothers, whether in this context, the court must first consider the best interest of the children. In reviewing the legislative history, the court concluded that the " 'best interests of the child' standard generally has no place in a proceeding to reconsider a paternity declaration. . . . To not allow testing now would violate . . . the Legislature's intent . . . to provide relief to putative fathers seeking review of potentially false paternity declarations entered against them."[29]

What Makes a Man a Father?

Underlying these decisions is the familiar struggle to arrive at an understanding of what makes a man a father. The two cases embody different understandings of the role that biology plays in determining fatherhood. By focusing on the developed relationship between Cheryl and her father, the SJC downgraded the importance of the biological link between a father and child in favor of relational considerations. However, it is possible that the court would have paid less attention to this connection if Cheryl's biological father had been standing in the wings, ready, willing, and able to assume a role in her life. In contrast, the Maryland court, in focusing on the vindication of the father's interest without regard to the impact of disestablishment on the children of these men, elevated the biological dimension of fatherhood over relational considerations.

■ Determining Paternity When the Genetic "Father" Is a Sperm Donor

In this section, we consider how questions of paternity are resolved where conception occurs through **donor insemination** rather than through sexual intercourse in the context of heterosexual couples, both married and unmarried, and single women. We take up the issue of donor insemination in the context of lesbian couples in the following section as this situation opens the door to a child having two legally recognized mothers, which clearly unsettles the long-standing assumption that parentage must be vested in a mother and a father.

Donor Insemination and the Heterosexual Couple

Where a married woman and her husband are unable to conceive due to his infertility (or possibly the risk of transmitting a genetic disease), one possibility is for her to be inseminated with the sperm of another man. Here, although she is married, the child is actually the biological offspring of two persons who are not married to each other. Under these circumstances, who is entitled to legal recognition as the father?

The previously discussed common law presumption of paternity, which operates to identify a woman's husband as the legal father of children born during the marriage, provides a partial answer. As we have seen, however, this common law presumption is not absolute, and can be rebutted by proof of infertility or the lack of a genetic link. To address this situation (along with other unresolved issues), in 1973, the influential National Conference of Commissioners on Uniform State Laws (NCCUSL) adopted the Uniform Parentage Act (UPA). To this end, the UPA included a donor cutoff provision, which established that "the donor is not a parent of a child conceived by assisted reproduction"; a corresponding provision served to vest legal fatherhood in a consenting husband. For these rules to apply, under this version of the UPA, the insemination had to be done under the supervision of a licensed physician.

In 2002, the NCCUSL amended the UPA. In relevant part, the rules regarding donor insemination were updated First, the requirement that the insemination had to be done under the supervision of a physician in order for the donor cutoff/paternal consent provisions to apply was dropped; second, the marriage requirement was dropped. Accordingly, a man who consents to the insemination of his partner "with the intent to be the parent, is the parent of the resulting child."[30] The Act further provides that the absence of a signed consent does not preclude a finding of paternity where a couple resides together during the first two years of a child's life and the man holds the child out as his own.[31] The 2002 UPA also adopted a gender-neutral mandate stating that the "[p]rovisions of this [Act] relating to determination of paternity apply to determinations of maternity."[32] As discussed in the section entitled "Same-Sex Couples and the Establishment of Legal Parenthood," below, this provision is particularly important when it comes to determinations of parentage in lesbian couples.

It is important to be aware that many states have not adopted the UPA, and of those that have, many have yet to adopt the 2002 version of the Act. Accordingly, where the original version is still in effect, the insemination must still occur under the supervision of a physician and the couple must be married in order for the cutoff/parental intent rules to take effect. Additionally, not all adopting states have followed the text of the UPA verbatim; accordingly, there is some variability even in adopting states. Moreover, other states have adopted their own version of the cutoff/parental intent rules. As a result, the law in this area varies from state to state. However, it is probably safe to say that most states have a statutory provision adopting some version of a paternal presumption, at least where married heterosexual couples are concerned.

Even in the absence of a statute, a court is likely to hold that a consenting husband is the legal father of a child. For instance, in the case of People v. Sorenson,[33] one of the earliest and still influential decisions on this issue, a husband who had consented to the insemination of his wife and had held himself out as the child's father argued upon divorce that he should not have to pay child support because the sperm donor, not he, was the child's legal father. In rejecting this position, the court stated:

> [W]here a reasonable man who because of his inability to procreate, actively participates and consents to his wife's artificial insemination in the hope that a child will be produced whom they will treat as their own, knows that such behavior carries with it the legal responsibilities

of fatherhood. . . . One who consents to the production of a child cannot create a temporary relation to be assumed and disclaimed at will. . . . [I]t is safe to assume that without defendant's active participation and consent, the child would not have been procreated.[34]

Accordingly, the husband's consent to the insemination was deemed to establish him as the legal father, and he was not permitted to disavow the relationship. Courts have similarly relied on the doctrine of equitable estoppel to reach the same result, finding that where a husband consents to the insemination of his wife and then treats the child as his own, he may be estopped from denying his paternity in order to avoid paying child support in the event of a separation or a divorce.[35]

When it comes to unmarried couples, the law is somewhat more variable in states that have not adopted the 2002 UPA or a cognate rule. Nonetheless, the clear trend of the law is in favor of vesting legal paternity in the consenting partner of a woman who has conceived by way of donor insemination, whether married or not.

Donor Insemination and the Single Woman

What about when a woman decides to have a child on her own by way of donor insemination? This raises a question regarding the potential rights of a sperm donor where there is no consenting male partner standing in the wings ready to take on the mantle of legal fatherhood. As discussed, in large part, the answer depends upon whether the sperm donor is known or unknown.

If sperm is obtained from a sperm bank, there is almost no chance of a future legal conflict over the establishment of paternal rights as most facilities promise the donors anonymity and maintain their records in such a way as to make the subsequent matching of sperm donor and birth mother very difficult. Moreover, it is unlikely that the donor was motivated by the desire to become a parent but was instead prompted by a wish to earn extra money and/or by altruism. Accordingly, his participation cannot reasonably be read as an indication of intended parenthood.

It should be noted that there is a growing push for greater openness in the process, and many programs now provide sperm donors with an identity-release option that allows children conceived with their sperm to obtain certain information about their biological fathers when they reach adulthood. Moreover, in 2000, a California appeals court, in a case involving a genetically transmitted disease, concluded that the donor's right to preserve his anonymity was outweighed by the state's compelling interest in protecting the health and welfare of minor children, including those born by donor insemination. Accordingly, the court ordered the disclosure of the donor's identity so that needed medical information could be obtained.[36] However, requiring the release of a donor's identity is a far cry from providing donors with the option of seeking parental rights.

Rather than relying on a sperm bank, a woman might instead prefer to use a known donor. This approach provides the recipient with more control over the process and greater knowledge of the child's origins. It also allows for the possibility that the donor can play a continuing role in the child's life. However, the potential downside of using a known donor is that the parties may not be able to control the legal outcome should a dispute arise, particularly if they do not have a written agreement setting out their intent. In contrast to the situation where sperm is obtained from an unknown donor, the law when it comes to the legal status of a known donor is far from settled and depends in part on whether or not the parties have a written agreement as well as on whether or not the jurisdiction has adopted the 2002 UPA or a cognate provision.[37]

Where the parties do not have a written agreement, the donor may well be able to bring a paternity action to establish his right to maintain a relationship with the child; likewise, the mother may be able to bring an action in order to secure child support. However, this result may be precluded in states that have adopted the 2002 version of the UPA, which, as we have seen above, cuts off the rights of donor, unless the parties have entered into an agreement granting him parental rights. Highlighting the complexity of the law in this regard, in the 2014 case of Jason P. v. Danielle S., a California appeals court concluded that the donor cutoff provision should only be read to preclude a donor from seeking to establish his paternity based upon a biological connection to the child, and should not be read to bar him from doing so based upon the development of a post-birth relationship with the child, even in the absence of any intent to be recognized as the father at the time of conception.[38] In short, his conduct was deemed sufficient to convert him from donor to father, regardless of his original intent.

In many cases, the respective parties do enter into an agreement embodying their intent. They may, for example, agree that the donor will relinquish all rights in exchange for a commitment from the mother not to seek child support. Alternatively, they may agree that the donor will have the right to participate in the child's life and correspondingly will contribute to the support of the child. The critical question, of course, is what happens if a party changes his or her mind and a donor who previously agreed to relinquish his rights decides he wants a relationship with the child or a woman who had agreed to let him participate in the child's life now wishes to cut off the relationship.

It is here that the law becomes particularly murky as jurisdictions are divided over the enforceability of these agreements, and one must proceed with great care in these situations. Believing that it is in a child's best interest to have an identifiable legal father, some courts are unlikely to enforce these agreements if the end result would be to sever the relationship between the donor and the child. However, other courts have been willing to enforce these agreements, based on the recognition that to do otherwise would discourage this form of assisted reproduction. As recently explained by the Supreme Court of Pennsylvania, a policy of non-enforceability would likely deter women from seeking "sperm from a man she knows and admires . . . whose background, traits, and medical history are not shrouded in mystery" in favor of an unknown donor.[39] Accordingly, the Court concluded that the presence of a genetic link was not of sufficient weight to override the clear intent of the parties that the donor not be regarded as a legal parent.

■ Same-Sex Couples and the Establishment of Legal Parenthood

As noted above, the question of determining parentage when it comes to same-sex couples is a more freighted terrain as these cases unsettle the long-standing normative assumption that a child's best interest is served by having a legally recognized mother and a legally recognized father. With this in mind, after a brief consideration of the traditional approach that courts have taken to the establishment of parental rights in the context of same-sex relationships, we first consider the potential use of the common law marital presumption and UPA's cutoff/parental intent provisions toward this end. We then look at how the doctrine of de facto parenthood has been used to gain at least partial rights for **co-parents**.

In this regard, it should be noted, that our focus is on lesbian couples. Not only does this continue our inquiry into the legal rights of sperm donors, but the majority of cases have involved lesbian, rather than gay male, couples. Moreover, the issues are quite different when it comes to sorting out parental rights where two men make the decision to have a child, as this necessitates the use of other assisted reproductive technologies, such as in vitro fertilization and gestational surrogacy, which raise a myriad of issues that are beyond the scope of this book.[40]

The "Other" Mother: The Traditional Legal Approach

Along with the fight for marriage equality, same-sex parents have also struggled for legal recognition of their relationships with their children. Critically, until recently, the law has regarded the non-biologically related partner, often referred to as a co-parent, as a legal stranger to the child, even where a couple has jointly decided to have a child and raise him or her together (unless, as discussed in Chapter 13, the co-parent has adopted the child). The failure to be recognized as a legal parent has multiple ramifications. For instance, a state may refuse to put her name on the birth certificate or a known donor might seek to seek to assert his rights as the child's other legal parent. Moreover, if the relationship ends, the legally recognized parent could potentially seek to prevent her partner from maintaining an ongoing relationship with the child based on the assertion that she is a legal stranger. In turn, this would require the co-parent, assuming she were found to have standing, to show something more than that preservation of the relationship would be in the child's best interest in order to be granted visitation or custodial rights (see Chapter 5).

The Extension of Parental Rights Based on Marriage and Consent

As we have just seen, when a married heterosexual couple relies on a sperm donor in order to conceive a child, a husband is virtually certain to be treated as the legal father of the resulting child based upon the common law marital presumption, a parentage statute, or case law that effectively treats his consent as a substitute for sexual intercourse. Although an unmarried man obviously does not have recourse to the marital presumption as the basis for establishing his legal parentage, in states that have enacted the 2002 UPA or a cognate provision, he will likewise be regarded as the legal father assuming he consented to the insemination with the requisite parental intent (or cohabits with mother and holds the child out as his during the first two years of the child's life). In either eventuality, it is important to recognize that these mechanisms serve to vest legal parenthood in a man in the absence of a biological connection with the child in question. The issue we now turn to is whether these approaches to establishing legal parenthood are likewise available where the spouse or partner of a woman who conceives by way of donor insemination is another woman. In short, will the law treat her as the child's other legal parent on the same basis as it does the husband or partner in a heterosexual union, or is a different standard applied? We begin this discussion with the common law marital presumption.

In the wake of the *Obergefell* decision, the common law marital presumption that treats a husband as the legal father of children born to his wife during their marriage should likewise govern the parental status of a married lesbian co-parent. However, it is important to keep in mind that this presumption is rebuttable, and one of the chief grounds for doing so is the lack of a biological relationship between the parent and child. Of course, the problem then becomes that the lack of a biological link could routinely be deployed for purposes of rebuttal. Recognizing this possibility, a New York appeals court recently held that not only does the marital presumption apply to same-sex couples, but that it "is not defeated solely with proof of the biological fact that, at present, a child cannot be the product of same-gender parents," and that to conclude otherwise would deny "children born to same-gender couples . . . the benefit of this presumption without compelling justification."[41]

In states that have adopted the 2002 UPA or a cognate provision, a same-sex co-parent should be able to rely on the operative provisions discussed above to establish her status as the other legal parent of the child born to her spouse or partner, assuming the requisite intent. This result is supported by the Act's gender-neutral injunction regarding parentage determinations. Leading the way in this regard, courts in both California and New Jersey were among the first to use this approach in order to recognize the reality of two-mother households. For instance, in the case of Elisa B. v. Emily B., the California court concluded that under the UPA, as adopted by California, just as a similarly situated man would be the presumed legal father, a woman who consents to the insemination of her partner, and then receives the child into her home and openly holds the child out as her own, is the presumed legal mother of that child.[42]

However, *Obergefell* notwithstanding, even where a couple is married some states appear to be resisting the application of these approaches to establish the parental rights of a lesbian co-parent. However, the Supreme Court's 2017 per curiam decision in Pavan v. Smith[43] may have some bearing on this matter, at least when it comes to married couples. In *Pavan*, the Court concluded that the refusal by the Arizona Department of Health to include the names of both same-sex spouses of a child born through donor insemination on the birth certificate unconstitutionally denied them access to " 'the constellation of benefits that the Stat[e] ha[s] linked to marriage' " in accordance with *Obergefell*'s equality mandate.[44] In short, this decision suggests that the right of marriage equality encompasses the right to equality with regard to parental rights — that the later cannot be severed and treated according to a different standard, although it is certainly possible that *Pavan* may be read somewhat more narrowly.

Although the trend is clearly in favor of recognizing the reality of two-mother families, the majority of states have not ruled on this issue. Accordingly, experts in the field continue to recommend that, even where a couple is married, they secure the parental rights of the co-parent through adoption or a judicial declaration of parentage.[45] A handful of states also permit same-sex parents to sign a voluntary acknowledgment of parentage (see the section entitled "Establishing Paternity," earlier in this chapter), which likewise establishes legal parentage in a co-parent.

De Facto Parental Status

Another approach that some courts and legislatures have adopted is to afford a co-parent some legal recognition based on her established relationship with the child whose upbringing she is sharing in. This approach is known under various names, including equitable parenthood, de facto parenthood, and parenthood by estoppel. For purposes of this discussion, we will use the term "**de facto parent**." Dating back before the advent of marriage equality, this approach has been adopted in a significant minority of states; however, it is important to recognize that in most recognizing jurisdictions, it does not vest a co-parent with full legal status. In short, although enabling a co-parent to maintain a relationship with a child she has helped to parent, which is a significant advance over the traditional legal stranger approach to co-parent rights, it typically is understood as falling short of declaring her a legal parent (see, however, the discussion below of the approach taken by the Washington Supreme Court).

In 1996, in the landmark case of Holzman v. Knott, the Supreme Court of Wisconsin became the first court to expressly extend de facto parental status to a lesbian co-parent.[46] In *Holzman*, a lesbian couple decided to have and rear a child together. Following the termination of the relationship, Holzman sought visitation rights when her former partner, the child's biological mother, refused to allow her to see the child. Rejecting the assertion that a biological parent has a constitutionally protected right "to determine who shall visit her child," the court concluded that a party with a "parent-like" relationship with a child that has been disrupted by the termination of that relationship has standing to seek visitation (note that this case did not involve custody). To determine if there is a parent-like relationship, a party must be able to establish the following elements:

1. The legal parent consented to and fostered the relationship.
2. She resided with the child in the same household.
3. She assumed the responsibilities of parenthood.
4. She was in the parental role long enough to establish meaningful connection with the child.[47]

Since *Holzman*, courts adopting this approach have stressed the importance of a couple's mutual decision to have and raise a child together. Thus, for example, in a subsequent case from Massachusetts, the parties sent out joint birth announcements; embodied their parenting intent in a range of legal documents, including a co-parenting agreement; gave the child both of their last names; and fully shared parenting responsibilities.[48] Similarly, in a case from Rhode Island in which the co-parent was granted visitation rights, the child was given a hyphenated name; the names of both parties appeared on the baptismal certificate and the birth announcements; and both parties fully participated in the raising of the child.[49]

This element of mutual consent ensures that this status is not one that a court can impose on a legal parent; rather, recognition of a co-parent honors a reality that would not have existed but for the consent and active cooperation of that parent. It also means that a court cannot be said to be encroaching upon the exclusive domain of the legal parent. As explained by the New Jersey Supreme Court:

> This opinion should not be viewed as an incursion on the general right of a fit legal parent to raise his or her child without outside interference. What we have addressed here is . . . the volitional choice of a legal parent to cede a measure of a parental authority to a third party. . . . In such circumstances the legal parent has created a family with the third party and the child, and has invited the third party into the otherwise inviolable realm of family privacy.[50]

This requirement also responds to the concern raised by some that a nanny or babysitter could somehow end up as a de facto parent simply by participating in the life of a child. Further responding to this concern, some courts have stressed that the caretaking functions must be performed "for reasons primarily other than financial compensation."[51] Once recognized as a de facto parent, a party is no longer a "legal stranger." However, the question still remains as to whether a de facto parent stands on equal footing with her former partner, much as a divorcing husband and wife would. For instance, the New Jersey Supreme Court stated that "[o]nce a third party has been determined to be a psychological parent to a child, under the previously described standards, he or she stands in *parity* with the legal parent." The court went on to emphasize, however, that "parity" does not require equality of treatment, and that because ". . . in the search for self-knowledge, the child's interest in his or her roots will emerge," if "the evidence concerning the child's best interests (as between a legal parent and psychological parent) is in equipoise," custody should be awarded to the legal parent.[52]

In contrast, in a more recent case, the Supreme Court of Washington made clear that once a party is found to be a de facto parent, he or she is in "legal parity" with the other parent, which places them in "equivalent parental positions." In rejecting the biological mother's argument that such a determination interfered with her fundamental rights as a parent, the court concluded that once a determination of parentage is made, both parents have a "fundamental liberty interest" in the "care, custody, and control" of their child.[53]

Chapter Summary

Once considered a child of no one, the legal status of children of unmarried parents has improved greatly since the colonial era. Today, laws that differentiate children based on the marital status of their parents are unconstitutional if the underlying purpose is deterrence of nonmarital sexual relations or the promotion of an idealized family type. However, laws that differentiate them for the narrow purpose of preventing fraud are generally allowed.

The rights of unwed fathers have also been expanded. Although biology alone does not give a man a protected interest in maintaining a relationship with his child, his rights cannot be unilaterally terminated where he has sought to develop a relationship with his child. However, where the mother is married to another man, the presumption of paternity may preclude the unwed father from seeking paternal rights.

Paternity cannot simply be assumed. It must be established either through a court proceeding (i.e., adjudication) or a voluntary acknowledgment of paternity. To improve paternity establishment procedures, states must now comply with federal requirements or risk the loss of federal funds. A court must order genetic testing if requested by one party, and states must have rules that create a rebuttable presumption of paternity if the tests establish that the man is the father of the child within a threshold degree of probability. States must also have simplified procedures in place, such as the availability of paternity affidavits, for the voluntary acknowledgment of paternity.

A highly contested issue is whether a man should be allowed to disestablish paternity based on scientific evidence that he is not the biological father. Some states focus on the effect that disestablishment will have on the child and take best interest into account in determining whether a father can disavow his legal relationship with the child, while others consider best interest to be irrelevant, focusing instead on the rights and status of the man who is contesting his paternal status.

Where conception is accomplished through sperm donation, the presumption of paternity and donor cutoff/parental intent provisions typically vest legal parenthood in a husband and may well do so with an unmarried male partner. In the situation of a single woman, the status of the sperm donor may turn on whether or not the woman and donor have entered into an agreement embodying their intent, although these agreements are not treated as binding in all states.

The same rules should apply in the context of same-sex couples; however, some states have expressed more ambivalence when it comes to the establishment of two-mother families. The de facto parent doctrine has also been used by co-parents in order to maintain an ongoing relationship with a child following the dissolution of her relationship with the legal parent.

Key Terms

Presumption of Paternity

Legitimation

Equal Protection Clause

Adjudication of Paternity

Acknowledgment of Paternity

Genetic Testing

Paternity Disestablishment

Donor Insemination

Co-Parent

De Facto Parent

Review Questions

1. What was the common law status of children of unmarried parents? Why were these children treated so harshly?
2. What is the presumption of paternity?
3. Describe the early U.S. reform efforts.
4. What underlying statutory purposes will invalidate a law that treats children of married parents and children of unmarried parents differently? What purpose will sustain differential treatment?
5. In the case of Stanley v. Illinois, how was the father treated differently from unwed mothers or married fathers? How did the Court respond to Stanley's challenge?
6. Based on the case of Lehr v. Robinson, when must an unwed father be given a voice in the adoption process?
7. Why did the dissent in *Lehr* disagree with the majority position? What did they think should be controlling?
8. On what basis did the *Nguyen* Court justify the differential treatment of mothers and fathers in the immigration context? How did the approach of the *Morales-Santana* Court differ?
9. Why was the biological father barred from pursuing his paternity claim in the case of Michael H. v. Gerald D.?
10. Explain current state approaches with respect to allowing a father to pursue a paternity claim where the mother is married to another man.
11. What is the significance of establishing paternity?
12. What are the two ways that paternity can be established?
13. What federal requirements are imposed on states in contested paternity actions?
14. What is a voluntary acknowledgment of paternity? What legal effect does an acknowledgment have?
15. What information must a state provide to persons who are thinking about acknowledging paternity?

16. What are the legal consequences of establishing paternity?
17. What does it mean to disestablish paternity? In what situations do these cases arise? What are the two basic approaches that courts use in these cases?
18. Where a married woman becomes pregnant through donor insemination with the consent of her husband, who is the legal father? What rules potentially apply here?
19. What is the likely outcome where a single woman uses an anonymous donor?
20. What are the possible outcomes when a single woman uses a known donor?
21. What are the potentially applicable rules when it comes to establishing parentage in lesbian couples?
22. What is a de facto parent and how is this status achieved?

Discussion Questions

1. Thinking back to the case of Michael H. v. Gerald D., do you think the biological father should have been permitted to establish his paternal rights, or do you think the Court was right to bar his claim? What competing rights and interests are at stake here?
2. Assume that a man and woman who know each other casually have sexual intercourse one time. As a result, she becomes pregnant and decides to have the baby. Based on this fleeting moment of intimacy, is it fair that the father be responsible for 18 years of child support? What if he offers to pay for an abortion? What if he already has a family? What if the woman lied and said she was using birth control when she was not?
3. If a woman who is not married becomes pregnant, do you think she and the father should have equal rights with respect to the child? Is your thinking influenced by the circumstances? For example, does it matter if they were in a long-term serious relationship or if the pregnancy resulted from a casual fling? Should the law take circumstances such as these into consideration?
4. Assume that, upon separation from his wife or partner, a man who has believed himself to be the father of the child he has been raising suddenly has doubts and wishes to have genetic testing done to determine if he is in fact the biological father. Do you think he should be allowed to do this and, if the tests show he is not the father, to disestablish paternity? What considerations do you think are important here?
5. Do you think paternity and maternity should be established using gender-neutral rules?

Assignments

1. For your state, locate the applicable paternity statute (and custody statute, if separate) and determine the following:
   a. What court are the proceedings held in?
   b. With respect to the use of genetic tests, at what percentage of probability of paternity is a man presumed to be the father?
   c. Does your state employ a rebuttable or a conclusive presumption of paternity?
   d. What is the legal standard for determining custody? Are there any differences in the treatment of married and unmarried parents?
2. Go to the appropriate court or other local agency and obtain the form your state uses for voluntary paternity acknowledgments. If explanatory information is not contained on the form, make sure that you obtain any supplementary documents.

   Now, assume that your office has a client who is contemplating executing the acknowledgment. You have been asked to send him the relevant documents with a cover letter explaining the process and its significance. In writing the letter, assume the client is young and has no familiarity with legal concepts.
3. Assume your office is representing an unmarried woman who is planning to be inseminated with the sperm of a known donor. You have been asked to draft an agreement between the parties to memorialize their intent. They have agreed on the following:
   - The donor waives all potential parental rights.
   - The donee agrees not to pursue any child support or other claims.
   - The donor may see the child as a friend of the family but agrees not to disclose his true relationship to the child or to anyone else.
   - The child is to have no established relationship with the donor's extended family.

   After drafting the agreement, draft a cover letter to the client explaining the legal provisions contained in the agreement.
4. Assume a lesbian co-parent has come to your office for guidance following the dissolution of her relationship with her wife, who is now preventing her from seeing their child. The attorney you work for has asked you to write a memo in which you set out all of the approaches that she may be able to use in seeking to establish her parental rights and/or maintain her relationship with the child.

Cases for Analysis

In the following case, the court considers whether, in dismissing his paternity action, the trial court violated the constitutional rights of a man whose genetic tests showed with virtual certainty that he was the biological father of a child born to a married woman,

IN RE THE PATERNITY OF A.R.R.
2015 WI App. 19, 360 Wis. 2d 388, 860 N.W.2d 538 (2015)

STARK, J.

Stuart S. appeals an order dismissing his paternity action against Heidi R. and Scott R. Stuart alleges he is the biological father of A.R.R., a child born to Heidi while she was married to Scott. The circuit court dismissed Stuart's paternity action, pursuant to Wis. Stat. §767.863(1m), concluding a judicial determination that Stuart was A.R.R.'s father would not be in A.R.R.'s best interest. . . . Stuart . . . asserts dismissal of the paternity action violated his constitutionally protected liberty interest in his putative paternity of A.R.R. . . .

We . . . conclude dismissal of the paternity action did not violate Stuart's constitutional rights as A.R.R.'s putative father because his relationship with A.R.R. was not substantial enough to give rise to a constitutionally protected liberty interest. We therefore affirm.

BACKGROUND

Scott and Heidi were married in 1990. Heidi gave birth to five children during their marriage. Scott initiated divorce proceedings in October 2012. Custody and placement of Scott and Heidi's two youngest children—five-year-old A.R.R. and three-year-old W.R.R.—were contested.

While the divorce was pending, Stuart filed the instant paternity action against Heidi and Scott on May 20, 2013, asserting he was A.R.R.'s biological father. The petition alleged that Heidi and Scott were married, but separated, at the time of A.R.R.'s conception. The petition also asserted that Heidi, Scott, and Stuart had "always known" Stuart was A.R.R.'s biological father, that A.R.R. also knew, and that Stuart had "maintained a father/daughter relationship with [A.R.R.] since she was born[.]" Finally, the petition alleged that Stuart, Heidi, and A.R.R. underwent genetic testing on April 29, 2013, and the results showed a 99.9999996% probability Stuart was A.R.R.'s biological father. . . .

Scott . . . testified he attended prenatal medical appointments with Heidi and helped her prepare their home for the new baby. He asserted he did not receive any money from Stuart during Heidi's pregnancy. A.R.R. was born in the car on the way to the hospital, while Scott was driving. Stuart was not present for the birth. After a short hospital stay, Scott and Heidi took A.R.R. home and introduced her to their other children. Stuart was not with them when they took A.R.R. home for the first time.

Scott testified he supported A.R.R. during her infancy, providing her with food, clothing, and shelter. He further testified he changed "almost every single diaper" and fed A.R.R. bottles when she was not breast-feeding. According to Scott, Stuart did not have any type of relationship with A.R.R. during her infancy and did not contribute any money for her care.

Scott testified his youngest child with Heidi—W.R.R.—was born when A.R.R. was about eighteen months old. Scott stated he developed close relationships with both girls, and they both referred to him as "daddy." He also testified that, because he worked from home, he was able to care for A.R.R. and W.R.R. "at all times and hours[.]"

Scott testified Heidi began taking A.R.R. to Stuart's farm when A.R.R. was about two years old. Around that time, Scott also began hearing rumors that Stuart was A.R.R.'s father. However, when he confronted Heidi about the rumors, she denied them.

Scott [also] explained that his family moved closer to Stuart's residence when A.R.R. was about three or four, and when A.R.R. was four, Heidi started sending her to Stuart's house alone. He also testified that, in about May 2012, A.R.R. started asking to use his phone "a couple times a week" to call Stuart and ask to visit his farm. A.R.R. began staying overnight at Stuart's residence sometime in 2012. Scott stated he was uncomfortable with these overnight visits, but he permitted them because he was in a "manipulative marriage[.]" . . .

Heidi testified A.R.R. was conceived in November 2006, and Stuart is her biological father. Heidi asserted she was separated from Scott at the time of conception, and she was between two and four months pregnant when she moved back into the family home. She also asserted Scott knew Stuart was A.R.R.'s father when they reconciled, and he agreed that Stuart could have access to A.R.R. in order to build a relationship with her.

Heidi conceded Scott attended prenatal medical appointments with her, and Stuart did not. She also conceded Stuart did not come to the hospital when A.R.R. was born, even though she invited him to do so. Heidi admitted she allowed her other children to believe Scott was A.R.R.'s father. She also admitted A.R.R. had a "great" relationship with her younger sister, W.R.R.

Heidi testified she first brought A.R.R. to Stuart's farm shortly after A.R.R. was born. She continued visiting Stuart's farm with A.R.R. "bi-daily" during the first year of A.R.R.'s life—both because she had animals there and because she wanted Stuart to see his daughter. Heidi testified she and Scott moved in across the street from Stuart when A.R.R. was two, and after that A.R.R. saw Stuart "almost daily." She also testified Stuart would visit her home and read A.R.R. books. In 2009, A.R.R. began staying overnight at Stuart's house on a regular basis.

Heidi conceded Stuart never fed A.R.R. when she was less than two years old and never changed her diapers. However, Heidi asserted Stuart later began feeding and bathing A.R.R. when she visited his farm. Heidi further testified Stuart paid her between $200 and $600 each month to support A.R.R., and Scott knew about the payments. She also stated Stuart purchased birthday and Christmas presents for A.R.R. after she turned two. . .

Heidi testified A.R.R. began referring to Stuart as "dad" when she was about two or three. As of February 2014, A.R.R. called both Scott and Stuart "dad," and she also referred to them by their first names. However, Heidi asserted A.R.R. had more father-daughter contact with Stuart than with Scott.

Stuart testified Heidi first brought A.R.R. to visit his farm when A.R.R. was three days old. He asserted Heidi and A.R.R. visited him every other day until A.R.R. was about one year old. He changed A.R.R.'s diapers "about two times[,]" but then he "said that's enough of that." A.R.R. began staying overnight at his house in 2009, when she was about two-and-a-half years old. They went swimming together and attended horse auctions, garage sales, flea markets, and church services. Stuart testified he paid Heidi cash on a monthly basis to support A.R.R., and he purchased birthday and Christmas presents for her. He also testified he and A.R.R. hug and kiss each other in a manner characteristic of a father and daughter.

Stuart conceded he did not attend any prenatal medical appointments while Heidi was pregnant with A.R.R., and he was not present for her birth. Although he had health insurance through his employer, he did not check to see whether that insurance would cover Heidi's birthing expenses. He never attempted to add A.R.R. to his health insurance. In addition, he never attended any of A.R.R.'s medical or dental appointments.

Stuart further conceded he did not have any overnights with A.R.R. during the first two and one-half years of her life, and, as a result, he was not responsible for middle-of-the-night feedings, and he did not care for A.R.R. when she woke with stomachaches or earaches. He admitted he was not present at A.R.R.'s baptism, and, in fact, he did not know whether she had been baptized. He also admitted he had never dropped A.R.R. off or picked her up from preschool, and he did not pay for her preschool. Finally, Stuart conceded he did not take any steps to claim paternity of A.R.R. until April or May of 2013, and before that time he never informed Scott he believed he was A.R.R.'s father. . . .

A.R.R.'s guardian ad litem (GAL) moved to dismiss the paternity action, asserting a judicial determination that Stuart was A.R.R.'s father would not be in A.R.R.'s best interest. The GAL emphasized that allowing the paternity action to proceed could result in Stuart receiving physical placement of A.R.R., which could result in "split[ting] up" A.R.R. and

W.R.R. The GAL opined the relationship between A.R.R. and W.R.R. was "of paramount importance[,]" and A.R.R. and W.R.R. had indicated they did not want to be separated. Scott joined the GAL's motion, arguing Stuart had not established a substantial parental relationship with A.R.R.

The circuit court granted the motion to dismiss . . . concluding a judicial determination that Stuart was A.R.R.'s father would not be in her best interest. The court noted A.R.R. was around six years old and had lived with Scott for the majority of her life. The court also observed that Stuart was not listed as the father on A.R.R.'s birth certificate, was not present at her birth, did not pay any birthing expenses, and did not take any legal steps to assert paternity until A.R.R. was five years old.

The court conceded there was "a substantial amount of testimony" establishing that Stuart had "developed a substantial relationship with [A.R.R.]." However, the court stated, "The real issue that the Court has to grasp is whether that relationship is substantial enough to rise to a level of establishing . . . a father-daughter relationship and to overcome the presumption that the marital father should be the one . . . declared to be the father[.]" The court concluded Stuart's relationship with A.R.R. was not substantial enough to rise to the level of a father-daughter relationship, reasoning Stuart was more like a "Dutch uncle"[1] or "father of convenience" than a true father.

In particular, the court observed that, for the first two and one-half years of A.R.R.'s life, Scott and Heidi "did the heavy lifting" by feeding her, changing her diapers, and being there when she woke in the morning and went to bed at night. In contrast, Stuart "got into the game pretty late." The court conceded Stuart had contact with A.R.R. during the first few years of her life, but it found that contact was "more by convenience or coincidence than anything else[,]" and there would have been significantly less contact "had Heidi not had horses over at his farm[.]"

The court also noted that Scott consistently provided financial support for A.R.R., whereas Stuart merely "[p]aid what he felt like, when he wanted to[.]" In particular, the court observed that Stuart had paid considerably less than he would have been required to pay pursuant to the relevant child support guidelines. . . . The court also observed that, if it allowed the paternity action to proceed and Stuart was determined to be A.R.R.'s father, A.R.R. and W.R.R. could ultimately be separated. The court agreed with the GAL that separating the sisters would not be in their best interest.

Finally, the court stated it was "mindful" of the timing of Stuart's paternity action, which was filed during the pendency of Scott and Heidi's divorce proceedings. The court suggested Stuart may have filed the paternity action to "give[] Heidi a leg up in terms of the custody battle, because

---

[1]The term "Dutch uncle" commonly means "[o]ne who admonishes or reprimands with great severity and directness[.]" Webster's Third New Int'l Dictionary 705 (unabr. 1993). However, it is undisputed that the circuit court used the term to mean a favorite uncle.

now if we have two different fathers involved that creates an argument for her to say well, if we are going to keep the kids together, I'm the logical choice." The court noted that, if Stuart's only goal was to preserve his relationship with A.R.R., he could have simply filed a petition for third-party visitation in the divorce case instead of initiating a separate paternity action.

For these reasons, the court concluded allowing the paternity action to proceed would not be in A.R.R.'s best interest. Accordingly, the court entered an order dismissing the paternity action on April 9, 2014. Stuart now appeals.

Discussion

. . . Stuart . . . argues dismissal of the paternity action violated his constitutionally protected liberty interest in his putative paternity of A.R.R. . . .

As a general matter, a parent has a "constitutionally protected liberty interest in the 'companionship, care, custody, and management of his or her children.'" *Randy A.J.*, 259 Wis. 2d 384, 655 N.W.2d 630, 636 (2004) (quoting *Stanley v. Illinois*, 405 U.S. 645, 651, 92 S. Ct. 1208, 31 L. Ed. 2d 551 (1972)). However,

> parental status that rises to the level of a constitutionally protected liberty interest does not rest solely on biological factors, but rather, is depend[e]nt upon an actual relationship with the child where the parent assumes responsibility for the child's emotional and financial needs. . . . As the Supreme Court has explained, the "paramount interest" is in the welfare of children so that the "rights of the parents are a counterpart of the responsibilities they have assumed." *Lehr v. Robertson*, [463 U.S. 248, 257, 103 S. Ct. 2985, 77 L. Ed. 2d 614 (1983)]. As Justice Stewart observed in *Caban v. Mohammed*, [441 U.S. 380, 99 S. Ct. 1760, 60 L. Ed. 2d 297 (1979)]: "Parental rights do not spring full-blown from the biological connection between parent and child. They require relationships more enduring." *Id*. [at 397] (J. Stewart, dissenting).

Randy A.J., 270 Wis. 2d 384, 395.

In *Randy A.J.*, the court concluded the putative father, Brendan, did not have a constitutionally protected liberty interest in his putative paternity, despite the fact that genetic tests showed a 99.99% probability he was the child's biological father. The court reasoned Brendan had failed to establish a "substantial relationship" with the child because he did not take "affirmative steps to assume his parental responsibilities for [her]." *Id*., 397-399. The court noted the child was six years old and had lived with another man as her father for her entire life; Brendan was not listed as the father on the child's birth certificate; he was not present at her birth; he did not pay for her birthing expenses; he took no steps to assert his paternity until she was fifteen months old; and he had never provided for her emotional or financial support. *Id*.

Here, the circuit court took judicial notice of genetic test results showing a 99.9999996% likelihood Stuart is A.R.R.'s biological father. The court also observed that this case was "significantly different" from *Randy A.J.* because the evidence showed that Stuart had developed a "substantial relationship" with A.R.R. Stuart argues these two findings establish that he had a constitutionally protected liberty interest in his putative paternity of A.R.R. As a result, he argues the circuit court erred by dismissing his paternity action "without regard to his constitutional rights."

Stuart seizes on the circuit court's use of the term "substantial relationship." However, while the court characterized Stuart's relationship with A.R.R. as "substantial," it ultimately concluded the relationship was not "substantial enough" to be afforded protection. The court highlighted the following facts in support of this conclusion:

- A.R.R. had lived with Scott for most of her life;
- Stuart was not listed as A.R.R.'s father on her birth certificate, was not present for her birth, and did not take any steps to assert paternity until she was five years old;
- Stuart did not perform any day-to-day parenting responsibilities during the first two and one-half years of A.R.R.'s life;
- Although Stuart provided some financial support for A.R.R., he paid "what he felt like, when he wanted to[,]" which was less than he would have been required to pay under the applicable child support guidelines;
- Stuart never provided health insurance for A.R.R.;
- The timing of the paternity action appeared to be motivated by a desire to give Heidi an advantage in the pending divorce case; and
- Stuart was more like a "father of convenience" than a true father.

These findings are amply supported by the record and compel a conclusion that Stuart's relationship with A.R.R. was not substantial enough to give rise to a constitutionally protected liberty interest in his putative paternity.

The circuit court made an unfortunate choice of words when it stated Stuart had shown a "substantial relationship" with A.R.R. However, it is the nature of the relationship, not the label given to it by a court, that gives rise to constitutional protection. Here, despite describing the relationship as "substantial," the circuit court clearly concluded the relationship was not "substantial enough" to warrant protection. We agree with that conclusion, based on the circuit court's factual findings, and, accordingly, we reject Stuart's argument that he established a constitutionally protected liberty interest in his putative paternity of A.R.R.

QUESTIONS

1. Why did the trial court dismiss Stuart's paternity case?
2. Why did Stuart argue that the court was in error in dismissing his complaint?
3. Why did the appeals court uphold the dismissal?
4. What role did consideration of A.R.R.'s best interest play in the court's decision?

The following case raises an important issue—whether a man who has voluntarily acknowledged paternity and participated in a child's life as her father can thereafter seek to revoke the acknowledgment based on tests showing that he in fact is not the biological father.

PATERNITY OF CHERYL
434 Mass. 23, 746 N.E.2d 488 (2001)

MARSHALL, C.J.

We consider in this case whether a father may move to set aside a judgment of paternity when, more than five years after he voluntarily acknowledged paternity, genetic tests established that he was not the child's biological father. . . .

. . . The mother gave birth to the child (Cheryl) on August 29, 1993. In November, 1993, the [Department of Revenue (department)] filed a complaint in the Probate and Family Court against the father on behalf of the mother and the Department of Public Welfare (now the Department of Transitional Assistance), seeking to establish his paternity. . . .

On December 16, 1993, the mother and the father executed an acknowledgment of parentage in which the father acknowledged that he was the father of Cheryl, that he understood his acknowledgment would have the effect of a judgment against him, and that the acknowledgment would obligate him to support Cheryl. . . . The mother, in turn, acknowledged and affirmed that he was the father of Cheryl. That same day, a judge in the Probate and Family Court entered a judgment of paternity. The father, who was not represented by counsel at the time, did not submit to genetic marker testing prior to the entry of the paternity judgment. Nothing in the record explains why. . . .

The mother and the father apparently were never married. In the years following the entry of the paternity judgment, the father behaved as though he were Cheryl's father. He and his family visited and bonded with Cheryl. In 1995 and again in 1996, the father, acting pro se, sought successfully to expand and enforce his visitation rights with his daughter. According to the mother, Cheryl, now seven years old, has always called the father "Daddy" and "is bonded to and loves him as her father." . . .

In April, 1999, the department filed a complaint seeking to increase the father's child support obligation, and on May 27, 1999, a Probate Court judge ordered the father to pay $90 per week, an increase of $33.50 each week. Five days later, on June 1, 1999, the father filed for the first time a motion requesting an order for genetic marker testing, and an amendment to the 1993 paternity judgment should the test results warrant it. The motion contained a number of unsworn statements, tending to suggest that he believed he was not Cheryl's biological father. More particularly, and of relevance to this appeal, the father's motion suggested that, as early as Cheryl's birth, he may have had reason to suspect that he might not be Cheryl's biological father. . . .

With his 1999 motion, the father submitted a doctor's letter stating that laboratory testing of the father's semen conducted in June, 1996, had revealed that he has a low sperm count. . . . The motion also stated that, in 1993, the father had acknowledged his paternity "based on misleading information and without the benefit of a paternity test of any kind."

On July 21, 1999, a judge, "after careful review," denied the father's motion for genetic marker testing. . . .

On November 12, 1999 . . . the father took Cheryl for genetic testing, without the knowledge of the mother. The test report, contained in the record, concluded that he was not the biological father of Cheryl. Relying on the report, on January 27, 2000, the father moved for a second time to amend or to vacate the paternity judgment. He also requested reimbursement for all of the child support that he had paid since the 1993 judgment of paternity. The department and the mother opposed the motion.

On May 30, 2000, . . . a judge in the Probate & Family Court filed a memorandum and order in which he ordered the mother, the father, and Cheryl to participate forthwith in blood or genetic marker testing. . . . [T]he judge said that if the tests established that the father was not the biological parent of Cheryl, he would be entitled to relief from the prospective application of the 1993 paternity judgment. . . . The judge explained that the father's "interests in no longer being obligated to support a child not his own" outweighed Cheryl's interests "in maintaining a relationship with someone she believed to be her biological father." He said that a contrary conclusion would prolong "an apparent fraud and falsehood."

[The father] argues that, because he now knows with "scientific certainty" that he is not Cheryl's biological father, the prospective application of the 1993 paternity judgment is no longer equitable. His motion is timely, he says, because he did not discover the mother's "deceit" until he received the results of the genetic marker tests in late 1999.

There is a compelling public interest in the finality of paternity judgments. . . . Where a father challenges a paternity judgment, courts have pointed to the special needs of children that must be protected, noting that consideration of what is in a child's best interests will often weigh more heavily than the genetic link between parent and child. . . . Like those courts, we have recognized that stability and continuity of support, both emotional and financial, are essential to a child's welfare. . . .

Social science data and literature overwhelmingly establish that children benefit psychologically, socially, educationally and in other ways from stable and predictable parental relationships. . . .

Where a father and child have a substantial parent-child relationship, as the father and Cheryl apparently have, and the father has provided the child with consistent emotional and financial support, an attempt to undo a determination of paternity "is potentially devastating to a child who has considered the man to be the father." Hackley v. Hackley, 426 Mich. 582, 598 n.11, 395 N.W.2d 906 (1986).

We assess the reasonableness of the five and one-half year interval between the entry of the paternity judgment in 1993, and the father's first motion for relief filed in 1999. . . . In 1993, the father had an opportunity to, but did not seek, genetic testing. . . . He never claimed, and the record, such as it is, does not establish that his decision to acknowledge paternity voluntarily at that time was conditioned solely on his understanding that he was Cheryl's biological father. A man may acknowledge paternity for a variety of reasons, and we cannot assume that biology is the sole impetus in every case. . . .

Moreover, the father failed to challenge the paternity judgment at the earliest reasonable opportunity, in the face of what he acknowledges was mounting evidence that he might not be Cheryl's biological father. He took no action in 1995 after he was informed, he says, by friends of the mother that he was not Cheryl's biological father. He took no action after the mother "unequivocally" confirmed, he says, that he was not Cheryl's biological father. He took no action after he observed that Cheryl did not share his, his parents', the mother's, or the mother's parents' physical attributes. He took no action in 1996 when he discovered that his low sperm count could explain his and his wife's fertility problems. During all those years, Cheryl knew and relied on him as her father, and he enjoyed her love and companionship. . . .

[W]e conclude that, as a consequence of the father's long delay before he challenged the paternity judgment, Cheryl's interests now outweigh any interest of his. . . . Our conclusion is consistent with our prior jurisprudence, and the decisions of numerous other courts, that a father's challenge to a paternity judgment may be untimely even though he may establish conclusively that he is not a child's genetic parent. . . .

. . . We harbor no illusion that our decision will protect Cheryl from the consequences of her father's decision to seek genetic testing and to challenge his paternity. We cannot protect Cheryl from learning about her genetic parentage. If Cheryl does not yet know of her father's challenge, he (or others) may disclose it to her. No judgment can force him to continue to nurture his relationship with Cheryl, or to protect her from whatever assumptions she may have about her father. But we can protect her financial security and other legal rights. . . . Relieving him of child support obligations might itself unravel the parental ties, as the payment of child support "is a strand tightly interwoven with other forms of connection between father and child," and often forms a critical bond between them. Bowen v. Gilliard, 483 U.S. 587, 617, 97 L. Ed. 2d 485, 107 S. Ct. 3008 (1986) (Brennan, J., dissenting). We can ensure that Cheryl, who may be deprived of her father's affection and long-held assumptions about her paternity, is not also deprived of the legal rights and financial benefits of a parental relationship. . . .

Our rejection of the father's claim for relief . . . is consistent with the Legislature's clear intention to limit the ability of a voluntary signatory to a paternity agreement to challenge the validity of that agreement at some later time. . . .

QUESTIONS

1. What was the nature of the relationship between the "father" and Cheryl?
2. Why did the father seek to set aside the paternity judgment? Why do you think he waited so long to act?
3. What role did genetic marker tests play in this case?
4. What did the trial court say the result should be if the tests showed the father was not Cheryl's biological father?
5. Why did this court decide that the father could not set aside the paternity judgment?
6. Do you think the result would have been different if the father had not delayed as long as he had?
7. What role does biology play in the outcome of this case?

The following case considers the applicability of a statutory marital presumption in the context of a same-sex marriage.

McLAUGHLIN v. JONES
243 Ariz. 29, 401 P.3d 492 (2017)

Chief Justice BALES:

Under A.R.S. §25-814(A)(1), a man is presumed to be a legal parent if his wife gives birth to a child during the marriage. We here consider whether this presumption applies to similarly situated women in same-sex marriages. Because couples in same-sex marriages are constitutionally entitled to the "constellation of benefits the States have linked to marriage," *Obergefell v. Hodges*, 135 S. Ct. 2584, 2601, 192 L. Ed. 2d 609 (2015), we hold that the statutory presumption applies. We further hold that Kimberly McLaughlin, the birth mother here, is equitably estopped from rebutting her spouse Suzan's presumptive parentage of their son.

I.

The facts are not in dispute. In October 2008, Kimberly and Suzan, a same-sex couple, legally married in California. After the couple decided to have a child through artificial insemination, Suzan unsuccessfully attempted to conceive using an anonymous sperm donor. In 2010, Kimberly underwent the same process and became pregnant.

During the pregnancy, Kimberly and Suzan moved to Arizona. In February 2011, they entered a joint parenting agreement declaring Suzan a "co-parent" of the child. The agreement specifically states that "Kimberly McLaughlin intends for Suzan McLaughlin to be a second parent to her child, with the same rights, responsibilities, and obligations that a biological parent would have to her child" and that "[s]hould the relationship between [them] end . . . it is the parties [sic] intention that the parenting relationship between Suzan McLaughlin and the child shall continue with shared custody, regular visitation, and child support proportional to custody time and income." Kimberly and Suzan also executed wills declaring Suzan to be an equal parent.

In June 2011, Kimberly gave birth to a baby boy, E. While Kimberly worked as a physician, Suzan stayed at home to care for E. When E. was almost two years old, Kimberly and Suzan's relationship deteriorated to the point that Kimberly moved out of their home, taking E. and cutting off Suzan's contact with him.

Consequently, in 2013, Suzan filed petitions for dissolution and for legal decision-making and parenting time in loco parentis. During litigation, Suzan challenged the constitutionality of Arizona's refusal to recognize lawful same-sex marriages performed in other states, and pursuant to A.R.S. §12-1841, provided notice to the State of her constitutional challenge. The State intervened in the litigation.

... Based on *Obergefell*, the court reasoned that it would violate Suzan's Fourteenth Amendment rights not to afford her the same presumption of paternity that applies to a similarly situated man in an opposite-sex marriage. Additionally, the court held that Kimberly could not rebut Suzan's presumptive parentage. . . .

Kimberly sought special action review in the court of appeals. That court accepted jurisdiction but denied Kimberly relief, concluding that, under *Obergefell*, §25-814(A) applies to same-sex spouses and that Suzan is the presumptive parent. . . . The court also reasoned that Kimberly was equitably estopped from rebutting Suzan's presumption of parentage. . . .

After the court of appeals issued its decision, another division of the court reached a contrary result in a different case. . . . A divided panel concluded that a female same-sex spouse could not be presumed a legal parent . . . because the presumption is based on biological differences between men and women and *Obergefell* does not require courts to interpret paternity statutes in a gender-neutral manner.

We granted review because the application of §25-814(A)(1) to same-sex marriages after *Obergefell* is a recurring issue of statewide importance. . . .

II.

Under Arizona law, "[a] man is presumed to be the father of the child if . . . [h]e and the mother of the child were married at any time in the ten months immediately preceding the birth or the child is born within ten months after the marriage is terminated. . . ." The "paternity" presumed by this statute, as explained further below, refers to a father's legal parental rights and responsibilities rather than biological paternity. . . . Kimberly argues the trial court erred when it applied this marital paternity presumption to Suzan, because the statute by its terms only applies to males and *Obergefell* does not mandate extending the presumption to females.

A.

As Kimberly correctly notes, the text of §25-814(A)(1) clearly indicates that the legislature intended the marital paternity presumption to apply only to males. In articulating the presumption, the legislature used the words "father," "he," and "man." . . . As written, §25-814(A)(1) does not apply to Suzan.

However, in the wake of *Obergefell*, excluding Suzan from the marital paternity presumption violates the Fourteenth Amendment. . . .

Denying same-sex couples the right to marry, *Obergefell* concluded, unjustifiably infringes the fundamental right to marry in violation of the Fourteenth Amendment's Due Process and Equal Protection Clauses.

Accordingly, the Court invalidated as unconstitutional state laws banning same-sex marriage "to the extent they exclude same-sex couples from civil marriage on the same terms and conditions as opposite-sex couples."

Despite *Obergefell*'s holding requiring states to provide same-sex couples "the same terms and conditions" of marriage, Kimberly urges this Court to interpret *Obergefell* narrowly. . . . Under this reading, *Obergefell* does not require extending statutory benefits linked to marriage to include same-sex couples; rather, it only invalidates laws prohibiting same-sex marriage. *Id.*

Such a constricted reading, however, is precluded by *Obergefell* itself and the Supreme Court's recent decision in *Pavan v. Smith*, 137 S. Ct. 2075, 198 L. Ed. 2d 636 (2017) (per curiam). In *Obergefell*, the Court repeatedly framed both the issue and its holding in terms of whether states can deny same-sex couples the same "right" to marriage afforded opposite-sex couples. . . .

"The Constitution . . . does not permit the State to bar same-sex couples from marriage on the same terms as accorded to couples of the opposite sex." Such broad statements reflect that the plaintiffs in *Obergefell* sought more than just recognition of same-sex marriages. Indeed, two of the plaintiffs were a female same-sex couple who challenged a Michigan law permitting opposite-sex couples, but not them, to both serve as adoptive legal parents for the same child. . . . And the benefits attendant to marriage were expressly part of the Court's rationale for concluding that the Constitution does not permit states to bar same-sex couples from marriage "on the same terms.". . . . It would be inconsistent with *Obergefell* to conclude that same-sex couples can legally marry but states can then deny them the same benefits of marriage afforded opposite-sex couples.

Pavan, decided after *Turner*, confirms our interpretation of *Obergefell*. In *Pavan*, an Arkansas law generally required that when a married woman gives birth, the name of the mother's male spouse appear on the birth certificate, regardless of the male spouse's biological relationship to the child. The Arkansas Supreme Court concluded that *Obergefell* did not require the state to similarly list the name of the mother's female spouse on the child's birth certificate, in part because the state law did not involve the right to same-sex marriage or its recognition by other states. . . . The United States Supreme Court summarily reversed, stating that such differential treatment of same-sex couples infringed "*Obergefell*'s commitment to provide same-sex couples 'the constellation of benefits that the States have linked to marriage.'" . . .

On its face, [the statute] authorizes differential treatment of similarly situated same-sex couples. Consequently, a female spouse in a same-sex marriage is only afforded one route to becoming the legal parent of a child born to her marital partner—namely, adoption—whereas a male spouse in an opposite-sex marriage can either adopt or rely on the marital paternity presumption to establish his legal parentage. . . .

Kimberly counters that §25-814(A)(1) is constitutional despite its disparate treatment of same-sex couples because it simply concerns identifying biological parentage. However, as the previous example illustrates, the marital paternity presumption encompasses more than just rights and responsibilities attendant to biologically related fathers. . . . Because the marital paternity presumption does more than just identify biological fathers, Arizona cannot deny same-sex spouses the benefit the presumption affords. . . .

In sum, the presumption of paternity under §25-814(A)(1) cannot, consistent with the *Fourteenth Amendment's Equal Protection* and *Due Process Clauses*, be restricted to only opposite-sex couples. The marital paternity presumption is a benefit of marriage, and following *Pavan* and *Obergefell*, the state cannot deny same-sex spouses the same benefits afforded opposite-sex spouses.

QUESTIONS

1. What statutory provision is at issue in this case?
2. What argument does Kimberly make about the law?
3. How does she use the *Obergefell* decision to support her position?
4. What reading does the court give *Obergefell*?
5. What result does the court reach? How does its reading of *Obergefell* support this result?

Endnotes

1. Michael Grossberg, Governing the Hearth—Law and the Family in Nineteenth-Century America 196-198 (1985). This text was extremely helpful in the development of this historical section.

2. Tapping Reeve, Law of Baron and Femme 274 (1816) (cited in Grossberg, *supra* note 1, at 200).

3. For a discussion of changing attitudes toward children, *see* John Demos, Past, Present and Personal: The Family and the Life Course in American History chs. 1-3 (1986); Steven Mintz and Susan Kellog, Domestic Revolutions: A Social History of American Family Life ch. 3 (1968). *See also* Chapter 6.

4. Grossberg, *supra* note 1, at 207-215.

5. *Id.* at 201-207.

6. *Id.* at 228-233.

7. Levy v. Louisiana, 391 U.S. 68, 72 (1968).

8. For further detail, *see* Laurence C. Nolan, "Unwed Children" and Their Parents Before the United States Supreme Court from *Levy* to *Michael H.*: Unlikely Participants in Constitutional Jurisprudence, 28 Cap. U. L. Rev. 1 (1999).

9. 405 U.S. 645 (1972).

10. Lehr v. Robinson, 463 U.S. 248, 262 (1983). *See also* Quillion v. Walcott, 434 U.S. 246 (1977) (challenge to Georgia law denying an unwed father the right to prevent the adoption of his child unless the child had been legitimated); Caban v. Mohammed, 441 U.S. 380 (1979) (challenge to New York law allowing adoption of a nonmarital child upon the consent of the mother only).

11. 533 U.S. 53 (2001).

12. *Id.* at 64-66. Interestingly, the Court did not require proof of an actual relationship but was satisfied that the establishment of paternity created the opportunity for the development of a relationship.

13. *Id.* at 90 (citing Miller v. Albright, 523 U.S. 420, 482-483 (1998), dissenting opinion of Justice O'Connor, joined by Justices Souter, Ginsburg, and Breyer). For a discussion of an earlier decision that raises similar issues, *see* Kif Augestine-Adams, Gendered States—A Comparative Construction of Citizenship and Nation, 41 Va. J. Intl. L. 93 (2000).

14. 137 S. Ct. 1678 (2017).

15. *Id.* at 1689 and 1691.

16. *Id.* at 1692, quoting the 1940 Hearings at 426-427.

17. *Id.* at 1692, quoting the 1940 Hearings at 431.

18. *Id.* (internal citations omitted). For an important critique of the Court's remedial approach in this case, *see* Kristen A. Collins, Equality, Sovereignty, and the Family in *Morales-Santana*, 131 Harv. L. Rev. 170 (2017).

19. 137 S. Ct. at 1694.

20. 491 U.S. 110 (1989).

21. *Id.* at 130.

22. *Id.* at 142 (dissenting opinion of Justice Brennan with Justices Marshall and Blackmun).

23. For detail on these efforts, including concerns about the potential for coercion, *see* Paula Roberts, Paternity Establishment: An Issue for the 1990s, 26 Clearinghouse Rev. 1019 (1993). *See also* Paula Roberts, The Family Law Implications of the 1996 Welfare Legislation, 30 Clearinghouse Rev. 988 (1997).

24. Mary R. Anderlik and Mark A. Rothstein, DNA-Based Identity Testing and the Future of the Family: A Research Agenda, 28 Am. J.L. & Med. 215, 221 (2002). *See also* Melanie B. Jacobs, When Daddy Doesn't Want to Be Daddy Anymore: An Argument Against Paternity Fraud Cases, 16 Yale J.L. & Feminism 193 (2004).

25. Anderlik and Rothstein, *supra* note 24, at 221. *See also* Jacobs, *supra* note 24.

26. Paula Roberts, Truth and Consequences: Part I—Disestablishing the Paternity of Non-Marital Children 2 (2003). *See also* Parts II and III of this series as well as the 2006 update, all of which can be found on the website of the Center for Law and Social Policy, http://www.clasp.org (accessed Oct. 7, 2012). As these articles makes clear, this is a complex and rapidly changing area of the law and the rules vary from state to state based on the interplay of number of considerations including who is bringing the action, whether the parties are married, and whether paternity has been adjudicated or acknowledged.

27. 434 Mass. 23, 746 N.E.2d 488 (2001).

28. *Id.* at 496-497, quoting Hackley v. Hackley, 426 Mich. 582, 598 n.11, 395 N.W.2d 906 (1986).

29. Langston v. Riffe, 359 Md. 396, 754 A.2d 389 (2000).

30. UPA §703 (last amended or revised in 2002).

31. UPA §704 (last amended or revised in 2002).

32. UPA, Article 1, §106 (2002).

33. 68 Cal. 2d 280, 437 P.2d 495 (1968).

34. *Id.* at 499.

35. *Id.*

36. Johnson v. Superior Court, No. B137002 (2000).
A related, although distinct, question that generated considerable controversy is whether a child who is conceived using donor insemination has a right to learn the identity of the donor. At present, donor anonymity is generally protected. For competing views on this issue, *see* Maya Sabatello, Disclosure of Gamete Donation in the United States, 11 Ind. Health L. Rev. 29 (2014), and Naomi Cahn, Do Tell! The Rights of Donor Conceived Offspring, 42 Hofstra L. Rev. 1077 (2014).

37. Regarding the unsettled and conflicting nature of the law in this regard, *see* Amy Leah Holtz, Daddy or Donor? Uncertainty in California Law in the Wake of Jason P. v. Danielle S., 68 Hastings L.J. 869 (2017); Deborah H. Forman, Exploring the Boundaries of Families Created with Known Sperm Donors: Who's In and Who's Out, 19 U. Pa. J.L. & Soc. Change 41 (2016).

38. Jason P. v. Danielle S., 226 Cal. App. 167, 177 Cal. Rptr. 3d 789, 795 (2014).

39. Ferguson v. McKiernan, 596 Pa. 78, 940 A.2d 1236, 1247 (2007).

40. Of course, much has been written on the subject of parental rights in the advent of assisted reproductive technologies. *See generally* Maureen McBrien and Bruce Hale, Assisted Reproductive Technology: A Lawyer's Guide to Emerging Law and Science (3d ed. 2018); Judith Daar, Reproductive Technologies and the Law (2d ed. 2012).

41. Matter of Christopher YY v. Jessica ZZ and Nichole ZZ, 2018 NY Slip Op 00495 (3d Dept., 2017).

42. Elisa B. v. Emily B., 117 P.3d 660 (Cal. 2005). The New Jersey case is In the Matter of the Parentage of the Child of Kimberly Robinson, 383 N.J. Super. 165, 890 A.2d 1036 (2005).

43. 137 S. Ct. 2075, 2078 (2017).

44. *Id.*, quoting Obergefell v. Hodges, 135 S. Ct. 2584 (2015).

45. *See, e.g.*, the National Center for Lesbian Rights, Protecting Your Family After Marriage Equality: What You Need to Know, http://www.nclrights.org/wp-content /uploads/2015/01/Protecting-Your-Family-After-Marriage-Equality.pdf (accessed Apr. 1, 2019).

46. Holzman v. Knott, 193 Wis. 2d 649, 533 N.W.2d 419 (1995), *cert. denied*, 516 U.S. 976 (1995).

47. *Id.* at 436-437.

48. E.N.O. v. L.M.M., 429 Mass. 824, 711 N.E.2d 886, *cert. denied*, 528 U.S. 1005 (1999).

49. Rubano v. DiCenzo, 759 A.2d 959 (R.I. 2000).

50. V.C. v. M.J.B., 163 N.J. 200, 748 A.2d 539, 553 (2000).

51. *E.N.O.*, 711 N.E.2d at 891, n.6.

52. *V.C.*, 748 A.2d at 554-555.

53. Carvin v. Britain (In re Parentage of L.B.), 155 Wash. 2d 679, 122 P.3d 151, 178 (2005), *cert. denied*, 547 U.S. 1143 (2006).

Chapter Twelve

Child Abuse and Neglect

In this chapter, we look at the difficult topic of child abuse and neglect. The enormity of the problem is overwhelming. Each year, countless parents inflict devastating injuries upon their children. The newspapers are filled with lurid stories of children who have been burned, beaten, suffocated, and locked in filthy apartments with no heat, food, or water.

In thinking about how the legal system should respond to these situations, one must confront the tension that exists between respecting family autonomy and protecting children from harm. Respect for family privacy is enshrined in our legal system. The due process clause of the fourteenth amendment protects the fundamental right of parents to the care and custody of their children based on the assumption that parents are in the best position to love and nurture their children. However, this right is not absolute, and at some point, the state may step in to shield children from maltreatment.[1]

Although it is clear that protection of children is an important social goal, how do we determine the point at which parental claims of autonomy can be overridden? How do we define "bad" parenting, and how do we compare the impact of bad parenting with the impact of disruption and dislocation, which may also result in lasting harm? How do we respect the multiplicity of views about appropriate ways to parent without abdicating responsibility to children? And how do we respond to the fact that many parents who harm their children are themselves victims of violence or other traumas and may be struggling desperately to care for their children in a way that is not hurtful to them?

To help frame the discussion, I would like to share a troubling incident that I witnessed a number of years ago. I was ice-skating at an outdoor rink in what could generally be described as a middle-class community. Two parents were skating with their child who looked about ten years old. The child was miserable. He was cold, tired, and wanted to get off the ice. When the child would ask to leave the rink, the father would insist that he continue skating—that he must master the basics before sitting down. Eventually, he began stumbling from fatigue and begged to leave the ice, but the father would still not permit him to stop skating. The father did not raise his voice or strike the child, but it was clear that the child felt he had no choice but to continue. During this time, the mother must have been aware of what was going on, but she continued to skate as if all was fine.

At one point, I cast a hostile glance at the father, who told me to mind my own business. When I left, the child was still on the ice despite his exhaustion and abject misery. This scenario raises troubling questions about how we evaluate parental behavior. Was this abuse? Alternatively, was this possibly an effective parenting technique: teaching a child how to push beyond obstacles and strive for perfection? It also raises difficult questions about what response is called for. Should I have said something to the father? To the mother? Should I have reported the situation to the rink manager? To the state child protection agency? Would outside intervention have been helpful? Intrusive? Destructive? By whose standards are these determinations to be made?

Defining an appropriate social and legal response to child abuse and neglect is not a new task, and so we begin with a historical overview. We then consider the kinds of behaviors that may constitute abuse or neglect. Finally, we focus on how states respond to families where child abuse or neglect is suspected.

■ Historical Overview

The Colonial Period

The role of the family in early America was well defined. It was the essential building block of a well-ordered society and was responsible for the moral character, education, discipline, religious training, and economic well-being of its members. The family was presided over by the husband, who, as the household governor, was vested with broad authority over both his wife and his children; as legal subordinates, they were expected to defer to his authority.[2]

Judged by today's standards, punishment of children was harsh, but according to the then-prevailing view, children required strict correction to stamp out the stain of sin that marked each child at birth. Parental authority was not absolute; theoretically, the community could step in where a parent either engaged in excess cruelty or failed to properly discharge his or her child-rearing responsibilities. In practice, however, intervention was rare due to deference to parental authority. When it did occur, the primary goal was the preservation of social order rather than the protection of the child. Most interventions were triggered by parental neglect (e.g., exposing children to drunkenness or immorality or failing to provide them with basic necessities)[3] rather than by physical cruelty because neglect was thought to pose a greater risk of harm to the social fabric.[4]

The Emergence of the Privatized Family

As we have seen, industrialization helped to usher in a new family ideal. No longer the locus of production, the family became less integral to community life; home became a refuge—a place of escape from the harshness of the external, rapidly changing world, a private realm associated with maternal nurture. Influenced by the Enlightenment and the ideals of the Revolution, the view that children were stamped with original sin and needed to have their spirits broken lost hold. Childhood was reconceived as a time of innocence when individual potential could flourish under the watchful and gentle guidance of the newly sentimentalized maternal figure.

As the home came to be viewed as a sanctuary from the public realm, family relations were sealed off from community scrutiny. Family privacy was enshrined as a cherished value, and future generations of reformers would have to struggle against this ideal as they sought to protect children from parental harm. This retreat into privacy was a middle-class family ideal that was unattainable for many families, notably the poor, especially in the newly emerging cities, and the enslaved, whose family life was subject to external scrutiny and control.[5]

Child Rescue: Preventing Cruelty to Children

In the late 1800s, the plight of one small child, Mary Ellen Wilson, drew public attention to the horrors of child abuse and led to the formation of the first Society for the Prevention of Cruelty to Children. This case penetrated the barrier of domestic privacy and ushered in an era of intense concern for the maltreated child.

The Rescue of Mary Ellen

In 1874, a New York charitable worker's attention was drawn to the plight of Mary Ellen, a ten-year old who was being brutalized by her foster mother,

Mrs. Connolly. Not knowing where to turn, the worker appealed to the American Society for the Prevention of Cruelty to Animals (ASPCA), in the belief that the society had the authority to intercede on behalf of maltreated children as well as maltreated animals. Moved by Mary Ellen's plight, the ASPCA decided to help. Lacking an obvious legal approach, the ASPCA's attorney petitioned to have Mary Ellen brought before the court under the authority of an old English writ that permitted a magistrate to remove a person from the custody of another. In court, Mary Ellen recounted the horrors she had suffered, including being gashed on the face with a large pair of scissors and almost daily beatings. Mrs. Connolly was convicted of assault and battery, and Mary Ellen was committed to an orphanage and subsequently entrusted to a new family.[6]

Mary Ellen's case built on reforms that had taken place in the early part of the century when a number of states had expanded their neglect laws to encompass grounds beyond parental poverty. Motivated by fear that children would become public charges or turn to a life of crime, removal became sanctioned in cases of parental immorality, drunkenness, or where a child was living in idleness. In upholding the constitutionality of these laws against claims that they abrogated family rights, the courts relied on the English common law doctrine of *parens patriae*, literally "parent of the country," which gives the state, as the sovereign power, the authority to protect those unable to care for themselves.

The Emergence of Societies for the Prevention of Cruelty to Children

Mary Ellen's case triggered a public outcry and generated an awareness that although many societies existed to help mistreated animals, none existed for child victims. Within a year of Mrs. Connolly's conviction, the ASPCA's attorney, who had helped Mary Ellen, founded the New York Society for the Prevention of Cruelty to Children (NYSPCC), the first organization dedicated to child cruelty work. Similar societies soon emerged in other cities and towns.[7]

In general, these child protection agencies regarded themselves as an arm of the police and were committed to seeing that existing laws were vigorously enforced. Agents could arrest offending parents, search homes for evidence of abuse or neglect, remove children, and initiate prosecutions. The focus of the agents was on the offending parent rather than on the child, and punishment rather than assistance was the likely result.

The societies reached the peak of their influence in the 1920s. The Depression brought a loss of funding and a shift in societal emphasis from concern about family violence to family economic survival. Protection of children from parental harm would not surface again as a significant social issue until the 1960s.[8]

The Rediscovery of Child Abuse and the Initial Legislative Response

In the late 1950s, child abuse was "rediscovered" as a social problem. Based mainly on advances in x-ray technology, doctors came to identify patterns of injuries in children that were inconsistent with parental explanations of accidental occurrences. Doctors were also faced with parents who disclaimed a history of past injuries, yet x-rays revealed old fractures in various stages of healing. In 1962, a major study entitled "The Battered Child Syndrome" was published; based on medical findings, the study detailed the harms that children suffer at the hands of their caretakers.[9] As with the case of Mary Ellen Wilson nearly a century earlier, this study triggered a public outcry and paved the way for a major reworking of abuse and neglect laws.

Within about five years after publication of "The Battered Child Syndrome," all states had enacted **abuse reporting laws**. Initially narrow in scope, these laws focused on physical abuse and generally imposed reporting requirements only on doctors. A variety of agencies—including the police, juvenile courts, and child protective agencies—were designated to receive reports, but, unfortunately, most of the reporting laws did not specify who was to assume responsibility once a report had been made. As a result, reports often fell into a void and were passed from agency to agency without any clear lines of accountability. This fragmentary approach resulted in the loss of vital information and a gross inattention to the children who had been identified as possible abuse victims.[10]

Frustrated by this fragmentation, reformers pushed for greater coordination of protective services, and in 1974, Congress responded by passing the Child Abuse Prevention and Treatment Act (CAPTA). Since 1974, CAPTA has been reauthorized and amended multiple times in order to refine and expand the scope of the law, and it remains at the center of the child protective system.[11]

Under CAPTA, states that developed a coordinated child protective system, in accordance with federal requirements, would become eligible for federal funding. In response, all states revised their existing laws and centralized responsibility in a single **child protection agency**. These agencies now stand at the forefront of what is intended to be a coordinated system to protect children from harm by parents or other caretakers. They are charged with responsibility for receiving and investigating reports of abuse or neglect, providing services to families, taking children into emergency custody, and initiating court dependency and termination proceedings. In some states, protection agencies may also be obligated to refer certain cases, such as those in which a child has been raped, has suffered serious physical injury, or has died, to the district attorney's office for investigation of possible criminal charges.[12]

■ The Child Protective System

In most cases, a family comes to the attention of a child protection agency when a report of suspected abuse or neglect is filed. The reporting triggers a complex responsive process that, in extreme cases, may ultimately result in a termination of parental rights. This section provides a general overview of this process.

Defining Abuse and Neglect

CAPTA provides a foundational definition of **abuse** and **neglect** as follows:

- any recent act or failure to act on the part of a parent or caretaker which results in death, serious physical or emotional harm, sexual abuse or exploitation; or
- an act or failure which presents an imminent risk of serious harm.[13]

With these minimal definitions as the operative floor, states are responsible for developing their own definition of abuse and neglect. Some statutes provide broad definitions and speak generally about conduct that poses a threat to a child's well-being, while others provide considerable definitional detail regarding the behaviors that come within the scope of the law.

Determining which behaviors meet the statutory definitions of "abuse" and "neglect" is a powerful act as it mediates the boundary between family autonomy and permissible intervention. Once parental behavior is defined as coming within the statute, the door is opened to ongoing state involvement. Accepting the premise that family autonomy is worth protecting, how do we decide when it must yield in order to protect children? What if one family's notion of acceptable punishment is a social worker's idea of abuse? What if the family's view is shaped by cultural values that differ from the social worker's? What if lack of food or inappropriate clothing is due to poverty rather than lack of parental concern? To what extent might decisions to remove a child be shaped by racial bias? These are difficult questions that highlight the pervasive tension between the need to protect children and the privacy rights of families.[14]

Physical Abuse

Physical abuse is generally defined as conduct that causes physical injury or endangers the health of a child. This definition clearly leaves room for some physical "correction." For example, slapping a child's hand would not support a finding of abuse, but submerging the hand in boiling water would. Between these acts, however, lies a range of behaviors that are more difficult to categorize, and a determination whether a child is being abused may involve multiple factors such as the frequency of punishment and the state of mind of the parent. For example, a parent who occasionally spanks a child in accordance with his or her understanding of the appropriate boundaries of parental authority is not likely to be considered abusive, whereas a parent who frequently spanks a child, especially if an instrument is used, may well be considered abusive.

Physical abuse can be difficult to prove. Often there are no witnesses, and parents may be able to provide a plausible explanation for their child's injuries. For example, a cigarette burn on an arm may be the result of an intentional act or an accidental occurrence. Complicating matters in cases of intentional injuries, the victim may be too young or too afraid to tell anyone what really happened. If a case reaches court, testimony from persons such as doctors, social workers, and teachers who observed the condition of the child as well as expert witness testimony on the battered child syndrome can be helpful in establishing that injuries were intentionally inflicted rather than accidental.

Sexual Abuse

Child sexual abuse encompasses a range of actions from inappropriate touching to penetration. Unlike sexual assaults by strangers, incest by a family member often begins with nonspecific sexualized touching and gradually evolves into more overt sexual acts. The child is usually sworn to secrecy and may be threatened with great harm if disclosure is made.

Because sexual abuse is cloaked in secrecy and obvious physical manifestations are often lacking, it can be difficult to detect. At some point, a child may reveal what has been happening or may inadvertently say something that suggests abuse has occurred. Sexual abuse may also come to light when a child complains about physical problems such as vaginal soreness; when physical manifestations such as vaginal scarring or a venereal disease are noticed during a physical examination; or when an adult becomes concerned about unusual or developmentally inappropriate behavior.

To provide additional guidance to the states, CAPTA defines sexual abuse to include the following:

> A. the employment, use, persuasion, inducement, enticement, or coercion of any child to engage in, or assist any other person to engage in, any sexually explicit conduct or simulation of such conduct for the purpose of producing a visual depiction of such conduct; or

> B. the rape, and in cases of caretaker or inter-familial relationships, stat-
> utory rape, molestation, prostitution, or other form of *sexual exploitation*
> of children, or incest with children.[15]

In turn, most states have defined sexual exploitation to include acts such
as allowing or inducing a child to engage in prostitution or the production
of child pornography.

Emotional Abuse and Neglect

Emotional abuse and emotional neglect are more recently recognized
forms of child maltreatment, and many statutes now include them as distinct categories of behavior that can trigger state intervention. These terms
are difficult to define, and many statutes refer generally to parental conduct that is causally linked to mental or emotional injuries in a child, such
as depression, self-destructive impulses, acute anxiety, withdrawal, and
uncontrollable aggression.

Emotional abuse frequently involves subjecting a child to intense and
recurring anger or hostility. The child may constantly be belittled, scape-
goated, threatened, insulted, and verbally assaulted. Prolonged isolation
or acts such as locking a child in a closet can also constitute emotional
abuse. *Emotional neglect* usually refers to the withdrawal of love and affection. The boundary between emotional abuse and neglect is often blurry,
and both may be present simultaneously.

State intervention is rarely based solely on emotional maltreatment
for a number of reasons: (1) it usually co-exists with other kinds of abuse
or neglect; (2) the symptoms identified with emotional harm are difficult
to identify and tend to emerge gradually over time; (3) it is difficult to
establish a causal link between the parent's conduct and the child's emotional suffering; and (4) it is difficult to determine the standard that parents
should be held to. How do we decide what is good enough parenting and
when a parent's failure to provide a secure, loving environment slides into
destructive behavior? These determinations require tremendous sensitivity and respect for a diversity of parenting styles so that an idealized vision
of the "good" parent is not imposed on nonconforming families.

Neglect

Neglect is the failure to provide for a child's basic needs. It is a broad concept that encompasses a range of acts, including the failure to provide
food, the provision of unsanitary or unsafe housing, the failure to obtain
adequate medical care and related services (most states have created a

limited first amendment exemption for parents who rely on faith healing to treat their child), lack of supervision, neglect of personal hygiene, and educational neglect.[16] Reports consistently indicate that more children suffer from neglect than from any other form of parental maltreatment, with one governmental report finding that 78 percent of the cases of child maltreatment that came to the attention of child protective services involve neglect.

To support a finding of neglect, most states require some degree of parental willfulness; thus, a parent's inability to meet a child's needs because of poverty should not be considered neglect. Nonetheless, advocates for the poor have raised serious concerns about whether poverty is too readily equated with neglect, as the overt manifestations may be similar. Thus, for example, if a parent sends a young child to school without breakfast because the parent has spent the last of her or his income on heating, that is not neglect, whereas if a parent does so because she or he stays up late partying and cannot get out of bed in the morning, that may be considered neglectful. An additional concern is that if a child is removed from the home, a family's poverty may influence a social worker's decision not to return the child, particularly if the family lacks adequate shelter.[17]

Another question that may arise in the context of family poverty is whether homelessness or unsafe housing conditions can support a determination of parental negligence. Of particular concern in this regard is whether a call to a homeless shelter in search of beds or a call to a landlord to report substandard or dangerous housing conditions might result in the filing of a report with protective services and the subsequent removal of a parent's children, despite the fact that very few statutes specify whether these conditions on their own constitute neglect.[18] This raises the concern that the expedited time frame for the termination of parental rights under the Adoption and Safe Families Act, discussed below, will have a disproportionately adverse impact on these families "because homelessness and housing insecurity are long-term problems. . . ."[19]

Establishing neglect usually requires evidence that the child has been harmed or faces a risk of serious harm due to the deprivation. In making this determination, the frequency of the neglectful act may be relevant. An occasional parental slipup, such as occasionally sending a child to school without his or her lunch, is not neglect, whereas a consistent failure to provide a child with adequate clothing in the winter might be (unless this is due to poverty). Also, where the risk of injury is great, such as where a child is left alone in an apartment with exposed wires, a single incident may constitute neglect.

A parent may also be considered neglectful for the failure to protect a child in his or her care from abuse; most commonly, in these situations, the abuse is committed by the parent's partner or the other parent. Thus, although the parent is not directly harming the child, the parent's failure to prevent maltreatment of a child may support a finding of neglect. It is not uncommon in these situations for the "passive" parent to also be a victim of abuse; in these cases, some courts are less likely to find that the parent was neglectful, recognizing that her ability to take action may be impaired by the abuse she is experiencing. Moreover, it would hold the wrong person accountable for the harms rendered to the family.[20]

Taking this rationale a step further, a recent trend has been to consider it neglect when a battered woman "exposes" her children to acts of domestic violence against her. In these situations, the neglect lies, not in failing to protect a child from actual physical injury, but rather in failing to protect the child from witnessing acts of violence. The characterization of failing to protect children from witnessing abuse as neglect, which can lead to the removal of children from their mothers, has emerged as the serious consequences of witnessing domestic violence have become better understood (see Chapter 5).

The practice of removing children from their mothers for neglect based on their failure to shield their children from exposure to domestic violence is quite controversial. Some argue that this approach is necessary to push women to leave their abusers. Others believe that this approach serves to punish the victim, by holding her, rather than the abuser, responsible for the impact of the abuse. It also ignores the fact that a woman may be at greater risk when she leaves. Moreover, the punitive nature of this approach may deter a woman from seeking the services she needs to safely extricate herself from an abusive environment.[21]

This approach has come under increased scrutiny following a 2004 decision by New York's high court concluding that it is not appropriate to remove children on the sole ground that they were exposed to domestic abuse. Although recognizing that witnessing violence can have a negative impact on children, the court ruled that a parent's failure to protect her children from exposure to such violence is not enough to establish, as required under New York law, that she failed to exercise a "minimum degree of care" and thus neglected her children.[22]

Another controversial issue that courts have struggled with is whether state intervention is appropriate in cases where a child is morbidly obese and the parents do not appear to be taking steps to address the situation. Given the serious comorbidities of obesity, which include "type two diabetes, obstructive sleep apnea, asthma, nonalcoholic fatty liver disease, cardiovascular conditions, such as hypertension and atherosclerosis, and psychological problems such as depression," some courts have begun to regard this type of situation as a form of medical neglect that justifies state intervention, including the possible removal of a child from his or her home.[23] Thus, for example, in 2007 a family court in New York concluded that the willful failure by the parents of a morbidly obese daughter to take affirmative steps to address her obesity constituted the neglectful failure to "exercise a minimum degree of care," thus exposing her to "severe life-limiting dangers."[24] It should be noted that the court was also concerned with the parents' failure to ensure that their daughter attended school on a regular basis. Accordingly, the court ordered that the daughter be placed in state custody until such time as "one or both parents [could] actually demonstrate an ability to provide appropriate home, school and community supports . . . including indicia of consistently affording an environment conducive to healthy eating habits [and] exercise regimens."[25]

Medical Child Abuse

An emerging concept is that of medical child abuse, although it is not yet expressly written into most child protective statutes. Situated at the opposite pole from medical neglect, which consists of failing to obtain needed medical care for a child, here, it is alleged that a parent has subjected a child to unnecessary and potentially harmful medical care based upon exaggerated or feigned symptoms or the actual inducement of illness in the child.[26] It perhaps comes as no surprise that this is a highly freighted terrain. On one hand, some commentators argue that this development represents an arrogant overreaching by doctors when they disagree with choices that parents have made about a child's treatment and instead wish to impose their own treatment plan; on the other hand, some medical professionals argue that making medical child abuse reportable is necessary in order to prevent "harm or potential harm to the child caused by the actions of [the] caregiver and the efforts of the medical personnel to diagnose and treat a nonexistent disease."[27]

Forced Child Marriage

As discussed in Chapter 3, the issue of forced child marriage has been gaining increased attention in this country, and a variety of different legal approaches have been proposed to address the problem, such as raising the minimal marital age, or allowing minors to seek a civil order of protection against the party (most commonly a parent) who is compelling her to marry. Another proposed approach is that where a parent is the coercive agent, the forcing of a child to marry against her will should be treated as reportable child abuse. At present, however, it is not formally recognized as such; accordingly, if a suspected forced marriage is reported to a child protective agency, it is likely to be screened out as a matter that falls outside of the agency's scope of authority.

Drug Use by Pregnant Women

In the mid-1980s, the plight of babies born to women who used drugs, most notably crack cocaine, while pregnant attracted much public attention. Frequently born at low birth weights, these infants may exhibit painful withdrawal symptoms and suffer from a host of serious medical and developmental complications.[28] In response, a number of states expanded the concept of abuse and neglect to include prenatal drug exposure—based on either the actual physical impairment caused by the exposure or the risk of future harm the mother was thought to pose to the child.[29]

Some states specifically require health care professionals to report suspected prenatal drug abuse to child protective services, and a handful of states mandate testing for exposure if there are indications that the woman used drugs during her pregnancy. Positive results must then be reported. The consequences of determined drug use during pregnancy varies from state to state: "[I]n some states [it] is supposed to trigger only an evaluation of parenting ability and the provisions of services, whereas in others it provides the basis for presuming neglect or qualifies as a factor to be considered in terminating parental rights."[30] In still others, it may itself be the basis of a parental termination proceeding. Regardless of approach, the immediate consequence is most likely the separation of mother and newborn and the placement of the infant into foster care.

Treating prenatal drug exposure as a form of child abuse or neglect is controversial. Supporters of this approach point to the potentially devastating effect of prenatal drug exposure and to the need to hold women accountable for their conduct during pregnancy. Many speak of a duty of care that a woman owes to her unborn child once she elects to carry a pregnancy to term, rejecting the idea that a woman's right of privacy bars the state from scrutinizing her conduct in order to protect the unborn.

Critics argue that this approach is unduly punitive and ignores the complex, underlying social reality of drug addiction. Rather than recognizing the often-desperate situation of these women, this approach portrays them as the purposeful destroyers of their children. By blaming the individual, it avoids social responsibility for ensuring that pregnant women have access to adequate educational, prenatal, and drug treatment services. In this regard, it is noted that many pregnant drug users do not have ready access to treatment programs because many of these programs do not serve pregnant women. Seeking to remedy this historic exclusion, a number of states have established drug treatment programs specifically for pregnant women, or now provide them with priority access to state funded services.[31] Critics also express the concern that, in addition to shifting attention away from the need to provide pregnant women with essential services, reporting laws will deter them from utilizing whatever services are available based on the fear that this will result in the loss of their babies.

The Reporting of Suspected Abuse or Neglect

Most families come to the attention of a child protection agency following a report of suspected child abuse or neglect. Far less frequently, a parent who is struggling to care for his or her children will contact a protective agency directly for assistance.

The reporting laws in most states distinguish between mandatory and permissive reporters. **Mandatory reporters** are specifically designated by statute and are usually professionals who are likely to encounter children in the course of their work, such as dentists, social workers, therapists, teachers, and physicians. Mandatory reporters are legally obligated to report suspected instances of abuse or neglect and may be subject to criminal sanctions for the failure to do so, although prosecutions are rare. Generally, these statutes abrogate professional privileges so that a reporter can disclose information without violating any duty of confidentiality. Mandated reporters are protected from liability for making a report, so long as it is made in good faith.

Any person not specifically identified as a mandatory reporter is considered a permissive reporter. **Permissive reporters** can, but are not obligated to, report suspected cases of abuse or neglect. To encourage these reports, most states permit them to be made on an anonymous basis. Because permissive reporters have no duty to report, the failure to act will not result in sanctions. However, as discussed above, parents may be legally responsible for failing to protect their children from harm inflicted by the other parent or caretaker. Accordingly, even where not required by statute, the duty to protect may effectively impose a reporting obligation on a parent.

Other states do not distinguish between mandatory and permissive reporters. In these states, a reporting duty is imposed on any person who has reasonable grounds to believe a child is being harmed.

Reports are generally made directly to the child protection agency, although in some locales, the reporter may have the option of filing with the police. Also, in specific circumstances such as where a child has been killed, the reporter may be required to contact both the protective agency and another party such as the police or the district attorney's office. As a rule, reports must be made immediately or as soon as practicable after the harm comes to the reporter's attention. Due to this timeliness requirement, reports are usually made by telephone and then followed up on in writing.

In the course of your work as a paralegal, you may face a situation where a client either tells you about abuse that is taking place or you become suspicious that his or her children are being abused or neglected. If this happens, you face the question of whether you must or should file a report. Attorneys and paralegals are almost never included in the list of mandated reporters, although they may be under a general duty to report in states that do not distinguish between mandatory and permissive reporters. Of course, even if not legally required, a report can always be made on a permissive basis. However, reporting raises difficult ethical questions regarding the duty to preserve client confidentiality, as most states do not abrogate the attorney-client privilege for this purpose. It is thus possible that reporting would breach the duty of confidentiality owed to a client. In short, regardless of any impulse you may have, under no circumstances should you take any action without consulting the attorney on the case, as he or she is most likely the appropriate person to make the decision about what should be done.

Screening and Investigation

When a report is received, it is either screened in for investigation or screened out (i.e., not accepted for investigation). Cases are screened out where

- the facts do not suggest abuse or neglect;
- the matter falls outside the agency's authority, such as where the perpetrator is not a parent or caretaker;
- there is not enough information to identify or locate the child in question;
- the report was made in bad faith; or
- the agency is already involved with the family.

If a case is screened in, a social worker will promptly conduct an investigation to determine if the allegations can be substantiated. The investigation typically includes a home visit so the investigator can speak with all involved parties and evaluate the child's living situation; where the parents refuse access, the investigator may need to enlist the assistance of the police and/or the courts. Other persons, such as neighbors, teachers, and health care providers may be interviewed as well. In an emergency situation, the investigation must be completed within a very short time period.

If the investigator cannot substantiate the allegations contained in the report, the case is closed, and no further action is taken, although voluntary services such as parenting classes or day-care referrals may be offered to the family. If, however, the investigator has reasonable cause to believe that the child is being abused or neglected, the case will remain open and under the authority of the protective agency.

If the social worker has cause to believe that a child is in immediate danger of serious harm, he or she may remove the child without a court order or prior notice to the parents. Emergency removal is supposed to be limited to situations where there is no other way to ensure a child's safety while the investigation is pending. Following removal, the agency must immediately initiate court proceedings. The parents are entitled to a hearing (usually within 72 hours of removal), at which time they can challenge the state's actions. The court may decide the removal was in error and return the child to the home, or it may decide to keep temporary custody in the agency.

Substantiated Cases: Federal Law and the "Reasonable Efforts" Requirement

If the allegations of abuse or neglect are substantiated, the child protection agency must, in most cases, make "**reasonable efforts**" to keep the family together before it can seek to remove a child from the home and place him or her in **foster care**. If a child is removed, the agency must again, in most cases, make a reasonable effort to reunite the child with his or her family.

The reasonable efforts requirement has been a cornerstone of the child protective system since the passage of the federal Adoption Assistance and Child Welfare Act of 1980 (CWA).[32] CWA was enacted in response to concerns that children who were removed from the homes ended up spending much of their youth adrift in the foster care system. By emphasizing **family preservation**, the Act sought to "replace the costly and disruptive out-of-home placements that had dominated child welfare practice with preventative and reunification programs."[33] Accordingly, a child protective agency could not remove children from their parents unless "reasonable efforts" had been made to keep the family together; if removal did become necessary, the rights of the parents could not be terminated until reasonable efforts had been made to reunify the family.

This required emphasis on family preservation soon came under increasing criticism for two primary reasons. First, it became apparent that some children were being left with or returned to abusive parents; notably, several high-profile cases focused public attention on the plight of children who had been killed by a parent following an agency decision to either leave a child with or return a child to his or her parents.[34] The second concern was the lack of permanency in children's lives, as many continued to spend extended periods of time in the foster care system while child protective agencies attempted to "rehabilitate" their parents, even in situations where family reunification was highly unlikely. Thus, although foster care was supposed to be a short-term intervention strategy, children were "languishing for years in a child welfare system that moved at a 'glacial pace.'"[35]

In 1997, in response to these mounting concerns, Congress passed the Adoption and Safe Families Act (ASFA),[36] which shifted the emphasis of the child protective system from family preservation to child safety. Although ASFA preserves the reasonable efforts requirement, it makes the "health and safety" of the child the paramount consideration in determining if the state has done enough to try and keep the family together. Closely related, to avoid having children languish in foster care while ongoing efforts are being made to "rehabilitate" the parents, the Act prioritizes the development of a permanent resolution to the family situation.

ASFA thus "fast-tracks" the permanency planning process so that children are either returned home or parental rights are terminated so the children can be freed for adoption within a much tighter time frame than previously was provided.[37] As a result, parents now have considerably less time in which to try to remedy the difficulties that brought them into the child protective system in the first place, which, as noted below, has raised serious concerns that ASFA unduly penalizes parents who may need more time to resolve a myriad of often complex problems, such as drug addiction and mental illness, which impair their ability to care for their children.[38]

Before looking at these rules in more detail, it should be noted that like CWA, ASFA is a federal funding law. This means that rather than directly imposing substantive requirements on states, ASFA instead establishes the standards that a state must comply with in order to receive federal funding for its child protective program; in short, if a state fails to comply with federal mandates, it is at risk of being sanctioned by way of a reduction in federal support. However, ASFA does leave some determinations to the discretion of a state. For example, although, as discussed below, states are subject to a "reasonable efforts" requirement, they are entitled to define for themselves what constitutes "reasonable efforts," which, of course, means that the definition is likely to vary from jurisdiction to jurisdiction.

Reasonable Efforts Prior to Removal

When allegations of abuse or neglect have been substantiated, under ASFA a state must make reasonable efforts to work with the family so the child can remain safely at home. However, because "reasonable efforts" under CWA was often understood to mean keeping a family together at all costs, reasonable efforts are no longer permitted to jeopardize a child's safety. Accordingly, in determining whether reasonable efforts have been made, a child's health and safety must be the dominant consideration. ASFA also identifies a number of exceptions to the reasonable efforts requirement, such as where a parent has "committed murder or voluntary manslaughter of another of his or her children (or aided in the commission of the same)" or has "subjected a child to aggravated circumstances," which may include torture, chronic abuse, or sexual abuse.[39]

To meet the "reasonable efforts" requirement, the protective agency (assuming no risk to the child) must offer supportive services to help parents care for their children more successfully. Services may include day care, parenting education classes, counseling, and respite care. A **service plan** outlining the services to be offered is usually developed. The service plan may also impose certain obligations on the parents; for example, they may be required to get the children to school on time or to attend Alcoholics Anonymous meetings on a regular basis. Plans must take the special needs of parents with disabilities into consideration and tailor services to meet those needs.

Although entry into a service plan is voluntary in the sense that a caseworker cannot force a family to accept services, an agency can initiate court proceedings against parents it considers noncooperative, thus subjecting them to the risk that their children will be removed and possibly their parental rights terminated. While the plan is in effect, the family is subject to ongoing monitoring and review until the agency decides either that the situation has improved and the case can be closed or that it has deteriorated and court intervention is necessary.

Removal of a Child

The Dependency Proceeding

In some instances, the child protective agency may decide that despite their efforts to keep a family together (which, of course, is not a consideration where exempted from the reasonable efforts requirement in the first place) a child's health and safety requires his or her removal from the home and placement in foster care. This is done through the filing of a **dependency proceeding**, in which the agency seeks to have the child adjudicated dependent or in need of care and protection. Essentially, the state is asking the court to find that the parents are currently unable to care for their child and that alternative arrangements for the child must be made. If the court agrees that the parents cannot presently care for the child, the child is adjudicated dependent. With this determination, custody is usually transferred to the agency, which then assumes primary responsibility for making decisions involving the child, and the child is placed in foster care.

If a child is adjudicated dependent, the case then moves into the dispositional phase during which time a plan is developed that sets out the reasonable efforts that must be made in order to try and reunite the child with his or her family, subject to the same exceptions that exempted the agency from having to make reasonable efforts to keep the family together in the first instance. Reasonableness is again determined in light of the child's health and safety needs. A reunification case plan—which usually includes services to help the parents address the problems that led to the removal in the first place—is developed. Unless contraindicated, visitation arrangements are usually incorporated into the plan in the hope that the maintenance of family connections will increase the likelihood of reunification.

Permanency Planning

To prevent the problem of "foster care drift" discussed above, once a child has been removed from his or her home, ASFA requires that a permanency plan be developed within an expedited time frame. If the agency has been able to bypass the reasonable efforts requirement based on one of the permitted exceptions, the **permanency hearing** is held within 30 days of this determination. Otherwise, the hearing is to be held no later than 12 months after a child has entered into foster care, although states are free to set a shorter time frame for this hearing, and a number have done so.[40]

The primary purpose of the hearing is to develop a "**permanency plan**" so the child is not left in limbo. By far the two most common outcomes are either a determination that the child can safely be reunited with his or her family or, if this is deemed not to be possible, the agency will seek to terminate the rights of the parents so the child can be freed for adoption. Both options can be pursued concurrently so the child is not left hanging if the preferred goal of reunification fails, as the state can only offer "time-limited" **reunification services**.[41] With limited exceptions, a state must file for the termination of parental rights if a child has been in foster care for 15 out of the most recent 22 months. This fast-tracking of cases, referred to by one scholar as a "fish or cut bait" approach,[42] may be the most significant change that ASFA has made to the child protective system. What this means is that parents now have significantly less time in which to "get their act together" before facing the possibility of the permanent loss of their child.

To appreciate the significance of this change, it is important to understand what is at stake here. **Termination of parental** rights is a drastic measure because it permanently severs the parent-child relationship (see, however, the discussion below regarding the reinstatement of parental rights). Upon termination, the child is freed up for adoption and can thus be permanently incorporated into a new family. Because termination results in an irrevocable change in parental status, it must be based on clear and convincing proof of **parental unfitness**. Unlike in a custody dispute between two parents, a court cannot extinguish the rights of a parent because it believes the child would be better off with a different parent, as this would give the state enormous discretion to reconfigure familial relationships in pursuit of idealized arrangements.

As discussed, in moving away from the emphasis on family preservation, ASFA sought to protect children from being left with or sent back to abusive parents and to limit the amount of time children spend languishing in the foster care system. Although these are admirable goals, some commentators have raised important concerns have been raised that ASFA has gone too far the other way and does not provide well-intentioned parents with an adequate opportunity to resolve serious problems, such as a drug or alcohol addiction, that would then enable them to resume caring for their children.[43] Specific concerns have also been raised that this approach penalizes parents who have been incarcerated by basing termination proceedings solely upon the length of time of the parent-child separation without a separate inquiry into whether there have been independent acts of abuse or neglect that would themselves support a termination of parental rights.[44] As one commentator explains in expressing concern about this new fast-track approach: "Typically, furthering a family's interests will also benefit the children who belong to that family. Children have an interest in maintaining a bond with their parents and other family members and are terribly injured when this bond is disrupted."[45]

Compounding these trepidations is the fact that this fast-track approach is thought to have a disproportionate impact on families of color, whose children are likely to spend extended time in foster care due to the lack of adequate supports for parents in need of services. As one commentator writes, "the lack of affordable housing options and the lack of substance abuse treatment for African American parents" may "directly contribute to the systemic racial disproportionality in the lengths of stay in the foster care system."[46] In turn, these lengthier stays may trip wire parental termination proceedings under the shortened ASFA time frames.

Legal Orphans and the Reinstatement of Parental Rights

The term "legal orphan" was coined in 1995 to describe the poignant situation where parental rights had been terminated, but no adoptive home was found for the now parentless child.[47] To address this issue, starting with California in 2005, a significant minority of states have adopted statutes that allow for the **reinstatement of parental rights** under limited circumstances. Although the reinstatement criteria vary from state to state, common considerations include:

> (1) whether there is a likelihood of permanency in the future for the child, (2) whether the parent has rehabilitated herself, (3) whether both the child and biological parent are freely consenting to the reinstatement, (4) the success of some period of trial reunification . . . and (5) if reinstatement is in the best interest of the child.[48]

Although this does not appear to be a very frequently used option, it nonetheless offers another path to permanency, assuming, of course, that the underlying problems which resulted in the termination of rights in the first place have been addressed.

The Federal Statutory Framework: The Indian Child Welfare Act (ICWA)

In 1978, Congress enacted the Indian Child Welfare Act in order to "address the Federal, State, and private agency policies and practices that resulted in the 'wholesale separation of Indian children from their families.'"[49] More specifically, congressional hearings revealed that "cultural ignorance and biases within the child welfare system" had resulted in the alarming failure of courts and administrative bodies to "recognize the essential tribal relations of Indian people and the cultural and social standards prevailing in Indian communities and families."[50] Perhaps most significant was the widespread assumption that Indian children were being neglected due to a lack of awareness that they often spent "considerable time with care-givers other than their parents; cousins grew up like sisters and brothers in the houses of their aunts and uncles or grandparents, where whatever food and supplies they had were shared amongst the group."[51]

Recognizing that "the very existence of Indian tribes in America was at risk due to the alarmingly high number of children being placed with non-Indian families and the risk of loss of such an important aspect of American culture,"[52] the ICWA established specialized rules for the removal and placement of children who are members of or are eligible for membership in a federally recognized Indian tribe.[53] We now consider three of the Act's key provisions aimed at stemming the disproportionate outflow of children from Native communities.

First, ICWA requires states to employ "active efforts," in order to prevent removal of a child or to reunify the family if a child is removed. This is a more robust standard than ASFA's reasonable efforts requirement. For example, while "a referral for services," might satisfy ASFA, under the active efforts standard, a state might be obligated to "arrange for the best-fitting service and help families engage in those services."[54] Second, subject to very limited exceptions, ICWA also vests exclusive jurisdiction over any state custody proceeding involving an Indian child (as defined by the Act) who resides or is domiciled on the reservation lands of the tribe, or is a ward of the tribe, in the tribal court. In other instances, state courts are expected to transfer jurisdiction when asked to do so by a parent, the tribe, or the tribal custodian, absent an objection by the parent.[55] Third, in the absence of good cause to the contrary, foster care, pre-adoption, and adoption placements are to be made in order of preference with (1) a member of the child's extended family; (2) other members of the Indian child's tribe; or (3) other Indian families.[56]

Chapter Summary

Child abuse and neglect are not recent phenomena, but a systematic legal response to these problems did not emerge until the latter half of the twentieth century following medical evidence revealing the seriousness and scope of the problem. Following the enactment of the federal Child Abuse Prevention and Treatment Act in 1974, all states enacted abuse reporting laws and established a coordinated child protective system under the authority of a single state agency.

A family usually comes to the attention of a protective agency when a report of suspected abuse or neglect is filed. If, after an investigation, the allegations are substantiated, the family remains under the authority of the agency. Subject to limited exceptions, reasonable efforts must be made to prevent the need to remove the child from the home; reasonableness is determined in light of the child's health and safety needs. If removal becomes necessary, a dependency proceeding is initiated, in which the state seeks a determination that the parents are presently unable to care for the child and that the child should be removed and placed in foster care. Following removal, reasonable efforts at reunification must be made, subject, again, to limited exceptions. The law now imposes strict time limits within which both permanency and parental termination hearings must be conducted, subject to limited exceptions.

The termination of parental rights is the most drastic form of intervention because it permanently severs the parent-child relationship. Once parental rights have been terminated, the child can be adopted by another family. However, where a child has not been adopted, some jurisdictions allow for the reinstatement of parental rights under narrow circumstances.

In 1978, Congress enacted the Indian Child Welfare Act to reverse long-standing policies and practices that resulted in the removal of many Native children from their families. Specialized rules are now in place that respect the tribal relations of Indian peoples.

Key Terms

Parens Patriae
Abuse Reporting Laws
Child Protection Agency
Abuse
Neglect
Mandatory Reporters
Permissive Reporters
Reasonable Efforts
Foster Care

Family Preservation
Service Plan
Dependency Proceeding
Permanency Hearing
Permanency Plan
Reunification Services
Termination of Parental Rights
Parental Unfitness
Reinstatement of Parental Rights

Review Questions

1. What role did the family play in colonial America?
2. Why was harsh discipline of children encouraged?
3. What was the justification for community intervention?
4. How did industrialization reshape family norms?
5. Who was Mary Ellen Wilson, and how did her situation lead to the birth of societies for the prevention of cruelty to children? How did these societies aim to protect children?
6. What is the doctrine of *parens patriae*?
7. What role did x-rays play in the rediscovery of child abuse in the 1960s?
8. Describe the first generation of reporting laws and explain their primary shortcoming.
9. How did the federal government first become involved in the child protection field?
10. Speaking generally, what is meant by the term "child protective system"? What role does a child protection agency play in this system?
11. What is the core meaning of physical abuse?
12. Why does sexual abuse often remain hidden?
13. What is emotional abuse and neglect?
14. What is neglect? Why is willfulness an important factor?
15. Explain the concept of failure to protect.
16. What is medical child abuse? How does it differ from medical neglect?
17. What is the relationship between the child protective system and partner abuse?
18. How have states responded to concerns about babies born to women who use drugs while pregnant?
19. What are the main arguments for and against treating prenatal drug exposure as a kind of child abuse or neglect?
20. How do reporting laws work?

21. Explain the difference between a mandatory and a permissive reporter.
21. Why might a report of suspected abuse or neglect be screened out?
23. What happens after a case is screened in?
24. Explain the concept of reasonable efforts. When is this obligation triggered?
25. What is a dependency proceeding?
26. What is a permanency hearing? When must such a hearing be held?
27. Generally speaking, how did ASFA change the approach to cases of substantiated child abuse or neglect?
28. What does it mean to terminate parental rights? What must the state prove at a termination hearing?
29. Under what circumstances might parental rights be reinstated?
28. What concerns was the ICWA intended to redress?
29. What specialized provisions does the Act put in place for cases involving the removal and placement of Indian children?

Discussion Questions

1. Some would argue that the current protective system is over interventionist and tends to disrupt families in pursuit of an idealized vision of family life. In particular, critics argue that the poor are most likely to suffer because their lives fall short of the middle-class norms that pervade protective agencies.

   Others argue that the protective system does not do enough to help children out of deference to parental authority and thus perpetuates the idea that children are a form of parental property.

   Which position do you favor? What kind of deference do you think parents are entitled to? How would you decide when intervention is appropriate? How do you account for different class and cultural styles?
2. Assume that the following report has been made regarding the Smith family: A neighbor knocked on the door of the Smith residence to see if anyone there had seen her missing cat. Upon being admitted to the home, she observed that the house was filthy. Garbage was piled all over, and rotten food was covering the counters. Both the mother and her four-year old child were dirty, although no symptoms of illness or injury were apparent. The neighbor departed after about five minutes and promptly called the state protective service agency to report what she had seen. Based on these facts, what do you think the agency should do? Is this neglect? Is intervention warranted? If so, what action is appropriate?
3. Do you think a parent should be held accountable for failing to protect his or her child from being abused by the other parent? What if the parent did not know what was going on? Does a parent have an obligation

to know? If a parent has knowledge of the abuse, should he or she be obligated to report his or her partner to a protective agency?

4. Do you think parents who have been extremely abusive deserve a second chance at parenting?

5. The Adoption and Safe Families Act has shifted the focus away from family reunification in favor of fast-tracking permanency planning for children in the foster care system. As a result of this shift in emphasis, parents may have less time to address the problems that brought the family into the protective system in the first place. Do you think this shift makes sense in order to protect children, or does it fail to account for the importance of family ties?

Assignments

1. Locate the statute in your state that governs child abuse and neglect cases as well as the applicable regulations. Answer the following questions:
   a. Who are mandated reporters?
   b. What are the sanctions for failing to report suspected abuse or neglect?
   c. What kinds of services must be offered to families?

2. Develop a set of questions and interview a person who is involved with child protection work, such as an attorney, a judge, or a protective service worker. Ask him or her to describe his or her role in the system. Ask him or her about some of the most difficult situations he or she have encountered and his or her perceptions of the major strengths and weaknesses of the protective system.

3. Assume you are representing a child who was removed from her home at age 3 because of extreme neglect. At the time, the parents had serious drug and alcohol problems. The child has been in foster care for 12 months. During this time, the parents have tried to get their act together, but until recently their efforts had fallen short. However, they have recently both completed intensive treatment programs. The father has been at a new, steady job for about three months, and the mother is working hard toward her high school degree. Both have completed a parenting class. The agency is pushing termination so the child can be adopted by her foster parents. The child has bonded with them and is thriving.

   The judge has asked you to submit a memorandum outlining your position on behalf of the child. In doing do, you should research relevant case law to determine how your state approaches this kind of case and incorporate the results of your research into the memo.

Cases for Analysis

The case below looks at whether a parent's conduct must be "knowing" in order to support a finding of parental abuse or neglect. It also considers the extent to which potentially mitigating circumstances, such as limited intelligence and a history of abuse, should be taken into account when determining if neglectful conduct, which in this case involves the failure to properly nourish prematurely born twins, is in fact "knowing."

TENNESSEE DEPARTMENT OF CHILDREN'S SERVICES v. TIKINDRA G.
347 S.W.3d 188, 2011 Tenn. App. LEXIS 111 (2011)
Appeal denied by In re Samaria S. and Samarion S., 2011 Tenn. LEXIS 701
(Tenn., July 14, 2011)

Roger A. Page, Judge.

. . .

Facts and Proceedings Below

On July 9, 2007, Respondent/Appellant Tikindra G. ("Mother"), twenty years old at the time, gave birth to twins, Samarion S. ("Boy Twin") and Samaria S. ("Girl Twin"). At the time, Mother already had two other children, ages one and two. Although Mother maintained an "on again and off again" relationship with the twins' father, Siarron S. ("Father"), Mother and Father were never married.

The twins were born four to six weeks prematurely, at about thirty-four weeks' gestation. Each weighed about four pounds at birth. Consequently, they spent their first two weeks in the Neonatal Intensive Care Unit ("NIC Unit") of the Jackson Madison County Hospital ("Hospital"). Initially, the newborn twins had difficulty feeding, but this problem largely resolved while they were in the Hospital. . . .

Mother was given extensive instruction on how to feed and care for them once she brought them home, including both written and verbal instructions by the NIC Unit. Mother indicated that she understood the instructions, and she signed an acknowledgement for the discharge nurse stating that she understood the care and feeding instructions.

The address Mother had given the Hospital was the address for Mother's grandmother at 2465 Steam Mill Ferry Road. Mother and her children were residing there temporarily, because the utilities in Mother's apartment had been cut off. On July 26, 2007, the day after Boy Twin was released, home health professionals came to the Steam Mill Ferry address to discuss with Mother the services that had been scheduled for her premature infants. In the meeting, Mother signed a consent form for further home health services. The next day, on July 27, 2007, Mother brought the twins to their pediatrician for a checkup. The checkup indicated no problems with the twin babies at that time.

During the next week, the home health professionals came to the Steam Mill Ferry address to provide Mother and the premature infants with the scheduled in-home services. When they arrived, Mother's grandmother told them that Mother and the children were no longer living there and that the grandmother did not know Mother's whereabouts. Consequently, the scheduled home health services were not provided to Mother and the babies.

Unbeknownst to either Hospital personnel or the home health services personnel, Mother had moved with her four children into the home of her friend, Quintora "Quinn" Miller ("Ms. Miller"), at 907 Park Place Apartments in Jackson, Tennessee. Ms. Miller lived at the Park Place Apartment with her own three children. After moving in with Ms. Miller, Mother returned to work at her hourly wage job, working about six hours a day. While Mother was at work, she left the twins in the care of either Father or Ms. Miller.

During the almost-two-week period following the babies' initial checkup with their pediatrician, the twins' health plummeted. By August 9, 2007, Boy Twin's condition had become dire; while at home with Mother, he went into respiratory distress and his eyes rolled into the back of his head. After Mother called 911, Boy Twin was transported to the Hospital. When Boy Twin arrived at the Hospital, he was near death. His temperature was 86 degrees, and he had no subcutaneous fat, only skin hanging on his bones. CPR was administered, and the child was intubated and placed on a ventilator in the pediatric intensive care unit ("PIC Unit"). He received blood transfusions on both August 9 and 10, 2007. Boy Twin was diagnosed with having had a life-threatening event and malnutrition/failure to thrive. Mother apparently did little or no visiting Boy Twin while he was hospitalized.

On August 14, 2007, while Boy Twin was still in the hospital, Petitioner/Appellee State of Tennessee, Department of Children's Services ("DCS"), received a referral on Girl Twin. Child Protective Services ("CPS") investigator Doretha Brice ("Brice") was assigned to the case. Initially, Brice was unable to locate Girl Twin because Mother was not visiting Boy Twin in the hospital. . . . On the morning of August 16, 2007, Brice finally located Mother and Girl Twin at the home of Ms. Miller. When Brice explained to Mother that the home health agency had been unable to locate her to assess Girl Twin, Mother admitted to Brice that she had not given the home health agency her new address.

While Boy Twin was being treated at the Hospital, Girl Twin's condition had continued to decline. Later during the same day that Brice visited

Mother, while Girl Twin was in Father's care, Girl Twin was taken to the Hospital. Upon admission, her condition was nearly the same as Boy Twin; she was severely malnourished and dehydrated, with so little subcutaneous fat that her skin was hanging on her bones. . . .

On August 23, 2007, DCS filed a petition in the Juvenile Court of Madison County, asking the court to find that the twins were dependent and neglected and to enter an order placing them in State protective custody. The next day, the juvenile court entered an order granting DCS's request. In the order, the juvenile court noted that both babies had been hospitalized for malnutrition and dehydration, that the family's utilities had been cut off and Mother had been living with a family friend, that the family did not participate in home health services, and that the parents had no reliable means of transportation. . . .

On November 20, 2007, the juvenile court entered an order noting that Mother had stipulated that the twins were dependent and neglected. The juvenile court subsequently ordered Mother to undergo a psychological evaluation ("CCP evaluation"). In the CCP evaluation, Mother indicated that she came from a broken home; her mother neglected her and her father was in and out of jail for selling and using marijuana. After Mother reached adulthood, she entered into a relationship with Father. Their relationship was abusive. . . .

The results of Mother's CCP psychological testing revealed that she has Low Average to Borderline Intellectual Functioning. Although she is a high school graduate, Mother's reading comprehension is only at a third grade level. Her verbal IQ was estimated at 75, which is in the 5th percentile, and her performance IQ was estimated at 80, in the 9th percentile. The evaluation did not find a formal thought disorder or psychosis. . . . The evaluation indicated that Mother at times does not fully grasp or appreciate what is being explained to her, but is reluctant to admit this. The evaluator determined that Mother had "some insight" as to the special needs Boy Twin would have as a result of his severe neglect, because she recognized that Boy Twin would need a variety of professional appointments throughout his childhood.

On November 26, 2008, the babies' guardian ad litem filed a petition in the juvenile court to terminate the parental rights of both Mother and Father based on severe child abuse, abandonment, failure to comply with the provisions of the DCS permanency plans, and persistent conditions.

Ultimately, after several hearings, on August 11, 2009, the juvenile court entered a final order finding that Boy Twin was the victim of severe child abuse, but that Girl Twin was not a victim of severe child abuse. . . .

On December 3, 2009, the circuit court below conducted a *de novo* hearing on Mother's appeal from the juvenile court's dependency and neglect findings. Mother again stipulated that both children were dependent and neglected, but challenged the finding of severe child abuse. Mother, DCS, and the GAL all stipulated that the circuit court should consider the issue of severe child abuse as it related to both Boy Twin and Girl Twin.

On appeal, Mother stipulates that both of her twin babies were dependent and neglected. She argues that the circuit court erred in concluding that clear and convincing evidence established that both twins were subjected to "severe child abuse." Specifically, she argues that, to support a finding of severe child abuse, the evidence must show clearly and convincingly that her acts or failure to act were "knowing." Mother contends that the evidence is insufficient to show that her conduct was "knowing" in light of her limited intellect and psychological profile, as reflected in her CCP evaluation and other evidence. Even assuming that she possesses the necessary intellect to appreciate the risks involved in her negligent conduct, Mother claims that the evidence did not clearly and convincingly show that she deliberately ignored the situation. She claims that her failure to update her address with the home health agency or to take her children to their checkups with the pediatrician does not rise to the level of severe abuse.

In response, DCS maintains that the evidence before the circuit court showed clearly and convincingly that Mother's abuse or neglect of the twins was "knowing." In addition, DCS claims that the definition of severe child abuse . . . does not require that the parent's conduct be "knowing"; rather, it is sufficient to show that the abuse or neglect of the child "will reasonably be expected to produce" the severe consequences to the child noted in that subsection. . . .

ANALYSIS

A biological parent's right to the care and the custody of his child is among the oldest of the judicially recognized liberty interests protected by the due process clauses of the federal and state constitutions. . . . While this right is fundamental and superior to the claims of other persons, it is not absolute. . . . It continues without interruption only so long as the parent has not relinquished it, abandoned it, or engaged in conduct requiring its limitation or termination. . . .

In this case, Mother stipulated that her babies were dependent and neglected, and the issue on appeal is whether the circuit court erred in making a further finding that they were subjected to "severe child abuse". . . .

[I]f there is a finding of severe child abuse, under the statutes, DCS is relieved of the obligation to use reasonable efforts to reunify the child with the parent, it is more difficult for the parent to regain custody, and one ground for termination of the parent's parental rights is effectively established.

Mother argues that the trial court erred in finding severe child abuse, because the evidence does not show that her neglect of her premature infants was "knowing," as required under the statutory definition. DCS argues that the provision of the statutory definition of "severe child abuse" at issue does not require DCS to prove that Mother's neglect was "knowing." We consider first whether "knowing" conduct or neglect is an element of the applicable provision of the statutory definition of severe child abuse. We then address whether clear and convincing evidence establishes that Mother's neglect in this case was "knowing." . . .

In the Tennessee statute, the definition of severe child abuse in subsection (B) explicitly focuses on the "injurious consequences" of the perpetrator's "specific" neglect, even going so far as to expressly require "the opinion of qualified experts" on those expected consequences. . . .

From our review, subsection (B) appears intended to address precisely the circumstance in this case, namely, child victims who are especially fragile and vulnerable and less able to survive the risk inherent in reunification. The failure to properly nourish a fourteen-year-old child for a two-week period, while abusive, would not have the catastrophic consequences of the failure to nourish a premature infant who is only days old. Subsection (B) appears intended to be broad enough to include a perpetrator's conduct toward an especially vulnerable child victim that, regardless of the perpetrator's knowledge or intent, creates "an unacceptably high risk to the health, safety and welfare of the child." . . .

PROOF OF KNOWING NEGLECT

[Note: In contrast to the above discussion regarding whether proof of "severe child abuse" requires evidence that the parent's conduct was "knowing," the applicable statute was clear that a finding of neglect requires that the conduct be knowing.]

Mother also argues on appeal that there is not clear and convincing proof in the record that her neglect of the twin babies was knowing. Mother argues that the circuit court erred in failing to consider the evidence on her intellect, specifically, the CCP test results that showed a verbal IQ of 75, in the 5th percentile, and a performance IQ of 80, in the 9th percentile, and an overall classification as Borderline Intellectual Functioning. Mother also notes the observations in the CCP evaluation that Mother often does not fully grasp what people are telling her, but is reluctant to say so because she wants to project the image of an intelligent, capable person who does not need assistance. As corroboration, Mother's counsel cites instances during Mother's trial testimony in which the questioner based questions on mistaken assumptions and Mother simply answered the questions without correcting the erroneous assumption.

Mother's counsel also argues that, even if she is found to have the intellectual ability to understand the directions given her on the care of her premature babies, Mother's testimony showed that she simply did not appreciate the risk to her children. Specifically, she did not recognize the importance of staying in contact with the home health care agency and taking the babies to follow-up appointments with the pediatrician, and did not realize the risks involved in failing to feed the infants every two hours. . . .

According appropriate deference to the circuit court's implicit determinations on the witnesses' credibility, we find ample evidence in the record to support the circuit court's finding that Mother's neglect was "knowing." The testimony at trial showed that the Hospital's NIC Unit personnel took great care in educating Mother about the needs of her premature infants and how to care for them. Mother acknowledged that she was trained at the hospital as to the proper care and feeding of the twins. She also conceded that a discharge nurse presented her with a form indicating that she was given proper instructions, and that she understood those instructions. Mother received one home health care visit before she moved from her grandmother's house, and also had one visit with the babies' pediatrician. Certainly Mother received plenty of instruction and training on caring for the infants. Most importantly, Mother acknowledged in her testimony that she understood the instructions, and even testified that she in fact fed the babies every two hours. . . .

Of course, Mother's assertion, that both of her premature babies were in fact fed in accordance with the instructions she had been given, was patently untrue. After a favorable checkup with the pediatrician on July 27, 2007, less than two weeks later, on August 9, 2007, Boy Twin was rushed to the Hospital "pretty much dead." The records and the undisputed testimony describe an infant whose appearance was shocking, with no fat whatsoever under his skin, skin hanging over his bones, and in respiratory distress. Clearly, Boy Twin had been consistently starved during the interval between July 27 and August 9. By the time Girl Twin was rushed to the Hospital, the evidence shows that she was in a similar state, with essentially no subcutaneous fat and skin hanging on her bones. The fact that Mother would assert falsely in her testimony that both babies had been fed appropriately and that Boy Twin looked like he was "doing fine" until he went into respiratory distress is also indicative of her "state of awareness." Moreover, after Boy Twin was hospitalized, Mother must have been aware of his dire condition, and nevertheless apparently continued to starve Girl Twin until she too was hospitalized. We find clear and convincing evidence in the record to support the circuit court's conclusion that Mother's neglect was "knowing. . . ."

QUESTIONS

1. What did the court conclude regarding whether parental conduct must be "knowing" in order to be considered "severe child abuse"?
2. Why did the mother argue that her failure to adequately nourish her newborn twins was not knowing?
3. Why did the court disagree with her position? On what did it base its conclusion that she acted knowingly?
4. Do you think the result would have been different if the mother had not been instructed in how to care for her newborns?

The following case involves a father's appeal of the trial court's approval to change the placement goal from reunification with his son to adoption with a concurrent goal of placing him with a legal custodian. It is a straightforward example of the kinds of considerations that a court takes into account when deciding if reunification is an appropriate goal.

IN THE INTEREST OF A.W.
162 A.3d 1117 (Pa. Super Ct. 2017)

Oττ, J.:

R.W. ("Father") appeals from the September 30, 2016 order in the Court of Common Pleas of York County changing the placement goal to adoption with a concurrent goal of placement with a legal custodian with respect to his son, A.W. ("Child"), born in July of 2015. We reverse and remand in accordance with the following decision.

The record reveals the following facts and procedural history. On September 15, 2015, the trial court placed Child in the legal and protective custody of York County Children, Youth, and Families ("CYF" or "Agency"). CYF then placed Child in kinship foster care. On September 24, 2015, the court adjudicated Child dependent, and his placement goal was return to parent with a concurrent goal of adoption.

At the time of Child's placement, Father was incarcerated. The order of adjudication required Father to comply with family service plan ("FSP") goals including but, not limited to, securing stable employment, housing, and in-home services.... With respect to visits with Child, the order provided, "Father may request supervised visitation upon approval from SCI [State Correctional Institution] or upon his release [from prison] and return to York County."

On December 17, 2015, a status review hearing occurred before a dependency master, who found that Father remained incarcerated at SCI

Coal Township, and, although he has had no telephone contact with CYF, he "telephones about once a week to speak with the child." . . .

On March 9, 2016, the trial court held a permanency review hearing, during which the CYF caseworker, Wanda Muhly, and Father testified *via* telephone from SCI Coal Township. Based on the testimony, the trial court found that Father has been moderately compliant with the permanency plan "in that [he] remains incarcerated at Coal Township SCI. He is eligible for parole in late April or early May, 2016. Father would like to be a resource for his son. He contacts the kinship parents once a week and writes letters to his son."

On April 25, 2016, Father was transferred to a halfway house in Harrisburg. Thereafter, on June 9, 2016, a status review hearing was held before the master, who found that Father "works with the Agency to arrange visits and with the Agency to arrange a home team. He opened with Catholic Charities yesterday." Further, the master found that Father is employed full-time at Old Country Buffet in Harrisburg, *inter alia*. . . .

The master held the next permanency review hearing on August 30, 2016, and found that Father was released from the halfway house in Harrisburg five days earlier, on August 25, 2016, and that he had moved to the York area. The master concluded that Father was in minimal compliance with the permanency plan based on finding that "Father was assigned a Catholic Charities Team on June 8, 2016, but that he missed appointments, and the therapeutic portion of the team closed out unsuccessfully." Further, the master found that "[t]he GAL notes that Father had the opportunity to visit the Child, attend doctor's appointments and call the Foster Parents regarding the welfare of the Child and did not."

However, the master recommended as follows on August 30, 2016.

> Father states that he has a lot on his plate since being out of prison and he wants to have the opportunity to try to work towards reunification now that he is in the York area. [Catholic Charities] is willing to reopen if the Agency makes a referral. The Agency will make the referral for the team to reopen with Father. Should there be a delay in [Catholic Charities] starting, the Agency is to work with Father to arrange supervised visitation through the Agency.

On September 30, 2016, the trial court . . . changed the goal to adoption with a concurrent goal of placement with a legal custodian. The court directed CYF "to start the termination of parental rights process."

Father presents the following issue for our review:

> 1. Whether the trial court abused its discretion in changing the dependent child's permanency goal from reunification to adoption following a status review hearing where the record did not support such a goal change[?]

ASFA promotes the reunification of foster care children with their natural parents when feasible. . . .

". . . Pennsylvania's Juvenile Act focuses upon reunification of the family, which means that the unity of the family shall be preserved 'whenever possible.'" As such, child welfare agencies are required to make reasonable efforts to return a foster child to his or her biological parent. When those efforts fail, the agency "must redirect its efforts toward placing the child in an adoptive home."

At permanency review hearings for dependent children removed from the parental home, a trial court must consider the following factors:

> **(f) Matters to be determined at permanency hearing.—**
> At each permanency hearing, a court shall determine all of the following:
>> (1) The continuing necessity for and appropriateness of the placement.
>> (2) The appropriateness, feasibility and extent of compliance with the permanency plan developed for the child.
>> (3) The extent of progress made toward alleviating the circumstances which necessitated the original placement.
>> (4) The appropriateness and feasibility of the current placement goal for the child.
>> (5) The likely date by which the placement goal for the child might be achieved.
>> (5.1) Whether reasonable efforts were made to finalize the permanency plan in effect.
>> (6) Whether the child is safe.

. . . We have stated that, "[s]afety, permanency, and well-being of the child must take precedence over **all** other considerations." . . . Moreover, "the burden is on the child welfare agency . . . to prove that a change in goal would be in the child's best interest."

. . . [T]he trial court stated that it changed Child's placement goal based on his "lack of a bond with the biological parents and the need for the child to have permanency." The court explained as follows, in part.

> The child has only ever lived [with] his foster family, and therefore, they are the only family the child has known. The child was adjudicated dependent approximately a year prior to the change of goal to adoption on September 30, 2016. During that year, minimal progress was made towards the prior goal of reunification. Father was incarcerated, but is now living with his aunt; however, he does not have satisfactory housing for reunification. Father has not made any effort to engage in the child's life since being released from prison; he has not visited, attended doctor's appointments, or even called on the child's birthday.

On appeal, Father argues that the trial court erred by failing to address all of the relevant factors set forth in Section 6351(f) before issuing the subject order. Specifically, Father asserts that the court "did not reference the timeframe set forth in the family service plan or otherwise determine the likely date by which the child's reunification with [Father] might be achieved. Nor did the court determine whether or not CYF had made reasonable efforts to finalize the permanency plan that was in effect." Further, Father argues that the record does not support the court's findings with respect to (1) the lack of a bond between Father and Child and (2) that Father "has not made any effort to engage in the child's life since being released from prison" and/or "has not visited" Child.

CYF and the Guardian Ad Litem filed a joint appellee brief in which they assert that Father has made no progress in addressing the issues that caused Child's placement, and that the goal change order is in Child's best interest. For the reasons that follow, we disagree.

By the time of the subject proceedings, Child was in placement for twelve and one-half months, and Father was released from prison during the last five of those months. Indeed, on April 25, 2016, Father was paroled to a halfway house in Harrisburg. On August 25, 2016, Father was released from the halfway house, and he immediately relocated to York County. Therefore, Father had been living in York County for approximately one month at the time of the September 30, 2016 hearing.

The record reveals that Father had made progress with the permanency plan from the time of his release from prison through the status review hearing on June 9, 2016. At the permanency review on August 30, 2016, the court found, in part, that Father had missed appointments with the Catholic Charities team, "and the therapeutic portion of the team closed out unsuccessfully." However, Father requested the opportunity to work towards reunification now that he has relocated to York County. As such, the August 30, 2016 order directed CYF to make "the referral for the [Catholic Charities] team to reopen with Father." Further, the order directed that "[s]hould there be a delay in [Catholic Charities] starting, the Agency is to work with Father to arrange supervised visitation through the Agency."

At the subject hearing one month later, on September 30, 2016, the court found that Catholic Charities reopened with Father on September 22, 2016, and that supervised visits with Child began on September 28, 2016. In addition, the court found that Father is employed full-time at Old Country Buffet. Thus, Father made progress in one month by reopening with Catholic Charities, having a supervised visit with Child, and working full-time.

With respect to housing, Father's counsel stated during the subject proceedings that Father resided with his aunt, which he stated was not appropriate for reunification with Child. However, Father's counsel stated, "I believe Catholic Charities is going to be assisting with search[ing] for appropriate housing."

In its Rule 1925(a) opinion, the trial court stated that, "while Father is making progress, the child cannot wait indefinitely on Father to become a resource." Trial Court Opinion[.] We deem the court's conclusion unreasonable when Father was released from prison for five months before the subject proceedings; he relocated to York County upon his release from the halfway house one month before the hearing; and he was making progress in the permanency plan. Further, there is no record evidence that Child has any physical, emotional, or developmental special needs. Therefore, based on the totality of the evidence, we conclude that CYF failed to satisfy its burden of establishing that a change in goal would be in Child's best interest. As such, we conclude that the court abused its discretion in changing Child's placement goal. Accordingly, we reverse the order, and remand this matter to the trial court to issue an order establishing reunification with Father as Child's placement goal with a concurrent goal of adoption.

Order reversed. Case remanded for proceedings consistent with this decision. Jurisdiction relinquished.

QUESTIONS

1. What was the initial placement goal in this case?
2. What change did the trial court make with respect to the placement goal?
3. Why did the trial court decide this change was appropriate?
4. What did the father argue in his appeal?
5. Why did the appeals court conclude that the trial court's conclusion was "unreasonable?"
6. What did the appeals court order?
7. Which court decision do you think is the correct one? Why?

Endnotes

1. *See* Prince v. Massachusetts, 321 U.S. 158 (1944); Pierce v. Society of Sisters, 268 U.S. 510 (1925); Meyer v. Nebraska, 262 U.S. 390 (1923); Wisconsin v. Yoder, 406 U.S. 205 (1972); Stanley v. Illinois, 405 U.S. 645 (1972).

2. Mary Beth Norton, Liberty's Daughters: The Revolutionary Experience of American Women 1750-1800, at 3-9 (1980).

3. Poverty was readily equated with neglect, and local authorities had the statutory authority to remove poor children from their parents and place them in almshouses or bind them out as apprentices. *See* Michael Grossberg, Governing the Hearth: Law and the Family in Nineteenth-Century America 263-268 (1985); Judith Areen, Intervention Between Parent and Child: A Reappraisal of the State's Role in Child Neglect and Abuse Cases, 63 Geo. L.J. 887, 899-902 (1975).

4. *See* Elizabeth Pleck, Domestic Tyranny: The Making of American Social Policy Against Family Violence from Colonial Times to the Present, ch. 1 (1987); Mason P. Thomas, Jr., Child Abuse and Neglect, Part 1: Historical Overview, Legal Matrix, and Social Perspectives, 50 N.C. L. Rev. 293, 300-301 (1972).

5. Pleck, *supra* note 4, at 47-48. *See also* John Demos, Past, Present, and Personal: The Family and the Life Course in American History 41-64 (1986).

6. For more on this case, *see* Pleck, *supra* note 4, ch. 4, and Thomas, *supra* note 4, at 307-313.

7. For the most part, the anti-cruelty societies were founded by upper-class, native-born reformers, while the families who became involved with the societies were generally poor and often immigrants. For an analysis of the tensions caused by the clash of these two worlds, including a discussion of the social control aspects of the child protection movement, *see* Linda Gordon, Heroes of Their Own Lives: The Politics and History of Family Violence (1988). *See also* Pleck, *supra* note 4, ch. 4.

8. Pleck, *supra* note 4, at 72-87.

9. C. Henry Kempe et al., The Battered Child Syndrome, 181 JAMA 17 (1962).

10. Douglas J. Besharov, "Doing Something" About Child Abuse: The Need to Narrow the Grounds for State Intervention, 8 Harv. J.L. & Pub. Poly. 539, 546-547 (1985); Brian G. Frasier, A Glance at the Past, A Gaze at the Present, A Glimpse at the Future: A Critical Analysis of the Development of Child Abuse Reporting Statutes, 54 Chi.-Kent L. Rev. 650, 661 (1978).

11. *See* Pub. L. No. 93-247, 88 Stat. 4 (codified as amended in scattered sections of 42 U.S.C.).

12. Although beyond the scope of this chapter, it is important to be aware that parents may also be criminally prosecuted for abusing or neglecting their children and that most states have a specific criminal abuse statute.

13. CAPTA, 42 U.S.C.A. §5106g, as amended by Pub. L. No. 111-320, the CAPTA Reauthorization Act of 2010.

14. For further discussion of some of these issues, *see* Kathleen B. Simon, Catalyzing the Separation of Black Families: A Critique of Foster Care Placements Without Prior Judicial Review, 51 Colum. J.L. & Soc. Probs. 347 (2018); Zachary Auspitz, The American Child Welfare System: The Inconspicuous Vehicle for Social Exclusion, 7 U. Miami Race & Soc. Just. L. Rev. Issue 59 (2017); David Pimentel, Fearing the Bogeyman: How the Legal System's Overreaction to Perceived Danger Threatens Families and Children, 42 Pepp. L. Rev. 235 (2015); Victor I. Veith, A Critical Look at Child Protection: From Sticks to Flowers: Guidelines for Child Protection Professionals Working with Parents Using Scripture to Justify Corporal Punishment, 40 Wm. Mitchell L. Rev. 907 (2014); R. Lee Strasburger, Jr., The Best Interests of the Child?: The Cultural Defense as Justification for Child Abuse, 25 Pace Intl. L. Rev. 161 (2013); William Y. Chen, Blue Spots, Coining and Cupping: How Ethnic Minority Parents

Can Be Misreported as Child Abusers, 7 J.L. Socy. 88 (2005); Michael Futterman, Seeking a Standard: Reconciling Child Abuse and Condoned Child Rearing Practices Among Different Cultures, 34 U. Miami Inter.-Am. L. Rev. 491 (2003).

15. 42 U.S.C. §5101, §111(4)(A) & (B), as amended by Pub. L. No. 111-320, the CAPTA Reauthorization Act of 2010.

16. With respect to medical neglect, most statutes include a religious exemption for parents who rely on spiritual means to cure their child. However, this exemption does not necessarily mean that a court is prohibited from ordering medical treatment if the child is in imminent danger, and, if the child dies, it may not shield the parent from criminal prosecution. For further detail and references, *see* Jennifer Stanfield, Current Public Law and Policy Issues: Faith Healing and Religious Treatment Exemptions to Child-Endangerment Laws: Should Parents Be Allowed to Refuse Necessary Medical Treatment for Their Children Based on Medical Beliefs?, 22 Hamline J. Pub. L. & Poly. 45 (2000). Religious-based exemptions may also exist for what might otherwise be considered educational neglect. *See* Wisconsin v. Yoder, 406 U.S. 205 (1972) (allowing Amish parents to remove their children from the public schools at age 14 for religious reasons).

17. *See generally* Sandra Bullock, Low-Income Parents Victimized by Child Protective Services, 11 Am. U. J. Gender Soc. Poly. & L. 1023 (2003).

18. *See* H. Elenore Wade, Preserving the Families of Homeless and Housing-Insecure Parents, 86 Geo. Wash. L. Rev. 871 (2018).

19. *Id.* at 896.

20. Parents may also be held criminally responsible for failing to protect a child from abuse. This is sometimes referred to as passive abuse. *See* Jeanne A. Fugate, Note: Who's Failing Whom? A Critical Look at Failure-to-Protect Laws, 76 N.Y.U. L. Rev. 272 (2001).

21. For a discussion of these issues, *see* Lynn F. Beller, When in Doubt, Take Them Out: Removal of Children from Victims of Domestic Violence Ten Years After Nicholson v. Williams, 22 Duke J. Gender L. & Poly. 205 (2015); Heidi A. White, Refusing to Blame the Victim for the Aftermath of Domestic Violence: Nicholson v. Williams Is a Step in the Right Direction, 41 Fam. Ct. Rev. 527 (2003); Melissa A. Trepiccione, Note: At the Crossroads of Law and Social Science: Is Charging a Battered Mother with Failure to Protect Her Child an Acceptable Solution When Her Child Witnesses Domestic Violence?, 69 Fordham L. Rev. 1487 (2001).

22. Nicholson et al. v. Scopetta, 820 N.E.2d 840 (N.Y. 2004).

23. Melissa Mitgang, Childhood Obesity and State Intervention: An Examination of the Health Risks of Pediatric Obesity and When They Justify State Involvement, 44 Colum. J.L. & Soc. Probs. 553, 555 (2011).

24. In re Brittany T., 15 Misc. 3d 606, 835 N.Y.S.2d 820, 840 (2007).

25. *Id.* at 840-841.

26. National Organization for Rare Diseases, https://rarediseases.org/medical-child-abuse/ (accessed Mar. 30, 2019). The actual inducement of illness in children is known as Munchausen Syndrome by Proxy.

27. John Stirling, Jr. and the Committee on Child Abuse and Neglect, The American Academy of Pediatricians, 119 Pediatrics 1026, 1029 (2007). *See generally* Maxine Eichner, Bad Medicine: Parents, the State, and the Charge of "Medical Abuse," 50 U.C. Davis L. Rev. 205 (2016).

28. Complicating the picture, a number of scientific studies now suggest that other factors, such as poverty, may be to blame for the results previously assumed to be caused by a pregnant woman's cocaine use. *See* Lynn M. Paltrow, Governmental Response to Pregnant Women Who Use Alcohol or Other Drugs, 8 DePaul J. Health Care L. 461 (2005). *See also* Ian Vanderwalker, Taking the Baby Before It's Born: Termination of the Parental Rights of Women Who Use Illegal Drugs While Pregnant, 32 N.Y.U. Rev. L. & Soc. Change 423 (2008);

Dorothy E. Roberts, Punishing Drug Addicts Who Have Babies: Women of Color, Equality, and the Right of Privacy, 104 Harv. L. Rev. 1419 (1991).

29. In some states, prenatal drug exposure may also expose a woman to criminal prosecution on a number of grounds, including child endangerment, manslaughter, and the delivery of illegal substances—in this case through the umbilical cord.

30. Paltrow, *supra* note 28, at 465.

31. Guttmacher Institute, State Policies in Brief: Substance Abuse During Pregnancy, 2010 (accessed Feb. 6, 2010).

32. Pub. L. No. 96-272, 94 Stat. 500 (codified in scattered sections of 42 U.S.C.).

33. Dorothy E. Roberts, Is There Justice in Children's Rights? The Critique of Federal Family Preservation Policy, 2 U. Pa. J. Const. L. 112, 113 (1999).

34. Catherine J. Ross, The Tyranny of Time: Vulnerable Children, "Bad" Mothers, and Statutory Deadlines in Parental Termination Proceedings, 11 Va. J. Soc. Poly. & L. 176, 195-196 (2004). *See also* Will L. Crossley, Defining Reasonable Efforts: Demystifying the State's Burden Under Federal Child Protection Legislation, 12 B.U. Pub. Int. L.J. 259, 274 (2003).

35. Ross, *supra* note 34, at 195-196.

36. Pub. L. No. 105-89, 111 Stat. 2115 (1997) (codified in scattered sections of 42 U.S.C.).

37. A possible alternative approach may be to establish a permanent placement with a guardian relative. For detail, *see* William Vesneski et al., An Analysis of State Law and Policy Regarding Subsidized Guardianship for Children: Innovations in Permanency, 21 U.C. Davis J. Juv. L. & Poly. (2017).

38. Much has been written about these Acts in terms of their requirements and the different philosophies that they embody. In addition to the Roberts article cited *supra* note 33, the Ross article cited *supra* note 34, and the Crossley article cited *supra* note 34, *see* Jean C. Lawrence, A Critical Look at Child Protection: ASFA in the Age of Mass Incarceration: Go to Prison—Lose Your Child?, 40 Wm. Mitchell L. Rev. 990 (2014); Kendra Huard Fershee, The Parent Trap: The Unconstitutional Practice of Severing Parental Rights Without Due Process of Law, 30 Ga. St. U. L. Rev. 639 (2014); Kathleen S. Bean, Reasonable Efforts: What State Courts Think, 36 U. Tol. L. Rev. 321 (2005); Libby S. Adler, The Meaning of Permanence: A Critical Analysis of the Adoption and Safe Families Act of 1997, 38 Harv. J. on Legis. 1 (2001); Stephanie Jill Gendell, In Search of Permanency: A Reflection on the First 3 Years of the Adoption and Safe Families Act Implementation, 39 Fam. Ct. Rev. 25 (2001).

39. *See* 42 U.S.C.A. §671(a)(15)(D).

40. Reinforcing ASFA's focus on expedition, a state is also required to initiate (or join) proceedings to terminate parental rights if a child has been in foster care for 15 of the previous 22 months unless the child is being cared for by a relative; initiation proceedings would not be in the child's best interest; or where the state has failed to provide services that would have enabled the child to return home safely.

41. ASFA includes other options as well, but reunification and adoption are the primary dispositional choices. *See* Adler, *supra* note 38, at 9-10.

42. Adler, *supra* note 38, at 10.

43. *See* Philip M. Gentry, Moving Beyond Generalizations and Stereotypes to Develop Individualized Approaches for Working with Families Affected by Parental Incarceration, 50 Fam. Ct. Rev. 36, (2012); Deseriee A. Kennedy, Children, Parents, and the State: The Construction of a New Family Ideology, 26 Berkeley J. Gender L. & Just. 78 (2011).

44. Regarding the status of incarcerated parents under ASFA, *see generally* Lawrence, *supra* note 38.

45. Roberts, *supra* note 33, at 117.

46. Auspitz, *supra* note 14.

47. Martin Guggenheim, The Effects of Recent Trends to Accelerate the Termination of Parental Rights in Foster Care—An Empirical Analysis in Two States, 29 Fam. L.Q. 121 (1995).

48. Meredith L. Schalick, The Sky Is Not Falling: Lessons and Recommendations from Ten Years of Reinstating Parental Rights, 51 Fam. L.Q. 219, 228-229 (2017). *See also* LaShanda Taylor Adams, Backward Progress Toward Reinstating Parental Rights, 41 N.Y.U. Rev. L. & Soc. Change 507 (2017).

49. Bureau of Indian Affairs, Guideline for State Courts and Agencies in Indian Child Custody Proceedings, 80 Fed. Reg. 10146, 10147 (2015), quoting H. Rep. 95-1978 at 9.

50. 25 U.S.C. 1901(4) and (5) (1988).

51. Kelsey Vujnich, A Brief Overview of the Indian Child Welfare Act, State Court Responses, and Actions Taken in the Past Decade to Improve Implementation Outcomes, 26 J. Am. Acad. Matrimonial Law 183, 187 (2013).

52. *Id.*

53. The ICWA does not apply to disputes between parents.

54. FAC, National Indian Child Welfare Association, http://www.nicwa.org/Indian_Child_Welfare_Act/faq (accessed Jan. 5, 2016).

55. 25 U.S.C. §1911(a) & (b).

56. 25 U.S.C. §1915(a) and (b). *See* subsection (b) for other applicable considerations in pre-adoption and foster care placements. For further detail on ICWA, *see* http://www.tribal-institute.org/lists/icwa.htm (accessed Jan. 5, 2016).

Chapter Thirteen

Adoption

Adoption allows for the creation of family relationships along nonbiological lines. Through adoption, the legal bond between a child and his or her birth parents is terminated, and a new relationship is established between the child and the adoptive parent(s). In effect, the legal bond substitutes for the biological connection as the child is enfolded into a new family. (For exceptions to this general rule regarding termination of the biological parent's rights, see the discussion later in this chapter on stepparent and co-parent adoptions.) After a brief historical overview, we examine the two major methods of adoption—agency adoption and independent or private placement adoption—and consider the adoption process. We then look at some of the issues that can arise in particular contexts, such as when a stepparent or a same-sex couple wishes to adopt a baby. (Please note that this chapter does not address the issue of international adoption, and you should be aware that other policy and legal considerations come into play when the adoption process crosses national borders.[1]) Finally, we consider what happens when adoptive parents are unhappy with the child they have adopted and wish to abrogate or undo the adoption. Note that the terms "adoptive parents" and "adoptive parent" are used interchangeably, since both single persons and couples can adopt.

Historical Overview

In ancient Rome, adoptions were for the benefit of the adopting family rather than the adopted child. A family approaching the end of its bloodline might adopt a male child or adult who could perform the sacred rites of ancestor worship as well as save the family from extinction. Or, as with

Julius Caesar, who adopted his nephew, adoption could be used for political ends by enabling rulers to handpick their successors. With the emergence of Christianity, adoption fell into disrepute due to its association with pagan religious practices and its utilitarian nature.[2]

Unlike many other Roman legal practices, adoption did not find its way into English common law. Beyond being associated with paganism, adoption was regarded as incompatible with the English emphasis on blood lineage in establishing family ties and ensuring the orderly succession of property. Many English children, however, spent portions of their childhood living with families other than their family of origin. Most lived as servants or apprentices, although some lived more as members of the host family.[3]

As in England, the children of many American colonists were sent to live with other families, most commonly as servants or apprentices. Apprenticeships were formal arrangements by which a child was indentured to a person who was supposed to teach the child a trade and provide him or her with a place to live in exchange for the child's labor. This person stood *in loco parentis* and assumed the rights and responsibilities of a parent for the duration of the apprenticeship. These arrangements were found in all social classes, with children from middle and upper classes being indentured to persons from similar backgrounds in which they could "complete their social and professional training . . . while multiplying their connections and possibilities for advancement."[4] However, for the poor, these arrangements were born more from necessity and represented less of an opportunity for advancement; moreover, indenture was frequently imposed by officials in order to reduce the cost to towns of caring for the poor. By the end of the eighteenth century, middle- and upper-class parents no longer indentured their children; however, indenture continued to be a reality for many poor children, including those who were placed in orphanages, which often placed out children in their care.[5] Additionally, children often joined families through less formal arrangements, such as where they were taken in by a friend or relative following the death of one or both parents.

Thus, in the early part of our nation's history, it was not uncommon for children to spend part, or even most, of their youth living apart from their family of origin. Historians generally believe that the widespread acceptance of this practice, particularly that of apprenticeship, helped pave the way for the more modern practice of adoption.[6]

Adoption was accepted earlier in this country than in England perhaps because there was less historical emphasis on blood lineage, class distinction, and the orderly succession of property. In 1851, Massachusetts passed the nation's first general adoption statute. It quickly became a model, and similar laws were enacted in a majority of states. Although a break with centuries of tradition, these statutes were passed with little fanfare. Scholars speculate that the lack of fanfare reflects the fact that these laws simply formalized the existing practice of incorporating nonbiological children into a household.

The Massachusetts law, which framed the modern approach, placed adoption under judicial control and made clear that adoption was intended to benefit the child in need of a home rather than the parents in search of an heir. Under the law, each prospective adoptive family was to be scrutinized to ensure they were "of sufficient ability to bring up the child . . . and that it is fit and proper that such adoption should take effect." Upon approval by the court, the child would "to all intents and purposes" become the legal child of the adoptive parents, and the bond with the natural parents would be forever severed.[7]

These newly enacted adoption laws were prompted by a number of considerations. First, the laws were passed to ensure that children living in de facto adoptive relationships would be able to receive a share of the parental estate if the parents died intestate. Second, related to child welfare reforms, these statutes responded to a growing criticism of the common practice of placing poor and orphaned children in institutions and perhaps indenturing them. Corresponding to the emphasis on domestic nurture, placement in homes became the preferred alternative for children not in the care of their parents. Moreover, with the development of a market economy, apprenticeship as a form of employment relationship was becoming obsolete. Accordingly, adoption represented a way for a child to become part of a new family as a member rather than as a quasi-servant.[8]

Although placement in a family was generally a humane alternative to institutionalization, many children were initially "put out" by their parents because of desperate poverty or taken from them because the family did not conform to the emerging middle-class view of the proper family. Moreover, families sometimes lost control of the process, and what was initially intended as a temporary arrangement would evolve into a permanent separation.

Approaches to Adoption

Adoption usually takes place in one of two ways. It can be accomplished either by an agency (**agency adoption**) or by the parents themselves acting with or without the assistance of a third-party intermediary (**independent** or **private placement adoption**). Agency adoptions are permitted in all states; however, due to some of the concerns discussed later in this chapter, a few states prohibit nonagency adoptions except where a stepparent or a close relative is the adopting parent. Before looking at the adoption process, this section begins with a brief overview of these two approaches and also takes a brief look at "safe haven" laws, which are intended to address the problem of infant abandonment.

Agency Adoptions

In an agency adoption, a state-licensed agency arranges the adoption and oversees the process. The precise contours of an agency's responsibilities are determined by the applicable state statutes, regulations, and licensing laws. An adoption agency can be either public, in that it is part of the state's child protective system, or private. In either instance, an agency can obtain custody of a child for purposes of adoption in one of two ways. First, an agency may obtain custody where a child has been freed for adoption following the involuntary termination of parental rights (see Chapter 12). Second, parents who wish to give up a child for adoption can surrender their child to an agency. Before accepting a **voluntary surrender**, an agency will usually provide the parents with counseling to help them understand their options and make sure their decision is fully informed. A range of other services, such as legal referrals and financial assistance for basic legal and medical services, may also be available. The agency is then responsible for finding a suitable adoptive home for the child.

Before placing a child with prospective adoptive parents, the agency will conduct a home study to determine the appropriateness of the placement. Once a placement has been made, the agency maintains some degree of supervisory responsibility to ensure the placement meets the needs of the child. State rules often require an agency to make a certain number of home visits at specified intervals and to take remedial action, including removal, if the child is not adjusting well. In some states, the agency remains legally responsible for the child until the adoption is finalized.

Independent Adoptions

In contrast, in an independent adoption (also known as private or direct placement adoptions), a child is placed directly with the adoptive parents without a prior surrender to a licensed adoption agency. Most involve healthy, white newborns who are placed with the adoptive parents immediately after birth. Accordingly, adoption arrangements are usually made during pregnancy, often after an extensive search for an adoptable baby. If state law permits, searching parents may well launch a public campaign, which can include advertising in the classified section of a local paper, to help them locate a potential birth mother and demonstrate their qualifications as parents.

Some prospective adoptive parents hire an intermediary, who is often an attorney, to help them to find a child and arrange the placement. Where this is the case, the child may initially be transferred to this third party; however, unlike in an agency adoption, this is not a formal surrender—rather, the intermediary is simply serving as a conduit between the birth and the adoptive parents.

Unlike with agency adoptions, the birth parents are not usually provided with counseling prior to the relinquishment of the baby, and the prospective adoptive parents are not required to undergo a preplacement home study, although some states now require adoptive parents to be certified before they can accept a child into their home. In further contrast, once a baby is placed, the placement is not usually supervised, although a postplacement home study must be done before a court can approve the adoption. (Most adoptions must be approved by a court.)

Although, as discussed below, birth parents must consent to the adoption, a number of concerns have been raised about the potential for exploitation that exists when adoptions occur without the involvement of a state-licensed agency, and a few states expressly prohibit independent adoptions. Other states have instead opted for increased control of the process, particularly with respect to the often closely related role of intermediaries and the payment of the birth mother's expenses.

With regard to intermediaries, a primary concern is that because they stand to gain financially from facilitating adoptions, they may resort to unscrupulous means to help prospective parents procure adoptable children. In response, many states have enacted laws imposing restrictions on intermediaries, such as by limiting the fees they can charge and requiring a strict accounting to the court. A few states have gone further and prohibit the use of intermediaries altogether or only permit licensed adoption agencies to function in this capacity.

Applicable to both intermediaries and prospective adoptive parents, a potentially worrisome means of attempting to persuade a pregnant woman to relinquish her child is through the promise of generous payments to cover all of her needs in exchange for a commitment to give up her child—an inducement that can be particularly coercive in certain situations such as, for example, where a young teen has been kicked out of her home and is facing living on the streets or in a shelter. Intended to draw a clear line between baby-selling, which is illegal in all states, and adoption, most states accordingly limit the kinds of payments that may be offered to a birth mother by the prospective adoptive parents in order to help ensure that her choice is not distorted by her economic circumstances. Thus, for example, although most states allow the prospective adoptive parents to pay some of the birth mother's living expenses, the trend is to place limits on these expenditures, by, for example, specifically delineating what can be included, and/or by setting a dollar cap on the expenditures, or imposing a durational restriction that is usually linked to a specific time period prior to delivery.[9]

Safe Haven Laws

In response to several highly publicized cases involving newborn babies who had been abandoned in dumpsters, garbage cans, and toilets, starting with Texas in 1999, most states have enacted what are known as "**safe haven**" laws (sometimes referred to as "Baby Moses laws"), which permit birth parents, or in some states only the birth mother, to leave a baby at a designated safe location, such as a hospital or fire station, as an alternative to abandonment. Some states also permit a party acting with the express consent of the birth parent(s) to surrender the child at the safe haven. Intended for the purpose of preventing the abandonment of newborns, as distinct from infants or older children from being dropped off at safe haven locations, all laws contain an express limit on how much time can elapse between birth and the surrender of the child. Limits usually range from 72 hours to 30 days, although a few states provide for a period of up to a year.

In this regard, it should be noted that the Nebraska law, which was originally drafted without an age limit, came under considerable scrutiny and criticism when parents began dropping off children and teenagers to safe haven locations claiming that they could no longer care for them. Needless to say, the law was quickly amended, but as one commentator noted, this tragic occurrence "cast a spotlight on the hidden extent of family turmoil in the country and what many experts say is a shortage of respite care, counseling, and especially psychiatric services to help parents in dire need."[10]

Several common statutory features are designed to encourage parents to surrender their babies to a designated safe haven location rather than abandoning them. First, they are all structured to protect parental anonymity, and permit a parent to surrender a child without having to provide any identifying information. Some laws, however, do require that inquiry be made of the baby's medical and family history, but the parent is not required to provide this information. Second, a majority of states offer parents who *safely* relinquish a child immunity from prosecution for child abandonment or neglect. In other states, however, the protection is not as comprehensive, and the statute simply gives parents the right to raise safe relinquishment in accordance with the law as an affirmative defense to criminal charges. However, these protections may be forfeited if there is evidence that the child was abused or neglected.

Following relinquishment, the safe haven provider turns the infant over to the appropriate child protective agency. In some states, a parent is given a brief window of opportunity within which to change his or her mind and reclaim the child. The agency is then responsible for making an adoption plan for the child. A potentially complicating factor is that it is not always clear what steps must be taken by the agency in order to terminate the rights of the parents—the safe haven law may have specialized provisions, or it might reference the applicable provisions of the child protection law—and a number of cases have arisen over whether the agency had done enough to provide notice to the birth parents regarding the termination of their rights. This is most likely to be an issue with regard to the father, who may not have participated in or known about the decision to relinquish the baby, as it is usually the mother who avails herself of the safe haven option.[11] To address this situation, a few states require the protective agency to check the putative father registry prior to the filing of a petition to terminate parental rights. (See the discussion regarding the rights of unmarried fathers in the section entitled "Unwed Fathers," later in this chapter.)

■ The Adoption Process

In this section, we will look at the stages of the adoption process. In the following section, we consider particular issues or exceptions to general principles that may arise in specific circumstances, such as where a same-sex couple wishes to adopt a child or the birth parents are unwed.

Adoption Based on Parental Consent or Relinquishment

Unless the rights of parents have been involuntarily terminated, an adoption cannot proceed without their consent. (See, however, the discussion below regarding unwed fathers.) In some states, the consent of the child also becomes necessary once he or she reaches a certain age, which is generally set somewhere between age 10 and 14. Although this section generally speaks in terms of the birth parents, it is important to recognize that the parents may not be participating in the adoption as a unit and that each may play a different role in the process.

Parental Consent to a Private Placement Adoption

Parental **consent** is an essential requirement in a private placement adoption. To be valid, consent must be fully informed and free from duress, fraud, or undue influence, and given in a manner that conforms with all applicable state regulations, such as that it be in writing and signed before a public official.

In some situations, it can be difficult to determine if the consent was truly voluntary. For example, a young birth mother who is under pressure from her parents and friends to give up the child may be ambivalent but feel as if she has no choice but to give up her baby to a married couple who appears to be in a better position to raise the child. Although there may not be undue influence or duress in a strictly legal sense, under some circumstances, it may not be able to characterize a decision to give up a child as a purely voluntary one.

In most states, a mother's pre-birth consent is not binding, and a legally valid consent cannot be obtained until sometime after the birth of the child; a typical waiting period is 48 or 72 hours after birth. This rule recognizes the impact of giving birth and the fact that it may be impossible to fully comprehend the import of a decision to give up a child until the child is actually born. Interestingly, in many states, a father's pre-birth consent is binding. This differential treatment reflects both conventional views about fathers as less impacted by the birth process and thus less likely to regret a prior decision to give up a child, as well as the practical concern that a father might not be around to give consent at the time of birth.

By itself, the consent does not actually terminate the rights of the birth parents or transfer them to the adoptive parents. In effect, by executing a consent, the birth parents are authorizing the court to proceed with the adoption.[12]

Relinquishment to an Agency

In an agency adoption, the operative legal act is the **relinquishment** of the child to the agency, rather than the giving of consent to the adoption itself. By relinquishing their child, parents are effectively transferring their right to consent to the adoption to the agency. In many states, the act of relinquishment automatically terminates the rights of the birth parents. In other states, this result is not automatic, but relinquishment enables an agency to seek an immediate court order terminating parental rights. (Note: Keep in mind that these adoptions begin with a voluntary act and are thus different from adoptions that result from an involuntary termination of parental rights—these adoptions are discussed below.)

What If a Parent Changes His or Her Mind?

What happens if, after either consenting to an adoption or relinquishing a child to an agency, a parent changes his or her mind about going forward with the adoption? Although this occurs only in a small number of cases, it can result in bitter litigation that pits the birth parents against the prospective adoptive parents.

Private Placement Adoptions.   Most states allow parents to revoke their consent within a specified time period, such as up until the time the adoption is approved by the court. Thereafter, consent is deemed irrevocable. In some jurisdictions, however, irrevocability is limited to validly obtained consents. This leaves open the possibility that even after the adoption has been finalized, a birth parent could seek to revoke his or her consent by establishing that it was improperly obtained.

In most states, the **revocation of consent** (including those within the applicable time period) requires court approval. The standards for determining whether to allow a revocation vary widely from state to state. Some states are fairly tolerant of parental changes of heart, and judges have considerable discretion. In other states, judges can approve revocations based only on specific statutory factors, which typically address the validity of the consent and do not allow for changes of heart that are not bound up with considerations of duress and the like. In these states, a birth mother who experiences profound regret about her decision would not be permitted to revoke her consent even if requested within the statutory time frame. But a young birth mother who could establish that the prospective adoptive parents in concert with her own parents repeatedly pressured her to give up the child might be allowed to revoke her consent.

Where a parent seeks to revoke his or her consent, the prospective adoptive parents may respond by asking the court to **dispense with the parental consent requirement**. In effect, the adoptive parents are asking the court to terminate the parental rights of the birth parents so the adoption can proceed without their consent. In evaluating this request, the court may treat the consent as evidence of an intent to abandon the child and count it against the biological parents in evaluating their fitness. Thus, what began as a voluntary process may result in litigation and a possible involuntary termination of parental rights. (See the discussion below for greater detail on involuntary termination.)

Agency Adoptions.   Most states are stricter about revocations where a relinquishment has been made to an agency, and in many states the relinquishment becomes irrevocable once the child has been placed with the prospective adoptive parents for a specified period of time. This stricter standard reflects the fact that greater safeguards, such as pre-relinquishment counseling for the birth parents, are built into the agency process.

Adoption Based on the Involuntary Termination of Parental Rights

If the rights of parents have been involuntarily terminated because of abuse or neglect, an adoption can proceed without their consent because the termination frees the child for adoption. Following termination, custody is generally transferred to the state or, more specifically, to a public adoption agency, which must then try to find an appropriate adoptive home for the child.

If the rights of both parents have been terminated, the placement is virtually risk-free because they have been divested of any say in the matter.[13] If, however, the rights of both parents have not been terminated, such as where one parent has vanished, the agency may not be able to proceed with the adoption until that parent's status is resolved. However, if allowed by state law, an agency may choose to make an **at-risk placement**. These placements are subject to the risk of disruption if a parent whose rights have not been terminated subsequently seeks to assert his or her right to the child.

Many children who are available for adoption following the termination of parental rights have been in the protective services system for considerable periods of time. Few are infants, and many have experienced severe abuse or neglect and have lived in a variety of foster homes and institutional settings.[14] Although desperate for homes, these children are often passed over in favor of infants who are generally more available through the independent or private agency adoption route.

In most states, parental rights can also be terminated within the context of the adoption proceeding itself. Unlike a separate termination proceeding, which is almost always initiated by the state, here the request, generally referred to as "a request to dispense with parental consent," is usually initiated by a private party. These requests are made under a variety of circumstances. For example, a child may be living with relatives who then decide they want to adopt him or her, but the parents are opposed. The relatives would file an adoption petition and ask the court to dispense with the need for parental consent. Or an unmarried mother who places her newborn with prospective adoptive parents might seek to have the court dispense with the father's right of consent. Similarly, if a child was relinquished to an agency by one birth parent, the agency might seek to dispense with the consent of the other parent. In order to prevail, it must be shown that the parent is unfit; otherwise, his or her consent is legally required.

The Adoption Placement

Before an adoption can be finalized, a child must live with the prospective parents in a **pre-adoption placement**; however, many states exempt close relative, stepparent, and co-parent adoptions from this requirement. The pre-adoption placement requirement applies to both agency and independent adoptions; however, as discussed below, important differences exist in the placement process.

The Home Study

Perhaps the most significant distinction in the placement process between agency and independent adoptions is the **home study**. Home studies, which are intended to weed out potentially unsuitable parents, are generally not required in independent adoptions, whereas an agency cannot place a child until a home study has been completed. During the home study, prospective parents are usually asked about the following:

- religious beliefs and practices;
- approaches to child rearing and discipline;
- child-rearing skills;
- the nature of relationships with extended family members;
- history of prior intimate relationships;
- career plans and how the child will be cared for;
- ability to provide for the child financially;
- history of criminal convictions; and
- emotional stability and maturity.

Most adoption professionals regard the home study as essential to protect the well-being of adoptive children. While recognizing its potential intrusiveness, it is widely believed that in the absence of a biological connection from which affective bonds are thought to naturally flow, prospective parents must be evaluated to determine their capacity for developing a loving relationship with an adoptive child.

However, the home study process has also been subject to two major criticisms: first, that the process often serves as a thinly disguised effort to rank prospective parents based on how closely they conform to an idealized vision of the perfect family. Through the use of highly subjective evaluative criteria, "nonconforming" adults, including single parents, same-sex couples, and low-income parents, are placed at the bottom of waiting lists or are offered only children no one else wishes to adopt.[15]

The other major criticism is that the process exemplifies the cultural bias that exists against adoptive families, as individuals who choose to become parents through biological reproduction are not subject to an evaluative process. As stated by Professor Elizabeth Bartholet, a leading proponent of this view and an adoptive parent herself:

> [T]hose seeking to retain the sense that they are normal rights-bearing citizens. No one asks them to prove that they are fit to parent. They are perceived as having a God-given right to reproduce if they are capable of doing so. . . .
>
> [R]egulation also sends a powerful message about the essential inferiority of adoption as a form of parenting. By subjecting adoptive but not biologic parents to regulation, society suggests that it trusts what goes on when people give birth and raise a child but profoundly distrusts what goes on when a child is transferred from a birth to an adoptive parent. The specific nature of adoption regulation constantly reinforces the notion that biologic parenting is the ideal, adoption a poor second best.[16]

Configuration of Relationships During the Placement

Private Placement Adoptions.   As noted above, in these adoptions, parental rights are usually not terminated until the adoption is approved by the court. This makes these placements somewhat riskier than agency placements because the possibility exists that a biological parent will change his or her mind and seek the return of the child. As discussed earlier, states vary in their approach to postplacement revocations—some are very strict, while others are more flexible and may permit a change of mind unless harm to the child can be shown.

Because the rights of the biological parents are not terminated until the adoption is approved, the authority of the prospective adoptive parents to make decisions on behalf of the child during the placement needs to be established. This is usually done through a voluntary transfer of temporary custody from the birth parents to the adoptive parents.

Agency Adoptions.   Unless it is an at-risk placement, the rights of both parents will have been terminated by the time the placement is made; accordingly, the agency usually has legal custody of the child, although it may delegate some decision-making authority to the prospective parents. As the repository of legal authority, the agency retains supervisory control over the placement, and a social worker will make periodic visits to evaluate how the placement is working out. The agency has the right to remove the child if it determines that the placement is not in the child's best interest. Most states place some limits on the authority of an agency to revoke a placement, and aggrieved adoptive parents may have a form of redress, such as the right to an administrative hearing.

The Social Study

Although preplacement home studies are characteristic of agency adoptions, a **postplacement social study** must be completed in both private placement and agency adoptions before an adoption can be finalized, although the requirement may be waived in certain situations, such as where a close relative or a stepparent is the adopting parent. These studies are intended to provide the judge with information to help him or her decide whether or not to approve the adoption. In some states, the evaluator must also make a specific recommendation in favor of or against the adoption. Although important, these studies tend to be less comprehensive than the initial preplacement home study.

The Adoption

Judicial Review and Approval

All adoptions must be approved by a judge, and proper notice of the proceeding must be given to all persons with an interest in the child, including, for example, foster parents, pre-adoptive parents, and relatives who have been caring for the child.[17] To protect the validity of the adoption, it is critical that notice rules be carefully followed.

The rights of the parents must be terminated before the adoption can be approved. As has been discussed elsewhere in this chapter, parental rights may already have been terminated in a separate proceeding, such as where the child has been in foster care, or termination may occur as part of the adoption proceeding itself. In a private placement adoption, termination is usually a formality, as the court is simply being asked to approve what the parties have agreed to; however, when a party is requesting that the court dispense with the parental consent requirement, the termination phase of the hearing may well be contested.

Once parental rights are terminated, the court determines whether the adoption is in the best interest of the child. If approved, the court may also at the same time approve an **open adoption** agreement, allowing for postadoption contact between the birth parents, the child, and the adoptive parents (see below). If the court concludes the adoption is not in the child's best interest, it is not approved. If it is an agency adoption, the underlying relinquishment remains in effect, and the agency can attempt a subsequent placement. However, in a private placement adoption, parents usually consent to an adoption by a specific person or couple, and if the adoption fails, the consent is nontransferable. This is a difficult situation, as the prospective adoptive parents lose the child they were hoping to adopt, and the birth parents may find themselves with custody of a child they were planning to relinquish.

The final decree of adoption is the last step in the process. However, under limited circumstances the decree may be challenged based upon, for example, fraud, misrepresentation, or the failure to provide an interested party with notice of the adoption proceeding (see the section below entitled "Unwed Fathers"). The standards and procedural rules vary greatly from state to state, but as a general rule, the requirements for setting aside a final decree are quite strict, as most jurisdictions "have generally decided that the need for stability during a child's developmental years outweighs parental rights."[18]

■ Lifting the Shroud of Secrecy: Post-Adoption Contact and Access to Records

Once the adoption is approved (subject to any rights of appeal or post-judgment challenges), a child's legal ties with his or her family of origin are severed, and the child is now legally incorporated into a new family. Completing this transformation, the records of the proceeding are sealed along with the original birth certificate, and a new birth certificate is issued, naming the adoptive parents as the child's parents. The sealing of the records and the issuance of the new birth certificate exemplify the secrecy in which adoptions have typically been shrouded. As a rule, no information was shared either before or after an adoption, and adoptive parents were counseled not to disclose the fact of adoption to the child. This secrecy was thought necessary to protect the interests of all participants; birth mothers would be protected from the taint of immorality or shame, adopted children could grow up with unquestioned ties to their adoptive parents, and adoptive parents would not be threatened with the lurking presence of a child's "true parents."[19]

However, this began to change in the 1960s in large part because secrecy was no longer thought to be in an adoptive child's best interest: "Social scientists accumulated evidence that attempts by adoptive parents to supplant the biological parents by pretending that the child had no biological ancestry could be damaging to the child's orderly, normal development as well as to the adoption family's stability."[20] Supporting these findings, adult adoptees began to speak out about how damaging and confusing the silence about their origins had been and of their deep longing to know of their past. Other considerations, such as the lessening of the stigma of unwed motherhood, also contributed to a lifting of the shroud of secrecy, and today, many states facilitate open adoption and increased access to adoption records.

Open Adoption

The central feature of an open adoption is that it anticipates some degree of continued contact between the birth parents and the adopted child, despite the severance of their legal bond. Open adoptions are generally associated with private placement adoptions and those in which parents voluntarily relinquish a child to an agency; however, in some states, an open adoption may be an option even if the rights of a parent have been involuntarily terminated, if continued contact is determined to be in the best interest of the child.[21]

Open adoption offers a wide range of post-adoption contact arrangements. For example, contact might simply consist of a yearly exchange of letters and photographs with no direct interaction between the child and his or her birth parents. On the other hand, it might consist of regular telephone calls or even regular visits. Where visits are involved, they are often arranged through an intermediary so there is no direct contact between the birth parents and the adoptive parents.

Historically, most state laws were silent on the issue of post-adoption contact between the birth parents and the adopted child. Accordingly, if the birth parents and the adoptive parents entered into an agreement giving the birth parents rights of contact with the child, the contract would not have been judicially enforceable. However, a growing number of states have adopted open adoption laws that permit birth parents and adoptive parents to enter into judicially enforceable agreements regarding post-adoption contact, if such contact is deemed to be in the best interest of the child. Some states further extend this right to other birth relatives; however, they may impose a threshold showing before a contact agreement will be enforceable, such as that the relative had enjoyed a substantial relationship with the child prior to the adoption. In addition to laws recognizing the validity of contracts for post-adoption contracts, in some cases, judges are authorized to order post-adoption visits even where not expressly agreed to by the adoptive parents.

In some states, the option of post-adoption contact is not available to parents whose rights were involuntarily terminated.

Although increasingly common and accepted, open adoption remains controversial. Proponents firmly believe that children will feel a greater sense of security and wholeness if they are permitted to retain a connection with their birth parents and that this will obviate the sense of longing and loss that some adopted children experience. But others believe that this continued contact will interfere with the ability of children to fully integrate into their new families; as a result, they may feel caught between two worlds and never wholly part of either. Accordingly, it is argued that children do best if they have a clean break with their family of origin.[22]

Access to Adoption Records

Beginning in the 1970s, adult adoptees began to call for the opening of sealed birth adoption records, both so that they could fill in the missing pieces of their past and possibly also search for their birth parents. Asserting a right to know about their past, adult adoptees brought several class action suits challenging the constitutionality of state laws requiring the sealing of adoption records. They argued that these laws violated their right to privacy, including a right to know one's identity, and their right to equal protection of the law by conditioning access to birth information upon one's adoptive status. Courts weighed these claims against the interests of the other parties in the "adoption triangle"—namely, the privacy rights of birth parents and the interest of adoptive parents in safeguarding the integrity of their newly constituted families—and generally concluded that the sealed record laws served valid state interests.

Thereafter, reform efforts shifted to the legislative arena, with considerably more success. Today, almost all states allow the release of nonidentifying information about the birth parents to both adopted children and adoptive parents. Typically, a child who has been adopted cannot access this information directly until she or he is 18. Depending on the state, nonidentifying information may include medical information; information about the birth parents, such as their age, race, and religion; and information about the birth and the adoption process.

The pattern is considerably more complex when it comes to information that "may lead to the positive identification of birth parents, the adoptee, or other birth relatives," such as "current or past names of the person, addresses, employment, or other similar records or information."[23] Some of this information can usually be found in the adoption records, while at least some of it is typically contained in sealed birth records.

States differ in the ease with which they permit adoptees to access their adoption records. At one end of the spectrum, a handful of states allow children who have been adopted to access their birth records once they reach adulthood, without needing either the consent of the birth parents or proof of good cause or best interest. Most of these states give birth parents who do not want to be contacted the option of filing a "contact veto," and states providing this option also subject adoptees who violate the veto to civil or criminal penalties.[24] At the other end of the spectrum, many states do not allow individuals who have been adopted to access their birth records without a court order, which typically must be premised upon proof of good cause or that disclosure is in the adoptee's best interest. In the middle of the spectrum, many states have created various kinds of registry systems through which adult adoptees and birth parents (and sometimes birth siblings and adoptive parents) may be able to access identifying information. Some states use a "passive" registry system, which requires that both parties register their consent to the release of information before a match can be attempted. In other states, search efforts can be initiated based on the request of one party. If the other party is located and gives his or her consent, identifying information can be released to the person initiating the search.

Adoption in Specific Situations

The section above traced the general stages of the adoption process. However, given the myriad kinds of family arrangements, certain situations involve more specialized rules or raise unique issues. In this section, we consider some, although certainly not all, of these situations.

Stepparent Adoptions

Many of the adoptions that take place each year involve stepparents. Typically, this occurs when a divorced custodial parent remarries, and the couple wishes to establish a formal parent-child relationship between the new spouse and the children from the previous marriage. Most states have a "streamlined" procedure that allows a judge to waive the home study requirement; however, in some states, the adoption cannot be approved until the parties have been married for at least a year.

The custodial parent must consent to the adoption, as must the noncustodial parent. If the noncustodial parent refuses to consent, the adoption can proceed only if there are grounds for dispensing with his or her consent (as discussed previously). Some states have relaxed the requirements for the dispensing of consent in the stepparent adoption context by either statute or judicial decision. Thus, for example, the failure of a parent to maintain communication with his or her children, although not usually by itself considered unfitness, may be enough in the stepparent context to allow the adoption to proceed over the objection of the noncustodial parent.

As you are now aware, adoption typically severs the legal rights of the birth parents. Thus, in a "regular" adoption situation, the custodial parent, by consenting to the adoption, is agreeing to a termination of his or her legal status. However, given that the entire point of a stepparent adoption is to create a new parental unit consisting of the custodial parent and his or her new spouse, it would make no sense to apply the **"cutoff" rule** in this situation. In recognition of the absurdity of this potential outcome, most statutes include an explicit exception to the cutoff rule for stepparent adoptions, making it clear that the parental rights of the biological spouse continue in full force and effect following the adoption.

As far as the noncustodial parent is concerned, adoption by a stepparent does result in the termination of that parent's rights. However, questions have been raised as to whether severing all ties with this parent makes sense in every situation, and courts appear increasingly willing to grant post-adoption rights to the noncustodial parent even though legal parenthood now resides in the adopting parent. These rights can range from a yearly exchange of letters and photographs to regularly scheduled visitation.

In support of this open adoption model, many experts believe that it is important for a child's sense of well-being to provide the child with a continued connection to a parent with whom he or she previously enjoyed a relationship, and that severing this relationship cuts the child off from a vital sense of continuity with the past. In contrast, other experts fear that this more flexible, open arrangement will jeopardize the ability of the new family to develop a coherent identity and will subject the child to competing loyalty claims and uncertainty about the stability of the family.

Adoption by Gay Men and Lesbians

As discussed in earlier chapters, over the past few decades, gay men and lesbians have struggled to secure legal recognition of their family relationships, including the right to become parents through adoption, both as individuals and as couples. Today, formal statutory bans on adoptions by same-sex individuals or couples are essentially a relic of the past. Moreover, it is also anticipated that with marriage equality now the law of the land, the historic bias that many adoption agencies have shown toward gay men and lesbians seeking to adopt will continue to weaken as the culture becomes increasingly accepting of same-sex households. However, a push in the opposite direction should be noted: As of October 2018, ten states had enacted a law allowing publicly funded adoption and foster care agencies to refuse to place children with gay men and lesbians based upon religious objections to their sexual orientation. These laws also permit placement refusals based upon objections to "nonconforming" gender identity.[25]

Single-Parent and Joint Adoptions

All states generally permit a single person to adopt. However, many agencies and birth parents prefer to place a child with a married couple, thus potentially making it more difficult for any unmarried individual— straight or gay—to adopt.

In a joint adoption, a couple, whether same-sex or heterosexual, seeks to adopt a child who is not related to either party. Although all states allow unmarried individuals to adopt a child, many do not permit adoption by unmarried couples, regardless of sexual orientation, which means that only one partner can adopt a child. As a result, legal parenthood is vested in that partner, which can potentially leave the other partner out in the cold if the relationship ends and the adoptive parent seeks to limit or cut off contact with the child. It is possible that the partner could seek to establish that she or he is a de facto parent who is entitled to maintain an ongoing relationship with the child. However, as we saw in Chapter 11, the majority of states do not recognize de facto parenthood. Moreover, even where recognized, a party may not fit the strict criteria; for example, if the adult relationship developed after the child was adopted, the claim would most likely founder on the requirement that the couple had initially made a mutual decision to *have* and parent the child together. Of course, now that same-sex couples have the option of marrying in all states and can accordingly adopt as a couple, which operates to vest legal parenthood in both spouses, this has become a less pressing issue.

Co-Parent Adoption

Co-parent adoption, or as it is sometimes known, second-parent adoption, involves a situation where a couple is raising a child together, but only one is recognized as the child's legal parent (through birth or a prior adoption). Accordingly, the couple seeks to have the second parent (or co-parent) adopt the child so both partners are fully recognized as legal parents.

In seeking adoptive rights for co-parents, the stepparent adoption cases have been drawn on as analogous since, as with a stepparent, legal recognition is being sought for an established parent-child relationship that exists within the framework of a committed relationship with the child's legal parent. Recognizing this structural similarity, a number of courts have recently approved co-parent adoptions as being in a child's best interest. As explained by a New York court in one of the first cases to allow a second-parent adoption:

> It seems clear that the proposed adoption is in Evan's best interest. He is part of a family unit that has been functioning successfully. . . . The adoption would bring no change or trauma to his daily life; it would serve only to provide him with important legal rights which he does not presently possess. It would afford him additional economic security because Diane would become legally obligated to support him. . . . He would also be entitled to inherit from Diane and her family under the law of intestate succession and be eligible for Social Security benefits in the event of her disability or death. He would also be able to participate in the medical and educational benefits provided by her employment. . . .
>
> Even if, as anticipated, the petitioners remain together, there is a significant emotional benefit to Evan from adoption which is perhaps even more crucial than the financial.[26]

As with stepparent adoptions, in approving these adoptions, courts have agreed that it would be absurd to apply the cutoff provisions to terminate the rights of the legal parent. To avoid this result, courts have either read in a statutory exception based on the absurdity of the result or extended the stepparent exception to the cutoff rule by analogy.

It should also be noted that, as discussed in Chapter 11, in a post-*Obergefell* world, a married co-parent should be entitled to rely on the common law marital presumption or on the donor cutoff/parental intent provisions of a state parentage statute, thus obviating the need for a formalized adoption. However, given the ongoing uncertainty of the law, as we saw, experts in the field continue to advise married co-parents to take the second-parent adoption route in order to fully secure their relationships with the children they are parenting.[27]

Unwed Fathers

Historically, many jurisdictions permitted the adoption of a child born to unmarried parents based solely on the consent of the mother. Although the legal status of unwed fathers has improved, they do not have the same adoption consent rights as unmarried mothers. For women, consent rights vest automatically at the time of birth, whereas, as we saw in Chapter 11, under the "biology-plus" rule, men must take some steps to demonstrate their parental commitment to the child. This differential treatment reflects a number of considerations:

- First, because the mother is always present at birth, maternal identity is readily determined and a maternal consent requirement does not introduce delays into the process. In contrast, if the consent of the father were always required, many adoptions would be delayed until the father could be located and his paternity established.

- Second, the automatic vesting of rights in women may also reflect the asymmetrical involvement of men and women during pregnancy. Since only women are directly involved in the gestational process, social motherhood is seen as taking root during this time; at birth, the mother may be regarded as already having demonstrated a commitment to being a parent, thus making her consent essential. This difference may be less significant where the father is involved with the pregnancy; on the other hand, the difference may be even more pronounced where the pregnancy resulted from a casual sexual encounter. A related consideration is the generally operative assumption that the mother is most likely to be the one to care for the infant, thus giving her a more direct and immediate stake in the decision-making process.

- Third, this differential treatment is also rooted in the recognition that women may become pregnant in the context of an abusive relationship or as a result of rape and that exclusive consent rights may be necessary to protect her safety and ensure that paternal rights do not automatically spring forth from an act of coerced sexual intercourse.

Consideration

Do you think unwed fathers should have the same rights as unwed mothers where adoption is concerned?

Within these parameters, states have been sorting out, with inconsistent results, how to provide a meaningful role for unwed fathers in light of potentially competing maternal interests and the goal of providing children who are to be adopted with immediate homes. At the simplest level, all states now provide consent rights to unwed fathers who have taken steps to actualize a relationship with their children. Once the right to consent attaches, an adoption cannot proceed over the father's objection unless he is proved unfit; at this point, he is legally indistinguishable from either an unmarried mother or a married father. Note that even if an unwed father has not demonstrated enough of a parental commitment to become a consenting party, he may still be entitled to receive notice of the adoption hearing as an interested party. As an interested party, although he lacks authority to approve or veto the adoption, he most likely will be permitted to give testimony on the issue of whether the adoption is in the best interest of the child.

States take a variety of approaches with respect to what an unwed father must do to acquire consent rights. Over half of the states have established what are known as **putative father registries**, which enable men who are or believe they may be the father of a child to register with the state in order to protect their potential interest in the child. Registration must usually be accomplished within a statutorily prescribed time period following a child's birth; once registered, a man is entitled, at a minimum, to notice of any adoption proceeding involving the child. In some states, the failure to register cuts off the father's rights. Exceptions may be included, though (see Exhibit 13.1), for situations in which a man did not have a reasonable opportunity to comply with the statutory requirements, such as where the mother moved to another state before he knew she was pregnant, or where he did not know about the birth of the child under circumstances that do not suggest abandonment.[28]

Some states employ a more open-ended approach and look to see whether an unwed father has demonstrated a substantial commitment to developing a relationship with his child. Just what is meant by a substantial commitment, however, is far from clear. In some states, a minimal level of involvement seems to be enough, while in others, the father must demonstrate that he participates in his child's life in a consistent, meaningful manner.

When the child is a newborn, there is considerable divergence over what constitutes the demonstration of a substantial parenting commitment. Some states will evaluate the father's conduct during pregnancy to determine if he demonstrated a commitment to becoming a parent through the financial and emotional support of the mother. A lack of involvement during the pregnancy may deprive him of consent rights, while an active, involved role may serve as the basis for finding a demonstrated commitment to the assumption of parental responsibilities. In other jurisdictions, the father's conduct during pregnancy is less important, and the focus is more on his conduct immediately following the birth of the child and whether he acted in a timely manner to demonstrate his commitment to assuming the responsibilities of parenthood.

What happens if the father has not been able to take advantage of the **"opportunity interest"** in developing a relationship with his child either because the mother has prevented him from developing a relationship with the child or if he did not know about the pregnancy? If he somehow learns about the proposed adoption, will he be given the opportunity to consent or object to it going forward?

Most courts have permitted a father to participate in the adoption proceeding in the absence of an established relationship with the child where he can show that he sought to establish a relationship in a timely manner, even if his efforts failed. Thus, his rights will generally not be defeated in situations where the mother actively prevented the relationship from developing, absent countervailing considerations, such as a history of intimate partner abuse. Even less clear is what the result should be in situations where the putative father has no knowledge of the pregnancy and thus made no attempt to establish a relationship with the child. If he has no idea, should that be regarded as evidence of a lack of interest in or commitment to parenting? As one court concluded, a biological father who was "not interested enough in the outcome of his sexual encounter . . . to even inquire about the possibility of . . . pregnancy" should not acquire constitutionally protected rights to participate in an adoption proceeding.[29] On the other hand, is it really fair to expect someone to grasp an opportunity that he knows nothing about? Should courts really impose an affirmative duty on men to inquire about pregnancy, or should they instead focus on protecting the opportunity itself even if not known about and therefore not acted upon?

These kinds of questions can also arise in the context of the safe haven laws (as discussed previously) if the father does not know either of the pregnancy or of the mother's decision to avail herself of this option. Many safe haven laws do not have clear notice provisions, and as a result, some courts have refused to terminate the father's rights. Others do include specific notice provisions, such as that a search be made for the father using any information that might be available; that service be made through publication in the paper, which includes any possible identifying information about the baby; and that a search be done of the putative father registry.[30]

Last, and perhaps raising the most difficult questions, what should happen in a situation where an unwed father does not learn about the child until after an adoption has been approved by a court? Should the adoption be set aside in order to vindicate a father's right to develop a relationship with his child? Does this approach elevate the biological claims of fatherhood over the best interests of the child? What weight should be given to the adoptive parents? Should the outcome turn on the conduct of the mother, in terms of whether or not she lied to the father about the existence of the child? Is her conduct relevant from the perspective of the child's needs? Should the outcome turn on the conduct of the father — whether he did what he could to learn about and connect with the child?

Exhibit 13.1   Intent to Claim Parental Rights

 **NOTICE OF INTENT TO CLAIM PATERNITY**

INSTRUCTIONS/INFORMATION

1. Carefully read the information provided on the reverse of this form. The information provided is not designed to be legal advice. Questions concerning paternity, presumptions of paternity, or rights and responsibilities of a parent should be directed to an attorney.

2. Please type or print neatly.

3. All information in Part 1 concerning the father is required. Do not leave any of these items blank.

4. Complete Part 2 and Part 3 to the best of your ability. If any item is unknown, leave the space blank.

5. The child's name, date of birth, place of birth, and mother's maiden name are very critical to linking the Notice of Intent to Claim Paternity with an actual child. The more complete the information you provide, the more effective the paternity registry can be.

Part 1 MAN'S INFORMATION TO BE INCLUDED IN PATERNITY REGISTRY:

1. FULL NAME FIRST	MIDDLE	LAST		
2. DATE OF BIRTH (MM/DD/YYYY)	3. SOCIAL SECURITY NUMBER	4. DRIVER'S LICENSE NUMBER STATE	NUMBER	
5. RESIDENCE ADDRESS NUMBER & STREET NAME		CITY	STATE	ZIP
6. MAILING ADDRESS NUMBER & STREET NAME		CITY	STATE	ZIP

Part 2 CHILD'S INFORMATION:

7. FULL NAME FIRST	MIDDLE	LAST	
8a. DATE OF BIRTH (MM/DD/YYYY)	8b. EXPECTED DATE OF BIRTH (MM/DD/YYYY)	9. SEX	
10a. BIRTHPLACE (HOSPITAL NAME)	10b. CITY OF BIRTH	10c. COUNTY OF BIRTH	10d. STATE OF BIRTH

Part 3 MOTHER'S INFORMATION:

11. FULL NAME FIRST	MIDDLE	LAST	MAIDEN	
12. DATE OF BIRTH (MM/DD/YYYY)	13. SOCIAL SECURITY NUMBER	14. DRIVER'S LICENSE NUMBER STATE	NUMBER	
15. LAST KNOWN ADDRESS NUMBER & STREET NAME		CITY	STATE	ZIP

I declare under penalty of perjury that I am the father of the above child. I understand my name and information will be included in the paternity registry maintained by the Vital Statistics, Texas Department of State Health Services. I further understand that:

- Placing this form on file with Vital Statistics, Texas Department of State Health Services, entitles me to notice of proceeding for adoption of the child named above or for termination of my parental rights;
- Placing this form on file does not establish legal paternity of the child and does not begin the process of establishing legal paternity of the child;
- The information contained in this form may be used in a legal proceeding to establish paternity of the child.

_____
SIGNATURE OF MAN

VITAL STATISTICS USE ONLY	
ACTUAL NAME OF CHILD _____	☐ NOTICE SENT TO MOTHER
DOB _____ STATE FILE # _____	☐ DENIAL RECEIVED

Exhibit 13.1   Continued

IMPORTANT INFORMATION CONCERNING
NOTICE OF INTENT TO CLAIM PATERNITY

BACKGROUND AND PURPOSE

HB1091, 75th Legislative session amended Section 160, Texas Family Code, creating a Paternity Registry in the Vital Statistics, Texas Department of State Health Services. The purpose of the registry is to permit a man alleging to be the biological father of a child to assert his parentage, independent of the mother, and preserve his right as a parent. This registry also may expedite adoptions of children whose biological fathers are unwilling to assume responsibility of their child.

A man is not required to register with the paternity registry if he is presumed to be the biological father. Presumptions under the Family Code include:

1. Man and biological mother are married to each other and the child was born during wedlock or within 300 days after the marriage was terminated;

2. Before the birth of the child, man and biological mother attempted to marry in compliance with law but the marriage is or was void and the child was born within 300 days of when the attempted marriage terminated;

3. After the birth, the man and biological mother married or attempted to marry, he voluntarily asserted his paternity of the child, and:
    a. The assertion is in a record filed with the Texas Vital Statistics;
    b. He is voluntarily named as the child's father on the child's birth certificate; or
    c. Is obligated to support the child by written promise or court order.

INFORMATION

- This notice of intent to claim paternity <u>must</u> be filed before the birth of the child or not later than the 31st day after the date of birth of the child.

- The Texas Vital Statistics will send a copy of the notice of the registration to a mother named on a notice of intent to claim paternity form.

- The information in this form is admissible in court proceedings.

- **Service to assist in establishing paternity can be obtained through the Office of the Attorney General, Child Support Division, or by hiring an attorney.**

- **If the conception or birth of the child occurred in another state, a man should also register with the registry of paternity in that other state.**

- **Information on registries in other states is available from the Texas Vital Statistics.**

- A man who fails to file a notice of intent to claim paternity by the 31st day after the date of birth of the child may not assert an interest in the child other than by filling a suit to establish paternity before the termination of a man's paternal rights.

- A man who files a notice of intent to claim paternity must promptly notify the registry in writing of any change in information including a change of address.

- **A man may rescind the notice of intent at any time by sending the registry a written statement signed and witnessed or notarized either stating to the best of the man's knowledge and belief that he is not the father or that a court has adjudicated another person to be the father of the child.**

- The registry address:

  Paternity Registry
  Vital Statistics Unit - 1966
  Texas Department of State Health Services
  P.O. Box 149347
  Austin, Texas 78714-9347

  Toll Free #: (888) 963-7111 Ext. 7782
  Fax #: (512) 458-7164

  http://www.dshs.state.tx.us/vs/patreg/default.shtm

- **Information in the registry is confidential and may only be released to certain individuals or entities.**

These are agonizing questions to which there are no simple answers, and these cases highlight the tension between the long-cherished rights of biological parenthood and the need to secure stable adoptive homes for children where there does not appear to be a birth parent who is ready and able to assume the responsibilities of parenthood. Some courts have focused on the harm to the father and have been willing to set aside an adoption to vindicate his right to develop a relationship with his child. Here, his underlying biological connection to the child is given priority in determining which parenting relationships will be permitted to continue. In contrast, other courts have refused to set aside an adoption in this situation if it determines that it is in the best interest of the child to maintain the continuity of the adoptive relationships.

The much publicized 1993 "Baby Richard" case exemplifies both judicial approaches.[31] In this case, an unwed mother placed her newborn for adoption without informing the father. During her pregnancy, the father had returned to Czechoslovakia to care for his dying grandmother. While he was away, the mother received a call from his aunt informing her that he had resumed a former romantic relationship with another woman. As a result of this news, the mother moved out of their shared home and gave birth in a different hospital than the couple had decided on.

Upon the father's return, the mother informed him that the child had died. He did not believe this and made a number of attempts to find out what had happened to the child, including checking with the hospital they had planned to use, checking birth and death certificates, and going through the garbage at the mother's house for signs that a baby was living there. About six months later, the parties married and subsequently sought the return of the child based on the fact that the father had not consented to the adoption.

The trial court held that the father was unfit because he had failed to demonstrate a reasonable degree of interest, concern, or responsibility during the first 30 days of the child's life as required by state law, and his consent to the adoption was therefore not required. The appeals court was similarly unimpressed with the father's efforts to determine what had happened to the baby and agreed that he had failed to demonstrate a reasonable degree of interest, concern, or responsibility for the child. However, in upholding the adoption, the court's primary focus was on the best interest of the child rather than on the rights of the father, as it powerfully explained:

> Fortunately, the time has long past when children in our society were considered the property of their parents. Slowly, but finally, when it comes to children even the law has rid itself of the *Dred Scott* mentality that a human being can be considered a piece of property "belonging" to another human being. To hold that a child is the property of his parents is to deny the humanity of the child. Thus, in the present case

we start with the premise that Richard is not a piece of property with property rights belonging to either his biological or adoptive parents. Richard "belongs" to no one but himself. . . .

. . . A child's best interest is not part of an equation. It is not to be balanced against any other interest.[32]

In evaluating Richard's best interest, the court found that he should remain with his adoptive parents with whom he had lived since four days after his birth.

The Illinois Supreme Court had a radically different view of the situation. It disagreed that the father's actions to discover what had happened to the child had been inadequate in light of the mother's dishonesty, which was compounded by the fact that the lawyer for the adoptive parents had also encouraged concealment of the truth. Finding that the father had been wrongfully deprived of an opportunity to express his interest in the child, the court focused on the "preemptive rights" of a natural parent in his own children. It held that these rights had to be considered apart from the best interest of the child:

If it were otherwise, few parents would be secure in the custody of their own children. If best interests of the child were a sufficient qualification to determine child custody, anyone with superior income, intelligence, education, etc., might challenge and deprive the parents of their right to their own children.[33]

Accordingly, wholly apart from any considerations of best interest, the adoption was overturned, and the child returned to his birth parents based on the primacy of the biological link and the potentiality it embodies.

Consideration

Do you think a child should be returned to his or her biological father where the father was deprived of his right to have a say in adoption proceedings?

Transracial Adoption

Significant controversy surrounds the issue of the role that race should or should not play in the creation of families by adoption.[34] Until the 1950s, many states had laws prohibiting the placement of children across racial lines, and, even where not expressly prohibited, most agencies had explicit policies against such placements. Similar to laws banning interracial marriage, this prohibition reflected racial animus and a belief in the desirability of maintaining white racial purity. As courts began to strike down racial classifications in the late 1950s, these laws were eventually declared unconstitutional.

This constitutional direction, combined with other factors — including the increased numbers of children in the foster care system, the decline in the number of white infants available for adoption, and a greater societal acceptance of interracial relationships — led to an upsurge in the number of **transracial adoptions** during the late 1950s and 1960s. An additional contributing factor was that social workers had also begun to question their generally held assumption that children should be placed in families that most closely matched their families of origin based on the belief that children would do best if they blended into their adoptive families.[35]

Most of these transracial adoptions involved the adoption of black children by white families.[36] In 1972, this trend was denounced by the National Association of Black Social Workers, and in an influential position paper they took an unequivocal stand against the adoption of black children by white families:

> The National Association of Black Social Workers has taken a vehement stand against the placement of Black children in white homes for any reason. We affirm the inviolable position of Black children in Black families where they belong physically, psychologically and culturally in order that they receive the total sense of themselves and develop a sound projection of their future. . . .
>
> Black children in white homes are cut off from the healthy development of themselves as Black people, which development is the normal expectation and only true humanistic goal. . . .
>
> In our society, the developmental needs of Black children are significantly different from those of white children. Black children are taught, from an early age, highly sophisticated coping techniques to deal with racist practices. . . . Only a Black family can transmit the emotional and sensitive subtleties of perception and reaction essential for a Black child's survival in a racist society.[37]

In short, a primary concern was the believed inability of white parents to foster a healthy sense of racial identity and pride in their adopted children and to equip them with the skills they would need to cope with a racist dominant culture.

In response to these concerns, the role of race in adoption placements was reconsidered and in-racial placements again became the preferred approach. However, in contrast to the earlier policies that embodied notions of white racial supremacy, racial matching was now based on positive concerns for the well-being of black children. Regulations and agency policies were amended to reflect this preference for in-racial placements, which often meant that a child would not be placed with white families unless it was clear that no black adoptive home was available.

However, this shift in favor of in-racial placements also generated significant concern because it often meant that children remained waiting in foster care or institutional settings until a particular type of home became available. Additionally, a number of studies indicated that where adoptive parents are sensitive to the issue, transracially adopted children can develop a clear sense of racial identity and may be particularly adept at functioning in a world that is gradually coming to embrace the benefits of diversity.

Accordingly, in 1994, Congress passed the Multiethnic Placement Act (MEPA), which was amended in 1996 by the Interethnic Placement Provisions. Together, these enactments prohibit agencies that receive federal funding from denying or delaying adoption (or foster care) placements based on considerations of race, color, or national origin.[38] The Act is thus clear that "[r]ace, culture or ethnicity may not be used as the basis for any denial of placement," nor may such factors be used as a reason to delay any foster or adoptive placement; however, according to an authoritative government memorandum, if, in an individual case, an agency determines that considerations of race, culture, or ethnicity are necessary in order to protect the best interests of that particular child, it may take them into account when making a placement decision. To ensure that the exception does not swallow the rule, the memo stresses that only "the most compelling reasons may serve to justify consideration of race and ethnicity as part of a placement decision. Such reasons are likely to emerge only in unique and individual circumstances. Accordingly, occasions where race or ethnicity lawfully may be considered in a placement decision will be correspondingly rare."[39]

Although strictly limiting the role of race in the placement process, MEPA does recognize the importance of having a diverse pool of prospective foster and adoptive parents. Accordingly, the Act imposes a duty on states to make a diligent effort to recruit foster and adoptive parents who reflect the ethnic and racial diversity of the children in their state for whom homes are needed.

MEPA has not put an end to the robust debates regarding the role of race in adoption placements. For instance, some commentators believe that transracial adoption "can be used as a means to attack both racism and the social construct of race through intentional and functional kinship relationships that serve the best interest of the child." In contrast, others argue that the practice "reinforces the privilege . . . of the potential parent's identity" as a parent can "choose what race child they are willing to raise . . . yet the average child awaiting adoption . . . is unable to state a racial preference."[40]

■
Adoption Abrogation and the Tort of Wrongful Adoption

Like any other parents, most adoptive parents are prepared to handle the daily vicissitudes that come with raising children. But what happens if they come to regret their decision because the experience proves far more difficult because, for example, unbeknownst to the adoptive parents, the child had previously experienced severe physical and sexual abuse or is genetically predisposed to a debilitating disease? Should they be permitted to abrogate or undo the adoption?

The majority view is that children cannot be sent back; that once finalized, adoptions cannot be undone based on parental dissatisfaction with the child. Underlying this position is the recognition that children are not goods who can be returned if they later are viewed as "damaged."[41] However, this position is not universal. A few states, either by statute or judicial decision, permit **adoption abrogation** in what are deemed extraordinary circumstances, such as where a child is facing a lifetime of institutional care; however, most judges are wary of these actions because they effectively orphan the child. Note, however, that as with any parent, if adoptive parents cannot care for their child, they may eventually lose their parental rights due to abuse or neglect.[42]

However, in contrast to situations involving an attempt to abrogate an adoption based upon the adoptive parents' dissatisfaction with the child or their concerns that they cannot provide the child with the kind of care needed, the law tends to be somewhat more lenient where the abrogation is premised upon procedural defects in the adoption proceeding. Most commonly in this category of case are claims by the adoptive parents that the agency engaged in fraud or deliberate misrepresentation by, for example, telling them that a child had no history of mental disorders when it knew the child had been institutionalized for mental illness in order to induce them to adopt a child that they might not have otherwise taken into their home. In this situation, some courts are willing to undo an adoption based upon their authority to vacate court judgments for fraud in accordance with the rules of civil procedure.

However, based on the recognition that this approach disregards the interests of the adopted child, a number of states no longer permit adoptive parents to set aside an adoption based upon fraud or misrepresentation, but, instead, permit them to sue the agency for **"wrongful adoption"** in order to recover damages for unanticipated expenses, which might include, for example, residential care or extraordinary medical treatments. In allowing these damage suits, courts have been careful to make clear that adoption agencies cannot be expected to guarantee that adopted children develop as happy and healthy children. At the same time, they have emphasized that adoptive parents are entitled to rely on the accuracy of the information they obtain from an agency when seeking to make an informed choice about whether or not they wish to proceed with the adoption of a particular child.

Chapter Summary

Through adoption, a child acquires new parents who assume all of the rights and responsibilities previously vested in the biological parents, and the child's legal relationship with his or her birth parents is extinguished. This cutoff rule is subject to limited exceptions, most commonly in stepparent and co-parent adoptions. Adoptions can be accomplished through an agency or by the parents themselves acting with or without the assistance of a third-party intermediary. In addition, most states now have safe haven laws, which permit birth parents to anonymously drop a newborn off at a designated location without fear of being prosecuted for abandonment.

An adoption cannot proceed without the consent of the birth parents, subject to a limited exception for some unwed fathers, unless parental rights have been terminated or the court has approved a request to dispense with parental consent. In private placement adoptions, the consent attaches to the adoption itself; in an agency adoption, the consent attaches to the relinquishment of the child to the agency, which in turn acquires the right of consent. Most states allow a birth parent to revoke consent under specific circumstances; some states give birth parents considerable latitude, while others are quite strict; however, in all jurisdictions, it is harder to revoke a relinquishment to an agency.

In most situations, the child must live with the prospective adoptive parents in a pre-adoption placement before the adoption can be finalized. In an agency adoption, placement will not be made until a home study has been completed, and the placement is supervised by the agency. Postplacement social studies are done in both agency and private placement adoptions in order to assist the judge in deciding whether to approve the adoption. This decision is based on the best interest standard.

A developing trend is to provide for greater openness in adoption. Many states now allow open adoptions, which permit post-adoption contact between the adopted child and the birth parents. Additionally, most states now permit the release of nonidentifying information to adopted children, and many now permit the release of identifying information in accordance with specific procedures, which may result in communication between an adult adoptee and his or her birth parents.

Stepparent adoptions account for a considerable number of yearly adoptions. Here, in a significant exception to the cutoff rule, the parental rights of the custodial spouse survive the adoption. This same exception has been made in co-parent adoptions involving gay and lesbian couples; however, all states do not permit these adoptions. Most states prohibit joint adoption by same-sex couples; however, in some states, gay men and lesbians can adopt a child as a single parent.

Unwed fathers now have considerably more rights in the adoption arena than they had in the past and may be entitled to consent rights based on a substantial parenting commitment, or an acknowledgment of paternity, or the filing of notice in a putative father registry. If a father comes forward after an adoption has been finalized, some courts may allow the adoption to be disrupted, while other courts refuse to do this based on the best interests of the child.

There has been considerable controversy over the role that race should play in adoption placements. Presently, federal law prohibits delays in or denials of adoption placements based on considerations of race, color, or national origin.

When an adoption does not live up to parental expectations, most courts will not permit the parents to abrogate or undo the adoption, although abrogation has been permitted by some courts under extraordinary circumstances. Where the agency has breached its obligation to properly disclose information, parents may be able to sue the agency in tort for wrongful adoption.

Key Terms

Adoption	Pre-Adoption Placement
Agency Adoption	Home Study
Independent Adoption	Postplacement Social Study
Private Placement Adoption	Open Adoption
Voluntary Surrender	Cutoff Rule
Safe Haven	Co-Parent Adoption
Consent	Putative Father Registry
Relinquishment	Opportunity Interest
Revocation of Consent	Transracial Adoptions
Dispensing with Parental Consent	Adoption Abrogation
At-Risk Placement	Wrongful Adoption

Review Questions

1. What purpose did adoptions serve in ancient Rome?
2. Why were adoptions not recognized under English common law?

3. When was the first adoption statute in this country passed? What factors prompted its passage?
4. What is an agency adoption?
5. What is an independent or private placement adoption?
6. What role do intermediaries play in independent adoptions?
7. What concerns have been raised about the potential for exploitation/coercion in the context of independent adoptions? What solutions have been suggested?
8. What are some of the major differences between these two types of adoption?
9. Explain how safe haven laws work.
10. What role does consent play in an independent or private placement adoption?
11. What is the legal significance of relinquishment of a child to an adoption agency?
12. What happens if a parent wishes to revoke his or her consent to an adoption?
13. Why are states generally stricter about the revocation of a relinquishment made to an agency as compared to the revocation of consent?
14. What is the purpose of the home study? When is it usually done? What is usually inquired into?
15. Why has the home study process been subject to criticism?
16. During an agency placement, who usually has legal custody of the children?
17. Does the execution of the consent document effectively transfer parental rights over to the adoptive parents?
18. During the placement in an independent adoption, who has authority to make decisions regarding the child?
19. What is the purpose of a postplacement social study?
20. What standard does the court use in deciding whether to approve an adoption?
21. Why have adoptions traditionally been cloaked in secrecy? Why has this been challenged?
22. What is an open adoption?
23. What approaches do states take with respect to open adoption?
24. What typically happens to the original birth records and the adoption records once an adoption is approved? Why has this traditional approach been challenged?
25. What approaches do states take to provide children who have been adopted access to their birth records?
26. Following a stepparent adoption, what is the status of the custodial parent?

27. What is a second-parent adoption? Why is this an advisable step for a same-sex spouse to take?
28. Historically, what rights did an unwed father have relative to the adoption of his child and why?
29. How are unwed mothers and unwed fathers treated differently with respect to consent rights? What accounts for this differential treatment?
30. Under what circumstances will an unmarried father be entitled to consent rights?
31. What did the Illinois appeals court decide in the *Baby Richard* case? What did the Illinois Supreme Court decide?
32. Historically, what accounted for the policy against transracial placements? When and why did this policy begin to change?
33. Under federal law, what role, if any, can race play in the adoption placement process?
34. How do courts generally respond when parents seek to undo an adoption?
35. Explain the concept of wrongful adoption. How does it differ from adoption abrogation?

Discussion Questions

1. Should persons who wish to become adoptive parents be screened and subject to either pre- or postplacement studies? Should we subject persons who wish to reproduce biologically to similar requirements? Do you agree with the argument that this differential treatment relegates adoptive families to a second-class status? Do the two situations warrant this differential treatment? Why or why not?
2. The *Baby Richard* case raises difficult questions about the meaning of biological parenthood and the weight that should be given to this connection. Do you think Baby Richard should have been returned to his birth parents, or would you have allowed him to remain with his adoptive parents? Assuming both that the father was wrongfully deprived of his opportunity to develop a relationship with his child and that removing the child from his adoptive family would be harmful to the child, how do you go about resolving this case? What factors take precedence? Can a child's best interest and a parent's rights be balanced against each other in order to arrive at a solution?
3. If you were an adoptive parent, how would you feel about an open adoption plan that allowed the child to visit regularly with his or her birth parents? How would you feel about this if you were a birth parent?

4. What role do you think race should play in the formation of adoptive families? What about the sexual orientation of the parents?
5. Do you think safe haven laws make sense? What arguments can you think of in favor of and against this approach?

Assignments

1. Determine whether private placement adoptions are permitted in your jurisdiction. If they are, determine the following by consulting the relevant statutory and/or regulatory provisions:
   a. Are prospective adoptive parents subject to a certification requirement?
   b. Is the use of intermediaries allowed?
   c. If so, are they subject to any legal requirements, such as limitations of fees and costs or accounting requirements?
2. Determine what the rules are in your jurisdiction governing when a parent can revoke his or her consent to an adoption. In developing your answer, please detail both the substantive standards as well as the procedural requirements. To do this, you may need to consult both the relevant statutory and regulatory provisions as well as case law.
3. Locate an adoption agency in your area and interview someone who works there. In your interview, see if you can determine the following:
   a. Does the agency specialize in a particular type of adoption?
   b. How does it screen parents who want to adopt?
   c. What is the cost of a typical adoption?
   d. How long does the typical adoption take?
   e. What areas of inquiry are of particular importance when conducting a home study?
   f. Does the agency ever revoke placements? Under what circumstances?
4. Assume that you are the judge in a *Baby Richard* situation. Please write your opinion setting out how you would decide the case and why.
5. Assume the attorney you work for has asked you to do some research on co-parent adoptions, as he is seeking to file a petition on behalf of one of his clients. As there is no law in your jurisdiction on co-parent adoptions, he has asked you to locate rulings from other jurisdictions that either permit or deny second-parent adoptions. Carefully read and analyze the cases you have located and prepare a memorandum setting out the essential reasons behind the court decisions.

Cases for Analysis

The following case is an important decision involving the constitutionality of a sealed records law. The case highlights the difficulty of sorting out the potentially conflicting interests of parties in what is often referred to as the "adoption triangle."

ALMA SOCIETY, INC. v. MELLON
601 F.2d 1225 (2d Cir. 1979)

This appeal presents the question whether adopted persons upon reaching adulthood ("adult adoptees") are constitutionally entitled, irrespective of a showing of cause, to obtain their sealed adoption records, including the names of their natural parents. Appellants are adult adoptees and an association of such persons; and they urge that the New York statutes that require the sealing of adoption records are . . . invalid on Fourteenth Amendment Due Process and Equal Protection grounds and on further basis that those statutes impose upon them badges or incidents of slavery in violation of the Thirteenth Amendment. The . . . District Court . . . dismissed appellants' complaint. We affirm.

Appellants argue that adult adoptees should be given access to the records of their adoptions with no showing of cause whatsoever. Their supporting affidavits . . . indicate that lack of access to such records causes some of them serious psychological trauma and pain and suffering, may cause in them or their children medical problems or misdiagnoses for lack of history, may create in some persons a consciousness of danger of unwitting incest, and in others a "crisis" of religious identity or what they feel is an impairment of religious freedom because they are unable to be reared in the religion of their natural parents. . . .

The attack upon the New York statutes is three-fold. Appellants first argue that the interests of an adult adoptee in learning from the State (or from agencies acting under compulsion of state law) the identity of his natural family is a fundamental right under the Due Process clause of the Fourteenth Amendment. . . .

Second, appellants argue that adult adoptees constitute a suspect or "quasi-suspect" classification under the Equal Protection clause of the Fourteenth Amendment. Under this view semi-strict or intermediate scrutiny of the New York statutes would be appropriate, and appellants maintain that such a review does not indicate that the statutes are based on sufficiently important state interests.

Finally, appellants argue that the Thirteenth Amendment also applies to this case because the statutes that require sealing of the adoption records as to adults constitute the second of the five incidents of slavery namely, the abolition of the parental relation. . . . Under appellants' view, the rights that the Thirteenth Amendment guarantees are not subject to balancing but are instead protected absolutely. We will discuss each of appellants' three arguments in turn.

SUBSTANTIVE DUE PROCESS

What appellants assert is a right to "personhood." They rely on a series of Supreme Court cases involving familial relationships, rights of family privacy, and freedom to marry and reproduce. As they put it, "an adoptee is someone upon whom the State has, by sealing his records, imposed lifelong familial amnesia . . . injuring the adoptee in regard to his personal identity when he was too young to consent to, or even know, what was happening." . . .

[W]e must look to the nature of the relationships and [recognize] that choices made by those other than the adopted child are involved. . . . [T]he State may take these choices into consideration and protect the natural mother's choice of privacy which not all have forsaken even if appellants are correct, as we are told, that many mothers would be willing in this day and age to have their adult adopted children to contact them. So, too, a state may take into account the relationship of the adopting parents, even if, as appellants assert, many of them would not object to or would even encourage the adopted child's seeking out the identity of or relationship with a natural parent. The New York statutes in providing for release of the information on a "showing of good cause" do no more than to take these other relationships into account. As such they do not unconstitutionally infringe upon or arbitrarily remove appellants' rights of identity, privacy, or personhood. Upon an appropriate showing of psychological trauma, medical need, or of a religious identity crisis though it might be doubted upon a showing of "fear of unconscious incest" the New York courts would appear required under their own statute to grant permission to release all or part of the sealed adoption records.

EQUAL PROTECTION

Appellants begin their equal protection analysis with the argument that adult adoptees are a suspect classification (and the correlative argument that the State has no compelling interests to support the validity of the sealed records laws). Appellants refer us to Trimble v. Gordon, 430 U.S. 762, 766 (1977), where the Court stated that classifications based on illegitimacy fall in a "realm of less than strictest scrutiny" although the scrutiny "is not a toothless one." By the citation of *Trimble*, appellants suggest that they are at least entitled to the same level of constitutional scrutiny as illegitimates who have been termed a "sensitive" or quasi-suspect category for which the appropriate level of scrutiny is "intermediate," not "strict." . . .

Even assuming that the classification here were subject to intermediate scrutiny, it would not violate equal protection; for we conclude that it is substantially related to an important state interest. . . .

[T]he New York sealed record statutes do not want constitutional validity. The statutes, we think, serve important interests. New York Domestic Relations Law §114 and its related statutes represent a considered legislative judgment that the confidentiality statutes promote the social policy underlying adoption laws. . . . Moreover, the purpose of a related statute, Section 4138 of the Public Health Laws, was to erase the stigma of illegitimacy from the adopted child's life by sealing his original birth certificate and issuing a new one under his new surname. And the major purpose of adoption legislation is to encourage natural parents to use the process when they are unwilling or unable to care for their offspring. . . . These significant legislative goals clearly justify the State's decision to keep the natural parents' names secret from adopted persons but not from non-adopted persons.

To be sure, once an adopted child reaches adulthood, some of the considerations that apply at the time of adoption and throughout the child's tender years no longer apply or apply with less force. Illegitimacy might stigmatize an adult less than a child, and the goal of encouraging adoption of unwanted and uncared for children might not be significantly affected if adult adoptees could discover their natural parents' identities. But the state does have an interest that does not wane as the adopted child grows to adulthood, namely, the interest in protecting the privacy of the natural parents. . . .

THIRTEENTH AMENDMENT

Appellants make the novel argument . . . that the Thirteenth Amendment's prohibition of slavery and involuntary servitude gives them an Absolute right to release of their adoption records. . . . The argument is that in abolishing slavery and involuntary servitude the Framers also intended to abolish five "necessary incidents of slavery." We address only the second point because we find that the Amendment is entirely inapplicable to this case.

Appellants refer us particularly to the speech of Senator James Harlan of Iowa of April 6, 1864, in which he set forth a number of such incidents. The second named was

> the abolition practically of the parental relation, robbing the offspring of the care and attention of his parents, severing a relation which is universally

cited as the emblem of the relation sustained by the Creator to the human family. And yet, according to the matured judgment of these slave States, this guardianship of the parent over his own children must be abrogated to secure the perpetuity of slavery.

1 B. Schwartz, *supra*, at 72. . . . Appellants liken their situation . . . to that of the antebellum South where a slave child was "sold off" while too young to remember his parents and grew up separated from them by inability to communicate as well as by distance. The analogy according to appellants is that however literate they may be, they cannot write to their natural parents, cannot visit them, and thereby wear a "badge or incident" of slavery. . . .

. . . Although it is doubtless true that an "incident" of slavery (in the original sense) was the abolition of the parental relation, i.e., the offspring of a slave was deprived of the care and attention of parents . . . the New York sealed records laws do not deprive appellants of their parental relation. It is the New York adoption laws themselves and not the sealed records laws that recognize the divestment by natural parents of their guardianship because of formal surrender, abandonment, or forfeiture by unfitness or jeopardy of the child's best interests; and it is the adoption laws that create a new parent-child relationship between appellants and their adoptive parents. Appellants do not challenge the constitutionality of the adoption laws; thus their challenge to the sealed records laws, even if cognizable under the Thirteenth Amendment in the absence of congressional legislation, is misdirected. Appellants are left to their remedies under the New York statute or with the New York legislature.

QUESTIONS

1. What statute did the plaintiffs challenge in this case? What harms did the plaintiffs say were caused by this law? What were they seeking?
2. What constitutional arguments did the plaintiffs make in challenging this statute?
3. How did the court respond to each one of the constitutional arguments? What themes run through the court's analysis? What competing interests does the court identify? How does the court balance these considerations?
4. In cases involving important policy issues, courts sometimes suggest possible legislative alternatives. Do you think it would be possible to craft a law that strikes a different balance between the competing interests, or do you think the balance struck by the New York law is the appropriate one?

This well-publicized case highlights the heartbreaking complexity of cases involving children caught between disputing families. It also reveals the potential vulnerability of immigrant parents who may not fully understand the consequences of their actions because of language barriers or unfamiliarity with local laws and customs.

IN RE ADOPTION OF A.M.H.
215 S.W.3d 793 (Tenn. 2007)

The parents of A.M.H. are citizens of China. Prior to the child's birth, her father, Shao-Qiang ("Jack") was a tenured college professor in China. He moved to the United States on a student visa. . . . In 1997, he enrolled in an economics doctorate program at the University of Memphis and was awarded a scholarship and a graduate assistant position with a stipend. The mother of A.M.H., Qin ("Casey") Luo, although unmarried, obtained a visa as the father's wife. The mother arrived in the United States on June 30, 1998; the parents did not marry immediately. The mother speaks little English and has used an interpreter throughout these proceedings.

The mother became pregnant in July of 1998. Soon after, a student at the University of Memphis filed a complaint with the university alleging that the father had attempted to rape her. Although the father . . . was eventually acquitted by a jury, this charge had severe consequences. Because of the charge, the father was terminated from his graduate assistant position in October of 1998. With no job or stipend, the parents had very little income and no health insurance; in late 1998, they decided to meet with a birth-parent counselor at Mid-South Christian Services (hereinafter "Mid-South"). . . .

On January 28, 1999, A.M.H. was born. Shortly after the birth, the mother told the Mid-South counselor that A.M.H. was not to be placed for adoption. . . . Instead, the parents desired help with the care of their child for six to twelve months while they tried to regain financial stability. Consequently . . . when A.M.H. was four weeks old, the parents went to juvenile court and explained that they could not afford to care for A.M.H. and wanted temporary foster care. . . .

After placing A.M.H. with the Bakers, the parents visited her regularly in the Bakers' home, consistently bringing food and gifts and taking photographs at every visit. . . .

Because their financial condition was not improving, the parents decided to send A.M.H. to China to have relatives care for her temporarily. The father testified that in May of 1999, Mr. Baker told the father that it was a bad idea to send A.M.H. to China and that the Bakers would keep A.M.H. until the father graduated from the university. . . . According to the Bakers' testimony, because the parents of A.M.H. would not agree to an adoption, they entered into an oral agreement. . . . Under the oral agreement, the Bakers would raise A.M.H. until she was eighteen, and the parents of A.M.H. would retain their parental rights. . . .

On June 4, 1999, Mid-South's attorney went with the Bakers and the parents of A.M.H. to the Juvenile Court of Shelby County to obtain a consent order transferring custody of A.M.H. to the Bakers. A juvenile court officer drafted the "Petition for Custody" and a "Consent Order Awarding Custody.". . . The juvenile court officer who drafted the consent order testified that the mother was very concerned that the arrangement be temporary and that the parents would continue to have "open visitation" with A.M.H. through the duration of the Bakers' custody.

Despite the mother's concerns that the arrangement be temporary, the juvenile court officer added a guardianship provision to the consent order so that the Bakers could obtain medical insurance for A.M.H. . . .

The Bakers testified that as part of the custody agreement, the parents agreed that the Bakers would raise A.M.H. until she was eighteen years old and that the child would refer to the Bakers as "mommy" and "daddy." Contrary to the Bakers' testimony, the juvenile court officer testified that the parents were not agreeing that the Bakers could raise A.M.H. until she was eighteen years old. Indeed, the juvenile court officer testified that the mother "was fairly adamant that at some point she wanted her child back." The mother testified as follows: "I was told I can get my daughter back at any time. I asked him three or four times about that." Finally, the juvenile court interpreter, Pastor Kenny Yao, testified that the mother understood the agreement to be temporary and for the purpose of obtaining medical insurance for A.M.H. An order transferring custody and awarding guardianship was entered by consent; there was no court hearing on the matter. . . .

In November of 1999, when A.M.H. was ten months old, the father of A.M.H. asked Mr. Baker to return A.M.H. to the parents' custody. Mr. Baker responded that he and Mrs. Baker did not want to return A.M.H. and told the father not to mention his request to Mrs. Baker because she was pregnant. Mr. Baker also stated that he would hold the father responsible if Mrs. Baker had a miscarriage because she was worried about the custody situation. The father testified that he felt threatened and intimidated. The parents decided to wait for the Bakers' child to be born before pursuing the return of their daughter. The relationship between the parties continued to deteriorate; nevertheless, the parents continued to visit consistently and bring gifts. . . .

On May 3, 2000, the parents went to the Juvenile Court of Shelby County and signed a petition alleging a change in circumstances and seeking custody of A.M.H. . . . At the hearing on June 28, 2000, the Court Appointed Special Advocate submitted a report recommending that the

Bakers retain custody and the parents be allowed supervised visitation twice a week for four hours each visit. . . .

The parents did not appeal the custody order. However, they continued to visit their daughter at the Bakers' home despite the increase in animosity between the parties. . . .

Prior to January 28, 2001, A.M.H.'s second birthday, the parents requested to take their daughter for a family picture; they invited the Bakers to go with them and made an appointment at a photography studio. When the parents arrived with their son at the Bakers' home, they were told A.M.H. could not go because she was sick. The father testified to the following:

> Number one that was our child—our first daughter's birthday—second birthday. That was a special day. Number two, according to Chinese culture, on birthday, family picture together is of much significance—whole family. . . . That was such a special day for us. We made appointment. If she was sick . . . why didn't you call me and tell me in advance, one day or two days, so that we made a rescheduled appointment. . . . They knew my phone number. . . . Jerry Baker was so—he was, oh, so upset. He was not very happy. . . . I said, "Today, we cannot accept any more excuses. We want the—we want to take our daughter to the studio for family to get a picture made, period." That's what I said, "Period," and he noticed that I was very pushy, very insistent, and he said, "you've got to leave here. You've got to leave here." I said, "I won't—not today, I won't leave here. Until we have picture made, I won't leave here." And then he said, "I'm going to call the police." I said, "Call the police. I won't leave here."

The police were called, and the officer told the parents not to return to the Bakers' house or they would be arrested. . . . On June 20, 2001, four months and five days later, the Bakers filed a petition to terminate parental rights to A.M.H. This four-month lapse in visitation is the ground upon which the chancery court found abandonment of A.M.H. and terminated the parents' rights to their daughter.

Although the parents no longer pursued a relationship with A.M.H. through visits in the Bakers' home, they soon contacted the juvenile court and asked for assistance in regaining custody of A.M.H. . . .

On June 6, 2001, the parents appeared in juvenile court for the hearing on their custody petition. Had the matter been heard that day . . . the four-month period required for statutory abandonment would not have run. The hearing was rescheduled, however, to accommodate the Bakers' attorney. . . . However, two days previously (which was four months and five days after the parents' last visit with A.M.H.), the Bakers had filed a petition for adoption and termination of parental rights in chancery court. Consequently, rather than hear the modification of the custody petition, the juvenile court transferred the custody case to chancery court. . . .

The filing of the petition for adoption and termination of parental rights by the Bakers began chancery court proceedings that would span thirty-two months and generate a technical record containing eleven volumes of motions, responses, and orders. . . . The grounds alleged in the original petition seeking termination of the parents' rights were the parents' abandonment of A.M.H. by willfully failing to visit and the parents' abandonment of A.M.H. by willfully failing to support the child financially. The petition was later amended to assert grounds of termination based on the father's lack of legal status as a parent, the parents' mental incompetence, and the persistence of conditions preventing the child's reunification with the parents. . . .

On February 7, 2002, upon the guardian ad litem's motion, the chancery court ordered the parents to surrender A.M.H.'s passport to the court. The order also appointed the Bakers as A.M.H.'s guardians as defined in section 36-1-102(24) and (25) of the Tennessee Code Annotated and ordered that the parents have no contact with their daughter.

None of the witnesses could explain why the court ordered that the parents have no contact with their daughter. It may have been intended as a means of forcing the parents to surrender A.M.H.'s passport; however, it is also possible that the court ordered no contact upon the advice of the guardian ad litem. The guardian ad litem testified that she did not recommend visitation because "the status quo was that the child had not seen her biological parents in a number of months, I didn't believe that throwing the child into something different than the status quo was necessarily in her best interest." The guardian ad litem continued to oppose visitation and reunification with the parents throughout the proceedings. She believed that A.M.H. was attached to the Bakers and considered them to be her parents, although the guardian ad litem had never seen A.M.H. with her biological parents. She further stated that she had read a book about Chinese girls being placed in orphanages and consequently was concerned that the parents wanted to return to China.

> From the very beginning of the case, it was very clear to me that [the parents'] intention was that if the child were returned to them, they wanted to go back to China:
> They have never said anything different than that. They have always said that when this case is over they would like to take her back. . . . I honestly can't tell the Court today I know to an absolute certainty what kind of life she would have there. This book that I read caused me some concerns. . . .

In July of 2002, Dr. Goldstein submitted a report that found that A.M.H., who by this time was three years old and had not seen her parents in over a year, considered the Bakers her psychological parents and concluded that a child who experiences loss in early childhood is at a greater risk of developing serious psychological disorders. . . .

At the trial, the parents of A.M.H. introduced evidence from . . . a Chinese culture expert. . . .

The Chinese culture expert testified to the importance of "family" to the Chinese and the practice among Chinese students of allowing family members to care for their children temporarily. The chancery court found that the Chinese expert lacked credibility, despite similar testimony given by Pastor Kenny Yao, who the court found to be honest and without bias. Pastor Yao, who served as the mother's interpreter on several occasions (including in juvenile court when the petition to transfer temporary custody to the Bakers was drafted) testified as follows: "There is substantial difference between temporary custody and adoption in the Chinese culture. Adoption is you're giving the parental rights of the baby . . . to someone else. . . . But temporary custody is someone is helping to take care of the baby while you are unable to take care of the baby." He also testified that when the consent order was signed by the mother in juvenile court, he understood and translated the term "temporary custody" to the parents as follows: "[C]ustody means taking care. Temporary means not permanent."

Additionally, the parents introduced expert testimony from Dr. Yih-Jia Chang, who spoke fluent Mandarin Chinese. Dr. Chang performed a psychological evaluation (based on Chinese norms) on A.M.H.'s parents. She testified that they were both within the normal range. . . . Dr. Chang's report also states that it is a common practice in China for a child to be placed temporarily in the care of extended family. Dr. Chang testified that she believed the evaluations were valid because the answers were consistent with her determinations while meeting with each parent. . . .

After considering this evidence, the chancery court concluded that the parents are manipulative and dishonest people who appeared to have no intent to raise A.M.H. but have used the child from birth for financial gain and to avoid deportation. The chancery court found that the parents willfully abandoned A.M.H. by failing to visit or provide support for the four months immediately preceding the filing of the Bakers' petition to terminate parental rights. The court concluded that it would be in A.M.H.'s best interest to terminate parental rights and allow her to remain with the Bakers. . . .

However, the Court of Appeals affirmed the termination based on the parents' willful failure to visit their daughter for four months and held that termination was in the best interest of A.M.H. . . . Consequently, the sole ground for termination presented in this Court is abandonment grounded on the parents' willful failure to visit A.M.H. for a period of four consecutive months immediately preceding the filing of the petition to terminate parental rights.

TERMINATION OF PARENTAL RIGHTS

The sole ground for termination presented in this appeal is the parents' willful abandonment of A.M.H. by failing to visit her for four months preceding the filing of the termination petition. It is well established that both the United States and Tennessee Constitutions protect parents' rights to the custody and care of their children. . . .

A parent who has abandoned a child by "willfully" failing to visit is "unfit" under constitutional standards. . . . Where the failure to visit is not willful, however, a failure to visit a child for four months does not constitute abandonment. We have held that a parent who attempted to visit and maintain relations with his child, but was thwarted by the acts of others and circumstances beyond his control, did not willfully abandon his child. . . .

Here, we are presented with a situation in which the parents of A.M.H. actively pursued legal proceedings to regain custody of A.M.H. during the "abandonment" period but failed to visit for a period of four consecutive months immediately prior to the filing of a petition for termination of parental rights. . . . We hold that the evidence in this case does not support a finding that the parents intentionally abandoned A.M.H.

Disregarding the witnesses that the trial court found to lack credibility, the record clearly shows the following undisputed facts:

1. On January 28, 2001, the parents visited A.M.H. in the home of the Bakers;
2. The parents became upset when they could not take A.M.H. with them to sit for a family portrait;
3. The parents refused to leave A.M.H. until a police officer arrived and told them to leave;
4. During the subsequent four months and five days prior to the filing of the petition for termination, the parents pursued help in regaining the custody of their child by contacting the juvenile court and the local media;
5. During this time, the parents initiated two juvenile court hearings on a petition to regain custody of A.M.H.;
6. The first hearing was thwarted by the Bakers' request for a continuance; and
7. The second hearing was thwarted by the Bakers' initiation of proceedings in chancery court.

This undisputed evidence does not support a finding that the parents' failure to visit A.M.H. was willful. Where, as here, the parents' visits with their child have resulted in enmity between the parties and where the parents redirect their efforts at maintaining a parent-child relationship to the courts the evidence does not support a "willful failure to visit" as a ground for abandonment. . . . Therefore, we hold that there has been no willful abandonment and reverse the termination of parental rights. Accordingly, the Petition for Adoption and Termination of Parental Rights is dismissed. . . .

This evidence overwhelmingly shows that the parents' voluntary relinquishment of custody was entered as a temporary measure to provide health insurance for A.M.H. with the full intent that custody would be returned. Therefore, we hold that the parents of A.M.H. did not voluntarily transfer custody and guardianship of A.M.H. to the Bakers with knowledge of the consequences and, therefore, are entitled to superior rights to custody. . . .

Accordingly, we hereby revoke the parental consent to the change of custody and guardianship, and consider the competing claims of the parties, giving due deference to the parents' superior rights to the care and custody of A.M.H.

Under the superior rights doctrine, "a natural parent may only be deprived of custody of a child upon a showing of substantial harm to the child." In re Askew, 993 S.W.2d 1, 4 (Tenn. 1999). Therefore, the determination of a custodial dispute between a parent and a non-parent rests on a determination of whether there is substantial harm threatening a child's welfare if the child returns to the parents. Only then may a court find a sufficiently compelling justification for the infringement of the parents' fundamental right to raise a child as they see fit. See *id.* at 3.

Here, the only evidence of substantial harm arises from the delay caused by the protracted litigation and the failure of the court system to protect the parent-child relationship throughout the proceedings. Evidence that A.M.H. will be harmed from a change in custody because she has lived and bonded with the Bakers cannot constitute the substantial harm required to prevent the parents from regaining custody. . . .

Additionally, we note that the testimony concerning the general conditions in China is not relevant to a finding of substantial harm. Financial advantage and affluent surroundings simply may not be a consideration in determining a custody dispute between a parent and a non-parent. . . . "[M]ere improvement in quality of life is not a compelling state interest and is insufficient to justify invasion of Constitutional rights" (internal quotation marks and citation omitted). The evidence at trial showed that the parents have overcome many obstacles to achieve financial stability and are ably taking care of their other two children. Given the lack of evidence of a threat of substantial harm to A.M.H. if she is returned to her parents, we conclude that physical custody of A.M.H. must be returned to the parents. . . .

The Juvenile Court of Shelby County is directed to consider, prepare, and implement a plan to resolve the pending custody matter with a view toward reunification of A.M.H. with her natural parents . . . in a manner that minimizes trauma to the child.

QUESTIONS

1. Explain the various stages in this case.
2. What was the issue before the appeals court?
3. What legal standard did the court use in deciding to return A.M.H. to her biological parents? Why?
4. What role do you think cultural differences played in this case?

The following case addresses the applicability of the Indian Child Welfare Act to a termination proceeding against a father where the mother, who was "half-Apache," had previously consented to the termination of her parental rights.

IN RE THE TERMINATION OF PARENTAL RIGHTS TO ARW
2015 Wyo. 25, 343 P.3d 407 (2015)

Appellant, DRW (Father), appeals from the district court's order terminating his parental rights pursuant to Wyo. Stat. Ann. §14-2-309(a)(iv). He contends the district court erred in finding that the Indian Child Welfare Act did not apply to the termination proceedings. . . .

FACTS

Appellant is the father of ARW, born in 2002. Appellees, DLP and MLP (Adoptive Couple), have been involved in ARW's life since she was three weeks old, when ARW's biological mother began living in Appellees' home. After Appellant and ARW's mother divorced in 2004, Appellees exercised mother's visitation with ARW under mother's shared custody arrangement with Appellant. Both Appellant and ARW's mother executed powers of attorney providing that Appellees could have physical custody of ARW. In August 2012, ARW's mother, who has had very little involvement in ARW's life, consented to termination of her parental rights and to adoption by Appellees.

During ARW's lifetime, Appellant was incarcerated several times for drug-related offenses. Due to his incarceration, he did not have contact with ARW until she was approximately nine months old. On multiple occasions, Appellant or his adult children requested that Appellees retrieve ARW from Appellant's home because Appellant was too intoxicated to care for ARW. Appellant consumed alcohol to the point of inebriation almost every day. On two occasions, the Department of Family Services contacted Appellees to take care of ARW due to the condition of Appellant's home. ARW knew what a marijuana pipe was and had learned how to mix Appellant's drinks by the time she was five years old.

On March 8, 2012, the mother of one of ARW's friends reported to the police that her daughter had been sexually assaulted by Appellant. . . . He was subsequently charged with two counts of sexual abuse of ARW's friend.

On July 26, 2012, Appellees were appointed permanent guardians for ARW without Appellant's consent. Appellees enrolled ARW in counseling, and the counselor recommended that Appellant have no contact with ARW. On February 8, 2013, Appellant pled guilty to two counts of sexual abuse of a minor stemming from his contact with ARW's friend. He was sentenced to serve concurrent terms of four to seven years on each count.

Appellees initiated this action to terminate Appellant's parental rights on April 8, 2013. The petition alleged that Appellant's parental rights should be terminated pursuant to Wyo. Stat. Ann. §14-2-309(a)(iv), which provides that parental rights may be terminated if it is shown by clear and convincing evidence that "The parent is incarcerated due to the conviction of a felony and . . . the parent is unfit to have the custody and control of the child.". . .

A hearing on Appellees' petition to terminate parental rights was subsequently held on February 11, 2014. . . . During the hearing, counsel for Appellant informed the court that, according to Appellant, ARW might be an Indian child, stating that ARW's mother was "half Apache." Accordingly, Appellant claimed that he was entitled to the protections, including the notice requirements, of the Indian Child Welfare Act.

Following the hearing, the district court entered an order terminating Appellant's parental rights. The court found that Appellees had proven by clear and convincing evidence Appellant was incarcerated for a felony conviction and that he was unfit to have custody and control of ARW. The court also found that the Indian Child Welfare Act was inapplicable. Appellant filed a timely appeal.

DISCUSSION

I. APPLICATION OF INDIAN CHILD WELFARE ACT

. . . Appellant contends the district court erred in determining that the Indian Child Welfare Act did not apply to the termination proceedings.

Ultimately, whether the ICWA applied to the termination proceedings is an issue of statutory interpretation. . . .

According to Appellant, the district court was required to apply the provisions of the Act after his counsel informed the court at the termination hearing that, according to Appellant, ARW's mother was "half Apache" and ARW was therefore an "Indian child" under the terms of the ICWA. Accordingly, Appellant asserts that, pursuant to Sections 1912(a) and (f) of the Act, the court was required to "notify the parent or Indian custodian and the Indian child's tribe . . . of the pending proceedings and their right of intervention," and Appellees were required to demonstrate beyond a reasonable doubt that "continued custody of the child by the parent or Indian custodian is likely to result in serious emotional or physical damage to the child." Appellees respond that, in accordance with the United States Supreme Court's recent decision in Adoptive Couple v. Baby Girl, 133 S. Ct. 2552, 2562, 186 L. Ed. 2d 729 (2013), because ARW's mother consented to the relinquishment of her parental rights, and because Appellant has not claimed any Native American heritage of his own, the termination of Appellant's parental rights would not precipitate the "breakup of the Indian family" as contemplated by the ICWA. We agree with Appellees.

In Adoptive Couple v. Baby Girl, . . . the U.S. Supreme Court determined, first, that the text of the Act demonstrated that it was designed primarily to counteract the unwarranted *removal* of Indian children from Indian families. *Id*. at 2561. In light of this purpose, the Court concluded that when "the adoption of an Indian child is voluntarily and lawfully initiated by a non-Indian parent with sole custodial rights, the ICWA's primary goal of preventing the unwarranted removal of Indian children and the dissolution of Indian families is not implicated." *Id*. . . .

We note that Appellant does not provide any discussion of the U.S. Supreme Court's decision in Adoptive Couple v. Baby Girl. In any event, however, we would agree with the reasoning of the Supreme Court and conclude that it applies with equal, if not greater, force in the present case. In this case, Appellant has not asserted that he has any Native American heritage that would qualify ARW as an "Indian child" under the ICWA. Rather, he claims that ARW "might be" an "Indian child" because ARW's mother is "half Apache." ARW's mother, however, relinquished her parental responsibilities to Appellees soon after ARW's birth, and she allowed them to exercise her custody and visitation rights after she was divorced from Appellant. Further, ARW's mother consented to termination of her parental rights in the adoption proceedings. Accordingly, as in *Adoptive Couple v. Baby Girl*, the "breakup" of an Indian family would not be precipitated by the termination of Appellant's parental rights. We find no error in the district court's conclusion that the ICWA did not apply to the termination proceedings.

QUESTIONS

1. What was the relationship of the birth mother to ARW at the time the proceeding was brought against the father?
2. Why did the father assert that the ICWA was applicable in this case?
3. If the Act had been applicable, what would the court have been required to do?
4. Explain why the court concluded that the ICWA was not applicable in the present case.

Endnotes

1. Elizabeth Bartholet, International Adoption: Thoughts on Human Rights Issues, 13 Buff. Hum. Rts. L. Rev. 151 (2007).

2. C.M.A. McCauliff, The First English Adoption Law and Its American Precursors, 16 Seton Hall L. Rev. 656, 657-659 (1986); Stephen B. Presser, The Historical Background of the American Law of Adoption, 11 J. Fam. L. 443, 445-448 (1971).

3. McCauliff, *supra* note 2, at 659-665; Presser, *supra* note 2, at 448-456.

4. Catherine J. Ross, Welfare Reform and Juvenile Courts: Families Without Paradigms: Child Poverty and Out-of-House Placements in Historical Perspective, 60 Ohio St. L.J. 1249, 1257-1258 (1999).

5. *Id.* at 1258-1259.

6. McCauliff, *supra* note 2, at 659-665; Presser, *supra* note 2, at 448-456.

7. Presser, *supra* note 2, at 465 (citing Act of 1851, ch. 324).

8. Presser, *supra* note 2, at 465-480. *See also* Michael Grossberg, Governing the Hearth—Law and the Family in Nineteenth-Century America 259-269 (1985).

9. For further discussion of some of these issues, *see* Andrea B. Carroll, Re-regulating the Baby Market: A Call for a Ban on Payment of Birth-Mother Living Expenses, 59 Kan. L. Rev. 285 (2011), and Barbara Fedders, Race and Market Values in Domestic Infant Adoption, 88 N.C. L. Rev. 1687 (2010).

10. Erik Eckholm, Older Children Abandoned Under Law for Babies, N.Y. Times, Oct. 3, 2008. http://www.nytimes.com/2008/10/03/us/03omaha.html.

11. For a discussion of some of the complexities of safe haven laws, *see* Susan Ayres, Kairos and Safe Havens: The Timing and Calamity of Unwanted Birth, 15 Wm. & Mary J. Women & L. 227 (2009); Jeffrey A. Parness, Deserting Mothers, Abandoned Babies, Lost Fathers: Dangers in Safe Havens, 24 Quinnipiac L. Rev. 335 (2006); Carol Sanger, Infant Safe Haven Laws: Legislating in the Culture of Life, 106 Colum. L. Rev. 753 (2006). For details on the laws in each state, *see* Infant Safe Haven Laws, https://www.childwelfare.gov/topics/systemwide/laws-policies/statutes/safehaven/?hasBeenRedirected=1 (accessed Jan. 7, 2016).

12. For a thoughtful discussion of some of the complexities inherent in the consent process, *see* Elizabeth J. Samuels, Time to Decide? The Laws Governing Mothers' Consents to the Adoption of Their Newborn Infants, 72 Tenn. L. Rev. 509 (2005).

13. Courts in several states have recently grappled with the complex interplay between termination and adoption proceedings in situations where the adoption of a child was approved while a parent's appeal of the termination of her parental rights was under review. For a discussion of these cases, *see* Kate M. Heideman, Avoiding the Need to "Unscramble the Egg": A Proposal for the Automatic Stay of Subsequent Adoption Proceedings When Parents Appeal a Judgment Terminating Their Parental Rights, 24 St. Louis U. Pub. L. Rev. 445 (2005).

14. Many of these children may be classified as having "special needs," thus making prospective adoptive parents eligible for financial assistance under the federal Adoption Assistance and Child Welfare Assistance Act, as well as under various state adoption assistance programs.

15. *See* Elizabeth Bartholet, Family Bonds Adoption and the Politics of Parenting ch. 5 (1993).

16. *Id.* at 33-34.

17. In interstate cases, the applicable jurisdictional requirements of PKPA, the UCCJA, and the UCCJEA must be complied with. For a general discussion of these Acts, see Chapter 9.

18. Justin Owens, Challenging Post-Adoption Decrees and the Convoluted Applications of State Courts, 31 J. Am. Acad. Matrimonial Law 209 (2018).

19. It should, however, be pointed out that the adoption process was initially more open, and that the emphasis on secrecy emerged over the course of the twentieth century as adoption became a more regulated practice. For further detail on both this history and some of the debates over open adoption, *see* Amanda C. Pustinik, Private Ordering, Legal Ordering, and the Getting of Children: A Counterhistory of Adoption Law, 20 Yale L. & Poly. Rev. 263 (2002); Jennifer R. Racine, A Fundamental Rights Debate: Should Wisconsin Allow Adult Adoptees Unconditional Access to Adoption Records and Original Birth Certificates?, 2002 Wis. L. Rev. 1453; Heidi Hildebrand, Because They Want to Know: An Examination of the Legal Rights of Adoptees and Their Parents, 24 S. Ill. U. L.J. 515 (2000); Naomi Cahn and Jana Singer, Adoption, Identity, and the Constitution: The Case for Opening Closed Records, 2 U. Pa. J. Const. L. 150 (1999); Lucy S. McGough and Annette Peltier-Falahahwazi, Secrets and Lies: A Model for Cooperative Adoption, 60 La. L. Rev. 13 (1999).

20. McGough and Peltier-Falahahwazi, *supra* note 19, at 41.

21. Although the term "open adoption" is usually identified with post-adoption arrangements, in a broader sense the term also applies to pre-adoption processes in situations where the birth parents and the prospective adoptive parents meet, share information, and, if the placement is agreed upon, determine how the post-adoption contact is to be structured.

22. For a discussion of some of these issues, *see* Cynthia R. Mabry, The Psychological and Emotional Ties That Bind Biological and Adoptive Families: Whether Court-Ordered Post-Adoption Contact Is in an Adopted Child's Best Interest, 42 Cap. U. L. Rev. 285, and McCough and Peltier-Falahahwazi, *supra* note 19, at 56-71.

23. Access to Adoption Records, Child Welfare Information Gateway, http://www.childwelfare.gov (accessed Jan. 6, 2016).

24. *See* Rosemary Cabellero, Open Records Adoption: Finding the Missing Piece, 30 S. Ill. U. L.J. 291 (2006); Caroline B. Fleming, The Open-Records Debate: Balancing the Interests of Birth Parents and Adult Adoptees, 11 Wm. & Mary J. Women & L. 461 (2005).

25. For detail, *see* Bewkes et al., Welcoming All Families: Discrimination Against LGBTQ Foster and Adoptive Parents Hurts Children, https://cdn.americanprogress.org/content/uploads/2018/11/07063534/WelcomingAllFamilies1.pdf.

26. In re Adoption of Evan, 153 Misc. 2d 844, 583 N.Y.S.2d 997, 998-999 (Sur. Ct. 1992).

27. Alternatively, as noted in Chapter 11, the rights of a co-parent can also be established by a judicial declaration of parentage or, where permitted, the joint signing of a voluntary acknowledgment of parenthood.

28. *See* Karen Greenberg, Daniel Pollack, and Andrea Maciver, A National Responsible Father Registry: Providing Constitutional Protections for Children, Mothers and Fathers, 13 Whittier J. Child & Fam. Advoc. 85 (2014); Robbin Pott Gonzalez, The Rights of Putative Fathers to Their Infant Children in Contested Adoptions: Strengthening State Laws That Currently Deny Adequate Protection, 13 Mich. J. Gender & L. 39 (2006); Kimberly Barton, Who's Your Daddy? State Adoption Statutes and the Unknown Biological Father, 32 Cap. U. L. Rev. 113 (2003); Mary Beck, Towards a National Putative Father Registry, 25 Harv. J.L. & Pub. Poly. 1031 (2002).

29. In re A.A.T., 287 Kan. 590, 196 P.3d 1180, 1195 (2008), citing In re Adoption of S.J.B., 294 Ark. 598, 600, 745 S.W.2d 606 (1988).

30. *See* articles cited in *supra* note 11.

31. The name of the case is actually In re Doe. The citation for the appeals court decision is 254 Ill. App. 3d 405, 627 N.E.2d 648 (1993). The citation for the Illinois Supreme Court decision is 159 Ill. 2d 347, 638 N.E.2d 181 (1994).

32. In re Doe, 627 N.E.2d at 651-652.

33. In re Doe, 638 N.E.2d at 182-183.

34. Most of the debate has focused on the adoption of black children by white families, and this chapter's discussion is based on the literature on this subject. Many of the same considerations will be present, though, whenever an adoption crosses racial or ethnic lines. *See* Twila Perry, Race, Color and the Adoption of Biracial Children, 17 J. Gender Race & Just. 73 (2014); David Ray Papke, Transracial Adoption in the United States: The Reflections and Reinforcement of Racial Hierarchy, 15 J.L. & Fam. Stud. 57 (2013); Stephanie R. Richardson, Strict Scrutiny, Biracial Children and Adoption, 12 B.U. Pub. Int. L.J. 203 (2002); Kim Forde-Mazrui, Black Identity and Child Placement: The Best Interests of Black and Biracial Children, 92 Mich. L. Rev. 925 (1994) (discusses placement issues relative to biracial children).

35. For detail, *see* Cynthia G. Hawkins-Leon and Carla Bradley, Mid-Atlantic People of Color Legal Scholarship Conference: Race and Transracial Adoption: The Answer Is Neither Simply Black Nor White or Wrong, 51 Cath. U. L. Rev. 1227 (2002); Valerie Phillips Herman, Transracial Adoption: "Child-Saving" or "Child-Snatching," 13 Natl. Black L.J. 147 (1993).

36. The gap between the number of black children needing homes and available black adoptive parents has been attributed in part to the failure of agencies to recruit black parents and to the use of screening criteria that are weighted in favor of white families. *See* Hawkins-Leon and Bradley, *supra* note 35, at 1233-1238.

37. National Association of Black Social Workers, Position Paper (Summer 1972), reprinted in Forde-Mazrui, *supra* note 34, at 926.

38. *See* the Multiethnic Placement Act of 1994, Pub. L. No. 103-382, 108 Stat. 405, as amended by the Removal of Barriers to Interethnic Adoption Provisions of the Small Business Job Protection Act of 1996, Pub. L. No. 104-188, 110 Stat. 1755, §1808.

39. Dennis Hayashi—Director Office for Civil Rights, and Olivia Golden, Principal Deputy Assistant Secretary, Administration for Children and Families Memorandum: Interethnic Adoption Provisions of the Small Business Job Protection Act of 1996 (1997), http://www.hhs.gov/ocr/civilrights/resources/specialtopics/adoption/jointguidancewacf.html (accessed Jan. 7, 2016). This topic remains very controversial, and the current federal approach to transracial adoption has again been the subject of public hearings. For discussion of some of the issues, *see* Evan B. Donaldson Adoption Institute, Finding Families for African American Families: The Role of Race and Law in Adoption from Foster Care (2008); Laura Briggs, Somebody's Children, 11 J.L. & Fam. Stud. 373 (2009); Ralph Richard Banks, The Multiethnic Placement Act and the Troubling Persistence of Race Matching, 38 Cap. U. L. Rev. 271 (2009).

40. Jessica Dixon Weaver, The Changing Tides of Adoption: Why Marriage, Race, and Family Identity Still Matter, 71 SMU L. Rev. 159 (2018).

41. For a discussion of an unregulated practice known as "rehoming," through which adoptive parents who no longer feel they can give their adopted child a good home sign over custody and legal authority of the child to a new guardian, *see* Emma C. Martin, A (Re) Adoption Story: What Is Driving Adoptive Parents to Rehome Their Children and What Can Texas Do About It?, 5 Tex. A&M L. Rev. 537 (2018).

42. *See generally* Margaret M. Mahoney, Permanence and Parenthood: The Case for Abolishing the Adoption Annulment Doctrine, 42 Ind. L. Rev. 639 (2009).

Glossary

Abuse. Broadly speaking, abuse refers to the physical, sexual, or emotional harm of a child by a parent/caretaker.

Abuse prevention laws. Laws that enable domestic violence victims to obtain emergency protective orders.

Abuse reporting laws. Laws that establish a mechanism for the reporting of suspected cases of child abuse and/or neglect to a state protective agency. *See also* Mandatory reporter; Permissive reporter.

Acceptance of service. Assent by a defendant to being presented with the summons and complaint, and the defendant's willing acknowledgment of the receipt of the same.

Acknowledgment of paternity. Voluntary acknowledgment by the parents of the paternity of the father. This is accomplished through the completion of a notarized paternity affidavit.

Active listening. An engaged way of listening, involving reflection back of informational and emotional content.

Adjudication of paternity. Paternity determined through a court action.

Adoption. The legal process by which someone becomes a parent to a child with whom he or she does not have a biological relationship and assumes all the rights and responsibilities of parenthood. Adoption is premised on the termination of rights in the biological parents unless a co-parent or a stepparent is adopting the child, in which case the parental rights of that party's partner will remain in effect. *See also* Adult adoption; Agency adoption; Independent adoption; Open adoption; Transracial adoption.

Adoption abrogation. The undoing of an adoption by the adoptive parent(s).

Adoption placement. *See* Pre-adoptive placement.

Adult adoption. The adoption of one adult by another.

Adultery. Voluntary sexual intercourse between a married person and someone who is not his or her spouse; a fault divorce ground.

Affidavit. A factual statement that is signed under the penalties of perjury; often submitted to a court in support of a motion.

Affirmative defense for relief. A response to an allegation in a complaint in which the defendant seeks to establish that the plaintiff is not entitled to recover on his or her claim.

Age of capacity. The minimum age below which a young person may not marry—commonly set at age 14.

Age of consent. The age at which a young person becomes eligible to consent to his or her own marriage—usually set at the age of majority.

Agency adoption. As distinct from an independent adoption, an adoption that is handled by a state or private agency. A key component of these adoptions is that a home study is done prior to the placement of a child with a prospective adoptive family.

Alimony. *See* Spousal support.

Alimony pendente lite. Temporary support paid to one spouse by the other during the pendency of a divorce.

All-property. States that allow a couple's accumulated assets to be distributed at divorce without a formal distinction between separate property and marital property.

Annulment. A decree establishing that spouses were never actually married because an impediment existed at the time the marriage was celebrated.

Answer. The pleading filed by a defendant in response to a plaintiff's complaint, in which he or she seeks to avoid liability; component parts include responses to the plaintiff's factual allegations, affirmative defenses, and counterclaims.

Appeal. Resort to an appellate court for review of a lower-court decision; usually involves questions of law rather than of fact.

Appellate court. A court with jurisdiction to review lower-court decisions.

Appreciation. The increase in value of an asset.

Arbitration. A dispute resolution mechanism whereby parties agree to submit their disagreement to a neutral decision maker. The arbitrator's authority derives from the party's agreement, and his or her decision is usually binding subject to a limited right of court review.

Arrearage. Money that is overdue or unpaid; in this context, an outstanding support obligation.

At-risk placement. An adoption placement that is made before the rights of both parents have been terminated.

Attributed income. *See* Imputed/attributed income.

Bankruptcy. The filing of a court action in which a party seeks to be discharged from responsibility for paying his or her debts.

Batterer intervention program. A treatment or counseling program that works specifically with abusers.

Best interest. The predominant legal standard for resolving custody disputes between parents; the standard is child-centered, focusing on the needs of the child rather than on the rights of the parents.

Bigamy. The unlawful act of contracting a second marriage while one or both of the partners is already married to someone else.

Change in circumstances. A future event that arguably makes an existing order unfair and serves as the basis for a request for modification.

Child protection agency. Usually a state agency with responsibility for handling cases of child abuse and neglect.

Child support. The duty of financial support owed by a noncustodial parent to his or her minor children and to children over the age of majority in limited situations, such as in cases of disability.

Child support guidelines. Mandated by federal law, guidelines employing numeric criteria used to calculate the amount of child support to be paid by the noncustodial parent; under certain circumstances, deviations from the resulting amount may be allowed.

Child tax credit. Credit against tax liability provided to parents. Available to the parent with the dependency exemption.

Civil union. A formal status that provides same-sex couples with the rights, benefits, protections, and responsibilities that are available to married heterosexual couples under state (but not federal) law.

Clean break. Refers to the view that upon divorce, obligations stemming from the marriage should be kept to a minimum, leaving each partner free to start life anew, unencumbered by claims from the past.

Cohabitation. Two unmarried persons living together in an intimate relationship. The term applies to both same-sex and heterosexual couples.

Collaborative divorce. An approach to the practice of law that stresses cooperation and the avoidance of litigation in contested divorce cases.

Collusion. Agreement by a couple to obtain a divorce in avoidance of the fault principle that requires a guilty and an innocent spouse.

Common law. The law of England as accepted by the colonies prior to the American Revolution; also refers to judge-made law.

Common law marriage. A marriage created by the conduct of the parties rather than through a formal ceremony. Creation usually requires agreement, cohabitation, and a reputation in the community as husband and wife.

Community property. A system of property ownership between husband and wife in civil law jurisdictions in which each spouse has a vested one-half ownership interest in all marital property regardless of title; excluded is all property classified as separate property.

Comparative rectitude. A doctrine that ameliorates the harsh effects of the traditional divorce defense of recrimination by allowing a divorce when one party's marital fault is regarded as less serious than the other party's.

Compelling state interest. A governmental interest of sufficient magnitude that it may justify limitations on fundamental rights.

Complaint. In a civil case, the pleading filed by the plaintiff to initiate a lawsuit; includes factual allegations, a statement of legal claims against the defendant, and a request for relief; called "petition" in some states.

Complaint for contempt. A parent's return to court following a divorce, to enforce existing arrangements about custody or visitation arrangements after a dispute.

Complaint for modification. A parent's return to court following a divorce, to change existing arrangements about custody or visitation arrangements after a dispute.

Condonation. A divorce defense, the essence of which is that the plaintiff has forgiven the acts of marital misconduct upon which his or her complaint for divorce is based.

Confidentiality. An ethical rule prohibiting attorneys and persons working with them from disclosing client information except under limited circumstances, such as to prevent the commission of a serious crime.

Connivance. A divorce defense, the essence of which is that the plaintiff consented to the wrongdoing upon which his or her complaint for divorce is based.

Consent. Relative to adoption law, the requirement that a biological parent must assent to the adoption of his or her child unless his or her parental rights have been terminated.

Consideration. The bargained-for exchange that underlies the formation of an enforceable contract; consideration serves to distinguish a contract from a promise.

Constructive desertion. Imputes the act of desertion to the spouse responsible for the other's departure.

Constructive service. Service of a summons and complaint on a defendant in a manner other than by delivering it to him or her in person, usually by publication, mailing, or both.

Contempt proceeding. A proceeding against a party who is in violation of a court order; contempt proceedings can be either civil or criminal in nature. The purpose of a civil contempt action is to obtain compliance with a court order, while the purpose of a criminal contempt action is to punish a party for his or her noncompliance.

Continuing jurisdiction. In the custody context, the continuation of the initial decree state's authority to modify a decree to the exclusion of other states.

Contract. A legally enforceable agreement between two or more parties. *See also* Express contract; Implied-in-fact contract.

Co-parent. A parent who shares the raising of a child with his or her partner in the absence of a formally recognized parent-child relationship.

Co-parent adoption. Adoption by a co-parent (*see above*); here, the adoption does not extinguish the rights of the biological parent.

Cost basis. The cost of an asset, used to calculate the amount of appreciation from the time of purchase.

Counterclaim. A claim made by the defendant against the plaintiff.

Covenant marriage. Developed in response to concerns about the prevalence and impact of divorce, covenant marriage laws emphasize the permanency of marriage and limit the availability of divorce.

Credit reporting. In the child support context, the provision of information to a credit agency about a party's failure to make child support payments.

Criminal nonsupport. The willful failure to pay child support when one has the ability to do so; may also apply to the willful failure to pay spousal support.

Cruelty. A fault ground for divorce based on mistreatment of a relatively serious nature; cruelty generally can include either physical or emotional wrongdoing.

Custody. Broadly, the care of and responsibility for a child. *See also* Joint custody; Legal custody; Physical custody; Sole custody.

Cutoff rule. A principle that operates to extinguish the parental rights of the biological parents at the time of adoption; may not be applied when a stepparent or a co-parent is adopting the child.

Cyberstalking. The use of the Internet or other mode of electronic communication to threaten or harass someone.

De facto parent. An individual who has no biological relation to a child but who has functioned as a family member; must show that he or she resided with the child and shared caretaking responsibilities with the consent and cooperation of the legal parent.

Decree *nisi*. A provisional judgment of divorce that automatically ripens into the final divorce decree absent a challenge or decision by the parties to vacate the divorce.

Default judgment. A judgment entered against a defendant who fails to respond to a complaint or otherwise defend the action.

Dependency exemption. Deduction that a taxpayer can take from gross income for a person who is principally dependent on the taxpayer for support.

Dependency proceeding. A court process to determine if a child's parents lack the present ability to care for him or her; may result in a transfer of custody to the state.

Deponent. The person whose deposition is being taken.

Deposition. A method of discovery in which the oral testimony of a witness is obtained through questions that are answered under oath.

Desertion. A fault ground for divorce; involves the voluntary, nonconsensual departure of one spouse without justification for a period of time defined by statute.

Diminished earning capacity. A decrease in a spouse's earning potential due to a lack of a sustained connection with the paid workplace, usually because of domestic responsibilities.

Discovery. The process by which each side is able to acquire information from the other side in advance of trial. *See also* Deposition; Interrogatories; Request for admissions; Request for physical and mental examination; Request for production of documents.

Discovery conference. A meeting at which the court develops a plan for how discovery will proceed in a case.

Dispensing with parental consent. In the course of an adoption proceeding, a decision by the court to proceed with the adoption without the consent of the parents based on a finding of parental unfitness.

Divisible divorce. A divorce in which the court has jurisdiction to dissolve the marriage based on a party's domicile but cannot resolve support and property matters because it lacks personal jurisdiction over the defendant.

Divorce. The legal dissolution of a marital relationship, such that the parties are no longer spouses. *See also* Divisible divorce; *Divorce a mensa et thoro*; Fault divorce; No-fault divorce.

Divorce a mensa et thoro. A common law term meaning a "divorce from board and bed"; this is a decree of separation that permits spouses to live apart without dissolving the marital relationship.

Divorce hearing. The court hearing at which a marriage is dissolved and collateral issues are resolved; results in a divorce judgment. If the case is uncontested, the hearing is usually simple; the judge will inquire into the circumstances underlying the request for divorce and review the parties' separation agreement. If the case is contested, a trial on the merits will be conducted.

Divorce judgment. The court decree that dissolves the marriage; a decree *nisi* may be entered initially.

Docket number. The number assigned to each case by the court; the number is used for organizational and reference purposes and is included on all papers filed in a case.

Domestic partnership. Usually refers to a municipal ordinance allowing unmarried couples to register as domestic partners; provides some legal recognition and possible eligibility for benefits. Domestic partnerships are also recognized by some private employers.

Domestic violence. Abusive behavior toward someone with whom one is in a dating, familial, household, or intimate relationship. *See also* Intimate partner violence.

Domestic violence courts. Specialized courts that take a coordinated approach to the handling of domestic violence cases in order to avoid fragmentation.

Domicile. A person's permanent home; the place to which the person intends to return when away.

Donor insemination. The process by which a woman is inseminated with or inseminates herself with sperm contributed by a donor, who may be known or unknown.

Dual property. States that distinguish between marital property and separate property for distribution purposes.

Due process clause. A clause found in both the fifth and fourteenth amendments to the U.S. Constitution that protects persons from arbitrary or intrusive governmental actions. The clause provides both procedural protections and substantive rights.

Economic self-sufficiency. The idea that after a divorce, both spouses should become self-supporting as quickly as possible.

Electronic monitoring. The use of a GPS tracking device that reports the unauthorized presence of a domestic violence perpetrator in an exclusion zone.

Emancipation. The point at which a child is no longer considered a dependent of his or her parents; generally occurs at the age of majority or upon the occurrence of certain acts, such as marriage of the child.

Emergency jurisdiction. A jurisdictional ground that permits a court to assert jurisdiction over a custody dispute when a child is physically present in the state and has been abandoned or needs immediate protection from abuse or neglect.

Enhanced earning capacity. An increase in a spouse's earning ability attributable to a marital division of labor that enabled that spouse to concentrate on career development without major domestic responsibilities.

Equal protection clause. A clause in the fourteenth amendment to the U.S. Constitution that prevents states from imposing arbitrary and discriminatory legislative classifications.

Equitable distribution. The division of property at divorce based principally on considerations of fairness and contribution rather than title.

Equitable parenthood. A doctrine used to extend parenting rights to a stepparent when there is a developed, consensual relationship between the child and the stepparent, and he or she wishes to assume the rights and responsibilities of parenthood; may also be applicable when a co-parent is seeking custodial or visitation rights.

Ex parte. A hearing that is held without prior notice to the other side due to the urgent nature of the proceeding or the harm that such notice would cause.

Exclusion zone. A designated area that a perpetrator of domestic violence is not permitted to enter.

Express contract. A contract that is created by the actual, articulated agreement of the parties. *See also* Implied-in-fact contract.

Extraordinary expenses. Large, discrete expenditures that do not recur on a regular basis, as distinct from the day-to-day expenses of raising a child.

Fair market value. The price that a willing buyer would pay to a willing seller when neither party is under compulsion to buy or sell.

Family preservation. A child welfare approach that stresses the use of "reasonable efforts" to keep family together or reunify them following a child's removal.

Fault divorce. A divorce that is premised on the marital fault of one spouse.

Federal Marriage Amendment (FMA). An amendment first introduced in Congress in 2003, stating that "[m]arriage in the United States shall consist only of the union of a man and a woman"; the FMA would prevent either the federal or any state constitution from being construed to require that "marriage or the legal incidents thereof be conferred upon any union other than the union of a man and a woman."

Filing fee. The administrative fee charged by a court for the filing of an action.

Financial affidavit. A document that discloses income and assets, which parties must complete in family court proceedings where property or support is at issue.

Foster care. The taking in and caring for a child who is unable to live at home, usually because of parental abuse and/or neglect.

Freedom of contract. The right of each individual to freely structure his or her own affairs.

Genetic testing. Performed when paternity is contested; can be done through a cheek swab and can prove or disprove paternity with virtual certainty. Unless an objection is made, the tests must be admissible without foundation testimony or proof of authenticity.

Gift. A voluntary transfer of property made with donative intent, meaning that the gift-giver (donor) simply wishes to give the recipient something without requiring anything in exchange. For a gift to be effective, the transfer must be complete—the donor must fully relinquish all vestiges of ownership and control.

Goodwill. An intangible asset, the good reputation of a business in the community that generates future patronage.

Guardian ad litem. A person who is appointed by a court to conduct a custody investigation; may also refer to a person appointed to provide legal representation to a child.

Harassment Order. Civil order that can be obtained by an individual who is being harassed without the requirement of a special qualifying relationship.

Home state jurisdiction. A jurisdictional ground that enables a state to assert jurisdiction over a custody dispute based on the fact that the child lives or had lived in that state for the six months prior to the initiation of the action.

Home study. An evaluation of a person or couple seeking to adopt a child to determine potential suitability, usually done only in agency adoptions.

Implied-in-fact contract. A contract that is inferred from the conduct of the parties. *See also* Express contract.

Imputed/attributed income. The attribution of income to a party who is deliberately unemployed or underemployed, based on earning capacity, for the purpose of establishing the amount of his or her support obligation.

In loco parentis. Common law doctrine conferring parental rights and responsibilities on someone who voluntarily assumes a parenting role.

In rem jurisdiction. The authority of a court to resolve a case based on the presence of property within its borders.

Inception of title rule. A rule fixing title at the time an asset is acquired.

Incest. Unlawful sexual relations between persons who are closely related to each other; marriages contracted in violation of incest provisions are invalid.

Incorporation. In the divorce context, upon approval of a separation agreement, the inclusion of its terms into the divorce judgment such that those terms become part of the judgment. *See also* Merger; Survival.

Independent adoption. An adoption that is accomplished without an agency; parents can either place the child directly or utilize an intermediary.

Indissoluble. In reference to marriage, the belief that the legal relationship between spouses is permanent and can never be terminated.

Initial custody determination. The first custody decision in a case, as distinct from subsequent modifications.

Innocent spouse. Pertaining to fault divorce, the requirement that the petitioning spouse not have engaged in marital misconduct.

Intangible assets. Property that lacks a physical presence and cannot be ascertained by the senses.

Interrogatories. A discovery method involving written questions to a party, which must be answered under oath.

Intimate partner violence. Violence between partners who are in a same-sex or heterosexual relationship, including dating relationships. *See also* Domestic violence.

Irreconcilable differences. A no-fault divorce ground, the essence of which is that the parties are no longer compatible and there is no hope of reconciliation.

IV-D agency. Under Title IV-D, the agency in each state responsible for administering that state's child support program.

Joint custody. As distinct from sole custody, the sharing of parental rights and responsibilities—can apply to legal or physical custody, or both.

Joint petition. A pleading filed in a no-fault divorce action by co-petitioners to initiate the divorce.

Judgment. *See* Default judgment; Divorce judgment.

Jurisdiction. The authority of a court to hear and resolve a case before it. *See also* Emergency jurisdiction; In rem jurisdiction; Personal jurisdiction; Subject matter jurisdiction.

Lack of capacity. Lack of ability of a party to enter into legally enforceable agreements.

Last resort jurisdiction. A relatively insignificant jurisdictional ground that enables a state to assert jurisdiction over a custody dispute when no other state has or is willing to assume jurisdiction and it is in the best interest of the child for the state to do so.

Legal custody. As distinct from physical custody, legal custody confers on a parent the authority to make major decisions related to his or her child's life; legal custody can be sole or joint.

Legal separation. A judicial decree permitting parties to live apart, usually for cause, without dissolving the legal relationship of spouses. *See also* Separate maintenance.

Legitimation. The process of altering the status of a child born to unmarried parents so that he or she is the legal equivalent of a child born to married parents.

Lien. A nonpossessory interest in the property of another that operates as a cloud against title.

Living separate and apart. A no-fault divorce ground that requires the parties to have lived apart for a statutory period of time, with the separation serving as proof of marital breakdown.

Long-arm statute. A statute that spells out when a state may assert personal jurisdiction over a nonresident.

Lump-Sum Support/Alimony in Gross. A support award of a specific amount of money, usually payable in a single installment, although it can also be made payable in periodic installments until the full amount of the order is reached.

Mandatory reporter. In contrast to a permissive reporter, a person, usually a professional who comes into contact with children in the course of his or her work, who is legally obligated to report suspected cases of child abuse or neglect pursuant to an abuse reporting law.

Marital breakdown. *See* Irreconcilable differences.

Marital fault. Acts of wrongdoing by one spouse toward the other that serve as the basis of a fault divorce. *See* Adultery; Cruelty; Desertion.

Marital property. As distinct from separate property, assets acquired during the marriage as a result of marital efforts or funds, which are subject to division at divorce.

Marital unity. A common law principle espousing that upon marriage a husband and wife become one, resulting in the suspension of the wife's legal identity.

Marriage restriction laws. Laws that prevent certain people, such as close relatives, from marrying each other.

Married Women's Property Acts. The series of statutory reforms that gradually improved the legal status of married women, principally through extending rights of property ownership and control that had been denied at common law.

Mediation. A nonadversarial approach to dispute resolution in which a neutral third party—the mediator—helps parties reach a mutually satisfactory resolution to a conflict; an increasingly popular option in divorce cases.

Merger. Going beyond incorporation, merger refers to when a separation agreement, once approved by the court, loses its separate identity and thereafter exists only as part of the court's judgment; this contrasts with the concept of survival.

Minimum contacts. A jurisdictional concept enabling a state to assert personal jurisdiction over a nonresident when he or she has a sufficiently developed relationship with that state.

Modification. The alteration of an existing order based on a change in circumstances.

Modification jurisdiction. The authority of a court to modify a custody or support decree.

Motion. In general, a request made to a court for some kind of relief during the pendency of an action.

Motion for a new trial. A post-trial request that the court set aside the judgment and order a new trial because of prejudicial errors during the trial.

Motion for relief from judgment. A post-trial request that the court vacate or modify its judgment, usually because of an error, unfairness, or newly discovered evidence.

Motion to compel. A request to the court that it order the other side to comply with a discovery request.

Motion to dismiss. A request to the court that it dismiss the plaintiff's case for lack of jurisdiction, improper service, or the plaintiff's failure to state a valid claim entitling him or her to relief.

Mutual consent. The idea that a no-fault divorce should require the agreement of both spouses.

Mutual orders of protection. Orders of protection granted by some courts to both parties where only one party has sought court intervention.

Neglect. Broadly speaking, the willful failure by a parent/caretaker to provide for a child's basic needs.

Negotiation. The process through which attorneys seek to resolve a case outside court; often done at a settlement conference at which the clients are present.

Nexus approach. As distinct from the per se approach, this approach requires that parental conduct have a demonstrated detrimental impact on a child before it will be taken into account in a custody determination.

No-contact order. A protective order that prohibits someone from having any contact with the party he or she has abused.

No-fault divorce. A divorce that is based on the breakdown of the marital relationship rather than on the marital fault of one spouse. *See also* Irreconcilable differences.

Noncustodial parent. A parent who has been divested of both legal and physical custody, but is still a legal parent with enforceable rights, such as visitation.

Open adoption. An adoption that permits some degree of contact with one or both biological parents.

Opportunity cost. The loss of earning potential attributable to a lack of a sustained relationship with the labor force, often due to a spouse's primary investment in the domestic realm.

Opportunity interest. The opportunity that the biological link provides to an unmarried father to develop a meaningful relationship with his child.

Parens patriae. The authority of the state, as a sovereign power, to protect those who cannot protect themselves, most notably children.

Parent locator service. A federal or state agency that is responsible for locating absent parents in order to establish or enforce a child support award.

Parental unfitness. Parental abuse or neglect that is severe enough to warrant a termination of rights.

Parenting coordinator. A person who is appointed to assist parents in implementing their parenting plan following a divorce.

Parenting plan. A written agreement in which the parents detail how they intend to care for their children following a divorce.

Paternal preference. The common law doctrine that vested fathers with the absolute right to care and custody of their children.

Paternity disestablishment. The undoing/revocation of a determination that a man is a child's legal father.

Pension. Deferred compensation payable at retirement.

Per se approach. As distinct from the nexus approach, the idea that some behaviors are so inherently harmful that they should be the basis for denying custody to a parent without proof of actual harm.

Permanency hearing. A hearing to determine if a child who has been removed from the home due to abuse or neglect can safely return home or whether parental rights should be terminated and the child freed for adoption.

Permanency plan. A plan that either calls for the return of a child home following removal for abuse or neglect or for the termination of parental rights.

Permanent alimony. An ongoing support award to a spouse who is unlikely to become economically self-sufficient; the award is subject to modification and is generally terminable upon death of either spouse or remarriage of the recipient.

Permissive reporter. In contrast to a mandatory reporter, a person who may report suspected cases of child abuse or neglect to a child protective agency but is not legally obligated to do so.

Personal jurisdiction. The authority of a court over the person of a defendant.

Personal property. Broadly, all property owned by an individual other than real property; includes both tangible and intangible assets.

Personal service. In contrast to constructive service, delivering the summons and complaint by hand to the defendant.

Petition. *See* Complaint.

Physical custody. As distinct from legal custody, physical custody refers to where a child lives; a parent with physical custody usually maintains a home for the child and is responsible for the child's day-to-day care. Physical custody can be either sole or joint.

Polygamy. The situation where an individual (most commonly a man) has multiple spouses at the same time.

Postmarital agreement. Similar to a premarital agreement, but entered after rather than before a marriage. *See* Premarital agreement.

Postplacement social study. An assessment of an adoption placement done to provide information to the judge who will be deciding if the adoption should be approved.

Prayer for relief. *See* Request for relief.

Pre-adoption placement. The specified period of time that a child must live with his or her prospective adoptive parents before the adoption can be approved.

Premarital acquisitions. Property owned by a spouse prior to marriage.

Premarital agreement. A contract entered into by prospective spouses in which they seek to establish their respective rights in the event the marriage fails; most commonly, provisions address spousal support and the allocation of property.

Premarital counseling. Using incentives such as a reduced marriage license fee, some states now encourage potential spouses to participate in counseling as a way to reduce the divorce rate.

Presumption of paternity. The legal assumption that the father of a child born to a married woman is the woman's husband.

Pretrial conference. A meeting held by a judge with counsel prior to trial, mainly to streamline issues and determine the possibility of settlement.

Pretrial statement. A memorandum prepared by each side in advance of a pretrial conference; a key purpose is the delineation of issues still in contention.

Primary caretaker. The parent who has been mainly responsible for the day-to-day care and nurture of a child.

Primary caretaker presumption. A legal rule that gives preference to the primary caretaker parent in the event of a custody dispute.

Private placement adoption. *See* Independent adoption.

Procedural fairness. Fairness of the parties in their treatment of one another in the process of negotiating an agreement, as distinct from fairness in the resulting terms (substantive fairness).

Professional goodwill. The reputation of a professional practice in the community that generates future patronage.

Protective order. 1. In domestic violence cases, a court order to shield the victim from harm; although civil in nature, violation of these orders is a criminal offense in many states. *See also* No-contact order; Restraining order; Stay-away order; Vacate order. 2. A court order limiting discovery that is unreasonable or oppressive.

Qualified Domestic Relations Order (QDRO). A court order that allows the distribution of pension benefits to a nonemployee spouse.

Qualified Medical Child Support Order (QMCSO). A court order requiring that a child be covered by the noncustodial parent's group health insurance plan.

Real property. As distinct from personal property, real property refers to land and that which is growing upon or affixed to it.

Reasonable efforts. The effort that a child protective agency must make (in most situations) to prevent removal of a child from his or her home, or if the child has been removed, the effort that the agency must put toward reunification.

Recapture. The recomputation of a support obligor's gross income to include amounts that had been improperly deducted as spousal support payments and the readjustment of his or her tax obligation.

Recrimination. A divorce defense that prevents a divorce from being granted on the basis that both parties are guilty of marital misconduct; may be ameliorated by the doctrine of comparative rectitude.

Rehabilitative support. Time-limited support intended to enable a spouse to obtain the education or training necessary to become economically self-sufficient.

Reimbursement alimony. A support award intended to reimburse a spouse for contributions to the professional education of the other spouse; in addition to reimbursing the financial contribution, it may also compensate for the loss of future income.

Reinstatement of Parental Rights. Where previously terminated parental rights are restored in order to prevent a child from becoming a "legal orphan."

Relinquishment. The surrender by a parent of a child to an adoption agency.

Relocation disputes. A disagreement arising during or after a divorce in which the custodial parent seeks to move to another state with the children and the noncustodial parent seeks to prevent the move.

Request for admissions. A discovery method in which a party asks the other side to admit to the truth of certain facts or to the authenticity of certain documents; done mainly to simplify matters for trial.

Request for mental or physical examination. A discovery method in which a party asks the court to order the other side to submit to a medical or mental evaluation, used when such information is arguably relevant to the outcome of the case.

Request for production of documents. A discovery method in which a party can obtain documents from the other side that are needed to prepare the case.

Request for relief. The portion of a complaint in which the plaintiff sets out the relief that he or she is seeking from the court.

Restraining order. A court order directing a perpetrator to refrain from committing further acts of domestic violence against the party seeking protection from abuse; may also protect the children.

Retroactivity. The application of a court decision backwards in time following the declaration that a statute is unconstitutional.

Return of service. The acknowledgment to the court by the person serving the defendant that service was made; usually includes a notation of how and when the service was made.

Reunification services. Services that a child protection agency provides to a family following the removal of a child for the purpose of enabling the child to return home.

Review and adjustment procedure. The periodic assessment and potential revision of a child support order by an IV-D agency.

Revival. The restoration of certain rights deriving from a prior marriage following the annulment of a subsequent marriage.

Revocation of consent. A parent's seeking to take back his or her agreement to an adoption.

Safe haven. These laws allow a birth parent, or an agent of the parent, to leave a baby at a safe location, such as a hospital or fire station, without fear of being prosecuted for child abandonment or neglect.

Second glance doctrine. Review by a court of the terms of a premarital agreement to determine whether they are fair as of the time of enforcement.

Separate maintenance. Similar to a legal separation, but here the essence of the action is a request for support. *See also* Legal separation.

Separate property. As distinct from marital property, property that belongs to the acquiring spouse and is not subject to distribution at divorce. It usually consists of gifts, inheritances, and premarital acquisitions.

Separation agreement. A contract between divorcing spouses in which they set out the terms of their agreement relative to all collateral matters, such as custody, support, and the distribution of property.

Service of process. Delivery of a summons and complaint to a defendant; provides the defendant with notice of the action and informs him or her that a default judgment may be entered unless an answer is filed within a specified time. *See also* Constructive service; Personal service.

Service plan. A plan developed by the child protection agency in cases of substantiated abuse that sets out the services to be provided to the parents to help them care for their children; may also impose certain obligations on the parents.

Significant connection jurisdiction. A jurisdictional ground that permits a court to assert jurisdiction over a custody dispute based on the fact that a child and at least one contestant have a meaningful relationship with that state and relevant evidence is available there.

Sole custody. The vesting of custodial rights in one parent—can apply to legal custody, physical custody, or both.

Source of funds rule. As distinct from the inception of title rule, an approach that ties the time of acquisition of an asset to the contribution of funds and permits the dual characterization of an asset as both marital and separate in proportion to contribution.

Special equity. A rule giving a spouse who contributed purchase funds to an asset titled in the name of the other spouse an interest in the asset, which is reachable at divorce; was relevant in jurisdictions that divided property according to title.

Spousal support. A monetary amount paid to one spouse by the other for support pending or after legal separation or divorce. *See also* Alimony pendente lite; Lump-sum support; Permanent alimony; Rehabilitative support; Reimbursement alimony.

Stalking. The malicious, willful, and repeated tracking down and following of another person; stalking is often a precursor to acts of serious bodily harm.

Standing. A jurisdictional concept requiring a person to have a sufficient stake in the outcome of a controversy in order to maintain a legal action.

Statute of frauds. A rule requiring that certain kinds of contracts be in writing in order to be enforceable.

Stay-away order. A court order, pursuant to an abuse prevention law, requiring the perpetrator to keep away from the victim's home or from other places where the victim regularly goes (e.g., work).

Stepparent. The legal relationship of a new spouse to the children of a prior marriage.

Subject matter jurisdiction. The authority of a court to hear a particular kind of case.

Subpoena. A writ commanding a witness to appear at a particular time and place to give testimony.

Subpoena duces tecum. A writ commanding a witness to produce books, papers, or other items, usually at a deposition or trial.

Substantive fairness. Fairness of the actual terms of an agreement, as distinct from procedural fairness.

Summons. Issued by the court at the commencement of an action for service on the defendant, a document that informs the defendant of the action and that he or she is required to respond within a certain period of time or risk the entry of a default judgment.

Support worksheet. A worksheet that is tied to child support guidelines and is used in calculating a support award.

Survival. In contrast to a merger, the incorporation of a separation agreement into the divorce judgment, but the retention of its significance as an independent agreement.

Tangible property. Property with a physical presence, which is capable of being felt and seen.

Temporary order. An order made during the pendency of a legal proceeding; temporary orders are superseded by the judgment.

Tender years presumption. The traditional custodial assumption that children of a young age should be raised by their mothers.

Termination of parental rights. The permanent severance of the parent-child relationship based on parental unfitness.

Testamentary capacity. The legal ability to dispose of one's property at death through the execution of a will.

Title. The right of exclusive ownership and control of an asset.

Title IV-D. A law that amends the Social Security Act to establish a cooperative federal-state program for the obtaining and enforcement of child support orders.

Tracing. The process by which a party seeks to establish the separate identity of an asset owned at the time of divorce so that it is not subject to distribution.

Transitional support. *See* Rehabilitative support.

Transmutation. The postacquisition change in the classification of an asset from marital to separate, or vice versa. Transmutation can occur through agreement, commingling, the taking of title in joint name, or use.

Transracial adoption. Adoption across racial lines.

Trial notebook. A binder containing everything needed to present a case in court.

Unallocated support. Child and spousal support awards combined in a single support amount without designation.

Unbundled legal services. Also referred to as "limited task representation." An attorney agrees to provide a client with limited assistance from a menu of options instead of providing the client with comprehensive representation. Typically, rather than entering into a retainer agreement, the client pays for each separate service at the time it is rendered. Unbundled services include the giving of legal advice, coaching on how to handle the case, assistance with drafting pleadings, and representation in court.

Unconscionability. When a contract is grossly unfair to one side; usually involves parties with a significant disparity in bargaining power.

Vacate order. A court order requiring a perpetrator of domestic violence to move out of the home that he or she shares with the party who has been abused; vacate orders do not affect title to property.

Valuation. The determination of what an asset is worth, most commonly by ascertaining its fair market value; usually done by an expert.

Venue. A geographical concept designating which locale an action is to be filed in.

Violence Against Women Act (VAWA). A federal law providing protection to victims of domestic violence and funding for antiviolence programs.

Virtual visitation. The use of electronic communication tools as a supplemental way for a child and a noncustodial parent to connect.

Visitation. The time that a noncustodial parent spends with his or her child.

Void. A marriage that is without any legal effect from its inception; a void marriage does not require a decree of annulment to invalidate it. *See also* Voidable.

Void as against public policy. The invalidation of a contract on the basis that it violates deeply held community beliefs.

Voidable. A marriage that is considered valid unless and until it is declared invalid by a decree of annulment. *See also* Void.

Voluntary surrender. *See* Relinquishment.

Wage withholding. An order directing a support obligor's employer to take support payments directly out of that party's paycheck.

Wrongful adoption. An action that an adoptive parent can bring against an adoption agency if the agency failed to tell the parents the truth about the child they adopted.

Index

Abandonment
  child neglect. *See* Child abuse and neglect
  as ground for divorce, 161–162
Abduction of children, international, 431–433, 437–441
Absent parents, locating, 273–274
Abuse. *See* Child abuse and neglect; Domestic violence
Abuse prevention laws, 96, 101–102, 109–110, 119–124, 131–133. *See also* Domestic violence; Protective orders; Violence Against Women Act
Abuse reporting laws, 607, 615–616
Acceptance of service, 467
Acknowledgment of paternity, 566–568
Active listening, 450–452
Adjudication of paternity, 555, 561–566
Admissions requests, 485–486
Adoption, 643–695
  abrogation, 672–673
  access to sealed adoption records, 658–659, 678–681
  agency adoptions, 646
    parental relationships and rights during placement, 654–655
    relinquishment, 650
    revocation by agency, 654–655
    revocation of consent, 651–652
    wrongful adoption, 672–673
  at-risk placements, 652

"best interest of the child" standard, 668–669
birth certificate, reissue of, 656
consent
  child's consent, 649
  prebirth consent, 650
  private placement adoptions, 650
  request to dispense with, 651–652
  revocation, 651–652, 654–655
  of unwed fathers, 650, 664–665
by co-parents, 661–662
cut-off rule, exceptions to, 661
by gay men, 660–661
historical perspective, 643–645
home study, 646, 653–655
Indian Child Welfare Act, 689–692
intent to claim parental rights, 666–667
intermediary roles, 646–648
joint adoption, 661
judicial review and approval, 655–656
by lesbians, 660–661
notice of proceedings, 655–656, 664
open adoption, 655–656, 657–658, 694n21
post-adoption contact, 657–658
post-placement social study, 655
pre-adoption placements, 653–655
private placement or independent adoptions, 646–648
  parental consent, 650
  parental relationships and rights during pre-placement, 654
  revocation of consent, 651–652, 654

Adoption (*continued*)
putative father registries, 664
registry systems, 659
relinquishment, 650
safe haven laws, 648–649
sealed records, 656–657, 658–659,
678–681, 694n19
by single parent, 661
special needs children, 693n14
by stepparents, 240–241, 659–660
support for adopted child, 302
termination of child support, 302
termination of parental rights
adoption by stepparents, 659–660
A.M.H., In re Adoption of (2007),
682–689
involuntary, 652, 693n13
opportunity interest requirement,
664–665
voluntary, 646, 650, 654
transracial, 669–671, 695n34, 695n36
unwed fathers' rights, 649, 650,
662–669
voluntary surrender, 646, 650, 654
wrongful adoption, 672–673
Adoption and Safe Families Act, 611
Adoption and Safe Families Act of 1997
(ASFA), 618–621, 640n40
Adoption Assistance and Child
Welfare Act of 1980 (CWA),
617, 693n14
Adult children, support of, 302–304
Adultery
as ground for divorce, 159–161
same-sex couples, 186–189
Advocates, domestic violence
cases, 110
Affidavits. *See also* Divorce
accompanying motions, 488
financial disclosure affidavit, 283,
284–289
motion for temporary custody and
supporting affidavit, 494–496
Affirmative defenses, 472
After-hour emergency protective
orders, 118
Agency adoptions
overview, 646

parental relationships and rights
during placement, 654–655
relinquishment, 650
revocation by agency, 654–655
revocation of consent, 651–652
wrongful adoption, 672–673
Age of capacity, marriage and, 18, 175
Age of consent, 18
AIDS
epidemic, 10
marriage licenses and, 21
Aid to Families with Dependent
Children (ADFC), 269–270
Alabama, alimony legislation, 7
Alaska
intimate partner violence, 133
same-sex marriage, 10, 57n18
separate vs. marital assets, 408–412
Alimony. *See* Spousal support
Alimony in gross, 339
Alimony pendente lite, 339
All property approach, 374
Alma Society, Inc. v. Mellon (1979),
678–681
Alternative dispute resolution
arbitration, 503–504
mediation, 498–503
domestic violence cases, 501–502
mediators, 498, 548n21
motions, diversion of, 489–490
overview, 498–499, 548n30
process, 499–501
American Bar Association Model Rules
of Professional Conduct, 448
American Indian women, domestic
violence, 133
American Law Institute (ALI)
child custody, approximation rule
for, 216–218
equitable compensation principle for
spousal support, 337
"marital status" approach to
cohabitation, 27
*Principles of the Law of Family
Dissolution*, 59n61, 216–217
role of, 266n49
American Society for the Prevention of
Cruelty to Animals (ASPCA), 606

A.M.H., In re Adoption of (2007), 682–689
Annulment of marriage, 174–178
  children, effect on, 176
  consequences, 176–177
  divorce, compared, 156, 174–175
  grounds, 175–176
  religious underpinnings, 156–157
  revival, 177–178
  spousal support, 177
Answer to divorce complaint, 468
  affirmative defenses, 472
  counterclaims, 472
  filing, 468
  forms, 473–475
  motion to dismiss, 472
Antenuptial agreements. *See* Premarital agreements
Anti-cruelty societies, 605–606, 638n7
Anti-miscegenation laws, 8–9, 31–34
Anti-stalking laws, 127–130, 133
Appellate procedure, 532
Appreciation of separate property, 389–390
Apprenticeships and indenture, 644
Approximation rule for child custody, 216–218
Arbitration, 503–504
Arizona
  Brush & Nib Studio v. City of Phoenix (2018), 49–56
  community property approach, 4, 372
  covenant marriages, 172
  same-sex marriage, opposition to, 15
Arkansas, covenant marriages in, 172
Arm's length relationships, 65
A.R.R., In Re Paternity of (2015), 585–591
Arrearages, 290–291
  interstate cases, 293–295
Arrest policies, domestic violence, 126–127
Artificial insemination. *See* Sperm donation
ARW, In re Termination of Parental Rights to (2015), 689–692
ASFA (Adoption and Safe Families Act of 1997), 618–621, 640n40

Assets, motion for protection of, 492
Assisted reproductive technologies. *See* Sperm donation
At-risk placements, 652
Attorneys, unbundled legal services, 506–508
Attorneys' fees, motion for payment of, 492
Attributed income, 276
A.W., In the Interest of (2017), 633–637

Baby Richard case (1993), 668–669
Bankruptcy, spousal support obligations and, 350–351
Bankruptcy Abuse Prevention and Consumer Protection Act of 2005, 351
Bartholet, Elizabeth, 654
"Bastardy" rules, 552
Battered child syndrome, 607
Battered wives. *See* Domestic violence
Batterer intervention programs, 108
Bedrick v. Bedrick (2011), 85–90
Berry v. Berry (2018), 183–186
Best interests of child
  adoption, 668–669
  A.R.R., In Re Paternity of (2015), 585–591
  child custody, 73, 195, 197–213, 218–222, 250–258
  child support, 315, 318
  critiques and alternative approaches, 214–218
  Danti v. Danti (2009), 250–258
  grandparents' rights to visitation, 238–239
  jurisdictional issues, 429
  Langston v. Riffe (2000), 571
  marriage as stability needed for, 38
  modification of custody and visitation, 230
  nonparents' rights to custody and visitation, 236–239
  parenting coordinator provisions, 227
  paternity determinations, 571
  relocation disputes, 232–233
  stepparent's rights to visitation, 240
  visitation rights, 223–226

Bigamy, 17–18, 175
Birth defects, incestuous marriages
    and, 16
Blackstone, William, 2, 3, 196
Blanchflower, In the Matter of (2003),
    186–189
Bottoms v. Bottoms (1995), 210
Brush & Nib Studio v. City of Phoenix
    (2018), 49–56

California
    anti-stalking legislation, 127–128
    biology-plus approach to paternity,
        559–560
    cohabitation, 25–26, 44–49
    community property
        approach, 4, 372
    Joint Petition for Summary
        Dissolution, 461
    no-fault divorce, 155, 164
    parental health and child
        custody, 213
    sperm donor's rights, 573
Capacity
    age of, 18
    Berry v. Berry (2018), 183–186
    lack of, 175, 183–186
    testamentary capacity of married
        women, 3
    voidable marriages and, 176
CAPTA (Child Abuse Prevention and
    Treatment Act of 2010), 607
Case registries. *See* Registries
Castle v. Castle (2018), 412–417
Catholic Church, view of divorce, 156
Change in circumstances
    child support, 299–300
    spousal support, 339, 346–348
Cheryl, Paternity of (2001), 571, 591–594
Child abduction, international, 431–
    433, 437–441
Child abuse and neglect, 603–641
    "abuse," defined, 608–610
    abuse reporting laws, 607
    A.W., In the Interest of (2017), 633–637
    child protection agencies, 607
    correlation to partner abuse, 205
    dependency proceeding, 619–620

emergency removal, 616–617
emotional abuse and neglect, 610
exposure to domestic violence,
    611–612
family preservation, emphasis on,
    617, 621
forced child marriage, 613
historical perspective, 604–607
knowing, 627–633
legal orphans, 621–622
mandatory reporters, 615
medical child abuse, 613
mitigating circumstances, 627–633
"neglect," defined, 610–613
obesity, 612
parental unfitness, consequences
    of, 621
passive abuse, 612, 639n20
permanency planning, 620–621
permissive reporters, 615–616
physical abuse, 608–609
prenatal drug exposure, 614–615
privacy and autonomy vs. child
    protection, 603–604, 605, 608
"reasonable efforts" requirement,
    618–619
reinstatement of parental rights,
    621–622
removal of child, 619–622
reporting, 607, 615–616
rescue of Mary Ellen Wilson, 605–606
reunification services, 620
screening and investigation, 616–617
service plan, 619
sexual abuse, 609–610
societies for the prevention of cruelty
    to children, 605–606
spanking, 609
*Tennessee Department of Children's
    Services v. Tikindra G.* (2011),
    627–633
termination of parental rights,
    620–621, 633–637, 640n40
Child Abuse Prevention and
    Treatment Act of 2010 (CAPTA),
    607, 608
Child abuse prevention laws. *See*
    Abuse prevention laws

Child custody. *See* Custody and
    visitation
Child protection. *See* Child abuse and
    neglect
Child protection agencies, 607
Children. *See* Minors
Children of unmarried parents. *See also*
    Paternity
    "child in common" protection
        provisions, 98
    common law status, 552
    constitutional developments,
        554–560
    early American reforms, 552–554
    equal protection of, 554–555
    "illegitimate" defined, 551
    inheritance rights, 555
    legal status of fathers, 553,
        555–560
    legitimation, 553
    presumption of paternity, 552,
        559–560
Child support, 269–325
    absent parents, locating, 273–274
    adopted children, 302
    annulment of marriage and, 177
    arrearages, 290–291
    change in circumstances, 299–300
    college students, 302–304
    Colonna v. Colonna (2004), 313–317
    custody and visitation, adjustments
        for, 282–283
    disabilities, adult children
        with, 304
    duration of, 300–304
    enforcement, 271–273, 290–291
    extraordinary expenses, effect of,
        280–281
    factors affecting, 278–283, 310–313
    financial disclosure affidavit, 283,
        284–289
    Flexibility, Efficiency, and
        Modernization in Child Support
        Enforcement Programs (Final
        Rule 2016), 271, 274, 277, 281,
        297, 300
    formulas
        income shares approach, 275–276

    Melson formula, 275
    percentage of income
        approach, 275
    guidelines, 274–283
    health insurance and, 281
    historical perspective, 270–271
    incarcerated parent, 317–321
    income considerations
        child's resources, 279
        of custodial parent, 279, 313–317
        defining income, 276–277
        imputed or attributed income, 276
        income base, determining, 277–278
        of new partner, 279
        withholding, 290–291
    jurisdiction, 423–424
    McLeod v. Starnes (2012), 310–313
    modification and adjustment,
        299–300
    multiple families, 279–280
    noncompliance
        absent parents, locating, 273–274
        arrearages, 290–291
        collection agencies, 294, 298–299
        contempt, 296–297
        credit reporting, 292
        criminal actions, 295–296
        federal enforcement, 271, 273–274,
            292–293, 322n8
        income withholding, 290–291
        interstate cases, 293–295
        license suspension or
            withholding, 292
        liens, 291–292
        passport denial, 293
        rates of, 269
        state enforcement, 271–272,
            290–291
        tax offsets, 292–293
    nontraditional family
        structures, 322n7
    paternity, establishing, 568, 570
    permanent awards, 274, 323n18
    in premarital agreements, 73
    public assistance and, 271–272
    qualified medical child support
        order, 281
    review and adjustment, 300

Child support (*continued*)
  tax considerations, 304–305
  temporary orders, 107, 274
  termination
    adoption, 302
    emancipation, 301
    parental death, 301
  unwed fathers, 568
  worksheet, 274
  Yerkes v. Yerkes (2003), 317–321
Child Support Enforcement and
    Establishment of Paternity Act of
    1974, 270, 271, 273–274, 560. *See
    also* Title IV-D agencies
Child tax credit, 305
Church of England, view of
    divorce, 157
Civil law
  community property, 4, 372
  contempt, 296–267, 349–350
  divorce and annulment, 156–157,
    174–175, 457
  violation of adoption contact veto,
    658–659
Civil unions, 58n54. *See also* Same-sex
    couples
Clean break approach, 329, 331–333
Clean hands doctrine, 430
Client confidentiality, 449, 616
COBRA (Consolidated Omnibus
    Budget Reconciliation Act of
    1986), 345
Cohabitation, 24–28
  dissolution of, 59n61
  domestic partnerships, 58n54
  durable power of attorney, 59n58
  formal status of, 59n59
  implied-in-fact contract theory, 26
  legal rights of, 24–28
  "marital-status" approach, 27
  Marvin v. Marvin (1976), 25–26, 27,
    44–49
  property acquisition, 386
  protective orders, 98
  spousal support and, 347
Collaborative divorce, 504–506
Collection agencies, child support, 294,
    298–299
College students, support of, 302–304
  McLeod v. Starnes (2012), 310–313
Collusion, as defense for divorce,
    163–164
Colonna v. Colonna (2004), 313–317
Colorado
  accrued vacation as marital
    property, 382
  freedom of religion, 15
  same-sex marriage, opposition to, 15
Commingling, transmutation of
    separate property by, 391
Common law
  annulment of marriage, 176
  children of unmarried parents, 552
  child support, 270, 300
  defined, 57n1
  grandparents' rights, 236–239
  husband's right to physical
    violence, 93–94
  marital property, 372
  presumption of paternity, 552
Common law marriage, 22–24
Community property. *See also* Marital
    property
  marital property determinations,
    372–373
  marriage and, 4
Comparative rectitude, 163
Compelling state interest, 57n18, 238
Complaints
  for contempt
    custody and visitation, 230
    divorce proceedings, 536
  for divorce. *See under* Divorce
  for modification of custody and
    visitation, 230
  for paternity, 561
Condonation, as defense for divorce,
    163, 189–191
Conferences, discovery, 486–487
Confidentiality, 449, 616
Confidential relationships, 65
Connecticut
  marital privacy, 7
  premarital agreements, 85–90
Connivance, as defense for divorce,
    162–163

Consent
  adoption
    child's consent, 649
    prebirth consent, 650
    private placement adoptions, 650
    request to dispense with, 651–652
    revocation, 651–652, 654–655
    of unwed fathers, 650, 664–665
  age of, 18
  divorce by mutual consent, 156, 171
  jurisdiction rule, 423
Consideration, premarital agreements, 64
Consolidated Omnibus Budget
    Reconciliation Act of 1986
    (COBRA), 345
Constitutional considerations. *See*
    Due Process Clause; Equal
    Protection Clause
Constructive desertion, doctrine of, 162
Constructive service, 465
Contemplation of marriage, property
    acquisition, 386
Contempt
  child support noncompliance,
    296–297
  civil contempt, 297–298
  criminal contempt, 297
  custody and visitation complaint, 230
  divorce proceedings, 536, 537–539
  motion for, sample form, 537–539
  spousal support arrearages, 349–350
Continuing jurisdiction, 429–430
Contracts. *See also* Premarital
    agreements
  arm's length vs. confidential
    relationships, 65
  consideration, 64
  fairness requirement, 64–71, 92n7
  freedom of contract principle, 64
  implied-in-fact contracts, 26
  by married women, 3
  second glance doctrine, 70
  spousal support modification,
    agreements to prohibit, 349
  statute of frauds, 64
  transmutation of separate property
    by agreement, 391
  unconscionability, doctrine of, 64–65

Co-parents, 576–577
  adoption by, 661–662
  marriage and consent rights, 577–578
  McLaughlin v. Jones (2017), 595–598
Corporal punishment, 609
Cost basis of marital property, 400
Counseling orders, 108
Counterclaims in divorce actions, 472
Court costs, motion for payment
    of, 492
Covenant marriages, 172–174,
    193n23, 193n38
Credit reporting, for child support
    arrearages, 292
Criminal penalties
  adoption contact veto, violation of,
    658–659
  child abuse, 607, 638n12, 639n20
  contempt, 296–297, 350
  domestic violence, 97, 130–131, 132
  ethical violations, 448
  failure to report child abuse, 615
  incest, 16–17
  multiple marriages, 17
  nonsupport, 296
  prenatal drug use, 640n29
  protective orders, violation of, 125,
    131, 492–493
  stalking, 127–128, 131
Cruelty as ground for divorce, 162
Cultural considerations
  adoption and, 653–654, 682–689
  child punishment, 603–604, 609
  client interviews, 547n1
  custody decisions, 208–209, 214
  transracial adoptions, 669–671,
    695n34, 695n36
Custody and visitation, 195–268
  adoption agencies, custody by, 646
  annulment of marriage, 177
  approximation rule, 216–218
  arrangements, types of, 218–222
  child support adjustments based on,
    282–283, 299–300
  client interview checklist, 229
  contempt, complaint for, 230
  Danti v. Danti (2009), 250–258
  determining factors, 198–199

Custody and visitation (*continued*)
   child's preference, 201–204
   domestic violence, 205–207
   interracial relationships, 208–209
   parental health, 213
   parental lifestyle, 207–213
   parental sexual activity, 209
   parental sexual orientation, 209–211
   parent-child bond, 200
   past caretaking, 200–201
   primary caretaker presumption, 200–201, 215–216
   religion, 211–213
   stability of environment, 201
   time availability, 201
  educational programs for children, 228
  grandparents' rights, 236–239
  historical perspective, 196–197, 216–217
  initial custody determinations, 427–429
  joint custody
   controversy about, 220–222
   relocation disputes, 232–235
   types of arrangements, 219
  judges' bias, 207–208, 265n34
  jurisdiction
   declining, 430
   deployed parents, 430
   emergency jurisdiction, 428, 430
   home state jurisdiction, 427, 430
   initial custody determinations, 427–429
   last resort jurisdiction, 429, 430
   modification or continuing jurisdiction, 429–430
   Parental Kidnapping Prevention Act, 431
   significant connection jurisdiction, 428, 430
   uniform legislation, 426–431
  legal custody, 219
  maternal preference, 197, 214
  modification, complaint for, 230
  nexus approach, 208, 210, 213
  noncustodial parent, rights of, 222–223
  parent-child relationships, fundamentals of, 236
  parent education programs, 228
  parenting plans, 226–228
  paternal preference, 196–197, 214
  paternity, establishing, 568
  per se approach, 210
  physical vs. legal custody, 218–219
  post-divorce disputes, 230–235
   custody, 230–231
   relocation, 232–235
   visitation, 231
  in premarital agreements, 73
  primary caretaker presumption, 200–201, 215–216
  relocation disputes, 232–235
  same-sex couples, 209–211
  shared custody
   controversy about, 220–222
   relocation disputes, 232–235
   types of arrangements, 219–220
  sole custody, 219, 225, 276
  standing, 237
  stepparents' rights, 240–241
  temporary orders, 106–107
  tender years presumption, 197
  terminology, 219
  unpredictability of decision making, 214–215
  visitation, 223–226
   determining factors, 223–224
   post-divorce disputes, 231
   restrictions, 225–226
   schedules and parameters, 224–225
   virtual visitation, 233–235
Cut-off rule, exceptions to, 661
CWA (Adoption Assistance and Child Welfare Act of 1980), 617, 693n14
Cyberstalking, 129–130, 131, 147–149

Dahlman, Jesse, 168
Damage awards as marital property, 388–389
Danti v. Danti (2009), 250–258
Databases

Federal Case Registry of Child
 Support Orders, 273
National Directory of New Hires,
 273, 291
 putative father registries, 664
State Case Registry, 273
State Directory of New Hires,
 273, 291
Dating relationships, protective orders
 in, 99–102
Deadbeat Parents Punishment Act of
 1998, 296
Decree *nisi,* 528, 529, 531
De facto parents, 579–580
 Holzman v. Knott (1996), 579
Default judgments, 468
 military personnel, 527
Defense of Marriage Act (DOMA), 10
 invalidation, 11–14
Defenses to divorce, 472
Denver boot, 290
Dependency exemptions, 305
Dependency proceedings, 619–620
Deployed parents, 430
Depositions, 478–479
Desertion, as ground for divorce,
 161–162
Diminished earning capacity, 331, 395
Disabled children
 adoption of, 693n14
 support of, 304
Discovery, 476–487
 admissions requests, 485–486
 child support financial disclosure
  affidavit, 283, 284–289
 conferences, 486–487
 defined, 476
 depositions, 478–479
 interrogatories, 479–481
 limiting, 486–487
 mental examination requests,
  484–485
 methods of, 477–485
 motion to compel, 486–487
 physical examination requests, 484–485
 protective orders, 486
 purposes of, 476

requests for production of
 documents, 481–484
 sanctions, 487
 scope of, 476–477
Disestablishment of paternity, 569–570,
 591–594, 600n26
Dismissal of action, motion for, 472
Dispensing with parental consent,
 651–652
Dispute resolution
 arbitration, 503–504
 mediation
  domestic violence cases, 501–502
  mediators, 498, 548n21
  motions, diversion of, 489–490
  overview, 498–499, 548n30
  process, 499–501
Dissolution of marriage
 annulment. *See* Annulment of marriage
 divorce. *See* Divorce
 legal separation. *See* Legal separation
District of Columbia, same-sex
 marriage in, 11
Divisible divorce, 423–424
Division of marital property. *See*
 Marital property
Divorce, 155–174, 445–549. *See also*
 Marital property
 admissions requests, 485–486
 affirmative defenses, 472
 alimony. *See* Spousal support
 alternative approaches, 496–504
  arbitration, 503–504
  collaborative law, 504–506
  mediation, 498–503
  negotiations, 496–498
  unbundled services, 506–508
 annulment, compared, 156, 174–175
 answer to complaint
  affirmative defenses, 472
  counterclaims, 472
  filing, 468
  form of, 473–475
  motion to dismiss, 472
 appellate procedure, 532
 arbitration, 503–504
 asset protection, motion for, 492

Divorce (*continued*)
attorneys' fees, motion for payment of, 492
Berry v. Berry (2018), 183–186
child educational programs, 228
clean break approach, 329, 331–333
client confidentiality, 449
collaborative divorce, 504–506
common law marriage and, 24
complaint, 457–463
 accompanying documents, 463
 amendment, 458
 answer to, 468, 472, 473–475
 default judgment, 468
 example, 459–460
 fees, 463
 fee waivers, 463
 filing, 461–463
 form, 459–460
 functions of, 458
 indigent status, application for, 464–465
 joint petition and affidavit, 462
 motion to dismiss, 472
 overview, 457
 request for relief, 458
contempt, complaint for, 536, 537–539
counterclaims, 472
court costs, motion for payment of, 491
default judgment, 468
depositions, 478–479
discovery. *See* Discovery
dismissal of action, motion for, 472
divisible divorce, 424
docket number of case, 461
emotional context, 376, 446–447
ethical considerations, 447–449
evaluator, motion for appointment of, 491
fault-based
 alimony concept, 328
 defenses to, 162–164
 grounds for, 158, 159–162
fee waivers, 463
filing fees, 463
grounds for, 158, 159–162, 189–191

guardian ad litem, motion for appointment of, 491
hearings, 526–530
 contested cases, 528–530
 requesting, 526
 uncontested cases, 526–528
historical perspective, 155–159, 164–166
initial client interview, 445–456
 client confidentiality, 449
 closed-inquiry questions, 454–456
 eliciting a client narrative, 453–454
 emotional context, 446–447
 ethical considerations, 447–449
 listening skills, 450–452, 547n1
 nonverbal communication, 450
 obtaining information, 453–456
 paralegal's role, 447
 parameters, establishing, 452–453
 three-stage approach, 452–457
 trust, creating an atmosphere of, 452–453
 unauthorized practice of law, 448–449
 wrapping up, 456
innocent spouse requirement, 158, 327–328
interrogatories, 479–481
investigator, motion for appointment of, 491
joint petitions, 461, 462
judgments
 appeals from, 531–532
 default judgment, 468
 modification of, 533
 motion for relief from judgment, 530–531
jurisdiction, 423–431
mediation
 domestic violence cases, 501–502
 electronic, 502–503
 mediators, 498, 548n21
 motions, diversion of, 489–490
 overview, 498–499, 548n30
 process, 499–501
mental examination requests, 484–485
modification, complaint for, 533

motion practice
  abuse, protection from, 492–493
  affidavits accompanying
    motions, 488
  assets, protection of, 493
  costs and fees, payment of, 492
  dismissal of action, 472
  diversion of motions to court,
    489–490
  ex parte relief, 488–489, 492
  motion for modification, 533
  new trial, 530
  overview, 487–488
  paralegal's role, 493
  preparation of motions, 488
  presentation of motions to
    court, 489
  relief from judgment, 530–531
  sample motion and supporting
    affidavit, 493, 494–496
  service of motions, 488
  temporary custody and supporting
    affidavit, 491, 494–496
  temporary orders, 488
  temporary support, 492
motion to dismiss, 472
negotiations, 496–498
new trial, motion for, 530
no-fault
  alimony concept, 329–333
  debate about, 168–170
  domestic violence, effect on,
    170, 193n26
  grounds for, 166–168
  historical perspective,
    164–166, 192n19
  marital property distribution, 329
  mutual consent requirement, 171
  reform efforts, 171–172
physical examination requests,
  484–485
premarital agreements, 61–62
pretrial conference, 528–529
pretrial statement, 529
proof of service, 469–471
relief from judgment, motion for,
  530–531
religious underpinnings, 156–157

requests for production of
  documents, 481–484
return of service, 467, 469–471
same-sex couples, 424
separation agreements, 508–526
  approval of, 527–528
  decree nisi, 529
  drafting, 508–509
  paralegal's role, 509
  sample agreement, with
    commentary, 509–526
service of process. *See* Service of
  process
spousal support. *See* Spousal support
subpoenas, 478
subpoenas duces tecum, 478
trial, 529
trial notebook, 529–530
unbundled legal services, 506–508
uncontested cases, 526–528
venue, 461
Divorce a mensa et thoro, 156, 178
DNA-based paternity testing, 561
Docket numbers, 461
DOMA (Defense of Marriage
  Act), 10–11
Domestic partnerships. *See also*
  Cohabitation; Same-sex couples
  registries for, 58n54
Domestic violence, 93–153. *See
  also* Abuse prevention laws;
  Protective orders; Violence
  Against Women Act
  arrest policies, mandatory, 126–127
  batterer intervention programs, 108
  child abuse and, 205
  as child custody consideration,
    205–207, 222
  child visitation restrictions and,
    225–226
  cruelty, as ground for divorce, 162
  cyberstalking, 129–130, 131
  "Domestic Violence Offender Gun
    Ban," 109–110
  effect of no-fault divorce on,
    170, 193n26
  emergency jurisdiction, 428–429
  emotional abuse, 103

Domestic violence (*continued*)
employment law and, 150n11
ex parte proceedings, 111, 135
exposure of children to, 205, 245–250, 265n20, 611–612
forced child marriage, 104
harassment, 103
historical perspective, 93–96
immigrant women, 132–133
Inter-American Court on Human Rights, 126
interference with liberty, 103
interspousal immunity, 151n26
interstate, 132
mandatory arrest policies, 126–127
mandatory prosecution policies, 126–127
mediation, appropriateness of, 501–502
Native American women, 133
physical abuse, 103
police officers, statutory obligations, 110, 126–127
prosecution policies, mandatory, 126–127
qualifying relationships, 97–102
sexual assault, 103, 206
specialized court programs, 130–131
stalking, 127–130, 132
statistics, 97
treatment orders, 108
tribal affairs, 133
Violence Against Women Act, 96
working with victims, 134–135
Domicile rule for jurisdiction, 422, 423–424, 442n4
Donor insemination. *See* Sperm donation
Driver's licenses, denial of for child support arrearages, 292
Drug use by pregnant women, 614–615
Dual property approach, 374
Due Process Clause
ex parte relief, 488–489
jurisdiction and, 422–423
marriage as fundamental right, 8–9

parental rights, 603
religion and, 211–213
right to notice, 463
Durable power of attorney, 59n58

Economic self-sufficiency assumption, 329, 330
Electronic monitoring, 108–109
Emancipated minors, support of, 301
E-mediation, 502–503
Emergency jurisdiction, 428–429, 430
Emergency protective orders, 111, 118
Emergency removal of children, 616–617
Emotional abuse. *See also* Child abuse and neglect; Domestic violence of children, 610–613
domestic violence, 103
Employee Retirement Income Security Act of 1974 (ERISA), 399, 420n45
Enforcement of protective orders, 126–130
Enhanced earning capacity, 331, 342–343
Equal contribution, presumption of, 405–408
Equal Protection Clause
Brush & Nib Studio v. City of Phoenix (2018), 49–56
children of unmarried parents, 554–555
differential treatment of fathers and mothers, 554–555
Levy v. Louisiana (1968), 554
marriage rights and responsibilities, 6–7
personal bias in custody cases, 208
Sessions v. Morales-Santana (2017), 558
Equitable distribution principles, 375–376, 394–395
Equitable parenthood, 240
Ethical considerations
client confidentiality, 449, 616
divorce cases, 447–449
suspected child abuse, 616
unauthorized practice of law, 448–449

Ethnicity. *See* Interracial couples;
    Racial issues
Expanded Access to Family Court Act
    (New York), 100
Ex parte proceedings
    domestic violence cases, 111, 135
    motion for ex parte relief, divorce
        cases, 492
    motion for relief, divorce cases,
        488–489
Experts, role in valuation, 393
Express contract, 25–26
Extraordinary expenses, 280–281

Fair market value, 392–394
Family courts, 421
Family preservation, 617, 621
Family residence, disposition of,
    397–398, 412–417
Fathers. *See also* Paternity; Sperm
    donation
    bias against in child custody
        decisions, 214
    biology-plus approach, 557,
        559–560, 662
    fatherhood, defining, 569–570,
        571–572, 585–591
    intent to claim parental rights,
        666–667
    paternal preference, 196–197, 214
    prebirth consent to adoption, 650
    presumption of paternity, 552,
        559–560
    unwed fathers, 585–591
        adoption and, 649, 650, 662–669
        biology-plus approach,
            559–560, 662
        child support, 568
        intent to claim parental rights,
            666–667
        legal status of, 554, 555–560
        paternity, establishing. *See* Paternity
        putative father registries, 664
        sperm donors, 572–574,
            600n36, 600n37
Fault-based divorce
    alimony concept, 328

defenses to, 162–164
grounds for, 158, 159–162
Federal Case Registry of Child Support
    Orders (FCR), 273
Federal Offset Program (FOP), 290,
    292–293
Federal Parent Locator Service (FPLS),
    271, 273
Federal Rules of Civil Procedure, 476,
    530–531
Fees
    attorneys' fees, motion for payment
        of, 492
    divorce complaints, filing, 463
    unbundled legal services, 506–508
FFCCSOA (Full Faith and Credit for
    Child Support Orders Act of
    1994), 295
Filing fees, 463
Financial disclosure affidavit, 283,
    284–289
Financial Management Service, 292
Firearms, relinquishment of in
    protection orders, 109–110
Flexibility, Efficiency, and
    Modernization in Child Support
    Enforcement Programs (Final
    Rule 2016), 271, 274, 277, 281,
    297, 300
Florida
    interracial marriage, 208
    pets and divorce, 379
    premarital agreements, 63, 78–80
    stalking, 147–149
Forced child marriage, 104, 613
Forms
    abuse prevention order, 119–124
    answer to complaint, 473–475
    complaint for contempt, 537–539
    complaint for paternity, 562–566
    divorce complaint, 459–460
    financial disclosure affidavit, 283,
        284–289
    indigent status, application for,
        464–465
    intent to claim parental rights,
        666–667

Forms (*continued*)
joint petition and affidavit, 462
marriage license, 22
motion for modification, 534–535
motion for temporary custody and supporting affidavit, 494–496
premarital agreements, schedule of assets, 67–68
proof of service, 469–471
request for protective order, 112–117
summons, 466–467
voluntary acknowledgment of paternity, 566–568
Formulas for child support
income shares approach, 276–283
Melson formula, 275
percentage of income approach, 275
Forum non conveniens doctrine, 430
Foster care, 617
Fourteenth amendment. *See* Due Process Clause; Equal Protection Clause
Fowler v. Fowler (2019), 138–143
FPLS (Federal Parent Locator Service), 271, 273
Fraud, voidable marriages, 176
Freedom of contract principle, 64
Freedom of religion, 49–56
Full faith and credit. *See also* Jurisdiction
Parental Kidnapping Prevention Act, 431
paternity acknowledgment, 568
Violence Against Women Act, 132, 427
Full Faith and Credit for Child Support Orders Act of 1994 (FFCCSOA), 295

Garrett v. Garrett (1995), 212–213
Garska v. McCoy (1981), 215–216
Gay men
adoption by, 660–661
couples. *See* Same-sex couples
marriage. *See* Same-sex marriage
Gay rights activism, 9–10
Gender differences. *See also* Married women
adoption, parental rights in, 662

in child custody decisions, 196–197, 214
marriage rights, 2–7
maternal preference, 197, 214, 553
paternal preference, 196–197, 214
premarital agreements, 63
spousal support obligations, 330, 331
unmarried parents' rights, 557–558, 599n10, 599n12
Genetic paternity testing, 561
Gifts, as marital property, 387–388
Gonzales v. Castle Rock (2005), 126–127
Goodin v. Department of Human Services (2000), 436–437
Goodridge v. Department of Public Health (2003), 10–11
Goodwill, professional, 382–383
Grandparents' right to custody and visitation, 236–239
Griswold v. Connecticut (1965), 7
Guardians ad litem, 204, 492
Gun Control Act of 1968, 109–110
Guns, relinquishment of in protection orders, 109–110

Hague Conference on Private International Law, 432
Hague Convention on the Civil Aspects of International Child Abduction, 432, 437–441, 443n24
Hague Convention on the Enforcement of Child Support and Other Forms of Family Maintenance, 295
Hamet v. Baker (2014), 379
Harassment, 103. *See also* Domestic violence
Hard-drop policies for prosecution in domestic violence cases, 127
Hawaii, same-sex marriage in, 10, 57n18
Hawk v. Hawk (1993), 238
Health insurance
child support, 281
COBRA, 345
provision of as spousal support, 344–345

Hearings
  divorce, 526–530
    contested cases, 528–530
    requesting, 526
    uncontested cases, 526–528
  paralegals, roles and
    responsibilities, 493
  permanency hearing, 620
  protective orders, 111, 125
Heckler, Margaret, 270
Henry VIII, 157
Holzman v. Knott (1996), 579
Home state jurisdiction, 427, 430
Home study for adoption, 646
Homicide, domestic violence and, 97
Homosexuals
  adoption by, 660–661
  couples. *See* Same-sex couples
  marriage. *See* Same-sex marriage
Huch v. Marrs (2003), 147–149

Idaho
  child custody, 210, 250–258
  community property
    approach, 4, 372
  "If, as, and when" approach, 398–399
Illegitimacy. *See* Paternity; Unwed
  fathers
Illinois
  cohabitation, 59n57
  interracial adoption, 208
  preemptive rights of natural
    parents, 669
  unwed fathers, rights of, 556
Immigrants, protection for battered
  women, 132–133
Immigration and Naturalization Act of
  1952, 557
Implied-in-fact contracts, 26
Imputed income for child support, 276
Incarcerated parent, child support
  from, 317–321
Inception of title rule, 385
Incest, 16–17, 175
Income considerations for child
  support
  child's resources, 279
  of custodial parent, 279, 313–317

defining income, 276–277
  imputed or attributed income, 276
  income base, determining, 277–278
  of new partner, 279
  withholding, 290–291
Income taxes. *See* Tax considerations
Income withholding, child support
  arrearages, 290–291
Incorporation and merger with spousal
  support exception, 525
Incorporation of separation agreement
  into divorce judgment, 528
Independent adoptions. *See* Adoption
Indian Child Welfare Act, 622–623
  termination of parental rights,
    689–692
Indigent status, application for,
  464–465
Indissoluble bond, marriage as, 156
Inheritance proceeds as marital
  property, 405–408
Inheritance rights. *See* Intestacy
Initial custody determinations,
  427–429
In loco parentis doctrine, 240, 644
Innocent spouse, 158, 327–328
In re _____. See name of party
In rem jurisdiction, 426
Insemination. *See* Sperm donation
Intangible assets, 376–377
Intent to claim parental rights form,
  666–667
Inter-American Court on Human
  Rights (IACCHR), 126
Interethnic Placement Provisions, 671
Internal Revenue Service (IRS). *See also*
  Tax considerations
  alimony recapture, 351
  Federal Offset Program, 292
International child abduction, 431–433,
  437–441
Interracial couples
  anti-miscegenation laws, 8–9
  child custody and, 208–209
  interracial marriage, 8–9, 31–34,
    208–209
Interrogatories, 479–481
Interspousal immunity, 151n26

Interstate cases. *See also* Jurisdiction
  child custody, 232–235, 426–431
  child support arrearages, 293–295
  common law marriages,
      recognition of, 24
  protective orders, recognition of, 132
  service of process, 467
Interstate Stalking Punishment and
      Prevention Act of 1996, 127–128
Intestacy
  adopted children's rights, 645
  of noncustodial parents, 222–223
  rights of children of unmarried
      parents, 555
Intimate partner violence. *See* Domestic
      violence
Iowa, spousal support in, 356–360
Irreconcilable differences, as ground
      for divorce, 166
IV-D agencies. *See* Title IV-D agencies

Jefferson, Thomas, 158
Joint adoptions, 661
Joint custody
  controversy about, 220–222
  relocation disputes, 232–235, 258–263
  types of arrangements, 219–220
Joint petition and affidavit,
      divorce, 462
Judgments
  appeals, 531–532
  default judgment, 468
  modification of, 533, 534–535
  motion for relief from judgment,
      530–531
Jurisdiction, 421–443
  child abuse and neglect, 623
  child custody cases, 426–431
    declining, 430
    emergency jurisdiction, 428, 430
    home state jurisdiction, 427, 430
    initial custody determinations,
        427–429
    international abduction, 437–441
    last resort jurisdiction, 429, 430
    modification or continuing
        jurisdiction, 429–430

    under Parental Kidnapping
        Prevention Act, 431
    significant connection jurisdiction,
        428, 430
  consent rule, 423
  divorce actions, 423–431
  domicile rule, 422, 423–424, 442n4
  Indian Child Welfare Act, 623
  in rem jurisdiction, 426
  international or tribal
      disputes, 442n10
  last resort jurisdiction, 429, 430
  long-arm statutes, 422–423, 425
  marital property division, 425–426
  minimum contacts rule,
      422–423, 442n4
  personal jurisdiction, 422–423, 425,
      436–437
  physical presence rule, 423
  subject matter jurisdiction, 421–422
  support, awarding, 424–425
  tribal courts, 623
Justice Department
  cyberstalking, 129–130
  partner violence statistics, 97
Juveniles. *See* Minors

Kentucky
  divorce education program for
      children, 228
  grandparent-grandchild
      relationship, 237
  leave time as marital property, 382
Kidnapping cases international child
      abduction, 431–433, 437–441
  Parental Kidnapping Prevention Act,
      426–427, 432
King v. King (1992), 237

Lack of capacity, 175, 183–186
  Berry v. Berry (2018), 183–186
Langston v. Riffe (2000), 571
Last resort jurisdiction, 429, 430
Lautenberg Amendment, Gun Control
      Act of 1968, 110
  ongoing viability of, 151n38
Lawrence v. Lawrence (2006), 189–191

Leave time as marital property, 382
Legal custody, 219
Legal orphans, 621–622
Legal separation, 178–179. *See also*
    Separation agreements
  nature of, 156, 178–179
  religious underpinnings, 156
  separate maintenance,
      distinguished, 179
Legal services, unbundled, 506–508
Legitimation of children, 553, 554.
    See also Paternity
Lehr v. Robertson (1983), 557
Lesbians
  adoption by, 660–661
  couples. *See* Same-sex couples
  marriage. *See* Same-sex marriage
Levy v. Louisiana (1968), 554
Licenses
  denial of for child support
      arrearages, 292
  marriage, 20–22, 171
Liens, for child support arrearages,
    291–292
Limited divorce. *See* Legal separation
Line Nang Baccam, In re Marriage of
    (2018), 356–360
Listening skills, developing, 450–452
Living separate and apart, as grounds
    for divorce, 167–168
Long-arm statutes, 422–423, 425
Lottery-winning intercepts, 290
Louisiana
  children of unmarried parents, rights
      of, 554
  community property
      approach, 4, 372
  covenant marriage, 172, 193n38
Loutts v. Loutts (2015), 363–367
Loving v. Virginia (1967), 8–9, 10,
    18, 31–34
Lump-sum spousal support, 339, 348

Mahoney v. Mahoney (1982), 343
Maine, married women's property
    rights in, 5
Malpractice, 448

Maltreatment of children. *See* Child
    abuse and neglect
Mandatory reporting of abuse, 615
Marital breakdown, as ground for
    divorce, 166–167
Marital fault. *See* Fault-based divorce
Marital property, 374–420. *See also*
    Separate property
  all property approach, 374
  annulment, 177
  classification of
    appreciation of separate property,
        389–390
    cohabitation, property acquired
        during, 386
    cost basis, 400
    cut-off point, 387
    damage awards, 388–389
    gifts, 387–388
    inception of title rule, 385
    personal injury awards, 388–389
    premarital acquisition, 385
    property in contemplation of
        marriage, 386
    property in exchange for separate
        property, 390
    Schmitz v. Schmitz (2004), 408–412
    separate property, 372, 374,
        384–385, 390
    sick leave, 382
    source of funds rule, 385–386
    time of acquisition, 385–386
    tracing the source, 390
    transmutation, 391–392
    vacation time, 382
  common law approach, 372
  community property approach, 372–373
  distribution of
    Castle v. Castle (2018), 412–417
    effectuating, 396–399
    equal vs. equitable division, 394–395
    factors affecting, 395–396
    family residence, 412–417
    marital residence, 397–398
    pensions, 398–399, 418n16
    Qualified Domestic Relations
        Order, 399

Marital property (*continued*)
  division of, general considerations,
    375–376
  dual property approach, 374
  emotional considerations, 376
  equitable distribution principles,
    375–376
  fair market value, 392–394
  family residence, 397–398, 412–417
  inheritance proceeds, 405–408
  jurisdiction, 425–426
  no-fault divorce and, 329
  Olesberg v. Olesberg (2006), 405–408
  pets, 377–380, 418n13
  professional degrees,
    342–343, 369n20
  professional goodwill, 382–383
  same-sex couples, 386–387
  special equity rule, 372
  tangible vs. intangible property,
    376–377
  tax considerations, 399–400
  title, division according to, 372
  unvested pensions, 380–381, 398–399
  valuation of, 392–394, 399–400
  virtual assets, 383–384
Marital residence, 397–398, 412–417
Marital unity doctrine, 2–3, 94
Marriage, 1–59
  age restrictions, 18–20
  annulment. *See* Annulment of
    marriage
  blood tests, 21
  civil law tradition, 4
  cohabitation and, 24–28
  common law marriage, 22–24
  common law origins, 2–4
  community property, 4
  covenant marriages, 172–174
  divorce. *See* Divorce
  forced child marriage, 104, 613
  formalities, 20–22
  as a fundamental right, 8–9
  incest laws, 16–17
  as indissoluble, 156–157
  lack of capacity, 175–176
  as legal act, 1–2

legal separation. *See* Legal separation
licenses, 20–22, 171
multiple marriages, 17–18
premarital counseling, 171–172
procedural flaws, effect of, 22
property acquisition in
    contemplation of, 386
regulation of, 2–7
restrictions, 15–20, 175
right of marital privacy, 7
rights and responsibilities, 2–4
same-sex. *See* Same-sex marriage
venereal disease, 21
void and voidable, 175–176
waiting periods, 21, 171
Marriage of ____. See name of party
Marriage restriction laws, 15–20, 175
Married women
  abuse of. *See* Domestic violence
  community property, 4
  contracts, 3
  earning capacity, 331
  economic self-sufficiency, 329, 330
  husband's right to use physical
    violence against, 93–94
  legal equality, 6–7
  legal subordination of, 2–4
  marital unity doctrine, 2–3
  maternal rights, 196–197
  personal property, 3, 4–6
  premarital agreements, 63
  real property, 3
  services of, husband's right to, 3, 5
  support, right to, 3–4
  testamentary capacity, 3
Married Women's Property Acts,
    4–6, 372
Marvin v. Marvin (1976), 25–26,
    27, 44–49
Mary Ann P. v. William R.P., Jr. (1996),
    245–250
Maryland
  adultery, meaning of, 160
  disestablishment of paternity,
    571, 572
Massachusetts
  abuse protection legislation, 99

adoption statutes, 644–645
de facto parents, 579
disestablishment of paternity, 571,
591–594
joint divorce petitions, 461
joint petition for divorce, 463
postnuptial agreements, 73–74
relocation custody and visitation
disputes, 258–263
same-sex marriage, 10–11
Maternal preference, 197, 214, 553
McCoy v. McCoy (2001), 233–234
McGriff v. McGriff (2004),
210–211, 265n39
McLaughlin v. Jones (2017), 595–598
McLeod v. Starnes (2012), 310–313
Mediation, 498–503
domestic violence cases, 501–502
electronic, 502–503
mediators, 498, 548n21
motions, diversion of, 489–490
overview, 498–499, 548n30
process, 499–501
Medical child abuse, 613
Medical insurance. *See* Health
insurance
Melson formula for child support, 275
Mental examination requests, 484–485
Mental health professionals, child
custody cases, 204
Mentally disabled children, support
of, 304
MEPA (Multiethnic Placement
Law), 671
Merger of separation agreement, 528
Michigan
"best interests of the child"
approach, 198
equitable parenthood, 240
gender roles in marriage, 6
spousal support, 363–367
Miller v. Miller (2018), 258–263
Mini-DOMA statutes, 10
Minimum contacts jurisdiction,
422–423, 442n4
Minors
abuse. *See* Child abuse and neglect

age of capacity for marriage,
18–20, 175
age of consent, 18
custody. *See* Custody and visitation
emancipation, 301
"illegitimate." *See* Children of
unmarried parents
income and resources, effect on child
support, 279
neglect. *See* Child abuse and neglect
protective orders, 101–102
teen dating relationships, protective
orders in, 101–102
visitation. *See* Custody and visitation
Mississippi
condonation as ground for divorce,
189–191
marital property, 412–417
personal jurisdiction and service of
process, 436–437
Missouri, prohibition on inmate
marriages in, 9
Modification
child support, 299–300
custody and visitation, 230
divorce judgments, 533, 534–535
jurisdiction, 429–430
spousal support. *See under* Spousal
support
Mormon Church, 17–18
Motion practice
abuse, protection from, 492–493
affidavits accompanying
motions, 488
assets, protection of, 492
costs and fees, payment of, 492
dismissal of action, 472
diversion of motions to court
conciliation or mediation services,
489–490
evaluator or investigator,
appointment of, 491
ex parte relief, 488–489, 492
modification, motion for, 533,
534–535
motion to compel, 487
new trial, 530

Motion practice (*continued*)
  overview, 487–488
  paralegal's role, 493
  preparation of motions, 488
  presentation of motions to court, 489
  relief from judgment, 530–531
  sample motion and supporting
    affidavit, 493, 494–496
  service of motions, 488
  temporary custody motion and
    supporting affidavit, 491,
    494–496
  temporary orders, 488
  temporary support, 492
Multiethnic Placement Law
  (MEPA), 671
Mutual consent to divorce, 156, 171
Mutual orders of protection, 118

National Association of Black Social
  Workers, 670
National Association of Legal
  Assistants, 448
National Conference of Commissioners
  on Uniform State Laws
  (NCCUSL), 426–427, 572–573
National Directory of New Hires,
  273, 291
National Divorce Reform League, 159
National Federation of Paralegal
  Associations, 448
National League for the Protection of
  the Family, 159
National Society of Genetic
  Counselors, 16
Native Americans
  domestic violence and, 133
  jurisdiction, 442n10
NCCUSL. *See* National Conference
  of Commissioners on Uniform
  State Laws
Nebraska, child custody, 212–213
Neglect. *See* Child abuse and neglect
Negotiations, divorce cases, 496–498
Nevada, community property
  approach in, 4, 372
New Hampshire, adultery, meaning of,
  160, 186–189

New Jersey
  de facto parents, 580
  disposition of marital property,
    395–396
  reimbursement alimony, 343
  virtual visitation, 233–234
New Mexico, community property
  approach in, 4, 372
New York
  co-parent adoptions, 662
  Expanded Access to Family Court
    Act, 100
  no-fault divorce, 164
New York Society for the Prevention
  of Cruelty to Children
  (NYSPCC), 606
Nexus approach to child custody, 208,
  210, 213
*Nguyen v. Immigration & Naturalization
  Services* (2001), 557
No-contact orders, 106
No-drop policies for prosecution in
  domestic violence cases, 126–127
No-fault divorce
  alimony concept, 329–333
  debate about, 168–170
  domestic violence, effect on,
    170, 193n26
  grounds for, 166–168
  historical perspective,
    164–166, 192n19
  marital property distribution, 329
  mutual consent requirement, 171
  reform efforts, 171–172
Noncustodial parent, rights of, 222–223
Nonmarital couples. *See also* Same-sex
  couples
  cohabitation. *See* Cohabitation
  protection of relational interests, 26
  trends in legal recognition of,
    24–25, 27–28
  unwed fathers. *See* Unwed fathers
Nonverbal communication, 450

Obergefell v. Hodges (2015), 12–14, 34–44
  parental rights, 597
  protective orders, 102
  retroactive application of, 23, 58n36

Obesity as child abuse, 612
Office of Child Support Enforcement
     (OCSE)
   establishment of, 271
   Federal Parent Locator Service,
     271, 273
   interception of tax refunds, 292–293
   state support, 324n33
Ohio
   arbitration, 504
Oklahoma, abuse protection
     legislation in, 99
Olesberg v. Olesberg (2006), 405–408
Open adoption, 655–656,
     657–658, 694n21
Opportunity costs, 339
Opportunity interest, 664–665
Oregon, presumption of equal
     contribution, 405–408
Orphans, legal, 621–622

"Palimony," 44–49
Palmore v. Sidoti (1984), 208
Paralegals, roles and
     responsibilities, 486
   appeals process, 532
   child abuse, reporting, 616
   child custody and visitation cases,
     client interviews, 229
   client confidentiality, 449, 616
   depositions, 479
   discovery, coordinating, 477–485
   divorce cases, client interview, 447,
     452–457
   ethical considerations, 447–449, 616
   filing complaints, 461
   hearings, 493
   interrogatories, 479–481
   jurisdiction, determining, 423
   listening skills, development of, 450–452
   motion practice, 493
   negotiations and settlement
     conferences, 498
   premarital agreements, 66
   requests for physical and mental
     examinations, 484–485
   requests for production of
     documents, 485

separation agreements, drafting, 509
spousal support cases, client
     interviews, 338
state regulation of, 547n7
trial preparation assistance, 529–530
unauthorized practice of law,
     448–449
Parens patriae doctrine, 606
Parental Kidnapping Prevention Act of
     1980 (PKPA), 426–431
   international cases, 432
Parental unfitness, 621
Parent education programs, 228
Parenting coordinator provisions, 227
Parenting plans, 226–228
Parent Locator Service, 271, 273
Parents and parenting. *See also*
     Adoption; Child abuse and
     neglect; Custody and visitation
   intent to claim parental rights form,
     666–667
   parent-child relationships,
     fundamentals of, 236
   parenting coordinator
     provisions, 227
   parenting plans, 226–228
   post-adoption contact, 657–658
   search for birth parents, 658–659
   termination of parental rights. *See*
     Termination of parental rights
   unfitness, consequences of, 621
   unwed fathers. *See* Unwed fathers
Passport denial, for child support
     arrearages, 293
Paternal preference, 196–197, 214
Paternity, 551–601
   adjudication of, 555, 561–566
   "best interest" standard, 571
   biology-plus approach, 557, 559–560,
     662
   Child Support Enforcement and
     Establishment of Paternity Act,
     270, 271, 560
   consequences of establishing, 568
   disestablishment of, 569–570,
     591–594, 600n26
   fatherhood, defining, 569–570,
     571–572, 585–591

Paternity (*continued*)
  genetic testing, 561
  presumption of, 552, 559–560
  sample complaint form, 562–566
  sperm donors, 572–576, 600n36
  voluntary acknowledgment, 566–568
    sample form, 567
Pennsylvania
  adoption, 633–637
  child abuse and neglect, 633–637
  child support, 313–317
  pets and divorce, 379
  premarital agreements, 63, 69–70,
    80–84
  sperm donor's rights, 576
  spousal support, 360–363
  termination of parental rights,
    633–637
Pensions, marital vs. separate property,
    380–381, 398–399, 418n16
Percentage of income approach to child
    support, 275
Permanency hearing, 620
Permanency planning, 620–621,
    633–637
Permanent spousal support, 338–339,
    356–360. *See also* Spousal support
Permissive reporting of abuse, 615–616
Per se approach to child custody, 210
Personal injury awards, 388–389
Personal jurisdiction, 422–423, 425,
    436–441
  *Goodin v. Department of Human
    Services* (2000), 436–437
Personal property
  marital property. *See* Marital
    property
  of married women, 3, 4–6
  in premarital agreements, 72
  separate property. *See* Separate
    property
Personal Responsibility and Work
    Opportunity Reconciliation Act
    (PRWORA), 270, 294
Personal service, 436–437, 465
Pets
  as marital property, 377–380, 418n13

protective orders, 107
Physical abuse. *See also* Child abuse
    and neglect; Domestic violence
  of children, 608–609
  domestic violence, 103
Physical custody. *See* Custody and
    visitation
Physical examination requests, 484–485
Physical presence rule for
    jurisdiction, 423
Pilgrims, view of divorce, 157
PKPA (Parental Kidnapping
    Prevention Act of 1980), 426–431
  international cases, 432
Police officers, statutory obligations
    in domestic violence cases, 110,
    126–127
Polygamy, 17–18
Posner v. Posner (1970), 63, 78–80
Postmarital agreements, 61
Postnuptial agreements, 73–74
Post-placement social study, 655
Poverty
  adoption and, 645
  child abuse and, 611, 638n3, 639n28
Pre-adoption placements, 653–655
Pregnant women
  drug use by, 614–615
  protective orders, 98
Premarital acquisition of property, 385
Premarital agreements, 61–92
  Bedrick v. Bedrick (2011), 85–90
  child custody and support
    provisions, 73
  consideration, 64
  disclosure requirements, 66, 67–68
  historical perspective, 61–62
  Posner v. Posner (1970), 63, 78–80
  procedural fairness, 65, 66–69, 71
  property provisions, 72
  schedule of assets
    example, 67–68
    sample questions, 67
  Simeone v. Simeone (1990), 63, 69–70,
    80–84, 92n7
  spousal support provisions, 72–73
  substantive fairness, 65, 69–71, 92n7

threshold requirements, 64
trends in, 63
unconscionability, 64–65
void as against public policy, 61–62
Premarital counseling, 171–172
Prenatal drug exposure, 614–615
Presence, jurisdiction based on, 423
Present value approach, 398
Presumption of paternity, 552, 559–560
Pretrial conference, 528–529
Pretrial statement, 529
Primary caretaker presumption,
    200–201, 215–216
*Principles of the Law of Family
    Dissolution* (ALI), 59n61, 216–217
Private adoption. *See* Adoption
Probate courts, 421
Procedural fairness, 65, 66–69, 71
Production of documents requests,
    481–484
Professional degrees, spousal support
    and, 342–343, 369n20
Professional goodwill, 382–383
Professional licenses, denial of for
    child support arrearages, 292
Proof of service form, 469–471
Property
    community, 4, 372–373
    marital. *See* Marital property
    personal. *See* Personal property
    real, 397–398, 412–417
    separate. *See* Separate property
Prosecution policies, domestic
    violence, 126–127
Protection of children. *See* Child abuse
    and neglect
Protective orders, 96. *See also* Abuse
    prevention laws; Domestic
    violence; Violence Against
    Women Act
    child custody and visitation, 106–107
    child support, 107
    covered conduct, 102–104
    electronic monitoring, 108–109
    emergency orders, 118
    enforcement, 126–130
    ex parte orders, 111, 118

firearms, relinquishment of, 109–110
forced child marriage, 613
Fowler v. Fowler (2019), 138–143
    limiting discovery, 486
    modification or termination of,
        138–143
    monetary compensation, 107
    mutual orders, 118
    no-contact orders, 106
    pets, 107
    procedure, 118
        advocate, role of, 110
        ex parte orders, 111
        failure to appear, 125
        hearings, 111, 118, 125
        lack of coordination with other
            proceedings, 130–131
        request for protective order, 111,
            112–117
        specialized courts, 130–131
        temporary orders, 118, 119–124
    qualifying relationships
        cohabitation, 98
        dating relationships, 99–102
        parents of child in common, 98
        pregnant women, 98
        same-sex couples, 102
        special relationships, 98
        teen relationships, 101–102
    remedies, 104–110
    restraining orders, 105, 119–124
    same-sex couples, 99, 102
    Silva v. Carmel (2014), 144–147
    stay-away orders, 105
    treatment orders, 108
    vacate orders, 105
Protestantism, view of divorce,
    156–157
PRWORA (Personal Responsibility
    and Work Opportunity
    Reconciliation Act), 270, 294
Public accommodation, places
    of, 59n63
Puritans
    domestic violence reforms, 95
    view of divorce, 157
Putative father registries, 664

Qualified Domestic Relations Order
(QDRO), 399, 420n45
Qualified Medical Child Support
Order (QMCSO), 281

Racial issues. *See also* Cultural
considerations
anti-miscegenation laws, 8–9
child custody and, 208–209
interracial marriage, 8–9, 31–34,
208–209
transracial adoptions, 669–671,
695n34, 695n36
Real property
family residence, disposition of,
397–398, 412–417
of married women, 3
"Reasonable efforts" requirement,
child abuse cases, 618–619
Recapture provisions for spousal
support, 351
Recreational and sporting licenses,
denial of for child support
arrearages, 292
Recrimination, as defense for
divorce, 163
Registries
adoption, 659
Federal Case Registry of Child
Support Orders, 273
putative father, 664
State Case Registry, 273
Rehabilitative spousal support,
340–341, 348–349
Reimbursement alimony, 343–344, 348
Reinstatement of parental rights,
621–622
Relief motions
ex parte relief, 488–489, 492
relief from judgment, 530–531
Religion
as basis for child custody decisions,
211–213
covenant marriages, 172–174
dissolution of marriage and, 156–157
medical neglect and, 639n16
Relinquishment of children, 650

Relocation custody and visitation
disputes, 232–235, 258–263
Remarriage
child support and, 279
spousal support and, 346–347
Removal of children, 619–622
Requests. *See also* Motion practice
in discovery. *See* Discovery
for production of documents,
481–484
for protective order, 112–117. *See also*
Protective orders
Residence, disposition of, 397–398,
412–417
Restraining orders, 105, 119–124.
See also Protective orders
Retirement Equity Act of 1984 (REA),
399, 420n45
Return of service, 467
Reunification services, 620, 622–623
Review and adjustment procedure, 300
Revival following annulment, 177–178
Revocation of consent, 651–652,
654–655
Rhode Island, de facto parents in,
579–580

Safe haven laws, 648–649
Same-sex couples. *See also*
Cohabitation; Same-sex marriage
adultery, 160
child custody, 209–211
co-parents, 576–577
de facto parent status, 579–580
divorce, 424
intimate partner violence, 102
joint adoption, 661
legal parenthood, 576–580
co-parents, 576–577
de facto parent status, 579–580
by marriage and consent, 577–578
marital property, 386–387
McLaughlin v. Jones (2017), 595–598
presumption of paternity, 595–598
protective orders, 99, 102
sperm donation, 576
Violence Against Women Act, 133

Same-sex marriage, 9–15
    backlash against, 10, 14–15
    Brush & Nib Studio v. City of Phoenix
        (2018), 49–56
    common law marriage
        recognition, 23
    Obergefell v. Hodges (2015), 34–44
    religious opposition to, 15
Sanctions for noncompliance with
        discovery requests, 487
Schaeffer, Rebecca, 127
Schedule of assets, premarital
        agreements
    example, 67–68
    sample questions, 67
Schmitz v. Schmitz (2004), 408–412
Sealed records adoption, 656–657,
        658–659, 678–681, 689–692
Second glance doctrine, 70
Seekins v. Hamm (2015), 437–441
Seneca Falls Convention, 5
Separate maintenance, complaint
        for, 179
Separate property. *See also* Marital
        property
    appreciation of, 389–390
    classification as, 384–385
    cohabitation, property acquired
        during, 386
    contemplation of marriage, property
        acquired in, 386
    damage awards, 388–389
    definition, 372–373, 374
    distinguished from community
        property, 372–373
    gifts, 387–388
    inception of title rule, 385
    personal injury awards, 388–389
    property received in exchange
        for, 390
    same-sex couples, 386–387
    source of funds rule, 385–386
    time of acquisition, 385–386
    transmutation to marital property,
        391–392
    valuation, 392–394
Separation agreements, 508–526

    approval of, 527–528
    decree *nisi,* 529
    drafting, 508–509
    paralegal's role, 509
    sample agreement, with
        commentary, 509–526
Separation of spouses. *See* Legal
        separation
Service of process, 463–467
    acceptance of service, 467
    constructive service, 465
    methods of, 463–465, 467
    motions, 488
    nonresident defendants, 467
    personal service, 436–437, 465
    proof of service, 469–471
    resident defendants, 465, 467
    return of service, 467
    summons, 463, 466–467
Service plans, child abuse cases, 619
Sessions v. Morales-Santana (2017), 558
Sexual abuse of children, 609–610.
        See also Child abuse and neglect
Sexual assault, 103, 206. *See also*
        Domestic violence
Shared custody
    controversy about, 220–222
    relocation disputes, 232–235, 258–263
    types of arrangements, 219–220
Sick leave as marital property, 382
Significant connection jurisdiction,
        428, 430
Silva v. Carmel (2014), 144–147
Simeone v. Simeone (1990), 63, 69–70,
        80–84, 92n7
Single-parent adoption, 661
Slaves, children of, 553
S.M.C. v. W.P.C. (2012), 360–363
Smith, Joseph, 17
Social Security Act of 1935, 269–270.
        See also Title IV-D agencies
Societies for the prevention of cruelty
        to children, 605–606, 638n7
Soft-drop policies for prosecution in
        domestic violence cases, 126–127
Soldiers and Sailors Relief Act of
        1940, 527

Sole custody, 219, 225, 276
Source of funds rule, 385–386
South Carolina, child support, factors
    affecting, 310–313
Spaht, Katherine Shaw, 172–173
Spanking, 609
Special equity rule, 372
Special needs children
    adoption of, 693n14
    adult children, 304
Sperm donation
    determining paternity, 572–576
    donor's legal status, 576,
        600n36, 600n37
    known donors, 576, 600n37
    heterosexual couples, 572–573
    lesbian couples, 577–578
    single women, 574–576
Spousal abuse. *See* Domestic violence
Spousal support, 327–370
    annulment of marriage, 177
    bankruptcy and, 350–351
    change in circumstances, 339,
        347–348
    clean break approach, 329, 331–333
    client interview checklist, 338
    compensatory principle, 337
    diminished earning capacity, 331, 395
    duty of, 3–4
    economic self-sufficiency,
        consideration of, 329, 330
    enforcement, 349–350
    enhanced earning capacity, 331,
        342–343
    factors determining, 333–335
    guidelines, 335–337
    health insurance, 344–345
    historical perspective, 327–328
    jurisdiction, 424–425
    Loutts v. Loutts (2015), 363–367
    lump-sum support, 339, 348
    Mahoney v. Mahoney (1982), 343
    Marriage of Line Nang Baccam, In re
        (2018), 356–360
    modification and termination,
        363–367
        agreements to prohibit, 349

changes in circumstances, 346–348
    cohabitation, 347
    complaints, filing, 345
    nonmodifiable types of
        support, 349
    remarriage, 346–347
no-fault reform, impact of, 329–333
opportunity cost, 339
permanent, 338–339
in premarital agreements, 72–73
professional degrees and,
    342–343, 369n20
protective orders, 107
rehabilitative support, 340–341,
    348–349
reimbursement alimony, 343–344, 349
separate maintenance, 179
shifting views of, 329–333
S.M.C. v. W.P.C. (2012), 360–363
tax considerations, 351, 352
temporary orders, 107, 339
transitional support, 340–341
unpredictability of awards, 332–333,
    335–336
Stalking, 103, 127–130, 132, 147–149.
    See also Domestic violence
Standing, custody and visitation
    cases, 237
Stanley v. Illinois (1972), 556–557
Stanton, Elizabeth Cady, 5
State Case Registry, 273
State Department, passport denial, 293
State Directory of New Hires, 273, 291
States. *See also specific state*
    child support
        enforcement, 271–272, 290–291
        guidelines, 275–276
    common law marriages,
        recognition of, 24
    community property approach, 4, 372
    declining jurisdiction, 430
    IV-D agencies, 271–272
    jurisdiction requirements, 422–423
    protective orders, recognition of, 132
Statute of Frauds, 64
Statutes of limitations, domestic
    violence tort actions, 105

Stay-away orders, 105
Stepparents
    adoption by, 240–241, 659–660
    child custody and visitation,
        240–241
Subject matter jurisdiction, 421–422
Subpoenas, 478
Subpoenas *duces tecum*, 478
Substantive fairness, 65, 69–71, 92n7
Summons, 463, 466–467
Support. *See* Child support; Spousal
        support
Support worksheet, 274
Survival of separation
        agreement, 528

TANF (Transitional Aid to Needy
        Families), 270, 322n12
Tangible property, 376–377. *See also*
        Marital property
Tax considerations
    alimony recapture, 351
    child support payments, 304–305
    child tax credit, 305
    dependency exemptions, 305
    Federal Offset Program, 292
    marital property, 399–400
    spousal support, 305, 351, 352
Tax refund intercept, 292–293
Teen dating relationships, protective
        orders in, 101–102
Temporary alimony, 107, 339
Temporary restraining orders, 118,
        119–124
Tender years presumption, 197
Tennessee
    adoption from immigrant parents,
        682–689
    child abuse and neglect, 627–633
    visitation rights of nonparents, 238
*Tennessee Department of Children's
        Services v. Tikindra G.* (2011),
        627–633
Termination of parental rights
    adoption
        A.M.H., In re Adoption of (2007),
        682–689

Indian Child Welfare Act, 689–692
    involuntary, 652, 693n13
    opportunity interest requirement,
        664–665
    by stepparents, 659–660
    voluntary, 646, 650, 654
    child abuse and neglect, 620–621,
        633–637, 640n40
    child support obligations, 302
Testamentary capacity, of married
        women, 3
Texas
    abuse protection legislation, 99
    community property
        approach, 4, 372
        safe haven legislation, 648
Threatened physical harm, 103
Time of valuation, 393–394
Title
    division of marital property
        according to, 372
    transmutation of separate property
        by, 391
Title IV-D agencies
    basic services, 271–272
    genetic paternity testing, 561
    legislative intent, 270
    spousal support, 350
Tort actions, domestic violence, 105
Tracing the source of marital asset, 390
Transitional Aid to Needy Families
        (TANF), 270, 322n12
Transitional spousal support, 340–341
Transmutation of separate property,
        391–392
Transracial adoptions, 669–671,
        695n34, 695n36
Treasury Department, Federal Offset
        Program, 292
Treatment orders, 108
Trials, divorce, 529
    notebooks, 529–530
Tribal affairs
    domestic violence and, 133
    jurisdiction, 442n10
Troxel v. Granville (2000), 238–239, 241
Turner v. Safley (1987), 9

Unauthorized practice of law, 448–449
Unbundled legal services, 506–508
Unconscionability, doctrine of, 64–65
Uncontested divorce, 526–528
Uniform Child Custody Jurisdiction
  Act (UCCJA), 426–431
Uniform Child Custody Jurisdiction
  and Enforcement Act (UCCJEA),
  426–431
Uniform Deployed Parents
  Custody and Visitation Act
  (UDPCVA), 430
Uniform Interstate Family Support Act
  (UIFSA), 293
  federal requirements for continued
    support, 295
  long-arm provisions, 294, 324n45,
    423, 425
  overview, 293–295
  personal jurisdiction under, 425
  remedies, 324n33
  spousal support, 350
Uniform Parentage Act (UPA),
  572–573, 576
Uniform Partner Act (UPA), 331
Uniform Premarital Agreements Act
  (UPAA), 92n6
Unmarried parents, children of. *See*
  Children of unmarried parents
Unvested pensions, 380–381, 398–399
Unwed fathers
  adoption and, 649, 650, 662–669
  biology-plus approach, 557,
    559–560, 662
  child support, 568
  intent to claim parental rights,
    666–667
  legal status of, 554, 555–560
  Lehr v. Robertson (1983), 557
  *Nguyen v. Immigration &
    Naturalization Services* (2001), 557
  paternity, establishing. *See* Paternity
  putative father registries, 664
  Sessions v. Morales-Santana (2017), 558

sperm donors, 576, 600n36, 600n37
Stanley v. Illinois (1972), 556–557
Use, transmutation of separate
  property by, 391–392
Utah, bigamy and polygamy in, 17–18

Vacate orders, 105
Vacation time as marital property, 382
Valuation of marital property, 392–394,
  399–400
Venue, 461
  motion to dismiss for improper
    venue, 472
Vermont, pets and divorce, 379
Violence Against Women Act of 1994,
  96, 126, 131–133
  full faith and credit, 427
Violence Against Women
  Reauthorization Act of 2013, 133
Virginia
  legitimation of children, 553
  marriage age restrictions, 20
Virginia, pets and divorce, 379–380
Virtual assets, 383–384
Visitation. *See* Custody and visitation
Voidable marriage, 176
Void marriage, 175
Void premarital agreements, 61–62
Voluntary surrender, 646, 650, 654

Wage withholding, child support
  arrearages, 290–291
Washington
  community property
    approach, 4, 372
  de facto parents, 580
  protective orders, 138–143
  same-sex marriage, opposition to, 15
  visitation rights of nonparents,
    238–239
Washington v. Arlene's Flowers (2017), 15
Whitehead, Barbara Defoe, 169–170
Wilson, Mary Ellen, 605–606
Windsor, United States v. (2013), 11–12

Wisconsin
 de facto parents, 579–580
 fatherhood, defining, 585–591
Women's rights movement, 95
Wrongful adoption, 672–673

Wrongful death actions, 554
Wyoming, termination of parental
 rights, 689–692

Yerkes v. Yerkes (2003), 317–321